PLATFORM 8

AN INDEX OF
DESIGN & RESEARCH

HARVARD UNIVERSITY GRADUATE SCHOOL OF DESIGN

Published by the Harvard University Graduate School of Design
& ActarD.

Printed by Die Keure, Belgium.

This book is set in Century Schoolbook and is printed on
Munken Lynx & Terraprint Gloss.

The Harvard GSD alphabet was designed by Mikhail Grinwald
& Zaneta Hong, in collaboration with Alexander Cassini, Vi Vu,
and Michael Leighton Beaman.

ISBN 978-1-940291-74-1

The Harvard University Graduate School of Design is a leading
center for education, information, and technical expertise on the
built environment. Its Departments of Architecture, Landscape
Architecture, and Urban Planning & Design offer masters and
doctoral degree programs, and provide the foundation for the
school's Advanced Studies & Executive Education programs.

ActarD
151 Grand Street, 5th Floor
New York, New York 10013
actar-d.com

Harvard University
Graduate School of Design
48 Quincy Street
Cambridge, Massachusetts 02138
gsd.harvard.edu

EDITORIAL & DESIGN

Zaneta H. Hong
Faculty Editor & Lecturer in Landscape Architecture

Alexander Louis Cassini
Mikhail Thomas Grinwald
Vi Vu
Student Editors

Laura Grey & Zak Jensen
Graphic Design Consultants

Steven Moore
Indexer

Eric Glenn Williams
Proofreader

PUBLICATIONS

Jennifer Sigler   Melissa Vaughn
Editor in Chief   *Senior Editor*

Meghan Ryan Sandberg Leah Whitman-Salkin
Publications Coordinator *Associate Editor*

PHOTOGRAPHERS

Adam DeTour & Matt Baldelli   Anita Kan & Raymond Vincent Coffey
Portrait Photographer & Assistant   *Photographer & Assistant*

Maggie Janik   Justin Knight & Hannah P. Gaengler
Multimedia Producer, Communications   *Photographers*

ACKNOWLEDGEMENTS

John Joseph Aslanian   Trevor D. O'Brien
Director of Student Affairs & Recruitment   *Assistant Manager, Building Services*

Michael Leighton Beaman   Ronee Saroff
Design Consultant   *Assistant Director of Digital Content & Strategy, Communications*

Dan Borelli
Director of Exhibitions   Matthew Smith
                                  Media Services Manager, User Services

Hal Gould
Manager of User Services, Computer Resources   Chelsea Spencer
                                  Coeditor of the Harvard GSD Student Guide

Mark Hagen
Windows System Administrator, Computer Resources   Daniel Widis
                                  Geographic Information Systems Assistant

Edwin Antonio Martinez   Inés Zalduendo
Help Desk Technician, Computer Resources   *Special Collections Archivist & Reference Librarian, Frances Loeb Library*

Janina Mueller
Design Data Librarian, Frances Loeb Library   David W. Zimmerman-Stuart
                                  Exhibitions Coordinator

HARVARD GSD LEADERSHIP

Mohsen Mostafavi
Dean of the Harvard University Graduate School of Design
Alexander & Victoria Wiley Professor of Design

Patricia J. Roberts
Executive Dean

Lauren Baccus
Director of Human Resources

W. Kevin Cahill
Facilities Manager,
Building Services

Stephen McTee Ervin
Assistant Dean for Information Technology

Rena Fonseca
Director of Executive Education & International Programs

Mark Goble
Chief Financial Officer

Beth Kramer
Associate Dean for Development & Alumni Relations

Theresa A. Lund
Managing Director, Office of the Dean

Jacqueline Piracini
Assistant Dean for Academic Services

Benjamin Prosky
Assistant Dean for Communications

Laura Snowden
Dean of Students & Assistant Dean for Enrollment Services

Ann Baird Whiteside
Assistant Dean for Information Services & Librarian,
Frances Loeb Library

Sara J. Wilkinson
Director of Human Resources

K. Michael Hays
Associate Dean for Academic Affairs
Eliot Noyes Professor in Architectural Theory

Iñaki Ábalos
Chair of the Department of Architecture
Professor in Residence

Martin Bechthold
Director of the Doctor of Design Studies Program
Professor of Architectural Technology

Pierre Bélanger
Codirector of the Master in Design Studies
Associate Professor of Landscape Architecture

Anita Berrizbeitia
Director of the Master in Landscape Architecture Program
Professor of Landscape Architecture

Felipe Correa
Director of the Master in Urban Design Program
Associate Professor of Urban Design

Ann Forsyth
Director of the Master in Urban Planning Program
Professor of Urban Planning

Grace La
Director of the Master of Architecture Program
Professor of Architecture

Rahul Mehrotra
Chair of the Department of Urban Planning & Design
Professor of Urban Planning & Design

Kiel Moe
Codirector of the Master in Design Studies
Associate Professor of Architecture & Energy

Mark Mulligan
Interim Curator for the Loeb Fellowship Program
Associate Professor in Practice of Architecture

Erika Naginski
Director of Doctoral Programs
Professor of Architectural History

Antoine Picon
Director of Research & G. Ware Travelstead
Professor of the History of Architecture & Technology

Charles A. Waldheim
Chair of the Department of Landscape Architecture
John E. Irving Professor of Landscape Architecture

PREFACE

Mohsen Mostafavi
Dean of the Harvard University Graduate School of Design
Alexander & Victoria Wiley Professor of Design

I have long been fascinated by the idea of variety within limits. How do you imagine something new within a constrained framework—similarity as a precondition of difference?

Each edition of *Platform*—the annual publication of the Harvard University Graduate School of Design—aims to present the diversity of design and research projects produced at the school. While bound by essentially the same format, each edition also puts forth a new context for reconsidering the work that it shows.

Each book has an editorial team, made up of a faculty member and a group of students, which bears the responsibility for selecting a representative sample of the outstanding recent work of the school. As editors, they also face the task of shaping the available content—literally hundreds of projects—into a book with its own coherence. In that sense, the making of this book is no different from any other year. But it is an exception, as they all have been.

Presenting a large number of projects in a publication is invariably a challenge. Part of this has to do with striking the right balance between a catalogue and a book—between the raw presentation of the work and its integration into an overarching interpretive model or taxonomic system. This year's *Platform* uses the concept of the index as a means to navigate the multiple layers of concepts incorporated within the work. By treating projects as exemplars, it subjects their readings and consequences to the logic of a larger context, that of the index.

The famous *Encyclopédie* of Diderot and D'Alembert, published between 1751 and 1777, was the Enlightenment's response to the prevailing religious orthodoxy. By challenging the historical authenticity of events documented in the Bible, it opened the way to a secularization of learning. In a similar fashion, *Platform: An Index of Design & Research* aims to partially decouple projects from the presupposed authenticity of their context and to relocate them within a broader nexus of affiliations and connections, so enriching the reader's knowledge of, and sensibilities toward, the design domain. And this, while always remaining mindful of Gustave Flaubert's musings in his unfinished satirical novel *Bouvard and Pécuchet* on the pitfalls of encyclopedic knowledge. Flaubert claimed to have read endlessly, perhaps over 1,500 books, in preparation for his intended masterpiece. The book is a great source for understanding the relationship between research and project, preparation and proposition.

The Harvard GSD is committed to the exploration of the creative imagination in aid of simultaneously advancing disciplinary knowledge and transformative social good. The work of our students and faculty, the cultural and intellectual life of the school, and its connections with the rest of the university are all manifestations of this aspiration. It is valuable to see individual projects with their own specific ideas and intentions set in relation to context of the school and to wider themes in the design domain. I am grateful to the editorial team, and to all the students, faculty, and staff whose efforts have made this edition of *Platform* such a rewarding and enriching experience.

LETTER FROM THE EDITOR

Zaneta H. Hong
Faculty Editor & Lecturer in Landscape Architecture

"Indeed, the purpose of an encyclopedia is to collect knowledge disseminated around the globe; to set forth its general system to the men with whom we live, and transmit it to those who will come after us, so that the work of preceding centuries will not become useless to the centuries to come; and so that our offspring, becoming better instructed, will at the same time become more virtuous and happy, and then we should not die without having rendered a service to the human race in the future years to come" —Denis Diderot & Jean le Rond d'Alembert, *Encyclopédie.*

The lineage of *Platform* is one of collecting, cataloging, and curating a rich, inspirational, and experimental body of research and design generated at the Harvard University Graduate School of Design. Within this framework, *Platform* provides a glimpse into the assemblage of diverse individuals, fields of inquiry, and modes of production that come to define the school over the course of a single academic year. *Platform 8* strives to not only extend this tradition, but also to make explicit its tacit role as an annual compendium of design knowledge and culture.

Incumbent upon each volume of *Platform* is the articulation of a criterion that guides the act of organizing and communicating both the products of design-research (the hundreds of projects, texts, and events) and the people that make them possible (the hundreds of students, faculty, staff, guest lecturers, and critics). Acknowledging the nature of design practice and research, which generates and refines knowledge by crossing disciplinary boundaries, *Platform 8* allows innate concepts and qualities organizational salience, uncovering new relationships, meanings, and potentials.

Structured as an encyclopedic survey in which entries are presented alphabetically, rather than hierarchically, *Platform 8* documents both scholarly discourse and material production as concomitant artifacts of contemporary practice, design education, and academic research. In keeping with the indexical approach of the publication, both text and image are presented as portraits of pedagogies, processes, and products of design.

Portraits are constructed representations, communicating a likeness of both actual and imagined subjects. The portrait's agency lies not only in its ability to capture and convey information, but also in its ability to supersede documentation by imbuing an authority and immortality to a specific reading of the subject's form, composition, and affect. In this sense, portraiture is not an act of replication, it is rather a process of selection and re-presentation—it is the creation of a new and coherent whole, both contingent upon and autonomous from its subject matter.

For me, this publication is an effort to simultaneously present an archaeological documentation into the working concepts of design and research—a reveal, exposing a particular moment of design culture at the Harvard GSD—and to provide a projective platform for defining new possibilities.

EXPLANATORY NOTES ON AN ENTRY

Seminars, Theses, Dissertations,
Lectures & Events, Exhibitions, Publications,
Centers, Initiatives, Research Labs, Student Groups

Entry heading ──────────────────────── PLATFORM

Entry definition(s)
Merriam-Webster Dictionary

1: Plan, design. 2: A declaration of the principles on which a group of persons stands, especially a declaration of principles and policies adopted by a political party or a candidate. 3: (a) A usually raised horizontal flat surface, especially a raised flooring; (b) a device or structure incorporating or providing a *platform*; especially such a structure on legs used for offshore drilling; (c) a place or opportunity for public discussion. 4: (a) A usually thick layer between the inner sole and outer sole of a shoe; (b) a shoe having such a sole. 5: (a) A vehicle used for a particular purpose or to carry a usually specified kind of equipment; (b) operating system, also the computer architecture and equipment using a particular operating system.

Entry type(s)
Book Launch
Campaign Launch
Colloquium
Competition
Conference
Exhibition
Film Screening
Lecture
(including Artist Talk,
Brown Bag Lunch,
GSD Talks Program,
Webinar Series)
Panel Discussion
Publication
Student Event
Symposium

Entry location(s)
7 Sumner
20 Sumner
40 Kirkland
42 Kirkland
Gund Hall
(including
Frances Loeb Library,
Piper Auditorium,
Stubbins, Chauhaus)

Entry category
Getty Art & Architecture
Thesaurus

Entry definition(s)
Getty Art & Architecture
Thesaurus

Platform mound, earthworks, engineering works: Artificial earthen mounds with a flat summit, intended to support a structure or activity. They were particularly prominent in the pre-Columbian American cultures. *Platform*, object genres by form: Flat surfaces, blocks, or floors, generally raised above the adjoining floor.

Date(s)

Entry title

Entry description

Usage of entry heading
in description

Platform. Publication. ActarD & Harvard GSD, 2009–2015.
The Harvard GSD has always recognized the indispensable importance and values of architecture, landscape architecture, urban planning, and urban design, yet has transcended their individual aspirations through intellectual cross-fertilization and collaboration. The Harvard GSD *Platform* series is reviewed and edited by a different faculty member every year. [§]

Participant(s)

Harvard GSD
GSD-related entry

Reference(s)
to related entry headings

See also FLOOR—see also INSTALLATION—see also LANDFORM—see also PRACTICE: Practice Platform Panel—see also PROJECT: South America Project—see also PUBLICATION—see also ROOF—see also SCALE—see also SURFACE—see also STRUCTURE.

The entries presented in *Platform 8* represent a terminology of topics and subject matter that are part of general design discourse. Each entry consists of a definition provided by the *Encyclopædia Britannica's Merriam-Webster Dictionary* and/or the *Getty Art & Architecture Thesaurus* (AAT). In addition, each entry definition is followed with specific usages of the term from selected course work, lectures, events, exhibitions, publications, research labs, centers, and initiatives at the Harvard University Graduate School of Design. The selection of entries were limited to the 2014–2015 academic year.

In particular to the entry definitions, the *Merriam-Webster Dictionary* was selected as it is the standard for the American English language and its usage. The Getty AAT, as an open-source classification system used by museum curators, librarians, archivers, cataloguers, researchers, and scholars, is a vocabulary that is specifically structured to the fields of architecture, fine arts, decorative arts, conservation, archeology, and material culture. Its 131,000 terms are organized by 34,000 organizing concepts, and each term is defined with descriptions and bibliographic citations.

EXPLANATORY NOTES ON AN ENTRY

Core & Option Studios

Entry heading ——————————————

CAMPUS

Entry category
Getty Art & Architecture Thesaurus

Entry definition(s)
Getty Art & Architecture Thesaurus

Campus, educational complexes: Grounds of colleges or universities, including the open space between or around the buildings. The term is also used to refer to the grounds of other building complexes with layouts similar to colleges.

Course title
2014–2015 course catalogue

A Campus for the 21st Century: The Purisima Alameda District of Monterrey. STU 1506. Department of Urban Planning & Design. Option Studio. Spring 2015. Instructors: Felipe Correa & Carlos Garciavelez Alfaro. Teaching Assistant: Jose Alexandro Medina (MAUD).

—— Course number

Department

Course type
*Core & Option Studios
Independent Study
Lecture
Seminar
Thesis
Workshop*

Semester & Year

Instructor(s)
(including coordinators, workshop instructors, speakers)

Teaching Assistant(s)
with degree program(s)

Course description
2014–2015 course catalogue and / or course syllabus

This option studio examined the role of the academic institution as a driver of an intermediate-scale urban project. The studio focused on how the *campus*, conceived as an open canvas for architectural and urban experimentation, can serve as a generator of new spatial relationships between institution and city within the Purisima Alameda District in downtown Monterrey, Mexico. For 2016, the Universidad Regiomontana has agreed to construct the first gateless university in Mexico. With the implementation of a new institutional model, the *campus* must reframe the relationship between the spaces of the academy, the neighborhood, and the city at large. A fresh institutional perspective, paired with significant investment in the university's *campus*, has an enormous potential to completely rethink the Purisima Alameda District and transform it into a new university city model for Monterrey and beyond.

Taking this new institutional development initiative as a point of departure, the students explored the agency of architecture and design in shaping a new *campus*—all in an effort to construct new spatial formats to rethink the space of the experimental *campus* for the 21st-century university.

—— Usage of entry heading in course description

Course roster
List of enrolled students with degree program(s)

Students: Radhya Ananta Adityavarman (MLA II), Hovhannes Balyan (MAUD), Joseph William Bivona (MLA II), Xiaoran Du (MLA I AP), Kevin Alton Gurley (MUP), Mary Angela Lange (MLA I AP), Mengdan Liu (MArch II), Lauren Gail McClellan (MArch I), Clayton C. Strange (MAUD), Stephen Sun (MArch II), Magdalena Valenzuela (MAUD), Yutian Wang (MAUD). §

—— Harvard GSD
GSD-related entry

Caption for entry figure(s)
with student(s) name(s) and degree program(s)

Figure. Model Inserts & Site Model (opposite page). Clayton C. Strange (MAUD).

See also EDUCATION—see also INSTITUTE—see also MODERN: More than Mere Practicality—see also WORK: Work Environments I.

—— Reference(s)
to related headings

LIST OF COLOR FIGURES

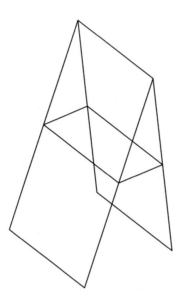

ACADEMIA

Academia, learning and scholarship concepts: The milieu and characteristics surrounding *academic* learning and university scholarship. Academies, educational institutions: Organizations or societies of learned individuals united for the advancement of art, science, or literature, intended to provide instruction, to engage in intellectual life or the practice of an art, to set standards, disseminate information, and to confer prestige on its members.

Harvard University Graduate School of Design. Since its founding, the Harvard University Graduate School of Design has been a crossroads of university learning and intellectual debate. Today, the school continues to build on that legacy, firm in the conviction that a multiplicity of voices and viewpoints is essential to its mission of imagining and shaping the future of the built environment. Just as the challenges we face are diverse, increasingly linked across cultural and geographic lines, so too must be our solutions and approaches. To foster innovation and bring about real change, we must ensure the expression of individual positions and come together across lines of difference. The simultaneous presence of these two conditions is at the heart of the Harvard GSD. To tackle the complex challenges of our time, students must be exposed to and understand a broad array of ideas, insights, and cultures. The Harvard GSD's degree and nondegree programs are built around the notion that cultural and contextual consciousness is essential to training the next generation of leaders. §

Academic Calendar. September 2, 2014: fall classes began. December 8–12, 2014: studio reviews. December 15–18, 2014: final exams. December 18, 2014: last day of fall semester. January 20, 2015: thesis reviews. January 26, 2015: spring classes began. May 4–8, 2015: studio reviews. May 11–12, 2015: final exams. May 13–15, 2015: thesis reviews. May 15, 2015: last day of spring semester. May 28, 2015: commencement. §

Academic Programs. Master in Architecture (MArch I, MArch I AP, and MArch II), Master of Architecture in Urban Design (MAUD), Master in Landscape Architecture (MLA I, MLA I AP, and MLA II), Master of Landscape Architecture in Urban Design (MLAUD), Master in Urban Planning (MUP), Master in Design Studies (MDes), Doctoral Programs (DDes & PhD), Loeb Fellowship Program, Executive Education, and History of Art & Architecture (HAA) undergraduate concentration. §

See also ARCHITECTURE—see also DESIGN—see also FACULTY— see also LANDSCAPE ARCHITECTURE—see also RESEARCH—see also STAFF—see also STUDENT—see also URBAN DESIGN—see also URBAN PLANNING.

ACHROMATIC

Achromatic color, hues or tints: Colors comprising hues that have been reduced in intensity by the addition of white, making pastel colors, such as cream and pink; or of black, producing the earth colors, such as mustard and moss green, or of both white and black, creating the neutralized hues, or color-tinged grays, such as oatmeal and charcoal.

ACOUSTICS

Acoustics, physics concepts, physical sciences concepts: Physics concepts dealing with the properties of sound.

ACTION

1: The initiating of a proceeding in a court of justice by which one demands or enforces one's right. 2: The bringing about of an alteration by force or through a natural agency. 3: The manner or method of performing, such as (a) an actor's or speaker's deportment or expression by means of attitude, voice, and gesture; (b) the style of movement of the feet and legs; (c) a function of the body or one of its parts. 4: An act of will. 5: (a) A thing done; (b) the accomplishment of a thing usually over a period of time, in stages, or with the possibility of repetition; (c) initiative, enterprise <a man of *action*>. 6: (a) An event or series of events forming a literary composition; (b) the unfolding of the events of a drama or work of fiction; (c) the movement of incidents in a plot. 7: (a) An operating mechanism; (b) the manner in which a mechanism or instrument operates. 8: The most vigorous, productive, or exciting activity in a particular field, area, or group <wants to be where the *action* is>.

Action, works of art: Direct, literal events carried out by artists, especially in Germany and Austria, attempting to destroy barriers between art and life; often brutal and obscene. *Action*, happenings, time-based works: Works from the 1950s and 1960s that were unique, unrehearsed events, often combining elements of theater, music, and the visual arts. Usually nonverbal, they may incorporate visual, tactile, and olfactory responses, chance, and audience participation. The term was coined by artist Allan Kaprow. Participatory *action* research, analytical functions: Collaborative research approach that incorporates those affected by the issues studied for the ends of education and taking *action* to effect change.

Design as Survival, Resistance & Transformative Action. Panel Discussion. Gund Hall, Piper Auditorium. November 20, 2014. Rouse Visiting Artist Fund. Lucy Orta, Joep van Lieshout, Rikke Luther, with Krzysztof Wodiczko (moderator).

The design practices that inspire social collaboration, participation, and coauthorship continue the avant-garde tradition of challenging outmoded thinking and perception while proposing and testing the visions of a beneficent social imagination. In this symposium, three artist-designers whose work critically reactivates this tradition presented and discussed their agendas, ideas, and projects. The panel explored methodological approaches and concepts such as critical design, discursive design, interrogative design, and transformative design: which are currently being investigated in the Art, Design and the Public Domain program at the Harvard GSD. ▧

See also ART—see also ADVOCACY—see also DOMAIN—see also FILM—see also PRACTICE—see also PROCESS—see also PROJECT—see also RESEARCH—see also TRANSFORMATION—see also VISIONARY.

ACTIVISM

1: A doctrine or practice that emphasizes direct vigorous action especially in support of or opposition to one side of a controversial issue.

See also ADVOCACY—see also BOOK: Books that Built Democracy—see also CONFLICT—see also DEMOCRACY—see also

FORUM—see also MATTER—see also PRACTICE—see also PROJECT—see also WORK.

ADAPTIVE REUSE

Adaptive reuse, use, functional concepts: The conversion of outmoded or unused structures, such as buildings of historic value, and objects, such as software, to new uses or application in new contexts.

Building Appreciation. Thesis. Tim Daniel Zeitler (MArch I), advised by Cameron Wu.

"*Adaptive reuse* navigates, interprets, and responds to existing buildings and their contexts. The resultant new work of architecture must confront and negotiate the realities of the existing built context. In *adaptive reuse*, it is usually advisable to start with a building worthy of *reuse*; perhaps it is solidly constructed, full of embodied energy, or built of materials that render it noble and worth preserving. Even when a sturdy starting point is given, the *adaptive reuse* of the project might be executed in a compliant, hesitant, or tentative manner. What happens when a temporary, cheaply constructed building is retained as the starting point instead? Typically, we might expect such a structure to simply be demolished to make way for an entirely new project, forgoing the process of *adaptive reuse*. But perhaps a building originally designed and constructed for expediency can, in its *reuse*, exert an unexpected influence on the architectural intervention that comes later.

If a simple building is given a new life through its reinterpretation, even the most unassuming building can come of age, appreciating to the level of architecture. We are used to appreciating works that we deem to be architecture, but we also might begin to change the way we look at the mundane buildings that exist everywhere in our world. Can an unremarkable, everyday building undergo, in its lifetime, an unpredicted period of appreciation—thereby gaining new value and agency in its new context? This thesis takes shape in the form of a new architecture school whose curriculum emphasizes the incorporation of a strong knowledge of building construction into the training of its students." ▧

See also BUILDING—see also COMPUTATION: Computation's Deep Ancestry—see also CONSTRUCTION—see also ECOLOGY: Projective Ecologies—see also ENERGY—see also MATERIAL—see also MEMORY—see also see also PERFORMANCE—see also PRESERVATION: Tax Credits & Adaptive Reuse—see also SUSTAINABILITY—see also TIME.

ADVENTURE

1: (a) An undertaking usually involving danger and unknown risks; (b) the encountering of risks <the spirit of *adventure*>. 2: An exciting or remarkable experience <an *adventure* in exotic dining>. 3: An enterprise involving financial risk.

Adventure story, document genres for literary works: Literary works in which action, physical danger, and suspense are key elements.

See also EXPERIENCE: Choose Your Own Adventure—see also RISK—see also WORK.

ADVOCACY

Advocacy, communication functions, functions by general context: Representing and supporting the interest of a person, group, project, or program.

Advocacy Student Groups. African American Student Union (AASU), American Society of Landscape Architects (ASLA) Harvard University Student Chapter, Community Development Project, Project Link, Queers in Design, Women in Design, and Working GSD. ֍

See also ACTION—see also COMMUNITY—see also JUSTICE— see also LINK—see also MATTER—see also PROJECT—see also REPRESENTATION—see also WORK.

AERIAL

Aerial photograph, photographs by picture-taking technique, visual & verbal communication: Photographs of the earth taken from aircraft.

Aircraft. Publication. The Studio Publications, 1935. Le Corbusier (author). Le Corbusier Research Collection, Frances Loeb Library. LeC NAC 8540 L496.
  "A celebration of flight: this book presents emerging aircraft technology through text and photography. Le Corbusier revels in the sheer beauty of airplanes, and in the advent of the *aerial* view. The book demonstrates man's conquest of the air and the possibility of a new way of looking at the world. The bird's-eye perspective enables a new 'plastic vision,' a new aesthetic. It also suggests a new scale of measurement, both in terms of space and time. For Le Corbusier, airplanes were the perfect demonstration of machinery and craftsmanship coming together." —Inés Zalduendo. ֍

See also AIR—see also AIRPORT—see also AVIATION: Flights of Imagination—see also COLLECTION—see also COMMUNI-CATION—see also DRONE—see also GEOGRAPHY—see also LANDFORM—see also MAPPING—see also OBSERVATION—see also PERSPECTIVE—see also PHOTOGRAPHY—see also POW-ER—see also REPRESENTATION—see also SCALE—see also TECHNIQUE.

AESTHETIC

Aesthetic concepts, philosophical concepts: Concepts related to perception of what is ideal or beautiful.

The Ruin Aesthetic: Episodes in the History of an Architectural Idea. HIS 4420. Department of Architecture. Seminar. Spring 2015. Instructor: Erika Naginski.
  Artifacts, fragments, vestiges, rubble, debris, detritus, wreckage: all this has prompted a venerable body of writings and objects that work the metaphor of ruin into anything from a template for the Sublime to a mechanism for iconoclastic violence. The course began by thinking about architecture and the vision of the past in the early modern period, considering a range of examples from the *Hypnerotomachia Poliphili* to antiquarian treatises. Students considered how the cult of the ruin has shaped nostalgia and dystopia in modern contexts. ֍

See also CONTEXT—see also DYSTOPIA—see also PERCEP-TION—see also SKYSCRAPER: Wood Skyscraper—see also STYLE—see also THERMODYNAMICS: Abalos + Sentkiewicz— see also VALUE—see also WRITING.

AFFORD

1: (a) To manage to bear without serious detriment <you can't *afford* to neglect your health>; (b) to be able to bear the cost of <can't *afford* to be out of work long>. 2: To make available, give forth, or provide naturally or inevitably <the sun *affords* warmth to the Earth>.

See also HOUSING.

AFFORESTATION

1: The act or process of planting a forest.

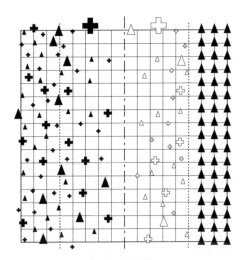

Colony & Homeland: Afforestation in Pre-State Israel. Thesis. Daniel Vladimir Rauchwerger (MDes, RR), advised by Sonja Dümpelmann.
  "Singular in its magnitude as a modern landscape architecture project, the process of Israel's *afforestation* in the 20th century is a deeply controversial one. Directly linked to Zionism, *afforestation* efforts in Israel were planned and executed by the Jewish National Fund (JNF), an organization established in Basel in 1901 as a land acquisition and development agency for future Jewish settlers in Palestine. It has since become a global fundraising machine that is responsible, among other things, for the planting of over 240 million trees in Israel.
  Even before the state was founded, the forest, in the case of the JNF, served as a state apparatus in the form of an infrastructural landscape—a projective, ecological network in its most simplistic form. To the European Zionist, the rocky terrain, sand dunes, swamps, and desertscapes that made up most of the indigenous Palestinian landscape seemed empty and barren. Biblical pathos and mythology of land redemption for the Jewish people relate to physical needs for shading and to a desire for an oasis in the Levant.

This thesis examines *ufforcstation* in pre-state Israel in its formative years of operation, until 1948. Linking the artificial and ideological foundation of the country's landscape to notions of memory, recreation, and security, it draws a map of forests that are hardly self-sustaining, much like Israel itself." §

Figure. Artifacts (previous page). Daniel Vladimir Rauchwerger (MDes, RR). Diagram (page 18). Christina Leigh Geros (MLA I AP & MAUD).

See also CONFLICT—see also CULTURE—see also DEVELOP-MENT—see also ENVIRONMENT—see also MEMORY—see also OPERATION—see also PLANT—see also SUSTAINABILITY.

AGENCY

1: (a) The office or function of an *agent*; (b) the relationship between a principal and that person's *agent*. 2: The capacity, condition, or state of acting or of exerting power. 3: A person or thing through which power is exerted or an end is achieved, instrumentality <communicated through the *agency* of the ambassador>. 4: An establishment engaged in doing business for another <an advertising *agency*>. 5: An administrative division, as of a government <the *agency* for consumer protection>.

New Geographies. Publication. Harvard University Press & New Geographies Lab.
New Geographies examines the emergence of the geographic—to articulate it to bear effectively on the *agency* of design. After more than two decades of seeing architecture and urbanism as the spatial manifestation of globalization, it is time to consider the expanded *agency* of the designer. Designers are increasingly compelled to shape larger scales and contexts, to address questions related to infrastructural problems, urban and ecological systems, and cultural and regional issues. These questions, previously confined to the domains of engineering, ecology, or regional planning, now require articulation through design. Encouraging designers to reexamine their tools and develop strategies to link attributes previously understood to be either separate from each other or external to the design disciplines, those questions have opened up a range of technical, formal, and social repertoires for architecture and urbanism.
In the past decade, different versions of landscape and infrastructural urbanism have emerged in response to similar challenges. This new condition of "the geographic" suggests more than a shift in scale. Much of the analysis in architecture, landscape, and urbanism—of emergent urban mutations and global changes on the spatial dimension—comes by way of social anthropology, human geography, and economics, and *New Geographies* extends these arguments by asking how design practice can have a more active and transformative impact on contemporary urban realities. The synthesizing role of geography—the physical, the economic, and the sociopolitical—is increasingly shared by design. *New Geographies* is interested in new associations or linkages between social and physical, form and context, the very large and the very small.
Through critical essays and design projects, the journal aims to open up discussions on the expanded *agency* of the designer, *agency* both as a form of capacity in relation to new techniques and strategies, and as a faculty of acting, power, and disciplinary repositioning. §

Social Agency Lab. Andy Gerhart, Brian Goldberg, Michael Hooper, and Andrew Perlstein. The Social *Agency* Lab studies the ways in which individuals, institutions, and organizations shape social outcomes in cities. §

See also ADAPTIVE REUSE: Building Appreciation—see also COM-PUTATION: Paradigms in Computing—see also DISCIPLINE—see also HYPEROBJECT: The Proximities of Nuclear Waste—see also IDENTITY—see also LAB—see also PRACTICE—see also PRODUC-TION: Tactics for a Coproduced City—see also SOCIAL.

AGE

1: (a) The time of life at which some particular qualification, power, or capacity arises or rests <the voting *age* is 18>; (b) one of the stages of life; (c) the length of an existence extending from the beginning to any given time. 2: A period of time dominated by a central figure or prominent feature <the *age* of Pericles>, such as (a) a period in history or human progress <the *age* of exploration>; (b) a cultural period marked by the prominence of a particular item <entering the atomic *age*>; (c) a division of geologic time that is usually shorter than an epoch. 3: (a) The period contemporary with a person's lifetime or with his or her active life; (b) a long time—usually used in plural <haven't seen him in *ages*>; (c) generation. 4: An individual's development measured in terms of the years requisite for like development of an average individual.

Aging & Place: Designing Housing and Communities for an Aging Population. Joint Center for Housing Studies Symposium. Gund Hall, Piper Auditorium. October 17, 2014.
According to the World Health Organization, the number of people aged 60 and over will double from 11 percent in 2006 to 22 percent by 2050; for the first time in history, older people will outnumber children. The world population is rapidly *aging*, and housing will play a central role in the well-being of older adults. This half-day event, organized by the Joint Center for Housing Studies, highlighted recent research and the latest innovations in design and policy, to understand and respond to the urgent needs of a global *aging* population. §

See also BODY—see also COMMUNITY—see also DEMOGRAPHY—see also DEVELOPMENT—see also HEALTH—see also HOUSING—see also PLACE—see also TIME—see also WELL-BEING.

AGORA

Agora, open spaces by location or context: In ancient Greek settlements, open spaces used as marketplaces or general public meeting places. For similar spaces in ancient Roman settlements, use "forums."

Agora MML: Reimaging La Merced Market as a New Landscape of Agricultural & Cultural Endeavors. STU 1406. Department of Landscape Architecture. Option Studio. Spring 2015. Instructor: Iñaki Echeverria. Teaching Associate: Adriana Chávez.
By 2050, about 30 cities will reach 20 million inhabitants each, but only three will be located in the so-called developed world. It may be argued that the future of the city and humanity is shared and not Western. This emergent condition demands new paradigms of city

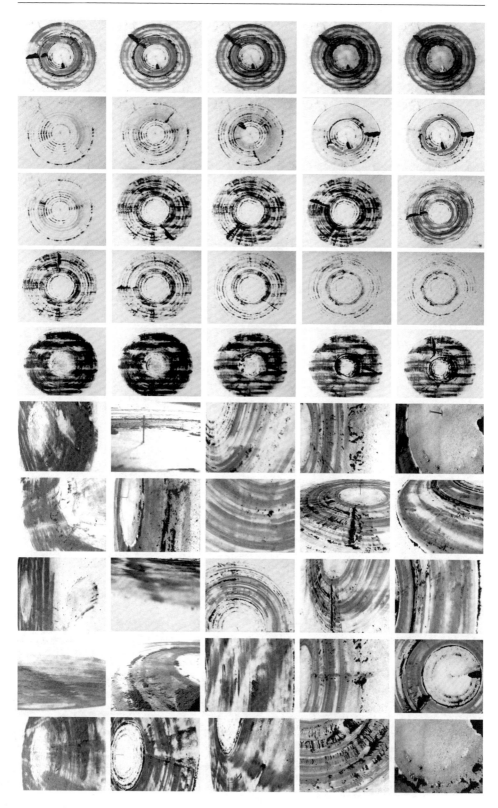

design, which architecture, landscape, and urbanism in a conventional sense cannot provide. In this context, multiple-scenario planning and hybridized techniques become potential fields for innovation. Students were expected to unlearn design techniques traditionally associated with landscape practice and city design. This openness granted the space to develop tools customized to their individual investigations. The proposed strategy sustained a dialogical relation rather than dialectic, both toward the site construct and to the aims of each individual investigation. A design without program emerged clearly at this stage. Probes of this design explored archetypal situations informal, spatial, and specific antropomorphical propositions that extended beyond the logic and mechanisms of conventional landscape design practice. Students addressed issues of atmosphere, form, culture, water and waste management, energy production and consumption, and responsible mobility.

Students: Shahab Yousuf Al Bahar (MLA I AP), Sourav Kumar Biswas (MLA I AP), Lisa Jane Caplan (MLA I), Bradley Paul Howe (MLA I), Hanul Kim (MLA I), Thomas Nideroest (MLA II), Natasha Emily Polozenko (MLA II), Dima Rachid (MLA II), Antonia Rudnay (MLA II), Flavio Stefano Sciaraffia Marquez (MLA I AP), Emily Elizabeth Wettstein (MLA I AP & MArch I), Hannes Zander (MLA II). ⌘

Figures. Drawings (page 21). Emily Elizabeth Wettstein (MLA I AP & MArch I). Section Elevation (previous spread). Thomas Nideroest (MLA II) & Hannes Zander (MLA II).

See also CITY—see also CULTURE—see also DEVELOPMENT—see also ECONOMY—see also FORUM—see also PLACE—see also PRODUCTION—see also SUPERMARKET—see also URBANISM.

AGRICULTURE

Agriculture, biological sciences, natural sciences: Science or art of cultivating the soil, harvesting crops, and raising livestock.

See also ECOLOGY—see also LAND USE—see also PLANT—see also SOIL—see also SURFACE: Dueling Surfaces—see also TERRAFORM: Terraforming Cultivation—see also WATER.

AIR

Air, atmosphere, combination inorganic/organic material: A mixture of gases comprising the Earth's atmosphere generally understood as that which is essential to the survival of land animals and plants.

Innovate. GSD Talks. Gund Hall, Stubbins. October 21, 2014. Iñaki Ábalos & Nerea Calvillo.

Contemporary ways of dealing with *air* pollution are generally focused on emissions and efficiency, on hygiene, and on control. This presentation aimed to open up other ways of taking *air* quality into account from an architectural perspective, questioning what is at stake from a conceptual, technical and design point of view. Thinking "with the *air*" challenged notions of sustainability, public space, digital infrastructures, and toxic environments, through steel boxes, bodies, markets, fines, maps, and many other agents of the aerial sociotechnical assemblage. ⌘

See also AERIAL—see also AIRPORT—see also BODY—see also ENVIRONMENT see also HYDROLOGY—see also PHENOMENON—see also PLANT—see also PROCESS—see also REPRESENTATION—see also SENSE—see also SYSTEM—see also TERROIR: Built Climates—see also TYPOLOGY: Air Frontier—see also VENTILATION: Supernatural Ventilation—see also WATER.

AIRPORT

Airport, air transportation complexes: Typically refers to large tracts of open, level land upon which runways, hangars, terminals, and other buildings have been constructed to allow for the takeoffs, landings, loading and unloading, and maintenance of aircraft. For smaller areas that have a runway but no or few additional facilities, use "airfields."

Airports in the Last Fifty Years. Lecture. Gund Hall, Piper Auditorium. March 3, 2015. Paul Andreu with Alastair Gordon & Charles A. Waldheim (moderators).

Airport designer Paul Andreu presented his work on *airports*. Alastair Gordon, architecture critic for the *Wall Street Journal* and author of *Naked Airport* engaged Andreu in conversation. ⌘

Airport Park Zurich: A New Park Typology. STU 1405. Department of Landscape Architecture. Option Studio. Fall 2014. Instructors: Martin Rein-Cano & Gareth Doherty. Teaching Associate: Jian He. Teaching Assistant: Eri Yamagata (MLA I).

Encircled by the rapid growth of the adjacent towns, the Zurich *airport* plays a broader role in the expanding urban development of the Glattal area. Due to its peculiar landscape situation and potential for new connections, the area offers the possibility to conceive a new typology of public space, an *airport* park, combining the *airport* with new program. The central task of the studio was to develop a new park typology related to the *airport*, envisioning this open space as an extension of the *airport* itself, developing a hybrid between city park and *airport* functionality. The studio explored the possibility for an *airport* to take a central role in urban development by proposing an *airport* park.

In the new *airport* park, innovative programs were introduced to link *airport* infrastructure to the urban fabric, overcoming the *airport* tendency for separation and bringing it closer to the city. The particular proximity of the site to the Zurich *airport* presents it as a possible generator of a new urbanity—as were 19th-century train stations, the *airport* can be understood as the new starting point of urban development. The adoption of a park as the first step in a city's development—similar to the role of the Central Park for the further settlement of New York—secures its open space quality. The new *airport* park serves as a gateway to the city and caters to the needs of both *airport* passengers and residents in nearby communities, mediating the separation between the *airport* and its city.

Students: Ian Scott Brennick (MLA I), Zheming Cai (MLA II), Sherry Szu Jung Chen (MLA I), Ken Chongsuwat (MLA I), Danika Cooper (MLA I AP & MDes, ULE), Peichen Hao (MLA I), Mary Angela Lange (MLA I AP), Zannah Mae Matson (MLA I), Lauren Elizabeth Micir (MLA I), Timothy Yung Wei (MLA I), Eri Yamagata (MLA I), Hyosun Yoon (MLA I AP), Sara Zewde (MLA I). ⌘

Figure. Models (opposite page). Peichen Hao (MLA I).

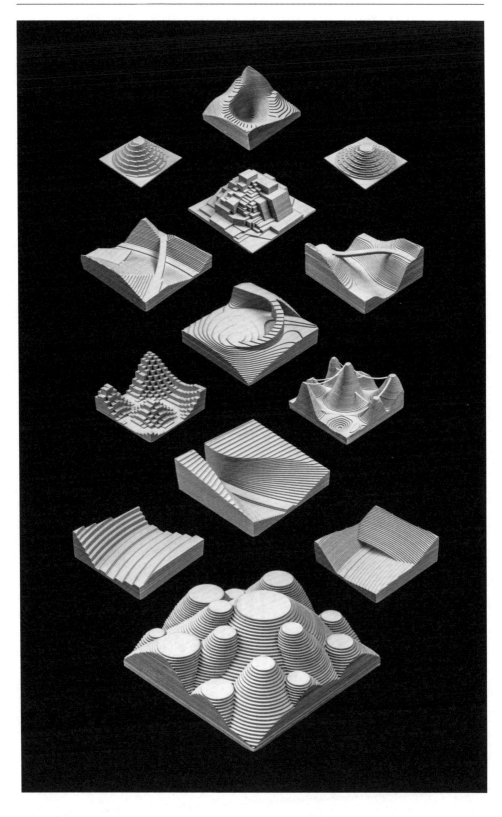

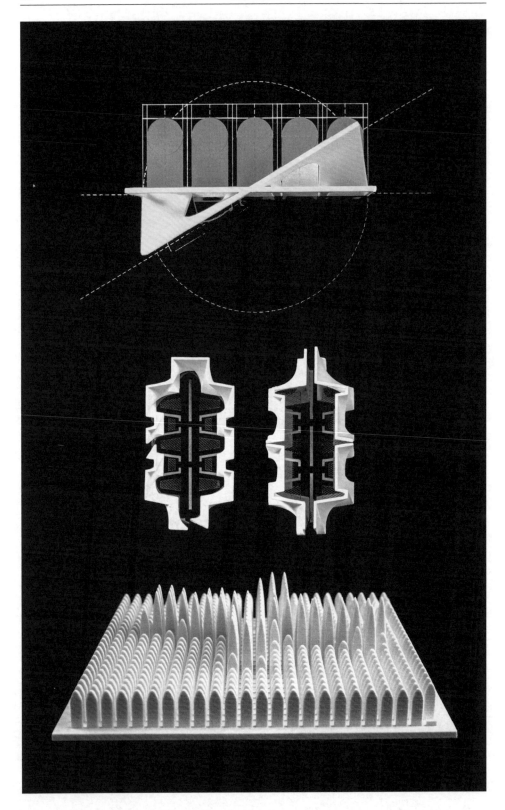

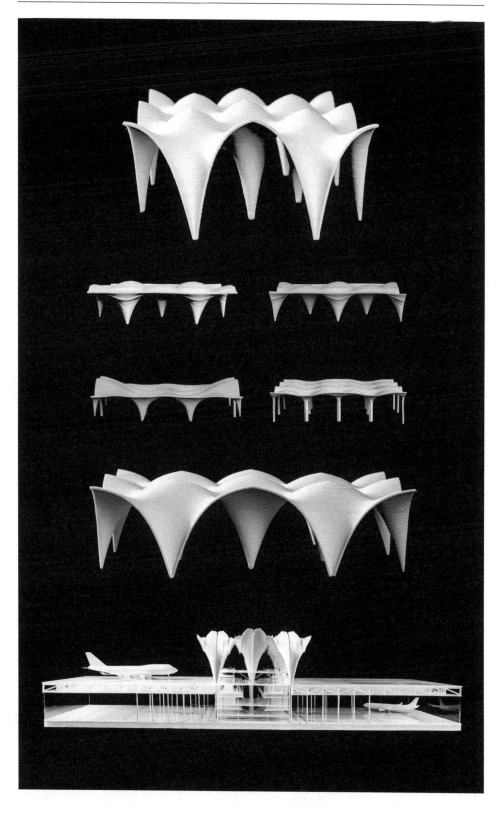

Dwelling in Stop-Over City: A Piranesian Guide.
Thesis. Joanie Tom (MArch I), advised by K. Michael
Hays & Eric Höweler.

"Piranesi's *Campo Marzio Ichnographia* portrays
simultaneously through fact and fiction a city more
ancient than ancient Rome and one that has yet to come.
Significantly, the map depicts not the heart of the ancient
capital but its western outskirts; Piranesi left the city
behind in order to reimagine it. Similarly, whereas it
began as an object situated in the hinterlands of important cities, the commercial *airport* has now expanded to
the point where an involution has occurred and the city
now finds itself both within the *airport* and shunted to
its periphery. The precise morphology of the *airport*-city
and the limits of its scale and contents remain unknown;
it is a proto-city in flux—a mutation of postmodern
hyperspace, which, according to Frederic Jameson, has
'finally succeeded in transcending the capacities of the
individual human body to locate itself.'

This thesis places Piranesi's *Campo Marzio* in dialogue
with the contemporary international *airport*. However,
rather than presenting a strictly backward-looking model
of historicism, a parity of sorts is reached between the
two subjects, eliding past and present. In this condition,
with past and present inextricably intertwined, the
abstractions of history are drawn out to impact design
of the present and to excavate latent mythologies of the
past." ⊕

Figure. Models (page 26). Joanie Tom (MArch I).

The New London Airport: Time & Space Reconsidered.
Thesis. Alexander Sarkis Karadjian (MArch I), advised
by Toshiko Mori.

"With Heathrow and Gatwick *Airports* operating at
almost 100 percent capacity, London is once again in
search of an alternative that would allow the city to
maintain its position as the leader in handling international air traffic. An additional runway at either of these
airports would only alleviate the situation temporarily,
which, when considered along with the fact that London's
air traffic is quite fragmented due to the use of five
airports serving the metropolitan area, clearly indicates
the pressing need for a more global solution than the
simple addition of a runway. It seems the right time for
the implementation of a radical new scheme for an
airport situated on the controversial site of the Thames
Estuary. With a projected capacity of 170 million passengers per year (almost twice the volume handled by
the busiest *airport* today, Atlanta Hartsfield-Jackson),
it is unreasonable to think that expanding *airports* or
constructing new ones can continue being a matter of
simple acquisition and development of more and more
land. My proposal, situated on the Hoo Peninsula in the
Thames Estuary, makes use of a sudden 30-meter drop
in the topography to position the runways at two different levels. Aircraft will taxi and park below and above
the ground, which will allow for an arrangement that
is twice as efficient as that of any current *airport* terminal building, thus ensuring a significant reduction in
flight-connection times. London will finally have an
airport that consolidates the region's air traffic and
operates 24 hours a day on a regular basis." ⊕

*Figure. Models (previous page). Alexander Sarkis Karadjian
(MArch I).*

See also AERIAL—see also AVIATION: Flights of Imagination—
see also BUILDING—see also CIRCULATION—see also CITY—see

also LAND USE—see also TRANSPORTATION—see also TYPOL-
OGY —see also URBANIZATION.

ALCOVE

Alcove, rooms and spaces by form: Use to designate small
recessed spaces off of larger rooms.

ALIENATION

1: A withdrawing or separation of a person or a person's
affections from an object or position of former attachment, estrangement <*alienation*...from the values of
one's society and family —S. L. Halleck>. 2: A conveyance
of property to another.

ALIMENT

1: (a) Food, nutriment; (b) sustenance <there was nothing
there of conversational *aliment*>.

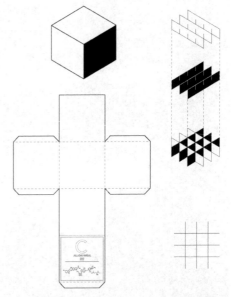

Alimentary Design. STU 1303. Department of Archi-
tecture. Option Studio. Fall 2014. Instructors: Shohei
Shigematsu & Christy Cheng. Teaching Assistant: Hung
Lai Wesley Ho (MArch I).

Food transcends cultural and temporal boundaries,
constitutes the largest industry in the world, and is an
inescapable and essential fundamental. Continuing the
work begun in Fall 2013, this studio investigated the
multiple scales and processes involved with food and
beverage, including specific topics such as the future of
agriculture and aquaculture, food security and the global
hunger epidemic, and culinary innovation in storage,
distribution, and production.

Rather than addressing one site or one program, each
student addressed an area of research to become the
authority on a particular issue related to architecture

and urbanism within the topic of food and beverage. Through this approach, the work became both diverse and comprehensive and enabled students to think beyond the typical boundaries of design. The research was developed in collaboration with the James Beard Foundation in New York, leading experts in the field, as well as with the Harvard Law School's Food Law and Policy Clinic.

Students: Cheuk Fan Au (MArch I), Sofia Blanco Santos (MArch II), Yu Chen (MArch I), Matthew Joseph Conway (MArch I), Christina Leigh Geros (MLA I AP & MAUD), Daniel Alexander Hemmendinger (MArch II), Patrick Kramer Herron (MArch I), Jina Kim (MArch II), Elizabeth Anna Lee (MArch I), Sicong Ma (MArch I), Paruyr Avetikovich Matevosyan (MArch I AP), Akihiro Moriya (MAUD), Haodi Grace Xu (MAUD). ⊛

Figures. Diagrams (page 28). Cheuk Fan Au (MArch I) & Patrick Kramer Herron (MArch I). Section (previous page). Haodi Grace Xu (MAUD).

ALLEE

Allee, walkways, open spaces by function: Walkways bordered by formally planted trees, clipped hedges, or shrubs; usually found in formal gardens or parks. For wide, straight, usually tree-lined roads or approaches, use "avenues." For walkways or narrow streets between and behind buildings in an urban environment, see "alleys (streets)."

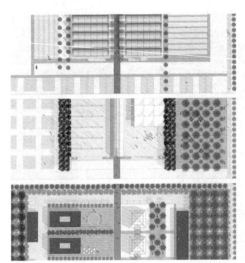

Figure. Plans (above). Lara Elisabeth Mehling (MLA I).

ALLEY

Alley, streets by form: Narrow streets, usually wide enough for only one vehicle or for pedestrians, passing between buildings or giving access off of main streets to back entrances or garages.

See also CIRCULATION—see also CITY—see also STREET—see also TRANSPORTATION.

ALTERNATIVE

1: *Alternate*. 2: Offering or expressing a choice <several *alternative* plans>. 3: Different from the usual or conventional, such as (a) existing or functioning outside the established cultural, social, or economic system <an *alternative* newspaper> <*alternative* lifestyles>; (b) of, relating to, or being rock music that is regarded as an *alternative* to conventional rock and is typically influenced by punk rock, hard rock, hip-hop, or folk music; (c) of or relating to *alternative* medicine <*alternative* therapies>.

Alternative Spatial Practices in Istanbul. Student Event. Gund Hall, Room 124. April 8, 2015. Club MEdiNA. ⊛

AMBITION

1: (a) An ardent desire for rank, fame, or power; (b) desire to achieve a particular end. 2: The object of *ambition* <her *ambition* is to start her own business>. 3: A desire for activity or exertion.

ANALOG

1: Of, relating to, or being an *analogue*. 2: (a) Of, relating to, or being a mechanism in which data is represented by continuously variable physical quantities; (b) of or relating to an *analog* computer; (c) being a timepiece having hour and minute hands.

See also COMMUNICATION—see also COMPUTER—see also DATA—see also DIGITAL—see also HYBRID—see also PHOTO-MONTAGE: Composite Landscapes—see also PROCESS—see also REPRESENTATION—see also SOFTWARE—see also SPACE: Terrestrial Analogues—see also TOOL—see also 2-D.

ANALYSIS

Analysis, analytic functions, functions by general context: Examining an object, action, material, or concept in detail by separating it into its fundamental elements or component parts, reducing something complex into its various simple elements. It is the opposite process to "synthesis." Spatial *analysis*: Statistical technique in which the spatial locations, distributions, and relations of designated factors are *analyzed*.

Market Analysis & Urban Economics. SES 5495. Department of Urban Planning & Design. Seminar. Fall 2014. Instructor: Raymond Torto.

This course was built upon the academic literature and the applied experiences that constitute the accumulated knowledge of urban and real estate economics and finance to address two questions: (1) How do urban land and real estate markets mature and function in the global macro-economy; and (2) how should a designer/developer/planner/investor *analyze* these markets both with regard to the macro and micro aspects of a specific project? The *analytical* tools introduced in the course are universal and need to be understood to know what the real estate market is telling us. The discussion of the tools and markets drew from current real estate market behavior and performance and examples from around the world. The course focused on the property and capital markets for the major commercial property types: residential, office, retail, and industrial. ֍

See also PRACTICE—see also PROCESS—see also QUALITA-TIVE—see also RESILIENCE: Creating Resilient Cities.

ANIMATION

Animation, image-making processes and techniques, techniques by type: Refers to the process of making still images appear to move, particularly by the technique of photographing drawings or objects in progressive stages of performing an action, so that movement is simulated when the images are projected as a series in quick succession.

Animation GSD. Student Group. *Animation* GSD is a collaborative experimenting with traditional and alternative spaces of visual storytelling. ֍

Animating Material. Thesis. Olga Lucia Mesa (MDes, Tech), advised by Allen Sayegh.
"The word *animation* comes from the Latin *animare*, 'to instill with life.' A sign associated with living organisms is transformation in response to external stimuli. Creating the illusion of movement in *animation* is thus central to conveying that something is alive. To actuate inanimate objects is a challenge not just for *animators* but also for designers across disciplines. Emerging technologies are pointing toward a reality in which objects respond to inputs around us. This thesis proposes *animation* technique as a medium for investigating an emergent approach to responsive material systems. Rather than seeking to achieve transformations by creating the illusion of movement, it is based on an understanding of the possibilities for actuation and response inherent within the system itself. In particular, it studies the potential that arises from coupling material composition, geometry, and the forces at play to achieve a particular behavior. I delve into the design limitations and possibilities granted by such an approach and explore its artistic expression. Following a discussion of fundamental concepts of action/reaction and an analysis of relevant precedents in both responsive systems and material-*animation* techniques, I offer a definition of principles and a methodology for implementing this technique. By manipulating paper with water to trigger transformation, a formal and performative vocabulary is developed and set into motion by a guiding narrative. Material affordances of kinetic nature are exploited to achieve nuances in the articulation of movement for the sake of formal expression and to convey emotional meaning. This effort intends to awaken our imagination and celebrate alternative ways of connecting to the world." ֍

See also ACTION—see also DRAWING: Animation Drawing—see also FILM—see also REPRESENTATION—see also TECHNIQUE.

ANTHROPOCENE

1: The period of time during which human activities have had an environmental impact on the Earth regard-ed as constituting a distinct geological age <Most scientists agree that humans have had a hand in warming Earth's climate since the industrial revolution—some even argue that we are living in a new geological epoch, dubbed the *Anthropocene.—Nature*, February 12, 2004>.

Eating in the Anthropocene. Lecture. Gund Hall, Room 124. October 8, 2014. Zack Denfeld & Cathrine Kramer.
Zack Denfeld & Cathrine Kramer of the Center for Genomic Gastronomy presented research and creative work on the organisms and environments manipulated by human food cultures. Project highlights included Glowing Sushi, Smog Tasting, the DeExtinction Deli, and the Spice Mix Super Computer. This lecture was organized in conjunction with the studio Alimentary Design, taught by Shohei Shigematsu & Christy Cheng. ֍

See also ALIMENT—see also BODY—see also FOOD—see also HUMAN—see also NUCLEAR: Fatal Vitality—see also SCALE—see also TIME.

ANTHROPOLOGY

Anthropology, behavioral sciences, social sciences, disciplines: The scientific study of human history in its biological, linguistic, and social aspects.

Design Anthropology: Objects, Landscapes, Cities. DES 3336. Department of Landscape Architecture. Seminar. Spring 2015. Instructor: Gareth Doherty.
In recent years, there has been a movement in *anthropology* toward a focus on objects, while design and planning have been moving toward the understanding of objects as part of a greater social, political, and cultural milieu. This seminar explored their common ethnographic ground. The course was both the *anthropology* of design and the design of *anthropology*.
Anthropologists were challenged to think about different forms of fieldwork by collaborating with non-*anthropologists* and working toward a collective ethnography; using visual information to represent ethnographic information and insights; and applying *anthropological* skills to the study of objects, materiality, and design processes. For designers, the goals were to learn thick ethnographic observation and description, to apply theoretical concepts in making connections between ethnographic data, and to move from ethnography to design proposals. ֍

APERTURE

1: An opening or open space.

Aperture, camera components, tool & equipment components: The opening that allows light to pass through an optical instrument, whether the image is to be fixed chemically on photographic materials or merely viewed as in a camera obscura. *Apertures* may be simple fixed holes, or of variable width or diameter achieved by mechanical means.

The Aperture Analyzed: The Form & Space of Openings. DES 3499. Department of Architecture. Seminar. Fall 2014. Instructor: Grace La.
This seminar focused on an essential component of architecture—the *aperture*—which has broad implica-

tions for our understanding of space. An *aperture* is commonly understood as a window or door, an element offering a controlled connection between interior and exterior in buildings. Simultaneously and more conceptually, an *aperture* is a frame, threshold, portal, passage, oculus, cleft, chasm, gap, valve, or void. Louis Kahn placed the *aperture* at the very center of our conception of space saying that, "architecture itself had begun 'when the walls parted and the columns became,' admitting light and creating a system of support at the same time." As a primary element of enclosure, the *aperture* frequently yields our most intimate contact with buildings, offering light, view, and ventilation. As a mechanism for engagement, the *aperture* provides a connection with the outdoors, both literal and phenomenal, serving as a conduit for movement through and access to architecture.

The term *aperture*, therefore, is profound and significant to our study. The seminar sought to explore the value of openings in three distinct, yet integrated ways: (1) functional power of illumination, ventilation, and view; (2) derivation of form and its relationship to structure and skin; and (3) the role in shaping public/private realms, defining spatial experience and the contours of our consciousness.

The course explored these issues through readings, analysis, and design. Students led and participated in discussions. Additionally, the seminar examined notions of the *aperture* in the work of such artists as Hopper, Vermeer, Turrell, and Pichler. Students then explored issues of the *aperture* through an *aperture* design project, focusing on the possibilities for the *aperture* to offer illumination and view, to develop tectonic and material conditions, and to imply territories of space and habitation. ▧

See also CIRCULATION—see also LIGHTING—see also OPENING—see also PHOTOGRAPHY—see also VENTILATION.

ARBOR

Arbor, garden structures, built works by location or context: Light, open structures either formed from trees, shrubs, or vines closely planted and twined together to be self-supporting or formed from a latticework frame covered with plants; generally less extensive and less substantial than "pergolas."

ARBORETUM

Arboretum, botanical gardens, gardens by function: Botanical gardens devoted to the cultivation and exhibition of trees and other woody plants, rare or otherwise.

The Arnold Arboretum. The Arnold *Arboretum* contributes to the advancement of society as an international center for the study of plants. Integrating eminent living and archival collections for discovery and dissemination of knowledge to the students of Harvard University, local educational institutions, and the public, the Arnold *Arboretum* is a premier destination for deepening understanding and appreciation of plants, horticulture, and biodiversity.

Established in 1872 and planned and designed in collaboration with Frederick Law Olmsted, the *arbore-*

tum is a National Historic Landmark and one of the best preserved of Olmsted's landscapes. Founded as a public-private partnership between the City of Boston and Harvard University, the Arnold *Arboretum* is a unique blend of respected research institution and beloved public park in Boston's Emerald Necklace.

Occupying 281 acres, the *arboretum's* living collection of trees, shrubs, and woody vines is recognized as one of the most comprehensive and best documented of its kind in the world. The living collection is supported by comprehensive curatorial documentation, herbaria containing more than 1.3 million specimens, extensive library and archival holdings, and a 43,000 square-foot state-of-the-art research center. These facilities and holdings, along with 75 full-time staff, provide the basis for research and education by Harvard faculty and students, *arboretum* scholars, and visiting scientists from around the world. Investigations focus on examining plant diversity from genomic, developmental, organismic, evolutionary, and ecosystem perspectives.

See also COLLECTION—see also DIVERSITY—see also ECOL-OGY—see also GARDEN—see also LANDSCAPE ARCHITEC-TURE—see also NEIGHBORHOOD—see also PALIMPSEST—see also PLANT—see also RESEARCH—see also SYSTEM—see also TECHNIQUE.

ARCADE

Arcade, structural assemblies, structural elements: Series of arches on the same plane and carried on piers, columns, or pilasters; either free-standing or attached to a wall (a "blind *arcade*"). The term is also used to denote a covered avenue with shops on one or both sides, which originally was set within an architectural *arcade*.

ARCH

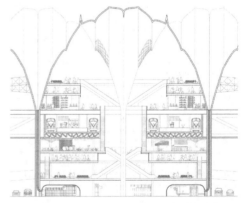

1: A typically curved structural member spanning an opening and serving as a support, as for the wall or other weight above the opening. 2: (a) Something resembling an *arch* in form or function, especially either of two vaulted portions of the bony structure of the foot that impart elasticity to it; (b) a curvature having the form of an *arch*. 3: *Archway*.

Figure. Section (above). Alexander Sarkis Karadjian (MArch I).

trust me
I'm an architect

ARCHITECT

Architect, people in the visual arts, people by occupation: People trained in or practicing architecture, which is the art of designing and building habitable structures, especially those considered to have aesthetic value.

Figure. Photograph (above). Renzo Piano.

ARCHITECTURE

Architecture, visual arts, disciplines: The art or science of designing and building structures, especially habitable structures, in accordance with principles determined by aesthetic and practical or material considerations. For a general term for the actual structures or parts of structures that were made by human beings, use "*architecture* (object genre)."

Architecture for Everyone. Open House Lecture. Gund Hall, Piper Auditorium. November 14, 2014. Tobias Armborst, Daniel D'Oca, and Georgeen Theodore.

Interboro, the New York City-based *architecture*, planning and research firm of three Harvard GSD graduates—Tobias Armborst, Daniel D'Oca, and Georgeen Theodore—welcomed prospective students and the Harvard community to the Harvard GSD with a call to arms in their lecture "*Architecture* for Everyone."

Interboro concluded with a powerful and provocative invitation, not only for prospective students but also for current students, practitioners, and professors in the audience: "We hope that if you decide to study *architecture*, landscape *architecture,* or urban planning and design, you will fully embrace the idea that these disciplines are more fun, more interesting, more relevant, and more fair when they meaningfully engage the opinions, practices, and idiosyncrasies of others." ⊛

Department of Architecture. The Department of *Architecture* is rich in diversity, creativity, and scholarship. With an international faculty prominent across the breadth of the field, students are exposed to many different approaches to design. Critics and theorists from around the world supplement the faculty, and together, they introduce students to issues and trends in contemporary *architectural* design.

List of Degrees: Master in *Architecture* (MArch I), Master in *Architecture* Advanced Placement (MArch I AP), and Master in *Architecture* Post-Professional (MArch II). Department Chair: Iñaki Ábalos. Program Director: Grace La. Program Coordinator: Ryan Gregory Jacob. Assistant to the Chair: Andrea Croteau. Staff Assistant: Kim Gulko. Students: 238 MArch I candidates, 36 MArch I AP candidates, and 89 MArch II candidates. ⊛

Vers une architecture. Publication. Éditions G. Crès, 1923. Le Corbusier (author). Le Corbusier Research Collection, Frances Loeb Library. LeC NA 2500 L496v 1923.

"Reyner Banham stated that *Toward an Architecture* is probably the most influential and least understood books on *architecture* of the 20th century. With a photograph of the steamboat *Aquitania* on its cover, the images and text are deliberately presented in combinations and oppositions intended to lead toward a different understanding of *architecture*. Concepts of volume, surface, and plan are followed by chapters on boats, planes, and cars. The book raises analogies between classical *architecture* and the logic of industrial production. The mistranslation of the title to English (and of much of the text) contributed to the timid reception of Le Corbusier's ideas in the English-speaking world in the 1930s. John Goodman's 2007 translation is a celebration of good translation, and includes an excellent introduction by Jean-Louis Cohen. This is the book that defines *Architecture* as the masterful, correct, and magnificent play of volumes in light." —Inés Zalduendo. ⊛

ART

Art, visual arts, disciplines: Refers to objects, environments, or experiences (as in performance *art*) that are visual in nature, were created by the use of skill and imagination, and possess an aesthetic that is valued and of a quality and type that would be collected by *art* museums. It may refer to the study or practice of the fine *arts* or the fine and decorative *arts* together. With reference to the visual and performing *arts* together, use "*arts*."

Post Facto. Master in Design Studies (MDes) Art, Design and the Public Domain and Loeb Fellowship Program Event. Gund Hall, Studio Trays. April 10, 2015. Michael Craig-Martin.

Master in Design Studies candidates from the *Art*, Design and the Public Domain concentration at the Harvard GSD "made the building sing" as part of their "Post Facto" collaboration with Senior Loeb Fellow and artist Michael Craig-Martin. Improvisational jazz musicians used Gund Hall's unique sonic and performative qualities to create a new architectural experience based on Bauhaus concepts of building a community through performance. Starting in scattered corners of the building, musicians playing brass, woodwinds, and strings navigated across the studio trays, shifting the collective focus toward the possibilities of what can transpire through spontaneity.

Musicians: Gabe Gladstein (FAS) on violin, Caetano

Hanta-Davis (FAS) on alto saxophone, Jacob Lurye (FAS) on drums, Ryan Park-Chan (FAS) on tenor saxophone, Jonah Philion (FAS) on alto saxophone, Aditya Raguram (FAS) on keyboard, Gary Smiley on trumpet, and Rose Whitcomb (FAS) on clarinet. The event was organized by students in the Art, Design and the Public Domain seminar, including: Kritika Dhanda (MDes, ADPD), Maria Jaakkola (Loeb), Tamara Jafar (MUP), Jiyoo Jye (MDes, ADPD), Marcia Soviak (FAS), Scott Michael Valentine (MDes, ADPD). §

Figure. Photograph (above). Post Facto. Gabe Gladstein (FAS) & Caetano Hanta-Davis (FAS).

See also AUDIOVISUAL—see also DOMAIN: Master in Design Studies (MDes) Art, Design and the Public Domain (ADPD)—see also EXPERI-ENCE—see also FOLLY: Torqueing Spheres—see also MUSEUM—see also PRACTICE—see also SOUND—see also WORK.

ARTICULATORY

1: Of or relating to *articulation*.

Articulatory Urbanism. Urban Planning & Design Lecture. Gund Hall, Room 124. April 20, 2015. Felipe Hernández & Rahul Mehrotra.

The concept of *articulation*, which has a long trajectory in geography, philosophy, social studies, and cultural theory, has had a much lesser impact on urban studies and architecture. In the work of Cities South of Cancer (CSC), the research group created and chaired by Felipe Hernández at the University of Cambridge, *articulation* has inherent potential for the study of the impact of subaltern agencies in the continuous development of cities. This talk explored the notion of *articulatory* urbanism, both theoretically and through the work of the CSC in various developing-world cities: Cali and Pereira (Colombia), Jakarta (Indonesia), Queretaro (Mexico), and Nanjing (China). The CSC proposes an approach to urbanism geared toward *articulation* rather then absorption

and eradication. It seeks to strategically *articulate* diverse and often antagonistic elements in order to reconfigure the notion of city, helping to improve conditions of life for people in conflict-ridden communities. §

ARTIFACT

Artifact, object genres, object classifications: Generally, objects made or modified by humans, typically manually portable products of human workmanship, such as tools, utensils, objects for personal adornment, or art, as distinguished from natural remains. In the context of technical and medical research, for a spurious result that is a product or effect resulting from the experimental technique or procedure itself, use "experimental *artifact*."

See also ANTHROPOCENE—see also ASSEMBLY—see also COL-LABORATION: The Calumet Collaborations—see also CONSTRUC-TION—see also EXPERIMENT—see also NATURE: Another Na-ture—see also OBJECT—see also PATTERN: R. Buckminster Fuller, Pattern Thinking—see also RESEARCH—see also RESPONSIVE: Responsive Environments & Artifacts—see also WORK.

ARTIFICE

1: (a) Clever or artful skill; ingenuity <believing that characters had to be created from within rather than with *artifice* —Garson Kanin>; (b) an ingenious device or expedient. 2: (a) An artful stratagem; (b) false or insincere behavior <social *artifice*>.

Maker, people by activity: Those who bring about or construct artifacts directly by their own labor, especially as their craft or profession. For industrialists who own or run a manufacturing plant, use "manufacturers." For those who practice an occupation, trade, or pursuit requiring manual dexterity or artistic skill, use "craftsmen."

ASSEMBLAGE

Assemblage, sculpture technique, processes and techniques: A contemporary technique of creating a three-dimensional work of art by combining various elements, especially found objects; may include elements painted, carved, or modeled by the artist. Originally coined in 1953 by artist Jean Dubuffet.

ASSEMBLY

1: A company of persons gathered for deliberation and legislation, worship, or entertainment. 2: A legislative body, specifically the lower house of a legislature. 3: A meeting of a student body and usually faculty for administrative, educational, or recreational purposes. 4: A signal for troops to *assemble* or fall in. 5: (a) The fitting together of manufactured parts into a complete structure or unit of a machine; (b) a collection of parts so *assembled*.

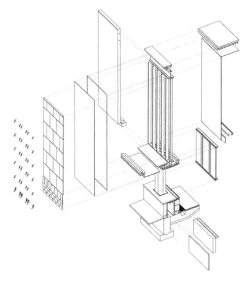

Figure. Exploded Detail (above). Yiliu Chen Shen-Burke (MArch I).

See also CONSTRUCTION—see also FORUM—see also GARDEN: *Third Natures*—see also LANDFORM: *Landformation Catalogue*—see also MACHINE—see also OBJECT: *Common Objects*—see also PROCESS—see also TECHNIQUE.

ATLAS

Atlas, cartographic materials, graphic document genres: Volumes of maps, with or without descriptive text, which may be issued to supplement or accompany texts or be published independently.

Form & Pedagogy: The Design of the University City in Latin America. Lecture. Gund Hall, Portico 123. October 28, 2014. Carlos Garciavelez Alfaro.

Of the 20th-century large-scale urban interventions inscribed into the Latin American city, the university campus is the most salient symbol of progress. Carlos Garciavelez Alfaro spoke about his research, examining the urban and architectural structure and legacy of the principal Latin American campuses built in the past 60 years. The culmination of his work is a campus *atlas* that traces and details the historical and current state of the University City and links these individual campuses in a de facto Pan-American project. ﹩

Territorial Organization beyond Agglomeration: Toward an Atlas of the Global Hinterland. SES 5406. Department of Urban Planning & Design. Seminar. Spring 2015. Instructor: Nikolaos Katsikis.

This research seminar began with an understanding of urbanization as a process of generalized territorial organization where cities, metropolises, and megalopolises are the focal points in the utilization of the whole Earth by humans. Building upon the agenda of Planetary Urbanization—under development at the Urban Theory Lab—the seminar investigated how the global system of agglomerations are responsible, through their multi-scalar metabolic interdependencies, for the organization of most of the 75 percent of the Earth's developed surface. The goal of the seminar was to challenge the agency of designers to systematically engage with, spatialize, and chart the organizational contours of this rather obscure "global hinterland"—the patterns, typologies, distribution, and equipment of specialized landscapes of production, extraction, and waste disposal, and their logistical coordination through dense infrastructural networks. ﹩

Urban India Atlas. Research Project. The Urban India *Atlas* project is a long-term critical assessment of emergent patterns of urban growth in India. The investigation applies a range of spatial analysis techniques to better understand the logic (or lack thereof) behind urban, regional, and national development, and arrive at conclusions regarding future patterns of growth. ﹩

ATMOSPHERE

Atmosphere, combination inorganic/organic material, materials by composition: The gas and aerosol envelope that extends from the ocean, land, and ice-covered surface of a planet outward into space; used especially in reference to the Earth where it is held by the force of gravity.

See also AIR—see also BUILDING: *High-Rise, High-Density*—see also ENVIRONMENT—see also SENSE—see also VISIONARY: *Grounded Visionaries*.

AUDIOVISUAL

Audiovisual materials, information artifacts by physical form: Nonprint materials, such as slides, transparencies, motion pictures, or filmstrips, that make use of sight and sound to convey information; refers especially to such materials when used for instruction.

Six Microphones. Exhibition. Carpenter Center for the Visual Arts. April 8–19, 2015. Robert Gerard Pietrusko.

"Six Microphones" was a piece composed entirely of *audio* feedback that explored the mutually-constitutive relationship between sound, space, and body. Departing from the simplest and most legible diagram of audio feedback. The installation transformed the gallery from a space in which sound simply propagates, to the medium required to bring sound into being. It became the interior of a complex oscillator whose sonic textures are dependent on the gallery's geometry and materiality.

AUGMENTED REALITY

Augmented reality, virtual reality, computer science concepts: The use of digital technology to overlay visual real-life representations, usually provided through video, with computer-generated data.

See also HOLOGRAM: Fragments of a Hologram House—see also PERCEPTION—see also REALITY—see also VIRTUAL.

AUTONOMOUSMOBILE

The (Love) Affair: Architecture & the Autonomousmobile. Thesis. Peter Duncan Sprowls (MArch I AP), advised by Jeffry Burchard.

"The love affair between architecture and the car cannot be stopped, only evolved. Over time, these two characters have affected and accommodated each other in many ways, producing cities like children—big and small, hyperactive and quiet, wide and tall. As we witness a radical shift in the design of the car toward autonomy and interconnectivity, it is architecture's responsibility to craft the physical environment of the driverless car's invisible system. The next love child will be like none before. It is best to glimpse the form of this new city through the moments when architecture and the *autonomousmobile* are most intimate or, put another way, when they see each other most often. This thesis proposes six projects that examine how specific architectural typologies could evolve to draw boundaries around a system that is illegible to the pedestrian and immune to the constraints of the driver. These boundaries propose new relationships between architecture and the street, redrawing the diagram of the city. Unbuckle and shift to drive." ※

Figure. Model (above). Peter Duncan Sprowls (MArch I AP).

AVIATION

Flights of Imagination: Aviation, Landscape, Design. Publication. University of Virginia Press, 2014. Sonja Dümpelmann (author). TL725.3.L6 D86 2014.

In *Flights of Imagination*, Sonja Dümpelmann follows the evolution of airports from their conceptualization as landscapes and cities to modern-day plans to turn decommissioned airports into public urban parks. Dümpelmann discusses landscape design and planning activities that were motivated, legitimized, and facilitated by the aerial view. She also shows how viewing the Earth from above redirected attention to bodily experience on the ground and illustrates how design professionals understood the aerial view as simultaneously abstract and experiential, detailed and contextual, harmful and essential.

Along the way, Dümpelmann traces this multiple dialectic from the 1920s to land-camouflage activities during World War II, and from the environmental and landscape planning initiatives of the 1960s through today.

See also AERIAL—see also AIR—see also AIRPORT—see also CIRCULATION—see also IMAGINATION—see also LANDSCAPE—see also MODERNITY—see also PHOTOGRAPHY—see also TRANSPORTATION.

AXIS

Axis, geometric concepts, mathematical concepts: Fixed reference lines for the measurement of coordinates. Vanishing *axis*, perspective-relating concepts, visual & verbal communication: The *axis* toward which parallel lines converge in an *axial* perspective system.

AXONOMETRIC

Axonometric projection, image: Refers to drawings or works in another two-dimensional medium, where the image is created by using *axonometric* projection, which is a system of portraying a three-dimensional object by depicting projectors parallel to each other and generally where at least one of the three spatial axes is inclined to the plane of projection. In modern architectural parlance, the term sometimes refers only to drawings depicted as if an orthographic rendering of the object has been tilted to the plane.

From Mono to Multi. STU 1320. Studio Project. Haotian Tang (MArch II), advised by Mack Scogin.

"By decentralizing the subject, the reading of a circular structure can be converted into a linear one. By synchronizing from the exterior, the interpretation of a linear structure can be transformed into a circular one. Within the changing procession of viewing the perception of the whole and the identity of parts, as well as through the aggregation of spectacles, the opposition and equilibrium between origin and its flow never cease. From one to multiple, the operation of transformation acts, blurring time and blurring lines.

The project is based on an ontological spatial description that reveals connections between memory, time, experience, methodological interpretation and design instinct. According to the narrative, the site we picked, the characters assigned to us, the entire design process spanned from rhetorical spatial narration to character-specific strategy, from the theoretical to the architectural, and from abstraction to the secondary reality." ※

Figure. Drawing (opposite page). Haotian Tang (MArch II).

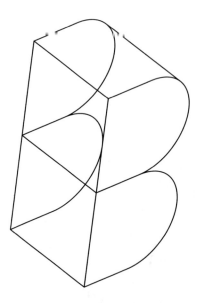

BALANCE

Balance, compositional concept: The impression of visual equilibrium in a composition. *Balance*, scales, weighing devices by form: Scales with a horizontal bar pivoting about a central fulcrum, creating equal-length arms; suspended from the ends of the arms are pans or baskets, in one of which is placed the item being weighed and in the other, a premeasured weight.

Balance. Lecture. Gund Hall, Piper Auditorium. October 2, 2014. Annabelle Selldorf.
   Annabelle Selldorf is known for outstanding new projects and sensitive restorations of existing buildings. She discussed recent projects that demonstrate the programmatic scope of Selldorf Architects, including the David Zwirner Gallery, the first LEED-certified commercial art gallery in the United States, and Sunset Park Material Recovery Center, a recycling plant and public education center on the Brooklyn waterfront. ⊛

BALCONY

Balcony, rooms and spaces by form: Railed platforms projecting from the exterior walls of buildings. Use also for similar interior features, when small. For larger platforms which extend the length of one side of a room or are recessed behind an arcade, use "galleries (upper level spaces)."

GSD Balconies. *Balconies* are located at the north and south ends of the Harvard GSD studio trays. ⊛

See also BUILDING—see also ELEMENT—see also GALLERY—see also PLATFORM.

BEAUTY

1: The quality or aggregate of qualities in a person or thing that gives pleasure to the senses or pleasurably exalts the mind or spirit. 2: A *beautiful* person or thing; especially a *beautiful* woman. 3: A particularly graceful, ornamental, or excellent quality. 4: A brilliant, extreme, or egregious example or instance <that mistake was a *beauty*>.

BEAUX ARTS

Beaux Arts, modern European architecture styles and movements, styles and periods: Refers to the style of architecture and city planning originally taught at the *Ecole des Beaux Arts* in Paris and at other schools in the United States in the 19th and 20th centuries. The style is characterized by an emphasis on the harmonious composition of elements that form a classical whole, the revival of baroque and neoclassical styles, and cities laid out geometrically with wide, grand streets.

Beaux Arts Ball. Student Event. The Liberty Hotel. Boston, Massachusetts. March 28, 2015.
   Each spring students pitch themes in the form of a poster contest for the *Beaux Arts* Ball, and the favorite is decided by popular vote. ⊛

BEE

Bee, Apoidea superfamily: Members of a superfamily containing more than 20,000 living species of flying insects in eight families, including primitive wasp-like

bees, solitary *bees*, and *bees* that live in colonies, some of which are valued by humans as pollinators and producers of honey and wax.

GSD Bees. Student Group. GSD *Bees* manages the health and productivity of the resident honeybees on the roof of Gund Hall, aiming to increase the beekeeping capacity of the university, advance knowledge of *bees* and beekeeping within the design disciplines, and act as a conduit to other beekeeping efforts and studies across Harvard University. ⑨

BEER

1: An alcoholic beverage usually made from malted cereal grain (as barley), flavored with hops, and brewed by slow fermentation. 2: A carbonated nonalcoholic or a fermented slightly alcoholic beverage with flavoring from roots or other plant parts <birch *beer*>. 3: Fermented mash. 4: A drink of *beer*.

Beer & Dogs. Student Group & Event. Gund Hall, Chauhaus, most Fridays at 6:30 p.m. *Beer* & Dogs is a student group committed to connecting Harvard GSD students to one another through a weekly Friday social event. It provides a break for students from the demanding and monotonous weekly schedule at the Harvard GSD as well as a way to meet students from other disciplines within the school. Free *beer*. ⑨

BIOPHILIA

1: A hypothetical human tendency to interact or be closely associated with other forms of life in nature.

Suspicious Biophilia: Organic Growth, Winning Proposal City of Dreams Competition. Event. Gund Hall, Room 121. April 17, 2015. Spain GSD & Ecological Thinking. Izaskun Chinchilla. ⑨

BLACK

Black, color, neutrals, hues or tints: Universal Color Language (UCL) standard color name identifying a range of *blackish* colors. More specifically, *black* is an achromatic color of maximum darkness, referring to objects having little or no hue owing to the absorption of almost all light in the visible spectrum. In the context of pigments, *black* is theoretically the mixture of all

colors. In the context of colors of light, *black* is the absence of light.

BLOCK

City *block*: Pieces of land within urban areas usually bounded on all sides by streets or other transportation routes, natural physical barriers, or public open space and not traversed by through streets. Gage *block*, size measuring devices, distance measuring devices: Hardened steel *blocks* having two flat, parallel surfaces with the parallel distance between the surfaces marked to a guaranteed accuracy of a few millionths of an inch; used in manufacturing processes as a precise measuring standard. Slab *block*: Medium- or high-rise buildings having smaller depth compared to their length and usually to their height; use to distinguish from "point *blocks*," which are usually tower-like in form and built around a central circulation core. Super *block*: Designates very large, usually residential, city *blocks* often formed by consolidating several smaller *blocks* and often barred to through traffic and crossed by pedestrian walks.

Figure. Diagrams (above). Shiyang Chen (MArch I).

See also CITY—see also FLOATING: Floating Cities—see also GRID—see also HEALTH: Life-Styled, China-Town—see also MEASURE—see also PRECISION—see also TYPE: Blob Block Slab Mat Slat—see also URBAN.

BLUR

1: A smear or stain that obscures. 2: Something vaguely or indistinctly perceived; especially something moving or occurring too quickly to be clearly seen.

Blur, conditions and effects by specific type: The condition, as it applies to optical phenomena and images in any medium or on any support, of being visually indistinct or hazy in outline or detail.

Blur. Thesis & James Templeton Kelley Prize. Meng Li (MArch I AP), advised by Mack Scogin.
"On Gerhard Richter's *Blur*: During Art Basel this summer, I visited Fondation Beyeler for the Gerhard Richter exhibition, curated by Hans Ulrich Obrist. The works of the artist, especially the *blurry* figurative paintings, are reflections of reflections, representations of representations and reproductions of reproductions. Such as in the work of *Annunciation After Titian* (1973), each incarnation loses more and more of its definition

and eventually, any figuration has altogether been reduced to a *blur* of color. The act of *blurring* is a process of the removal

For Richter, a person or an event of the past in an atlas fades from the memory and is eroded by anonymity precisely because it is 'correctly' recorded. Today we can hardly recall who the person portrayed in yesterday's photograph is supposed to be; 'Did grandma really look like that?' The photograph of the young girl is supposed to be of a grandmother 60 years earlier, or so the parents tell the grandchild. In another 60 years the photograph will merely show an anonymous portrait of a young girl, no longer a grandmother, for nobody will know whether the photograph bears any resemblance to the original person. In contrast, the portrait of a young girl is out of focus, is free of a preexisting reference and therefore becomes immediately present. Where form ends, aura returns.

On Architecture: However, unlike paintings, if architecture fundamentally consists of the making of three-dimensional spaces, it is, then, problematic to reduce architecture to mere visual representations and it is dangerous for architects today to unconsciously equate the art of space-making to the making of two-dimensional surfaces. Therefore, the *blur* for architecture, cannot be reduced to a mere technique of literally creating fog around the building to dissolve its form. Architecture is the most archaic act of constructing. Let it be a mountain, a cave, or a hut. It cannot escape from form. The goal of a *blur* in architecture is not to overcome form. Instead, to *blur* is to bring back the lost aura of the place.

Martin Heidegger used a bridge to explain how a building gathers the seemingly contradictory notions of earth and sky, of mortality and the divine, which allow a location to come into existence. Heidegger's bridge is physical, in allowing the body to experience the crossing of a river or an abyss, but it is also an intellectual construct that renders the ambiguity of connectedness and separation visible. Neither a mere phenomenon nor a thing-in-itself, it is constituted as antinomy between the two. This is the *blur*." §

Figure. Drawing (previous spread). Meng Li (MArch I AP).

BODY

1: (a) The main part of a plant or animal *body* especially as distinguished from limbs and head; (b) the main, central, or principal part. 2: (a) A mass of matter distinct from other masses <a *body* of water>; (b) something that embodies or gives concrete reality to a thing, a sensible object in physical space; (c) aggregate, quantity <a *body* of evidence>. 3: (a) The part of a garment covering the *body* or trunk; (b) the main part of a literary or journalistic work; (c) the sound box or pipe of a musical instrument. 4: A group of persons or things, such as (a) a fighting unit or force, (b) a group of individuals organized for some purpose <a legislative *body*>. 5: (a) Fullness and richness of flavor (as of wine); (b) viscosity, consistency—used especially of oils and grease; (c) denseness, fullness, or firmness of texture; (d) fullness or resonance of a musical tone.

BODY. Student Group. *BODY* is a forum for exploring the role of movement in constructing space. Through drawing and exercises adapted from the fields of dance and movement awareness, the group enhances percep-

tion and opens up possibilities for spatial design. In weekly sessions, group members participate in movement exercises while others respond to their movements in drawing. This hybrid practice nourishes the connection between vision and the other senses. As both maker and model, students gain an integrated sense of the interplay of anatomical structure and function. §

The Room for Hiding the Body In. Thesis. Annie Yuxi Wang (MArch I), advised by Mack Scogin.

"A puritanist-led disgust toward our *bodies* was born in the 16th century and never went away. The taboo of scatalogic and *bodily* practices led to the denial and clinicization of everything the *body* touched and ultimately to their encasement in architecture (later known as the bathroom). The loss was twofold: the public *body* was hidden, and the private *body* was no longer discussed. Soon, bathrooms were designed to be completely ascetic, thoroughly bland, inoffensive, and code abiding, or they were conceived as lavishly decorated, rococo throne rooms (hence the euphemism). The denial-fetishization dichotomy can only be explained by a general immaturity toward the content of the bathroom. And so we return to adolescence to recover our losses. A boarding school is the site of inquiry—a microcosmic institution for the maturation of prepubescents into independent adults. First is to reestablish the language of the public *body*, the construction of a spatial etiquette. Only through this can the realm of the private *body* be defined, whereby the procedural maintenance of the *body* becomes a space for the nurturing of intimacy. Where we once chased the tacit ghosts of norms, we now fly in headfirst, with a newfound sincerity." §

Figure. Rendering (opposite page). Annie Yuxi Wang (MArch I).

Standard Deviations. Thesis. Christopher Michael Johnson (MArch I AP), advised by Mariana Ibañez.

"Architecture's efficacy can be measured in terms of consideration for the comfort of the people who inhabit it—that is, its users. Spatial design is embedded within the physiological and psychological characteristics of inhabitants, and over time, architectural theories and practitioners have molded these characteristics into a series of disparate architectural users.

Architectural users span from the ideal and proportioned *body* of the Vitruvian Man to Henry Dreyfuss' dynamic and dimensioned representations and, more recently, to biological and thermally considered models. They are encoded with taste, biological concerns, philosophical inclinations, and dimensional data. Their constraints utilize norms and specificities, creating an index of highly varied and often oppositional architectural inhabitants.

Le Corbusier initially based the Modulor on the average height of the French male, 1.75 meters; he later raised it to 1.83 meters, claiming that, 'in English detective novels, the good-looking men, such as policemen, are always six feet tall.' The depicted architectural user is an idiosyncratic tool made by the designer, for the designer. It exists as a means of rationalization for the architect, who outfits the inhabitant with a series of carefully chosen norms around which to design. These norms may correctly apply to some of the actual inhabitants of the space, but the designer must always oscillate between the norm and the specific. This thesis intends to explore the interface between the perceived architectural inhabitant, the specific inhabitant, and their spatial consequences. Through a series of historical studies and forward projections, in the form of a health club, this project tests a new framework for designing civic space that addresses the evolution of the specific user and the stasis of the architectural user." ◈

Figure. Diagram (previous page). Christopher Michael Johnson (MArch I AP).

See also AGE—see also AUDIOVISUAL: Six Microphones—see also ERGONOMICS—see also GAZE: Subverting the Gaze—see also HEALTH—see also IMAGINATION: Architectural Imagination After May '68—see also MEASURE—see also PERCEPTION—see also PROPORTION—see also SCALE—see also SENSE—see also SPACE: Spaces of Living for the Subsystem Human Being.

BOOK

1: (a) A set of written sheets on skin, paper, or tablets of wood or ivory; (b) a set of written, printed, or blank sheets bound together into a volume; (c) a long written or printed literary composition; (d) a major division of a treatise or literary work. 2: Something that yields knowledge or understanding <her face was an open *book*>. 3: (a) The total available knowledge and experience that can be brought to bear on a task or problem <tried every trick in the *book*>; (b) the standards or authority relevant in a situation.

Books that Built Democracy, Public Patronage, Civic Significance, and Regional Identity in 1980s Valencian Architecture. Exhibition. January 31– March 15, 2015. Gallery Talk. April 6, 2015. Gund Hall, Frances Loeb Library, Special Collections. Manuel Lopez Segura (PhD) & Real Colegio Complutense.

This exhibition presented a collection of *books*, artifacts, and graphic works charting the contribution of architecture to the construction of democracy and the welfare state, and to the recovery of regional identity in 1980s Spain—specifically in the Valencian Country, an area on its Mediterranean shores. The items displayed were instrumental in elaborating and campaigning for a progressive political program aimed at forging a public space of civic significance through institutional patronage. Through its contents it brought nuance to prevailing views on postmodernism and politics, cast new light on the urban incarnation of social-democratic programs, and reformulated the definition of regionalism in architecture. ◈

BOTANY

Botany, biological sciences, natural sciences, disciplines: The scientific study of all plant life, including their structure, properties, and biochemical processes.

BOUTIQUE

1: (a) A small fashionable shop; (b) a small shop within a large department store. 2: A small company that offers highly specialized services or products <*boutique* wineries> <an independent investment *boutique*>.

America's Boutique City. STU 1409. Department of Landscape Architecture. Option Studio. Spring 2015. Instructors: Adriaan Geuze, Claire Agre, and Rachel Laszlo Tait. Teaching Assistant: Lauren Elizabeth Micir (MLA I).

With the rise of new economies and the influx of millennials and empty nesters, it seems there is a new urban biotope. Some American cities are undergoing a renaissance, and suddenly a new cityscape has emerged, which is complex, layered, and multifunctional. In new and old cities—New Orleans, Santa Monica, the Portlands, and Toronto, to name a few—the boundaries between residential, industrial, and cultural districts do not exist anymore. Is this evolution happening incrementally? Was there ever an overarching theory for this movement? Is this the birth of the new American *Boutique* City? This studio developed a complex, multilayered urbanism promoting overlap and exchange. Public space was equally distributed between bicycles, pedestrians, public transit, and vehicles. The ground level became an incredible interface where people meet and find new subcultures. Architecture, public space, and form all worked together. Although this *Boutique* City seems inevitable, the great American legacy of engineering seems far behind. The sad truth is, every light rail or bus lane is delivered as a high-speed rail corridor. Is it true that American ingenuity is incapable of delivering integrated, smart, urban infrastructure for trams, bicycles, skaters, pedestrians, and drivers? The cultural leadership of Miami Beach offered the studio their city as a laboratory. The studio asked: What kinds of strategies can promote multifunctionality? What kinds of designs can be imagined for identity, architecture, public landscapes, and ecology? Students analyzed Miami Beach, where catalytic points might be, and what kind of transit could be integrated.

Students: Erica Hope Blonde (MUP), Jordan Boan (MLA I AP), Shaunta Rene Butler (MLA II), Sherry Szu Jung Chen (MLA I), Yuxin He (MLAUD), Stephanie Hsia (MLA I), Meng Jia (MLA I AP), Alejandro Lara (MAUD), Zachery Max LeMel (MUP), Marcus Pulsipher (MLAUD), Rui Qian (MLA I AP), Rituparna Simlai (MLA I AP), Vi Vu (MLA I), Samuel Joseph Wright (MUP). ◈

Figure. Perspective & Diagrams (opposite page). Sherry Szu Jung Chen (MLA I).

BOX

1: (a) A rigid typically rectangular container with or without a cover <a cigar *box*>; (b) an open cargo container of a vehicle; (c) coffin. 2: The contents of a *box* especially as a measure of quantity. 3: A *box* or *box*-like container and its contents, such as (a) an automobile transmission; (b) television; (c) a signaling apparatus <alarm *box*>; (d) usually self-contained piece of electronic equipment; (e) boom *box*. 4: An often small space, compartment, or enclosure, such as (a) an enclosed group of seats for spectators <a theater or stadium>; (b) a driver's seat on a carriage or coach; (c) a cell for holding

mail. b: A usually rectangular space that is frequently outlined or demarcated on a surface, such as (a) any of six spaces on a baseball diamond where the batter, coaches, pitcher, and catcher stand; (b) a space on a page for printed matter or in which to make a mark. 6: Predicament, fix. 7: A cubical building. 8: The limitations of conventionality <trying to think outside the *box*>.

Boxes for America. STU 1316. Department of Architecture. Option Studio. Spring 2015. Instructor: Kersten Geers. Teaching Assistant: Ali Ismail Karimi (MArch I).

This studio was the 13th incarnation of Architecture without Content, which started as research on the Big *Box* in 2010. The idea was that architecture is reducible to its perimeter, where the economy of the envelope determines the success of the building. From the start, the studios have been interested in scale, turning even the most mundane of gestures into monumental presences. A big *box* transforms the territory it inhabits, despite a complete ignorance toward its immediate surroundings. If one considers the architecture of the United States, the Big *Box* is undoubtedly part of its DNA. This was so in 1960s corporate America, but is perhaps today—due to recent developments within the champions of American distribution and technology—more than ever the case; Big *Boxes* provide a mirror image. So perhaps, portraits of Big *Boxes* do, in one way or another, represent the country they support.

Students: Hamed Bukhamseen (MAUD), Ali Ismail Karimi (MArch I), Helen Edith Kongsgaard (MLA I), Daniela Angie Leon (MArch I AP), Raffy Mardirossian (MArch I AP), Paruyr Avetikovich Matevosyan (MArch I AP), Chong Ying Pai (MArch I AP), Ivan Ruhle (MArch I), Adelene Yu Ling Tan (MArch I), Tiantian Wei (MArch II), Tong Wu (MAUD).

Outside the Box: Spaces are Where We Move. Thesis. Jun Wang (MArch I AP), advised by Iñaki Ábalos.

"Having been an architecture student for seven years, I find myself struggling with the dichotomy between the codification of space and the fragmentation of time. Spatial creativities are superseded by social and legal standardizations across different scales, while ideology and technology provide us the appearance of choice. Our behaviors are no longer (or never really were) bounded by the spaces they contain; a designed space does not blur the boundary between the public and private, but rather that boundary is already blurred by the introduction of new social norms and technology. In searching for a way to address this issue architecturally, I aimed to look outside the *box* of thermally and legally closed systems—outside the *box* of buildings—for an answer. Circulation outside buildings is where we are in between spaces—in between living and working—where we may choose to work, connect, or simply move, with other people or just on our own. To explore circulation space for a kind of architectural experience other than itself, we do not need space that moves but rather spaces that allow fluid actions—spaces that are light, flexible, and engageable."

BRANDING

Branding, economic and financial functions, functions by context: The promotion of consumer awareness of particular goods or services, often through merchandise packaging or trademarking.

Branding in Architecture. Lecture. Gund Hall, Room 109. March 10, 2015. Spain GSD. Montse Zamorano.

In the constantly and rapidly changing panorama of the architecture profession, it is the responsibility of young architects to reinvent professional practice, generate new visions, improve and sharpen existing ones, and open the range of possible applications to our creative capacity. The lecture addressed the observation and interchange of new modes, models, and frameworks of contemporary practice, first analyzing photography as communication by comparing the work of Julius Shulman and Ezra Stoller, and then using these observations to generate a discussion on contemporary approaches to communication in recently created firms.

BROWNFIELD

Brownfield, sites & locations, complexes by function: Sites considered for development that already have some form of development on them or that are derelict and thus would require clearance before redevelopment could take place.

Brownfields Practicum: Regeneration of Brownfield Lands. SCI 6323. Department of Landscape Architecture. Seminar. Spring 2015. Instructor: Niall G. Kirkwood.

This course studied the reclamation of sites altered by prior industrial or commercial uses and in particular those that are derelict, environmentally hazardous, and located in neighborhoods and/or close to residential communities. The subject matter addressed recent advances in the legal, regulatory, environmental, economic, and community landscape as well as the remediation of despoiled land in a manner that reclaims and redevelops these sites for future sustainable uses. The course introduced students to the foundations of *brownfield* regeneration and reuse as well as the science and applied technology of waste, site cleanup, and connected *brownfield* redevelopment to broader issues in environmental policy and planning such as environmental justice, public health, and sustainable development.

BUILDING

Building, construction, assembling: The process of creating something by combining parts or elements, and also for the manner in which the thing has been put together. High-rise *building*: *Buildings* over nine or ten stories and served by elevators, especially when such *buildings* stand out in a skyline. Slab block: Medium- or high-rise *buildings* having a smaller depth compared to their length and usually to their height; use to distinguish from "point blocks" which are usually tower-like in form and built around a central circulation core. *Building*, structures: Structures, generally enclosed, that are used or intended to be used for sheltering an activity or occupancy.

Harvard GSD Buildings. 7 Sumner, 40 Kirkland, 42 Kirkland, and Gund Hall.

Building & Planning for Climate Change. Climate Week at Harvard University. Lecture. Gund Hall, Stubbins. April 8, 2015. Harvard Center for Green Buildings & Cities. Kairos Shen.

The Harvard Center for Green *Buildings* & Cities partnered with the Harvard GSD and the Harvard Center for the Environment to host Kairos Shen, architect, urban planner, and Director of Planning at the Boston Redevelopment Authority. Shen shared his unique perspective as both builder and planner to discuss the climate change resiliency of the built environment at multiple scales, from the building envelope to the greater urban landscape of Boston. He also discussed how Boston's planning, development review, and permitting procedures have been modified to promote sustainability, adaptation, and resilience. ⊕

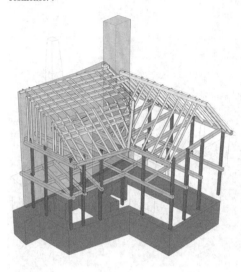

Buildings, Texts, and Contexts I. HIS 4121. Department of Architecture. Seminar. Fall 2014. Instructors: K. Michael Hays & Erika Naginski.

This course was structured as a dialogue between the historical and theoretical frameworks that have shaped the formulation of architectural principles—what the architectural historian Rudolf Wittkower called the "apparatus of forms"—by means of selected case studies. The organizing principle was thematic and synoptic rather than chronological and factual, treating a selected range of concepts developed by philosophers and historians to explain the classical and baroque as dialectical systems of thought that arise in history but transcend this history to mark modern and postmodern practices. ⊕

Buildings, Texts, and Contexts II. HIS 4122. Department of Architecture. Seminar. Spring 2015. Instructor: Edward Eigen.

Any account of architecture's history over the course of the 18th and 19th centuries is faced with the challenge of addressing the general rupture caused by the rise of modernity—that is, by the social, economic, technological, and ideological transformations accompanying the political and industrial revolutions marking the end of the European Enlightenment. The transition of architecture to the modern world gave rise to a series of fundamental questions: How did historical conditions place pressure on the time-honored foundations of architecture, on its origins, theories, and pedagogies? How did new conditions of scientific possibility actively reconfigure architecture's relation to engineering? And finally, how did aesthetic conceptions and approaches, which followed an arc from Beaux-Arts eclecticism and historicism to modernist avant-gardes, intersect with society

and politics? This course explored these questions through topics and themes ranging from technology and utopia to ornament and nationalism beginning with late baroque polemics and the academic foundations of architecture as discipline. ⊕

Buildings, Texts, and Contexts III: Rethinking Architecture. HIS 4223. Department of Architecture. Seminar. Fall 2014. Instructor: Neil Leach.

This course looked at several iconic *buildings* and architectural texts from the beginning of the 20th century to the present day and offered a critique of these *buildings* through the lens of essays on architecture and urbanism by key philosophers and cultural theorists. The idea was not only to introduce students to these key *buildings* within their contexts, but also to provide theoretical tools from outside the discipline of architecture in order to rethink architectural discourse. The iconic *buildings* included the Sagrada Família, Bauhaus, Barcelona Pavilion, Villa Savoye, Fallingwater, Sydney Opera House, Centre Pompidou, Parc de la Villette, CCTV Headquarters, and the Guggenheim Museum, Bilbao, along with other works by Le Corbusier, Mies van der Rohe, Walter Gropius, Frank Lloyd Wright, Bernard Tschumi, Peter Eisenman, Rem Koolhaas, Herzog & de Meuron, and Frank Gehry. ⊕

High-Rise, High-Density. Studio Reports. Publication. Harvard GSD, 2014. Stephen Bates & Jonathan Sergison (studio instructors). NA7862.M37 H54 2014.

The high-rise, multistory *building* is a very American invention, the result of high land values in rapidly developing cities, an abundance of iron ore, and Elisha Otis's invention: the elevator. In "The Tall Office *Building* Artistically Considered," written in March 1896, Louis Sullivan argues for an approach to high-rise *buildings* that combines appearance with pragmatism, architectural and architectonic qualities, and technical performance. More than 100 years after he wrote this seminal text, we considered what it might mean to build a high-rise *building*. ⊕

Figure. Structural System Diagram (left). Sasha S. Bears (MArch I), Shiyang Chen (MArch I), Chieh Chih Chiang (MArch I), Grace McEniry (MArch I), Ho Cheung Tsui (MArch I), and Hanguang Wu (MArch I).

BUILT

Built: Includes the *built* and natural environment, covering constructed works and natural landscapes, forming a continuum from the largest natural landscapes and settled areas to the smallest of individual *built* works. *Built* environment: Refers to the aggregates of human-made structures, infrastructural elements, and associated spaces and features.

See also ANTHROPOCENE—see also BOX: Outside the Box—see also BUILDING—see also CONSTRUCTION—see also ELEMENT—see also ENVIRONMENT—see also GARDEN: Third Natures—see also GALLERY: Kirkland Gallery—see also LANDSCAPE—see also PROJECT: Nose-to-Nose—see also REAL ESTATE: Master in Design Studies (MDes) Real Estate & the Built Environment (REBE)—see also RESPONSIVE: Socio-Environmental Responsive Design—see also SIMULATION: Building Simulation—see also STYLE: The Function of Style—see also TERROIR: Built Climates—see also THERMODYNAMICS: Ábalos + Sentkiewicz—see also TRANSITION: The Forms of Transition—see also UNBUILT—see also URBAN.

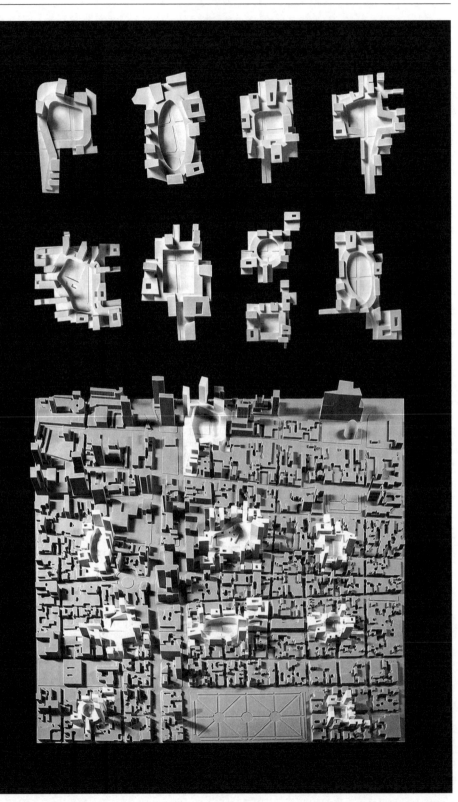

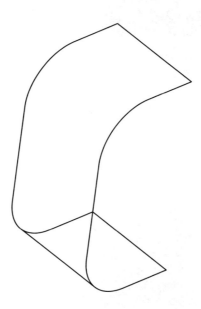

CAMPUS

Campus, educational complexes: Grounds of colleges or universities, including the open space between or around the buildings. The term is also used to refer to the grounds of other building complexes with layouts similar to colleges.

A Campus for the 21st Century: The Purisima Alameda District of Monterrey. STU 1506. Department of Urban Planning & Design. Option Studio. Spring 2015. Instructors: Felipe Correa & Carlos Garciavelez Alfaro. Teaching Assistant: Jose Alexandro Medina (MAUD).

This option studio examined the role of the academic institution as a driver of an intermediate-scale urban project. The studio focused on how the *campus*, conceived as an open canvas for architectural and urban experimentation, can serve as a generator of new spatial relationships between institution and city within the Purisima Alameda District in downtown Monterrey, Mexico. For 2016, the Universidad Regiomontana has agreed to construct the first gateless university in Mexico. With the implementation of a new institutional model, the *campus* must reframe the relationship between the spaces of the academy, the neighborhood, and the city at large. A fresh institutional perspective, paired with significant investment in the university's *campus*, has an enormous potential to completely rethink the Purisima Alameda District and transform it into a new university city model for Monterrey and beyond.

Taking this new institutional development initiative as a point of departure, the students explored the agency of architecture and design in shaping a new *campus*—all in an effort to construct new spatial formats to rethink the space of the experimental *campus* for the 21st-century university.

Students: Radhya Ananta Adityavarman (MLA II), Hovhannes Balyan (MAUD), Joseph William Bivona (MLA II), Xiaoran Du (MLA I AP), Kevin Alton Gurley (MUP), Mary Angela Lange (MLA I AP), Mengdan Liu (MArch II), Lauren Gail McClellan (MArch I), Clayton C. Strange (MAUD), Stephen Sun (MArch II), Magdalena Valenzuela (MAUD), Yutian Wang (MAUD). ⊗

Figure. Models & Site Model (opposite page). Clayton C. Strange (MAUD).

See also EDUCATION—see also INSTITUTE—see also MODERN: More than Mere Practicality—see also WORK: Work Environments I.

CANOPY

Artificial *canopy*: Rooflike ornamented projections, suspended from one wall or from the ceiling, used in architecture or furniture design, typically placed over a niche, door, window, tomb, etc., to protect it from the sun or elements, or to draw attention to the feature. *Canopy*, trees: Trees which form an overhanging shade or shelter.

Vegetal City: Projecting Urban Canopy. ADV 9135. Department of Landscape Architecture. Seminar. Spring 2015. Instructors: Gary R. Hilderbrand & Sonja Dümpelmann.

This seminar explored an under studied but crucially important urban realm—the designed, adapted, and vegetative *canopy*—through descriptive, analytical, and projective methods. Students built an interpretive and systematic archive of planted formations in urbanizing regions throughout modern history and into the present. Specific case studies documented the variable conditions that both sustain and challenge designed vegetative morphologies and their mutations; soils and microcli-

01 : axis

02 : ground

mate; adjacencies and ecological connectivity; responses to pathologies and adaptations to climatic change; and administrative management and stewardship. Students produced a close reading of how these plantations were conceived and implemented. How have they adapted, and how can their performance characteristics be optimized? In the projective portion of the study, students wrote speculative proposals that would augment ecological and spatial performance, and modeled potential outcomes. ⊛

Figure. Photomontage (opposite page). Eri Yamagata (MLA I).

CARBON

Carbon, inorganic material: Element that forms the framework for all tissues of plants and animals. Chemical symbol *C* and atomic number 6. *Carbon* may appear in many forms, including diamond, graphite, charcoal, *carbon* black, and fullerene. High quantities of *carbon* occur in coal, coke, oil, gasoline, and natural gas. Proteins such as hair, meat, and silk contain *carbon* and other elements. More than six and a half million compounds of the element *carbon* exist, including sugar, starch, and paper.

CARBONURBANISM

Carbonurbanism: Projective Futures. DES 3338. Department of Landscape Architecture. Seminar. Fall 2014. Instructor: Chris Reed.
   Carbon C is ubiquitous—it is one of the primary elements supporting life on Earth, the fourth most abundant element in the universe, and it makes up 18.5 percent of the human body. Global economies have increasingly relied on *carbon*-based resources since the industrial revolution (fuel, plastics, paving, building materials, etc.), and its steady increase in release into the atmosphere is one of the major contributing factors to climate change. From the Environmental Protection Agency: "*Carbon* dioxide is naturally present in the atmosphere as part of the Earth's *carbon* cycle (the natural circulation of *carbon* among the atmosphere, oceans, soil, plants, and animals). Human activities are altering the *carbon* cycle—both by adding more CO_2 to the atmosphere and by influencing the ability of natural sinks, like forests, to remove CO_2 from the atmosphere. While CO_2 emissions come from a variety of natural sources, human-related emissions are responsible for the increase that has occurred in the atmosphere since the industrial revolution." Within the discussions on sustainability and energy neutrality, few have probed the relevance or development of a *carbon*-based framework for framing and informing individual projects or, more appropriately, the broader projects of *urbanism*. The work of this research seminar attempted to do just this, answering: (1) what are the implications of a *carbon*-based future? (2) how do we define and measure such a thing? and (3) what are its implications for how we live? ⊛

CARDBOARD

Cardboard, pasteboard, paper, paper by form: A type of stiff pasteboard that is thicker than 0.006 inches, typically consisting of good-quality chemical pulp or rag pasteboard, and varying greatly in type and stability. High quality archival *cardboard* is made from rag pulp and has a low acid content, used for mounting prints, drawings and watercolors. Other grades of *cardboard* are used for cards, signs, printed materials, and high-quality boxes. Inferior grades of *cardboard*, such as corrugated board, are made from coarsely ground sulfite treated wood pulp; for this board, use "corrugated board." The first *cardboard* box was produced in England in 1817. Corrugated *cardboard* was patented in 1871.

See also MATERIAL—see also MODEL—see also PAPER—see also STUDY—see also TECHNIQUE.

CARTOGRAPHY

Cartography, discipline: The science surrounding the calculation and representation of a geographical area, usually on a flat surface such as a map or chart. It may involve physical or geographical features, the superimposition of political, cultural, or other nongeographical divisions, or the distribution of socioeconomic, political, agricultural, meteorological, or other information. Each point in the representation corresponds to an actual geographical position according to a fixed scale or projection. Digital mapping: *Cartography* in which the points and lines that comprise a map are digitized as computer data.

Figure. Map (above). Christina Leigh Geros (MLA I AP & MAUD).

See also GEOGRAPHY—see also MAPPING—see also PATTERN: R. Buckminster Fuller, Pattern Thinking—see also REPRESENTATION.

CATALOGUE

Book *catalogue*, documents: *Catalogues* containing the surrogate descriptions of books or other bibliographic material in a collection. *Cataloging* system, information systems: Systems for describing and indexing works or images, particularly in a collections management system or other automated system. *Catalogue*, documents:

Enumerations of items, such as a file of bibliographic records or a list of art objects, usually arranged systematically and with descriptive details; may be in book or pamphlet form, on cards, or online. *Catalogues* are created according to specific and uniform principles of construction and under the control of an authority file.

See also COLLECTION—see also EXHIBITION—see also FUNDAMENTAL: 14th International Architecture Exhibition—see also INFORMATION—see also LANDFORM: Landformation Catalogue.

CEILING

Ceiling, surface element, architectural element: Overhead surfaces of interior spaces, sometimes constructed to mask building systems or structural elements.

See also ELEMENT: Architecture at the Human Scale.

CENTER

Center, geometric, mathematical concept: The middle point, especially of a line, circle or sphere, equidistant from the ends or from any point on the circumference or surface. *Central* city, urban areas: Largest core areas within the incorporated limits of metropolitan areas; often used to distinguish the *center* from the suburban or newer outlying sections of metropolitan areas; generally excludes the *central* business district and inner city sections. Cultural *center*: Public buildings, sites, or complexes set aside for activities related to the culture of an area, such as music, dance, drama, or fine arts. Research *center*: Buildings or spaces housing organizations or corporate, industrial, or educational facilities for research.

Berkman Center for Internet & Society. Harvard University's Berkman *Center* for Internet & Society explores all aspects of cyberspace, its development and dynamics and seeks to assess the need or lack thereof for laws and sections.

Center for Geographic Analysis. Harvard University's *Center* for Geographic Analysis develops GIS tools—like WorldMap—and hosts an annual conference on the topic.

David Rockerfeller Center for Latin American Studies (DRCLAS). DRCLAS (pronounced "Dr. Class") seeks to increase knowledge about Latin American culture and strengthen ties between the region and Harvard University.

Harvard Asia Center. The Harvard Asia *Center* funds student research and study in Asia, as well as the activities of Asia-focused student groups.

Harvard University Center for the Environment. The Harvard *Center* for the Environment focuses on the environment and its many interactions with human society.

Joint Center for Housing Studies. The Joint *Center* for Housing Studies was originally formed in 1959 as the Joint *Center* for Urban Studies of MIT and Harvard University. It took the challenge of addressing intellectual and policy issues confronting a nation experiencing

widespread demographic, economic, and social changes, with dramatic and far-reaching effects on cities. ❦

Mahindra Humanities Center. Mahindra Humanities *Center* is a crossroads of discussion between the humanities, social sciences, and sciences.

See also CULTURE—see also GEOMETRY—see also LINE—see also PERSPECTIVE—see also RESEARCH—see also URBAN.

CHALLENGE

1: To demand as due or deserved <an event that *challenges* explanation>. 2: To order to halt and prove identity <the sentry *challenged* the stranger>. 3: To dispute especially as being unjust, invalid, or outmoded <new data that *challenges* old assumptions>. 4: To question formally the legality or legal qualifications of. 5: (a) To confront or defy boldly, dare <he *challenged* his critics to prove his guilt>; (b) to call out to duel or combat; (c) to invite into competition <he *challenged* his brother to a tennis match>. 6: To arouse or stimulate especially by presenting with difficulties <she wants a job that will *challenge* her>.

Launch: Harvard Center for Green Building & Cities Inaugural Challenge Conference. Gund Hall, Piper Auditorium. November 7, 2014. Ali Malkawi, Richard Freeman, Iñaki Ábalos, Martin Bechthold, Stephen McTee Ervin, Eric Höweler, Jerold S. Kayden, Panagiotis Michalatos, Kiel Moe, Toshiko Mori, Richard Peiser, Antoine Picon, Spiro N. Pollalis, Chris Reed, Holly Samuelson, and Allen Sayegh.

Celebrating the Harvard Center for Green Buildings & Cities, this conference brought together a diverse set of scientists, designers, and economists to consider issues whose eventual solution will transform the way we design, build, and live. As the center works toward a multidisciplinary plan for the future of the built environment that will respect and respond to the intricacies of an increasingly complex global landscape, the annual conference continued the inquiry into effective strategies for shifting the frontier of knowledge and practice. ❦

See also COLLABORATION: The Calumet Collaborations—see also COMPETITION—see also LAUNCH—see also REVIEW.

CHANGE

1: (a) To make different in some particular, alter <never bothered to *change* the will>; (b) to make radically different, transform <can't *change* human nature>; (c) to give a different position, course, or direction to. 2: (a) To replace with another <let's *change* the subject>; (b) to make a shift from one to another, switch <always *changes* sides in an argument>; (c) to exchange for an equivalent sum of money <*change* a 20-dollar bill>; (d) to undergo a modification of <foliage *changing* color>; (e) to put fresh clothes or covering on <*change* a bed>.

Surface or structural *change*: Describes processes that transform the surface or structure of an object.

See also CLIMATE CHANGE—see also OBJECT—see also PROCESS—see also TRANSFORMATION.

CHAPEL

Chapel, religious building spaces: Rooms or small buildings that serve as sanctuaries or places of worship. A *chapel* may be used for private worship in or attached to a church, palace, house, prison, monastery, or school. It may alternatively be used for public worship of the established church, subordinate to or dependent upon the parish church, the accommodation supplied by which it in some way supplements. The Latin *cappella* or the French-derived *chappelle* or *chapelle* are occasionally used for "*chapel*" in English texts.

Ronchamp. Publication. Hatje, 1957. Le Corbusier (author). Le Corbusier Research Collection, Frances Loeb Library. LeC NA 5200 Ronc L496bg.
   "Le Corbusier's last two books were published by Gerd Hatje. This one, dedicated to his *Chapel* of Nôtre-Dame-du-Haut at Ronchamp (1950–1955), is illustrated with beautiful photographs (he encourages the reader to look at them from different angles and upside down). It also included sketches of the hilltop sanctuary commanding the surrounding landscape. It surprises above all because of its plastic qualities, particularly in the name of modern architecture." —Inés Zalduendo. ❦

See also BUILDING—see also CHURCH—see also CULTURE—see also PHOTOGRAPHY—see also STRUCTURE.

CHARETTE

Charette, educational event: Periods of intense final effort made by architectural students to complete their solutions to a given architectural problem within an allotted time.

CHARTER

1: (a) A written instrument or contract (as a deed) executed in due form. 2: (a) A grant or guarantee of rights, franchises, or privileges from the sovereign power of a state or country; (b) a written instrument that creates and defines the franchises of a city, educational institution, or corporation; (c) constitution.

Charter, legal documents, visual & verbal communication: Documents, usually sealed, granting specific rights, setting forth aims and principles of a newly established entity, and often embodying formal agreements and authorizing special privileges or exemptions.

La charte d'Athènes. Publication. Plon, 1943. Le Corbusier (author). Le Corbusier Research Collection, Frances Loeb Library. Rare NAC 250 C76.
   "The fourth CIAM meeting was held partly aboard the S.S. *Patris* bound for Athens. It was here that the members set forth the aims and principles for urban interventions that would later be codified and incorporated into what would become the Athens *Charter*. In the midst of World War II, one of Le Corbusier's main concerns was putting in writing the CIAM doctrine as an underlying agreement among the international group of architects. Their resolutions had to be organized, edited, and made publicly available. He did so in 95 points that summarized their agreements and considerations related to the city and its region, habitation, leisure, work, traffic, and historic heritage. As explained by Eric Mumford, Eugène Claudius Petit, Minister for Reconstruction and Urban Planning in 1948 and strong supporter of Le Corbusier, believed this document could be used as a basis for reconstruction projects." —Inés Zalduendo. ❦

CHAUHAUS

The *Chauhaus* is in many ways the heart of the Harvard GSD. Much more than a school cafeteria, it is visited by nearly everyone at the GSD (and other schools) and used for informal meetings between faculty and students, and is the site of Beer & Dogs. ❦

CHROMATIC

Chromatic color, hues or tints: Colors which have hue. All colors have hue except for black, white, and shades of gray.

CHURCH

1: A building for public and especially Christian worship. 2: The clergy or officialdom of a religious body. 3: A body or organization of religious believers, such as (a) the whole body of Christians; (b) denomination <the Presbyterian *church*>; (c) congregation. 4: A public divine worship <goes to *church* every Sunday>. 5: The clerical profession <considered the *church* as a possible career>.

Nicholas Hawksmoor: London Churches. Publication. Lars Müller Publishers, 2015. Mohsen Mostafavi (author) & Hélène Binet. NA5497.H39 M67x 2015.
   British architect Nicholas Hawksmoor (ca. 1661–1736) is recognized as one of the major contributors to the traditions of British and European architectural culture. Nevertheless, there is insufficient visual documentation and analysis of his work. *Nicholas Hawksmoor: London Churches* reconsiders his architecture in relation to urbanism. The publication focuses on a series of important London *churches* the architect designed during the early part of the 18th century. The key distinguishing features of these *churches* are their spires, each designed with different qualities and motifs. While Hawksmoor was inspired by the ancient history of architecture, his work was considered radical and contemporary in its day. Photographer Hélène Binet was commissioned to document the various aspects of the seven remaining London *churches*. Her immaculate black-and-white photographs demonstrate the beauty of Hawksmoor's architecture with special attention to the variety of scales, sites, interiors, textures, and materials.

See also BUILDING—see also CULTURE—see also PHOTOGRA-PHY—see also TYPOLOGY—see also URBANISM.

CIRCULATION

Circulation, functional concepts: A continuous flow of space linking the parts of a building or buildings, or

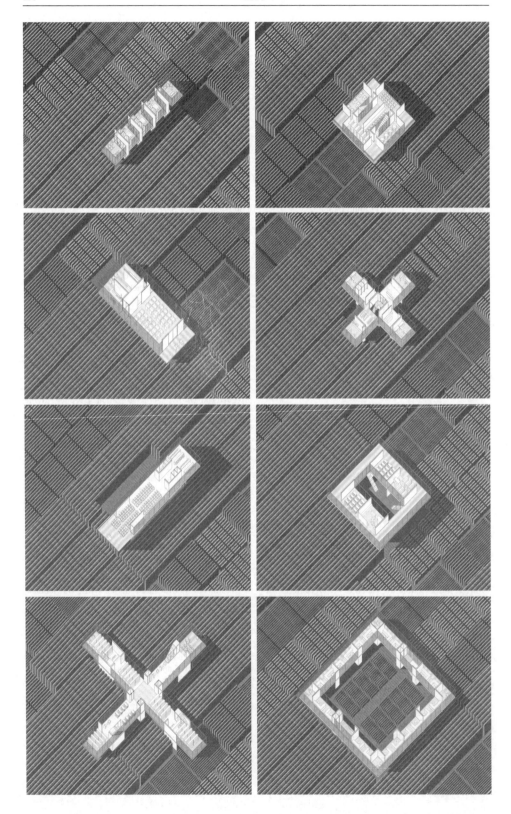

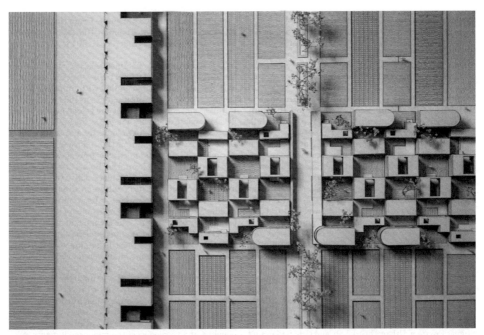

through any series of interior or exterior spaces. Used often with reference to traffic patterns through areas or buildings, including the means of travel through a building, such as doors, corridors, stairs, or elevators.

See also MEMORIAL: Abstracted Geologies—see also SPACE: Outside the Box—see also TRANSPORTATION.

CITY

City, settlement by form: Distinctions among villages, towns, and *cities* are relative and vary according to their individual regional contexts. Generally, *cities* designate large communities with population, status, and internal complexity greater than most towns in the region.

The Countryside as a City. STU 1503. Department of Urban Planning & Design. Option Studio. Fall 2014. Instructor: Christopher C. M. Lee. Teaching Associate: Simon Whittle.

The studio was premised upon two fundamental ambitions, the recuperation of an idea of the *city* as a project and the pursuit of alternative forms of urbanization in response to the challenges posed by the developing *city* in China. The former treats the project of the *city* as a cultural, political, and aesthetic act; the latter as a strategic project for urbanization, articulated through its architecture, landscape, and infrastructure. The studio's research focused on the transformation of China's rural villages into towns. With China's rate of urbanization reaching 51 percent in 2011, the next phase of economic and social development will now be focused on the urbanization of its rural areas. In Premier Le Keqiang's announcement, the state's urbanization target of 70 percent, affecting 900 million people by 2025, will not come from the further expansion of large *cities*, but will instead be focused on the growth of rural towns and small *cities*. As a continuation of the Building a New

Socialist Countryside program of 2006, developed against the backdrop of rural unrest and urgent need to secure food production, this drive attempts to reverse the migration of the rural populace to the *city*, uplift the living standards in the rural areas, and safeguard farmland from further speculative developments. This is manifest in the demolition and reconstruction of substandard housing in villages, and the wholesale demolition and merging of several villages, to share new communal amenities, as an approximation of life in the *city*.

China's rural urbanization should not be mistaken with the process of suburbanization of the United States nor the creation of low-density, picturesque, garden *cities* in Britain. It should neither be mistaken for the transformation of rural areas into dense urbanized cores, with the glut of speculative housing as the primary economic driver. Beyond the upgrading of basic infrastructure and sanitation, the challenge here is to imagine a self-sufficient place that can support a dynamic economy in the countryside, provide cultural and intellectual stimulation, and offer a respite to the inequalities and divisions that plague the developmental *city*; the *city* as a space of equal and plural coexistence.

Students: Radhya Ananta Adityavarman (MLA II), Carly J. Augustine (MArch II), Jyri Antti Mikael Eskola (MArch I AP), Siwei Gou (MLA I AP), Shaoliang Hua (MArch II), Nicolas Lee (MArch II), Ho Wai Wilfred Leung (MAUD), Jose Alexandro Medina (MAUD), Feng Shen (MAUD), Pg Human Smit (MLAUD), Dimitris Venizelos (MAUD), Zhenhuan Xu (MArch II), Bicen Yue (MArch II). ❀

Figures. Axonometric Drawings (opposite page). Siwei Gou (MLA I AP). Site Model (above). Carly J. Augustine (MArch II) & Nicolas Lee (MArch II).

Expeditions in the Contemporary City. Lecture. Gund Hall, Piper Auditorium. February 12, 2015. Jeanne Gang.

Today's *cities* must cope with lapsed industrial spaces and inherited infrastructure. Through the lens of Studio

Gang's most recent and noteworthy projects, cofounder Jeanne Gang considered how architectural practice might be refocused to reimagine these territories and initiate transformation, and professed her longstanding interest in the new ways that cultural and science-based aspects of natural systems can be of use in defining the *city*. ֍

Identity, Sovereignty, and Global Politics in the Building of Baghdad: From Revolution through the Gulf War and Beyond. Conference. Gund Hall, Piper Auditorium. September 18–20, 2014.

Using the history of urban development in Baghdad as a reference point, this conference examined the extent to which interventions intended to modernize and integrate different populations in the *city* were part of a larger process of negotiating competing visions of political economy, sovereignty, and identity in post-World War II Iraq. By gathering political scientists, architectural and urban historians, and scholars of Iraq and the larger Arab world, the conference engaged theoretical and empirical questions about the ruptures and continuities of Baghdad's urban and political history, using the built environment of the *city* as a canvas for understanding struggles over Iraq's position in a global context shaped by ongoing war tensions (from the Cold War to the Gulf War and beyond) to more recent Middle East conflicts. This event was cosponsored by the Aga Khan Program, MIT Center for International Studies, Master in Design Studies Program, Urban Theory Lab, and Urban Planning & Design Interdisciplinary Urbanism Initiative. ֍

Macau: Cross-Border City. Studio Reports. Publication. Harvard GSD, 2014. Christopher C. M. Lee (editor). HT384.C6 M38 2014.

Common Frameworks: Rethinking the Developmental City in China documents the second year of a three-year research and design study on the future of the Chinese *city*. A collection of essays and design conjectures, this report focuses on the *city* of Macau and particularly on the challenges faced by *cities* in *city*-regions and the effects of cross-border urbanization. Asserting that the tropes used to describe and understand the border and its architecture fall short, the studio projects present an alternative urban strategy, conceiving a common framework for the border and its supporting facilities. The critique reconceptualizes the inherent architecture and spatiality of the cross-border *city*, its implicit ambition to bring about a *city* that is plural and equitable. It sows the seed for an alternative idea of the *city* for China. ֍

Manière de penser l'urbanisme. Publication. Éditions de l'Architecture d'Aujourd'hui, 1946. Le Corbusier (author). Le Corbusier Research Collection, Frances Loeb Library. LeC NAC 250 L496f.

"This study, together with *Les trois établissements humains*, was produced by Le Corbusier while he was a member of the Assemblée de constructeurs pour une rénovation architecturale (ASCORAL), the French group he founded within Congrès internationaux d'architecture moderne (CIAM) that would later develop, the direction of the official CIAM grid of 1947 for the comparative study of *cities*. In *Manière de penser l'urbanisme*, Le Corbusier proposes a new kind of urbanism based on linear *cities* of 50 to 100 kilometers long, which would link concentric *cities* of greater density but limited growth. Here, architecture and urbanism come together through unités d'habitation, unités de travail, unités de loisirs, unités de circulation, and unités de paysages."
—Inés Zalduendo. ֍

Structuring Urban Experience: From the Athenian Acropolis to the Boston Common. HIS 4362. Department of Architecture. Seminar. Fall 2014. Instructor: Christine Smith.

This lecture course examined selected cities between the 5th century BCE and the 17th century CE, beginning with ancient Athens and ending with proposals for rebuilding London after the great fire in 1666. Each of the lectures considered one *city* at one golden moment of its development to exemplify a theme or themes. The course, therefore, was both chronologically and thematically structured. The first half of the semester treated the ancient and late antique *city*, beginning with Athens and continuing with Alexandria, Rome, Constantinople, and Antioch. This section concluded with a consideration of the effects of Christianization on urban form, the widespread decline of urban habitation in the early Middle Ages, and the rising importance of ideal or symbolic "cities of the mind." The second half of the semester looked at selected instances of Renaissance and Baroque urban interventions, beginning with Florence, returning again to Rome, and then moving to Venice, Madrid, Paris, and London. The last lecture was on Boston, from its founding in 1630 up to the Revolution, giving students the opportunity to reflect on to what extent new cities do or do not learn from historical patterns of settlement. Lectures covered urban layout and topography, infrastructure, patterns and types of housing, and typologies of the major monuments. ֍

The Mixed-Reality City: The Urban Fabric as Landscape, Network, and Platform. DES 3448. Department of Architecture. Seminar. Fall 2014. Instructor: Jeffrey Schnapp.

The contemporary *city* is constituted by multiple overlapping, intermixing realities articulated across built form and imagined space, individual experience and collective memory, and embodied sensation and digital mediation. Often, these multiple realities are invisible or illegible, with certain narratives dominating particular environments. However, realities always leave traces to be excavated and reconstructed. The Mixed-Reality *City* was an exploratory research seminar and workshop in which students studied urbanism-in-the-making through means and methods emerging in the digital arts and humanities, including data narrative, digital ethnography, adversarial design, and critical technical practice. The course focused in equal parts on unpacking discourses and developing interpretative digital artifacts. ֍

Unplugged City: The Obsolescence of the Physical Grid & Imagining the Future of the Urban. Lecture. Gund Hall, Stubbins. April 23, 2015. Iñaki Echeverria.

By the year 2050, about 30 *cities* worldwide will grow beyond 20 million inhabitants and only three will be located in the so-called developed world. Already in China, a metropolitan area of 120 million inhabitants is growing in the Pearl River Delta. This conglomerate incorporates three *cities* with separate legislations (Guangzhou, Foshan, and Zhaoqing). Known as Guangfo Metropolis, it challenges every notion of the original meaning of *city*. Whether these new conglomerates should still be called *cities*, or a more appropriate term is needed to name and understand these constructed landscapes, is yet to be determined. Yet, one could argue that the viability of the megacity is the viability of the idea of the *city*, and that the future of the *city* is intrinsically linked to the future of mankind. Already more than 50 percent of humans

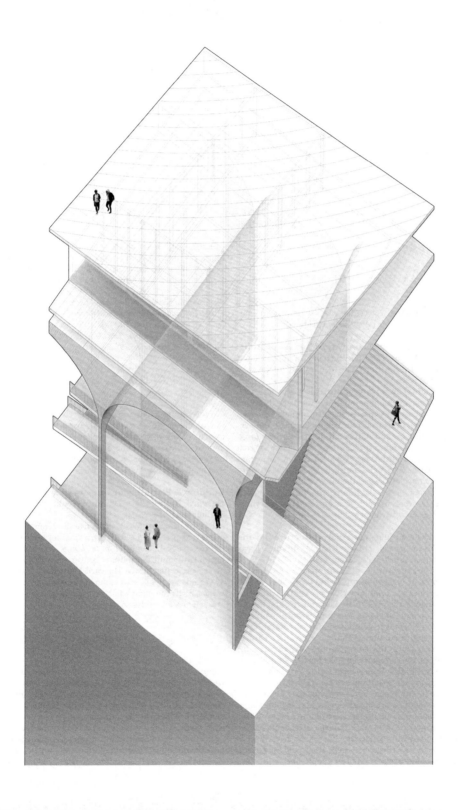

Inhabit some sort of urbanized reality. Issues that may redefine today's *city* in relation—to the environment at large, to water, and to the mutually exclusive categories of urban versus landscape or production versus consumption—become urgent. ※

See also AIRPORT: Dwelling in Stop-Over City—see also AUTONOMOUSMOBILE: The (Love) Affair—see also CAMPUS: A Campus for the 21st Century—see also CIVIC: Starbucks & Spiderman—see also COLOR—see also EDGE: The Barracks of Pion—see also FLOAT: Floating Cities—see also GRID—see also HEALTH—see also LIFESTYLE: Redefining Urban Living—see also MIGRATION—see also MORPHOLOGY—see also OBJECT: Object Studio—see also PARK—see also PRODUCTION: Tactics for a Coproduced City—see also RADICAL: Radical Cities—see also REAL ESTATE—see also RESILIENCE: Creating Resilient Cities—see also RESPONSIVE: Socio-Environmental Responsive Design—see also SPECTACLE—see also SPECULATION: Practices in the Turbulent City—see also SYSTEM—see also TERRITORY: Territorialism—see also TRANSPORTATION—see also TYPOLOGY—see also URBANISM—see also URBAN DESIGN—see also URBAN PLANNING—see also VISION: Toulouse—see also VISIONARY: Grounded Visionaries—see also WELL-BEING.

CIVIC

1: Of or relating to a citizen, a city, citizenship, or community affairs <*civic* duty> <*civic* pride>.

Designing the American City: Civic Aspirations & Urban Form. DES 3302. Department of Urban Planning & Design. Spring 2015. Seminar. Instructor: Alex Krieger.

This course took an interpretive look at the American city in terms of changing attitudes toward urban life. City and suburb are experienced as the product of design and planning decisions informed by cultural and economic forces, and in relationship to utopian and pragmatic efforts to reinterpret urban traditions in search of American alternatives. Topics included persistent ideals such as the single-family home, attitudes toward public and private space, the rise of suburbs and suburban sprawl, cycles of disinvestment and renewed interest in urban centers, and impacts of mobility and technology on settlement patterns. ※

Starbucks & Spiderman: An Architecture Beyond New Civic Ideals. Thesis. Kevin William Murray (MArch I), advised by Eric Höweler.

"*Civic* architecture is disconnected. As antiquated anonymity or masked in prosthetic technology, it fantasizes relevance. Contemporary city centers are overwhelmed with the prostitution of economy and leisure alike. Consumerism is a tactic to feign a populous; technology, a plot to combat emptiness. Familiarity is essential to comfort. What do Piccadilly Circus, Potsdamer Platz, and Times Square have in common? Starbucks, the caffeinated mark of urban significance. To the world, these places are representations of the city, but to that city, they are representations of the world. The surface is engulfed by tourists demanding re-pedestrianization of the street. Locals bury themselves underground, preferring to endure labyrinthine infrastructures, and only emerge at inconspicuous and peripheral stairwells. Kitsch is key. Why is Spiderman here? Because, where else would Spiderman be? He is a superhero for the people and so he goes

where the people are. Perhaps the governmental center enjoys no longer being *civic*. It maintains an image that depends on peacefulness and in so doing propagandizes peacekeeping. Emptiness, axiality, sterility, massiveness, oppression, and history—*civic* institutions set themselves away from the fourth estate: 'We are history, we are stability, we are control,' a protest against the eternal and familiar newness of technology and mass media. Cognizance is the only child of a long and spiteful divorce between mass media and authority, the respective mother and father of the crowd, claiming custody of the public sphere and determining which parent the holidays will be spent with; liberty convenience, equality consumerism, and justice comfort. *Civic* architecture is the execution of cognizance." ※

Figure. Drawing (previous page). Kevin William Murray (MArch I).

CLIMATE

Climate, weather and related phenomena, earth science concepts: The long-term total of atmospheric variations at a specific geographical location. Regarding shorter-term atmospheric conditions, use "weather."

See also ATMOSPHERE—see also CHANGE—see also EXTREME: Housing in Extreme Environments—see also HABOOB: Dust Kingdom—see also RESPONSIVE: Socio-Environmental Responsive Design—see also TERROIR: Built Climates—see also TRANSITION: The Forms of Transition.

CLIMATE CHANGE

Climate change, environmental concepts: Any alteration in regional or global *climate* as during the five glacial periods of the past 450,000 years. The term is often applied to the recent changes in global climatic patterns, attributed to emission of greenhouse gases, also known as global warming.

Building & Planning for Climate Change. Lecture. Harvard University's Climate Week. Gund Hall, Stubbins. April 8, 2015.

Harvard Climate Week was a five-day, campus-wide event that presented a wide variety of perspectives on critical issues driven by *climate change*. In an effort to host a truly multidisciplinary conversation, colleagues at key programs across Harvard University gathered at various venues across campus to engage in conversations with prominent scholars, politicians, policy-markers, scientists, and leaders. ※

CLUB

1: (a) A heavy usually tapering staff especially of wood wielded as a weapon; (b) a stick or bat used to hit a ball in any of various games; (c) something resembling a *club*. 2: (a) A playing card marked with a stylized figure of a black clover; (b) the suit comprising cards marked with *clubs*. 3: (a) An association of persons for some common object usually jointly supported and meeting periodically, also a group identified by some common characteristic <nations in the nuclear *club*>; (b) the

meeting place of a *club* <lunch at the *club*>; (c) an association of persons participating in a plan by which they agree to make regular payments or purchases in order to secure some advantage; (d) nightclub; (e) an athletic association or team.

Architects' Club: Clerkwell, London. STU 1302. Department of Architecture. Option Studio. Fall 2014. Instructor: Sir Peter Cook.

As London has the world's highest number of international working graduates in the field of architecture, there is need for an independent *club* where they can meet and have semiformal or informal gatherings, or feel that they can just drop by. This can include lectures, seminars, eating, drinking, indoor sport, and chilling out. Pursuit of the project involved: (1) defining a new institution that was not institutional in the narrow sense; (2) capturing the essence of a place of relaxation; (3) overlaying this with facilities that are identifiable, but not inflexible; (4) dealing with a simple, linear site near a vibrant area; and (5) absorbing an equivalent quantity of residential volume into the building in addition to the *club* as described.

Students: Sonya Chao (MArch I), Jaewoo Chon (MArch I AP), Brian Y. Chu (MArch II), Conor Coghlan (MArch II), Mircea Eni (MArch II), Raffy Mardirossian (MArch I AP), Christine Min (MArch II), Matthew Lee Montry (MArch II), Yina Ng (MArch I), Yi Ren (MArch I), Annie Yuxi Wang (MArch I), Wenxin Ye (MAUD), Ying Zhang (MAUD). ֎

Figure. Rendering (previous page). Annie Yuxi Wang (MArch I).

CMYK

CMYK, color model, color systems, color & color-related phenomena: Color model used in printing; based on mixing *Cyan*, *Magenta*, and *Yellow* pigments in a subtractive method to create *Key* (black) and all other colors through light absorption.

See also COLOR—see also LIGHTING—see also PLOT—see also PRINT.

COASTAL

Coastal environment, object groupings: Environments along shores of bodies of water, affected by factors of both the land and the water. Regarding the geology or geography of *coastal* areas, use "shores (landforms)" or "coastlines."

Changing Natural & Built Coastal Environments. SCI 6337. Department of Landscape Architecture. Seminar. Fall 2014. Instructors: Steve Apfelbaum & Katharine Parsons.

This course examined natural and anthropogenic processes affecting the *coastal* zone and near-shore environment. Ecological principles and their application to design and planning were emphasized. Topics included *coastal* wetland development; sediment movement in estuaries and long-shore, natural disturbance regimes; *coastal* storms, flooding and erosion; applications of ecological principles for landscape design, planning, restoration, recreation, management, and conservation

at regional scales with regard to storm water management, hardened coastlines, sediment and toxics management; and marsh restoration. ֎

See also ENVIRONMENT—see also HYDROLOGY—see also ONTO-CARTOGRAPHY: Cyborg Coasts—see also RESILIENCE: Coastal Resilience, Sustainable Development of the Spanish Atlantic Coast.

CODE

1: A systematic statement of a body of law, especially one given statutory force. 2: A system of principles or rules <moral *code*>. 3: (a) A system of signals or symbols for communication; (b) a system of symbols (as letters or numbers) used to represent assigned and often secret meanings. 4: Genetic *code*. 5: A set of instructions for a computer.

Code, culture-related concepts: Systems of symbols, sounds, or gestures used for translating a piece of information in a source language, such as a symbol, letter, word, or phrase, into a target language according to a strict rule, in order to achieve some purpose, such as disguising the message or facilitating its transmission or reception. *Code*, regulations: Systematically arranged and comprehensive collections of laws, or, more generally, systematic collections of regulations and rules of procedure or conduct.

Code without Frontiers. Student Group. The aim of this group of volunteers is to help mentor students at the Harvard GSD with technical questions; *code* problems; and provide one-on-one assistance with digital tools and workflows. ֎

COFFEE

Coffea, Rubiaceae family: Genus containing over 90 species of shrubs and small trees native to subtropical Africa and southern Asia. Seeds of several species are the source of a popular beverage. It was first cultivated in southern Arabia in the 15th century, then spread to Indonesia in the 17th century. By the 18th century, *coffee* plants were also being grown in Central and South America. *Coffee*, food, dye: Aromatic, dark brown liquid prepared from the aqueous extract of the seeds of several species of the genus *Coffea*, particularly C. arabica. *Coffee* is used as a beverage and as a brown dye. On wool, it produces a dark yellow-tan color with a chrome mordant and a tan with an aluminum mordant. Both colors have fair light fastness. *Coffee* colors on cotton are not fast. Some restorers have used *coffee* to tint bleached papers or repair regions to a shade that corresponds to surrounding areas.

Coffee Cups. 56,000 cups of *coffee* are consumed at the Chauhaus every year. ֎

COLLABORATION

Collaboration, organizational functions: Refers to any venture in which individuals or organizations work together, especially in an intellectual endeavor.

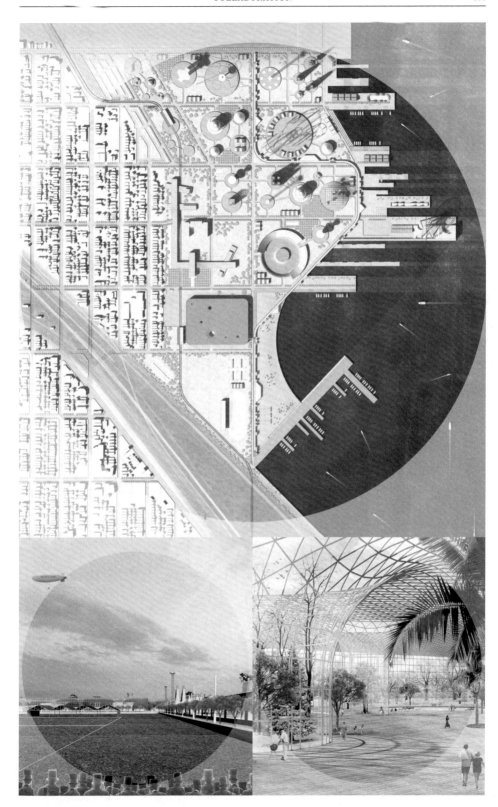

The Calumet Collaborations: Daniel Burnham Meets Andre Breton on the South Side of Chicago. STU 1508. Department of Urban Planning & Design. Option Studio. Spring 2015. Instructor: Michael Sorkin. Teaching Assistant: Moises Garcia Alvarez (MAUD).

Chicago, lake-sided and magnificently flat, gridded to the horizon, studied and troubled, is ever ready for reimagining. What better moment than the impending 119th anniversary of the Burnham Plan? While the city no longer butchers hogs for the planet, its shoulders remain broad and its sense of its own practicality and possibility abides. But it is also a place of mesmerizing abstraction. The inflections of its Cartesian substrate by big ideas, by slashing highways, by demographic disaster, by fringing skyscrapers, by corruption and genius: here is Chicago.

So what next? While architectural culture is still thick with ambivalence about big plans, we know we love them—if only in secret—as the stuff of our most febrile dreams, even when they spring from mosaic collusions of an infinity of independent tininess. Perhaps we realize them too much as a form of negative capability, patching up somebody else's disaster-driven tabula rasa. Bring on Katrina! Bring on white flight! Bring on the collapse of Detroit! Bring on the fall of U.S. Steel! Bring on the flattening of miles of public housing! Bring on the rising seas! But bring it on! Can we meet the challenge, whether by confrontation, embrace, or avoidance? The duty of urban designers is to enlarge the conversation, to try the impossible, to assure that no speculation is forbidden. The vocation is to invent the new forms of urban organization that will lead to sustainable, equitable, and beautiful futures. The studio attempted to produce a new urban pattern and a new way of designing, using Chicago as the site for our research.

Here's the skinny. An academic consortium—including the City College of New York, the University of Illinois at Chicago, the Illinois Institute of Technology, Science Applications International Corporation, the University of Chicago, and the Harvard GSD—combined forces to operate on a huge site in Calumet, on the far south side of the city. Collectively, the studio pursued the kind of ambitious intervention that characterized the optimistic age of Burnham and the Columbian Exposition, while rejecting the idea of producing any strict singularity of vision. The ambition was to accumulate alternatives and to invent new forms of reciprocity and concord.

Students: Clare Adrien (MArch I), Mikela De Tchaves (MAUD), Moises Garcia Alvarez (MAUD), Ethan Lassiter (MUP), Andrew Michael Nahmias (MArch II), Nadia Perlepe (MArch II), Dai Ren (MAUD), Gabriella Solange Rodriguez (MLAUD & MLA I), Jeenal Mulchand Sawla (MUP), Dana Shaikh Solaiman (MAUD), Trax Yinan Wang (MAUD), Ran Wei (MAUD), Yiying Yang (MAUD). ▨

Figure. Perspectives (previous page). Ran Wei (MAUD). Plan (opposite page, above). Dai Ren (MAUD). Perspective (opposite page, below). Andrew Michael Nahmias (MArch II).

COLLAGE

Collage, technique, image-making processes: Refers to the technique of making compositions in two dimensions or very low relief by gluing paper, fabrics, photographs, or other materials onto a flat surface. If heavy three-dimensional objects dominate, use "assemblage (sculpture technique)." If the constituent fragments form a somewhat unified image, see "montage."

See also ASSEMBLAGE—see also COMMUNICATION—see also FABRICATION—see also IDEA—see also MODEL—see also MONTAGE—see also PHOTOCOLLAGE—see also PHOTOGRA-PHY—see also REPRESENTATION—see also 2-D.

COLLECTION

Collection, object groupings: Refers to accumulated groups of objects or materials having a focal characteristic and that have been brought together by an individual or organization. Examples include a selected set of artworks in a museum or archive, or separate literary works that do not form a treatise or monograph on a subject but have been combined and issued together as a whole.

Le Corbusier Research Collection. Gund Hall, Frances Loeb Library. "The Le Corbusier Research *Collection* is held in the Special *Collections* of the Frances Loeb Library. It was established when the library was dedicated in 1972 and consists primarily of printed materials by and about Le Corbusier (1887–1965). In addition, it includes original materials by Le Corbusier: a group of paintings and drawings in a variety of media, a tapestry, and an unpublished sketchbook. The collection is the focus of ongoing acquisition and collection development, and currently holds over 1,100 titles (including republications, translations, and new editions).

Interspersed in the pages of *Platform 8* are single entries for each of the 35 monographs and monographic series published by Le Corbusier during his lifetime (and designated by himself as the bibliography of his published work). Within the encyclopedic structure of *Platform 8*, this bibliography is indexed by associated topics or terms, and briefly annotated. If we understand the books authored by Le Corbusier (and collected at the Harvard GSD) as both writing and design practice since many of his projects were developed in this format, they belong somewhere in our collective disciplinary (and institutional) memory. The bibliography is presented here as an homage à Le Corbusier, 50 years later." —Inés Zalduendo. ▨

Special Collections. Gund Hall, Frances Loeb Library. The Special *Collections* department of the Frances Loeb Library includes the Rare Book *Collection*, the Le Corbusier Research *Collection* both searchable online, and the Special *Collections*—the archival *collections* of original materials. A number of the Special *Collections* inventories can be accessed through Harvard's Online Archival Search Information System (OASIS) database. In addition, the collection is a site for exhibitions and other library-related meetings, presentations, and activities. ▨

Visual & Materials Collections. Gund Hall, Frances Loeb Library. The Visual & Materials *Collections* hold non-print digital images, videos, DVDs, maps and plans, photographs, and specialized equipment, including a slide scanner and copy stand. Many of the digital images and slides can be accessed through Visual Information Access (VIA). The Harvard GSD Materials *Collection* is a collection of over 600 materials ranging from innovative, new materials to those found everyday in the built environment. The *collection* allows users to rethink conventional applications and promote material experimentation in design practice. ⊛

See also BOOK—see also CATALOGUE—see also EXHIBITION—see also ICON—see also INFORMATION—see also MATERIAL—see also OBJECT—see also PUBLICATION—see also RESEARCH—see also WRITING.

COLLECTIVE

Collective, artists' collectives, associations, organizations: Associations of artists, wherein members of each group collaborate in a formal manner.

COLLOQUIUM

Colloquium, conferences, meetings: Meetings at which academic specialists deliver addresses on a topic or on related topics and then participate in a discussion on the topics.

See also CONFERENCE—see also SYMPOSIUM—see also WOOD: Wood Urbanism.

COLOR

Color, colorfastness, physiochemical attributes & properties: The property of a *coloring* matter or material containing a *coloring* matter to retain its original hue or intensity. Refers especially to the ability to resist running or fading, which most frequently results from cleaning or exposure to light. *Color, perceived attribute, color & color-*related phenomena: Refers to a general perceived attribute of an object or light resulting from the response of vision to the wavelength of reflected or transmitted light. The principal dimensions of *color* when discussing painting are the variables or attributes of hue, tone, and intensity. When referring to individual chromatic *colors* and achromatic *colors* or neutrals, use "*colors* (hues or tints)." Primary *color, color* types, hues or tints: Generally refers to the traditional primary *colors* of pigment (red, yellow, blue) that cannot be made from mixtures of other *colors*, and from which theoretically all other pigment *colors* may be produced. When two primary *colors* are mixed together, the result is a secondary *color*; for example, mixing red and yellow makes orange. Secondary *color, color* types, hues or tints: *Colors* which result from mixing two primary *colors* (orange, green, violet). Spectral *color*, perceived attribute, *color & color-*related phenomena: *Color* seen when a beam of light is split into its component parts. The *colors* of the rainbow that correspond to the electromagnetic waves of the visible spectrum (violet, blue, green, yellow, orange, red), illustrated by shining white light through a prism. Tertiary *color*: *Colors* produced by mixing a primary *color* with an adjacent secondary *color*; examples are red-orange and blue-green.

Almanach d'architecture modern. Publication Éditions G. Crès, 1925. Le Corbusier (author). Le Corbusier Research Collection, Frances Loeb Library. LeC NA 680 L496.

"Le Corbusier's *Almanach* contains a diversity of information: documents, theories, proposals, histories, short stories, data, standards proposed, apologies, and idealizations about standards organizations and the industrialization of buildings, all written in response to the critiques of the 'Pavilion de L'Ésprit Nouveaux.' It also serves as a source of information related to projects where he was experimenting with *color*, and more specifically, the housing project at Pessac where Le Corbusier used sienna, yellow, gray, green, blue, and aquamarine. These *color* studies may have influenced his text 'Polychromie architecturale' (published posthumously), in which he states that in architecture one should 'let elements speak through *color*.' As described by Arthur Rüegg, the palette of *colors*, or *color* keyboards, that Le Corbusier later designed for Salubra wallpapers, denoted different atmospheres (sometimes related to the landscape: earth, sky, sand) and enabled the use of two or three *colors* in harmony. For Le Corbusier, *color*— on flat surfaces or volumes—was an intrinsic component in the conception of architecture. Ada Louise Huxtable wrote about Pessac saying: 'If this is so bad, how can it be so good?'" —Inés Zalduendo. ⊛

See also LIGHTING—see also MATERIAL—see also OBSERVATION—see also PHOTOGRAPHY—see also PRINT—see also REPRESENTATION.

COLUMN

Column, architectural elements: In the discipline of architecture, refers to cylindrical or slightly tapering vertical members made to either give support or to appear to give support. They usually comprise three sections: base, capital, and shaft. The term also refers to all uprights in steel frame or concrete frame structures. *Columns* may occasionally stand alone as a monument, for example Trajan's *Column* in Rome or Nelson's *Column* in London. *Columns* may be used as decorative elements on furniture. For square or rectangular members, either in masonry construction or classically treated, use "piers (supporting elements)." For wooden square uprights, use "posts."

COMMENCEMENT

Commencement, academic ceremonies: Ceremonies at which degrees or diplomas are conferred by an educational institution.

Harvard University Commencement. Harvard University has 12 degree-granting schools in addition to the Radcliffe Institute for Advanced Study. The university has grown from nine students with a single master to an enrollment of more than 20,000 degree candidates including undergraduate, graduate, and professional students. There are more than 360,000 living alumni in the United States and over 190 other countries.

Academy Award-winning actress Natalie Portman addressed graduating seniors at Harvard University's Senior Class Day ceremony on May 27, 2015 at the Tercentenary Theater. Former Massachusetts governor Deval L. Patrick gave his address on the following day. Public artist and MacArthur Fellow Rick Lowe (LF, 2002) was the Harvard GSD Class Day Speaker. He gave his address on May 27, 2015 in Piper Auditorium.

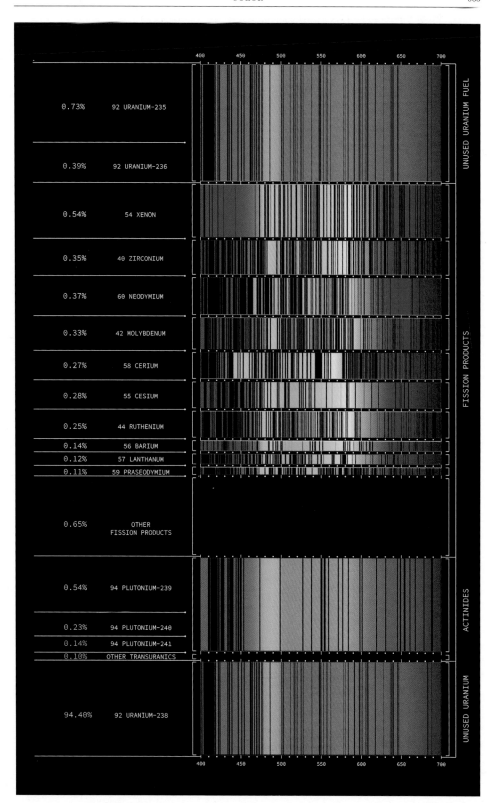

		400	450	500	550	600	650	700	
0.73%	92 URANIUM-235								UNUSED URANIUM FUEL
0.39%	92 URANIUM-236								
0.54%	54 XENON								FISSION PRODUCTS
0.35%	40 ZIRCONIUM								
0.37%	60 NEODYMIUM								
0.33%	42 MOLYBDENUM								
0.27%	58 CERIUM								
0.28%	55 CESIUM								
0.25%	44 RUTHENIUM								
0.14%	56 BARIUM								
0.12%	57 LANTHANUM								
0.11%	59 PRASEODYMIUM								
0.65%	OTHER FISSION PRODUCTS								
0.54%	94 PLUTONIUM-239								ACTINIDES
0.23%	94 PLUTONIUM-240								
0.14%	94 PLUTONIUM-241								
0.10%	OTHER TRANSURANICS								
94.40%	92 URANIUM-238								UNUSED URANIUM
		400	450	500	550	600	650	700	

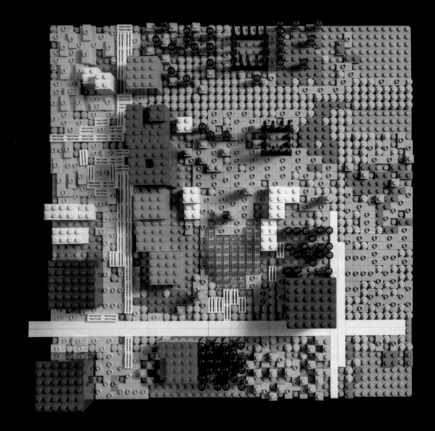

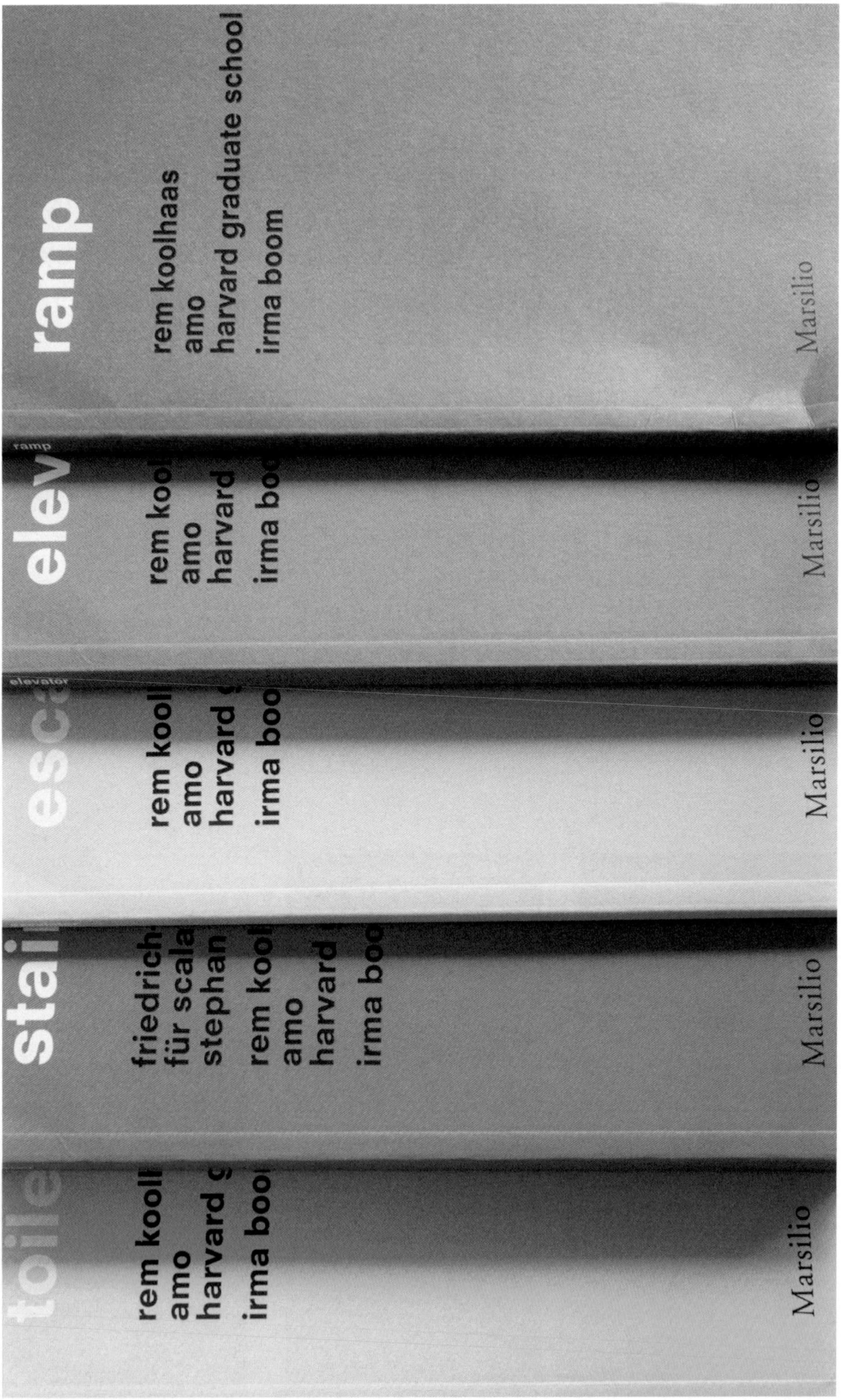
ramp
rem koolhaas
amo
harvard graduate school
irma boom
Marsilio

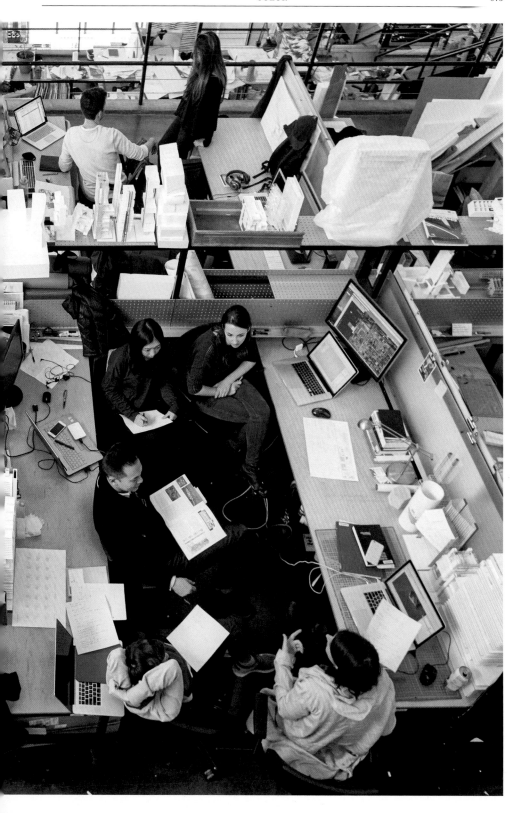

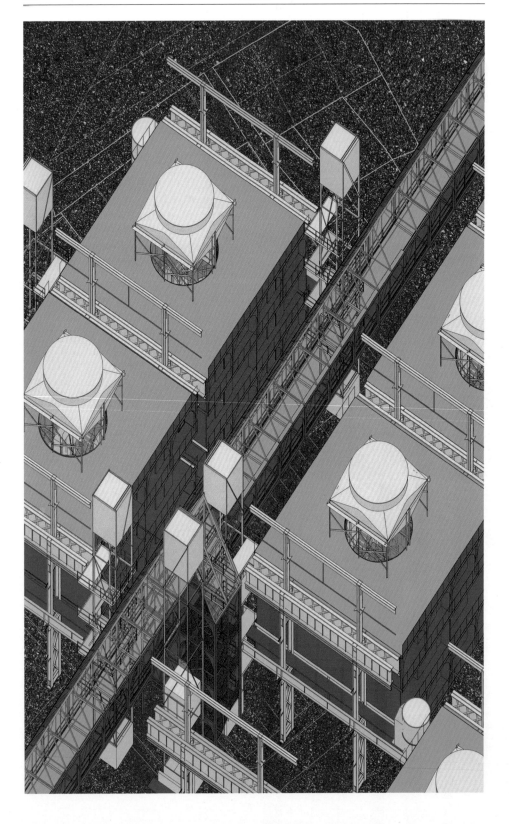

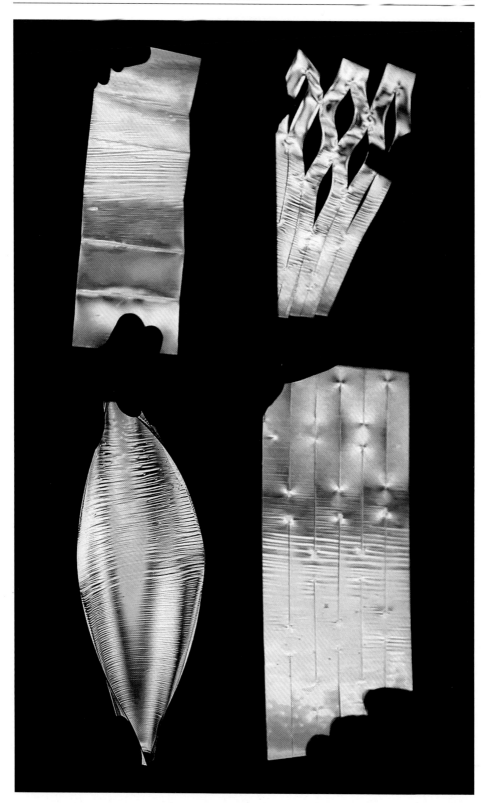

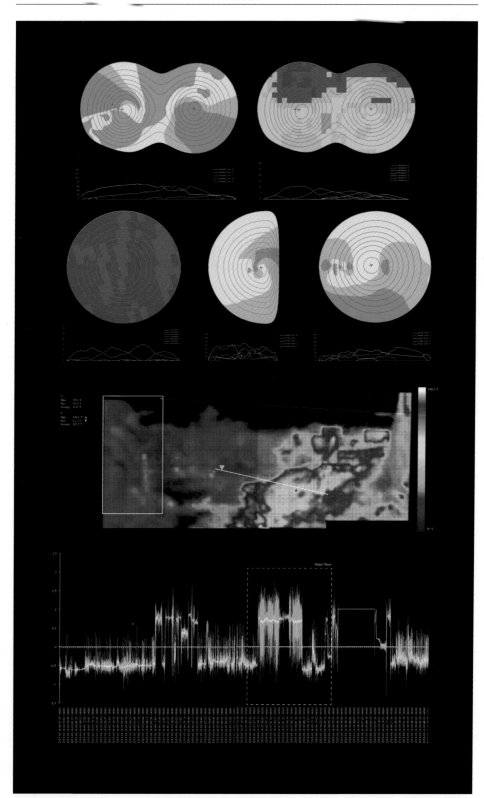

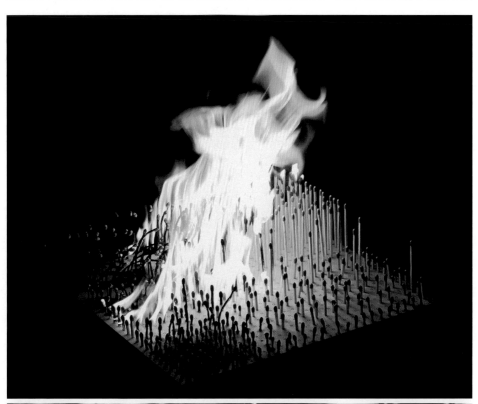

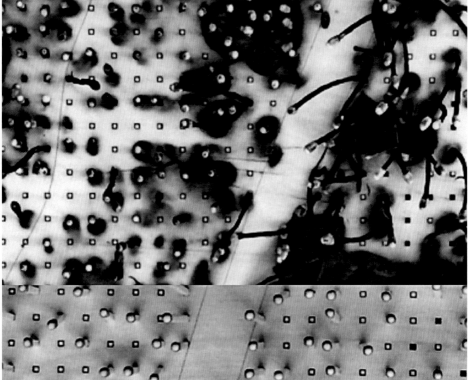

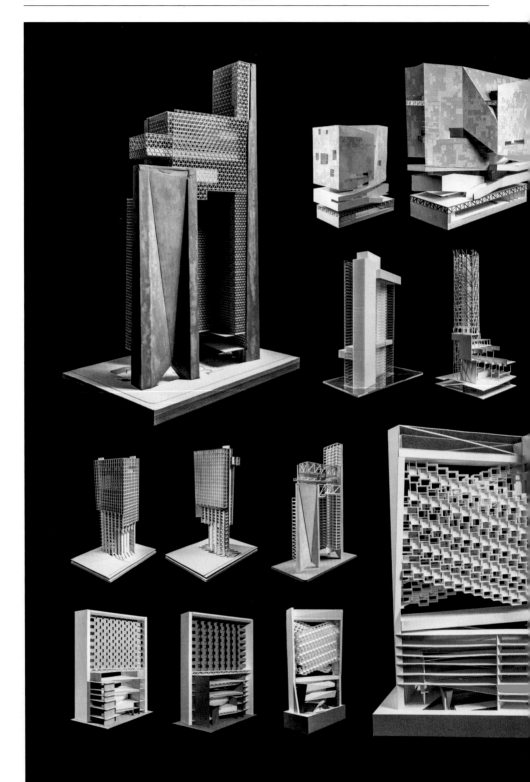

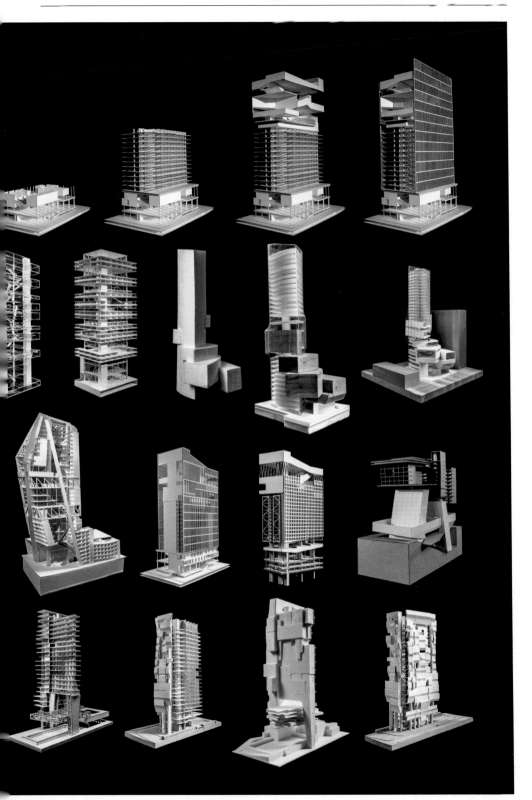

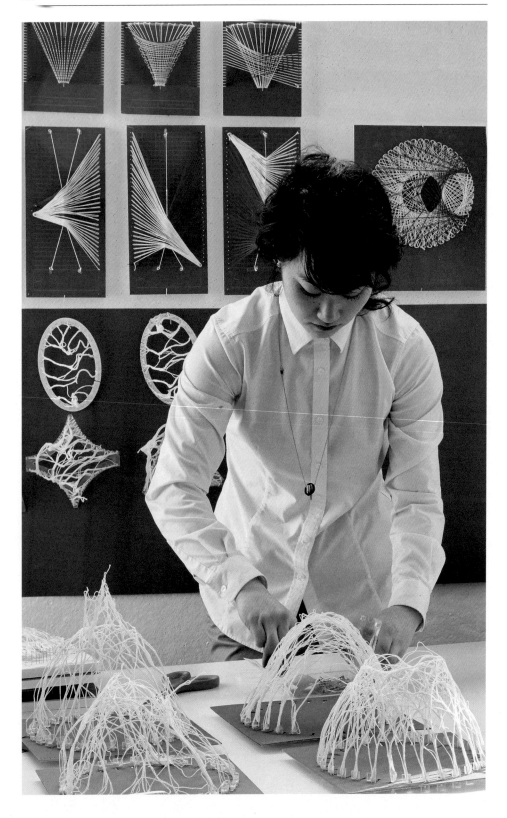

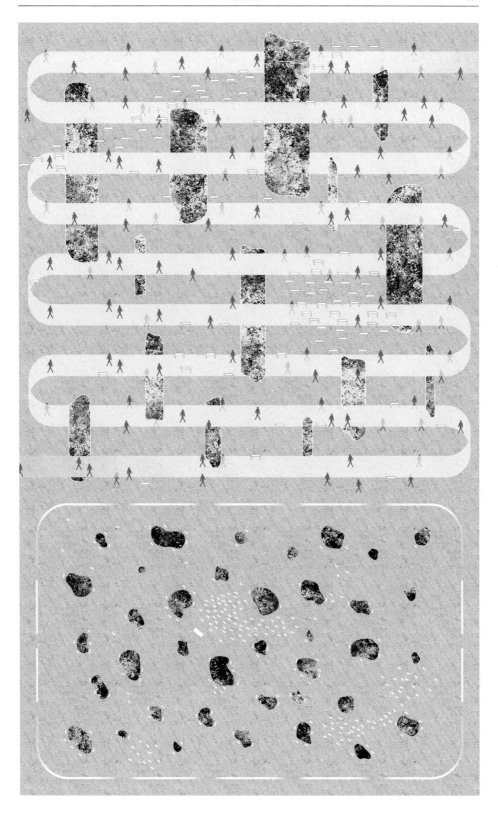

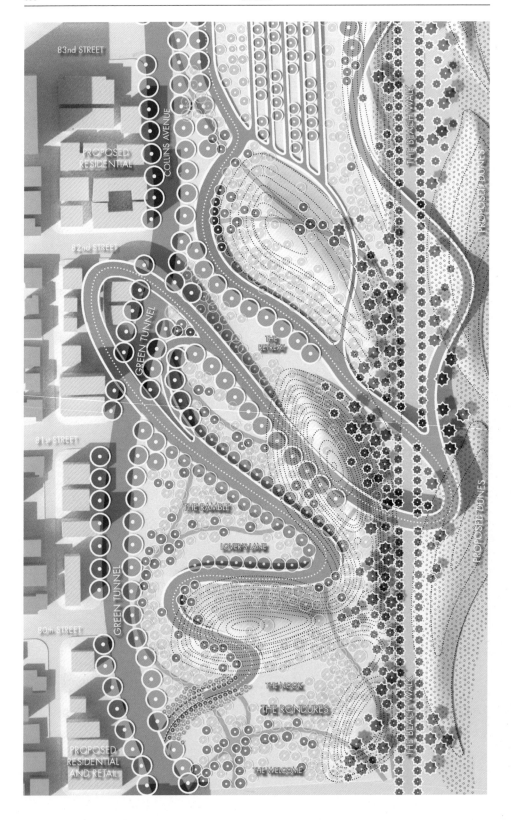

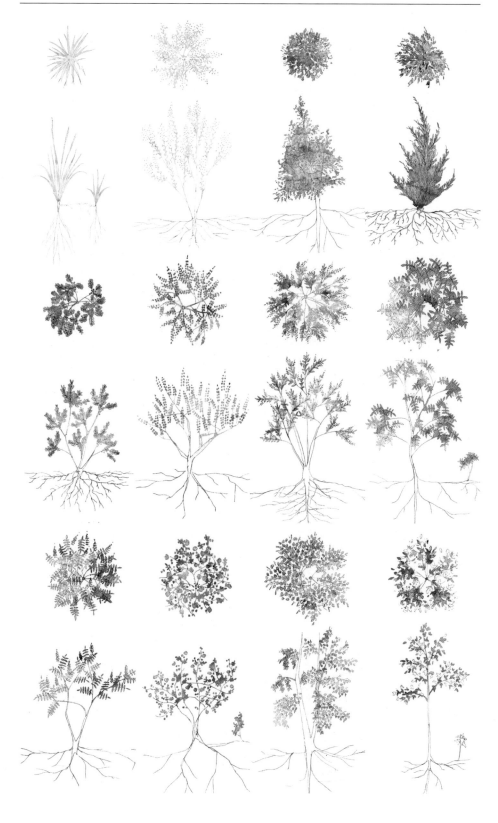

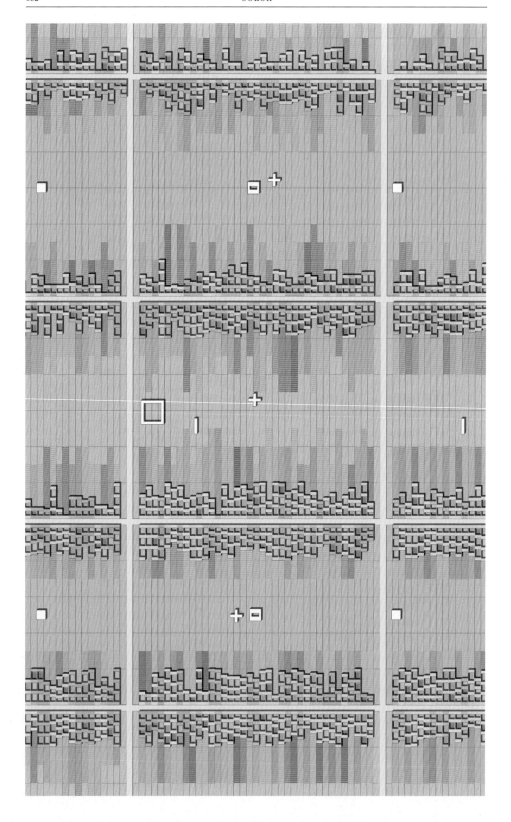

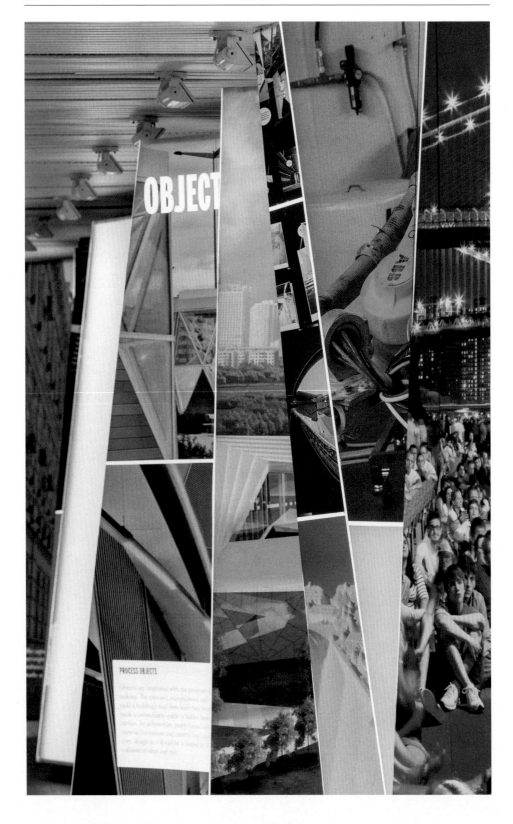

COMMERCIAL

Commercial building, single built works by function: Use broadly to refer to buildings associated with any aspect of the various activities and business relationships of industry and trade; when referring to structures associated with the purchase, sale, or exchange of goods in business, use "mercantile buildings." *Commercial* complex, complexes by function, buildings: Buildings or complexes constructed for or serving businesses, merchants, and other *commercial* purposes.

See also PRACTICE: From Roots to Routes—see also RETAIL: Prestige Retail.

COMMITTEE

Committee, organizations, groups: Groups of persons delegated to consider, investigate, or take action upon and usually to report concerning some matter or business.

Design by Committee: Digital Interfaces for Collaborative & Participatory Design. SCI 6468. Department of Architecture. Seminar. Fall 2014. Instructor: Panagiotis Michalatos.

This seminar looked into the design and technical challenges involved in the development of web-based interfaces for collaborative and participatory design scenarios where more than one agent is involved. The designer, in a sense, is given the chance to design and experiment with the communication architecture and temporality of the design process itself. Students were introduced to web technologies for front-end and back-end development (javascript, webGL, nodeJS, MongoDB) and related APIs for data mining, visualization, mapping, and interaction. ₪

COMMON

Common, open space by location or context: Expanses of land, paved or green, owned by the community as a whole.

Boston Common. Boston, Massachusetts. The starting point of the Freedom Trail, Boston *Common* is the oldest park in the country. The park is almost 50 acres in size. Today, Boston *Common* is the anchor for the Emerald Necklace, a system of connected parks that winds through many of Boston's neighborhoods. The *"Common"* has been used for many different purposes throughout its long history. Until 1830, cattle grazed the *Common*, and until 1817, public hangings took place there. British troops camped on Boston *Common* prior to the Revolution and left from there to face colonial resistance at Lexington and Concord on April, 1775. Celebrities, including Martin Luther King Jr., Pope John Paul II, and Gloria Steinem (advocate of the feminist revolution), have given speeches at the *Common*.

Cambridge Common. Cambridge, Massachusetts. The Cambridge *Common* is a major city park as well as a National Historic Landmark. The 16-acre park which is centrally located outside of Harvard Square surrounded by Massachusetts Avenue, Garden Street, and Waterhouse Street has a long and colorful history, and

is an important local resource as well as a tourist attraction. The *Common* contains the popular Alexander W. Kemp Playground re-built in 2009, a playing field, lawns, historic monuments, and pathways. The park acts as a haven for neighborhood people who want a place to relax in the sun or on a bench under a tree. The *Common* is also significant in that over 10,000 pedestrians and cyclists use the paths and sidewalks on a daily basis.

The Holler: The Cosmopolitan Roots of the Appalachian Scene. Thesis. Christina Leigh Geros (MLA I AP & MAUD), advised by Rosetta S. Elkin.

"Views into and through the Appalachian landscape have prioritized the geologic and atmospheric qualities of the region. By way of road and trail, the ridge lines have become the primary viewing platforms from which this landscape is both traversed and understood. Historically, these lands served as a forest *commons* for the people of the region, providing resources that enabled social and economic movement for a marginalized population.

This project proposes a network of easements within the Appalachian landscape to both amplify and expose the cultural specificity of the region and strengthen an existing grassroots movement to return privatized land to a public *commons*. By connecting, isolating, and highlighting the thresholds between land uses, this network explicates seemingly minor narratives found within plant species as instrumental in the construction of cultural image and artifact. This thesis thus contends that the vegetal material of the region is in continual negotiation with the culture of its human counterpart and offers this pattern as a site for design—building from the regional narrative of conservation through stewardship rather than preservation through isolation." ₪

COMMUNICATION

Communication, social science concept: Concepts related to the science and technology of the transmission and reception of information.

Interactive Games for Risk Communication. Master in Design Studies Risk & Resilience Lecture. Gund Hall, Piper Auditorium. October 14, 2014. Pablo Suarez.

Pablo Suarez conducted a workshop, where students, professors, and practitioners encountered new methods to integrate risk information, better understand the implications of implementing policies and plans through systems oriented scenarios, and engage in thought-provoking discussions that critically consider past and future solutions. This event was a foundational opportunity for those from the varied fields of risk and resilience, urban planning, public policy, *communications*, development, science, humanitarian relief, design, and others to comprehensively contribute to an improved environment for actionable decisions. ₪

See also DATA—see also INFORMATION: New Geographies 07—see also REPRESENTATION—see also RISK.

COMMUNITY

Community, inhabited places: Groups or bodies of people who live in the same place and are usually united by a common way of life, cultural or ethnic identity, or other factors. Usually reserved for smaller groups that have not organized into a village or town.

Agitating Communities. Meet the Loebs Seminar Week. Loeb Fellowship Program. Andrew Howard, Shahira Fahmy, and Kolu Zigbi. ⊛

Community: What is the City but the People? Lecture. Gund Hall, Stubbins. October 23, 2014. Suketu Mehta.
    Cities can be resilient—not just in their physical structure, but in their spirit. In the absence of a functioning government, they survive through a series of solidarity networks that sustain the populace—small solutions for the big city. What role does the state have in fostering them? How do we fashion a city that may not include everybody, but excludes nobody? ⊛

See also FELLOWSHIP: Community Service Fellowship Program—see also INFRASTRUCTURE: Lively Infrastructures—see also MODEL: Architecture & the Territory—see also POWER: Community Power & Leadership.

COMPARATIVE

1: Of, relating to, or constituting the degree of *comparison* in a language that denotes increase in the quality, quantity, or relation expressed by an adjective or adverb. 2: Considered as if in *comparison* to something else as a standard not quite attained, relative <a *comparative* stranger>. 3: Characterized by systematic *comparison* especially of likenesses and dissimilarities <*comparative* anatomy>.

See also INFORMATION—see also LIVELIHOOD: Livelihoods & Urban Form—see also QUALITATIVE—see also QUANTITATIVE.

COMPASS

Compass point, positional attributes: Refers to directions as referenced on a *compass*, which is an instrument for measuring a horizontal reference direction relative to magnetic north. The four basic points are at the top, bottom, right, and left sides of a *compass*, corresponding to north, south, east, and west. Points between the four basic points are described by combining terms, for example, northeast, southeast, etc. *Compass* rose, document genres by form: Circular representations on maps and navigational charts of the points of the *compass*, often including both true and magnetic directions; originally used to assist mariners in navigation, now most commonly decorative in nature. *Compass*, drawing instruments: Instruments for drawing circles and measuring the distance between two points; consisting of two pointed legs, movable on a joint or pivot, usually made so that one of the points can be detached for the insertion of a pen or an extension. Sun *compass*, direction indicators, horizontal angle measuring devices: Navigational devices that utilize the shadow of a pin and accompanying dial to facilitate use of the sun in measuring direction.

See also CIRCULATION—see also DRAFTING—see also GEOMETRY—see also LINE—see also ORIENTATION—see also REPRESENTATION—see also TOOL.

COMPETITION

Competition, contests, activities: Events during which parties compete for an honor, job, or the like. A prime example is in the context of art and architecture, where a *competition* is a formal process by which *competing* architects or artists submit plans, budgets, and other information to a client or patron for an architectural or artistic project.

The Design Competition. Conference. Gund Hall, Piper Auditorium. April 23–24, 2015. Jerold S. Kayden & David van der Leer (conference cochairs).
    Design *competitions* are increasingly used to procure the design of just about anything. Governments, philanthropies, advocacy organizations, developers, and even celebrities are offering ever-larger awards and visibility for buildings, landscapes, and products, as well as for solutions to complex economic, social, and ecological problems. *Competitions* can mobilize thousands of talented people across disciplines to creatively tackle pressing challenges in publicized—if not public—settings. They can also be wasteful, less-than-fully transparent, and even exploitative.
    The Design *Competition* Conference reviewed the state of design *competitions* today and their impact on *competitors*, sponsors, design, and public interest. Using the lens of professional, ethical, business, legal, aesthetic, and public policy perspectives, the participants asked: Do *competitions* enhance creativity and excellence in the production of built and landscape environments? Do they advance the skills and interests of the designers who participate in the process? Does the public get to participate and benefit? Do they make for better financial outcomes and, if so, for whom? Is it an ethical method for securing design given the mechanics of the process? Do *competitions* strengthen or weaken the design professions as a whole? Do they identify new talent? These and other questions emerged through discussion of case studies and thematic presentations. ⊛

DesignOFF GSD. Student Group. In an effort to explore architectural ideas and concepts that are discussed within the student body, but may not be part of the design curriculum, DesignOFF proposes *competitions* to bare these issues to light. ⊛

Une maison—un palais. Publication. Éditions G. Crès, 1928. Le Corbusier (author). Le Corbusier Research Collection, Frances Loeb Library. LeC NA 2500 L496a.
    "Both as propaganda for Le Corbusier's project for the League of Nations in Geneva, and as framework for his ideas on architecture from the private house to the public building (Palace of Nations), this book was originally written as a lecture delivered in Zurich on November 9, 1927. Le Corbusier also gave this lecture in Madrid on May 11, 1928; Barcelona on May 16, 1928; and ETH Zurich in summer 1928. The 1926 international *competition* for the League of Nations received 377 entries. Le Corbusier was awarded a prize, among others, but the jury did not immediately recommend the execution of the project. This sparked an international controversy with attacks from both modernist and classicist camps. The modernist projects of Le Corbusier, Hannes Meyer, Richard Neutra, and Rudolf Schindler were later exhibited by the Werkbund in 1927." —Inés Zalduendo. ⊛

See also DRAWING: Competition Drawing—see also PAVILION: Design Miami / Harvard GSD Pavilion.

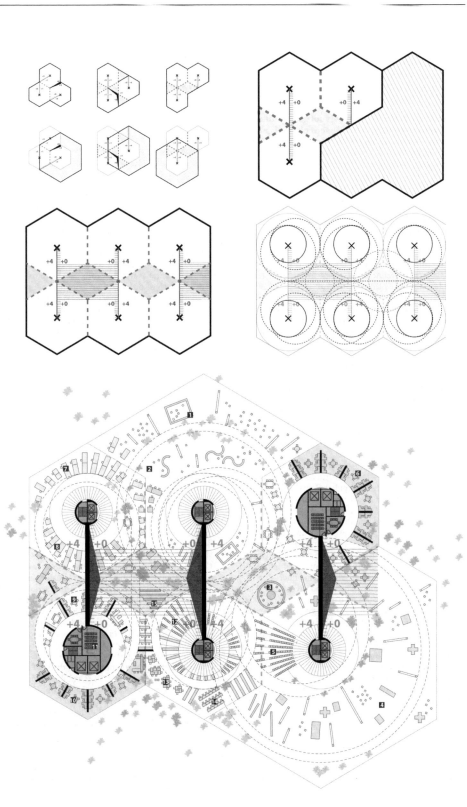

COMPLEX

Complex, buildings: Aggregations of buildings, other structures, and/or open spaces, often multifunctional, and more extensive than single built works, usually shaped over a longer period of time by more participants.

Cambridge Talks IX—Infrastructure, Media, and Power-Knowledge: The Research University. Lecture. Gund Hall, Piper Auditorium. April 2, 2015. Reinhold Martin.

Beginning with Michel Foucault's elusive and omnipresent "power-knowledge" couplet, this talk examined the aesthetic and technical properties of certain infrastructures through which this couplet is manifest. These infrastructures, which could be called architectural, are mainly found in research universities in the United States during the late 19th century, with genealogical ties to the business corporation. Martin discussed the limits of transferring the Foucauldian analytic directly onto architecture. Likewise for the "new materialism" that has more recently shed significant light on the multifarious life of things. Instead, a "gay science" of corporate power, centered on the university, can only arise during those brief intervals when architecture appears repeatedly as one among many media.

Cambridge Talks is the annual conference organized by students in the PhD program at the Harvard GSD. ⊕

The Function of Time: Cultural Complex. STU 1301. Department of Architecture. Option Studio. Fall 2014. Instructors: Farshid Moussavi & James Khamsi.

This studio was one of a series at the Harvard GSD focused on exploring the architectural potentials of time and uncertainty in large cultural *complexes* to generate interior urbanism. The previous two studios investigated these in the context of a large contemporary art museum.

This studio explored these potentials in the context of Olympicopolis—a large cultural and education *complex*, the size of the Pompidou Centre in Paris, currently being planned for London. This will house the Victoria and Albert Museum, Sadler's Wells Theater, University of the Arts London, and a contemporary art museum in a single building. These institutions are required to both share space and maintain independence within the building. Instead of the universal and autonomous space of the Pompidou Center, which leaves change to chance, and where its stacked floors can vary only through subdivision. The studio investigated how a large interior can be designed as an operational matrix that can change in radically different ways over time by incorporating switch-spatial elements such as moveable building parts, multi-static spatial grids, as well as strategically planned free spaces (atriums). By embracing change as a core component of the *complex*, the studio aimed to use the dynamics of the *complex* to generate interior urbanism.

The students' initial research examined Mies van der Rohe's experiments with "universal space" and Cedric Price's Fun Palace as two alternative proposals for large, flexible interiors, Walter Gropius's Total Theater, and Bernard Tschumi's discussions of cross-programming. The studio also examined the history of the atrium as an alternative element for change that is not autonomous in itself.

Students: Joon Hyuk Choe (MArch II), Jeongmo Kwon (MArch I), Mengdan Liu (MArch II), Chen Lu (MArch

I), Xuanyi Nie (MArch I), Fani-Christina Papadopoulou (MArch II), Jee Hyung Park (MArch I), Sizhi Qin (MArch II), Bingjie Shi (MLA I AP), Fan Wang (MArch II), Jiaqi Wang (MAUD), Ping Wang (MArch I), Xi Yi (MAUD). ⊕

Figure. Diagrams (previous page). Jee Hyung Park (MArch I).

See also ASSEMBLY—see also BUILDING—see also CAM-PUS—see also CULTURE—see also MUSEUM—see also STRUC-TURE—see also TIME.

COMPOSITE

1: Made up of distinct parts, such as (a) relating to or being a modification of the Corinthian order combining angular Ionic volutes with the acanthus-circled bell of the Corinthian; (b) of or relating to a very large family of dicotyledonous herbs, shrubs, and trees often considered to be the most highly evolved plants and characterized by florets arranged in dense heads that resemble single flowers; (c) factorable into two or more prime factors other than one and itself <eight is a positive *composite* integer>. 2: Combining the typical or essential characteristics of individuals making up a group <the *composite* man called the Poet —Richard Poirier>. 3: A statistical hypothesis specifying a range of values for one or more statistical parameters.

COMPOSITION

Composition, artistic arrangement: Structure or arrangement of the internal elements of a work of art, such as a drawing, sculpture, or written or musical work. *Composition,* material: Refers to various aggregate materials formed artificially from two or more substances, such as whiting, resin, and size used for modeling ornament in the late 18th century, or plaster of Paris, sawdust, bran, and glue used for doll-making, or plastic cement-based mortars used in construction.

Après le cubisme. Publication. Éditions des Commentaires, 1918. Le Corbusier (author). Le Corbusier Research Collection, Frances Loeb Library. LeC NA 1053.J4 A515x.

"Considered the manifesto of Purism, *Après le cubisme* is a declaration of principles by Le Corbusier, in collaboration with Amedée Ozenfant. Aimed at a revision of art beyond Cubism, the work strives toward 'constants' as opposed to 'variants' in the search for an art expressive of the times. This new approach to painting was based on a rational, almost mathematical, logic of *composition* (and the role that art could play in the social fabric). Here, bottles, guitars, and pipes are new *objet* types representing the virtues and products of the new industrial age. *La Cheminée* (1918), exhibited one month after this manifesto, is considered Le Corbusier's first painting. Shortly after Le Corbusier and Ozenfant began *L'esprit nouveau*, the journal they launched together in 1920, and where they further articulated their theories." —Inés Zalduendo. ⊕

See also AUDIOVISUAL: Six Microphones—see also BALANCE—see also FORM—see also GASTRONOMY: The Architecture of Taste—see also HARMONY—see also OEUVRE—see also PAINT-ING—see also REPRESENTATION.

COMPOST

Compost, residue materials: A mixture of decaying organic material generally from plant residue.

Harvard University Office for Sustainability. Annually, Harvard University recovers 4,000 tons of food waste, yard waste, and coffee grounds. Food waste is taken to nearby Brick Ends Farm. This *compostable* material is turned into rich fertilizer and used on over 80 acres as part of Harvard University's organic landscaping effort.

COMPUTATION

1: (a) The act or action of *computing*, calculation; (b) the use or operation of a computer. 2: A system of reckoning. 3: An amount computed.

Adaptive Technologies: Computation's Deep Ancestry. Panel Discussion. Gund Hall, Piper Auditorium. October 14, 2014. Mario Carpo, George L. Legendre, Greg Lynn, Cameron Wu, with Andrew Witt (moderator).

This discussion featured designers, historians, and experimentalists who study the resonance and conflict between design and exact science. The panel explored the attraction, limits, amplifications, and subversions of exactness and deduction. As designers have turned to physics and mathematics as models for technique or knowledge in *computational* design, what have they learned? What might be of hidden or pathological ancestors and antecedents to our current and future design technology? ֍

Paradigms in Computing: Making, Machines, and Models for Design Agency in Architecture. Publication. eVolo, 2014. David Jason Gerber & Mariana Ibañez (editors). NA2728 .P37 2014.

Paradigms in Computing investigates critical, theoretical, and practical research and design that illustrate the plurality of *computing* approaches within the broad spectrum of design and mediated practices. With exploration of critical discourse in the form of theoretical work, as well as design projects illustrated through the coupled nature of *computing* and digital theory with modes and models of design research and production, this book argues for and against the plurality of paradigms of *computing* within contemporary research and architectural practice. Through this combination, the book investigates the digital as a form of agency within architecture and the expanding design disciplines akin and adjacent to it. Arguably, the convergence of the cyber, physical, and social is producing a potent set of possibilities that challenge and foster an open polemical debate of the notions of design agency and the pluri-potent *Paradigms in Computing* for design practice.

See also COMPUTER—see also MACHINE—see also PROCESS— see also TECHNOLOGY—see also TOOL.

COMPUTER

Computer equipment, data processing equipment: Electronic devices or systems capable of automatically performing prescribed sequences of operations on digitized data to achieve a desired end result. *Computer*-generated: Use to describe something, as an arrangement of visible forms or of data, that is produced by a *computer*, especially when the programming generates automatically a relatively large number of the steps between what is input and what is produced. *Computer*-Aided Design (CAD): Refers to the process by which a *computer* is used as a tool in designing architecture, landscape design, cities, transportation infrastructure, engineering projects, automobiles, *computer* chips, or other objects of any size. The process uses a *computer* program to provide an interactive drawing tool, with an interface to allow simulation and analysis. In architectural design, the *computer* typically allows the user to virtually walk through three-dimensional spaces, to view the architecture in position on the proposed site, and to test aspects of stress and support. It is also used to reconstruct ruined buildings and cities, and to depict archaeological sites at different periods of time. *Computer*-Aided Machine (CAM): Manufacturing using *computer* systems and techniques to track and control the flow of information, materials, energy, and labor throughout a factory, completely or in part. *Computer* modeling: The development of *computer* models to represent concepts or dynamic systems.

Computer Resources Group (CRG). Gund Hall, Room 520. "Design studies require substantial *computer* use well beyond basic word-processing, spreadsheets, and social media. Advanced *computer* literacy skills— including familiarity with 2-D and 3-D *Computer*-Aided Design (CAD) modeling software, animation, video, multimedia, image processing, Geographic Information Systems (GIS), structural, thermal, financial and other analysis packages, and programming and algorithmic approaches—are increasingly required of students and professionals in all design and planning disciplines.

CRG maintains an environment in which information technology is easily available and easily accessible to all the members of the Harvard GSD community. CRG manages a complex *computer* network, supporting Windows, Macintosh, and Linux operating systems, providing a variety of services students for course work and independent study, as well as to staff, faculty, and visitors for research. Most of the Harvard GSD campus is bathed in high-bandwidth wireless infrastructure, and every student desk is provided with a high-speed network connection. Each student has access to state-of-the-art software, licensed over the network, as well as to the Internet. This account also provides access to input and output devices including large format digitizers, flatbed scanners, large format color plotters, high quality color printers, video and multimedia equipment, and CAD/CAM fabrication equipment." —Stephen McTee Ervin. ֍

Computer-Numerical-Control (CNC) Machine Tools. Gund Hall, Room L32. CNC machine tools are the workhorses of CNC-manufacturing technology and are responsible for assisting with the manufacture of virtually everything produced today—from toothbrushes and running-shoe soles to furniture. CNC has been applied to two-axis tools such as lathes, cut-off tools, and slitting operations, but perhaps the most significant applications are found in three-axis, four-axis, and five-axis tools such as milling machines, stone cutting equipment, grinders, router tables, robotic welders, material handlers, and a astonishing variety of other tools. These tools require sophisticated CAD-CAM soft-

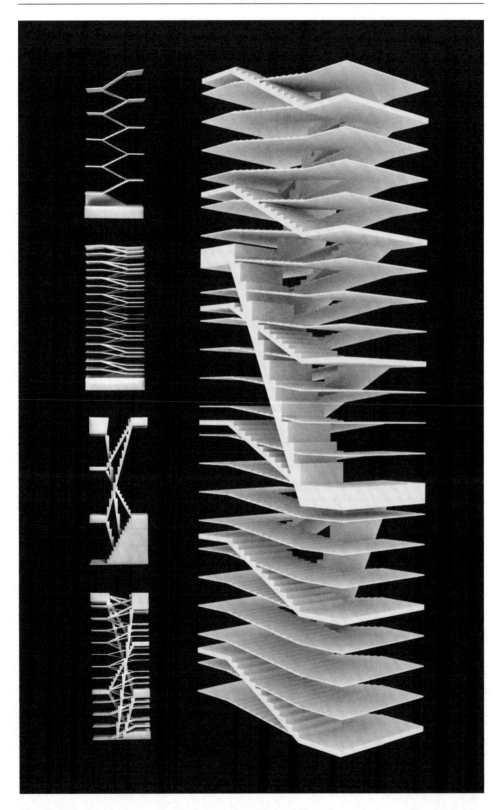

ware to translate three-dimensional models into simple text files that control the tool through combinations of linear and rotational motion, such as .TAP and .CNC file formats. ⊕

CONCEPT

Concept, first drafts, versions of documents: Rough or preliminary proposed texts of documents, not yet in definitive form, usually subject to review, revision, rejection, approval, or adoption. Formal *concept*, artistic *concepts*: Artistic *concepts* concerned with form, as opposed to content. Functional *concept*: General *concepts* that are related to activities, statuses, or modes of actions, particularly as related to such activities, statuses, and actions having to do with fulfilling a purpose or having to do with basic, utilitarian functions. In this sense, references to functional *concepts* in the realm of art, architecture, and cultural heritage usually differ from physical attributes, many of which (such as weight) are often considered functional *concepts* by certain disciplines in other contexts. Geometric *concept*, mathematical *concepts*: Mathematical *concepts* related to geometry. Philosophical *concept*: *Concepts* related to knowledge, learning, and scholarship.

CONFLICT

Conflict, general sense: The action of clashing or being in a state of variance between opposed principles, statements, arguments, or the like.

Ad Absurdum. Thesis. Naomi Maki (MArch I AP), advised by Iñaki Ábalos.

"I: Absurdism is the irreconcilable *conflict* that arises between the tendency to seek meaning and the inability to find any. II: Indifference toward convention and value liberates forms to operatively pursue their emergent potentials. Forms establish autonomous methodologies driven by the evolving syntax of their internal properties. III: Scale is an instrument of absurdity. Its transformative capacities are compounded to produce an array of amalgamated absurdities. As a potentially infinite set, these quasi-architectures evolve to form an archive—a constellation of singularities composing and unfolding totality." ⊕

Figure. Models (opposite page). Naomi Maki (MArch I AP).

See also ADVOCACY—see also GEOGRAPHY: Geographies of Social Conflict and Cohesion—see also POST-CONFLICT: May Kabul Be without Gold, Rather without Snow—see also POST-SUBURB—see also TIME.

CONNECTION

Connection, joints: The apparatus used or the manner of joining two or more parts of an object or structure. In bookbinding, the term describes the flexing exterior junctions of the spine and covers of a book. Distinguished from "hinges (fasteners)," which use strips of fabric or paper placed between the two halves of an endpaper where the body of the book is fixed to its cover.

Connections Studio II. HAA 96B. Undergraduate Architecture Studio. Spring 2015. Instructor: Zaneta H. Hong. Teaching Assistants: Hillary Jane Archer (MLA I), Paloma Garcia Simon (MLA I), and Joshua Michael Jow (MArch II).

Over half of the world's inhabitants live in urban environments. Understanding, engaging, and reimaging the urban condition, with all its complexities, structures, processes, and idiosyncrasies, has become a pressing issue for architects, landscape architects, and urban designers alike. This studio focused on the urban condition as a byproduct of the *connections* between both human and nonhuman frameworks (systems and environments). Using diagramming and mapping processes, both iteratively and speculatively, students investigated system-environment relationships through the examination of qualities, behaviors, and territories for a select set of urban agents. Each investigation revealed latent, suppressed, emerging, provisional, and otherwise unmapped *connections*, which influence the formation of urban spaces, infrastructures, and technologies. Course material was presented through a series of exercises, lectures, workshops, and reviews, which introduced students to the application of foundational design principles and critical design strategies. This course fostered the development of a design methodology founded on thoughtful, creative, ethical and sustainable practices, and explored meaningful expressions for the built environment.

Students: Katherine Ingersoll (FAS), Hee Young Angie Jo (FAS), Samia Kayyali (FAS), Larkin McCann (FAS), Matthew Ricotta (FAS), Hoo In Linda Song (FAS), James Thurm (FAS), Liesl Ulrich-Verderber (FAS), John Wang (FAS), Gianina Yumul (FAS). ⊕

Figure. Models & Diagrams (next page, above). Hoo In Linda Song (FAS). Model (next page, below). Hoo In Linda Song (FAS) & James Thurm (FAS).

See also ASSEMBLY—see also CITY—see also HISTORY: Temporary Accumulations—see also MAPPING.

CONSERVATION

Conservation, discipline: The discipline involving treatment, preventive care, and research directed toward the long-term safekeeping of cultural and natural heritage. For actions taken to halt changes or deterioration in objects, sites, or structures, see "preservation (function)"; for changes made to an object or structure so that it will closely approximate its original or other past state, see "restoration (process)."

Master in Design Studies (MDes) Critical Conservation (CC). Critical *Conservation* applies issues of culture, history, and identity to design and development, transcending outdated dialectics as past-future, traditional-modern, and us-them. By engaging 21st-century questions of environmental, social, and economic sustainability, Critical *Conservation* serves a pluralist and global society. It provides designers, real estate professionals, and planners, among others, with a foundation to understand the cultural systems that frame conflicts inherent in making progressive places. Unlike preservation programs that presume the permanence of architecture and use top-down regulation to reinforce existing power structures, Critical

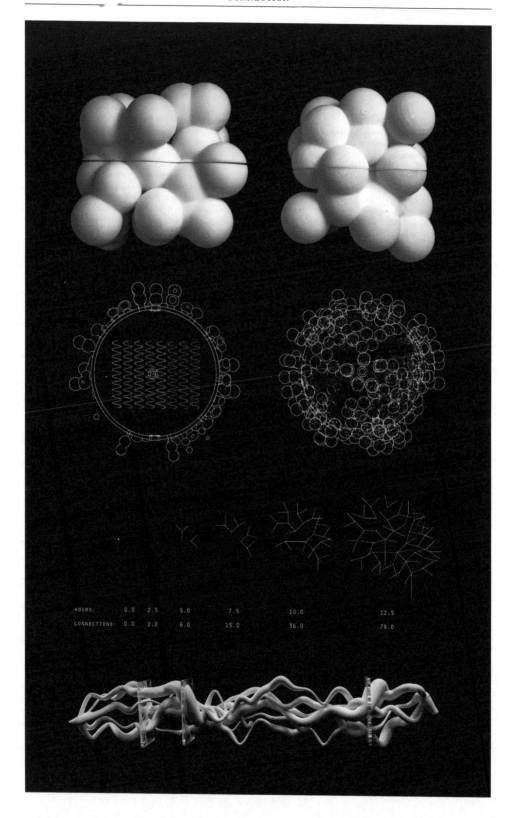

CONNECTIONS: 0.0 2.0 6.0 15.0 36.0 79.0

Conservation extends beyond issues of age, history, and aesthetics to offer a framework of theory and research tools encompassing social, political, and cultural meaning. This enables students to make nuanced decisions about the impact of *conservation* in complex urban and natural places. ⸙

Case Studies in Critical Conservation: Strategies for Curating the Built Environment. HIS 4475. Departments of Architecture and Urban Planning & Design. Seminar. Spring 2015. Instructor: Jana Cephas.

This course analyzed case studies in *conservation* as a means of developing projective strategies for interpreting and curating buildings, landscapes, and cities. More specifically, the course examined the use of design to *conserve* and convey the significance of sites. Students conducted in-depth research and analysis of sites and their social landscapes with the aim of curating aspects of the built environment to reveal its inner histories. The course tackled the controversies inherent to urban *conservation* and attempted to develop proposals that engaged in these controversies rather than dismissing them. The first part of the course focused on theoretical and historical readings and case studies to identify core issues relevant to interpretation planning, including material culture analysis, intangible heritage and cultural intimacy, visitor accessibility, assisting the public experience of significant sites, and policies affecting the interpretation and planning of sites. The second part of the course focused on the interpretation of urban sites, the various meanings of *conservation* in an urban context, and, in particular, the curation of the urban environment as an act of critical *conservation*. ⸙

See also CONSERVATION: Critical Conservation—see also PRESERVATION—see also SOCIAL—see also TECHNIQUE—see also TOOL—see also URBANISM: Extreme Urbanism III.

CONSTRUCTION

Construction, discipline: The art and science of constructing architecture. *Construction,* assembling: The process of creating something by combining parts or elements.

Cases in Contemporary Construction. SCI 6230. Department of Architecture. Seminar. Fall 2014. Instructors: Mark Mulligan & Andreas Georgoulias.

As the final component in the required sequence of technology courses, this professionally-oriented course developed an integral understanding of the design and *construction* of buildings and their related technologies: structural, *constructional,* and environmental. Building on fundamentals covered in SCI 6123: *Construction* Systems, the course looked in detail at examples of innovative *construction* techniques in wood, steel, and concrete structures, introducing the fundamentals of managing design and *construction* projects as well as the principal project delivery methods and scheduling techniques. Aspects such as risk management and environmental and social impacts were introduced, as well as topics related to facilitating innovation and developing talent. ⸙

Construction Lab. SCI 6121. Department of Architecture. Seminar. Fall 2014. Instructor: Salmaan Craig.

This course was an introduction to materials in both science and *construction*. The motivation was to equip the next generation of architects with the means to make sense of the rapid changes occurring in material culture today. The lectures were divided into three parts. The aim of the first part was to establish a qualitative grounding in some key aspects of physics. This was done through a history of measurement, materials, and thermodynamics. It turns out that the secret to understanding materials is scale. Materials have an internal architecture that can be designed to control a variety of phenomena in surprising ways. The second part introduced the science of materials. This included: how to categorize materials, the mechanics of materials, the relationship of materials to heat; how to design new materials; and what makes biological materials special. The third part contextualized this knowledge. Subjects for lectures included: the ecology of materials, the history of their use in *construction,* why only certain materials dominate in *construction,* and the status of materials science now and in the near future. ⸙

Construction Systems. SCI 6123. Department of Architecture. Seminar. Spring 2015. Instructor: Billie Jo Faircloth.

This course introduced a framework for the instantiation of architecture through *construction* systems. *Construction* systems were discovered through the methods of dissection, drawing, and building selected systems to reveal their materials and attributes, their logics of assembly, their detailing and manufacture, and their performance in the presence of environmental flows. *Construction* systems, and by association, wall, roof, envelope, and foundation systems, were further examined for specificity where they are shaped by regimes of culture, climate, tools, time, and design philosophy. ⸙

Figure. Exploded Axon (next page). Yiliu Chen Shen-Burke (MArch I).

Innovative Construction in Japan. SCI 6311. Department of Architecture. Seminar. Spring 2015. Instructor: Mark Mulligan.

Modern Japanese architecture has been much admired in the West for its attention to materials, its refined *construction* details, and its ability to simultaneously integrate traditional design principles and push the forefront of technology. This lecture course looked in-depth at significant works by modern Japanese architects, particularly those of the last quarter-century, analyzing both their detailed *construction* and the larger historical, cultural, and theoretical contexts in which they are produced. Individual buildings therefore served as vehicles for exploring the relationship between design theories and *construction* technique. ⸙

Poetics of Landscape Construction. SCI 6454. Department of Landscape Architecture. Seminar. Fall 2014. Instructors: Niall G. Kirkwood & Alistair McIntosh.

This seminar promoted advanced understanding of and executive skill in the design development of landscape architecture. Speculative in nature, it required students to take part in a joint exploration with the instructors on themes relating to conceptual ideas, development, making in landscape architecture, and the accompanying practices of seeing, judging, and thinking by the individual designer. It was also accompanied by an examination of the various theories, conditions, forms, and styles that inform contemporary construction design and implementation practices. Each semester, the course focuses on a different aspect of the landscape design

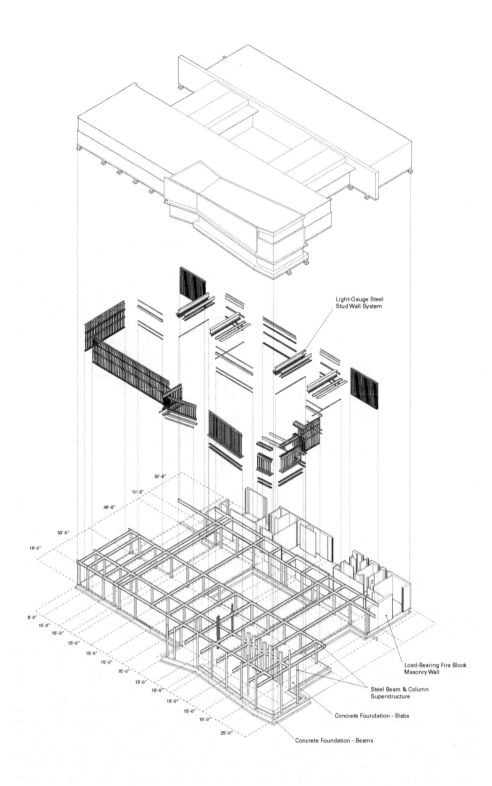

Light-Gauge Steel
Stud Wall System

30'-6"

10'-3"

46'-6"

33'-0"

16'-0"

8'-0"

15'-0"

15'-0"

15'-0"

15'-0"

15'-0"

15'-0"

15'-0"

15'-0"

15'-0"

25'-0"

Load-Bearing Fire Block
Masonry Wall

Steel Beam & Column
Superstructure

Concrete Foundation - Slabs

Concrete Foundation - Beams

process. The topic for the Fall 2014 seminar was detail design. The assumption that was presented and tested during the semester was that a landscape design and detail design is conceived, developed, and made tangible within the formal structures and technical practices of a poetics of *construction*.

The manipulation of the medium gives birth to and shapes ideas. The seminar explored the viability of this conception in the contemporary practice of landscape architecture. The ambition of the course was to engender in each participant a critical understanding of, and skill in, conceiving and developing built landscapes that will endure, are socially accommodating, and expressively potent. It examined the concerns of place and genus loci, style, fashion, design inspiration, and referencing in landscape detail, as well as the pragmatic issues of materials, material combinations, detail design language, and identity. ❧

See also ADAPTIVE REUSE: Building Appreciation—see also ART: Post Facto—see also ASSEMBLY—see also BUILDING—see also COLOR—see also DRAWING: Construction Drawing—see also ENERGY—see also EXTREME: Housing in Extreme Environments—see also FABRICATION—see also ICON: Icons of Knowledge—see also LAB—see also MATERIAL—see also ROBOTICS: Informal Robotics—see also SKYSCRAPER: Wood Skyscraper—see also SUSTAINABILITY—see also SYSTEM—see also TECHNIQUE.

CONTEMPORARY

Contemporary, style of art: Styles of painting, sculpture, graphic arts, and architecture dating from the recent past and present. It differs from modern art in that the term "*contemporary* art" does not carry the implication of a nontraditional style, but instead refers only to the time period in which the work was created. Modern and *contemporary* are inherently fluid terms. The term *contemporary* is sometimes more narrowly used to refer to art from ca. 1960 or 1970 up to the present. To refer to the current time period without reference to style of art, use "*contemporary* (generic time frame)."

Contemporary Practices in Urbanism. PRO 7441. Department of Landscape Architecture. Seminar. Spring 2015. Instructors: Christopher Eaton Glaisek & Mark R. Johnson.

This course provided an in-depth study of the range of practice issues, methods, and strategies for achieving built works in the urban context, including the public realm. Success in the urban environment requires an understanding of the full range of activities that are required—from both public and private sector perspectives. The course presented a range of topics including the roles of the designer, identifying issues, selecting talent/aligning expertise, methods for success, engaging the community, governance models, using public funds, securing approval, and implementation. ❧

Frameworks of Contemporary Practice. PRO 7408. Department of Architecture. Seminar. Fall 2014. Instructor: Paul Nakazawa.

The purpose of the course was: (1) to examine architecture through the lens of the discipline, profession, and practice—the issues of knowledge domains, development of technique, analytics, and technologies; ethics, social responsibility, and regulation; value and innovation as they relate to different social, economic, political,

and environmental conditions; (2) to explore the range of *contemporary* and emergent practices as they relate to the reframing of our participation in and impacts on changing social, political, economic, cultural, technological, and material landscapes; (3) to develop analytic frameworks and tools for critically examining different approaches to and modes of practice, including their respective organizations, operations and business models; and (4) to challenge students to think about their present and future participation in practice, and assist in their visualization of possibilities. ❧

Untitled. Daniel Urban Kiley Lecture. Gund Hall, Piper Auditorium. April 20, 2015. Adriaan Geuze.

As a cofounder of West 8, Adriaan Geuze has established an international reputation based on a unique approach to design, relating *contemporary* culture, urban identity, architecture, public space, and engineering in the individual project, always taking the context into account. With an international team of 70 architects, urban designers, landscape architects, and industrial engineers, West 8 has implemented projects such as Schouwburgplein in Rotterdam, Governor's Island in New York, and SoundScape Park in Miami Beach.

The Daniel Urban Kiley Lecture is an annual honorific lecture on landscape architecture. ❧

See also AIRPORT: Dwelling in Stop-Over City—see also ARCHITECTURE—see also CITY—see also CIVIC: Starbucks & Spiderman—see also COMPUTATION: Paradigms in Computing—see also EXHIBITION: Exhibiting Contemporary Architecture—see also HISTORY—see also INTENSITY: Urban Intensities—see also LISTEN: Symphony of the Air—see also MODERN—see also PHOTOMONTAGE: Composite Landscapes—see also RADICAL: The Grounds of Radical Nature—see also REPRESENTATION—see also STYLE—see also TECHNIQUE: Design Techniques II—see also TERRITORY—see also TIME: TIon—see also URBANISM: Ecological Urbanism—see also WORK.

CONTENT

1: (a) Something contained—usually used in plural <the jar's *contents*> <the drawer's contents>; (b) the topics or matter treated in a written work <table of *contents*>; (c) the principal substance (as written matter, illustrations, or music) offered by a World Wide Web site <Internet users have evolved an ethos of free *content* in the Internet —Ben Gerson>. 2: (a) Substance, gist; (b) meaning, significance; (c) the events, physical detail, and information in a work of art. 3: (a) The matter dealt with in a field of study; (b) a part, element, or complex of parts.

CONTEXT

1: The parts of a discourse that surround a word or passage and can throw light on its meaning. 2: The interrelated conditions in which something exists or occurs, environment, setting <the historical *context* of the war>.

King's Cross: Social, Economic, Environmental, and Cultural Context. Lecture. Sustainable Real Estate Series. Gund Hall, Room 124. October 29, 2014. John McAslan.

As part of the Sustainable Real Estate Series, John McAslan discussed the King's Cross Station project, broadening the definition of sustainability to focus on issues of social, economic, and cultural longevity in addition to environmental sensitivity. ֍

See also BUILDING: Buildings, Texts, and Contexts—see also CONTEMPORARY—see also ENVIRONMENT—see also HOUSING: Craft, Politics, and the Production of Housing in Oaxaca, Mexico—see also REPRESENTATION: Dweller on the Threshold.

CONTINUITY

1: (a) Uninterrupted connection, succession, or union; (b) uninterrupted duration or *continuation,* especially without essential change. 2: Something that has, exhibits, or provides *continuity,* such as (a) a script or scenario in the performing arts; (b) transitional spoken or musical matter especially for a radio or television program; (c) the story and dialogue of a comic strip. 3: The property of being mathematically *continuous.*

CONTOUR

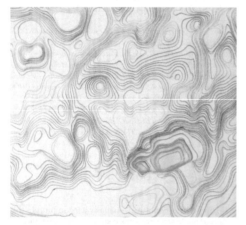

Contour, linear forms, form & composition concepts: The outer boundary of an object or shape, especially when it suggests volume or mass.

Figure. Model (above). Nuith Morales (MLA I).

COPY

1: An imitation, transcript, or reproduction of an original work (as a letter, a painting, a table, or a dress). 2: One of a series of especially mechanical reproductions of an original impression, also, an individual example of such a reproduction. 3: (a) Matter to be set especially for printing; (b) something considered printable or newsworthy—used without an article <remarks that make good *copy*—Norman Cousins>; (c) text especially of an advertisement. 4: Duplicate <a *copy* of a computer file> <a *copy* of a gene>.

Copy as Method. Thesis. Nuith Morales (MLA I), advised by Sonja Dümpelmann.

"This thesis explores the *copy* as a design method that allows us to change the way we understand a site by

viewing it through the lens of another. The *copy* is omnipresent in the history of landscape: Dan Kiley appropriated the splendor of Le Nôtre for his water-filtration plant in Chicago, Le Corbusier imitated the Mughal gardens for the Governor's Palace in India, the Villa Papiri in the Getty Museum is a recreation of an ancient Roman country house, and so on. This thesis tests design as a form of *copying* to explore how the ideas and meaning of an existing place inform a design in a different context.

The two sites chosen for this study are drastically different, yet both are iconic in their time and space. The Agdal Garden in arid Morocco is an Islamic orchard garden in which the transformation of water into fruit is a manifestation of paradise itself. The Meadowlands in New Jersey are brackish wetlands fragmented by centuries of industry and landfill. Today, in the time of climate change and severe weather events, the Meadowlands Commission faces the task of restoring the wetlands. Looking at the Meadowlands through the frame of the Agdal Garden expands the current discussion about the ecology of the Meadowlands site to include cultural and aesthetic values. My method of *copying* analyzes the elements of the Agdal Garden and their role in creating paradise in the context of the Qur'an, and uses these same elements to create paradise in the mud, ice, and culture of the Meadowlands." ֍

CRAFT

Craft, paperwork, visual works: Designs, patterns, or images created by removing small portions from the interior or edges of a piece of paper. *Craft,* field of study: Refers to the field of study that aims at developing manual skills and familiarity with tools and machinery or acquaintance with industrial processes.

See also HOUSING: Craft, Politics, and the Production of Housing in Oaxaca, Mexico—see also MODEL—see also TECHNIQUE.

CREATIVITY

Creativity, concepts relating to the *creative* process, artistic concepts: The quality of being *creative;* or the ability to use original ideas and imagination when thinking or producing work.

Teaching Creativity: Landscape Architecture, Originality & Autobiography. ADV 9136. Department of Landscape Architecture. Seminar. Fall 2014. Instructor: Michael Van Valkenburgh.

This seminar was an exploration into *creativity* in landscape architecture—what it is, where it comes from, what feeds it, and, crucially, whether and how it can be taught or nurtured. The methodology was that of a masterclass—assembling some of the most accomplished contemporary practitioners of landscape architecture to engage in a close reading of two or three of their built projects through the lens of their autobiography, professional trajectory, and working process. Landscape practitioners included: Julie Bargmann, James Corner, Toru Mitani, Shannon Nichol, Laurie Olin, and Mario Schjetnan. The filmmaker Wes Craven was the seventh guest. The course sponsored six Harvard GSD students to travel to see the built work of the guest designers. ֍

CRISIS

1: (a) The turning point for better or worse in an acute disease or fever; (b) a paroxysmal attack of pain, distress, or disordered function; (c) an emotionally significant event or radical change of status in a person's life <a midlife *crisis*>. 2: The decisive moment (as in a literary plot). 3: (a) An unstable or crucial time or state of affairs in which a decisive change is impending, especially one with the distinct possibility of a highly undesirable outcome <a financial *crisis*>; (b) a situation that has reached a critical phase <the environmental *crisis*>.

See CONFLICT—see also POWER: Cambridge Talks IX—see also VISIONARY: Grounded Visionaries.

CRITICISM

Criticism, analytical functions: Analyzing and evaluating the characteristics of man-made objects, literary works and documents, actions, or projects. For critical descriptions or analyses of relatively recent works or events, use "reviews."

See also AIRPORT: Airports in the Last Fifty Years—see also CONTEMPORARY—see also DISPLACEMENT: Global Displacement—see also HISTORY—see also PARK: Urban Parks—see also REVIEW—see also THEORY—see also WORK—see also WRITING.

CULTURE

Culture, culture & related concepts: The sum total of ways of living, artifacts, customs, and so on, built up by a group of people and transmitted from one generation to another.

Aga Khan Program for Islamic Architecture. The Aga Khan Program for Islamic Architecture at the Harvard GSD is dedicated to the study of Islamic art and architecture, urbanism, landscape design and conservation, and the application of that knowledge to contemporary design projects.

Asia GSD. Student Group. Asia GSD bridges divergent groups of students, faculty, and professionals committed to design issues relevant to Asia. The group's mission is to promote an awareness of architecture, landscape architecture, urban planning and design, and related disciplines in the visual and design arts within an Asian context.

By fostering dialogues focused on professional and scholarly concerns between students, academics, and professionals from around the world, Asia GSD creates an open community with a broad regional framework for Asians and non-Asians alike. ֍

Canada GSD. Student Group. Canada GSD is focused on promoting North American design issues and fostering connections between Canadians, past and present, studying and teaching at the Harvard GSD. In addition to highlighting Canadian topics in architecture, landscape, and urban design within the North American context, the group sponsors social events in conjunction with the wider Harvard community through the Harvard Graduate Students Canada Club. ֍

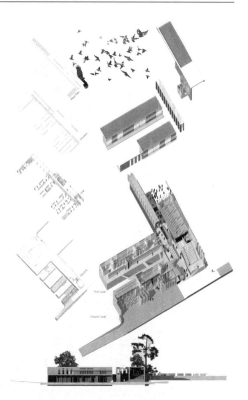

Chamamé: The Intangible Rhythms of the Guaraní Region. STU 1314. Department of Architecture. Option Studio. Spring 2015. Instructor: Jorge Silvetti. Teaching Assistant: Christian Lavista (MArch II).

This was the second of three architecture studios to study and develop proposals in an area of South America that will be affected by major multinational, infrastructural interventions. Specific sites, along a segment of the Paraná River, sit within a vast geographical area where the overlapping *cultural*, natural, and historic maps of different eras, peoples, and natural conditions have produced a layered, complex, and rich hybrid fabric of coexisting, heterogeneous substances. This area, both physical and intellectual, is called Territorio Guaraní: the geology, flora and fauna, water courses and bodies, multicultural migrations and religions, diverse languages and literature, music, crafts and architectures that constitute the site on which the studio operated. Tying this together is a distinctive *culture* of water spread throughout the Cuenca del Plata system, and sitting on the Aquifer Guarani—one of the two largest freshwater reservoirs of the world. The singularities that compose this zone were experienced and surveyed in order to approach, conceptualize, and create specific design solutions for the proposed needs. Under the emblematic title of "Chamamé"–the Guaraní name of a musical genre that emerged in this region in the 20th century as a result of the hybridization of aboriginal music, the rhythms of the Central-European polka, and Guaraní lyrics–the students examined the *cultural* heritage as a totality: not of an ethnic group, of a single language, a specific art form or a particular historical period or style. The task was to conceive, program, and resolve the architecture of a museum of the future, involving both the tangible and intangible *cultural* heritage of the Territorio Guaraní.

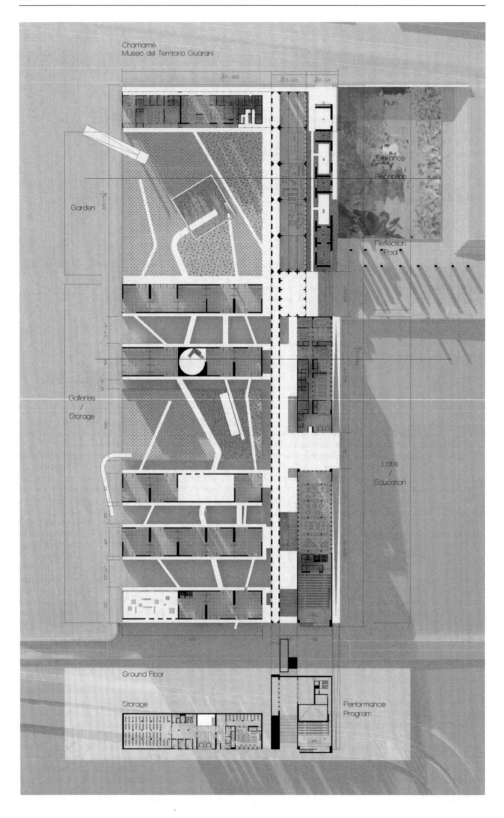

Chamamé
Museo del Territorio Guaraní

Ruin

Entrance

Reception

Garden

Reflection
Pool

Galleries
/
Storage

Labs
/
Education

Ground Floor

Storage

Performance
Program

Students: Joshua Bremner Feldman (MArch I), Paul Daniel Fiegenschue (MArch I), Arianna Mirielle Galan Montas (MArch I), Mazyar Kahali (MArch I), Christian Lavista (MArch II), Patrick Michael Mayfield (MArch I AP), Thien Nguyen (MAUD), Carolina Sendoda Yamate (MAUD), Jeronimo Van Schendel Erice (MArch II), Haoxiang Yang (MArch II), Yufeng Zheng (MArch I AP). ֎

Figures. Exploded Axon (previous page) & Plan (opposite page). Thien Nguyen (MAUD).

China GSD. Student Group. China GSD provides a platform for Harvard GSD students who are interested in issues of design and urbanization in China. The group promotes a comprehensive understanding of China and its transformation within the Harvard GSD community through various social and academic events, including academic lectures. China GSD cultivates a fresh outlook on contemporary China, promotes *cultural* and social understanding, and adds international diversity to the Harvard GSD student body. ֎

Club MEdiNA. Student Group. Club MEdiNA is a student organization at the Harvard GSD for students interested in design issues in the Middle East and North Africa. Its aim is to engage in a better understanding, current and historical, of the architectural and urban dynamics of the region. The group also aspires to become a platform for the promotion of dialogue and the establishment of links between the academic and professional milieus. ֎

Culture, Conservation, and Design. DES 3333. Department of Architecture. Seminar. Fall 2014. Instructors: Susan Nigra Snyder & George Earl Thomas.
This seminar addressed the theoretical foundations of critical conservation as an evolving discipline that bridges between *cultural* meaning, identity, and context. The goal was to enable students to understand how we use and misuse the past; and how we value the present to make nuanced decisions about conservation and change. Critical conservation is not about rules and opposition to change, but rather about understanding underlying forces and agendas to more effectively negotiate socially constructed meaning. The course was organized around three topics. First, "Conservation, *Cultural* Meaning, and Context" addressed the social construction of dynamic *cultural* meaning associated with places, artifacts, and history. It investigated the questions about the past, history, permanence, temporality, obsolescence, and authenticity and applied them to how we characterize the identity of places. Second, "Conservation, *Cultural* Identities, Power, and Exclusion" addressed the role of modernity and tradition in creating personal and group identities that are embedded, transportable, and temporal. Issues included history/heritage, nostalgia/tourism, ecological identity/nature. The roles of ancestor worship, government use of racial zoning, urban renewal, stigmatization of the other, and private use of exclusionary amenities were examined in relationship to how *cultural* groups use underlying agendas to manifest power, identity, and control of places. Third, "Conservation, Values, and Regulation" addressed the mechanisms of advocacy groups, legislation, and regulation to control context by design and identity narratives. ֎

Digital Culture, Architecture, and the City. DES 3428. Department of Architecture. Seminar. Spring 2015. Instructor: Antoine Picon.
Some 20 years ago, when Bernard Tschumi and young instructors like Greg Lynn and Ali Rahim launched the so-called Paperless Studio, based upon the intensive use of the computer, the endeavor was considered at best highly experimental. Today, computers have literally invaded schools of architecture and design offices. Their introduction has been accompanied by the emergence of new methods and forms. Moreover, their use is representative of a much broader phenomenon: the influence of digital *culture* on architectural and urban design. Beyond the design world, digital *culture* appears as a fundamental feature of our contemporary society. Ubiquitous computing constitutes one of the expressions of its pervasive presence.
This course envisaged the complex set of relations that have been established between the computer and architecture, as well as between digital *culture*, as a social phenomenon, and architecture and the city. Its aim was to contribute to a better understanding of what is at stake in a process of change that is still going on today. Whereas we are no longer fascinated by blobs, new subjects of interest have emerged such as the development of parametric design, the new possibilities offered by digital fabrication, the rising challenges of sustainability, and the role digital technologies will play to address them. In order to foster this better understanding of what is at stake in the digital, the course began by providing a series of historical points of reference regarding the development of digital *culture*. From history the course quickly turned to the present and to the various issues it raises. One passed thus from history to theory. Following almost 20 years of accelerated technological developments, the time has come to assess what they represent in terms of the way we define architecture, urban design, and even urban planning. Indeed, they are challenging a number of received ideas about these disciplines. ֎

GSD Christian Fellowship. Student Group. The GSD Christian Fellowship seeks to support Christians in the practice of their faith at Harvard, to be a forum for Christians to ask questions about the relationship between design and faith, to act as a resource for those interested in the Christian faith, and to provide opportunities for people of all faiths to dialogue. ֎

GSD West. Student Group. GSD West promotes an awareness of architecture, landscape architecture, urban planning, real estate, and design within the context of the North American West. United by big skies and the biggest ocean on the planet, GSD West promotes traffic between two sides of a continent; and represents Alaska, Arizona, California, Colorado, Hawaii, Idaho, Montana, Nevada, New Mexico, Oregon, Utah, Washington, Wyoming, and British Columbia. ֎

Greece GSD. Student Group. Greece GSD aims to inform the Harvard GSD and the broader Harvard community about contemporary academic, social, and professional initiatives that concern Greece and the broader region of the eastern Mediterranean. ֎

India GSD. Student Group. India is an ancient civilization and a young nation. Crucial to understanding India, not only as a rapidly developing socioeconomy and urbanscape, but as a bristling *cultural* phenomenon, is the knowledge of the incredible array of influences that impact its multidimensional personality. As contemporary design in the subcontinent continues to discover its identity and direction, India GSD celebrates its strengths and confronts its inhibitions with a critical eye. The student group brings the flavor of the world's largest democracy through academic, social, and *cultural* initiatives. ❦

Japan GSD. Student Group. Japan GSD is a social group open to all students interested in deepening their appreciation of Japanese *culture* and design. Members meet regularly for informal conversations about the state of contemporary Japanese design and invite outside scholars and practitioners to provide context and expertise. ❦

JewSD. Student Group. Jewish Students of Design (JewSD) is a nondenominational social group that connects Jewish students to each other and to events happening elsewhere on Harvard's campus. The group plans events that celebrate Jewish history and *culture* with a special emphasis on the contributions of Jewish designers to contemporary *cultural* discourse and the relationship of our tradition to the designed environment. ❦

Korea GSD (KGSD). Student Group. Korea GSD is an organization that connects the Harvard GSD with the Korean community at home and abroad. The group focuses on two goals: to serve as a platform for the greater student body to engage *cultural*, professional, and academic practices of contemporary Korea, and to establish relationships with the larger academic community, including the 500-member Harvard Korea Society, as well as alumni and industry leaders. ❦

Latin GSD. Student Group. Latin GSD is a student organization that discusses current topics relevant to the design and planning disciplines in Latin American countries. Latin GSD organizes lectures inviting faculty, practitioners, and policymakers from Latin America for discussions and brainstorming sessions as well as social activities that integrate and to enhance initiatives for students interested in the Latin American region. ❦

Queers in Design (QD). Student Group. Queers in Design is a reframing of the former LGBTQ student group, OutDesign, at the Harvard GSD. QD's goal is to build on the foundations established by OutDesign to elaborate on the issues concerning the umbrella term "queer" to include issues of gender, sexuality, and identity in the built environment. QD is a vehicle to dismantle, discuss, interrogate, and provoke change in spaces that are without the voice of inclusion. Though QD is founded by the LGBTQ community, it is not the primary aim to discuss these topics alone. The group believes in inclusion. As the future designers of space, armed with this perspective of queer identity, it is the group's agenda to design safe spaces for all populations seeking asylum. ❦

Spain GSD. Student Group. Spain GSD aims to promote the work of Spanish scholars, architects, planners, and institutions within the Harvard Community and beyond. The group organizes events promoting Spanish *culture*, with the objective to create enriching dialogue and exchange leading to innovation and a better understanding among designers. ❦

See also AGORA—see also BUILDING: Buildings, Texts, and Contexts—see also CHURCH: Nicholas Hawksmoor—see also CITY—see also COLOR—see also COMPLEX: The Function of Time—see also CONTEMPORARY—see also CONTEXT—see also ECOLOGY: Projective Ecologies—see also ELEMENT—see also GAZE: Subverting the Gaze—see also GEOGRAPHY—see also HISTORY: Temporary Accumulations—see also LISTEN: Symphony of the Air—see also MEMORY: Ecologies of Memory—see also MORPHOLOGY: Between

Geometry & Geography—see also ORNAMENT. Structure, Infrastructure, and Ornament—see also PROSTHETIC: Architecture of Cultural Prosthetics—see also RESPONSIVE: Socio-Environmental Responsive Design—see also SUSTAINABILITY: The Return of Nature—see also THEORY—see also VISIONARY: Grounded Visionaries.

CURB

1: An enclosing frame, border, or edging. 2: Check, restraint <a price *curb*>. 3: A raised edge or margin to strengthen or confine. 4: An edging (as of concrete) built along a street to form part of a gutter. 5: A market for trading in securities not listed on a stock exchange.

The Re-Rise of the Curb: Toward New Street-Design Methodologies. Thesis. Chungseok Baek (MLA I AP), advised by David Mah.

"This design project for Market Street in San Francisco challenges existing standards for traditional road-*curb* systems and explores an integrated vision for future streetscapes, with deeper analyses of each component of the street, including *curb* extensions, sidewalk trees, and raised crosswalks. The project proposes a new street code that adds to the current functions of roadside *curbs* by integrating poetic, cultural, and political dimensions with their current hydrological functions. The road-*curb* system was introduced as a solution to the conflict between horse-drawn vehicles and pedestrians. A symbol of modernity, the *curb* was recognized as a design innovation, and it had a variety of shapes and uses that corresponded with its various economic and aesthetic roles. This thesis argues that the *curb* is not only a flexible infrastructure that reflects the needs of different modes of transportation, but also an in-between space that bridges sociopolitical elements of the city. Located between 12-foot rights-of-way, *curbs* function as responsive boundaries that facilitate multimodal movement and social events along the street." ❦

CYBORG

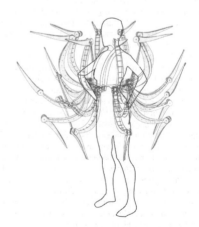

1: A bionic human.

Figure. Drawing (above). Chrisoula Kapelonis (MArch II).

See also ARTIFACT—see also ONTO-CARTOGRAPHY: Cyborg Coasts: Responsive Hydrologies.

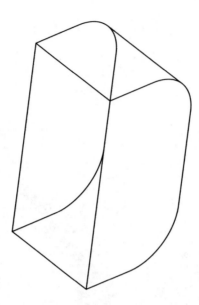

DATA

Data, information, multidisciplinary concepts: Information, especially digital information. In common usage in computer science, used as a singular noun to refer to information that exists in a form that may be used by a computer, excluding the program code. In the sciences and other contexts, "datum" is the singular and "*data*" is the plural, referring to facts or numbers in a general sense. For general reference to facts, use "information."

Figure. Animation Still Frame (previous page). Jili Huang (MDes, Tech).

Data across Scales: Reshaping Design. Doctor of Design Studies Program Conference. Gund Hall, Piper Auditorium. April 17, 2015.
   Harvard GSD and the Doctor of Design Studies program hosted the international interdisciplinary conference, "*Data* across Scales: Reshaping Design." Bringing together design researchers and practitioners, the conference inquired into the role of *data* in design and how it has steered its practice across all scales. ⑨

See also COMPUTATION—see also INFORMATION—see also MAPPING—see also SENSE: Remote Sensing in Mumbai—see also SOFTWARE—see also TOOL—see also TWIPOLOGY—see also VALUE.

DATUM

1: Something given or admitted especially as a basis for reasoning or inference. 2: Something used as a basis for calculating or measuring—plural *datums*.

DAYLIGHTING

1: Illumination of indoor spaces by natural light. 2: The uncovering and exposing of underground utilities and pipelines to *daylight*.

Daylighting. SCI 6479. Department of Architecture. Seminar. Fall 2014. Instructor: Holly Samuelson.
   Picture a space, one that feels vibrant, comfortable, warm, and healthy. Now visualize someplace cheerless, depressing, and dull. What changed in your mind's eye? Most likely, lighting—specifically natural lighting—plays a significant role. Yet, none of these terms explicitly relate to light or darkness. This is the emotive power of *daylighting*. In addition to enlivening a space, *daylight* can connect us to nature, mark the passage of time, maintain circadian rhythms, and save energy. Conversely, poorly considered *daylighting* can lead to overheating, visual discomfort, and wasted energy. This course explored the theme of *daylighting* in architecture. Because *daylight* design can be an unintuitive process, and because today's computerized tools allow designers to evaluate their ideas, this course included a detailed focus on *daylight* simulation. Other topics included design precedents, rules of thumb, shading strategies, and the technical fundamentals of light, sun position, solar heat gain, and glare. ⑨

DECAY

1: Gradual decline in strength, soundness, or prosperity or in degree of excellence or perfection. 2: A wasting or wearing away, ruin. 3: (a) Rot, specifically aerobic decomposition of proteins chiefly by bacteria; (b) the product of *decay*. 4: A decline in health or vigor. 5: Decrease in quantity, activity, or force, such as (a) a spontaneous decrease in the number of radioactive atoms in radioactive material; (b) a spontaneous disintegration.

DECORATION

Decoration, ornaments, object genres by function: Embellishments, adornments, or ornamentation, often specifically those that are temporarily put up on a holiday or another special occasion. *Decoration*, processes & techniques by specific type: The overall approach to and techniques of embellishing architecture, furniture, or other objects. See "ornaments" in reference to specific forms, such as fluting, finials, or monograms, that embellish and are part of the building or object, but are not structurally essential to it.

L'art décoratif d'aujourd'hui. Publication. Éditions G. Crès, 1925. Le Corbusier (author). Le Corbusier Research Collection, Frances Loeb Library. LeC NK 1390 L496.
"This book began as a series of articles written for *L'Esprit nouveau*, brought together here under one title. The book represents Le Corbusier's attack on the French *decorative* arts, which he assessed was on the decline because of industrial manufacture. He argues that the manufacture of standardized objects shifted production and *decoration* out of the hands of artists into those of an anonymous industry (with different economic interests). This book, like much of his early writing, demonstrates a strong didactic rhetoric and novel use of images, both of which may be credited to Le Corbusier's journalistic tenor." —Inés Zalduendo. 🖉

DEMOCRACY

Democracy, political administrative bodies by governing person: Political entities with a government in which people either rule themselves or elect representatives to rule in their interests.

See also ADVOCACY—see also BOOK: Books that Built Democracy—see also DISPLACEMENT: Global Displacement—see also FORUM: Student Forum—see also MATTER—see also PROCESS: Communicating Architecture.

DEMOGRAPHY

Demography, social science, disciplines: Statistical study of the characteristics of human populations especially with reference to size and density, growth, distribution, migration, vital statistics, and the effect of all these on social and economic conditions.

See also DENSITY—see also DIASPORA—see also ECONOMIC—see also GEOGRAPHY—see also MAPPING—see also MIGRATION—see also POPULATION—see also SOCIAL.

DENSITY

Density, attributes & properties by specific type: The distribution of something per unit area; can be, for example, the measure of the mass of a substance per unit volume, or the number of dwelling units per acre.

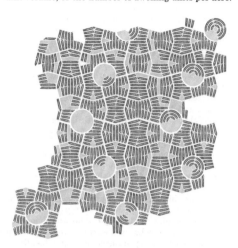

Figure. Diagram (above). Grace McEniry (MArch I).

See also COLLABORATION: The Calumet Collaborations—see also ELEMENT: Elements of Urban Design—see also INTENSITY: Urban Intensities—see also MATERIAL—see also MATTER.

DEPOSITION

1: An act of removing from a position of authority. 2: (a) Testifying, especially before a court; (b) declaration, specifically testimony taken down in writing under oath; (c) out-of-court testimony made under oath and recorded by an authorized officer for later use in court. 3: An act or process of *depositing*. 4: Something *deposited*, a deposit.

Fused *deposition* modeling: Type of rapid prototyping whereby filaments of heated thermoplastic are gradually extruded onto a platform, creating cross-sections of an object and eventually creating a 3-D object prototype out of plastic.

See also HABOOB: Dust Kingdom—see also PROCESS—see also PROTOTYPE: Rapid Prototyping.

DESIGN

Design, concept: Specific conceptual schemes for the organization or appearance of graphic works, objects, structures, or systems. For proposed undertakings or creations in general, including works of art or architecture, or for the actual carrying out of such proposals, use "projects." *Design*, discipline: Discipline comprising the creation of conceptual schemes for the organization or appearance of graphic works, objects, structures, or systems.

Harvard University Graduate School of Design. The Harvard Graduate School of *Design* upholds two primary responsibilities: to educate designers to be bold thinkers, pragmatic idealists, societal catalysts, and leading practitioners; and to make major contributions to the body of *design* knowledge through speculative thinking and research activities. A successful designer must have the tools, techniques, and methods that articulate and enhance the ideas constructed through imagination. Projective drawings, handmade and digitally fabricated models, animations, and other forms of visualization are all catalysts through which projects are developed. The Harvard GSD provides a context that allows *designers* the creative space to articulate their ideas and offers the framework through which these ideas can be expressed.

For this pedagogical work to have maximum impact on the field of *design*, the Harvard GSD is the vital locus for the creation of knowledge about our built environment. It continues to develop the technologies, processes, and functions that improve how our buildings, landscapes, and cities perform for their users. Rigorous and research-based, *design* is shaped by many criteria. *Design* is greater than analysis; it is empirical as well, testing new ideas against measured reality, in areas such as biomechanical feedback, energy efficiency, and economic stimulus. With *design*, what was chaotic can become organized, what was wasteful can become efficient, and what was unjust can become equitable. *Design* is projective. What exists in the present becomes imagined as something better in the future. ❧

DESIGN-BUILD

Design-build, contracting, legal functions: A contracting arrangement in which a person or organization assumes responsibility under a single contract for both the design and construction of a project.

Architect-Led Design-Build. Project Delivery Lecture. Gund Hall, Piper Auditorium. February 11, 2015. Peter Gluck. ❧

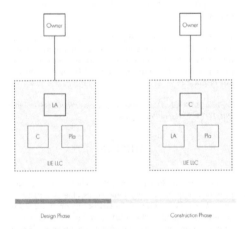

Design Phase   Construction Phase

Figure. Diagram (above). Vi Vu (MLA I) & Timothy Yung Wei (MLA I).

DESIGNER

Designer, people in the visual arts: People who create conceptual schemes for the organization or appearance of graphic works, objects, structures, or systems.

DESCRIPTION

Description, analytical functions: Representing in spoken, written, or signed language the attributes or qualities of something or someone.

Innovate. Lecture. Gund Hall, Stubbins. March 26, 2015. Maria Langarita & Victor Camilo Navarro Rios.

Every *description* of the world opens up an order of possibilities. This order allows for a set of diverse coherences. These coherences, understood as programs of intervention, are projects, and each of these projects, in turn, contain a distinct view of the world. To *describe* is to design and to *describe* in a new way is to establish the foundations of innovation, because the new is not the different; the new is what exists after a transmutation of value. ❧

DESK-CRIT

Desk-crit. *Desk-crits* are one-on-one project critiques given by an instructor at a student's desk during studio time. These can be the most enriching conversations students have about their projects. Students learn a tremendous amount not only from critics, but also from their peers simply by observing how the same design problem may be attacked and resolved in many different ways. ❧

DETAIL

Detail, components: Refers to minute parts of a larger structure, object, or image. For architectural drawings of design or construction *details*, use "*detail* drawings." For preparatory studies of pictorial or design *details*, use "*detail* studies."

See also ASSEMBLY—see also DRAWING: Detail Drawing—see also MODEL—see also STUDY: Detail Studies—see also TECHNIQUE.

DEVELOPER

Developer, people in engineering, building trade & planning: Individuals, companies, or corporations engaged in the development and improvement of land for construction purposes.

The Architect as Developer. Real Estate Development Club Panel Discussion. Gund Hall, Stubbins. November 5, 2014. Alex Barrett, Jared Della Valle, and Cary Tamarkin.

In contemporary practice, architects often find themselves relegated to the role of consultants, having to cede project leadership to *developers* who may or may not understand the importance of a well-designed product. A handful of architects, however, have decided to buck this trend and work as their own clients. By integrating the design and the development aspects of project delivery, the architect-as-*developer* business model allows the architect greater control in the project delivery process, resulting often in projects that are not only financially successful but beautifully designed as well. ❧

DEVELOPMENT

Community *development*: Activity of solving or ameliorating a community's social and economic problems, organized and controlled mainly by the community itself. Economic *development*: *Development* of low-income economies into industrial economies. Rather than strictly referring to economic growth, economic *development* refers to improvements in national economies that are both quantitative and qualitative. *Development*, function: Change over time in human activities, institutions, or settlements, usually in the sense of improvement or expansion. Housing *development*: Commercially *developed* real estate tracts commonly consisting of one- to four-unit dwellings. Mixed-use *development*: Relatively large-scale real estate projects incorporating several revenue-producing functions, having a highly intensive use of land, and developed from a coherent plan. Sustainable *development*: *Development* designed to ensure that the utilization of resources and the environment today does not damage prospects for their use by future generations. Urban *development*: Improvement and *development* of urban areas including infrastructure, especially by building.

Economic Development in Urban Planning. SES 5339. Department of Urban Planning & Design. Seminar. Spring 2015. Instructor: Donald Emanuel Zizzi.

This course introduced students to the theories, analytic frameworks, and financial tools used to encourage local economic *development* in the United States. Students investigated the key debates in the field and examined the different roles that practitioners play in the economic *development* process.

The goal of this course was to ensure that students gained a basic understanding of the economic issues affecting communities. The course was organized around the basic themes of urban economics and focused on the allocation of scarce resources and the global competition for private investment. Students left with a clear understanding of locational and investment decisions, private sector market forces, and public policies that can shape local economic systems. ✸

On the Theoretical & Practical Development of Landscape Architecture. Frederick Law Olmsted Lecture. Gund Hall, Piper Auditorium. October 28, 2014. Joseph Disponzio.

Joseph Disponzio discussed the intellectual origins of landscape architecture in relation to the new garden practices that emerged during the 18th century, the key texts that codified these practices, and Enlightenment-era changes in the understanding of nature. ✸

Public & Private Development. SES 5103. Department of Urban Planning & Design. Seminar. Spring 2015. Instructor: Jerold S. Kayden.

This course explored the analytic frameworks, skills, and bodies of knowledge required to understand, evaluate, plan, and implement public and private *development* within cities and surrounding regions. Using lectures, discussions, case studies, and individual and team exercises, the course taught students how to measure the complex blend of public and private actions promoting growth and change against financial, economic, legal, institutional, political, and other planning metrics.

The planning techniques specifically explored included, among others, public subsidies (grants and loans), public land acquisition and disposition through Requests For Proposals (RFP), strategic provision of physical infrastructure, inclusionary zoning, linkage, and business improvement districts. ✸

See also CITY—see also COMMUNITY—see also DIASPORA—see also HOUSING—see also LAND USE—see also LANDSCAPE ARCHITECTURE—see also MAPPING: Digital Mapping and Design Choices for International Development—see also MODEL: Architecture & the Territory—see also REAL ESTATE—see also RESILIENCE: Coastal Resilience, Sustainable Development of the Spanish Atlantic Coast—see also RETAIL: Prestige Retail—see also SUSTAINABILITY: Environmental Planning & Sustainable Development—see also TRANSPORTATION: Transportation Planning & Development—see also URBANIZATION.

DIALOGUE

Dialogue, document genre for literary works, literature: Written compositions in which two or more characters are represented as conversing.

Landscape Architecture Dialogues: Walter Hood & Anuradha Mathur. Lectures. Gund Hall, Room 124 & Frances Loeb Library. November 3 & 5, 2014. Walter Hood & Anuradha Mathur, with Anita Berrizbeitia, Preston Scott Cohen, K. Michael Hays, Niall G. Kirkwood, and Charles A. Waldheim.

The purpose of these gatherings was to understand how two landscape architects with very different backgrounds, locate their own work, and how their interests extend to their teaching. The speakers engaged in conversation thinking about the future of the academy in relation to landscape architecture, and how we prepare the next generation of landscape architects. ✸

DIASPORA

1: (a) The movement, migration, or scattering of a people away from an established or ancestral homeland <the black *diaspora* to northern cities>; (b) people settled far from their ancestral homelands <African *diaspora*>; (c) the place where these people live.

21st Century Architecture of Africa and the Diaspora. STU 1306. Department of Architecture. Option Studio. Fall 2014. Instructors: David Adjaye. Teaching Assistant: Charlotte Lipschitz (MArch I, 2015)

In the last 500 years, Europe and the West saw dramatic shifts in the nature and shape of their civilizations, from the Renaissance to the Enlightenment, empire to industrialization. Africa too experienced its own radical changes in population, cultural patrimony, and the scope of its encounters with the rest of the world. Africa's internal and external relations were in many ways defined by power struggles and exploitation, most notably in the form of the slave trade. Consequently, the continent experienced major shifts in and evolutions of identities, the culmination of which was the period between the Berlin Conference of 1884 and the achievement of independence in the 20th century. In the wake of these events, Africa has had to face even more extraordinary changes under complex circumstances. African nations and their *diasporas* have, from the second half of the

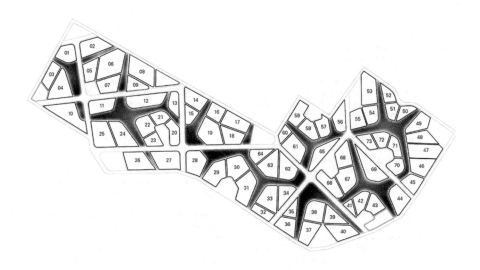

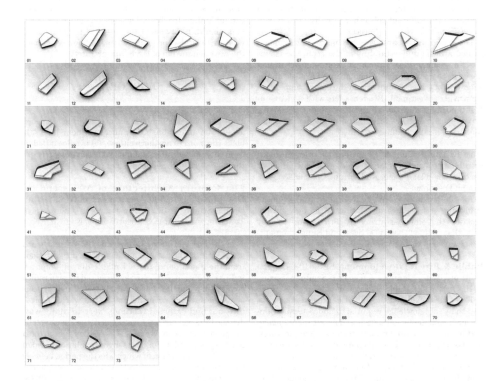

20th century to today, had to explore fundamental questions of sovereignty, identity, and culture as they emerge as distinct entities in the international community.

The aim of the studio was to investigate and examine latent qualities of African geographies, and urban and social histories in the latter part of the 20th century to today. The studio explored ways of charting possible narratives about urban identities within newly formed African contexts. This represents a break from the existing paradigm of importing foreign frameworks. Students sought to identify potential new identities in contemporary Africa and its *diaspora*, given modern complexities such as population explosion, energy concerns, political and socioeconomic security, and considerations for the natural environment. The study of Africa and its *diaspora* communities has much to offer in the way of understanding the core issues and conditions of urbanism. Examination of the skeletal forms of many of the continent's cities, as well as the histories and patterns involved in the formation of its communities, is key to understanding Africa's civic, commercial, residential, and planning qualities across its diverse geographies and climate.

Students: Patrick Burke (MArch I AP), Michael Ryan Charters (MArch II), Tiffany Chen (MArch II), Jose Pablo Cordero (MArch II), Elena Cecilia Hasbun (MArch II), David Wolf Himelman (MArch I), John Christopher Kirsimagi (MArch I), Ranjit John Korah (MArch II), Patrick Michael Mayfield (MArch I AP), Tristan Daniel McGuire (MArch II), Giancarlo Vengco Montano (MArch I), Thena Jeanhee Tak (MArch II), Georgia Williams (MArch I). ❧

Figure. Plan & Catalogue (opposite page). Thena Jeanhee Tak (MArch II).

The Diasporic Return of Capital: Diasporas as Investment Channels for Public-Oriented Projects in the Philippines. Thesis. Frank Refuerzo (MDes, ULE & MUP), advised by Michael Hooper.

"The primary purpose of this project is to advance an understanding of the multidimensional nature of migration and development as it relates to transnational money flows and to offer recommendations for realizing the potential for *diasporas* to finance development projects in their home countries. In particular, I look at the Philippines—a country whose 28 billion dollars in remittances account for more than 10 percent of the national gross domestic product—and ask, how can the Filipino *diaspora* finance public-oriented development projects in the Philippines?

Many scholars and government officials point to the positive effects of remittances, including the reduction of severe poverty, boosted domestic consumption, and new opportunities for entrepreneurship and savings. But remittances are private money transfers and studies show that much of these funds stay within the senders' family networks, raising questions as to whether these private funds actually promote exclusive development. I use this tension as a point of entry to explore the potential for *diaspora* communities to become effective actors in development. I extend prior research on transnational financing mechanisms, migration, and *diaspora* identity to investigate whether advances in technology or changes in cultural context, demographics, or policy can allow new opportunities for financing to emerge.

Through interviews with key development actors and researchers, I map out prior *diaspora* financing initiatives. These interview responses guide the design of a *diaspora* survey, which is used to determine the preferences, motivations, and reservations of the Filipino *diaspora* in investing in the Philippines. The results of the survey form the basis of a set of recommendations for capturing *diasporic* resources to finance development projects that promote inclusive growth in developing countries." ❧

DIGITAL

Digital file formats: Standardized means of organizing and storing files created using a binary numerical system electronically stored in the form of encoded image elements, or pixels. *Digital* imaging: The recording, storage, and manipulation of images in computer systems in the form of electronically encoded picture elements.

See also COLLECTION: Special Collections, Visual & Material Collections—see also COMPUTATION: Paradigms in Computing—see also CULTURE: Digital Culture—see also FABRICATION—see also HOLOGRAM: Fragments of a Hologram House—see also LAB: Excess Laboratory—see also LANDFORM: Landformation Catalogue—see also LIBRARY: Digital Library—see also MAP: Digital Map—see also MAPPING—see also MEDIA—see also MODEL: Digital Terrain Modeling—see also ORNAMENT: Structure, Infrastructure, and Ornament—see also PHOTOGRAPHY: Digital Photographer—see also PHOTOMONTAGE: Composite Landscapes—see also PROJECTION: Digital Projection—see also REPRESENTATION—see also TWIPOLOGY—see also WORKSHOP: Digital Media Workshops.

DIGNITY

1: The quality or state of being worthy, honored, or esteemed. 2: (a) High rank, office, or position; (b) a legal title of nobility or honor. 3: Formal reserve or seriousness of manner, appearance, or language.

Design with Dignity. African American Student Union Lecture. Gund Hall, Room 109. November 13, 2014. Phil Freelon.

Phil Freelon discussed how he has navigated the highly competitive industry as an African-American entrepreneur, from his time as a Loeb Fellow to the transformation of his practice by the acquisition of one of the most significant commissions on the National Mall in Washington, DC. ❧

DIMENSION

Size/*dimension*, form attributes, attributes & properties: Measurable or spatial extent of any kind, such as length, breadth, thickness, area, volume, measure, magnitude, or size. Describes attributes that are measurable by spatial or temporal extent.

DIRT

1: (a) A filthy or soiling substance (as mud, dust, or grime); (b) something worthless; (c) a contemptible person <treated me like *dirt*>. 2: Loose or packed soil or sand <a

mound of *dirt*> <a *dirt* road>. 3: (a) An abject or filthy state, squalor <living in *dirt*>; (b) corruption, chicanery <vowed to clean up the *dirt* in the city government>; (c) licentiousness of language or theme; (d) scandalous or malicious gossip <spreading *dirt* about his ex-wife>; (e) embarrassing or incriminating information <trying to dig up *dirt* on her political rivals>.

DISCIPLINE

1: Punishment. 2: Instruction. 3: A field of study. 4: Training that corrects, molds, or perfects the mental faculties or moral character. 5: (a) Control gained by enforcing obedience or order; (b) orderly or prescribed conduct or pattern of behavior; (c) self-control. 6: A rule or system of rules governing conduct or activity.

Discipline: Branches of learning, professions, and areas of professional specialization.

See also ARCHITECTURE—see also LANDSCAPE ARCHITEC-TURE— see also OPPORTUNITY: Innovate—see also UNDISCI-PLINED—see also URBAN DESIGN—see also URBAN PLANNING.

DISCOURSE

1: The capacity of orderly thought or procedure, rationality. 2: Verbal interchange of ideas, especially conversation. 3: (a) Formal and orderly and usually extended expression of thought on a subject; (b) connected speech or writing; (c) a linguistic unit larger than a sentence. 4: A mode of organizing knowledge, ideas, or experience that is rooted in language and its concrete contexts <critical *discourse*>.

DISCOVERY

1: The act or process of *discovering*. 2: Something *discovered*. 3: The usually pretrial disclosure of pertinent facts or documents by one or both parties to a legal action or proceeding.

Career Discovery. Summer Program. The six-week Career *Discovery* program at the Harvard GSD welcomes students—from recent high school and college graduates to seasoned professionals—who are not only considering a career in design or planning, but a broad spectrum of interests and remarkably diverse plans and goals. Participants in the program participate in intensive studio work, lectures, workshops, and field trips. Deeply immersed in a culture that is both challenging and rewarding, they experience what education and work are like in the design and planning professions. ⍟

DISPLACEMENT

1: (a) The act or process of *displacing*; (b) the state of being *displaced*. 2: (a) The volume or weight of a fluid *displaced* by a floating body of equal weight; (b) the difference between the initial position of something and any later position. 3: (a) The redirection of an emotion or impulse from its original object to another; (b) the substitution of another form of behavior for what is usual or expected especially when the usual response is non-adaptive—called also *displacement* activity, *displacement* behavior.

Global Displacement: Why Architects & Planners Should Be Very Concerned. Lecture. Gund Hall, Stubbins. April 7, 2015. Miloon Kothari. ⍟

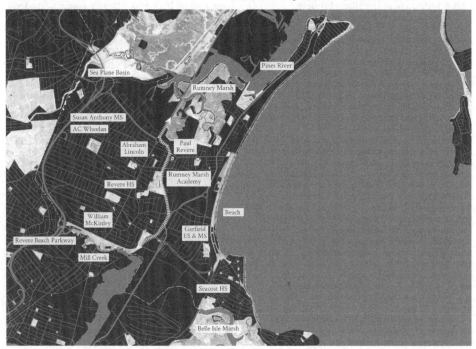

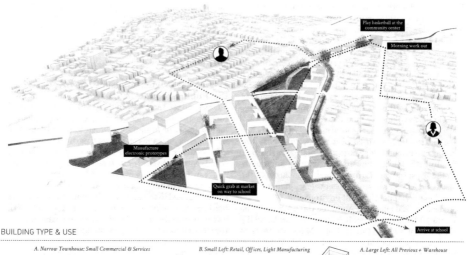

BUILDING TYPE & USE

A. Narrow Townhouse: Small Commercial & Services
Footprint: 22.5 x 60 ft
Lot size: 22.5 x 120 ft
FAR: 1.5
Total Area: 4,050 sf
3-story, 48 ft max height
Examples: Barber shop, therapist, graphic design studio

B. Small Loft: Retail, Offices, Light Manufacturing
Footprint: 45 x 80 ft
Lot size: 45 x 120 ft
FAR: 2 to 3
Total Area: 10,800 to 16,200 sf
3-story, double height w/ mezzanine, 54 max height
Examples: Law office, digital fabrication, bank, apparel, restaurant

A. Large Loft: All Previous + Warehouse
Footprint: 90 x 100 ft
Lot size: 90 x 120 ft
FAR: 3.5 to 5
Total Area: 36,000 to 54,000 sf
4-story, double height w/ mezzanine, 72 max height
Examples: clothing & textiles, electronics, green technologies

DISSECTION

1: The act or process of *dissecting*, the state of being *dissected*. 2: An anatomical specimen prepared by *dissecting*.

Step 7: Spatial Dissection. Bigger than a Breadbox, Smaller than a Building. Installation. Boston Society of Architects Space. June 17–October 4, 2015. Mariana Ibañez & Simon Kim (IK Studio).

Architecture is approaching a new state where agency and adaptability bring the environment and occupant together in a new synthetic relationship. "Step 7: Spatial *Dissections*" presents an aspect of this agenda via a series of environments that are reactive and active. The installation belongs to a family of components that produce new architectural characteristics that are self-supporting and expressive.

DISTORTION

Distortion, visual & representational concepts, formal concepts: The quality or state in a painting or of an object due to the use of optical illusions, manipulated surfaces, or discordantly juxtaposed images.

DISTRIBUTE

Distribute, function: Sending out or apportioning something from a central source to a community, group, or individuals. *Distributed* load: A load that is diffused over a large area of a structure.

Material Distributions: Gradients of Compliance. SCI 6425. Department of Architecture. Seminar. Spring 2015. Instructor: Panagiotis Michalatos.

This course explored the role of computational structural analysis and form finding methods in design and fabrication problems. Such techniques can offer hints on how to assemble and *distribute* materials in a structurally consistent way with implications in the geometric, aesthetic, and tectonic expression of the structure.

In a series of experiments, students reinterpreted and materialized digital structural models. These methods enable a high level of control over material behavior provided the designer has a good understanding of the underlying principles. ֍

DISTURBANCE

1: The act of *disturbing*, the state of being *disturbed*. 2: A local variation from the average or normal wind conditions.

DIVERSITY

Diversity, cultural pluralism: Cultural condition of the coexistence of numerous distinct ethnic and cultural groups within one society. For the cultural movement, use "multiculturalism." For the broader philosophical concept, use "pluralism." *Diversity*, economic & financial functions: Act or practice of manufacturing a variety of products, selling a variety of merchandise, or investing in a variety of securities, for example, so that failure in or economic slump affecting one of them will not be disastrous.

Second Semester Core Urban Planning Studio. STU 1122. Department of Urban Planning & Design. Core Studio. Spring 2015. Instructors: Melissa Sue Alexander (guest critic), Baye Adofo-Wilson, Janne Carmen Corneil, Daniel D'Oca, Alex Krieger (coordinator), and Kathryn Madden. Teaching Assistants: Ning Pei (MUP), Marcus Pulsipher (MLAUD), and Robert William Wellburn (MUP).

The second semester core planning studio expanded the topics and methodologies studied in the first semester core studio with the aim to prepare students for the mix of analytical and creative problem solving needed to address planning issues at the advanced level of the option studios. The studio centered around a single large-scale planning problem with a regional, intermunicipal scope, and addressed the following concerns, all of which are central to planning: the pattern and development nature of settlement form; the visual and scenic impact of development either at the fringe or in built-up areas; accessibility, walkability, and the relationship between transit and automobiles; the location and utility of open space, particularly with respect to development; how planning can promote development of places, businesses, and cultural activities; how to interact with and appreciate the perspectives of *diverse* constituencies; and the respective roles of large-scale concepts (e.g., plans) versus regulation in shaping the built environment.

Students: Faisal bin Ayyaf Almogren (MUP), Shani Adia Carter (MUP), Elena Chang (MUP), Sohael Chowfla (MUP), Katherine Anabel Curiel (MUP), Isabel Margarita De Leon Cantada (MUP), Megan Mahala Echols (MUP), Marco Luigi Gorini (MUP), Fernando Granados Franco (MUP), Carolyn J. Grossman (MUP), Tamara Jafar (MUP), Nathalie Maria Janson (MUP), Elliot Kilham (MUP), Russell P. Koff (MUP), Francisco Lara Garcia (MUP), Samuel Pike LaTronica (MUP), Alexander C. Lew (MUP), Paul Andrew Lillehaugen (MUP), Stephany Yu-Zhu Lin (MUP), Dana Elise McKinney (MUP & MArch I), Meghan L. McNulty (MUP), Marcus Antone Walter Mello (MUP & MArch I), Andres E. Mendoza Gutfreund (MUP), Alexander John Mercuri (MUP), Vanessa Park Moon (MUP), Yvonne G. Mwangi (MUP), Paige E. Peltzer (MUP), Lucy Forbes Perkins (MUP), Nina Denise Phinouwong (MUP & MLA I), Rebecca Marie Ramsey (MUP), Carlos Felipe Reyes (MUP), Jennifer Athena Saura (MUP & MLA I), Emma L. Schnur (MUP), David Schoen (MUP), Laurel M. Schwab (MUP), Courtney Dominique Sharpe (MUP), Apoorva Narayan Shenvi (MUP), Brodrick Charles Spencer (MUP), Annie White (MUP), Sarah Madeleine Winston (MUP & MLA I). ֍

Figures. Diagrams (previous pages, left & right). Vanessa Park Moon (MUP).

DOMAIN

Domain, computer networking concepts, information technology: Locations on the Internet or any network that may contain sub-*domains*, and that are defined by a unique address. A *domain* is maintained by an individual or organization. A "*domain* name" is the part of the *domain* address that identifies any part of it as belonging to the *domain*. A "*domain* name server," or DNS, is the computer that contains the programs and files that populate the *domain*. Eminent *domain*: The right of the state to seize private property for public purposes, normally without compensation. Public *domain*: Land owned and controlled by the state or federal government. Also, the status of publications, products, and processes that are not protected under patent or copyright.

Art, Design and the Public Domain. VIS 2482. Department of Architecture. Seminar. Fall 2014. Instructor: Krzysztof Wodiczko.

The course focused on informed review and discussion on contemporary transformative, analytical, critical,

and interventional art and design practice that engages public spaces and lives of people in cities. Student interests and instructor suggestions became a base for assigned readings, research, and presentation projects. Seminar sessions included appearances by invited artists, curators, and critics, as well as film screenings and site visits. ֍

Master in Design Studies (MDes) Art, Design and the Public Domain (APD). Among the remarkable developments in contemporary culture has been the convergence of practices that once unambiguously belonged to art or design, but which today happily share methods, means, and concerns. Of particular importance are practices that seek to engage with the public and social realm—physical or virtual—with a view to shaping and transforming human action and historical experience. The phrase "spatial practice"—once a term of idiosyncrasy that applied to the margins of architectural activism—has become a confident and widely-used term to describe a variety of architectural and artistic engagements with the city and society and with aesthetic practice in general. In many ways it defines the new and moving boundary of the design discipline. The MDes program in Art, Design and the Public *Domain* seeks creative and ambitious individuals from all backgrounds and academic disciplines with a keen interest in contemporary issues of urban, historical, aesthetic, and technological culture and with a predilection for intervention, exhibition, and public work. This program seeks practicing architects, artists, filmmakers, and cultural producers wishing to develop a practice of creative and imaginative speculation, or art-related work, with an emphasis on sophisticated thinking, advanced fabrication methodologies and techniques, and social and aesthetic engagement. ֍

DONUT

1: A small usually ring-shaped cake fried in fat. 2: Something that resembles a *doughnut* especially in shape <a mathematical torus>.

The Donut. Gund Hall, Lobby. "The *Donut*" is the nickname for the security desk in the lobby of Gund Hall, named so for its hole in the middle. ֍

DRAFTING

Drafting, drawing technique: Graphical representations of structures, machines, and their component parts that communicate the engineering intent of a technical design to the craftsman or worker who makes the product. *Drafting* is based on the concept of orthographic projection, which in turn is the principal concern of the branch of mathematics called descriptive geometry.

DRAWING

Animation *drawing*: Refers to original *drawings* that are created by an animator as a model from which animation cells or other animation will be made. Architectural *drawing*, visual works: *Drawings* of architecture and *drawings* for architectural projects, whether the project was executed or not. The term may also refer to any image in a two-dimensional medium that serves this same purpose, including prints and computer images. Competition *drawing*: *Drawings* done to express proposed designs in a competition, which is a formal process by which competing architects or artists submit plans to the same client or patron for the same architectural or artistic project. Computer *drawing*: Visual works that focus on the delineation of form in two dimensions and that are created using a computer, software, and input hardware. Conceptual *drawing*: Designates architectural *drawings* done early in the design process; often not to scale and may include diagrammatic elements. Construction *drawing*: *Drawings* that are used to communicate information about buildings, specifically the mechanics of their construction, and used by the team tasked with erecting an edifice. Contour *drawing*: Distinct from "outline *drawings*" in that the lines in contour *drawings* also follow major spatial edges within an outline; distinct from "contour maps," which delineate contours at regular intervals of elevation; distinct from "cross-contour *drawings*," in which the lines follow contours across the surface of the form. Design *drawing*: *Drawings* intended to work out the scheme of a project, whether the project is expected to be executed or not; more finished than sketches. Detail *drawing*: *Drawings* of construction or design details. For minute parts of a larger structure, object, or image, use "details." For preparatory studies of pictorial or design details, use "detail studies." Mechanical *drawing*: *Drawings* produced with the aid of instruments such as compasses or T-squares." Schematic *drawing*, design *drawings*, *drawings* by function: Diagrammatic *drawings* done early in the design process of an architectural project, usually *drawn* to scale and showing the entire project." Technical *drawing*: The broad class of *drawings* that are intended for constructional, mechanical, or mapping purposes and that follow precise conventions of scale and projection, including cross-sections, details, diagrams, elevations, perspectives, plans, etc., made for use in a technical context. *Drawing*, visual work: Visual works produced by *drawing*, which is the application of lines on a surface, often paper, by using a pencil, pen, chalk, or some other tracing instrument to focus on the delineation of form rather than the application of color. This term is often defined broadly to refer to computer-generated images as well.

Figure. Drawing (above). Ester Mira Bang (MArch I).

Drawing for Designers. Artist's Talk. Gund Hall, Room 111. September 25, 2014. Joanna Malinowska. ֍

Visual Studies. VIS 2121. Department of Architecture. Seminar. Fall 2014. Instructor: Ewa Harabasz.

The course objective was to develop and improve students' skills in freehand *drawing* based on direct observation, and to encourage them to incorporate *drawing* into their design process. Architects who are fluent in various kinds of freehand *drawing* are able to generate, refine, and evaluate design ideas more effectively than architects who depend on the computer for visualization. Along with other hand processes like painting, sculpting, and bricolage, *drawing* is a complement to computer-based and conceptually based design methods. In this course priority was given to line *drawing* and learning its various forms, methods, techniques, and materials. The projects included *drawing* a human body in action and in space—in interior and exterior conditions and situations. Students learned how to draw natural forms and human-made objects and to visually articulate their structure—see architectural forms in nature and natural forms in architecture—using charcoal, pencil, markers, graphite, ink, and other *drawing* materials. ֍

See also AXONOMETRIC—see also DIGITAL—see also DRAFTING—see also MATERIAL—see also OBLIQUE—see also ORTHOGRAPHIC—see also PERSPECTIVE—see also PROJECTION—see also REPRESENTATION—see also SCALE—see also TECHNIQUE—see also TOOL: Drawing Instruments.

DRONE

Drone aircraft, aircraft by function: Unmanned aircraft, often guided by remote control, used for strategic reconnaissance, aerial surveys or to deploy weaponry.

Hover GSD. Student Group. *Hover* GSD is a platform for student-led research on drone technology and its application within the design fields. *Hover* GSD functions as a lab—researching new applications for Unmanned Aerial Vehicles (UAV) within the fields of architecture, landscape architecture, urban planning and design—as well as a resource for the school. By providing both aerial services and instruction on how to use drones as a design tool, *Hover* GSD aims to make drone technology more readily available to the Harvard GSD community. Sponsored guest lectures introduce contemporary drone research and practices and generate discussion on UAV's current and future role in design. ֍

DUALISM

Dualism, philosophical movements & attitudes, philosophical concepts: Doctrine that the universe is under the dominion of two opposing principles, one of which is good and the other evil.

Dualisms: Ábalos + Sentkiewicz Arquitectos. Exhibition. Gund Hall, Lobby. January 19–March 8, 2015. Iñaki Ábalos & Renata Sentkiewicz.

Historic architecture takes its composite tension from two theoretically incompatible morphological organizations that correspond to different disciplines or languages. This composite-tension technique usually involves the union of two organizations that possess both a degree of compatibility and incompatibility, leading to the appearance of a certain kind of Frankenstein's monster—a hybrid characterized by *dualism*. These types of unions between different forms and materials can be carried out physically—and in this case the assemblage will probably display seams and scars—or by processes of chemical fusion, which, in the organic world gives the monster the appearance of a unique organism whose greatest visual effect will then possess a new, surprising naturalness.

The word *dualism* may appear as a misnomer relative to its standard definition. In this new sense, its meaning extends beyond the reductive view that there is a struggle between two disciplines (for example, architecture and landscape). More accurately, it refers to the limited scopes (for example, the geometry used in each part) that can expand and infect almost all the scenarios intrinsic to a project. *Dualism* can also help to describe the typological outline that makes a project both an infrastructural and public facility. It also alludes to the way a project incorporates material, formal, and geometric contradictions (for example, the use of two materials whose logics and compatibilities do not fit together simplistically). Likewise, space can be conceived by introducing tension between the lower and the upper parts, or between the interior and exterior, or by means of intrusions of varying depths and differing configurations. ❧

Figure. Drawing (below). Dualisms: Ábalos + Sentkiewicz Arquitectos Exhibition. Iñaki Ábalos & Renata Sentkiewicz.

On Dualisms. Lecture. Gund Hall, Piper Auditorium. February 5, 2015. Iñaki Ábalos, Renata Sentkiewicz, with Enrique Walker (moderator). ❧

DURATION

1: Continuance in time. 2: The time during which something exists or lasts.

Indeterminately Bound. Thesis. Ingrid Kestrel Bengtson (MArch I), advised by Toshiko Mori.

"In *De architectura,* Vitruvius identifies *firmitas,* or 'durability,' as one of the three principles of good buildings. But we can also trace a longstanding trend in architecture toward ephemerality, from Ise Grand Shrine to Junya Ishigami's 'Architecture as Air.' Each of these positions is an extreme approach to the issue of *duration* in architecture. While the durable withstands the ravages of time, the transitory submits to it. In our contemporary moment, the relationship of architecture to *duration* has become more complicated. The architectural discipline has attempted to equate the durable with the complex; elaborate and overwrought forms and building systems, promising resolutions for programmatic and environmental contingencies over unverifiable futures, are the norm. The result is architecture that claims *duration* but is in fact deadened by its determinism. Might architecture operate on a third plane, beyond the myopia of the binary and the flat fussiness of systems-driven design? This thesis approaches the insurmountability of *duration* not through resolution but through ambivalence. It takes the position that architecture, wavering between extremes, has the potential to contain great heterogeneity and intricacy while preserving ambiguity. The proposal is for an architectural intervention in the ruins of the Battersea Power Station in London. The program, a new concert space, is contextually both necessary and excessive. The project unfolds in time through serial representation,

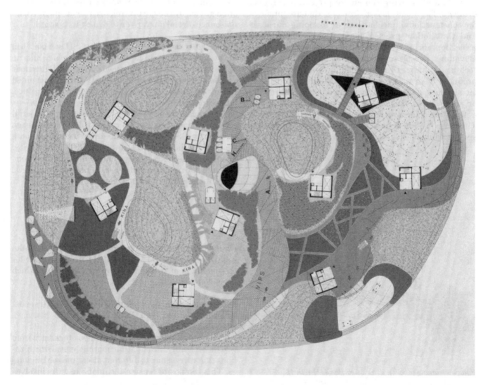

oscillating between the poles of permanent and temporary, monolithic and ephemeral, thus unseating the omniscience of the construction drawing." ⊛

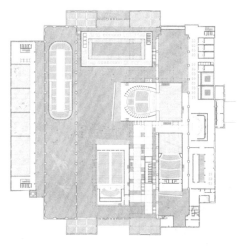

Figure. Plan (above). Ingrid Kestrel Bengtson (MArch I).

DWELLING

Dwelling, residential structures, single built works by function: Accommodations designed or adapted for residential occupancy, usually but not always intended for human occupancy rather than for animals. For hotels or other buildings intended for use by transients, see "public accommodations." For the locale which constitutes the center of an individual's domestic life, personal relationships, and interests, together with the feeling of comfort and satisfaction that it conveys, use "home (concept)." For the collective concept referring to types of living arrangements of a particular group, use "housing."

La maison des hommes. Publication. Plon, 1942. Le Corbusier & François de Pierrefeu (authors). Le Corbusier Research Collection, Frances Loeb Library. LeC NAC 5550 P614.

"Written in collaboration with François de Pierrefeu (while together at Vichy), the book is peculiar as it bears two signatures, two parts that can be read independently. The first part of the book is the text by Pierrefeu and the second includes illustrations by Le Corbusier. However, as they indicate in the introduction, the illustrations are not comments on the text, nor is the text a comment to the illustrations. The message they convey is that, through crisis and upheaval, society has arrived at the point of an era of construction. New *dwellings* are needed, and the authors are the ones that can lead that new horizon towards a new attitude of life, towards an optimism they believe is to come." —Inés Zalduendo. ⊛

Study Abroad: "Poor but Sexy"—Berlin, The New Communal. STU 1601. Departments of Architecture and Urban Planning & Design. Option Studio. Spring 2015. Instructors: Frank Barkow & Arno Brandlhuber.

Former Berlin Mayor Klaus "Wowi" Wowereit's claim that Berlin is "Arm aber Sexy" (poor but sexy), set the tone for a post-reunification milieu where cheap rents,

radically changing demographics, and a burgeoning art and music scene set the stage. Bogged down in large infrastructure projects, such as the long-delayed and over-budgeted new airport, Wowereit missed the needs of everyday citizens, that is, the urgent need for new affordable housing, and was ousted. Increasing friction between market-driven speculation and the need for affordable housing is rising in a context where 30,000 new apartments are needed within a current legislative period of five years with a yearly demand of 6,000. Berlin, as a growing metropolis, needs housing after much commercial and cultural expansion. The opportunity lies in creating density in a diffuse multicentered and layered city. What new sustainable typologies can give form to a new residential urban landscape? The current political and speculative climate suggests a proactive one, that is, where planners, architects, and developers propose housing solutions that can interface in a historical city, but without direct precedents or master planning to guide them, anticipating and provoking new experimental ideas for an immediate and urgent future. What could be new models for these typologies, where proactive speculation is given the opportunity to remap economic, zoning, and density, and as negotiated not preordained? The city of Berlin has decided to build thousands of new *dwellings* in response to an obvious lack of affordable housing. But how should these *dwelling* look? For whom are they built? How can they challenge the ongoing zombification (the blatant urban reimaging) of the city? How can post-nuclear family mass housing become a domain for experimentation and investigation?

Students: Oliver Appling Bucklin (MArch I), Julian Ryan Funk (MArch I), Nan Liu (MAUD), Shiqing Liu (MAUD), Gregory Joseph Logan (MArch I), Giancarlo Vengco Montano (MArch I), Nancy Ellen Nichols (MArch I), Elizabeth Anne Pipal (MArch I), Christopher J. SooHoo (MArch I), Dana Yao Yao Wu (MArch I). ⊛

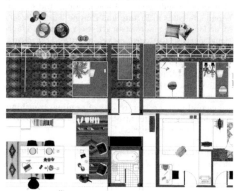

Figure. Collage (above). Teng Xing (MAUD), Man Su (MAUD), and Yuxiang Luo (MArch II).

See also *AIRPORT: Dwelling in Stop-Over City*—see also CON-STRUCTION—see also DEVELOPMENT—see also HOUSING—see also LIFESTYLE—see also STRUCTURE—see also ZOMBIFY.

DYSTOPIA

Dystopia, political concepts, social science concepts: Imaginary places where inhabitants lead fearful lives, and conditions are as bad as possible.

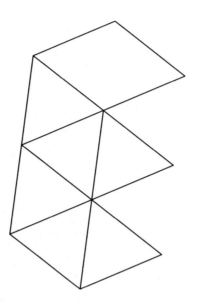

EARTHWORK

Earthwork, engineering works: Formations made of *earth*, resulting from the grading, trenching, or embanking of *earth* for utilitarian or ceremonial purposes. Examples include medieval fortifications and ancient ceremonial sites in Britain and Europe. For *earth* constructions having more of an artistic, rather than functional, purpose, use "*earthworks* (sculpture)." *Earthwork*, sculpture, environmental art: Artist works that manipulate natural *earth* and stone, altering the terrain of the land itself for artistic purposes. For large-scale outdoor works that otherwise exploit or incorporate aspects of their sites, use the more general term "environmental art." For the results of grading, trenching, or embanking *earth*, for utilitarian purposes, use "*earthworks* (engineering works)."

See also CONTOUR—see also LANDFORM—see also MEMORIAL: Abstracted Geologies—see also TERRAIN—see also TOPOGRAPHY.

ECOLOGY

Ecology, biological sciences, natural sciences, disciplines: Branch of biology dealing with the relations and interactions between organisms and their habitat, including other organisms. For aggregates of physical things, conditions, and influences surrounding and affecting given organisms or communities of organisms at any time, use "environments (object groupings)." For the concept of the external world, including the forces at work in it and the nonhuman life inhabiting it, perceived by human beings as separate and independent from themselves, their activities and civilization, use "nature."

Ecological Thinking. Student Group. Given the current urgency of the prospect of planetary environmental degradation, *ecology* has risen to the forefront, not only as an academic field but as a way of thinking. It has permeated areas beyond the natural sciences; and in the last 20 years, we have seen an unfolding of *ecology* into novel fields as diverse as industrial *ecology*, urban political *ecology*, and *ecological* economics. Design has not been the exception. Under the banners of sustainable, green, or environmentally friendly, *ecology* has become central to the agenda of design; yet *ecology* is not a smooth body of knowledge. Its various strands do not always overlap and sometimes even stand in contradiction. The frictions and tensions inherent to *ecological* thinking are rarely questioned. This group provides a much needed space to critically question the implications of the incorporation of ecological knowledge in design and how design in turn can shape *ecology*. ❧

Ecologies, Techniques, Technologies I. SCI 6141. Department of Landscape Architecture. Seminar. Fall 2014. Instructors: Rosetta S. Elkin & Matthew L. Urbanski.
  Recognizing that plants are one of the essential mediums in landscape architecture, this class introduced students to two basic relationships: the relationship between plants and people (horticulture), and the relationship between plants and environment (*ecology*). The class focused on topics and objectives including: (1) concepts and practices necessary for using plants as a design medium; (2) demonstrations on how to identify individual plants, their landscape communities, the *ecological* factors that define these communities; and (3) introductions to spatial, visual, functional, temporal, and sensorial qualities. ❧

Figure. Planting Sections (opposite page). Jeremy Kamal Hartley (MLA I).

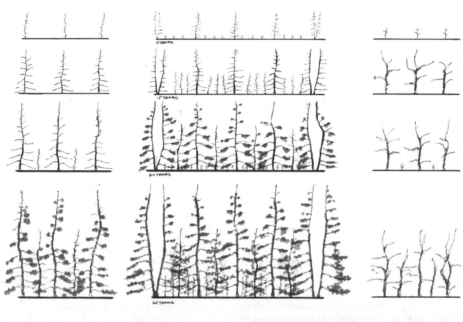

DECREASE IN TSUGA DENSITIES AS YOU APPROACH PIT BURIAN

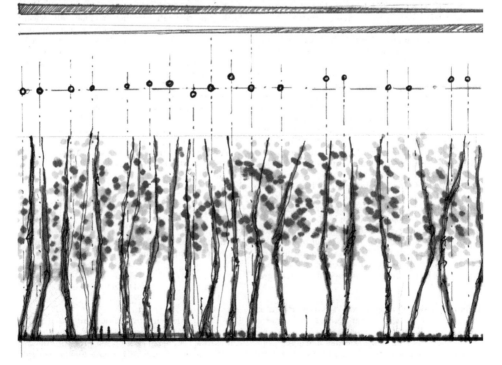

Ecologies, Techniques, Technologies III: Introduction to Energy. SCI 6241. Department of Landscape Architecture. Seminar. Fall 2014. Instructors: Erle C. Ellis, Thomas Richard Ryan, Laura J. Solano, and Peter Del Tredici.

This course introduced the science of *ecology* through the lenses of local sites, urban regions, and broad landscapes. The course covered basic *ecological* principles, spatial patterns and field observations, as well as the practical application of these principles to real-world situations. Understanding how spatial patterns link to functional flows and movements is critically important to *ecological* studies, as is the study of how ecosystems change over time. The functional biology of plants and their dynamic interaction with animals and people in both managed and unmanaged ecosystems received special emphasis. The goal of this course was for students to develop a solid understanding of the basic principles of *ecology*, especially those that are directly relevant to the practice of landscape architecture. Emphasis was placed on direct observation, analysis, and application of the *ecological* principles at different spatial scales to all types of habitats. ⚘

Projective Ecologies. Publication. ActarD & Harvard GSD, 2014. Chris Reed & Nina Marie Lister (editors). HT241 .P75 2014.

The past two decades have witnessed a resurgence of *ecological* ideas and thinking in discussions of urbanism, culture, and design. The field of *ecology* has moved from classical determinism and a reductionist Newtonian concern with stability and order in favor of more contemporary understandings of dynamic systemic change and the related phenomena of adaptability and resilience. *Projective Ecologies* takes stock of the diversity of contemporary *ecological* research and theory—embracing Félix Guattari's broader definition of *ecology* as at once environmental, social, and existential—and speculates on potential paths forward for design practices. ⚘

Research Seminar on Urban Ecology. SCI 6451. Department of Landscape Architecture. Seminar. Fall 2014. Instructor: Peter Del Tredici.

The course focused on the structure, function, and history of spontaneous urban ecosystems. They are a common feature of cities worldwide and form without being planted or maintained by humans. These emergent ecosystems are cosmopolitan in their composition and resilient in terms of their ability to tolerate the chronic environmental stress and disturbance that characterize modern cities. In recent years, there has been an increased recognition of the important *ecological* services that spontaneous ecosystems provide in terms of the improvement of air and water quality, the mitigation of soil contamination, and the promotion of biological diversity. In the context of shrinking park maintenance budgets, there is an opportunity for landscape architects to think creatively about how to manipulate spontaneous landscapes so as to increase their *ecological*, aesthetic, and recreational functionality. The course utilized the 24-acre Bussey Brook Meadow section of the Arnold Arboretum and the nearby Allendale Woods as a research studio site. ⚘

Urban & Town Ecology. SCI 6318. Department of Landscape Architecture. Seminar. Spring 2015. Instructor: Richard T. T. Forman.

Wildlife, vegetation, soil, air, water, and aquatic ecosystems, together with their human uses, are related to the distinctive, especially spatial, attributes of suburban and urban landscapes. The course addressed topics with *ecological* emphases including: urban region; suburbanization, growth, and sprawl; planned community and city; suburban town; greenway and greenbelt; large and small open-space types; rail line and trail; road and vehicle; fire and flood; groundwater, wetland, stream, river, and shoreline; commercial and industrial areas; development and neighborhood; house lot; building; and green space. ⚘

See also GARDEN: Third Natures—see also HYDROLOGY—see also LANDSCAPE—see also MATERIAL: Material Ecologies Workshop—see also NATURE—see also PLANT—see also PROCESS—see also SYSTEM—see also TECHNIQUE—see also TECHNOLOGY.

ECONOMIC

Economic, social science concepts: The management or administration of the money, financial resources, or material resources of a community, a nation, or the world. *Economic* concepts, social science concepts: Social science concepts related to *economics*. *Economic*, urban development: Improvement and development of urban areas including infrastructure, especially by building. *Economic* development, function: Development of low-income *economies* into industrial economies.

Environment, Economics, and Enterprise. SES 5370. Departments of Architecture and Urban Planning & Design. Seminar. Spring 2015. Instructors: Frank Peter Apeseche & Holly Samuelson.

How can we optimize the benefits of environmental or social sustainability while generating a higher return on investment in buildings? Where are the opportunities for real estate initiatives that are highly functional, healthy, aesthetically pleasing, and financially rewarding? The challenge for designers, developers, environmental consultants, policy-makers, and other professionals lies in finding and communicating these synergies. This cross-disciplinary course gave students an approach to problem solving to help contribute thoughtful, high-impact decisions about design and construction that are both environmentally and socially impactful and *economically* effective. ⚘

See also CONTEXT: King's Cross—see also DEVELOPMENT—see also FOOD: Surviving, Sustaining, and Shaping Urbanization—see also OUT-MIGRATE: On the Edge—see also SPECULATION: Practices in the Turbulent City—see also URBANIZATION—see also VALUE.

ECOSYSTEM

1: The complex of a community of organisms and its environment functioning as an ecological unit.

EDGE

Edge city, settlements by location, inhabited places, built environments: New settlements created in once rural areas, near major cities, primarily as destinations for office jobs, shopping, and entertainment, generally having a sprawling, car-based layout encompassing vast amounts of lease-able and retail space, but usually lacking social and community-based activities, clearly defined *edges*, a central government, or centralized growth patterns that characterize traditional cities. *Edge*, shaping & guiding tool, furnishings & equipment: Any of various tools, usually long bars or strips of wood or metal, having straight and true *edges* and used for drawing or cutting accurate straight lines or for testing levelness or the evenness of surfaces.

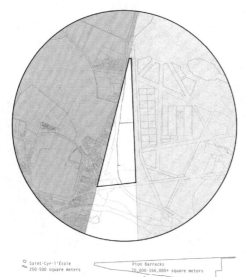

Saint-Cyr-l'École
250-500 square meters

Pion Barracks
70,000-166,000+ square meters

Versailles Agricultural Fields
6,600-25,000 square meters

Versailles Gardens
25,000-200,000 square meters

The Barracks of Pion: Developing the Edge of the Park of Versailles. STU 1408. Department of Landscape Architecture. Option Studio. Spring 2015. Instructors: Michel Desvigne & Inessa Hansch. Teaching Assistant: Samantha Maria Solano (MLA II).

Versailles is often considered the place of the invention of the classical city. Strikingly, the shapes of the city respond to those of the Park of Versailles, themselves territorial expressions. This link between geography, agrarian structures, and urban forms in the design of a park is an extraordinary reference for the actors of the contemporary city.

This studio focused on a site adjacent to the park—the former military barracks of Pion. This site forms a hinge between a historical landscape and an urban territory in flux including the Cluster of Paris-Saclay. The city of Versailles is planning to develop a new neighborhood on this 50-acre site. The studio intervened within the framework of a real project. The construction of peri-urban areas, their inclusion in an agricultural territory, the deciphering and transposition of historical traces, the invention of urban forms in relation to the creation of public spaces across the landscape were at the center of this study.

Like the creation of the city of Versailles during the 17th century, the studio overlapped landscape, public space, and urban form. Ultimately, because of its relatively small size, the site of the barracks was

considered as an experimental prototype for concrete and controlled solutions. Students proposed a small district with its built typologies, and its network of public areas at multiple scales.

Students: Hillary Jane Archer (MLA I), Joshua Ackermann Brown (MLA I), Zheming Cai (MLA II), John Frey (MLAUD & MLA I), Courtney Goode (MLA I), Qiyi Li (MLA II), Lara Elisabeth Mehling (MLA I), Maria Catalina Picon (MLA I AP), Bingjie Shi (MLA I AP & MAUD), Samantha Maria Solano (MLA II), Sonja Vangjeli (MLA I AP), Evelyn McLaurin Volz (MLA I), Xiaodi Yan (MLA II). ֍

Figure. Diagrams (left). Lara Elisabeth Mehling (MLA I). Site Plan (next spread). Bingjie Shi (MLA I AP & MAUD).

See also FORM—see also OUTLINE—see also SURFACE: Surface & Depth—see also TOOL.

EDUCATION

Education, social science, disciplines: Discipline that concerns the entire process of imparting knowledge, attitudes, skills, or socially valued qualities of character or behavior.

Executive Education. "For professionals in our incredibly dynamic fields, keeping both current and connected is an integral part of every job. Our carefully curated Executive *Education* programs extend the Harvard GSD's teaching and research excellence to practitioners actively working to build a better future." —Mohsen Mostafavi. ֍

Talca, Matter of Education. Lecture. Frances Loeb Library. March 10, 2015. Jose Luis Uribe Ortiz with Felipe Correa.

Jose Luis Uribe Ortiz discussed the academic experience of the School of Architecture of the University of Talca, Chile, followed by a conversation with Felipe Correa. ֍

EFFECT

Effect, conditions & *effects* by general type: The physical results of an action, process, physical circumstances, or spontaneous physical or chemical change; usually observable with the eye, other senses, or with specialized equipment, and typically having a measurable quantity, dimension, or other measurable characteristics. Greenhouse *effect*, environmental concepts: Phenomenon whereby the surface and the lower atmosphere of a planet are maintained at a relatively high temperature owing to the greater transparency of the atmosphere to visible radiation from the sun than to infrared radiation from the planet. It is so-called because the heating of Earth's atmosphere is loosely analogous to the glass of a greenhouse letting light in but not letting heat out. The term is often used to refer specifically to the increased magnitude of this *effect* occurring in the modern age in the context of global warming: gases from the burning of fossil fuels and other sources, including water vapor, carbon dioxide, methane, and chlorofluorocarbons, absorb infrared radiation and prevent its energy from leaving the Earth, resulting in the increasing mean global surface temperature.

Josef Albers: Minimal Means, Maximum Effect.
Lecture. Gund Hall, Piper Auditorium. November 18, 2014. Nicholas Weber & Toshiko Mori.

Nicholas Fox Weber, director of the Josef and Anni Albers Foundation, evoked the personality and sensibilities of Josef Albers through reflections on his personal acquaintance with Albers as well as descriptions of recent projects by the Albers Foundation that affirm the Bauhaus spirit of design and its commitment to improving human life generally. Toshiko Mori shared her recent projects for a health care facility, a cultural center in Senegal, and student projects from recent Harvard GSD studios in collaboration with the Albers Foundation. This lecture was part of the series "Then & Now: Walter Gropius and the Lineage of the Bauhaus," sponsored by the Breger Fund in Honor of Walter Gropius. ❦

See also CHANGE—see also CLIMATE—see also ENVIRONMENT—see also PHENOMENON—see also SENSE.

EFFICIENCY

Thermal *efficiency*, heat-related concepts, energy-related concepts: The ratio of the amount of work performed by a heat engine in one cycle to the amount of energy input required to operate the engine over one cycle.

See also AIRPORT: The New London Airport—see also CONSTRUCTION—see also EXERGY: Low-Exergy Communities—see also INSULATION.

EGO

1: The self especially as contrasted with another self or the world. 2: *Egotism.* 3: Self-esteem. 4: The one of the three divisions of the psyche in psychoanalytic theory that serves as the organized conscious mediator between the person and reality especially by functioning both in the perception of and adaptation to reality—compare to id and *superego.*

Ego: The Architecture of Freedom. Thesis. Marshall William Ford (MArch II), advised by Mack Scogin.

"*Ego* is freedom. Arrogance is imprisonment—self-imposed captivity in a signature. Architecture is about discovering an intrinsic human sound that pierces contemporary architectural white noise desperate for listeners. The discipline now begs for those who make architecture without question, hesitation, or anxiety; a call for a fragile architecture, personal to a point that makes things slightly off-disciplinary. Personal origins unground the visionary, make possible the untouchable, and shift disciplines.

An *ego* intrinsically doing something right is embedded in origins and is destined to create something permanent, while the arrogant lust to shape the discipline is doomed to anxious failure. Love for architecture lies in the *egotistically* selfless—an architect (an architecture) that projects the signature of a childish necessity to create. This architectural project is rooted at the origins (home), between the cliffs and the hill, between the inherently personal will of one and the cold vacuous weight of many—at the intimate intersection of the powerful *ego* (self) and the one we desperately want to satisfy, who we know we never will." ❦

ELEMENT

Architectural *element*, components by specific context: Forms, structural or decorative, developed originally or primarily as components of architecture, often adapted to other habitable spaces, such as in large vehicles, and often borrowed or imitated for structural or decorative use on other objects. Compositional *element*, form & composition concepts: Parts or aspects of compositions, such as foreground and background. Design *element*: The design *elements* hierarchy contains descriptors for conventionalized and recurring shapes and arrangements of forms used in the design of many types of objects and their ornament. Site *element*, open spaces and site *element*, built environment: *Elements* of the built environment that are not part of a built environment, yet are used or exist on sites. Trace *element*, chemical substances, materials be chemical form: *Elements* found in minute quantities in minerals, not essential to their composition but found in their structure or adsorbed on their surface, conventionally held to constitute significantly less than one percent of the mineral. Use also for *elements* found in plant and animal tissue in concentrations of one percent or less, which are physiologically essential to the organism.

Architecture at the Human Scale. Exhibition. Gund Hall, Dean's Wall. September 8–October 19, 2014. Rem Koolhaas, James Westcott, Stephan Trüby, Manfredo Di Robilant, and the Harvard-AMO Studio Rotterdam.

"*Elements*" is a 15-volume publication released in 2014 as part of the 14th International Architecture Exhibition: "Fundamentals." This gathering of exhibitions, events, and publications was curated by Rem Koolhaas, a founding partner of the Office for Metropolitan Architecture (OMA) and Professor in Practice of Architecture and Urban Design at the Harvard GSD.

The publication and exhibition are the result of a two-year collaboration between OMA, its research arm AMO, the book designer Irma Boom, and the Harvard GSD. In Fall 2012 and Fall 2013, two groups of students enrolled in the Studio Abroad program convened at OMA's Rotterdam office where they worked with AMO editors to formulate, research, and write the initial drafts of the books. Work with the school continued through independent studies and internships until the final product was realized—15 books, totaling almost 2,400 pages on the subject of a particular selection of critical architectural *elements*. Each volume is a dense exploration of floors, walls, ceilings, roofs, doors, windows, facades, balconies, corridors, fireplaces, toilets, stairs, escalators, elevators, and ramps—what Koolhaas describes as the "inevitable *elements* of all architecture." Buildings all over the world and throughout time are comprised of these *elements*. Each book was given a respective room inside the Central Pavilion on the Biennale grounds as part of the curated AMO exhibit that portrayed selections and artifacts from each of the *elements*. The images, texts, interviews, and essays found within the books expound upon the beginnings, critical points of transformation, and apotheoses of each *element*. The intention of this collection was not to provide an exhaustive architectural history, but rather to present a critical parsing that has implications extending beyond the physical boundary of each *element*. In isolation, each *element* takes on new political, social,

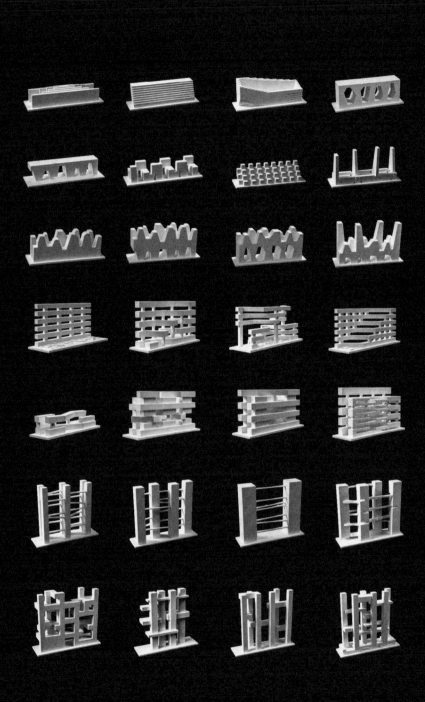

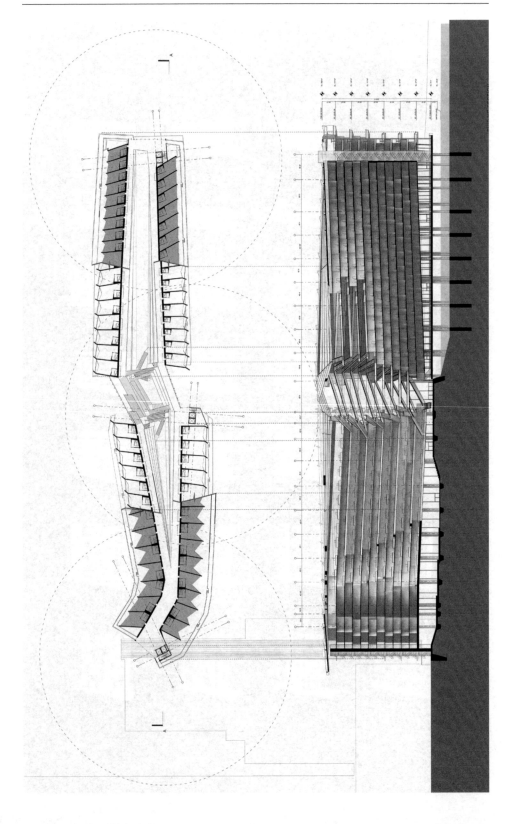

and economic relevance, which reinvigorate their architectural potential, both as the individual *elements*, as well as in their aggregation into architecture. ❧

Elements. Publication. Marsilio Editori Spa, 2014. Rem Koolhaas, James Westcott, Ben Davis, Stephan Trüby, and the Harvard-AMO Studio Rotterdam. NA 2840 .E447 2014.

Architecture is a strange mixture of persistence and flux, an amalgamation of *elements*—some that have been around for over 5,000 years and others that were reinvented yesterday. The fact that these *elements* change independently of each other, according to different cycles and economies, and for different reasons, turns each building into a complex collage of the archaic and the current, the site-specific and the standard, mechanical smoothness and spontaneity. Only by looking at the *elements* under a wide lens can we recognize the cultural preferences, forgotten symbolism, technological advances, mutations triggered by intensifying global exchange, climatic adaptations, political calculations, regulatory requirements, new digital regimes, and somewhere in the mix, the ideas of the architect that constitute the practice of architecture today.

Harvard-AMO Studio Rotterdam 2012: Heather Dunbar (MArch I, 2013), Elizabeth Echels (MArch I, 2014), Lauren Gerdeman (MArch I, 2014), Patrick Hamon (MArch I, 2014), Jenny Hong (MArch I, 2014), John Arthur Liu (MArch II, 2013), Lielu Lu (MArch I, 2014), William Lambeth (MArch I, 2013), Kurt Nieminen (MArch II, 2013), Tiffany Maria Obser (MArch I, 2014), Nicholas Potts (MAUD, 2013), Max Wong (MArch I, 2014).

Harvard-AMO Studio Rotterdam 2013: Cynthia Dehlavi (MLA I AP, 2014), Stefan Dileo (MAUD, 2014), Andrew Richard Gipe (MArch I AP, 2015), See Jia Ho (MArch I, 2015), Jingheng Lao (MAUD, 2014), Alison Ledwith (MArch II, 2014), Elizabeth MacWillie (MAUD, 2014), Alison Hinpei Kung (MArch I, 2015), Difei Ma (MLA I AP, 2014), Kangil Ji (MArch I, 2014), Annie Yuxi Wang (MArch I, 2015), Eric Glenn Williams (MArch II, 2015). ❧

Elements of Urban Design: Third Semester Urban Planning Core Studio. STU 1221. Department of Urban Planning & Design. Core Studio. Fall 2014. Instructors: Anita Berrizbeitia, Felipe Correa (coordinator), Carlos Garciavelez Alfaro, Michael Manfredi, Rahul Mehrotra, Carles Muro, Robert Gerard Pietrusko, and Richard Sennett. Teaching Assistants: Amanda Huang (MDes, RR & MAUD), Maynard Hayden Leon (MArch I AP & MUP), Ho Wai Wilfred Leung (MAUD), and Clayton C. Strange (MAUD).

This studio introduced critical concepts, strategies, and technical skills associated with current thinking on urbanism, and speculated on the designer's role in analyzing and shaping complex metropolitan systems. Applied research and lectures informed a series of interrelated exercises that constructed diverse hypotheses about new formal and experiential urbanities, across multiple scales of intervention and development. The studio focused on how an expanded notion of housing and domestic space in the city can serve as the backbone of a much more integral urban project. The studio tested the capacities of the Manhattan block to accommodate greater densities with experimental typologies that reshape conventions of urban life.

Students: Clayton Kelley Adkisson (MAUD), Hovhannes Balyan (MAUD), Mikela De Tchaves (MAUD), Moises Garcia Alvarez (MAUD), Seunghoon Hyun (MAUD), David Jimenez (MAUD), Michael Peter Keller (MAUD & MLA I

AP), Jeffrey Mark Knapke (MAUD), Yasamin Omar Mayyas (MAUD), Chi Yoon Min (MAUD), Nishiel R. Patel (MAUD), Dai Ren (MAUD), Gabriella Solange Rodriguez (MLAUD & MLA I), William Rosenthal (MAUD), Gaby Rebeca San Roman Bustinza (MAUD), Dana Shaikh Solaiman (MAUD), Man Su (MAUD), Magdalena Valenzuela (MAUD), Trax Yinan Wang (MAUD), Yutian Wang (MAUD), Ran Wei (MAUD), Mengchen Xia (MAUD), Ruoyun Xu (MAUD), Ting Yin (MAUD), Bin Zhu (MAUD). ❧

Figures. Models (previous page, top 3 rows). David Jimenez (MAUD). Models (previous page, middle 2 rows). David Jimenez (MAUD) & Yutian Wang (MAUD). Models (previous page, bottom 2 rows). Mikela De Tchaves (MAUD).

Portmanian Architecture. STU 1313. Department of Architecture. Option Studio. Spring 2015. Instructor: Preston Scott Cohen. Teaching Associate: Carl D'Apolito-Dworkin.

Portmanian Architecture is architecture characterized by the tropes that constitute the famed atrium hotels and office complexes of John Portman. These included: the glass elevator, the gondola aerial lift rotated into the Z-axis; the elevator shaft turned inside out, revealing its inner workings; the lifts passing periodically in and out of open space, solid concrete tubes, glass tubes and normal elevator shafts; the transverse spatial sequences produced by escalators and ceremonial spiral stairs; the hyperarticulated railings composed of horizontal and vertical patterns of porosity and plantings; the blurring of automobile and pedestrian thresholds; the suppression of the symbolic significance of any entrance; the introduction of pavilions and sculptures as isolated architectural figures in the plein-air within the interiorized urban space of the atrium; the revolving panoramic restaurant, invisible from the atrium and expressed on the outside as an airborne device, albeit anchored to the main building; the discreet articulation of reflective, transparent, and textured opaque components of the exterior; the aggregation of vertically attenuated masses to produce wide office buildings; and the cylindrical tower form used as a means to reduce the apparent scale of the comparably narrow hotel annex.

The properties inherent to Portmanian Architecture were prevalent in large-scale private developments from the 1970s to 1990s. Aesthetic and political theorists regarded the commercial atrium to be the apotheosis of postmodern space. Today, the atrium is no longer a dislocated and monumental component of suburban space. Interiorized environments have been reconfigured to integrate with the exterior spaces of residential developments and pedestrian oriented streets. The atrium type has been rescaled and adapted to the concept of the boutique: hotels and retail centers for small-scale vendors as opposed to mega-hotels and department stores. This studio transformed and reapplied Portmanian architectural *elements* to new urban and architectural configurations in intensely familiar contexts.

Students: Patrick James Baudin (MArch I), Yu Chen (MArch I), Jaewoo Chon (MArch I AP), Matthew Joseph Conway (MArch I), Yinjia Gong (MLA I AP), Ranjit John Korah (MArch II), Sicong Ma (MArch I), Katie MacDonald (MArch II), Michael C. Piscitello (MArch II), Sizhi Qin (MArch II), Harsha Sharma (MArch II), Wen Wen (MArch I). ❧

Figure. Plan & Section (opposite page). Michael C. Piscitello (MArch II).

See also BALCONY—see also BUILDING—see also COLOR—see also DOOR—see also ELEVATOR—see also EXHIBITION—see

also FACADE—see also FLOOR—see also PUBLICATION—see also RAMP—see also STAIR—see also WALL.

ELEVATION

Elevation, orthographic projection: Drawings or works in another medium showing the arrangement of vertical elements of a building, either exterior or interior, as a direct projection to a vertical plane. Street *elevation*: Particular arrangements of vertical elements of a building as seen by observers from the primary street view.

ELEVATOR

Elevator, vertical conveying systems, object groupings & systems: Cars, cages, or platforms and associated machinery for the vertical conveying of goods or people to and from different levels.

EMERGENT

1: (a) Arising unexpectedly; (b) calling for prompt action, urgent. 2: (a) Rising out of or as if out of a fluid <*emergent* coastal islands>; (b) rooted in shallow water and having most of its vegetative growth above water <an *emergent* plant>. 3: Arising as a natural or logical consequence. 4: Newly formed or prominent <*emergent* nations>.

Planning for the 21st Century: Emerging Trends, Challenges, and Opportunities. SES 5338. Department of Urban Planning & Design. Seminar. Fall 2014. Instructor: Mitchell J. Silver.
   What role does design play in the planning process? How will demographic and other *emerging* trends influence how we design and plan communities for present and future generations? The seminar provided an overview and implications of 20th- and 21st-century trends with a focus on planning for place, as well as planning for people. The seminar addressed the ethics and values in planning with an emphasis on social equity and other aspects of sustainability, both domestically and internationally. ֍

EMPIRICAL

1: Originating in or based on observation or experience <*empirical* data>. 2: Relying on experience or observation alone often without due regard for system and theory <an *empirical* basis for the theory>. 3: Capable of being verified or disproved by observation or experiment <*empirical* laws>. 4: Of or relating to *empiricism*.

ENCLAVE

Enclave, land use districts, districts by function, built environments: Distinct territories that are surrounded by foreign dominions.

Leftover Moments. Thesis. David Wolf Himelman (MArch I), advised by Jorge Silvetti.
   "The site is double: a linear stretch of Beverly Hills flanked by North and South Santa Monica Boulevards, its unity upset by Wilshire, which obliquely cleaves it in two. Abrupt changes in scale. An intersection wide like a piazza but treacherous to pedestrian and automobile alike.
   The site, without a doubt, is a mess. Maybe it is just another hazy nonmoment in the endless continuum of nonmoments that constitute the vehicular city of Los Angeles. Or maybe it is highly specific, the exhilarating encounter of Los Angeles's two major boulevards. Situated in the fissures between *enclaves* of extreme specificity, the site could be their epicenter. But these surrounding *enclaves*, similarly serviced and bounded by the two boulevards, have little to do with the site, nor do they care to associate with each other. The site is a ward of the infrastructure that produces, services, and encases it.
   A leftover: the product, but not the manifestation, of the *enclaves'* juxtaposition. It is a dilemma. An anomaly within the urban continuum. A point when the supposedly seamless fabric breaks down. It suggests a roadside architecture conceived as a node within a network, but also another *enclave* formation. It is a test demanding a figure that figures, a frame that frames, a perimeter that creates edges, not boundaries—something autonomous that brings it all together. An ambiguous architecture that draws out the site's latent qualities to establish a common ground. The leftover becomes occasion for threshold." ֍

Figure. Plan (below). David Wolf Himelman (MArch I).

ENERGY

Energy & related concepts, physics concepts: Generally, the capacity to do work; precisely, any quantity with dimensions that can be represented as mass times length squared divided by time squared.

Energy, Environments & Design Lab. Kiel Moe & Jane Hutton. The *Energy*, Environments & Design Lab expands and deepens our understanding of *energy* in relation to buildings, environments, and design. ֍

Energy in Architecture. SCI 6122. Department of Architecture. Seminar. Fall 2014. Instructor: Kiel Moe.

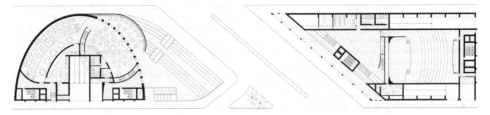

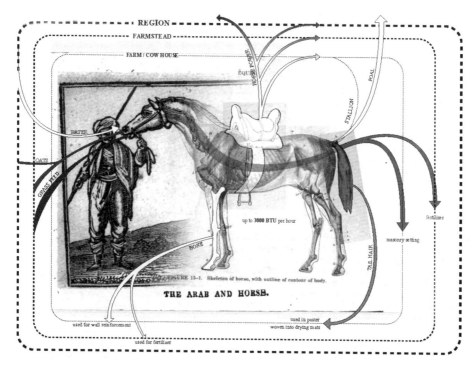

Figure 15–1. Skeleton of horse, with outline of contour of body.

THE ARAB AND HORSE.

This course introduced students to *energy* and environmental issues, particularly those that must be faced by the discipline of architecture. An overview of the basic principles of *energy* generation and *energy* use were provided, and the fundamental climatic precursors and patterns discussed. Building design issues in relation to basic *energy* needs and interior environmental requirements were briefly outlined, and students were exposed to the underlying complexity of developing solutions that address a wide range of local and global concerns. In addition, the technological responses to interior environmental control were contextualized within the larger framework of the scientific and socio-cultural influences that shaped the building systems we currently use. ❦

Forms of Energy: Nonmodern. SCI 6430. Department of Architecture. Seminar. Spring 2015. Instructor: Kiel Moe.

The course focused on nonmodern forms of *energy* and design. Nonmodern refers to those forms and formations of *energy* that are not modern in their constitution. A nonmodern constitution for *energy* begins with the implications of the second law of thermodynamics: the non-isolated propensities and capacities of our far-from-equilibrium world wherein form emerges to dissipate *energy* in the most powerful ways possible. Whether archaic or contemporary, a nonmodern formation of *energy* maximizes its intake, transformation, and feedback of matter and *energy* in landscape, architecture, and urbanization systems by design. This involves forms of *energy* that reflect how the aggregation of small-scale systems reinforces large-scale systems, and vice versa. This eschews the parochialism of modern system boundaries and methodologies for *energy* and thereby imagines more totalizing and deliriously vital alternatives to the recidivist posture of modern methods for *energy*. Students

examined a swath of intellectual history, ranging from the ancient to the contemporary, and constructed a genealogy of the intellectual tools by which people in history have attempted to quantify, qualify, understand, and manipulate forms of *energy*. In parallel, the course looked closely at several nonmodern examples to illustrate their design, behaviors, and principles. The course collectively developed a nonmodern praxis for *energy* in architecture, landscape architecture, and urbanization. Using a technical but humanist framework in understanding large and small forms of *energy*, this course questioned the current technocratic mindset of design professions, and carefully considered the intellectual legacy of the practice of building that existed prior to, and after, the radical transformations that occurred during modernization and industrialization. ❦

Figure. Diagram (above). Jacob Wayne Mans (MDes, EE), Benjamin Lee Peek (MDes, EE), Lance Smith (MArch I), and Alexander R. Timmer (MArch I).

Master in Design Studies (MDes) Energy & Environments (EE). The existing discourse on sustainable design inadequately frames questions of *energy* and environment. Whether one considers the narrowly defined system boundaries of buildings or landscapes, incomplete interpretations of the thermodynamics that support life today, or the externalities of contemporary sustainability, a more ambitious and totalizing praxis for *energy* and environments is necessary today. The *Energy & Environments* concentration focuses on buildings and landscapes as both small- and large-scale thermodynamic systems that aim to maximize *energy* intake, use, and feedback, achieving broad design and ecological impacts. Rather than focusing on the constrained principles of efficiency, conservation, and optimization, students examine the capacities and propensities of material and *energy* systems along with their historical and socioecological entanglements. This approach is necessary for a more thermodynamically cogent, ecologically exuberant, and vitally civilizing method of practice for the 21st century. *Energy* & Environments allows students to examine material and *energy* issues—broadly defined, from the molecular to the territorial—across disciplines and scales. It is closely associated with the *Energy, Environments,* and Design Lab, a way to couple theory with applied research. ⸙

See also ENVIRONMENT—see also EXERGY: Low-Exergy Communities—see also HOUSING: Creating Evidence-Based Healthy & Energy-Efficient Housing—see also SUSTAINABILITY—see also VENTILATION—see also WALL: Working Matter.

ENGAGEMENT

1: (a) An arrangement to meet or be present at a specified time and place <a dinner *engagement*>; (b) a job or period of employment especially as a performer. 2: Something that *engages*. 3: (a) The act of *engaging*, the state of being *engaged*; (b) emotional involvement or commitment <seesaws between obsessive *engagement* and ambiguous detachment —Gary Taylor>. 4: The state of being in gear. 5: A hostile encounter between military forces.

ENGINEER

Engineer, people in engineering, building trades & planning, people by occupation: Persons trained in a branch of engineering. In some jurisdictions the designation is legally restricted in technical use to persons who have completed a prescribed course of study and complied with requirements concerning registration or licensing.

In Search of Design through Engineers. SCI 6328. Department of Architecture. Seminar. Spring 2015. Instructors: Andreas Georgoulias & Hanif Kara.
    This course aimed to teach, stimulate, and demonstrate design-led opportunities that exist in the practice of architecture. Positioned between interdisciplinary boundaries, the course invited both Harvard GSD and MIT students to pioneer a joint interdisciplinary discourse, to learn how projects are won, designed, and built. Ten high-profile projects, won as design competitions and subsequently constructed, acted as the platform to expand the thinking on issues such as: (1) how each architectural practice reacts to and delivers design; (2) pioneering technical solutions; (3) establishing a variety of aesthetic positions; (4) exploring transformational research in both design methodologies and technological developments; and (5) pushing the client's brief. ⸙

ENGINEERING

Engineering, science, disciplines: The discipline of applying technical, scientific, and mathematical knowledge to the design and construction of architecture, machines, systems, processes, and the like.

Harvard School of Engineering & Applied Sciences. *Engineering* & Applied Sciences at Harvard has a long and

distinguished history, beginning with the creation of the Lawrence Scientific School in 1847. During the 19th and 20th centuries, the structure to support faculty and research in *Engineering* & Applied Sciences underwent several reorganizations and names; and in 2007, in recognition of the growing preeminence of *Engineering* & Applied Sciences, the university transitioned the former Division of *Engineering* & Applied Sciences into a school.

ENTROPY

Entropy, dynamics, mechanics concepts: Includes both the quantity that is a measure of the amount of energy in a system not available for doing work, and the ultimate state in the degradation of matter and energy in the universe.

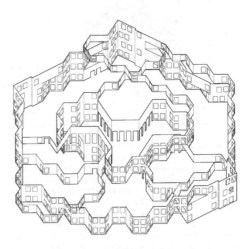

ENVELOPE

Building *envelope,* zoning concepts: Three-dimensional space within which a structure is permitted to be built on a zoning lot; used especially in relation to zoning regulations concerned with land use and access to light and air.

Figure. Diagram (above). Grace McEniry (MArch I).

ENVIRONMENT

Built *environment,* object groupings & systems: Refers to the aggregates of human-made structures, infrastructural elements, and associated spaces and features. *Environmental* design, planning disciplines, social sciences: The planning discipline concerned with the physical *environment* and any and all human involvement with it, with the general objective of assuring proper habitat for people, animals, and plants, and the resources upon which they depend. For the branch of architecture that deals with the design of the scenic *environment,* including green spaces, accompanying structures, and roadways, with the aim of creating a natural setting for human structures and settlements, use "landscape architecture." Urban *environment*, object groupings & systems: *Environments* affected by conditions characteristic of cities, including conditions of atmosphere, heavy use, and vandalism. Workplace, *environmental* psychology concepts: Locale where work is done, usually when referring to a place of employment.

The Built Environment. Grounded Visionaries Design Weekend. Lecture. Gund Hall. September 13, 2014. Michael Van Valkenburgh & Peter Walker. ⊛

REAL: Genome of the Built Environment/Measuring the Unseen. ADV 9140. Departments of Architecture and Urban Planning & Design. Seminar. Spring 2015. Instructor: Allen Sayegh.

The built *environment* is one of the most fascinating yet enigmatic artifacts of the human being. We perceive it as a complex entity resulting from the juxtaposition of spaces, flows, experiences, objects, and events. Each *environment* has certain qualities, and—even though shared characteristics do exist—those qualities vary from place to place. Although a variety of criteria, parameters, and indicators attempt to capture key figures of places, they are far from depicting the more qualitative aspects that constitute the real experiential character of built *environments*. And far less is known of the role of new media and digital tools in understanding these qualities. Articulating criteria of investigation and speculating on the role of design technology, this course introduced the "Genome of the Built *Environment*" as a new paradigm for understanding the built *environment*. How one might perceive it, and thus evolve it. Putting the human being at the center and forefront, the class investigated the role of new technologies in articulating, mapping, and exploiting the specificities of places through a multisensory approach. ⊛

Studies of the Built North American Environment: 1580 to the Present. HIS 4105. Department of Landscape Architecture. Seminar. Fall 2014. Instructor: John R. Stilgoe.

North America as an evolving visual *environment* was analyzed as a systems concatenation involving such constituent elements as farms, small towns, shopping malls, highways, suburbs, and as depicted in fiction, poetry, cartography, television, cinema, advertising, and cybernetic simulation. ⊛

See also BUILT—see also COASTAL: Changing Natural & Built Coastal Environments—see also CONTEXT: King's Cross—see also ECONOMIC: Environment, Economics, and Enterprise—see also ECOSYSTEM—see also ENERGY—see also FOOD—see also HOUSING—see also LANDSCAPE—see also MANAGEMENT: A Sustainable Future for Exuma—see also NATURE—see also NUCLEAR: Fatal Vitality—see also RESPONSIVE—see also SPACE—see also SYSTEM—see also URBANISM—see also WORK: Work Environments I.

EPHEMERAL

Ephemeral community, plant or animal communities: Communities of animals or plants that are temporary or in a constant state of flux. *Ephemeral* community, inhabited places: Inhabited places of any size that are populated on a temporary basis. Temporary structures, single built works by design: Buildings, monuments,

and other structures that are intended to be non-permanent, sometimes transportable.

ERGONOMICS

Ergonomics, social science, discipline: Study of human physiological and psychological capacities, limitations, and needs in relation to the human environment. In modern usage, the term is used particularly to refer to the workplace, regarding the spaces, objects, and systems that people use.

See also BODY: Standard Deviations—see also MEASURE—see also OBJECT—see also OFFICE—see also PROPORTION—see also PROSTHETIC: Architecture of Cultural Prosthetics—see also SCALE—see also SYSTEM—see also WORK: Work Environments I.

EROSION

Erosion, alveolar weathering, surface or structural changes: A distinctive effect of weathering, often affecting stone, characterized by a pattern of small cavities. *Erosion*, surface or structural changes, condition changing processes: Process whereby materials are worn away and removed by natural causes including weathering, solution, corrosion, or transportation. *Erosion* protection work, hydraulic structures by function: Protective walls, pipes, or other structures designed to allow water to flow from an area in order to avoid *erosion* of the soil.

ERROR

1: (a) An act or condition of ignorant or imprudent deviation from a code of behavior; (b) an act involving an unintentional deviation from truth or accuracy; (c) an act that through ignorance, deficiency, or accident departs from or fails to achieve what should be done <an *error* in judgment>; (d) a mistake in the proceedings of a court of record in matters of law or of fact. 2: (a) The quality or state of *erring*; (b) an instance of false belief. 3: Something produced by mistake <a typographical *error*>. 4: (a) The difference between an observed or calculated value and a true value, specifically variation in measurements, calculations, or observations of a quantity due to mistakes or to uncontrollable factors; (b) the amount of deviation from a standard or specification.

The Architecture of Error: Matter, Measure, and the Misadventures of Precision. Book Launch. Gund Hall, Frances Loeb Library. February 12, 2015. Francesca Hughes & Erika Naginski. ⊛

ESCALATOR

Escalator, diagonal & multidirectional conveying systems: Refers to continuously operating, power-driven, moving stairways used as transportation between floors or levels in subways, buildings, and other mass pedestrian areas. An inclined belt for passengers riding on cleats was invented by Jesse W. Reno of the United States in 1891; it was inclined at an angle of 25 degrees, and in the first model, the handrail was stationary. The name *escalator* was first applied to a moving stairway shown at the Paris Exposition of 1900, originally a trademark of the Otis Elevator Company.

Figure. Diagram (above). Timothy Yung Wei (MLA I).

ESPALIER

1: A plant trained to grow flat against a support. 2: A railing or trellis on which fruit trees or shrubs are trained to grow flat.

ETHICS

Ethics, philosophical concepts: System of moral principles or rules of conduct for voluntary human action. *Ethics*, philosophy, humanities: Branch of philosophy dealing with values relating to human conduct, with respect to the rightness and wrongness of certain actions, and to the goodness and badness of the motives and ends of such actions. Social *ethics*, philosophical concepts: *Ethics* that have as their utilitarian end the well-being and fair treatment of the entire community.

EVALUATION

Evaluation, analytical functions, functions by general context: Determining qualitative or quantitative worth or significance.

Under One Roof: New Findings from USAID Post-Disaster Shelter Projects Evaluations (Haiti, Four Years on, and the Philippines). Student Event, Master in Design Studies Risk & Resilience. Gund Hall, Room 109. April 17, 2015. Charles A. Setchell. ⌗

EVOLUTION

Evolution, biological concepts, scientific concepts: Refers to the gradual development of living organisms over successive generations, from lower to higher forms,

especially as articulated in Darwinian theory or in alternatives to or modifications of Darwinian theory.

See also LANDSCAPE: An Evolution of Practice & Theory—see also TRANSFORMATION.

EXERGY

Exergy is a measure of the maximum work potential in a system before it reaches equilibrium.

Low-Exergy Communities: An Exercise in Energy & Material Flows. Thesis. Kanika Arora (MDes, EE), advised by Kiel Moe.
"From redevelopment sites in thriving cities to rapidly urbanizing green fields in developing regions, urban environments have become the top consumers of energy in the world. Buildings are perhaps the most significant urban components. In addition to replacing natural systems, buildings spew large quantities of material and energy waste during the process of development and construction. With the advent of building simulations and energy-rating systems, there is a push toward energy-saving measures to achieve increased efficiency in all forms of energy utilization. Yet, despite these efforts, little progress has been made. A fundamental flaw associated with this kind of thinking is that it considers buildings as though they were in a closed energy-flow system. However, buildings are fundamentally open systems, constantly exchanging energy and matter with their surroundings. Moreover, the concept of energy efficiency in itself is also incomplete, given that in thermodynamic terms it deals only with the quantity of energy and not the quality of energy. The combination of these two properties is represented by the thermodynamic concept of *exergy*. Within an energy-production system in a building, *exergy* gain occurs in the form of useful heat, while *exergy* loss occurs in the form of nonuseful heat. In most inefficient buildings, this nonuseful heat is dissipated, causing other problems such as the urban heat island effect. This research uses an *exergy*-and-energy approach, rather than an energy-efficiency approach, to suggest ways that nonuseful heat can be captured and fed back into the energy-production system as useful heat. It seeks to initiate a conversation around buildings that, while individually *exergy* inefficient, can nevertheless have higher *exergy* efficiency within a community system." ⌗

EXHIBITION

1: An act or instance of *exhibiting*. 2: A public showing, as of works of art, objects of manufacture, or athletic skill <a one-man *exhibition*> <an *exhibition* game>.

Exhibiting Contemporary Architecture. Lecture. Gund Hall, Piper Auditorium. April 21, 2015. Ulrich Müller.
Despite the complexity of *exhibitions* and the easy availability of information online, a growing number of architects are *exhibiting* their works in private galleries. Any curator must confront the question of why to *exhibit* contemporary architecture, and how this seemingly old-fashioned format might measure up in the context of the new media. Using examples from Architecture Gallery Berlin as illustrations of current trends, Ulrich Müller, founder and director of Architecture Gallery Berlin, examined the *exhibition* as a means for architects to reflect publicly on their own work. ⌗

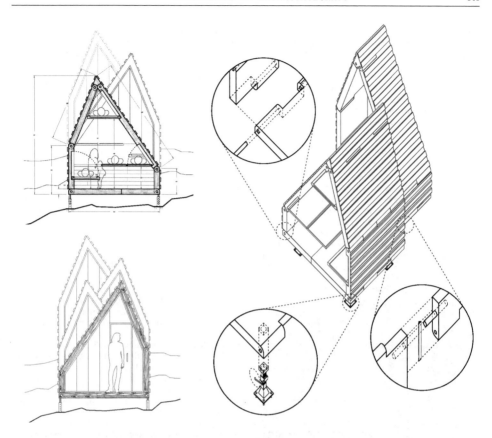

EXPERIENCE

1: (a) Direct observation of or participation in events as a basis of knowledge; (b) the fact or state of having been affected by or gained knowledge through direct observation or participation. 2: (a) Practical knowledge, skill, or practice derived from direct observation of or participation in events or in a particular activity; (b) the length of such participation. 3: (a) The conscious events that make up an individual life; (b) the events that make up the conscious past of a community or nation or humankind generally.

Choose Your Own Adventure. Thesis. Emily Eleanor Russell (MArch I), advised by Mack Scogin.
"In deciding their destination, travelers select a fantasy: what stories do they want to engage in, *experience*, and share? Using the tools of a production designer, this thesis aims to explore architecture's ability to create a spatial framework that allows a series of events and stories to unfold. Using the 827-mile journey of the Ring Road around the island of Iceland, this thesis parallels the cadence of a road trip with the rhythm of a story structure to generate a network of support spaces that facilitate an intimate adventure through the stark landscape.

Working with the belief that 'storytelling is the most fundamental interaction among humans …[and forms] part of human continuity,' this thesis tests the potential of architecture to generate, support, and elevate a common story. Architecture stands at the intersection between fact and fantasy, where reality becomes fiction." ⸶

EXPERIMENT

1: (a) Test, trial; (b) a tentative procedure or policy; (c) an operation or procedure carried out under controlled conditions in order to discover an unknown effect or law, to test or establish a hypothesis, or to illustrate a known law. 2: The process of testing, *experimentation*.

EXTRASTATECRAFT

Extrastatecraft. Lecture. Gund Hall, Piper Auditorium. April 7, 2015. Keller Easterling.
Keller Easterling addressed the theme of her book, *Extrastatecraft*: that repeatable formulas such as spatial products and free-zone cities make up most of the space in

the world. Some of the world's most radical changes are being written in the language of this almost infrastructural spatial matrix. It generates de facto forms of polity that can outpace law, and it is the secret weapon of some of the world's most powerful players. Infrastructure space is itself an information system—a spatial operating system for shaping the city. However unlikely it may seem, this space can bring to our art a new relevance, as well as additional aesthetic pleasures and political capacities. ✿

EXTREME

1: (a) Existing in a very high degree <*extreme* poverty>; (b) going to great or exaggerated lengths, radical <went on an *extreme* diet>; (c) exceeding the ordinary, usual, or expected <*extreme* weather conditions>. 2: Situated at the farthest possible point from a center <the country's *extreme* north>. 3: (a) Most advanced or thoroughgoing <the *extreme* political left>; (b) maximum. 4: Of, relating to, or being an outdoor activity or a form of a sport that involves an unusually high degree of physical risk <*extreme* mountain biking down steep slopes>.

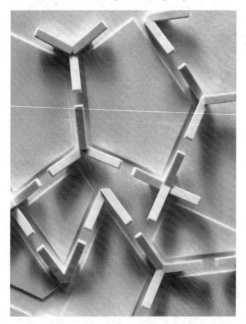

Housing in Extreme Environments. STU 1309. Department of Architecture. Option Studio. Fall 2014. Instructors: Rok Oman & Spela Videcnik. Teaching Assistant: Joshua Barton Schecter (MArch I).

The first part of the studio investigated architectural solutions and responses within *extreme* climatic conditions. Students researched traditional building designs that respond to risks associated with avalanches, heavy snowfalls, strong winds, and low temperatures, and constructed several prototypical designs of a smallest-possible habitable unit that became a temporary living space for mountaineers and hikers. The process involved structural engineers and elements of sustainable architecture to produce a shelter with strict design constraints, minimum energy consumption, minimum envelope exposure, lightweight structure, and adherence to limits of remote transportation.

Students: Myrna Josephine Ayoub (MArch II), Oliver Appling Bucklin (MArch I), Zheng Cui (MArch II), Frederick Chando Kim (MArch I), Katie MacDonald (MArch II), Lauren Gail McClellan (MArch I), Michael Ernest Meo (MArch I), Erin Anne Pellegrino (MArch II), Nadia Perlepe (MArch II), Elizabeth Anne Pipal (MArch I), Tianhang Ren (MAUD), Xin Su (MArch II), Elizabeth Y. Wu (MLA I AP). ✿

Figures. Axonometric Detail, Section & Elevation (previous page). Frederick Chando Kim (MArch I), Katie MacDonald (MArch II), and Erin Anne Pellegrino (MArch II). Model (left). Myrna Josephine Ayoub (MArch II) & Nadia Perlepe (MArch II).

See also BUILDING—see also EXHIBITION—see also HABITATION: Housing in Extreme Environments—see also PUBLICATION—see also RISK—see also TRANSITION: The Forms of Transition—see also URBANISM: Extreme Urbanism III—see also VISIONARY: Grounded Visionaries.

EXTRUSION

Extrusion, forming, processes & techniques by specific type: The process of shaping a heated or unheated material, by forcing or pressing it through a dye or other shaping device.

City of Artificial Extrusions. STU 1308. Department of Architecture. Option Studio. Fall 2014. Instructors: Sharon Johnston & Mark Lee.

The studio investigated the urban model of the detached city through the design of a mixed-use, high-rise tower situated around an existing shopping mall in Redondo Beach, California. While research has generated a set of theoretical inquiries into the dissolution of boundaries, this trajectory is being countered by the phenomenon of privatized, isolated programs. Rather than viewing autonomous and detached monocultures as fissures within the inclusive mentality of globalization, the studio embraced these models as opportunities to promote form of connectivity through precise demarcation and delineation of borders. The tower and socle were utilized as the primary building types to investigate the detached city. Although assembly techniques in high-rises have been evolving steadily, the programmatic effects caused by economics, zoning regulations, cultural identities, and geographies have been in a state of flux. These two trajectories propagated two design predilections. The first adhered to the efficiencies gained from repetition and interchangeability. The second relied on the idiosyncrasies gained from simulation and dynamics. In seeking to explore a third, alternative model, the studio proposed the exacerbation of *extrusion* for the massing of the tower and socle type, one that privileged the investment of the plan over the section. Instead of treating the tower and the socle type as directionally neutral, the vertical predilection intrinsic within this type was explored to the extreme.

Students: Ingrid Kestrel Bengtson (MArch I), Dong ah Cho (MArch II), Jaime Daroca Guerrero (MArch II), Julian Ryan Funk (MArch I), Gunho Kim (MArch II), Dayita Sanjay Kurvey (MArch II), Erin Jennifer Ota (MArch II & MDes, RR), Jim Peraino (MArch I), Harsha Sharma (MArch II), José Ramón Sierra Gómez de León (MArch II), Isaac James William Smith (MArch I), Han Wang (MAUD), Dana Yao Yao Wu (MArch I). ✿

Figure. Plan & Perspective Rendering (opposite page). Harsha Sharma (MArch II).

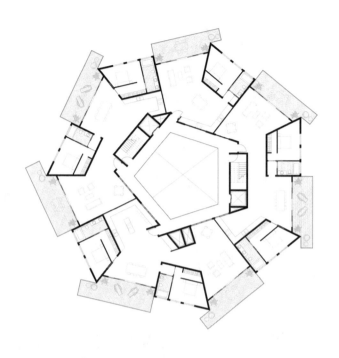

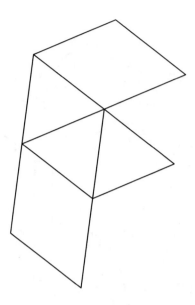

FABRICATION

1: The act or process of fabricating. 2: A product of *fabrication.*

Material Practice as Research: Digital Design & Fabrication. SCI 6317. Department of Architecture. Fall 2014. Seminar. Instructors: Leire Asensio Villoria & Carlos Felix Raspall Galli (DDes).

The translation between architectural design and the subsequent actualization process is mediated by various tools and techniques. Through the adoption of computation and information technologies in architectural practice, with their capacity for a relatively seamless transition between design and *fabrication,* a more integrated workflow across design and actualization processes is made more accessible. In recent years, designers have become increasingly able to move effortlessly between digital modeling, performance simulation, and physical realization. As technology evolves, this evolving field continually presents architects and designers with new challenges and opportunities for creative exploration and a materially intelligent practice. ❧

Rethinking Refabricating Architecture. Project Delivery Lecture. Gund Hall, Piper Auditorium. April 6, 2015. Stephen Kieran. ❧

FACADE

Facade & facade components, exterior walls: Exterior surfaces or faces of a building that are substantially in one plane, particularly those perceived to be the principal or most architecturally ambitious ones, designed with special regard to their conspicuousness or associ-

ation with an entrance and looks onto a street or open space. For the external areas of buildings, potentially including the *facade* and other features, but not necessarily restricted to surface features, use "fronts (architectural)." For the vertical arrangements of exterior or interior features, use "elevations (building divisions)."

See also BUILDING—see also ELEMENT: Architecture at the Human Scale—see also ELEVATION—see also ENVELOPE—see also SKYSCRAPER: Wood Skyscraper—see also SURFACE—see also VENTILATION—see also WALL.

FACULTY

1: Ability, power, such as (a) an innate or acquired ability to act or do; (b) an inherent capability, power, or function <the *faculty* of hearing>; (c) any of the powers of the mind formerly held by psychologists to form a basis for the explanation of all mental phenomena; (d) natural aptitude <has a *faculty* for saying the right things>. 2: (a) A branch of teaching or learning in an educational institution; (b) something in which one is trained or qualified. 3: (a) The members of a profession; (b) the teaching and administrative staff and those members of the administration having academic rank in an educational institution; (c) *faculty* plural: *faculty* members <many *faculty* were present>.

Harvard GSD Faculty. *Faculty* are responsible for academic policies, required courses of study, and the granting of degrees. The Harvard GSD *Faculty* of Design include professors, professors in practice, non-tenured professors in practice, senior lecturers, associate and assistant professors in practice, associate and assistant professors, lecturers, design critics, instructors, and visiting professors.

Iñaki Ábalos
Chair of the Department of Architecture & Professor in Residence

Martin Bechthold
Director of the Doctor of Design Studies Program & Professor of Architectural Technology

Pierre Bélanger

Codirector of the Master in Design Studies Program & Associate Professor of Landscape Architecture

Silvia Benedito
Cochair of the Sensory Media Platform & Assistant Professor of Landscape Architecture

Anita Berrizbeitia
Director of the Master in Landscape Architecture Program & Professor of Landscape Architecture

Preston Scott Cohen
Gerald M. McCue Professor in Architecture

Felipe Correa
Director of the Master in Urban Design Program & Associate Professor of Urban Design

Salmaan Craig
Lecturer in Architecture, Environmental Technology

Diane Davis
Charles Dyer Norton Professor of Regional Planning & Urbanism

Sonja Dümpelmann
Program Coordinator for MDes History and Philosophy of Design & Associate Professor of Landscape Architecture

Edward Eigen
Associate Professor of Architecture & Landscape Architecture

Rosetta S. Elkin
Assistant Professor of Landscape Architecture

Ann Forsyth
Director of the Master in Urban Planning Program & Professor of Urban Planning

Ewa Harabasz
Lecturer in Architecture, Landscape Architecture, and Urban Planning & Design

K. Michael Hays
Associate Dean for Academic Affairs & Eliot Noyes Professor of Architectural Theory

Gary R. Hilderbrand
Professor in Practice of Landscape Architecture

Zaneta H. Hong
Platform 8 Faculty Editor & Lecturer in Landscape Architecture

Mariana Ibañez
Associate Professor of Architecture

Jerold S. Kayden
Frank Backus Williams Professor of Urban Planning & Design

Grace La
Director of the Master in Architecture Program & Professor of Architecture

Ali Malkawi
Director of the Harvard Center for Green Buildings and Cities & Professor of Architectural Technology

Rahul Mehrotra
Chair and Professor of the Department of Urban Planning & Design

Kiel Moe

Codirector of the Master in Design Studies Program & Associate Professor of Architecture and Energy

Mohsen Mostafavi
Dean of the Harvard Graduate School of Design & Alexander and Victoria Wiley Professor of Design

Carles Muro
Design Critic in Architecture and Urban Planning & Design

Erika Naginski
Director of the Doctoral Program & Professor of Architectural History

Antoine Picon
Director of Research & G. Ware Travelstead Professor of History in Architecture and Technology

Robert Gerard Pietrusko
Assistant Professor of Landscape Architecture & Urban Planning

Jorge Silvetti
Nelson Robinson Jr. Professor of Architecture

Charles A. Waldheim
Chair of the Department of Landscape Architecture & John E. Irving Professor of Landscape Architecture

Andrew Witt
Codirector of the Geometry Lab & Assistant Professor in Practice of Architecture

Krzysztof Wodiczko
Professor in Residence of Art, Design and the Public Domain

The total number of *faculty* teaching at the Harvard GSD during the 2014–2015 academic year was 201, including 100 Department of Architecture *faculty*, 59 Department of Landscape Architecture *faculty*, and 49 Department of Urban Planning & Design *faculty*. ❧

See also *ACADEMIA—see also ARCHITECTURE—see also CLUB—see also DISCIPLINE—see also EDUCATION—see also HOUSING—see also LANDSCAPE ARCHITECTURE—see also PRACTICE—see also RESEARCH—see also URBAN DESIGN—see also URBAN PLANNING—see also WORK—see also WRITING.*

FELLOWSHIP

Fellowship, subsidies, financial aid: The financial grants awarded to members of a college or university graduate community for a limited number of years, on condition of pursuing some specified branch of study.

China Scholarship Council Exchange Scholarships. An agreement between Harvard University and the China Scholarship Council of the Ministry of Education of the People's Republic of China provides Harvard undergraduate and graduate students with the opportunity to study or conduct research in China for one academic year.

Community Service Fellowship Program (CSFP). The Community Service *Fellowship* Program provides opportunities for Harvard GSD students to extend their design education beyond the walls of the school through direct involvement with projects that address public needs and community concerns at the local level. ❧

Daniel Urban Kiley Teaching Fellowship. The Daniel Urban Kiley Teaching *Fellowship* is awarded to an emerging designer whose work articulates the potential for landscape as a medium of design in the public realm. ❧

Ecole Normale Superieure Exchange Fellowship. An agreement between Harvard University and the Ecole Normale Superieure (ENS) in Paris provides *fellowships* for Harvard College seniors and Harvard graduate students interested in studying at ENS for one academic year.

Frank Knox Memorial Fellowship. The Frank Knox *Fellowship* supports research and study in Australia, Canada, New Zealand, South Africa, or the United Kingdom.

Frederick Sheldon Fellowship. The Frederick Sheldon *Fellowship* supports research, study and travel abroad or within the United States.

Loeb Fellowship Program. The Loeb Fellows represent the broadest spectrum of accomplished design practitioners from countries around the world. In the middle of promising careers shaping the built and natural environment, Loeb Fellows step away from their professional lives.
For one academic year, they engage with students and faculty at the Harvard GSD, strengthen their leadership skills, audit classes throughout the university, and undertake independent study projects aimed at having social impact.

In 2014–2015 the *fellowship* continued the tradition of engaging with a core studio. The *fellows* interacted with Rahul Mehrotra's Extreme Urbanism III studio. They traveled to Agra, India with the studio and Master in Design Studies Critical Conservation students, mentored the students, participated in pin-ups and reviews, and provided multiple perspectives for the students to synthesize into their projects. The 2014–2015 Loeb *Fellows* were Gísli Marteinn Baldursson, Jamie Blosser, Scott Campbell, Shahira Fahmy, LaShawn Hoffman, Andrew Howard, Maria Jaakkola, Marc Norman, Edwin Thaddeus Pawlowski, and Kolu Zigbi. ❧

Luce Scholars Program. The Luce Scholars Program is an enterprise of the Henry Luce Foundation, which invites Harvard University to nominate three students (College seniors, graduate students, and/or recent alumni) as part of its national search for 15 to 18 Luce Scholars. The goal of the program is to enhance the understanding of Asia among potential leaders in American society and allows Luce Scholars to gain new perspectives and cultural insights through immersive living and working experiences in Asia.

Sinclair Kennedy Fellowship. The Sinclair Kennedy *Fellowship* supports research outside of the United States. Students enrolling at foreign universities are not eligible for these funds.

See also *ACADEMIA—see also CULTURE—see also FACULTY—see also POWER: Community Power & Leadership—see also PRIZE—see also RESEARCH—see also STUDENT.*

FENCE

Fence, open space & site elements, built environment: Roofless enclosures, barriers, defenses, or bulwarks, such as a hedges, walls, railings, or palisades, constructed along the boundary of a field, park, yard, or another place for the purpose of defending from intruders or keeping livestock or people within.

FIELD

Field, airfields, air transportation spaces: Areas prepared for the landing and takeoff of aircraft; may or may not be provided with associated buildings, equipment, or other installations. Athletic *field*, sport & recreation spaces, open space by function: Expanses of generally level open space intended primarily for highly organized games and sports, often supplied with spectator seating and delimiting fences or walls. For buildings with tiers of seats surrounding such *fields*, use "stadiums." Cross- & interdisciplinary *field*, disciplines: *Fields* that are interdisciplinary. Depth of *field*, visual & representational concepts, formal concepts, artistic concepts: Range of distances, near and far, within which objects appear in sharp focus. *Field*, land, cultural landscapes by development practices: Open land as opposed to woodland or land occupied by buildings; for land appropriated for pasture or tillage, use "agricultural land." *Fieldwork*, research: Studying or investigating a particular subject in its natural setting. *Field*, geomagnetism, magnetism & related concepts: Studying or investigating a particular subject in its natural setting.

See also AGRICULTURE—see also COLLABORATION—see also DISCIPLINE—see also GRID—see also LANDSCAPE ARCHI-TECTURE—see also OBSERVATION—see also RESEARCH—see also SURFACE—see also TRANSPORTATION—see also WORK.

FIGURE-GROUND

Figure-ground perception, visual & representation concepts, formal concepts: In an image, the way in which an object or shape is related to the background against which it is seen.

FILM

Film, material by form: A thin coating or thin sheet of material. *Film*, performing arts: The art and form of expression of *film*making and motion pictures, which are produced in the media of *film* or videotape, on which a series of pictures are presented to the eye in such rapid succession as to give the illusion of natural movement. It may also refer to art created in digital media. The art form is typically characterized by conveying drama, evoking emotion, and utilizing a complex array of contributions from other performing and visual arts, combined with numerous technical skills. It proliferated enormously throughout the 20th century. For the actual works created on *film*, use "motion pictures (visual works)."

Assistance Mortelle. *Film* Screening. Gund Hall, Piper Auditorium. November 13, 2014. Raoul Peck, with Pierre Bélanger and Michael Hooper (moderators).

Assistance Mortelle (Fatal Assistance) examines the process and legacy of humanitarian aid in Haiti following the 2010 earthquake. After the *film* screening, director Raoul Peck discussed the significance of fieldwork and the potential for media and representation to shed light on development and governance. ❦

Film GSD. Student Group. *Film* GSD seeks to promote design discourse through movies concerning architects, architecture, and broader issues of urbanism. Many screenings are followed by discussions with *filmmakers*, critics, and professors at the school. *Film* GSD also exhibits homegrown talent at Opening Night, an event for screening *films* made by and about the Harvard GSD and its people. ❦

FILTER

Filter, lighting device components: Transparent devices often of gelatin or glass which are placed in front of a light source and serve to diminish the intensity or alter the color of the light. *Filter*, materials by function: Any porous material through which a gas or liquid is passed to separate out matter in suspension.

FLOAT

Float glass, glass by technique, material: Sheet glass made by *floating* a ribbon of hot glass on a bath of heated liquid, usually molten tin. The process was developed in 1959 by Pilkington Brothers and is now the principal method of manufacturing good quality sheet glass which is clear and flat with parallel and fire polished sides. *Float*, freewheeled vehicle by form or function: Decorated platforms, either built on a vehicle or towed behind a vehicle or horse, often bearing a display or tableau and drawn in a parade or procession for a festive or solemn occasion.

Floating Cities. Wheelwright Prize Lecture. Gund Hall, Piper Auditorium. April 16, 2015. Gia Wolff.

On the eve of Rio de Janeiro's famous Carnival, the line of *floats* stretching from Samba City to the Sambadromo creates new city blocks that challenge our typical understanding of the sidewalk-street-block stratum. This slow-moving parade of architecturally scaled objects raises the question: who is actually performing, the carnavalesco or the pedestrian? The building or the *float*? The city or the procession? These visually magnificent *floats*, among the largest in the world, possess an intangible power that draws from their deep-rooted relationship to the urban fabric and to the diverse communities that build them. As part of Gia Wolff's ongoing research devoted to carnival constructions, this lecture focused on the surprising temporary urban transformations seen in Rio de Janeiro, and additional small-scale projects inspired by this long-term investigation. ❦

FLOOR

Floor plan, buildings plans, orthographic projections: Drawings or works in another two-dimensional medium that represent a horizontal section through a building taken above a *floor* to diagrammatically illustrate the enclosing walls, interior spaces, doors, and windows of a building. *Floor*, surface elements: The surfaces of rooms or spaces on which one walks. Floating *floor*, surface elements: *Floor* slabs or *floor* assemblies which are completely separated from (and mechanically isolated from) the structural *floor* by a resilient underlayment or resilient mounting devices; used to isolate the vibration of machinery from the building structure. Typical *floor* plan, building plans: Plans of one story of a building that has numerous stories in that form, thus illustrating what is typical or usual in the *floor* plans of this building.

See also BUILDING—see also CIRCULATION—see also ELE-MENT: Architecture at the Human Scale—see also PLAN—see also REPRESENTATION—see also STRUCTURE—see also SURFACE.

FLOW

Flow chart, graphic documents: Graphic representations of symbols connected with lines showing the successive steps in a procedure or systems. *Flow*, heat transmission, heat-related concepts, energy-related concepts: Transfer of heat from one point to another due to the tendency of heat to *flow* from an area of higher temperature to an area of lower temperature. Mud *flow*, earth movements, natural events: Occurrences of moving masses of soil made fluid by rain or melting snow, or masses of

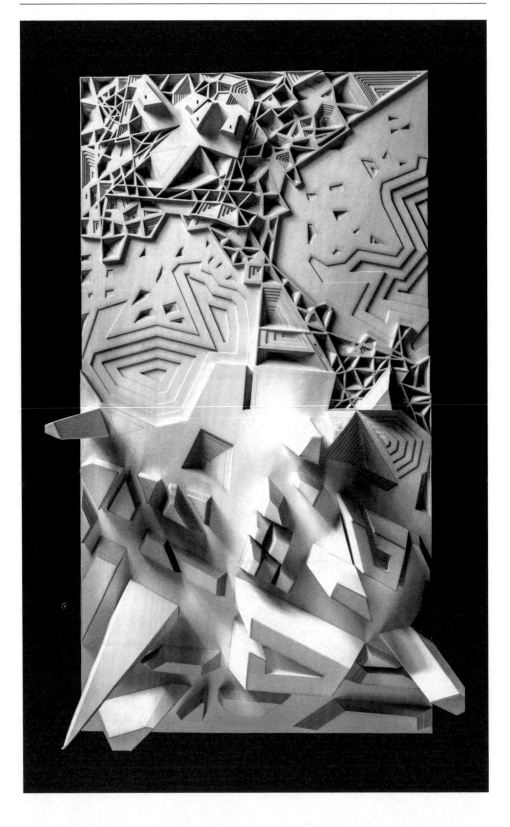

mingled volcanic particles and water that *flow* like lava from volcanoes. *Flow*, physics, dynamics, mechanics concepts: The movement of electrical charges, gases, liquids, or other materials or quantities. *Flow*, traffic, transportation-related concepts: The passage of people or vehicles along routes of transportation.

See also CIRCULATION—see also ENERGY—see also ERO-SION—see also EXERGY : Low-Exergy Communities—see also FLUX—see also HYDROLOGY—see also PROCESS—see also REPRESENTATION—see also TRANSPORTATION—see also WATER.

FLUX

1: A continuous moving on or passing by. 2: A continued flow, flood. 3: (a) *Influx*; (b) change, fluctuation <in a state of *flux*>. 4: A substance used to promote fusion, especially one applied to surfaces to be joined by soldering, brazing, or welding to clean and free them from oxide and promote their union. 5: The rate of transfer of fluid, particles, or energy across a given surface.

Flux City: Fourth Semester Core Landscape Architecture Studio. STU 1212. Department of Landscape Architecture. Core Studio. Spring 2015. Instructors: Silvia Benedito, Bradley Earl Cantrell, Sergio Lopez-Pineiro, David Mah (coordinator), and Chris Reed (coordinator). Consultants: Jason Bobowski, Timothy John Dekker, Kevin Hively, Alexander Lehnerer, and Jason Schrieber. Teaching Assistants: Christina Leigh Geros (MLA I AP & MAUD), Yinjia Gong (MLA I AP), Courtney Goode (MLA I), Siwei Gou (MLA I AP), and Peichen Hao (MLA I).

This studio focused on the development of urban form as driven by ecology and environmental dynamics, introducing students to methods and representational techniques for describing urban form and the underlying ecologies that might be invoked to shape the urban fabric. Representational strategies began with mapping and diagramming larger ecological processes and dynamics on an urban brownfield site, and then focused on the description of built form, urban infrastructure, and the relationships between the city and its reconstituted riverine setting.

Students: Weaam Hussain Alabdullah (MLA I AP), Rawan Aaah Alsaffar (MLA I AP & MDes, ULE), Maria Isabel Arroyo (MLA I), Rachel Nara Bedet (MLA I), Larissa Lea Kristina Belcic (MLA I), Christianna Bennett (MLA I AP), Elise N. Bluell (MLA I AP), Lee Ann Sheridan Bobrowski (MLA I), Sarah Marcela Bolivar (MLA I), Jessica Booth (MLA I), Andrew Gregory Boyd (MLA I), Sarah Morgan Canepa (MLA I), Alexander Louis Cassini (MLA I), Azzurra Shani Cox (MLA I), Devin Dobrowolski (MLA I), Alberto Embriz de Salvatierra (MLA I AP & MDes, ULE), Leif Tobias Estrada (MLA I AP & MDes, ULE), Enrico Evangelisti (MLA I), Yufan Gao (MLA I), Matthew Joseph Gindlesperger (MLA I AP), Jia Joy Hu (MLA I AP), Clementine InHye Jang (MLA I), Mark Turibius Jongman-Sereno (MLA I AP), Brett Keese (MLA I AP & MArch I), Gyeong Wanee Kim (MLA I AP), Lyu Kim (MLA I AP), Yong Uk Kim (MLA I), Bradley Kraushaar (MLA I), Liza Langer (MLA I AP), Ruichao Li (MLA I AP), Xinhui Li (MLA I), Yuanjie Li (MLA I), Ambrose Ka Yiu Luk (MLA I), Mailys Meyer (MLA I AP), Alica Meza (MLA I), Mary Catherine Miller (MLA I AP), Timothy Nawrocki (MLA I AP), Althea Jane Northcross (MLA I), Ivy Pan (MLA

I), Linh Kim Pham (MLA I AP), Christopher James Reznich (MLA I AP), Rachel Louise Schneider (MLA I), Max Elliot Sell (MLA I), Michelle Shofet (MLA I), Vipavee Sirivatanaaksorn (MLA I), Elaine Tyler Stokes (MLA I AP), Chella Jade Strong (MLA I), Carly Alexandra Troncale (MLA I), Foad Vahidi (MLA I), Gege Wang (MLA I), Hui Wang (MLA I), Daniel Widis (MLA I), Zehao Xie (MLA I), Han Xu (MLA I). ▧

Figures. Models (previous page, top to bottom, left to right). 1 Model (first row)—Xinhui Li (MLA I) & Gege Wang (MLA I). 12 Models—Alberto Embriz de Salvatierra (MLA I AP) & Christopher James Reznich (MLA I AP). 1 Model (second row)—Jia Joy Hu (MLA I AP) & Linh Kim Pham (MLA I AP). 1 Model (second row)—Han Xu (MLA I) & Hui Wang (MLA I). 3 Models—Mark Turibius Jongman-Sereno (MLA I AP) & Timothy Nawrocki (MLA I AP). 1 Model (third row)—Yong Uk Kim (MLA I) & Vipavee Sirivatanaaksorn (MLA I). 1 Model (third row)—Alexander Louis Cassini (MLA I) & Ambrose Ka Yiu Luk (MLA I). 1 Model—Mark Turibius Jongman-Sereno (MLA I AP) & Timothy Nawrocki (MLA I AP). 3 Models—Han Xu (MLA I) & Hui Wang (MLA I). 1 Model—Weaam H. H. Kh II. Alabdullah (MLA I AP) & Mailys Meyer (MLA I AP). 1 Model (fourth row)—Mark Turibius Jongman-Sereno (MLA I AP) & Timothy Nawrocki (MLA I AP). 1 Model—Alexander Louis Cassini (MLA I) & Ambrose Ka Yiu Luk (MLA I). 1 Model (fourth row)—Jia Joy Hu (MLA I AP) & Linh Kim Pham (MLA I AP). Model (opposite page) & Axonometric Drawing (above). Alberto Embriz de Salvatierra (MLA I AP) & Christopher James Reznich (MLA I AP). Sectional Perspective (next page). Xinhui Li (MLA I) & Gege Wang (MLA I).

See also BROWNFIELD—see also COLOR—see also ECOSYS-TEM—see also ENVIRONMENT—see also FABRICATION—see also INDETERMINACY—see also MAPPING—see also NEIGH-BORHOOD—see also PALIMPSEST—see also REPRESENTA-TION—see also SYSTEM—see also TRANSFORMATION—see also URBANISM.

FOLLY

Architectural *folly*, single built works by design:
Structures characterized by a certain excess in terms
of eccentricity, cost, or conspicuous inutility; often found
in gardens or parks.

Torqueing Spheres. Installation. Socrates Sculpture
Park. May 17–August 30, 2015. Mariana Ibañez & Simon
Kim (IK Studio).
   "Torqueing Spheres" combines a simple concept—a
straight line—with complex spherical pods, which become
deep, self-supporting chambers to create experiences for
both the collective and the individual. To construct the
voluminous curves of "Torqueing Spheres," IK Studio
implemented a material technique that uses a cost-
effective method of bending plywood while maintaining
a system of control and delivery. By blending *folly*
formalism with innovative material techniques, IK Studio
played off traditional architectural geometries to create
new construction spaces that allow for exploration.

FOOD

Food, materials by function: Any material that can be
digested or absorbed by the body of a human or other
animal and used as a source of energy or some essential
nutrient, to build and replace tissue, or to relieve hunger.

**Surviving, Sustaining, and Shaping Urbanization:
Manual of Informal Food Provision in Shanghai.**
Thesis. Haodi Grace Xu (MAUD), advised by Carles
Muro, Diane Davis, and Rahul Mehrotra.
   "A growing body of literature highlights the importance
of the informal economy in sustaining the formal city
and alludes to the disruptive effects of top-down spatial
redevelopments that further marginalize the urban poor
and their livelihood. Using *food* as a lens, this thesis
builds on this research by examining the role of traditional economies and microenterprises in surviving,

shaping, and sustaining the rapid urbanization of
Shanghai. The goal of this action-based research is to
examine informal tactics of space production in reimagining a hybrid urban typology and to stimulate interactions across the making and building of the city." §

FOREST

Forest, plant communities: Plant communities that are
dominated by trees and other woody vegetation. A typical
forest is composed of the over-story and the under-story;
the under-story may be subdivided into the lower tree
layer, shrub layer, herb layer, moss layer, and soil mi-
crobes. Today *forests* occupy approximately one-third of
the Earth's land area. For *forests* in the sense of cultural landscape rather than as a plant community, use
"*forests* (cultural landscapes)." Urban *forest*: *Forests*
comprised of the aggregate of all trees and associated
vegetation found in and around a given urban area,
including both individual street and park trees, and
groupings of trees, whether on public lands such as
greenways, or on private property.

*See also AFFORESTATION: Colony & Homeland—see also
CANOPY—see also PLANT—see also VEGETATION—see also
WILDING.*

FORM

Form, composition concepts: Use with reference to works
of art and architecture to mean the arrangement of
visual elements such as line, mass, shape, or color. *Form*
of expression, artistic concept: General term for artistic
approaches, practices, or doctrines.

*See also APERTURE: The Aperture Analyzed—see also COMPOSI-
TION—see also CONCEPT—see also CONFLICT: Ad Absurdum—
see also EDGE: The Barracks of Pion—see also ENERGY: Forms
of Energy—see also LANDFORM: Landformation Catalogue—see*

also MATERIAL—*see also* OBJECT: *Object Studio*—*see also* REPRESENTATION—*see also* TERRITORY: *Territorialism*—*see also* TRANSITION: *The Forms of Transition*—*see also* TYPE: *Blob Block Slab Mat Slat*—*see also* URBAN.

FORUM

1: (a) The marketplace or public place of an ancient Roman city forming the center of judicial and public business; (b) a public meeting place for open discussion; (c) a medium of open discussion or expression of ideas. 2: A judicial body or assembly. 3: (a) A public meeting or lecture involving audience discussion; (b) a program involving discussion of a problem usually by several authorities.

Forum, open spaces: In ancient Roman settlements, open spaces used as marketplaces or general public meeting places and places for judicial and public business. For similar spaces in ancient Greek settlements, use "agoras." *Forum*, Italian Medieval styles: Refers to a distinctive style of early Medieval glazed pottery produced in the Roman Campagna.

Harvard East Asia Urban Forum. Student Group. The Harvard East Asia Urban *Forum* is an academic group that provides a platform to discuss urban planning, design, development, and related urbanization issues in East Asian cities. It brings together advanced researchers, professors, practitioners, and politicians and provokes innovative ideas that may contribute to better cities and human settlement. It also links students, professors, professionals, and enterprises and creates a close collaboration between academia and practice. ⊛

Student Forum. Student Group. Student *Forum* is comprised of students elected annually from each degree program. Student *Forum* works to improve student life at the Harvard GSD and serves as a liaison between the student body and the school administration. Members of *Forum* participate in the meetings of the Student Affairs Committee and meet weekly with Student Services to foster a continuous dialogue between students and the administration.

Student *Forum* meets regularly with the Dean, the Visiting Committee, and the Alumni Council to communicate students' issues. Members of Student *Forum* represent the Harvard GSD on the university-wide Graduate Student Council and other ad-hoc administrative and student committees. Officers are elected by the Harvard GSD student body each December. They serve one-year terms starting in the beginning of the spring semester and continuing until the end of the fall semester.

Student Forum Members (2014–2015): President Stephen Sun (MArch II), Vice President Lauren Gail McClellan (MArch I), Academic Chair Aaron David Charles Hill (MLA I), Treasurer Gerrod M. Kendall (MArch I), Student Group Relations Ramzi Naja (MArch II), Executive Events Chair Shani Adia Carter (MUP), Social Cochairs Qi Xuan Li (MLA I) Nadia Perlepe (MArch II) & Bryan Yang (MArch I), External Relations Coofficers Jeronimo Van Schendel Erice (MArch II) & Aman Singhvi (MDes, EE), Alumni Relations Courtney Dominique Sharpe (MUP) & Yi Li (MArch I AP), Infrastructure Cochairs Michael Ryan Charters (MArch II) & Christopher Michael Meyer (MArch II). ⊛

FRAGMENT

Fragment, object portions: Portions of objects that are torn, broken off from, or dislocated from their original whole.

Ilium. Thesis. Gabriel Buxton Tomasulo (MArch I), advised by Iñaki Ábalos.
"There were huge factories in Schenectady, New York, and nothing else. The city defined itself through the products made in its workshops, pulled by its locomotives, preserved or catalyzed by its chemicals. The Electric City. The City that Lights and Hauls the World. Now the factories have gone. We can clearly see the marks they left: how the city was carved into units with single functions, how nobody ever lived downtown, how workers pushed farther and farther out into the suburbs. Neither the outskirts nor the center ever had the clarity of form or diversity of function necessary to inoculate them against the retreat of industry, a predatory financial sector, or the social isolation that comes with sprawl.
All that Schenectady has left are its history and the resources that made it possible: a river, well-connected regional infrastructure, and a lot of pieces. These pieces—building *fragments*, machines, containers—are the raw material from which this project is made. Spread out across the city, they carry with them a certain scale, rigidity, and territorial authority—vestiges of the ambitious and expansive logic of mass production. The architectural power that once fractured the city is now asked to claim space for public program—affordable housing, gathering spaces, and circulation. *Fragments* are arranged, divided, and assembled according to need; they make buildings, parts of buildings, pavilions, and infrastructures." ⊛

See also ART—*see also* ASSEMBLY—*see also* BUILDING—*see also* COLLAGE—*see also* CONNECTION—*see also* CONSTRUCTION—*see also* MATERIAL—*see also* OBJECT—*see also* PAVILION—*see also* STRUCTURE.

FRAME

A-*frame*, houses by form, massing or shape: Houses with steep gable roofs that extend to ground level on two sides. Door *frames* & door *frame* components: Assemblies built into a wall, consisting of two upright members (door jambs) and a horizontal member (door head), and providing support on which to hang the door. *Frame* construction: Type of construction in which walls, partitions, floors, and roof are wholly or partly made of wood. *Frames*, motion picture components: The successive individual images that comprise a motion picture, or the spaces such images occupy on a length of film, each separated by a horizontal bar. Space *frames*, trusses by construction: Trusses in which members are arranged three-dimensionally rather than in one plane. Steel *frame* construction, construction by form: Refers to a building technique used primarily in bridges and buildings, in which a skeleton *frame* of vertical steel columns and horizontal I-beams are constructed in a rectangular grid. The grid is used to support floors, roof, and walls. The development of this technique made the construction of the skyscraper possible. Structural *frames*, structural systems & elements: All the members of buildings or structures required to transmit loads to the ground.

FRAMEWORK

1: (a) A basic conceptional structure <the *framework* of the United States Constitution>; (b) a skeletal, open-work, or structural *frame*. 2: *Frame* of reference. 3: The larger branches of a tree that determine its shape.

See also CONTEMPORARY: Frameworks of Contemporary Practice.

FRINGE

Fringe, trimming, material: Trimming consisting of long or short lengths of straight or twisted thread, cord, or tassel, often grouped or knotted in various designs. Urban *fringes*, urban areas, districts by location or context: Settlement areas lying at the periphery of cities or suburbs where urban land uses meet rural land uses.

Homeownership on the Fringes: Understanding Tenure Security as a Tool of Slum Clearance in Modern Manila. Joint Center for Housing Studies Lecture. Gund Hall, Portico 123. February 17, 2015. Nancy Kwak.

With roughly four million residents living in informal settlements in Metro Manila, the Philippine government has reasons to experiment with large-scale clearance. The politics of eviction and forcible removal require a justification beyond the greater good, however. This talk explored how homeownership has become a critical tool in the government's relocation and resettlement programs for thousands of informal dwellers in the city. ⊛

See also BOUNDARY—see also CONTEXT—see also DWELL-ING—see also EDGE—see also FABRIC—see also SETTLEMENT.

FRONT

Fronts, architectural: The external areas of buildings, including the facade and other features, but not necessarily restricted to surface features. Often used with cardinal direction references, such as "west *front*" or "north *front*." For the vertical arrangements of exterior or interior features, use "elevations (building divisions)." *Front*, positional attribute: Attribute used to describe something situated at or near the forward or most important part of something. For the sense of facing the viewer, as a figure in a picture, use *"frontal." Front* view, view by vantage point or orientation: Refers to depictions with a point of view from in *front* of the subject, as contrasted to depictions taken from the side or back. Riverfronts, waterfronts: Spaces, land, or part of a city or town on the edge of a river. Storefronts, facades: Facades of store buildings *fronting* a street and usually containing window display spaces.

FUNCTION

1: Professional or official position, occupation. 2: The action for which a person or thing is specially fitted or used, purpose. 3: Any group of related actions contributing to a larger action. 4: An official or formal ceremony or social gathering. 5: (a) A mathematical correspon-

dence that assigns exactly one element of one set to each element of the same or another set; (b) a variable that depends on and varies with another <height is a *function* of age>. 6: Characteristic behavior of a chemical compound due to a particular reactive unit, also a functional group. 7: A computer subroutine, specifically one that performs a calculation with variables provided by a program and supplies the program with a single result.

FUNCTIONALISM

Functionalism, forms of expression, artistic concept: Doctrine or practice that emphasizes practical utility or *functional* relations in the design and construction of structures, objects, and systems. Use also when referring to the contemporary design philosophy, relating chiefly to architecture and furnishings.

FUNDAMENTAL

1: (a) Serving as an original or generating source, primary <a discovery *fundamental* to modern computers>; (b) serving as a basis supporting existence or determining essential structure or function, basic. 2: (a) Of or relating to essential structure, function, or facts, radical *<fundamental* change>, also of or dealing with general principles rather than practical application *<fundamental* science>; (b) adhering to *fundamentalism*. 3: Of, relating to, or produced by the lowest component of a complex vibration. 4: Of central importance, principal *<fundamental* purpose>. 5: Belonging to one's innate or ingrained characteristics, deep-rooted <her *fundamental* good humor>.

Fundamentals: 14th International Architecture Exhibition. Publication. Marsilio, 2014. Rem Koolhaas (editor). NA687 .I57 2014.

The official Venice Biennale catalogue was a global overview of architecture from the last 100 years, and the exhibition emphasized this architectural history. Each country was asked to narrate its history in relation to the idea of modernity, and answering the question: Has national identity been sacrificed at the altar of modernity?

See also ELEMENT: Architecture at the Human Scale—see also EXHIBITION—see also PUBLICATION—see also SCALE.

FUTURE

1: That is to be, specifically existing after death. 2: Of, relating to, or constituting a verb tense expressive of time yet to come. 3: Existing or occurring at a later time <met his *future* wife>.

Future cities, settlements by planning concept: Use especially with reference to the urban designs of the *Futurists* of the early 20th century; may also be used in general for projected forms or lifestyles of settlements in the *future.*

See also CARBONURBANISM—see also RESILIENCE: Creating Resilient Cities—see also MANAGEMENT: A Sustainable Future for Exuma—see also URBANISM: Ecological Urbanism.

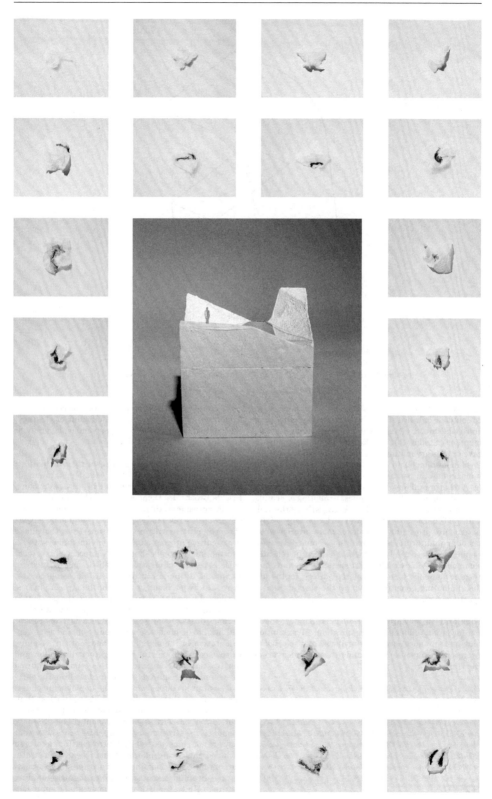

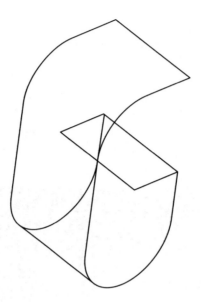

GALLERY

1: (a) A roofed promenade, colonnade; (b) corridor. 2: (a) An outdoor balcony; (b) a platform at the quarters or stern of a ship. 3: (a) A long and narrow passage, apartment, or corridor; (b) a subterranean passageway in a cave or military mining system, also a working drift or level in mining; (c) an underground passage made by a mole or ant or a passage made in wood by an insect. 4: (a) A room or building devoted to the exhibition of works of art; (b) an institution or business exhibiting or dealing in works of art; (c) collection, aggregation <the rich *gallery* of characters in this novel —H. S. Canby>. 5: (a) A structure projecting from one or more interior walls (as of an auditorium or church) to accommodate additional people, especially the highest balcony in a theater commonly having the cheapest seats; (b) the part of a theater audience seated in the top *gallery*; (c) the undiscriminating general public; (d) the spectators at a sporting event.

Kirkland Gallery. Kirkland *Gallery* is an independent, not-for-profit, student-run organization. All exhibition and event proposals are peer-reviewed and selected to represent the diverse design and research endeavors of the Harvard GSD. ▩

Figure. Photographs & Models (previous page). Ken Chongsuwat (MLA I).

See also ART—see also BALCONY—see also COLLECTION—see also EXHIBITION—see also GLOBAL WARMING: Nescient Hues/Meltwater—see also HISTORY: Temporary Accumulations—see also HORIZONSCOPE—see also INSTALLATION—see also LANDSCAPE: Vast Minute Landscapes—see also MEASURE: Seven Studies—see also MEMORY—see also PLATFORM—see also PROJECT: Inevitable Errors.

GAME

Game, public & interactive activities: Forms of competitive play, usually involving an element of strategy, especially to interfere with an opponent's play; may or may not require physical skill.

Immersive Landscapes: Representation through Gaming Technology. VIS 2449. Department of Landscape Architecture. Seminar. Fall 2014. Instructors: Eric de Broche des Combes & Chad Oppenheim.

The course investigated new ways to interpret, conceive, and describe landscape. While traditional methods of representation will prevail for some time, they make the cognitive process a one-way circumstance with an emitter and a listener that barely interact. *Game* technologies permit the creation of realistic, oneiric, utopian, as well as dystopian universes. It is possible to use, disregard, twist, bend, or reinvent the laws of physics, the flow of time, the hazards of weather, the perception of depth, but most importantly, it permits absolute freedom. Just as Rome was not built in a day, connections will need to be made through studies of landscape representation in the arts, movies and, not surprisingly, video *games*. Through the investigation, conception, and construction of virtual altered states, students acquired the techniques required to develop ideas from the early stages of preparatory work to the deployment phase, bearing in mind that technical skills matter less than the search for smart and imaginative solutions. *Game* fabrication was envisaged as a mental layout where elements are structured and organized in a way that they are not perceived as being intrusive. Topics covered included: mastering, planning, and researching strategies of representation; finding of a graphic style; creating meshes and textures for *game* engines; building nature in Unity, realistic versus nonrealistic approaches; sound designing, navigation and interaction; documenting, writing, and targeting different platforms; and having fun—while it is not exactly technical, it is a fundamental notion that should not be lost, especially when speaking of *games*. ֍

Interactive Games for Risk Communication. Lecture. Gund Hall, Piper Auditorium. October 14, 2014. Pablo Suarez.

Pablo Suarez conducted a workshop on "Interactive *Games* for Risk Communication" where students, professors, and practitioners learned new methods to integrate risk information, better understand the implications of implementing policies and plans through systems-oriented scenarios, and engaged in thought-provoking discussions that critically considered past and future solutions. ֍

Video Game GSD. Student Group. Video *Game* GSD is a student group dedicated to bringing the secret and public *gamers* of the Harvard GSD together. The group hosts tournaments, invites local developers to beta-test, and hosts "*game* jams" where students design their own *games*. The group investigates and develops discourse on the impact of immersive technology on architectural design and the profession. ֍

See also INTERACTION—see also TABLE: GSD Table Tennis—see also WELL-BEING—see also WORK: Work Environments I.

GARDEN

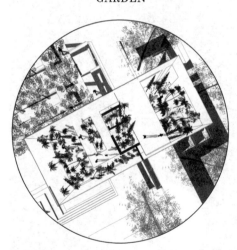

Botanical *garden*, *gardens* by function, open spaces: Primarily outdoor areas where a variety of plants are grown and displayed for scientific, educational, or artistic purposes. Community *garden*, *gardens* by ownership, open spaces: Areas of green space within communities or neighborhoods available for cultivation, usually by residents, and managed by local committees. Formal *garden*, *gardens* by form, open spaces: *Gardens* whose plantings, walks, pools, fountains, and other features follow a definite, recognizable plan, frequently symmetrical, emphasizing geometrical forms. Hanging *garden*, *gardens* by form, open spaces: *Gardens* or plantings that are on a steep slope, on a stepped pyramid or ziggurat, on the top of a wall, on a roof, or otherwise situated so

as to hang over the ground below or to appear to float. The most famous example was the hanging *gardens* of Babylon, one of the seven wonders of the ancient world. Healing *garden*, *gardens* by function, open spaces: *Gardens* designed to improve or maintain the physical and mental health of the ill or injured, including *gardens* serving as clinical tools in horticultural therapy. For *gardens* designed for use by the handicapped or the elderly, use "enabling *gardens*." Landscape *garden*, *gardens* by form, open spaces: Grounds laid out so as to produce the effect of natural scenery. *Garden*, open spaces: Area of ground or open space where flowers, shrubs, trees, vegetables, or fruits are grown and cultivated. Pleasure *garden*, *gardens* by function, open spaces: *Gardens*, whether public or private, intended for enjoyment and amusement. Public *garden*, *gardens* by ownership, open spaces: Planned spaces that are open to the public, usually located outdoors, and focused on plants and other natural or landscaped features. Roof *garden*, *gardens* by location or context, open spaces: *Gardens*, situated on rooftops, typically in urban areas above private houses or commercial buildings. The depth of soil is limited to keep the weight low and the plants are usually set in tubs or similar containers, but elaborate roof *gardens* have been constructed with small pools and beds.

Figure. Diagram (left). B. Cannon Ivers (MLA II).

Boston Public Garden. The Boston Public *Garden* is the oldest public botanical *garden* in the United States, established in 1837.

A Natural History of English Gardening: 1650–1800. Publication. Yale University Press, 2015. Mark Laird (author). SB457.6 .L35 2015.

Inspired by the pioneering naturalist Gilbert White, who viewed natural history as the common study of cultural and natural communities, Mark Laird unearths forgotten historical data to reveal the complex visual cultures of early modern *gardening*. Ranging from climate studies to the study of a butterfly's life cycle, this original and fascinating book examines the scientific quest for order in nature as an offshoot of ordering the *garden* and field. Laird follows a broad series of chronological events—from the Little Ice Age winter of 1683 to the drought summer of the volcanic 1783—to probe the nature of *gardening* and husbandry, the role of amateurs in scientific disciplines, and the contribution of women as *gardener*-naturalists. Illustrated by a stunning wealth of visual and literary materials—paintings, engravings, poetry, essays, and letters, as well as prosaic household accounts and nursery bills—Laird fundamentally transforms our understanding of the English landscape *garden* as a powerful cultural expression.

Studies in the History of Gardens & Design Landscapes 34, No. 3. Publication. Taylor & Francis, 2014. Edward Eigen & Charles A. Waldheim (editors). SB451 .J76

Third Natures: London Pleasure Gardens. STU 1321. Department of Architecture. Option Studio. Instructors: Cristina Diaz Moreno & Efren Garcia Grinda. Teaching Assistant: Carly J. Gertler (MArch I AP & MLA I AP).

The notion of the building as a "Third Nature" explored the possibility of artificially modifying our environments to form complex assemblies or ecologies in which living and inert materials, different social groups, and technological objects are brought together in a state of constant

interaction. Integrating strange subcultures, classical temples, natural ecologies, rituals, parties, and contemporary culture into architectural proposals, the studio redefined creativity, while exploring alternative forms. Conceived as distinct enclaves dedicated to pleasure along the banks of the Thames, the pleasure *gardens* were in-walled worlds of small wonders where social classes and hierarchies were put under discussion and flattened. Shifting programs and types from the private realm to the public, they became fertile grounds for extravagance, alternative activities, and social constructs. During their 200-year existence beginning in the 17th century, they redefined leisure and pleasure by putting together and reinventing menageries, rotundas, music halls, supper-boxes, kitchen *gardens*, pavilions, lighting and fireworks, public houses, lay temples, fountains, panoramas, immersive world maps, and conservatories to recreate a series of alternative counter-microcosms opposed to the daily routines and miseries of the big city. By revisiting the notion of pleasure *gardens*, the studio developed a set of medium-scale interiorized public buildings. Students tested the relevance of programs, typologies, languages, organizations, and spatial conditions to create a family of rare new species of public artifacts in the form of renewed Pleasure *Gardens*.

Students: Myrna Josephine Ayoub (MArch II), Erin Golden Cuevas (MArch II), Jyri Antti Mikael Eskola (MArch I AP), Carly J. Gertler (MArch I AP & MLA I AP), Patrick Kramer Herron (MArch I), Junyoung Lee (MArch II), Timothy Robert Logan (MArch II), Jana Marie Masset (MArch II), Julia Michalski (MArch II), Stefan Stanojevic (MArch II), Alexander R. Timmer (MArch I), Dimitris Venizelos (MAUD). ֍

Figure. Models (opposite page). Dimitris Venizelos (MAUD).

GASTRONOMY

1: The art or science of good eating. 2: Culinary customs or style.

Gastronomy, connoisseurship: The practice or art of choosing, cooking, and eating good food.

The Architecture of Taste. Publication. Harvard GSD, 2015. Pierre Hermé, with Savinien Caracostea and Sanford Kwinter. TX773.H47 A73 2015.
The Architecture of Taste recaptures the "lecture de pâtisserie" that renowned pastry chef Pierre Hermé delivered at Harvard University. Presenting his work as layered experiments in *gastronomy*—as well as in design and time—Hermé lays the foundations of a new theory of the architecture of taste. The book contains the conversations of this night, providing a rare glimpse into the conceptual and physical creation of Hermé's work. Commentary from architect and culinary consultant Savinien Caracostea and theorist Sanford Kwinter draws out points of engagement between *gastronomy* and architecture—such as the importance of sequence and layering in time and space, illustrated by the vertical cut of Hermé's Plaisir Sucré, a napoleon-like composition of chocolate and hazelnut. "Pastries are buildings just as buildings are pastries," Caracostea notes. The conversation is mapped, bite-by-bite, through precise sensory descriptions, while original "taste diagrams" and recipes tapped directly into Hermé's perspective and creative approach. ֍

GATE

Gates & *gate* components: Swinging or sliding barriers used to fill or close a *gateway* between two exterior spaces, often made of a grating, open framework, or heavy and rough structure. Also, interior barriers resembling these. For barriers of more solid and finished construction, usually leading to interior spaces, use "doors."

GAZE

Gaze, psychoanalytical concept: Psychoanalytical concept and theory surrounding a supposed anxious state that comes with the awareness that one can be viewed: the subject loses a degree of autonomy upon realizing that he or she is a visible object. In the context of art, literature, film, and other arts, a way of regarding people or things so as to embody certain aspects of the relationship between the observer and the observed.

Subverting the Gaze: Redefining the Object Role. Thesis. Tatjana Crossley (MArch II), advised by Jana Cephas and Krzysztof Wodiczko.
"Jerusalem is a city consumed by the *gaze*. Tourism, varying cultures, and political tensions foster an environment in which the *gaze* plays a crucial role in the development of cultural judgment, control, and identity between subjects and objects. The *gaze* inherently produces a subject and an object, and the relationship between the two is in constant flux. By designing an architecture that plays on nuances of visibility, we can allow the *gaze* to manifest at particular moments and deny it at others, forming new experiential relationships between bodies. This thesis begins by seeking to understand the individual through the implications of a *gaze*-subversion helmet and applies these concepts to cultural identity and architecture. The project's intention is to develop a labyrinth that disorients the user by creating a spatial procession through which the user can pass, leaving notions of judgment and preconception behind. The space becomes a spiritual succession from which one reemerges into the real world, where, it is hoped, this newfound awareness is borne. The architectural labyrinth subverts the *gaze* in order to dismember judgment and control, aspects common in our society of surveillance." ֍

GEOGRAPHY

Geography, social sciences, disciplines: Science dealing with the Earth and its life, especially the description of land, sea, air, and the distribution of plant and animal life, including human beings, their activities and territorial organizations.

The Distributed Winter & Other Edible Geographies. Alimentary Design Lecture. Gund Hall, Room 124. November 5, 2014. Nicola Twilley.
Writer and curator Nicola Twilley narrated a journey through the refrigerated warehouses of China, the smellscapes of Sheffield, and other edible *geographies*, describing her ongoing research tracing the way food shapes and is shaped by the built, natural, and cultural environment. ֍

Marrikka Trotter
PhD Candidate, Architecture, Landscape, and Urbanism
Harvard University GSD/GSAS

Project Statement

In the late 18th and early 19th centuries, discoveries in the earth sciences contributed to a new and deeply challenging picture of the planet as an entity with a history of its own-one that dwarfed both human history and that of all life forms. Collectively described by the historian of science Martin Rudwick as the rise of "geohistory," these developments had a profound impact on architecture. My dissertation focuses on this phenomenon in Britain, where the intensive exploration and exploitation of mineral wealth simultaneously contributed to the rapid development and popularization of earth science and furnished capital for major architectural commissions. The central argument is that architecture and geology shared not only the same physical landscape, but also the same inorganic spectrum of materials, the same methodology initially borrowed from antiquarianism, and the same representational conventions established by the orthographic sequence of plans, sections, and elevations. These overlapping concerns and areas of expertise allowed architecture to mitigate the temporal diminishment of human history in the face of geological time by highlighting the connections between cultural endeavors and natural activity. Although scholars in literature and art history have examined the impact of geohistory on their fields, little attention has been paid to the encounters between the geological sciences and architecture. This dissertation documents this connection in a series of chronologically organized case studies.

1. Temporal Sublime: Robert Adam's Castle Style
The first case study analyzes the late "castle-style" projects and landscape watercolors of the 18th-century Scottish architect Robert Adam in light of his exposure to the radical proposal made by the father of modern geology, James Hutton, that the Earth was almost infinitely old. Adam's approach to these projects was one that erased historically specific ornament and allowed architectural massing to emerge as ancient yet abstracted from human history. The proposal here is that Adam's work follows a uniquely Scottish philosophy of the Sublime as an overpowering apprehension of time; as David Hume put it, "a removal in the past, when very great, increases our passions." In Adam's hands, the temporal sublime can be understood as an attempt to mediate between the timescale of the terrain and that of architecture. This case study also establishes the reciprocity between architectural and geological discourse by examining Hutton's reliance on architectural terminology to describe his theory.

2. Historical Drift: Soane and Gandy's Precarious Neoclassicism
The second case study, on John Soane and his collaborator, Joseph Gandy, explores their connected yet distinct approaches to the newly unmoored foundations of history. Soane turned to the geologist and paleontologist Georges Cuvier as a model for formulating a comparative taxonomy of architectural relics while Gandy constructed his own mythography of architecture around the Noachian flood. Both architects explored novel strategies of architectural ornamentation as they attempted to address the new context of an old Earth. Works culminating in Charles Lyell's *Principles of Geology* (1830–1833) revealed even the most ancient aspects of human culture to be chronologically recent compared to the vast duration of the planet. In this scheme of things, architecture became either an exercise in proleptic ruination due to inevitable natural disasters (the example is Soane's Bank of England), or a form to be stripped of its newly inconsequential history (as is the case with Gandy's cottage designs).

3. Stratigraphic Architecture: High Victorian Development
The third case study describes the efforts of High Victorian architects William Butterfield and G. E. Street to create an architectural "stratigraphy" that would document and foster human development as a part of the overall maturation of the Earth. As opposed to Soane and Gandy's fraught engagement with deep time, the High Victorians worked within a more optimistic perspective on the era's geological turn. William Buckland, the Oxford geologist and theologian, and Robert Chambers, author of the influential *Vestiges of Creation* (1844), domesticated geohistory by describing the nonhuman past as a teleological prelude to a more perfect human future. Theirs was a directional vision of Earth's history (rather than the cyclical model proposed by Hutton), and it dovetailed with the 19th-century myth of progress. Armed with the notion of development over extended periods of time, the High Victorians eschewed "copyism" in favor of improving precedents from architectural history. In the context of one of the great ecclesiastical building campaigns in British urban history, these architects formulated a popular architectural idiom that responded to the diffusion of geological knowledge in the public domain.

4. Geological Ethics: John Ruskin's "Truth of Essences"
The closing case study examines John Ruskin's attempt to connect the essential workings of geology to architectural production by revealing a preexisting ethics common to both. Ruskin was an amateur geologist of considerable skill, but his scientific efforts must be understood in the context of his larger project to preach that the fundaments of physical nature, accurately observed and correctly interpreted, corresponded to principles of social integrity. Such principles were never merely

Geographies of Social Conflict & Cohesion. Latin GSD Lecture. Gund Hall, Room 510. February 20, 2015. Ricardo Truffello.

This lecture discussed different issues within the same territory by explaining the methodological and interdisciplinary processes for an adequate urban diagnosis through multiple approaches. The explored *geographies* revealed an effective tool for the surveying and targeting of public policy through the generation of multiscale functional indexes, segregation special indexes, spatial statistics and different spatial analysis techniques. The lecture was part of the class, "Territorial Intelligence in Landscapes of Production." ▧

Geography GSD. Student Group. *Geography* GSD is a collective for graduate students at Harvard University who seek to explore the gap between spatial discourse and practice. ▧

New Geographies Lab. The New *Geographies* Lab focuses on urban transformations in the Muslim world, casts them in the larger regional and territorial landscapes, and proposes alternatives for the improvement in design. ▧

Conservation Past and Present. Sylvester Baxter Lecture. Gund Hall, Piper Auditorium. November 17, 2014. David Lowenthal, with George Earl Thomas and Susan Nigra Snyder.

Geographer David Lowenthal is Professor Emeritus of the Department of *Geography* at the University College London, and a prolific writer on nostalgia, heritage, and the spatial outcomes of concepts of the past and future. In several books on the politics of preservation, the meaning and value of landscape, society in the West Indies, and conceptions of nature, he has focused on the landscape and built environment as palimpsests of cultural attitudes to history. Lowenthal taught landscape history and studied urban environmental perception at Harvard GSD between 1966 and 1969. Susan Nigra Snyder and George Thomas, lecturers in architecture, and Natalia Escobar (PhD) hosted the event on behalf of the Critical Conservation program at the Harvard GSD. ▧

See also AGENCY: New Geographies Journal—see also AIR—see also INFORMATION: New Geographies 07—see also LAND—see also MAPPING: Geographic Representation and Speculation—see also METABOLISM: New Geographies 06—see also MORPHOLOGY: Between Geometry & Geography—see also REPRESENTATION—see also SPACE: Terrestrial Analogues—see also WATER.

GEOLOGY

Geology, earth sciences, physical science, disciplines: Science that deals with the physical history of the Earth, the rocks of which it is composed, and the physical changes which it has undergone and is undergoing.

Abstracted Geologies: Content of Containment from an American Concentration Camp. Exhibition. Kirkland Gallery. April 20–May 1, 2015. Megan Jones Shiotani (MLA I).

Topaz, Utah, is the ruin of a Japanese American internment camp at the bottom of a barren, brine-soaked, prehistoric ocean bed. Abandoned since 1944, the sandy terrain is sculpted with cryptobiotic soil crusts, frost-fueled lichens, and microbia that cling to the remnants of internment for shade and moisture. In situ casting, material samples, and photographic catalogs used the surface of the ground to recall a city imprisoned in a remote alkaline desert. ▧

Shifting Foundations: Geology & the Architectural Imagination in Britain (1750–1890). Dissertation. Marrikka Maile Trotter (PhD), advised by Erika Naginski & Antoine Picon.

"The discovery of deep time profoundly challenged architectural thought and practice in the Romantic period. The real extent of Earth's history suddenly eclipsed the importance of Greco-Roman antiquity, and along with it, the cultural authority it had bestowed on architecture. Stone emerged as a formational process rather than an inert architectural material, and the formerly passive landscape became an active and unstable substrate. This dissertation examines how British architects and *geologists* responded to this upheaval, first by attempting to mediate between *geological* time and architectonic scale, then by positioning *geology* as a potential model for social, aesthetic, and national development." ▧

Figure. Text (opposite page). Marrikka Maile Trotter (PhD).

See also GROUND—see also LANDSCAPE—see also MEMORIAL: Abstracted Geologies—see also PROCESS—see also REFUGE: Refugia—see also SOIL.

GEOMETRY

Geometry, mathematics, science: Branch of mathematics dealing with the measurement, relationships, and properties of points, lines, curves, angles, surfaces, and solid figures.

Geometry Lab. Andrew Witt & Cameron Wu. The *Geometry* Lab engages with core questions of architectural *geometry* and computational design—addressing issues of digital fabrication, infrastructural optimization, and the history of *geometry* in design. ▧

See also AUDIOVISUAL: Six Microphones—see also FORM—see also MORPHOLOGY: Between Geometry & Geography.

GEOPOLITICS

Geopolitics, political science, social science, discipline: Study of the geographic aspects of political phenomena, including the geographical bases of the power of nations, and geographic influences on power relationships in international politics.

GEOTHERMAL

Geothermal power, energy resources: Energy supplied by the heat of the Earth's interior.

GESTURE

Gesture drawing, technique: Capturing in a few strokes the major forms of a figure, object, or composition. A method of drawing in which the artist responds to the action, *gesture*, and movement of the subject, not the details of structure. *Gesture*, visual & representational concepts, formal concepts, artistic concepts: Use of motion of limbs or body as means of intentional expression.

Trace of Emotion: Expression of Gesture in Social Media Communication. Thesis. Jili Huang (MDes, Tech), advised by Panagiotis Michalatos.

"In recent years, increasing attention has been given to the emotional aspects of human-computer interaction. There are many studies on emotion recognition and the expression of *gesture*, and yet we still feel ill-equipped in social media communication (e.g., person-to-person communication through machines) and that our emotion has been split and filtered. As Jonathan Safran Foer wrote, 'The problem with accepting—with preferring—diminished substitutes is that over time, we, too, become diminished substitutes.' To emphasize the emotional aspects of media and allow it to better promote human association and affairs, this thesis aims to develop a prototype to capture emotional information (e.g., movement) and integrate its expression (e.g., artistic imagery) into communications. The expression of this information is more about conveying the trace of emotion to other people than about arbitrarily judging or categorizing the emotion itself. With the addition of this emotion-expression layer, our communication can achieve an empathetic dimension that brings people closer together." §

Figure. Animation Still Frame (above). Jili Huang (MDes, Tech).

GLITCH

1: (a) A usually minor malfunction <a *glitch* in a spacecraft's fuel cell>; (b) bug; (c) a minor problem that causes a temporary setback. 2: A false or spurious electronic signal.

Responsive Environments: Glitchy Food. VIS 2314. Department of Architecture. Seminar. Spring 2015. Instructor: Allen Sayegh.

Today, more than ever before, we feel a technological presence as part of our everyday life. The all-pervasive nature of digital information and technological interaction affects all scales—from our bodies to the larger urban contexts we occupy and the infrastructures that support them. This technological presence has a strong impact on our perception of the urban environment, and on the way we embed technology in design. Current models tend toward performance and efficiency-driven urban systems, architectural spaces, and human interactions. A contextual and cultural implementation of new

technologies standardize the evolution of our built environment, leaving no room for imperfections and anomalies. But how can spaces, infrastructures, and places that define the social experience of tangible environments not incorporate elements of inherent spontaneity, creativity, and even error? This course looked at the concept of *glitches* as a strategy to embed serendipity and potential for creativity in design using responsive technologies. A *glitch* is defined as a temporary, transient fault in a system that corrects itself. *Glitches* are cracks, frictions that create openings in a particular system, revealing new meanings of the system itself. By looking at the opportunities that can be found in errors, the class explored design strategies that created the conditions for serendipity to emerge, sparking creativity and fostering innovation. §

GLOBAL

Globalism, philosophical movements & attitudes: The approach to social, cultural, scientific, ecological, or humanistic questions involving an orientation to the world as a single interacting system, and the placing of its interests above individual regions or nations. *Globalization*, sociological concepts: Refers to the *global* integration of economic, political, cultural, and social institutions as motivated by objectives, which include fostering international cooperation and coordination, universalizing regulatory standards, and enabling free flow of capital and free trade.

See also CITY: Identity, Sovereignty, and Global Politics in the Building of Baghdad—see also CULTURE—see also DISPLACEMENT: Global Displacement—see also ECONOMIC—see also EXTREME: Housing and Urbanization in Global Cities—see also LEADERSHIP: Global Leadership in Real Estate & Design—see also POLITICAL—see also POST-DISASTER: Understanding Tension around the Application of Global Standards in Post-Disaster Scenarios—see also TOWARD: Territorial Organization Beyond Agglomeration—see also VISIONARY: Grounded Visionaries.

GLOBAL WARMING

Global warming, climate change, environmental concepts: The gradual increase over time of the average temperature of the entire Earth's lower atmosphere. *Global warming* has occurred in the distant past as the result of natural influences, but the term is most often used to refer to the warming predicted to occur as a result of emissions of greenhouse gases directly and indirectly caused by the burning of fossil fuels. An increase of the Earth's temperature by only a few degrees results in dramatic climate change, loss of habitat and species, sea-level rise, and alteration of the oceans' currents.

Nescient Hues/Meltwater. Exhibition. Kirkland Gallery. October 20–29, 2014. Ken Chongsuwat (MLA I) & Eri Yamagata (MLA I).

Within everyday habits, what we do and what we see becomes invisible. The senses paralyze with repetition as the world around us becomes invisible. "Nescient Hues" was an experiment to identify and catalogue what has been neglected, visualizing that which has been treated as mundane. "Meltwater" explored the relationship between water, glaciers, and melt ponds associated with *global warming*. It raised awareness of the melting and forming of melt ponds within glaciers through a series of paper models. ⊛

See also CLIMATE CHANGE—see also CONFLICT—see also ENVIRONMENT—see also EXHIBITION—see also FLUX—see also SKYSCRAPER: Wood Skyscraper—see also TRANSFORMATION.

GRADIENT

1: (a) The rate of regular or *graded* ascent or descent; (b) a part sloping upward or downward. 2: Change in the value of a quantity with change in a given variable and especially per unit distance in a specified direction. 3: The vector sum of the partial derivatives with respect to the three coordinate variables x, y, and z of a scalar quantity whose value varies from point to point. 4: A *graded* difference in physiological activity along an axis (as of the body or an embryonic field). 5: Change in response with distance from the stimulus.

See also DISTRIBUTE: Material Distributions: Gradients of Compliance—see also ENERGY.

GREEN

Green, color, chromatic colors: Hue name for the color representing that portion of the spectrum that is intermediate between blue and yellow, with wavelengths between 520 and 570 nanometers. The term may refer to any of this group of colors that vary in lightness and saturation. An example of *green* color in nature is that of growing grass. It is a secondary pigment color (made by combining yellow and blue) and one of the three additive primary colors. *Green*, design, environmental concept: Methods of design that are conscious of the ozone-depleting and polluting effects of building materials and processes, that encourage energy and natural resource conservation and recyclability, and are, on the whole, ecologically sound. *Green*, open spaces by location or context: Grassy, public open spaces near the center of a town and used for a variety of community functions, found especially in New England and Mid-Atlantic states.

Harvard Center for Green Buildings & Cities. The Harvard Center for *Green* Buildings & Cities aims to transform the building industry through a commitment to a design-centric strategy that directly links research outcomes to the development of new processes, systems, and products. ⊛

See also CHALLENGE: Launch—see also SUSTAINABILITY—see also TECHNIQUE: Design Techniques.

GRID

Grid, layout features, information form components: Networks of horizontal and vertical lines used to guide the layout of graphic material.

Rethinking Urban Grids in Hangzhou. STU 1505. Department of Urban Planning & Design. Option Studio.

Spring 2015. Instructor: Joan Busquets. Research Fellow: Pablo Pérez-Ramos (DDes). Teaching Assistant: Yujun Yin (MArch II & MLA I AP).

The construction of modern Hangzhou can be seen as a laboratory of urban projects and planning strategies. Its recent development has occurred at unprecedented rates, as in many other cities in Asia. It is important to remember that this is a city with a long history. The historic city originated beside Xi Hú or West Lake and the Yangtze River, and followed the regularity established by an urban *grid* of canals and streets that mark urban blocks, housing the different urban functions within the city wall. Subsequent extensions reinterpreted the original model until the urban explosion of recent decades, when the application of a functional *grid* of big streets and motorways has produced a more anonymous city, the repository of complexes of large blocks of economic or residential activity, defining a generic city with no major defining values. The objective was to interpret the urban evolution of Hangzhou in order to draw conclusions for the hypothetical development of new residential districts in the metropolis. The aim was to explore the development of a creative program and residential and mixed-use sectors. These innovative developments offered a basis for comparison and contrast with hypotheses of systems that combine landscape and public spaces, achieving the harmony needed to consolidate this emerging sector. Work in the studio was part of Revisiting Urban *Grids*, at the Harvard GSD, and invited discussion of the tradition of urban *grids* in Chinese culture, comparing and contrasting them with other international examples to verify the applicability of some updated types of "regular city."

Students: Daniel Feldman (MAUD), David Jimenez (MAUD), Kyriaki Thalia Kasabalis (MAUD), Michael Peter Keller (MAUD & MLA I AP), Jeffrey Mark Knapke (MAUD), Weimao Kong (MLA I AP), Wenling Li (MLA II), Yasamin Omar Mayyas (MAUD), Chi Yoon Min (MAUD), Gaby Rebeca San Roman Bustinza (MAUD), Tin Hung Tsui (MAUD), Ping Wang (MArch I), Ting Yin (MAUD), Yujun Yin (MArch II & MLA I AP). ⊛

Figure. Drawings (next page). Michael Peter Keller (MAUD & MLA I AP) & Wenling Li (MLA II).

See also BLOCK—see also CITY—see also COMPOSITION—see also FORM—see also GEOMETRY—see also PLAN—see also REPRESENTATION—see also URBAN.

GROPIUS

Walter Gropius. "If there's one name associated with the reputation of Harvard GSD as the cradle of American modern architecture, it is that of Walter *Gropius*. His tenure at Harvard—from 1937 to 1952—marked the end of the academic French Beaux-Arts method of educating architects. *Gropius's* philosophy grew out of his leadership of the German Bauhaus: an emphasis on industrial materials and technology, functionality, collaboration among different professions, and a complete rejection of historical precedent." —*Harvard Magazine.*

Harvard GSD Registrar's Online Portal for Information & User Services (GROPIUS). *GROPIUS* is on online resource that provides students and faculty with the tools they need to access course, grade, and degree requirement information. Grade access and entry,

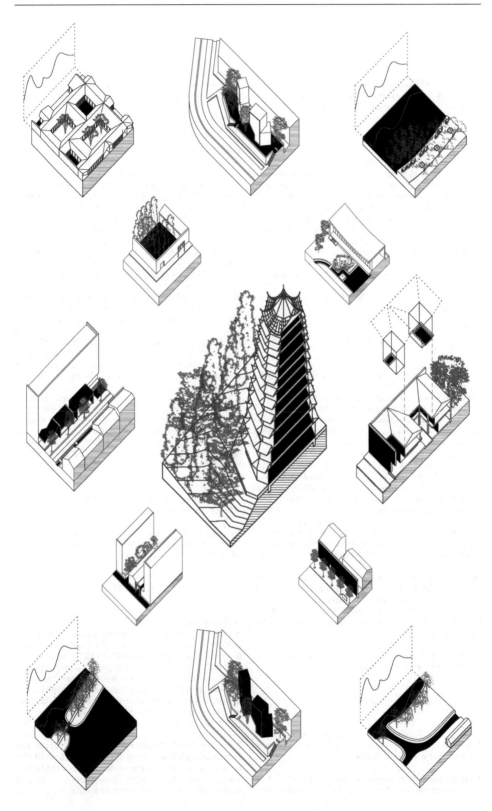

enrollment transactions, course evaluations, and studio option and limited enrollment lotteries are among the transactional functions that are available to students via *GROPIUS*. ⊛

GROTTO

Grotto, cave architecture: Refers to caves that are utilized, generally having been excavated or otherwise altered, for sheltering humans or animals, or for storage, worship, or another use. This term may overlap in meaning with "rock-cut architecture," but cave architecture is not necessarily rock-cut, and rock-cut architecture is not necessarily designed around a cave. *Grotto*, garden structures: Refers to artificially constructed garden features, common since the 16th century in French and English landscapes. A *grotto* is an excavation or structure made to imitate a rocky cave, often adorned with shell-work, colorful stones, etc., and serving as a place of recreation or a cool retreat. For natural features, use "caves" or "caverns."

GROUND

Ground plan, building plans, visual & verbal communication: Floor plans taken near *ground* level and showing the foundation and *ground* floor of the building. *Groundcover*: Plants with prostrate or low spreading growth that cover the surface of the Earth. Generally used in landscaping in place of turf. *Ground*, open space: Delimited portions of land, usually as lawn, plantings, or left natural surrounding and belonging to a house or other building. *Ground*, material, surface preparation material: Substance used to prepare the surface on which or from which an image is made.

Harvard GSD Grounded Visionaries. The Harvard Campaign. "Our school's faculty, students, alumni, and friends think big, imagine alternative futures, and implement their vision within a complex global society. We strive to create a better world, a more humane world, and yes, a more beautiful world. For over 75 years, we have successfully lived up to these values, and we will continue to do so. Unprecedented challenges require design leadership and innovation like never before. The Harvard GSD explores vital, global issues with authority, supplementing our core design pedagogy with research, both in traditional building fields and entrepreneurial ventures. We continually reach beyond the limits of our core disciplines to collaborate across sectors, including business, technology, the arts, health, and public policy. However, our purpose is not to sustain the work that is done at the Harvard GSD—significant and impactful though it is—but to transcend it, moving into new, even unfamiliar, levels of accomplishment. The Harvard GSD needs engagement and support, both for this campaign and as we move forward with our ambitious agenda. With help, we can seize the moment and contribute to the future of our planet in ways we have never before imagined." —Mohsen Mostafavi. ⊛

See also ENCLAVE: Leftover Moments—see also FLOOR—see also LAND—see also LANDFORMATION: Landformation Catalogue—see also MEMORY: Dirty Stories—see also PLAN—see also RADICAL: The Grounds of Radical Nature—see also SOIL—see also SPACE—see also SURFACE—see also VISIONARY.

GROWTH

Growth, biological concepts: The act or process of increasing in size or substance through natural development. Population *growth*, demographics: An increase in the total number of individuals of a given species or other class of organism in a defined area. Smart *growth*: Community development that focuses on minimizing urban sprawl and environmentally damaging development, promoting green-belt protection, pedestrian and rural areas, and restoring vitality to center cities and older communities through adaptive reuse and the use of infill development. Suburban *growth*, urbanization: The increase in population of the suburbs of large cities, spurred on in part by the spread of highways and rail systems.

Las Ciudades del Boom: Economic Growth, Urban Life and Architecture in the Latin American City, 1989–2014. Lecture. Gund Hall, Room 505. November 12, 2014. Latin GSD & the David Rockerfeller Center for Latin American Studies (DRCLAS). Fabrizio Gallanti.

Fabrizio Gallanti presented his research, titled *Las Ciudades del Boom: Economic Growth,* on urban life and architecture in the Latin American city from 1989 to 2014. This talk was part of the Harvard GSD course "Territorial Intelligence: Toward an Evidence Based Design" taught by DRCLAS Visiting Scholar Luis Valenzuela. The presentation explored the differences between causality and correlation, analyzing a series of case studies where the transformation of economy, phenomena of urban *growth,* and novel forms of architectural design constitute new narratives about the Latin American contemporary city. Gated communities in Rosario, office compounds in Panama City, intensive residential densification in Mexico, and new factories around Santiago de Chile are some of the physical traces of complex economic, political, and social processes redefining urban life. ⊛

See also BIOPHILIA: Suspicious Biophilia—see also BODY—see also DEVELOPMENT—see also DWELLING: Poor But Sexy—see also FORM—see also HOUSING: Craft, Politics, and the Production of Housing in Oaxaca, Mexico—see also PHENOME-NON—see also POPULATION—see also POST-SUBURB—see also SKYSCRAPER: Wood Skyscraper—see also SPRAWL—see also SUBURB: The Storm, the Strife, and Everyday Life—see also TERRAIN: Mountain Valley Urbanism—see also TRANSPORTA-TION—see also URBAN—see also URBANIZATION.

GUIDELINE

1: A line by which one is guided, such as a cord or rope to aid a passer over a difficult point or to permit retracing a course. 2: An indication or outline of policy or conduct.

Guideline, instructional materials, document genres by function, visual & verbal communication: Books or other documents containing recommendations and often examples, laying out best practice or advice regarding a certain procedure, activity, or topic. For documents containing more prescriptive instructions, use "rules (instructional materials)."

See also GRID—see also HEALTH: Planning and Design Guidelines and Prototypes for Healthier Places—see also LINE—see also MATERIAL—see also PRACTICE—see also REPRESENTATION.

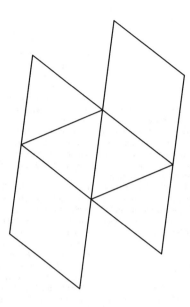

HA-HA

Ha-ha, landscape elements, site elements, built environment: Barriers in the form of trenches or sunken fences; usually used to prevent livestock from crossing.

HABITATION

Habitation, biological concepts, scientific concepts: Ecological or environmental areas that are *inhabited* by particular species of animals or plants and contain the materials and conditions necessary for survival. For the aggregates of influences affecting organisms, use "environments (object groupings)." For areas set apart as protected for plants or animals, use "wildlife refuges."

Habitation in Extreme Environments. Studio Reports. Publication. Harvard GSD, 2015. Spela Videcnik & Rok Oman (studio instructors). NA 2542. C75 H33 2015.

Extreme climates introduce a design challenge for architects. In a context of harsh environments, it is especially important to design buildings that respond to prevailing conditions—not only as a protective measure but as a benefit for future generations. Given dramatic climate shifts, housing design translates into a matter of immediate life safety for existing populations. In response to these demands, remote settlements in the North must be designed and constructed in accordance with ideas of self-sufficiency and backup energy systems. Many vernacular building traditions can serve as a reference for designing environments that are holistically sustainable within the extreme climatic conditions that challenge comfortable human *habitation* in the North.

This situation requires incisive designs that respond to irregular loading from strong winds, heavy snowfall, avalanches, and extreme cold. These phenomena are often sudden and unpredictable. Risk of severe weather increases the vulnerability of human *habitation* to the natural surroundings. The dichotomy between vernacular housing traditions and the latest innovation in building technology suggests an interesting terrain for the design of comfortable living environments. Housing, in particular, must achieve levels of self-sufficiency in such environments to decrease dependency on links to external infrastructure networks that can be severed during periods of harsh weather. At the same time, complications in material provision and inaccessible, remote terrain introduce ideas of prefabrication and economy of construction within these challenging contexts. Designing inhabitable environments must therefore respond effectively to scarcity, inaccessibility, and unpredictability with innovation particular to extreme climates. §

Housing in Extreme Environments. Exhibition. Gund Hall, Experiments Wall. February 2–March 22, 2015. Spela Videcnik & Rok Oman.

The extreme climatic conditions of the North introduce a design paradox for architects. The fragile environmental conditions require incisive designs that respond to irregular loading from strong winds, heavy snowfalls, avalanche risk zones, and extreme cold. These phenomena are often instantaneous, sudden, and unpredictable. Risk of severe weather increases the vulnerability of human *habitation* to the natural surroundings. Housing, in particular, must achieve levels of self-sufficiency in such environments in order to decrease dependency upon external infrastructure networks that can be severed during periods of harsh weather. At the same time, complications in material provision and inaccessible, remote terrain introduce ideas of prefabrication

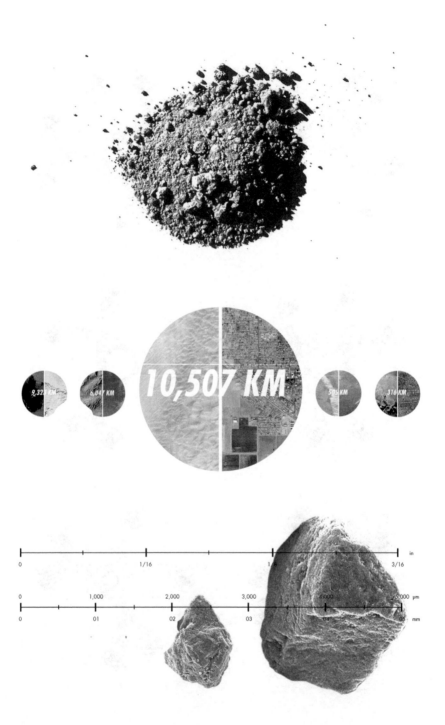

and economy of construction within these very particular contexts. Designing living environments must therefore consolidate solutions to scarcity, inaccessibility, and self-sufficiency with innovation particular to extreme climates. The existing dichotomy between vernacular housing traditions and the latest innovation in building technology establishes an interesting terrain for the design of comfortable living environments in the most harsh weather conditions. §

Figure. Diagrams (previous page). Lauren Gail McClellan (MArch I).

See also CLIMATE—see also DWELLING—see also EXTREME: Housing in Extreme Environments—see also HOUSING—see also IMAGINATION: Architectural Imagination after May '68—see also REFUGE.

HABOOB

1: A violent dust storm or sandstorm especially of Sudan.

Dust Kingdom: Harnessing Moving Material. Thesis. Danika Cooper (MLA I AP & MDes, ULE), advised by Sonja Dümpelmann.

"The wall of dust rolled in from the Sierra Madre Occidental in Northern Mexico, gathering speed as it moved northwest through the Santa Cruz River Valley. It ransacked the arid Sonoran Desert of its loose particles, before swiftly engulfing Pinal and Maricopa counties in a haze of dust and debris. The *haboob*, over 5,000 feet high, and about 100 miles wide, traveled through the territory at nearly 60 miles per hour.

Dust Kingdom elaborates the materiality of dust, from its unstoppable and inevitable omnipresence to its power as an emboldened landscape-scale phenomenon. The project expands the material palette of landscape architecture to include dust, acknowledging its potentials to literally create, contour, and destroy land. Given the material's strong connection to climate and meteorology, dust raises questions of control and ephemerality in landscape architecture. Dust Kingdom uses our inability to precisely predict its movement and behavior as an opportunity to employ sedimentation as design methodology, pushing back upon traditional conceptions of design as anticipated and measured. Dust Kingdom, sited in the Sonoran Desert, finds openings for harnessing the storm's inherent process of moving and depositing large amounts of material across vast territories. Because these storms are responsible for lifting the most nutrient-rich particles from the ground, Dust Kingdom is synchronized with the ecological, environmental, and social rotations of the region to encourage deposition, such that particles are stabilized, harvested, and made productive. The creation of a stabilized dune system not only mitigates but also creates a registration of the phenomenon on the ground to invoke the sublime." §

Figure. Photomontage (opposite page). Danika Cooper (MLA I AP & MDes, ULE).

HARMONY

Harmony, artistic concept, formal concept: In art, refers generally to a pleasing, orderly, and consistent arrangement of the parts of a whole. The concept of aesthetic description in which architectural proportion or artistic design displays congruity.

See also COLLABORATION: The Calumet Collaborations—see also COMPOSITION—see also OEUVRE—see also RHYTHM.

HEALTH

Health & related concepts: State of well-being of an organism or part of one, characterized by normal function and unattended by disease. Public *health*, social issues, sociological concepts: Protection and improvement of community *health* by organized community effort.

Harvard Design Magazine No. 40: Well, Well, Well. Publication. Harvard GSD, 2015. Jennifer Sigler (editor in chief).

Health, and the information around it, is messy. As are our bodies and the systems intended to help sustain them. No anatomical chart, in its immaculate precision, can articulate the ooze of our fluids and secretions, or our sensations of pain and fear; or the strain of accumulating medical bills; or the clash between the cult of wellness and rampant addiction; or the inequality of access to basic hygiene, nutrition, and medical care. Like *health* itself, our power—as individuals, citizens, and designers—to heal or to harm ourselves and the spaces in which we dwell is full of contradictions. "Well, Well, Well" explores some of the tensions and transformations of the landscape of *health* and illness. As both designers and inhabitants, we create this landscape, and in turn, must navigate our own well-being within it. And as the rules of wellness continue to change—along with political events, science and technology, and nature itself—design and planning must adapt and respond accordingly. Architecture's panaceas are not without expiration dates, and might even turn out to do more harm than good—ultimately design has the power to promote and support *health* and healing in preemptive and progressive ways. §

Life-Styled: China-Town. STU 1403. Department of Landscape Architecture. Option Studio. Fall 2014. Instructors: David Mah & Leire Asensio Villoria. Teaching Assistant: Yujun Yin (MArch II & MLA I AP).

Adopting the 1-9-6-6 model (one central city, nine new cities, 60 new towns, and 600 central villages), Shanghai's 1999 "One City, Nine Towns Development Plan" and its 10th five-year plan (2001–2005) contributed to the rapid development of a number of satellite locations in the city's rapidly urbanizing outskirts. Songjiang New City, one of nine towns pegged for conversion into a satellite city for Shanghai, underwent a dramatic transformation in this period. Its role as a means to alleviate pressure on the main Shanghai city center was reflected in its conceptualization, not as a dormitory town but as a city center able to sustain itself both socially and economically. It also reflected an ambition for projected lifestyles that manifested in the transplantation of various development and neighborhood types, borrowed and adapted from numerous global sources, with the sprawling Thames Town (a one square kilometer residential development replicating English towns) being among the most visible examples. Part of this wider ambition, Songjiang University Town was also initiated to operate as the largest education hub in

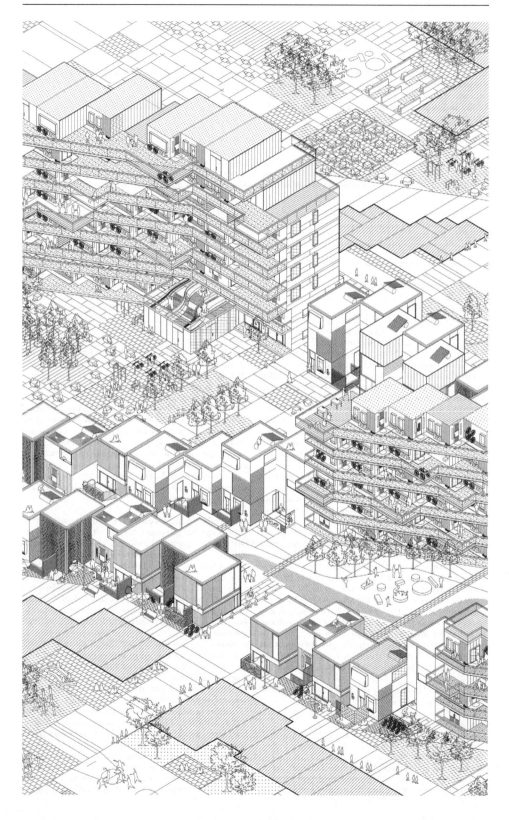

the country, offering Songjiang a clear role within this constellation of new towns and cities.

As part of the *Health* & Places Initiative (HAPI) research group at the Harvard GSD, the studio engaged with Songjiang New City to speculate on the construction of urban environments responding to projected and emerging lifestyles that are anticipated for Songjiang's citizens. The studio became invested in the systematic definition of small-scale urban environments, focusing on the development of neighborhood models restrained to the scale of the typical Songjiang superblock. Through focused study and investment at the neighborhood scale, the studio aimed to provide proposals that offered urban models and prototypes with potential to operate as tools for restructuring the wider urban developmental patterns practiced within a number of Chinese contexts. Students strategized ways in which architecture, landscape architecture, and urban design elements may be designed and arranged to both enable and express various projected and emerging lifestyle concerns.

Students: Whitney Elaine Hansley (MArch I), Ali Ismail Karimi (MArch I), Justin M. Kollar (MArch I AP), Alejandro Lara (MAUD), Yi Li (MArch I AP), Wei Lin (MAUD), Zhe Peng (MArch II), Dima Rachid (MLA II), Won Joon Seol (MLAUD), Rituparna Simlai (MLA I AP), Clayton C. Strange (MAUD), Wen Wen (MArch I), Yujun Yin (MArch II & MLA I AP). ❧

Figures. Drawing (opposite page). Yi Li (MArch I AP) & Clayton C. Strange (MAUD). Models (above). Zhe Peng (MArch II) & Yujun Yin (MArch II & MLA I AP).

Planning & Design Guidelines and Prototypes for Healthier Places. *Health* & Places Initiative Webinar Series. March 11, 2015. Leire Asensio Villoria, Ann Forsyth, David Mah, and Laura Smead.

Members of the *Health* & Places Initiative presented evidence-based guidelines for *healthier* places, introducing conceptual proposals operating at multiple scales: urban and local residential development as well as at the scale of specific buildings and typologies. The guidelines are based on a synthesis of existing research on the multiple dimensions connecting *health* and place, focusing on effective strategies most relevant to urban planners, and the built environment. Topics included accessibility to *health* services, air quality, water quality, opportunities for physical activity, universal design, access to community resources, the connections between green space and mental *health*, *healthy* food access, noise, *health* effects of disasters, and safety. ❧

Planning & Design Health Assessment Tools. *Health* & Places Initiative Webinar Series. March 24, 2015. Ann Forsyth, Emily Salomon, and Laura Smead.

Drawing on the research in other parts of the *Health* & Places Initiative project, including visits to China, this webinar presented new *health* assessment tools and their application to test both existing and planned neighborhoods. The discussion included the research and development of a scoping checklist to assess whether *health* impacts are likely to be large enough to warrant further analysis; and a workshop-based method for interactively assessing *health* impacts, engaging stakeholders in modifying an initial technical assessment to take account of local conditions. This is a variation of what is commonly termed the "rapid assessment"; a comprehensive checklist of key issues to consider and basic indicators of better *health*. ❧

See also BODY—see also HEALTH: Healthy Places—see also HOUSING: Creating Evidence-Based Healthy & Energy-Efficient Housing—see also INITIATIVE: Health & Places Initiative—see also VISIONARY: Grounded Visionaries—see also WELL-BEING.

HEDGE

Hedgerow, landscaped elements, site elements: Lines of closely spaced *hedges* typically interspersed with trees, usually planted on a low earthen wall or base and trained to form a barrier or mark the boundary of an area, particularly in fields or between properties. *Hedge*, landscaped elements, site elements: Plantings of bushes or woody plants in a row as a formal element of a landscape or as a barrier.

HERITAGE

Cultural *heritage*, culture & related concepts: The belief systems, values, philosophical systems, knowledge, behaviors, customs, arts, history, experience, languages, social relationships, institutions, and material goods and creations belonging to a group of people and transmitted from one generation to another. The group of people or society may be bound together by race, age, ethnicity, language, national origin, religion, or other social categories or groupings. Historic building, single built works by function: Buildings that are significant in the history of architecture, that incorporate significant architectural features, or that played significant historic roles in local cultural or social development; may or may not be officially designated. For buildings that are abandoned but not considered necessarily historic, use "abandoned buildings."

Save Beirut Heritage. Lecture. Gund Hall, Portico 124. October 6, 2014. Club MEdiNA. Giorgio Tarraf. ⊕

See also BUILDING—see also CONSERVATION—see also CULTURE—see also HISTORY—see also PRESERVATION.

HIGH-RISE

1: Being multistory and equipped with elevators <*high-rise* apartments>. 2: Of, relating to, or characterized by *high-rise* buildings.

HIKING

Hiking, walking, personal & passive activities: Walking long distances, especially through rural areas, as for pleasure, exercise, or military training.

Wanderwege. Exhibition. Kirkland Gallery. May 4–9, 2015. Eliana Dotan (MArch I).
  "Wanderwege" was an exhibition of photocollages. Together with an accompanying text, the images offered a critical reading of Switzerland's collective consciousness of its landscape. ⊕

See also BODY—see also CIRCULATION—see also MAPPING—see also NATURE—see also ORIENTATION—see also WILDERNESS.

HISTORY

Architectural *history*, arts-related disciplines: Study of the development over time of the human built environment. *History*, visual works: Pictorial or three-dimensional representations in any medium of an event or story, including *historical* and fictional events. *History*, discipline: Discipline that studies the chronological record of events, such as affecting a nation, community, individual, object, or place, based on a critical examination of source materials and usually presenting an explanation of their causes. Urban *history*: The *history* of cities and towns, the urbanization of human life, and all aspects of urban life over time.

Master in Design Studies (MDes) History & Philosophy of Design (HPD). *History* & Philosophy of Design is a platform for scholarly inquiry into design in the disciplines of architecture, urbanism, and landscape architecture and in other aesthetic, spatial, and technological practices. The aim of the program is to advance design knowledge through *historical* research into social, cul-

tural, and political contexts, through theoretical explorations, and through the formulation of critical perspectives. The program provides a thorough preparation for the subsequent pursuit of the PhD degree in the *histories* of design, architecture, urbanism, or landscape architecture, or in the many adjacent fields that incorporate the study of the built environment. The program also provides the intellectual training to pursue careers in criticism, media, or curatorship in established institutional settings or in newly emerging forms. ⊕

Temporary Accumulations. Exhibition. Kirkland Gallery. February 14–28, 2015. Daniel Solomon Koff (MDes, ADPD) & Scott Michael Valentine (MDes, ADPD).
  "Temporary Accumulations" considered the connections between personal and cultural *histories*. It presented performances and an installation to encourage participants to connect to and examine their own understandings of the past. ⊕

See also AIRPORT: Dwelling in Stop-Over City—see also BUILT—see also CONNECTION—see also CULTURE—see also DEVELOPMENT—see also DISCIPLINE—see also FUNDAMENTAL: 14th International Architecture Exhibition—see also GARDEN: Studies in the History of Gardens & Design Landscapes—see also GROWTH—see also MODERN: Women, Modernity, and Landscape Architecture—see also REPRESENTATION—see also TECHNOLOGY—see also THEORY—see also TIME—see also TRANSFORMATION—see also URBANIZATION—see also VISION: Toulouse.

HOLOGRAM

Hologram, positives, photographs by form: Three-dimensional images formed by exposing a negative image with monochromatic radiation from a laser while it is positioned in a second laser beam. The direct beam and the image scattered beam combine to form an interference pattern that is viewed as a three-dimensional image. The technique for making *holograms* was invented in 1947 by Dennis Gabor of Hungary, but was not widely used until after the laser was invented in 1960. Salvador Dalí used *holography* to make works of art.

Fragments of a Hologram House. Thesis. Cory Everett Seeger (MArch I), advised by Jeffry Burchard.
  "The private house is rife with contradiction. The need for privacy, the separation of life and work, the importance of family, and the desire for domesticity are outdated social norms that have driven the development of the traditional private house for the past few centuries. The cultural parameters by which we design our living spaces have drastically changed in recent decades; no other advancement affects the way we live quite like the invention of the digital world. As technology continues to grow and develop, the ability for architects to incorporate digital representation into the physical world will become much more profound.
  Previously, architects could only control experience through physical form and function, but as technology evolves, it yields greater agency to the abstract digital world of representation by giving it scale, context, and experiential properties of the physical through augmented, virtual, and *holographic* overlays. The addition of augmented reality into our everyday lives will not only inherently change the way we use space, but ultimately the way architects design. Architects will have new opportunities to introduce perception—and not just

vision—into the realm of experience, to use representation to produce spatial, organizational, material, and affective impressions, and to make an architecture that is both material and immaterial. Only by questioning the way we live now can we hope to reimagine the way we live in the future." 🙟

See also AUGMENTED REALITY—see also COLOR—see also EXPERIENCE—see also LASER—see also PERCEPTION—see also PHOTOGRAPHY—see also REPRESENTATION—see also TECHNIQUE—see also 3-D.

HORIZON

Horizon line, perspective-related concepts, visual & representational concepts: Use with reference to perspective systems for the line in which the horizontal plane containing the eye meets the picture plane and for the line containing the vanishing points of horizontal planes in the picture.

See also BODY—see also DRAWING—see also HORIZONSCOPE—see also LINE—see also OBSERVATION—see also PERSPECTIVE—see also REPRESENTATION.

HORIZONSCOPE

Horizonscopes. Exhibition. Kirkland Gallery. November 14–21, 2014. Lara Elisabeth Mehling (MLA I).

A line surrounds us, follows us at every point and with every step, draws and redraws the boundary of our sight until it ultimately marks site—the furthest extent of our visual field. But this bounding circle, a skyline, known to us as horizon, is never fixed. Weather and light transform it. Location and time determine view as much as our movement. The shifting horizon is what these optical instruments reveal. Each of the five horizonscopes, named for its operative effect, mechanized one landscape phenomenon for a handheld device that reanimates the landscape through the viewer's participation. 🙟

HORIZONTAL

Horizontal, form & composition concepts: Parallel relationships to a horizontal axis in designs for graphic works, objects, and structures.

HOUSE

House, dwellings, residential structure: Individual dwellings designed to be occupied by a single tenant or family. May also refer to a building for human occupation, for some purpose other than that of an ordinary dwelling; with this usage, "house" is generally prefaced (e.g., "cowhouse," "almshouse").

Une petite maison. Publication. Éditions Girsberger, 1954. Le Corbusier (author). Le Corbusier Research Collection, Frances Loeb Library. LeC NA 7592 Vevey L496.

"This book published by Le Corbusier in 1954 describes the house that was built for his parents on Lake Geneva.

He describes his mother as a musician, and his father as a lover of nature. His plan for them, a total of 60 square meters on a single level, was a minimal 'machine à habiter.' It required a lake and a view of the Alps: narrow and long, it had a single 11 meter long window. Le Corbusier talks about space, but above all, he writes about the act of dwelling—of having shelter." —Inés Zalduendo. 🙟

HOUSING

Affordable housing, housing by development practice: Designates housing for people who are unable to purchase or rent homes through normal marketplace mechanisms; includes such options as low-cost housing, low-income housing, shelters for the homeless, or mobile homes. Cooperative housing, housing by ownership: Housing owned by a legal entity that permits a group of members to mutually own all, or agreed-upon parts, of the complex and to share mutually in the benefits derived by the group under provisions of the entity's rules. Emergency housing, temporary housing, housing by function: Housing provided consequent upon a sudden state of danger or calamity that has made people's regular housing inaccessible or unsafe. Housing development, housing complexes by development practice: Commercially developed real estate tracts commonly consisting of one- to four-unit dwellings. Housing project, housing complexes by development practice: Planned residential developments, generally publicly built and operated, intended for low- and moderate-income tenants. Low-income housing: Housing units available to occupants whose income does not exceed certain maximum income limits set by local housing authorities.

Affordable & Mixed-Income Housing Development, Finance, and Management. SES 5490. Department of Urban Planning & Design. Seminar. Spring 2015. Instructor: Edward Henry Marchant.

The course explored issues relating to the development, financing, and management of housing affordable to low- and moderate-income households, examining community-based development corporations, public housing authorities, housing finance agencies, private developers, and financial intermediaries. Students identified, defined, and analyzed development cost, financing, operating, rental assistance, tax credit, entitlement, and project-generated cross-income subsidy vehicles and assessed alternative debt and equity funding sources for both rental and for-sale, mixed-income housing, and the now common practice of aggregating multiple subsidies into a single financial package. The course reviewed other aspects of the affordable housing development process, including assembling and managing the development team, preparing feasibility studies, controlling sites, gaining community support, securing subsidies, establishing design objectives, coordinating the design and construction process, selecting residents or homeowners, providing supportive services, and managing the completed asset. 🙟

Berlin Study Abroad Seminar: Plattenbau versus the New Communal. Mass Housing, Alternative Dwelling Models, and a Theory of Shared Spaces in Germany. DES 3601. Department of Architecture. Seminar. Spring 2015. Instructor: Niklas Maak.

With equal emphasis on historical and theoretical analysis, this seminar investigated the potential of various forms of historic alternative dwelling, and new ways to

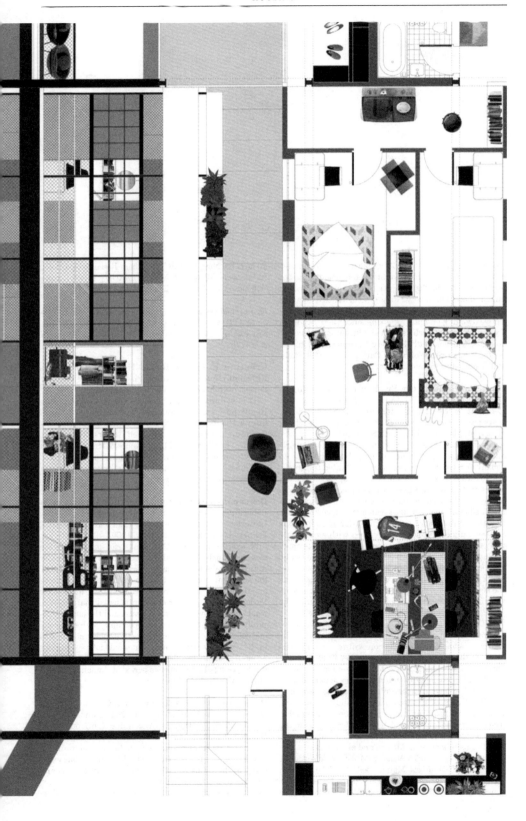

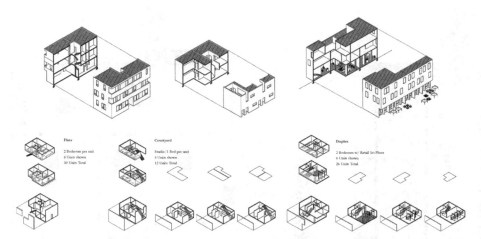

conceptualize mass *housing*. At a time when major crisis—including the urgent need for affordable *housing*, global warming, and the 2008 mortgage crisis—are directly linked to problematic dwelling typologies, this seminar began with an introduction to Germany's history of collective dwelling and mass *housing* since 1900. Students investigated six of Berlin's most significant mass *housing* projects—Gartenstadt Falkenberg, Siedlung Schillerpark, Großsiedlung Britz, Wohnstadt Carl Legien, Weiße Stadt, and Großsiedlung Siemensstadt. §

Craft, Politics, and the Production of Housing in Oaxaca, Mexico. STU 1504. Department of Urban Planning & Design. Option Studio. Spring 2015. Instructors: Diane Davis & Jose Castillo. Teaching Assistant: Margaret Elizabeth Scott (MUP).

For the second year in a row, this studio asked important questions about what can and should be done to densify or retrofit urban areas and evaluated the potential role that new or existent *housing* stock (or related infrastructures) could play in this process. The studio addressed these concerns in the context of Oaxaca, a midsized locale in a southern region of Mexico known for its cultural diversity, a strong tradition of indigenous heritage, a local economy associated with small-scale craft and agricultural production, and a history of opposition to the modernist project of the center. The studio used *housing* as a lens to understand the developmental history of Oaxaca while also conceptualizing *housing* as the key to transforming the built environment, achieving sustainable urbanism, and politically accommodating the social, cultural, and urban priorities of its residents.

In Oaxaca in particular, craft is the operative concept around which questions of *housing* and sociopolitical as well as economic transformation will revolve. Politics refers to the power structures—whether local, state, or national—that impact the territory and set limits on what is politically possible through regulatory actions undertaken in the form of urban planning and governance. "Craft and politics" framed an understanding of *housing* production in Oaxaca and laid a foundation for the studio's focus on urban planning and design interventions in the context of larger regional, national, and global economic trends affecting cities in Mexico and elsewhere.

Students: Clayton Kelley Adkisson (MAUD), Kyle Waldemar Belcher (MAUD), Jesica Marina Bello (MAUD), Duncan James Corrigall (MArch II), Allison Camille Green (MUP), Amanda Huang (MDes, RR & MAUD), Yuxiang Luo

(MArch II), Ning Pei (MUP), William Rosenthal (MAUD), Aliza Sovani (MLA I AP), Man Su (MAUD), Allyssa Petrina Williams (MLA II), Teng Xing (MAUD). §

Figures. Collage (previous spread). Teng Xing (MAUD), Man Su (MAUD), and Yuxiang Luo (MArch II). Diagrams (above). Kyle Waldemar Belcher (MAUD) & Amanda Huang (MDes, RR & MAUD).

Creating Evidence-Based Healthy & Energy-Efficient Housing. Health & Places Initiative Webinar Series. March 17, 2015. Gary Adamkiewicz.

This webinar, given by Harvard School of Public Health professor Gary Adamkiewicz presented findings from a 10-city *housing* study in China in order to understand the key *housing*-based drivers of occupant health. The China, Children, Homes & Health (CCHH) study provided a unique and valuable evidence-base and model for future studies of the linkages between urbanization and health. §

Des canons, des munitions? Merci! Des logis... s.v.p. Publication. Éditions de l'architecture d'aujourd'hui, 1938. Le Corbusier (author). Le Corbusier Research Collection, Frances Loeb Library. LeC NAC 1200 L496.

"Canons? Ammunition? No Thanks! *Housing*, please' is the message of this book, as an alternative proposal to rearmament. Anticipating the reconstruction work to be undertaken after the imminent war, Le Corbusier argues in favor of *housing* and the aims of the Congrès Internationaux d'Architecture Moderne (CIAM). Le Corbusier anticipated that the War would ultimately lead toward peace, and the opportunistically saw the situation as an opportunity for technicians and politicians to engage in a dialogue (that he could direct) in the reconstruction of cities that would follow—war announced ultimate transformation. This bellicose atmosphere would presage Le Corbusier's period of changing political alliances." —Inés Zalduendo. §

Housing & Urbanization in Global Cities. SES 5337. Department of Urban Planning & Design. Seminar. Spring 2015. Instructors: Alexander Von Hoffman & Deidre Schmidt.

This course analyzed *housing* policy and planning in developing urban societies around the world but especially in the Global South. Through presentations and lectures by distinguished guests, texts, and discussions, the course examined the significance of shelter and its production in urban contexts ranging from informal settlements to booming neighborhoods. To understand the effects of different national and cultural environments, students studied the ways private developers, planners, designers, nongovernmental organizations, and government officials work within local systems of land use, law, and finance to produce homes for people. After exploring urban development and residential practices and policies around the world, the class delved into particular *housing* and planning issues for four global cities: Mumbai, Bogota, Johannesburg, and Beijing. ▓

Institutional Strategies for Upholding Affordable Housing Agreements: New York City as a Case Study. Thesis. Owen Deutsch (MUP), advised by Michael Hooper.

"The failure of private *housing* providers to remain compliant with affordability agreements is a threat to the continued provision of affordable *housing*. The potential for affordable *housing* tenants to be overcharged, and the inability of regulators to ensure they are not, is a major but understudied problem. This thesis conducts a case study of rent-stabilized and subsidized *housing* in New York City. I was interested in the accountability and factors contributing to noncompliance and determining the best approaches to these issue. My research method involved interviewing a range of administrators, *housing* providers, legal experts, and other professionals. I found that estimates of the incidence of noncompliance are approximate at best, though monitoring and enforcement activities varied significantly across programs. Interviewees attributed noncompliance to a variety of primary and secondary causes, but some common narratives emerged as to what approaches might be beneficial for all stakeholders, and productive for improving the administration and performance of *housing* programs." ▓

Surplus Housing: Models of Collective Living in South America. ADV 9138. Department of Urban Planning & Design. Seminar. Spring 2015. Instructor: Felipe Correa.

This research seminar examined the legacy of *housing* as an architectural and urbanistic project in post-World War II South America. Since the late 1940s, the provision of *housing* has occupied a paradoxical position in the continent. On the one hand, architects have tested and refined models of *housing* through experimental design projects, inscribing new forms of domestic space and urban life. From the Copan Building in São Paulo and the Juscelino Kubitschek Complex in Belo Horizonte in the 1950s to John Turner and the Previ experiments in Lima of the 1970s to more recent initiatives like Elemental Chile in the early 2000s, *housing* has been front and center to the architect's agenda. On the other hand, this expansive instrumental and methodological diversity in *housing* design has not fully participated within the larger institutional frameworks—primarily government sponsored programs and public-private partnerships—put in place for the delivery of mass *housing*.

Through a series of canonical case studies, paired with the larger government programs that instigated them, this seminar investigated the paradoxes of *housing* in South America. In an effort to bridge these conflicting conditions and construct new models of implementation and replication, the course looked at the affinities and disconnects between experiments in *housing* design and those implemented by government and public-private partnerships. ▓

See also AFFORD—see also AGE: Aging & Place—see also BUILD-ING—see also COLOR—see also COMMUNITY—see also DENSI-TY—see also DEVELOPMENT—see also DISPLACEMENT: Global Displacement—see also DWELLING: Poor But Sexy—see also EXTREME: Housing in Extreme Environments—see also GRID: Rethinking Urban Grids in Hangzhou—see also HOUSING: Craft, Politics, and the Production of Housing in Oaxaca, Mexico—see also INTENSITY: Urban Intensities—see also LAND USE—see also LIFESTYLE: Re-Defining Urban Living—see also NEIGHBOR-HOOD—see also PHOTOGRAPHY: The Neighborhood Ketchup Ad—see also POST-DISASTER—see also REAL ESTATE—see also also TYPOLOGY—see also URBAN—see also URBANIZATION— see also VISIONARY: Grounded Visionaries—see also WELL-BE-ING: The Entwinement of Housing & Well-Being.

HUMAN

Human, Homo sapiens species: Members of the species to which all modern *human* beings belong. Homo sapiens is one of several species grouped into the genus Homo, but it is the only one that is not extinct. The name "Homo sapiens" was applied in 1758 by Carolus Linnaeus, who distinguished *humans* from their close cousins, the apes. The large fossil record now contains numerous extinct species that are much more closely related to *humans* than to today's apes and that were presumably more similar to us behaviorally as well.

Assessing Human Comfort in Urban Public Places in China. Health & Places Initiative Webinar Series. March 4, 2015. Jianxiang Huang & Jack Spengler.

Content research is focused on the modeling and measurement of thermal comfort in public places. The CityComfort+ model can be used to assess factors of building massing, shading, vegetation on radiant heat balance, and the sensation of *human* comfort. Using climate forcing methods, future conditions of public places can be used to evaluate alternative designs. During this webinar, Jack Spengler and Jianxiang Huang reviewed case studies and publications—assessing the relationship between efficient energy use and levels of resident satisfaction in China. ▓

See also AGENCY—see also ANTHROPOCENE—see also BODY— see also ELEMENT: Architecture at Human Scale—see also ERGO-NOMICS—see also PROPORTION—see also THERMODYNAM-ICS—see also VENTILATION—see also WOMAN.

HUMANITARIAN

1: A person promoting human welfare and social reform.

See also ADVOCACY—see also FILM: Assistance Moretelle—see also MATTER—see also POST-DISASTER: Understanding Tension around the Application of Global Standards in Post-Disaster Scenarios.

HYBRID

1: An offspring of two animals or plants of different races, breeds, varieties, species, or genera. 2: A person whose background is a blend of two diverse cultures or traditions. 3: (a) Something heterogeneous in origin or composition, composite <*hybrids* of complementary DNA and RNA

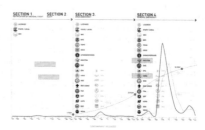

strands>; (b) something that has two different types of components performing essentially the same function.

HYDRAULIC

Hydraulic, physics, physical science: Science that deals with practical applications of water or other liquids in motion, such as the transmission of energy or the effects of flow.

Satec HVL 60 Universal Testing Machine. Gund Hall, Room L33. The *hydraulic* machine tests small specimens in tension or compression, and can apply a force up to 60,000 pounds. It can record both current force as well as peak force. The compression fixtures can be used for almost any material, including concrete. There is also a simple fixture for three-point bending tests. Testing data is sent directly to the computer-based data acquisition system and can be exported to other applications. §

HYDROLOGY

Hydrology, earth science, physical science: Generally, the study of the Earth's water. Specifically, the science that studies the occurrence and movement of water on and over the surface of the Earth. The main processes with which *hydrology* is concerned are precipitation, evaporation and transpiration, stream flow, and ground-

water flow. Applications include flood control and the supply of water for domestic and industrial purposes, irrigation, and hydroelectric power.

HYPEROBJECT

The Proximities of Nuclear Waste: A Reorientation of Proximal Perception. Thesis. Chris Bennett (MDes, ULE), advised by Robert Gerard Pietrusko.

"Timothy Morton defines *hyperobjects* as things that are massively distributed in time and space in ways that baffle humans and make interactions fascinating, disturbing, problematic, and wondrous. *Hyperobjects* operate on time-scales that are profoundly different than what humans are used to. A unique *hyperobject* worth examining is nuclear waste. Considering the fact that the half-life of plutonium-239 registers at 29,000 years, the idea of how to interact with an extreme nuclear waste *hyperobject* requires new methods of understanding. Nuclear waste challenges human notions of time, space, and proximity. A report released in 1957 by the National Academy of Sciences notes that 'the most promising method of disposal of high-level waste at the present time seems to be in salt deposits.' If, instead of viewing nuclear waste as a material to be regulated, we view it as an object-oriented agent operating within its own agency, we gain a new lens through which to view nuclear waste." §

Figure. Artifacts, Diagram, and Sectional Perspective (above). Chris Bennett (MDes, ULE)

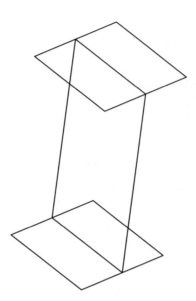

ICON

Icon, devotional images, religious works, visual & verbal communication: In general, images that portray a sacred entity and that are themselves regarded as sacred. In specific meaning, the term is typically used particularly for Christian images produced in the Eastern Rite churches, since the 6th century, according to prescribed formulas of subject (Christ, the Virgin, saints, and the great feasts) and composition, for devotional use in the church or home. Most commonly comprising tempera on panel, but they may be in any two-dimensional or relief medium, including fresco. For a non-Christian image that is sacred or embodies a deity, use "idol" or "cult image." *Icon*, script & type sign: A small picture, pictogram, or symbol on a computer display or in a graphical user interface used to represent a file or function.

Icons of Knowledge: Architecture & Symbolism in National Libraries. Exhibition. Frances Loeb Library. February 2–March 22, 2015. Noam Dvir & Daniel Vladimir Rauchwerger (MDes, RR).

Monumental in scale, dominated by nationalistic ambitions and overwhelming with architectural details, national libraries are amongst the most symbolic *icons* of modern day countries. Despite the rapid digitization of print, nations are vehemently investing resources in the construction of buildings that will project their cultural legacy and house the most precious treasures of their written history.

National libraries are a direct outcome of the establishment of sovereign countries and the emergence of national movements. The contemporary surge of library construction began in the 1990s in countries now independent after the fall of the Soviet Union, and was reinforced by the rise of new economies in the Persian Gulf and East Asia. Similar waves of construction frenzy

propagated through history—first, when national libraries initially appeared in parallel with printing innovation in the 15th and 16th centuries; later in the 19th century, at the same time as the decolonization of South America, the collapse of the French Napoleonic Empire, and the "Spring of the Nations"; and finally, in the turn of the 20th century, when the library came to be a performative symbol of identity in postcolonial contexts. Architecturally, national libraries transformed from glorified corridors lined with manuscripts, to neoclassical palaces, to functional modern edifices, and most recently to objects of exuberant form.

The comparative nature of this exhibition highlighted an exceptional and persistent formal similarity that spans across history and geography. In search of an architectural typology, one found designs that unfold the question of how nations wish to be read. ⊛

Figure. Icons of Knowledge Exhibition Diagrams (previous page). Noam Dvir (MAUD, 2014) & Daniel Vladimir Rauchwerger (MDes, RR).

See also BOOK—see also BUILDING—see also CHURCH—see also COLLECTION—see also CULTURE—see also DATA—see also EXHIBITION—see also GEOGRAPHY—see also HISTORY—see also KNOWLEDGE—see also MODERN—see also MONUMENT—see also REPRESENTATION—see also SCALE.

IDEA

1: (a) A transcendent entity that is a real pattern of which existing things are imperfect representations; (b) a standard of perfection, ideal; (c) a plan for action, design. 2: (a) An image recalled by memory; (b) an indefinite or unformed conception; (c) an entity actually or potentially present to consciousness. 3: A formulated thought or opinion. 4: Whatever is known or supposed about something <a child's *idea* of time>. 5: The central meaning or chief end of a particular action or situation.

See also AESTHETIC: The Ruin Aesthetic—see also OBJECT: Object Studio—see also PLAN: First Semester Core Urban Planning Studio—see also STYLE: The Function of Style—see also TYPOLOGY: The Fourth Typology.

IDENTITY

Identity, metaphysical concepts, philosophical concepts: Those characteristics or conditions of a thing, person, or group that remain the same amid change or that distinguish a thing, person, or group from another.

See also AGENCY—see also BOOK: Books that Built Democracy, Public Patronage, Civic Significance, and Regional Identity in 1980s Valencian Architecture—see also CITY: Identity, Sovereignty, and Global Politics in the Building of Baghdad—see also CONTEMPORARY—see also GAZE: Subverting the Gaze—see also ICON: Icons of Knowledge—see also RADICAL: The Grounds of Radical Nature—see also STUDENT—see also VISION: Toulouse—see also WRITING.

IKEBANA

Ikebana, placing processes & techniques: Japanese art form and spiritual discipline that involves the formal placement and arrangement of flowers, branches, and sometimes other natural objects. Those who practice *ikebana* organize the objects according to strict rules.

Untitled. Lecture. Gund Hall, Room 110. April 6, 2015. Reischauer Institute of Japanese Studies, Frances Loeb Library Materials Collection, and Japan GSD. Hiroki Ohara.

Ikebana is an aesthetic system allowing infinite variation and experimentation. Its fundamental principles of balance, contrast, abstraction, and metaphor foreshadowed the development of 20th-century abstract art by several centuries. Assembling plant materials cut at precise stages of growth, bloom, and decay, the *ikebana* artist fashions a deceptively natural arrangement through artificial means.

See also COMPOSITION—see also FORM—see also PLANTING—see also TECHNIQUE.

ILLUSION

Optical *illusion*: Deceptive visual phenomena induced by the refraction of light as it passes through one substance to another or by atmospheric conditions that manipulate light rays. *Illusion*, psychological concepts, social science concepts: In psychological studies, refers to the condition based on pseudohallucinations that occur when feelings of fear or anxiety are projected onto external objects and experiences, or are imagined, invented, or wrongly ascribed.

See also ANIMATION—see also LIGHTING—see also OBSERVATION—see also PHENOMENON.

IMAGINATION

Imagination, creativity, concepts relating to the creative process: The capacity to form or the state of forming mental images or ideas of people, objects, and situations that are not truly present to the senses, including both remembered and constructed ideas and images. In modern philosophy, *imagination* is the power or capacity by which the mind integrates sensory data in the process of perception.

Architectural Imagination after May '68. GSD Talks. Frances Loeb Library. September 17, 2014. Łucasz Stanek, Eve Blau, K. Michael Hays, Tom Conley, Stuart Elden with Neil Brenner (moderator).

Toward an Architecture of Enjoyment is the first book devoted to architecture by Henri Lefebvre. Written in 1973 but only recently discovered in a private archive, this work extends Lefebvre's influential theory of urban space to the question of architecture. Taking the practices and perspective of habitation as his starting place, Lefebvre redefined architecture as a mode of *imagination* rather than a specialized procedure or a collection of monuments. He called for an architecture of jouissance—of pleasure or enjoyment—centered on the body and its rhythms and based on the possibilities of the senses. Author Łucasz Stanek spoke about his book and engaged in a discussion with faculty and students.

Modélisations des imaginaires, innovation et création. La ville des réseaux: un imaginaire politique. Publication. Manucius, 2014. Antoine Picon (author). HT166.P425 2014.

In his book, Antoine Picon focuses on two moments in the evolution of networked cities. The first is the new Paris of Haussmann, conceived as the ultimate 19th-century networked city and the prototype of its many subsequent realizations. The second is the contemporary emergence of the smart city, a transition marked by the intensification of the dialectics of control and freedom. In response to this ongoing transition, Picon insists that there is a relative lack of critical perspective on this fundamental shift in the way we envisage, plan, and manage cities.

See also AVIATION: Flights of Imagination—see also CITY: Unplugged City—see also CREATIVITY—see also IDEA—see also PERCEPTION—see also SPACE: Terrestrial Analogues.

IMPACT

Environmental *impact*, environmental concepts: Change in one or more of various socioeconomic and biophysical characteristics of a given environment as a result of site development or new government regulation. *Impact* load, structural analysis concepts: The dynamic effect on a structure, either moving or at rest, of a forcible momentary contact with another moving body; also, a mathematical fraction of a calculated live load used to account for additional stresses resulting from movement of that load. Visual *impact*: The degree of change in the appearance of the visible environment caused by a development project or planning policy, and viewer response to these changes.

Learning from the Americas: Gropius & Breuer in the New World. Lecture. Gund Hall, Piper Auditorium.

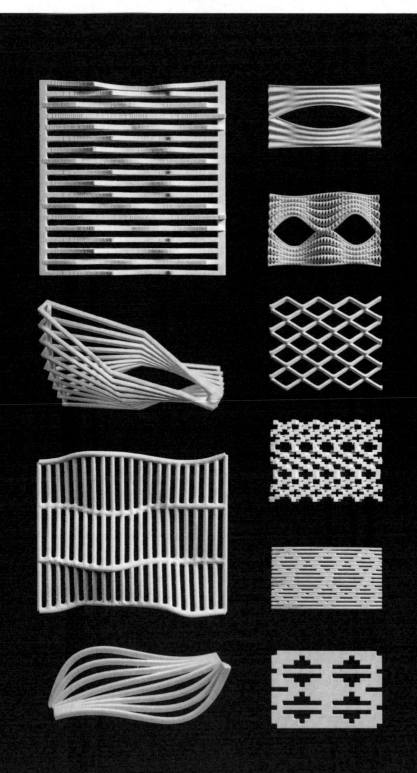

April 9, 2015. Barry Bergdoll with K. Michael Hays & Mohsen Mostafavi.

Barry Bergdoll presented a lecture on Walter Gropius and Marcel Breuer, arguing that the Bauhaus emigrés not only have an *impact* at Harvard University, but that they were types and models for the New World in general. This lecture was part of the series "Then and Now: Walter Gropius and the Lineage of the Bauhaus." ▧

See also COMPETITION: The Design Competition—see also ENVI-RONMENT—see also OBSERVATION—see also STRUCTURE.

IMPLEMENT

1: An article serving to equip <the *implements* of religious worship>. 2: A device used in the performance of a task, tool, utensil. 3: One that serves as an instrument or tool.

The Urban Design Group: Why Implementation Matters. Panel Discussion. Gund Hall, Piper Auditorium. October 9, 2014. Jacquelin Robertson, Richard Weinstein, Jonathan Barnett, Donald Elliott, with Jerold S. Kayden (moderator).

Formed in the late 1960s as part of New York City's Lindsay administration, the Urban Design Group (UDG) became famous for *implementing* district plans through innovative zoning approaches. Nearly 50 years later, this event convened several of the founding members to discuss their contributions to urban design history.

The UDG championed the theory and practice of enmeshing design with politics and law. Architects Jaquelin Robertson, Jonathan Barnett, and Richard Weinstein, cofounders of the UDG, along with lawyer Donald Elliott, then chair of the New York City Planning Commission, used incentive zoning, special districts, and transfer of development rights, among other legal techniques, to *implement* their vision of a vibrant, walkable city. The contributions of the UDG to a pluralist vision of urban design that incorporated strategies and tactics of *implementation* along with other design approaches are as valid today as they were 50 years ago. ▧

See also PLAN: First Semester Core Urban Planning Studio—see also PRACTICE—see also TECHNIQUE—see also TOOL.

INCUBATOR

1: One that *incubates*, such as (a) an apparatus by which eggs are hatched artificially; (b) an apparatus with a chamber used to provide controlled environmental conditions especially for the cultivation of microorganisms or the care and protection of premature or sick babies; (c) an organization or place that aids the development of new business ventures especially by providing low-cost commercial space, management assistance, or shared services.

Urbanity Incubator: Provided the Architecture for Social Technologies, Urbanity Naturally Follows. Thesis. Rossitza Dimitrova Kotelova (MArch I), advised by Carles Muro.

"Urbanity *Incubator* investigates the potential of architecture to transform the declining economic conditions of monoculture-producing communities in the countryside. Building upon Henri Lefebvre's theory that society has been completely urbanized, this thesis examines the Gotse Delchev region in Bulgaria as a case study of 60 tobacco-producing settlements treated as a city of fragmented neighborhoods. Architectural interventions programmed for social technologies—research, knowledge sharing, and business development, in combination with small-scale production—strategically puncture clusters of neighborhoods. The interventions are tied together as part of an urban system in order to act as a catalyst for economic transformation." ▧

Figure. Models (opposite page). Rossitza Dimitrova Kotelova (MArch I).

INDEPENDENT

1: (a) Not dependent; (b) not subject to control by others, self-governing; (c) not affiliated with a larger controlling unit <an *independent* bookstore>; (d) not requiring or relying on something else, not contingent <an *independent* conclusion>; (e) not looking to others for one's opinions or for guidance in conduct; (f) not bound by or committed to a political party; (g) not requiring or relying on others <*independent* of her parents>; (h) being enough to free one from the necessity of working for a living <a person of *independent* means>; (i) showing a desire for freedom (an *independent* manner); (j) not determined by or capable of being deduced or derived from or expressed in terms of members <as axioms or equations> of the set under consideration, having linear *independence* <an *independent* set of vectors>.

INDETERMINACY

1: The quality or state of being *indeterminate*.

First Semester Core Landscape Architecture Studio. STU 1111. Department of Landscape Architecture. Core Studio. Fall 2014. Instructors: Peter Beard (workshop instructor), Silvia Benedito, Gary R. Hilderbrand (coordinator), Zaneta H. Hong, and Jane Hutton (coordinator). Teaching Assistants: Marissa Ashley Angell (MLA I), Leo Raphael Miller (MLA I), Paloma Garcia Simon (MLA I), Courtney Goode (MLA I), Bradley Paul Howe (MLA I), and Thomas Nideroest (MLA II).

This studio problematized issues of orientation and experience, scale and pattern, topographic form, climatic and vegetative influences, and varied ecological processes that help define urban public space. As the first of a four-term sequence of design studios, the studio helped students develop spatial literacy and proficiency in diverse modes of inquiry in landscape architecture. The studio exercises investigated a set of typological models rooted in historical and contemporary urban landscape precedents. These underwent sequential transformations aimed at devising hybrid solutions to common conceptual design problems: conditions of stasis and movement, material composition and expression, conditions of solidity and porosity, and change over time. Later in the semester, these studies advanced to greater specificity on an urban waterfront site in Boston. A week-long workshop focused on specialized analog techniques of surface description. Students also participated in workshops built around focused interventions through the school's Sensory Media Lab. Throughout the course, emphasis was placed on the design studio

as a performative venue for conceiving, interrogating, and elaborating concrete ideas about the role of the biophysical landscape in shaping urbanization and urban life.

Students: Jonathan James Andrews (MLA I), Emily Anne Ashley Blair (MLA I), Lanisha Blount (MLA I), Laura Faith Butera (MLA I), Jenna Lee Chaplin (MLA I), Timothy Pittman Clark (MLA I), Tiffany Kaewen Dang (MLA I), Sara Giles Douglas (MLA I & MArch I), Emily Ballou Drury (MLA I), Ellen E. Epley (MLA I), Siobhan Elizabeth Feehan (MLA I), Ana Cristina Garcia (MLA I), Sophia Georgine Benet Geller (MLA I), Emma Freeman Goode (MLA I), Jeremy Kamal Hartley (MLA I), Aaron David Charles Hill (MLA I), Rayana Purnata Hossain (MLA I), Dana E. Kash (MLA I), Qi Xuan Li (MLA I), Annie J. W. Liang (MLA I), Rebecca A. Liggins (MLA I), Ho-Ting Liu (MLA I), Maria Gloria Robalino (MLA I), Louise Shannon Roland (MLA I), Kira Maria Sargent (MLA I), Keith L. Scott (MLA I), Yun Shi (MLA I), Jonah Susskind (MLA I), Diana Tao (MLA I), Carlo P. Urmy (MLA I), Lu Wang (MLA I), Yifan Wang (MLA I), James Toru Watters (MLA I), Eunice Wong (MLA I), Malcolm Blair Wyer (MLA I), Yuan Xue (MLA I), Xin Zhao (MLA I & MDes, ULE). ⊛

Figures. Pencil Drawing (opposite page). Sophie R. Maguire (MLA I), Keith L. Scott (MLA I), and Diana Tao (MLA I). Models (next page, top to bottom, left to right): 1 Model—Keith L. Scott (MLA I). 1 Model—Xin Zhao (MLA I & MDes, ULE). 2 Models—Ho-Ting Liu (MLA I). 1 Model—Jeremy Kamal Hartley (MLA I). 1 Model— Aaron David Charles Hill (MLA I). 1 Model—Siobhan Elizabeth Feehan (MLA I). 1 Model—Jonathan James Andrews (MLA I). 1 Model—Diana Tao (MLA I). 1 Model—Kira Maria Sargent (MLA I). 1 Model—Keith L. Scott (MLA I). 1 Model—Xin Zhao (MLA I & MDes, ULE). 1 Model—Emily Ballou Drury (MLA I). 1 Model—Carlo P. Urmy (MLA I). 1 Model—Ana Cristina Garcia (MLA I). 1 Model—Diana Tao (MLA I). 1 Model—Tiffany Dang (MLA I). 1 Model—Jenna Lee Chaplin (MLA I). 1 Model—Louise Shannon Roland (MLA I). 1 Model—Annie J. W. Liang (MLA I). 1 Model—Ellen E. Epley (MLA I).

INFILL

Infill, real estate development, economic development: Real estate development which aims to maintain the character of an older area by adding new buildings that are architecturally similar to those already there. For the insertion of material to fill a hole or area of loss, see "filling."

See also DEVELOPMENT—see also HOUSING—see also REAL ESTATE.

INFORMATION

Building *Information* Modeling (BIM), computer modeling, computer-use functions: Refers to a process of planning and managing construction projects from inception of a facility to its eventual demolition through digital *information* models (e.g., 4-D CAD) placed in shared knowledge resources. Geographic *Information* Systems (GIS), geographic systems, systems by function: Refers to combined software and hardware systems that relate and display collected *information* concerning phenomena associated with location relative to the Earth. They often have the ability to overlay temporal

information or *information* related to geology, ecology, weather, land use, demographics, transportation, or other data on top of existing geographic base data. The data are typically presented in the form of maps or tables, displayed in color on a computer screen or printed out. *Information* Technology (IT), technology & related concepts: The application of microelectronics, computers, telecommunication, and other automation methods or technology to the organization, storage, retrieval, and dissemination of *information*, including aural, pictorial, textual, and numeric *information*. *Information*, multidisciplinary concepts: Data, ideas, and imaginative works that have been communicated, recorded, published, and/or distributed formally or informally in any format.

Geographies of Information. Student Group. *Information* and communication technologies have become integral parts of design practice. While architecture and design have always been interested in the spatiality of *information*, they have for the most part circled around the topic rather than probing and examining it in detail. This group is a venue for discussions around *information* and communication technologies and their spatial manifestations. Through a series of talks, lectures, and discussion events, the group engages students and faculty at the Harvard GSD with the major issues facing designers and scholars of the spatial fields, linking them to the larger discussions around the space-making role of contemporary *information* and communication technologies. ⊛

New Geographies 07: Geographies of Information. Publication. Harvard University Press, 2015. Taraneh Meshkani (DDes) & Ali Fard (DDes) (editors).

Understanding the contemporary networks of *information* and communication as inherently geographic, *Geographies of Information* attempts to realign design's relationship to *information* and communication technologies by expanding on the multiscalar complexities and the contextual intricacies underlying their various footprints. *Geographies of Information* suggests an emphasis on the impure, messy, and dynamic characteristics of our contemporary society, as a more productive way of studying the hybridities that support the networked materialities and sociotechnical relationships of *information* and communication networks. This volume of *New Geographies* presents a new set of frameworks that refrain from the generalizations prevalent in modern scientific thought to highlight the complexity of sociotechnical constructions, processes, and practices that form the spaces of *information* and communication. ⊛

See also BUILDING—see also DATA—see also LAB: Excess Laboratory—see also EXTRASTATECRAFT—see also GEOGRAPHY— see also GESTURE: Trace of Emotion—see also MODEL—see also PROCESS—see also REPRESENTATION—see also SYSTEM— see also TECHNOLOGY—see also WRITING: Writing Architecture.

INFRASTRUCTURE

Infrastructure, technology-related concepts: Refers to the underlying foundation or basic framework of a system or organization, especially the services and facilities which are an integral part of the life in an urban community. Transportation *infrastructure*: General term for facilities that allow the movement of people and

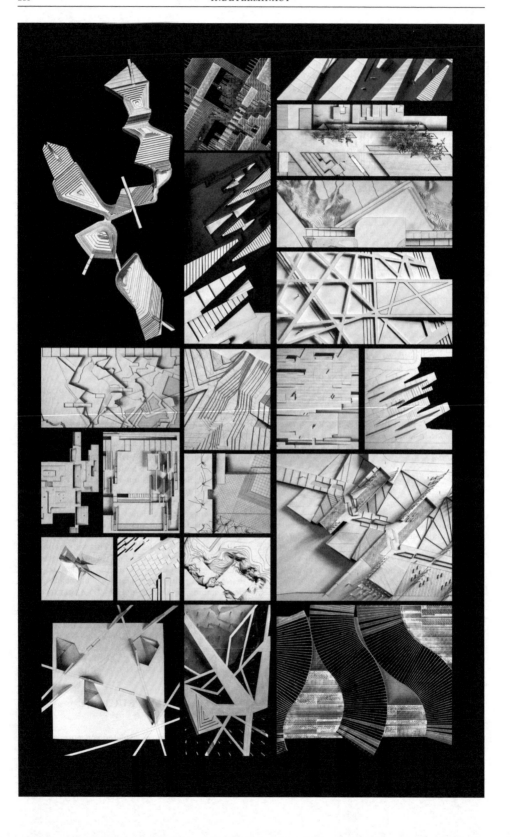

goods from one location to another, including rails, roads, bridges, and other facilities for air, rail, road, water, cable, pipeline, and space transport and travel.

Lively Infrastructures. Lecture. Gund Hall, Piper Auditorium. March 26, 2015. Ash Amin.

This lecture examined the social life and sociality of urban *infrastructure*. Drawing on a case study of land occupations and informal settlements in the city of Belo Horizonte, Brazil, where the staples of life such as water, electricity, shelter, and sanitation are coconstructed by the poor, Ash Amin argued that *infrastructures*—visible and invisible—are deeply implicated not only in the making and unmaking of individual lives but also in the experience of urban community, solidarity, and struggle.

See also CITY—see also COMMUNITY—see also ECOLOGY: Infrastructural Ecologies—see also EXTRASTATECRAFT—see also LANDSCAPE: Theories of Landscape as Urbanism, Landscapes as Infrastructure—see also ORNAMENT: Structure, Infrastructure, and Ornament—see also POWER: Cambridge Talks IX—see also RADICAL: The Grounds of Radical Nature—see also RESILIENCE: Ocean State—see also SETTLEMENT—see also SYSTEM—see also TRANSPORTATION—see also TYPOLOGY: Air Frontier—see also URBAN.

INHABIT

1: To occupy as a place of settled residence or habitat, live in. 2: To be present in or occupy in any manner or form <the human beings who *inhabit* this tale —Al Newman>.

INITIATIVE

1: Of or relating to *initiation*; introductory, preliminary.

Future of Energy Initiative. Research *Initiative*. Harvard's Future of Energy *Initiative*, under the umbrella of the Harvard Center for the Environment, was founded on the premise that the complex challenges we face in the areas of energy and climate require coordinated and multidisciplinary responses. This *initiative* brings together faculty and students from around the university who are engaged in research on major energy-related problems—including global climate change, urban air pollution, technologies for pollution abatement and renewable energy, energy security, and economic growth in developing countries—and exposes them to the perspectives of other disciplines and collaborative opportunities. By promoting partnerships and learning across Harvard, this *initiative* seeks to raise the quality and relevance of energy-related scholarship at Harvard University and to prepare the next generation of researchers, policymakers, and corporate leaders for developing workable solutions and adaptive strategies to energy and climate challenges.

Harvard Initiative for Learning & Teaching (HILT). Gund Hall, Room 522. The HILT space is an experimental, technology-rich space for teaching and learning through design, funded in part by the Harvard *Initiative* for Learning & Teaching.

Health & Places Initiative (HAPI). Research *Initiative*. The Health & Places *Initiative* investigates how to create healthier cities for the future, with a specific emphasis on China. By bringing together experts from the Harvard GSD and the Harvard School of Public Health, it creates a forum for understanding the multiple issues that face cities in light of rapid urbanization and an aging population worldwide.

Real Estate Academic Initiative (REAI). Research *Initiative*. The Real Estate Academic *Initiative* at the Harvard GSD contributes to the quality of urban development in the United States and internationally through multidisciplinary research and education in real estate and urban development.

See also ACTION—see also ADVOCACY—see also FUTURE—see also HEALTH—see also REAL ESTATE—see also VISION.

INNOVATION

1: The introduction of something new. 2: A new idea, method, or device; novelty.

Innovation in Practice: The Harvard Journal of Real Estate. Publication. Real Estate Academic Initiative (REAI), 2015. Brian Patrick Vargo (MDes, REBE), Alexander Akel (MDes, REBE), Shani Adia Carter (MUP), Matthew Alexander Ciccotti (MDes, REBE), Luis Eduardo Gil (MDes, REBE), Margaret Elizabeth Scott (MUP), and Enoch Wong (MArch I) (editors).

The 2015 issue of the *Harvard Journal of Real Estate* features 11 student authors from programs across Harvard University, each with distinct approaches to the various facets of the real estate industry. The authors investigate a range of subjects under the umbrella of *innovative* practice, including opportunistic investment strategies, creative financing mechanisms, progressive public policy, and case studies in unique approaches to real estate development.

See also AIR: Innovate—see also CREATIVITY—see also DESCRIPTION: Innovate—see also IDEA—see also IMAGINATION—see also LAB: Harvard Innovation Lab—see also OPPORTUNITY: Innovate—see also PROCESS—see also REAL ESTATE: Disruptive Innovation in Real Estate—see also VISIONARY.

INPUT

Input device, peripherals, computer equipment: A device that transfer data, programs, or signals into a processor system.

INSCRIPTION

Inscription, document genres by form: Lettering marked on something, especially for documentation or commemoration. Regarding material from the ancient period, includes most preserved written matter of any length, other than papyri. For standardized symbols or notations on objects that convey official information, use "marks (symbols)."

Cambridge Talks IX: Inscriptions of Power; Spaces, Institutions, and Crisis. Cambridge Talks Conference. Gund Hall, Piper Auditorium. April 2–3, 2015.

See also CRISIS—see also ICON—see also INSTITUTION—see also POWER—see also REPRESENTATION—see also SPACE—see also WRITING.

INSPIRATION

1: (a) A divine influence or action on a person believed to qualify him or her to receive and communicate sacred revelation; (b) the action or power of moving the intellect or emotions; (c) the act of influencing or suggesting opinions. 2: (a) The quality or state of being *inspired*; (b) something that is *inspired*. 3: An *inspiring* agent or influence.

Natural & Unnatural/Kong: Inspiration from Nature and Tradition. Lecture. Gund Hall, Piper Auditorium. March 11, 2015. Pei Zhu. ֍

INSTALLATION

Installation, exhibitions: Collectively, the physical elements that constitute an exhibition, including the exhibit design, graphics, lighting, labels, audiovisual components, and exhibit cases, as well as the objects on display. Sound *installation*, *installations*, visual works by material or technique: Interdisciplinary art *installations* that incorporate sound into physical environments.

See also ART—see also ASSEMBLY—see also AUDIOVISUAL—see also CONSTRUCTION—see also DISSECTION: Step 7—see also ELEMENT—see also EXHIBITION—see also FOLLY—see also GALLERY—see also LIGHTING—see also OLFACTORY: Fossa Olfactoria—see also PAVILION—see also PROXY—see also SPACE—see also TEA: Project TEAhouse.

INSTITUTE

Institute, groups: Organizations, societies, or regular meetings for the promotion of a particular literary, scientific, artistic, professional, or educational endeavor.

Harvard Global Health Institute (HGHI). The Harvard Global Health *Institute* seeks to unite cross-disciplinary professions in a common understanding of global health and a goal of worldwide well-being.

South Asia Institute (SAI). The Harvard South Asia *Institute* engages faculty and students through interdisciplinary programs to advance the teaching of and research on global issues relevant to South Asia.

INSULATION

1: (a) The action of *insulating*; (b) the state of being *insulated*. 2: Material used in *insulating*.

Insulating Modernism: Isolated & Non-Isolated Thermodynamics in Architecture. Publication. Birkhäuser, 2014. Kiel Moe (author). TH1715 .M54 2014.

No other concept has disturbed and disfigured our understanding of energy more than the seemingly innocent idea of isolation. Further, no other material practice in architecture has systemically reinforced this errant idea than *insulation*. In too many cases, architects and engineers treat buildings as increasingly efficient isolated systems without a regard to energy hierarchies for a building. This is the exact opposite of how architects should engage energy. This book is a history of the most common material and energy practice in architecture: heat transfer and *insulation*. Much more than walls were insulated in modernity, *insulation* became a highly active physical, conceptual, and historical agent in the determinant habits of 20th-century architectural design and associated construction practices. Non-isolated, non-equilibrium thermodynamics drive every building, city, and form of life. Their understanding helps architects grasp century-old thermodynamic concepts that position designers to finally capture, channel, intercept, store, accelerate, and modulate the total energetic dissipation of buildings through design.

INTEGRATE

1: To form, coordinate, or blend into a functioning or unified whole, unite. 2: To find the *integral* of. 3: (a) To unite with something else; (b) to incorporate into a larger unit.

Integrate: Third Semester Core Architecture Studio. STU 1201. Department of Architecture. Core Studio. Fall 2014. Instructors: Iñaki Ábalos, Preston Scott Cohen, Eric Höweler (coordinator), Max Kuo, Jonathan Sinclair Lott, and Maryann Thompson. Teaching Assistants: Kathryn Leigh Blackstock (MArch I), Matthew Joseph Conway (MArch I), Mark William Eichler (MArch II), Cory Everett Seeger (MArch I), and Joanie Tom (MArch I).

Integration was the agenda for the third semester architecture core studio. Architecture is fundamentally a part-to-whole problem, involving the complex *integration* of building components, systems and processes into a synthetic whole. Structural systems, envelope design, and environmental and thermodynamic processes were systematically addressed in the development of a single project during the semester. The building type consisted of a multiprogram urban building, requiring careful consideration of access and exchange (circulatory, visual, and energy), between programs. During the studio, students worked in consultation with engineers and scientists.

Students: Cari A. Alcombright (MArch I), Nastaran Arfaei (MArch I), Sofia Balters (MArch I), Taylor John Brandes (MArch I), Jacob Joseph Bruce (MArch I), Yaqing Cai (MArch I), Maria Carriero (MArch I), Ruth H. Chang (MArch I), Sean Chia (MArch I), Shani Eunjin Cho (MArch I), Collin Stephens Cobia (MArch I AP), Stephanie Kristina Conlan (MArch I), Allison C. Cottle (MArch I), Elizabeth Marie Cronin (MArch I AP), Carly Linda Dickson (MArch I), Anna Rose Falvello Tomas (MArch I), Evan Robert Farley (MArch I), Johanna Marja Faust (MArch I), Justin Gallagher (MArch I), John Morris Going (MArch I), Christian Alexander Gonzalez (MArch I), Yun Gui (MArch I), Fabiola Guzman Rivera (MArch I), Michael Haggerty (MArch I), Benjamin David Halpern (MArch I), David Benard Hamm (MArch I), Spencer Taylor Hayden (MArch I), Anna Karolina Hermann (MArch I), Olivia Jiang Yi Heung (MArch I), Gu Jia (MArch I), Justin Jiang (MArch I), Chase Mitchell Jordan (MArch I), Sarah

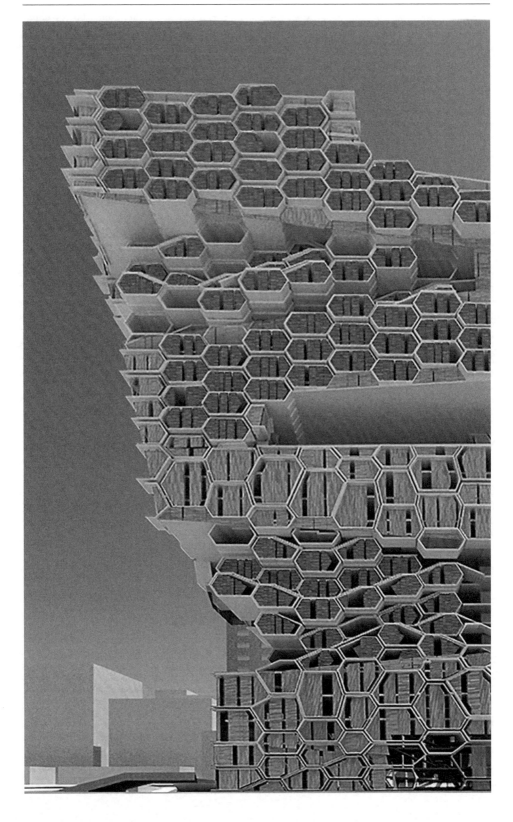

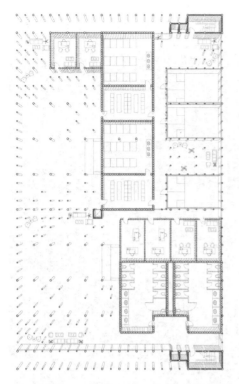
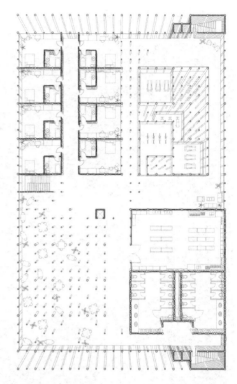

Kantrowitz (MArch I), Andrew Wade Keating (MArch I), Jason Hwan Kim (MArch I), Yurina Kodama (MArch I & MLA I AP), Claire Kuang (MArch I), Yixin Li (MArch I), Yanchen Liu (MArch I), Yan Ma (MArch I & MLA I), Emily Margulies (MArch I), Patrick Alexander McKinley (MArch I & MLA I), Thomas Michael McMurtrie (MArch I), Dasha Draginia Mikic (MArch I), Niki Murata (MArch I), James Francis Murray (MArch I), Duan Ni (MArch I), Felipe Oropeza (MArch I), Kimberly Orrego (MArch I), Davis Shimon Owen (MArch I), Sophia Panova (MArch I), Maia Sian Peck (MArch I), Haibei Peng (MArch I), Jiayu Qiu (MArch I), See Hong Quek (MArch I), Benzion Isaac Rodman (MArch I), Gavin Ruedisueli (MArch I), Anne MacDonald Schneider (MArch I), Anita Sellers Helfrich (MArch I), Scott March Smith (MArch I), Kathryn Leigh Sonnabend (MArch I), Constance Blair Storie Johnson (MArch I), Chang Su (MArch I AP), LeeAnn Liang Suen (MArch I), Lilian Mae Taylor (MArch I), Xuezhu Tian (MArch I AP), Enoch Wong (MArch I), Bryan Yang (MArch I), Guowei Zhang (MArch I), Snoweria Zhang (MArch I). ▩

Figures. Rendering (previous page). Felipe Oropeza (MArch I). Perspective Plans (above). Yaqing Cai (MArch I).

INTEGRATION

1: The act or process or an instance of *integrating*, such as (a) incorporation as equals into society or an organization of individuals of different groups; (b) coordination of mental processes into a normal effective personality or with the environment. 2: (a) The operation of finding a function whose differential is known; (b) the operation of solving a differential equation.

High-Performance Buildings & Systems Integration. SCI 6450. Department of Architecture. Seminar. Fall 2014. Instructor: Ali Malkawi.

The interrelationships of environmental control systems as they relate to high-performance and well-*integrated* buildings was explored in detail. The course addressed the main principles of buildings and allowed participants to develop a critical view about buildings' environmental performance. Projects such as residential, educational, and commercial buildings were analyzed. Systems *integration* and innovations were also studied. Other factors affecting high-performance buildings such as energy standards and how they relate to current sustainability rating systems globally were discussed. The relationship between energy conservation and principles of initial building cost versus life-cycle costs were also be presented. ▩

INTELLIGENCE

1: (a) The ability to learn, understand or deal with new or trying situations, also the skilled use of reason; (b) the ability to apply knowledge to manipulate one's environment or to think abstractly as measured by objective criteria; (c) mental acuteness, shrewdness. 2: (a) An *intelligent* entity; (b) intelligent mind or minds <cosmic *intelligence*>. 3: The act of understanding, comprehension. 4: (a) Information, news. 5: The ability to perform computer functions.

Artificial *intelligence*, computer science, disciplines: The study of the capacity of machines to simulate human behavior such as reasoning, learning, or the understanding of speech.

See also COMPUTER—see also HUMAN—see also INFORMA-
TION—see also MACHINE—see also STUDY—see also TOWARD:
Territorial Intelligence.

INTENSITY

Intensity, color property, perceived attribute: Strength
or purity of a color, determined by the quality of light
reflected from it; a vivid color is of high intensity, a dull
color of low intensity. Intensity, strength: The strength
or amount of a quality, condition, or phenomenon, such
as of an electric field, magnetization, or radiation.

**Urban Intensities: Contemporary Housing Types
& Territories.** Publication. Birkhäuser, 2014. Peter
Rowe & Har Ye Kan (authors). NA 9051.R69 2014.

This book combines the architectural and urban scales
to demonstrate that it is a specific quality, urban intensity, which determines the success of housing. The
authors provide a typology of housing according to the
ways in which diversity and density are created.
Comparisons with historical models and critical appraisals based on the authors' unique standing give ample
information on the pros and cons of major types of
housing, their pitfalls and successful examples. Newly
created sets of drawings, from floor plans to spectacular
3-D aerial views of the buildings in their urban contexts,
accompany each of the more than 20 case studies that
are described and analyzed in detail. The approach taken
here relates to many pressing issues in contemporary
housing, including the avoidance of urban sprawl, the
revival of city centers, and the ongoing search for innovative housing types.

INTERACTIVE

Interactive, operational attributes: Used to describe
two-way systems involving feedback from a viewer or
user, to obtain data or commands and to give immediate
results or updated information. Generally used to describe computer-based systems.

See also COMMUNICATION: Interactive Games for Risk Communication—see also COMPUTER—see also INFORMATION.

INTERNSHIP

Internship, training, educating: The activity and state
of being trained in the capacity of an intern, who is a
student obtaining practical professional experience.

INTERVENE

1: To occur, fall, or come between points of time or events
<only six months intervened between their marriage
and divorce>. 2: To enter or appear as an irrelevant or
extraneous feature or circumstance <it's business as
usual until a crisis intervenes>. 3: (a) To come in or
between by way of hindrance or modification <intervene
to stop a fight>; (b) to interfere with the outcome or
course especially of a condition or process; (c) to occur

or lie between two things. 4: (a) To become a third party
to a legal proceeding begun by others for the protection
of an alleged interest; (b) to interfere usually by force
or threat of force in another nation's internal affairs
especially to compel or prevent an action.

History & Theory of Urban Interventions. HIS
4115. Department of Urban Planning & Design. Seminar.
Fall 2014. Instructor: Neil Brenner.

This course provided a high-intensity introduction of
the history and theory of urban planning practice under
modern capitalism. Building upon an interdisciplinary
literature drawn from planning theory and history as
well as urban social science (geography, sociology, political science, and history), the course explored the
emergence, development, and continual transformation
of urban planning in relation to changing configurations
of capitalist urbanization, modern state power, and
sociopolitical struggle. The course also explored: (a) the
changing sites and targets of planning intervention, from
the neighborhood, city, and regional scales to those of
the metropolis, national economy, and beyond; and (b)
the evolution of political and institutional struggles
regarding its instruments, goals, and constituencies. ⊛

INVENTION

Invention, concepts relating to the creative process,
artistic concepts: The quality of original and productive
creativity. Use with reference specifically to art theory,
especially during the Renaissance, to mean the selection
and utilization of subject matter.

See also CONCEPT—see also CREATIVITY—see also IDEA—see
also INNOVATION—see also PATTERN: R. Buckminster Fuller,
Pattern Thinking.

INVESTIGATE

1: To observe or study by close examination and systematic inquiry. 2: (a) To make a systematic examination;
(b) to conduct an official inquiry.

See also OBSERVATION—see also PLAN: First Semester Core
Urban Planning Studio—see also PROCESS.

ISLAND

Artificial island, single built works by location, topographical: Human-made islands; examples are those
created by landfill or by diking and filling in a wetland,
bay, or lagoon. Island, landforms, landmasses, terrestrial: Landforms smaller than a continent, completely
surrounded by water at high water. Islands appear in
oceans, seas, lakes, or rivers.

Basel Study Abroad Seminar: Islands. DES 3602.
Department of Architecture. Seminar. Fall 2014.
Instructor: André Bideau.

Either consciously deployed or a product of difference,
the island is a recurring theme and metaphor. It can be
identified either as the expression of an intentional
community or as an instrument of discipline and control.

Both a product and a symptom of the urbanization process, it entertains a distinct relationship to power. Within the present postmodern condition, the urban has itself been framed as a condition of landscape. Here the *island* resurfaces in a new light. It is no coincidence that a metaphor of multiple *islands*, conjured by a group of architects around O. M. Ungers in 1977, has been revisited in the past years. Inspired by the loose fabric of West Berlin, the "Green Archipelago" addressed issues of habitation, identity, and place. The *island* metaphor has since gained significance in the physical transformation of cities where the production of themed difference dictates the performance of architecture. *Islands* become operative in an age of rampant difference that has vested the concept of landscape with new meanings.

Against a historical and socioeconomic backdrop, the seminar addressed authors, discourses, and work by not only investigating the spatial logic of design strategies, but also how various contexts have nurtured spatial metaphors. ⊛

Hydraulic Islands. Thesis. Sean William Connelly (MDes, REBE), advised by Kiel Moe and Sanford Kwinter.

"In 40,000 BCE, oceanic peoples were already cultivating areas of ocean larger than continents, navigating and planting *islands* in movements of swells, waves, and stars. In 1778, the first recorded European observation of Hawaii described the oceanic settlements as scattered—without order or respect to distance or position in any direction. Hawaiians were seen as a society without a city. Yet it was in the appearances of planetary chaos that Hawaiians discovered insights into feeding, clothing, sheltering, and inspiring a population nearing one million on Earth's most fragile, isolated landmasses (and without completely destroying their environs). Here on the ocean—where space is actively reversed in time that is perceived not in minutes and seconds but as living currents—Hawaiians coevolved with a pristine, fluid ecology, an immersive milieu without continental clock time. The proximity of available resources and the protection of the *islands'* enclosed coastlines led to distributed markets and

political economies in magnitudes of nested orders. Emerging on consistencies of soil, ocean, and atmosphere, the dispersed cities of Hawaii achieved something larger in time and scale than cities today have yet to actualize technically (though satellites and ocean sensors may potentially lead us toward something similar).

The Hawaiian settlement is an example of a technics and economy based in a conception of the cycles and surfaces of water as sources of place and value. It is in these original and essential actions that oceanic *islands* like Hawaii invite significant consideration in confronting the changing possibilities of human survival and equality on Earth." ⊛

Figure. Diagram (above). Sean William Connelly (MDes, REBE).

See also CLIMATE CHANGE—see also COLLABORATION: The Calumet Collaborations—see also GEOGRAPHY—see also INFILL—see also LANDFORM—see also TERRITORY—see also TOPOGRAPHY—see also WATER.

ISOMETRIC

Isometric projection, technique: Axonometric projection in which the three spatial axes are equally inclined to the plane of projection or drawing surface.

See also AXONOMETRIC—see also DRAFTING—see also DRAW-ING—see also PROJECTION.

ITERATION

1: The action or a process of *iterating* or repeating, such as (a) a procedure in which repetition of a sequence of operations yields results successively closer to a desired result; (b) the repetition of a sequence of computer instructions a specified number of times or until a condition is met—compare recursion. 2: One execution of a sequence of operations or instructions in an *iteration*.

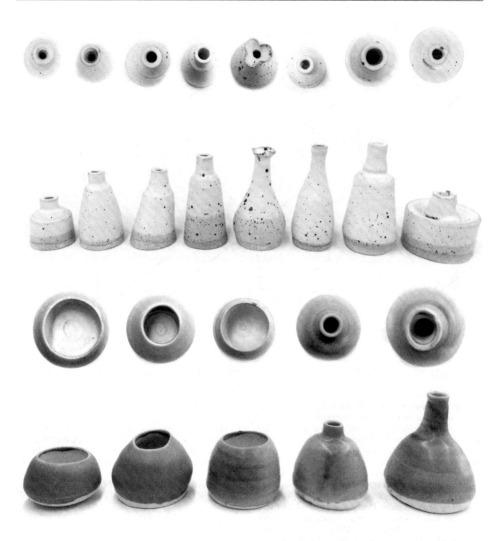

3: Version, incarnation <the latest *iteration* of the operating system>.

Identity Through Iteration: Seven Studies of Multiples in Clay. Independent Study. Michelle Shofet (MLA I), advised by Zaneta H. Hong.

"How far can an object's form, surface, or composition deviate from that of its counterparts and still speak to the group identity? How does one negotiate differentiation while working in a consistent formal language? This independent study is an exploration of object identity through the medium of clay. Each of the series of multiples introduces a different framework for approaching the concept of the multiple. Each series also introduces new tools and methods of manipulation. Some series rely only on the hand and its impressions while others incorporate the wheel, reference paintings or make use of traditional ceramic tools. The objects are perceived not as the products of this study, but rather as the process.

The objects created through the studies are not models, representations, projections, simulations, or abstractions. Unlike the majority of work produced in the design studio, they are 1:1 objects—complete works. In this sense, they are static in their objecthood. This condition speaks to the boundary between the disciplines of design and craft. But while fundamentally different in practice, much is shared in terms of process. *Iteration*, the translation of 2-D into 3-D, the space between projected outcome and reality, and the act of giving form to an idea are a few of the moments of overlap between respective practices. There is an inherent predictability in this work. One can exercise control only until a form is generated. The processes that come thereafter—glazing and firing—yield unpredictable results. We can be sure of the glaze we use, or of the temperature at which we fire, but chemical reactions that occur in the kiln are beyond our control. Glaze bleeds, reacts differently when dipped twice, when dipped over another glaze. These reactions further vary by firing techniques. The object, in its glazed but unfired state, is therefore a projection. It is not until the object has been fired again with glaze that it reaches its ultimate state." ❦

Figure. Clay Objects (above). Michelle Shofet (MLA I).

J-TERM

J-Term (January Term). Workshop. January 5–16, 2015. *J-Term* is an opportunity for students, staff, and faculty to hone skills, learn new ones, or just have fun. Workshops are noncredited courses held in January and are taught by the Harvard GSD community for the Harvard GSD community.

Courses included: Drawing to See the Outer & Inner World, LEED Certification Preparation, Creating A Simple Book, A Project a Day: Architectural Tours, Drawing Architecture: Feeling & Form, Data from Infrastructure Systems for Urban Algorithmic Modeling, Printing Design–Designing Print, Transit Route Planning & Scheduling, Getting Down with the Business of Design, Creating an Online Portfolio, Boston Living with Water: Design Charrette, The Poetics of Wood: Design & Carpentry System of Chinese Traditional Architecture, Quantified Self & Fabrication, Experiencing Blue–Green Infra, Design & Territory: Qualitative Tools for a New Phase of Infrastructure-Led Urbanization, Cultural Entrepreneurship: Translating Ideas into Action, Bruce Mau Design: Edit to Amplify. ⊛

See also SOFTWARE—see also TOOL—see also TECHNIQUE—see also WORKSHOP.

JOURNAL

Journal, accounts, document genres by form, visual & verbal communication: Books containing accounts of an individual's or organization's occurrences or transactions, including records of financial transactions. Use "diaries" when referring to personal accounts of the writer's experiences, attitudes, or observations. *Journal*, periodi-cals, publications, visual & verbal communication: Periodical publications, particularly those containing scholarly articles or otherwise disseminating information on developments in a particular subject field.

See also AGENCY: New Geographies Journal—see also COMMUNICATION—see also DISCIPLINE—see also EXPERIENCE—see also INFORMATION: New Geographies 07—see also INNOVATION: Innovation in Practice—see also METABOLISM: New Geographies 06—see also PROCESS—see also PUBLICATION—see also REAL ESTATE—see also WRITING.

JOYRIDE

1: A ride taken for pleasure, especially an automobile ride marked by reckless driving. 2: Conduct or action resembling a *joyride* especially in disregard of cost or consequences.

Joyriding in Riyadh. Club MEdiNA Event. Gund Hall, Portico 124. April 15, 2015. Pascal Ménoret. ⊛

JUSTICE

Justice, philosophical concepts: The quality, principle, or habit of being morally *just* or righteous, striving to render to each and to all what belongs to them. It is one of the four cardinal virtues.

Informing Justice: A Conversation about the Role of Design in Building Equitable Communities. Panel Discussion. Gund Hall, Piper Auditorium. April 8, 2015. African American Student Union, Joint Center for Housing Studies, and Loeb Fellowship Program.

Kimberly Dowdell, Theresa Hwang, Seitu Jones, with K. Michael Hays (moderator).

In the wake of the events in Ferguson, Staten Island, and elsewhere around the country, three organizations at the Harvard GSD came together to host a conversation about the role of urban design in social *justice* and equity. The event featured a dialogue among leading design, architecture, and planning professionals, exploring the power of urban form and the responsibility of design professionals in the creation of more *just* communities.

The panel was followed by a brainstorming session where attendees collaborated on effective design responses to racial injustice and concentrated poverty. §

See also ADVOCACY—see also AGENCY—see also COMMUNITY— see also ETHICS—see also INFORMATION—see also MATTER.

KEY

Key plan, orthographic projections, images, visual & verbal communication: Plans designed for locating details that appear on other drawings, typically small-scale plans of a building or group of buildings that indicate the placement of principal elements of the scheme, which may each be represented in greater detail on other plans.

KNOWLEDGE

Knowledge, psychological concepts, social science concepts: Refers to the fact or condition of *knowing* something with familiarity gained through experience or association, as in the acquaintance with or understanding of a science, art, or technique. Also refers to the body of *knowledge*, or range of information acquired by study, investigation, observation, or experience.

See also DATA—see also EXPERIENCE—see also ICON: Icons of Knowledge—see also INFORMATION—see also OBSERVATION— see also POWER: Cambridge Talks IX—see also PRACTICE—see also TECHNIQUE—see also VISIONARY: Grounded Visionaries.

LAB

Laboratory, research buildings, research structure: Rooms, buildings, or groups of buildings equipped with apparatus for scientific experiments or other research, testing, and investigations.

Harvard GSD Design Labs. Energy, Environments & Design *Lab*, Geometry *Lab*, Material Processes & Systems Group, metaLAB, New Educational Environments, New Geographies *Lab*, Responsive Environments & Artifacts *Lab*, Social Agency *Lab*, and Urban Theory *Lab*. §

Excess Laboratory: Surplus Storage beyond Efficiency. Thesis. Krystelle Andree Denis (MArch I AP), advised by Leire Asensio Villoria.

"Excess has become a driving force of technological advancement and the complex serialization processes that regulate digital and material information. Storage and distribution centers have become important mediators between producers and consumers, exacerbating

the proliferation of surplus (or excess) and simplifying transactions. Hyper-consumerism (a relatively new escalation in consumerism, which has reached an abnormal intensity that far surpasses its earlier forms) is the accelerated progression of the production, consumption, and disposal of excess resources. Today, the instant gratification of disowning the old runs parallel to the instant gratification of owning the new—a process that, on one hand, legitimizes the production of excess and, on the other, prevents overproduction.

Similar to the architect who designs an organizational system of prefabricated architectural parts, there are industries that specialize in the logistics of machinery and human tasks required for the efficient handling of material excess. What is the role of the architect in an architecture of pure efficiency designed by engineers, mathematicians, computer scientists, and researchers of industries that focus on the assembly and organization of storage and distribution centers? What can the architect extract from such systematized coordination in which the human element is stripped down to a mere extension of the serialization process of storage and distribution? How can built and digital environments function as organizational frameworks to reinforce and systematize relationships between people and objects as a means to counteract a society designed to consume and discard? In other words, how can architecture conceptualize and instrumentalize the very notion of excess?" §

Figure. Model Dioramas (next page). Krystelle Andree Denis (MArch I AP).

Fabrication Lab (Fab Lab). Gund Hall. L19, Robot Room; L31, Project Room; L31a, Metal Shop; L32, CNC Router; L33a, Machine Shop; L35, Wood Shop; L40 & L40e, Laser Cutters; L43, Fab *Lab* Store; L40a–L40c, 3-D Printers.

Experimentation with materials, prototyping and testing, physical mock-ups, and the exploration of new fabrication processes are integral parts of the design culture at the Harvard GSD. In support of these pursuits, the Fabrication *Lab* features a wide range of equipment—from cutting-edge robotic work cells, rapid prototyping and CNC milling machines to metal-working and material-testing machines. Students and faculty of all programs and departments can produce scale models and full-size prototypes using foam, wood, metal, plastics, composites and smart materials. §

Harvard Innovation Lab. Batten Hall. The Harvard Innovation *Lab* is a university-wide initiative fostering team-based and entrepreneurial activities to deepen interactions among Harvard students, faculty, entrepreneurs, and members of the Allston and Greater Boston communities.

Photo Lab. Gund Hall, Room L41. The Photo Lab is available for students to photograph their models and other work. The school maintains a collection of equipment—lights, light stands, solid color backdrops, screens, and umbrellas—for this purpose. §

See also AGENCY: Social Agency Lab—see also ENERGY: Energy, Environments & Design Research Lab—see also EXPERIMENT—see also GEOGRAPHY: New Geography Lab—see also GEOMETRY: Geometry Lab—see also MATERIAL: Material Processes & Systems (MaPS) Group—see also META: metaLAB—see also QUANTITATIVE: The Fisher Lab & Its Legacy—see also RESEARCH—see also RESPONSIVE: Responsive Environments & Artifacts Lab—see also THEORY: Urban Theory Lab.

LABYRINTH

Labyrinth, built works, single built works by form, massing, or shape: Structures of any material having a plan consisting of a number of intercommunicating passages arranged in bewildering complexity, through which it is difficult or impossible to find one's way without guidance. The term was derived from structures so-named in classical Antiquity, perhaps derived from *"labrys"* (Greek for "double axe" or "place of the double axes"), because the structures were labeled with the sign of a double axe. The earliest use of the term is usually associated with the mythical *labyrinth* at Knossos, Crete, in which Theseus killed the Minotaur. *Labyrinth,* maze gardens, geometric gardens, formal gardens: Gardens focused on a *labyrinthine* design having many intricate turnings and windings that are defined by flowers, hedges, or other plants. *Labyrinth,* motifs, design elements: Motifs depicting on a flat surface a path that twists around itself but never crosses itself, usually leading from an outer edge to the center.

See also CIRCULATION—see also ELEMENT—see also FORM— see also GARDEN—see also GAZE: Subverting the Gaze—see also GEOMETRY—see also LINE—see also ORNAMENT—see also PATTERN—see also STRUCTURE—see also SURFACE.

LAND

1: (a) The solid part of the surface of the Earth, also a corresponding part of a celestial body; (b) ground or soil of a specified situation, nature, or quality <dry *land*>; (c) the surface of the Earth and all its natural resources. 2: A portion of the Earth's solid surface distinguishable by boundaries or ownership <bought *land* in the country>, such as (a) country <the finest cheese in all the *land*>; (b) a rural area characterized by farming or ranching, also farming or ranching as a way of life <wanted to move back to the *land*>. 3: Realm, domain <in the *land* of dreams>—sometimes used in combination <TV-*land*>. 4: The people of a country <the *land* rose in rebellion>. 5: An area of a partly machined surface that is left without machining.

See also ENVIRONMENT—see also LANDFORM—see also MAP—see also SETTLEMENT—see also SPECULATION: Practices in the Turbulent City—see also URBAN.

LAND USE

Land use, demographics, social & economic geography concepts: Type of *use* of a lot or parcel of real property. *Land use* map, maps by subject type: Maps showing the existing conditions of a given area.

Land Use & Environmental Law. SES 5206. Department of Urban Planning & Design. Seminar. Fall 2014. Instructor: Jerold S. Kayden.
As a scarce and necessary resource for earthly activity, *land* triggers competition and conflict over its possession, *use,* development, and preservation. For privately owned *land,* the market manages much of the competition through its familiar allocative price-setting features. At the same time, because *use* of *land* in one

location affects the interests of neighbors and the general public and because market mechanisms alone do not always protect or advance such interests, government has enacted *land use* and environmental laws that significantly affect how *land* is handled. Expressed through local ordinances, higher-level legislation, constitutions, discretionary governmental decisions, administrative regulations, judicial opinions, and private agreements, these laws affect the look, feel, character, and composition of cities, suburbs, and rural areas everywhere.
This course introduced students to the content and controversies of *land use* and environmental laws. The purpose of the course was to provide students with a basic understanding of the theories, rationales, techniques, and implementing institutions involved in legally controlling the possession, *use,* development, and preservation of *land.* Particular attention was paid to law's intended and unintended impacts on the physical pattern of built environments and resulting social and economic outcomes, on the increasing overlap of *land use* law and environmental law regimes especially when climate change and urban resilience are front and center, and on the tensions between individual rights and asserted socioeconomic goals often resolved within the context of constitutional law by the courts. The legal techniques explored in the course included laws dealing with zoning, subdivisions, growth management, transfer of development rights, exactions and impact fees, form-based codes, environmental impact reviews, wetlands and water, endangered species, clean air, solid and hazardous waste disposal, design review, environmental justice, climate change, historic preservation, energy siting, billboard/ sign/cell tower controls, eminent domain, building codes, and private homeowner associations. ❦

See also MAPPING—see also PLOT—see also REAL ESTATE.

LANDFILL

Landfill, dumps, refuse areas, open spaces by function: Dumps where refuse is collected, usually low-lying ground, and often as a means to reclaim the land.

Systematic Landfill Reclamation: Designing a New Public Space for Edge Cities. Thesis. Hyosun Yoon (MLA I AP), advised by Bradley Earl Cantrell.
"There are two primary goals for the thesis: first, to study the distribution pattern of old, closed, and abandoned *landfills* within urban areas and to compose a framework for approaching them at the city scale; second, to reclaim and design these sites for reuse as new public spaces for edge cities. Urban sprawl and the substantial decrease in the total number of operating *landfills* in the United States—from 7,300 in 1990 to 1,967 in 2000—indicates a need to understand, manage, and design these forgotten spaces beyond their individual existence and reuse. San Antonio has the highest density of old, closed, and abandoned *landfills* in Texas and thus serves as a suitable city for analysis and design. Based on an analysis of San Antonio's *landfill* distribution, hydrology, and land use, this thesis builds a framework for systematic *landfill* reclamation that could be applied to other cities. As valuable open space and urban transition zones, *landfills* hold great potential to become a new typology of public space that could provide opportunities for social and ecological connection that benefit the edge city in

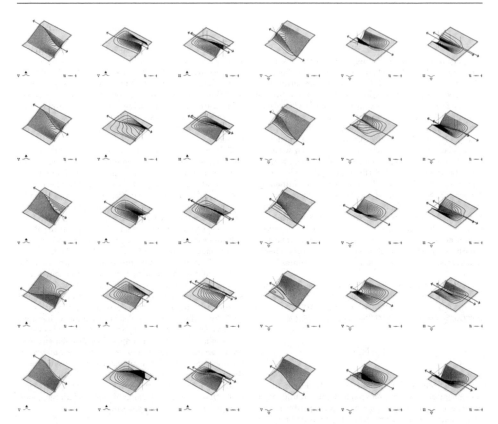

various aspects. For the design project, a selection of *landfills*, outlined by the proposed framework, are designed as a prototype study. Prioritizing the urban water environment, the project focuses on sites within critical proximity to streams and takes advantage of the growing Howard W. Peak Greenway trail to establish the transformed *landfill* sites as a network of public spaces." ⊗

LANDFORM

Landform, terrestrial, natural landscapes, environments: Geomorphic features of the Earth's surface formed by natural processes and that have definable composition and range of characteristics, which recur wherever the features are found and that reflect similar surface and subsurface conditions. Typically reserved for features above water. For marine *landforms*, use "undersea *landforms*."

Landformation Catalogue. Exhibition. Gund Hall, Frances Loeb Library. March 26–May 15, 2015. Zaneta H. Hong & Michael Leighton Beaman with Sarah Morgan Canepa (MLA I), Joshua Michael Jow (MArch II), Foad Vahidi (MLA I), and Phoebe White (MLA I, 2014).

Ground is both site and material for design intervention. Through a systematic manipulation of the landscape, humans account for the fastest geological transformation of the Earth's surface in its 4.54 billion year history. Anthropogenic activity is responsible for the re-formation of more of the Earth's surface than all other mechanisms combined. Agricultural and industrial

practices such as mining, farming, grazing, and damming impact a majority of the Earth's surface. Combined with formations and programs traditionally held within the domain of design practice—spaces of habitation, occupation, protection, and labor—humans have steadily increased the depth of the Earth's anthropocentric event layer to span over 2,000 meters. Human beings operate at the scale of geomorphic agents, relocating 120 billion metric tons of earth annually, twice the volume of Mount Fuji. Directly reshaping the surface of the Earth to provide capacities not immediately or adequately available, extracting energy and materials, and affecting behaviors and phenomena are results of human-driven interventions. This collection of operations, technologies, and forms constituted a catalogue of Earth's re-formation potentials. "*Landformation* Catalogue" examined the generative methodologies of *landform* manipulation, revealing correlations between the histories, morphologies, assemblies, materials, and affordances of landscape practice. It analyzed the resulting spatial artifacts of humanity's larger Earth transformation project. ⊗

Figure. Landformation Catalogue Exhibition (above). Zaneta H. Hong, Michael Leighton Beaman, Sarah Morgan Canepa (MLA I), Joshua Michael Jow (MArch II), Foad Vahidi (MLA I), and Phoebe White (MLA I, 2014).

See also ANTHROPOCENE—see also CATALOGUE—see also CONTOUR—see also DATA—see also FLUX—see also FORM—see also GEOLOGY—see also INFORMATION—see also OPERATION—see also REPRESENTATION—see also SURFACE—see also TERRAFORM: Terraforming Cultivation—see also TOPOGRAPHY—see also TRANSFORMATION.

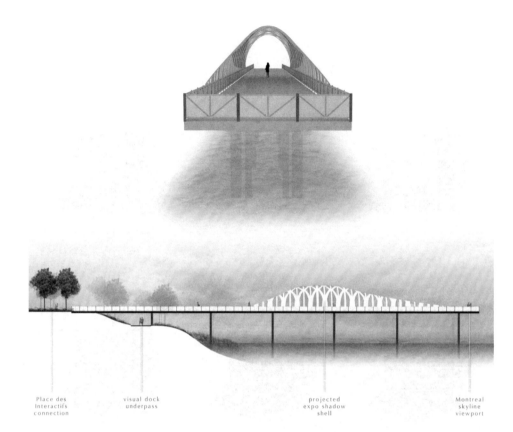

Place des   visual dock   projected   Montreal
Interactifs   underpass   expo shadow   skyline
connection   shell   viewport

LANDMARK

Landmark, historic buildings, single built works by function: Buildings that serve as points of reference because their height, siting, distinctive design, use, historic significance, or other feature sets them apart from surrounding buildings. *Landmark*, markers, monuments: Conspicuous monuments, fixed objects, or markers that serve as guides in the direction of one's course, characterize a neighborhood, or establish the location of land boundaries or property.

Montreal Is Back: It's Time to Say Goodbye to Place des Nations. STU 1407. Department of Landscape Architecture. Option Studio. Spring 2015. Instructors: Renée Daoust & Aisling Marie O'Carroll. Teaching Assistant: Alice Wan Chai (MArch II).

Place des Nations was built as part of Man & His World, the major development project of the Universal Exhibition of 1967. Located near the metro station, it hosted foreign dignitaries and thousands of participants in numerous ceremonies and cultural events during the World's Fair. Intended for temporary use during Expo 67, the square constitutes a symbolic site from this global event that marked the centennial of Canada. Liberated from the symmetry of the classical amphitheater, its innovative composition perfectly embodies the modern spirit of Expo 67. The only reason Place des Nations has not been torn down already is sentimentality. It may be

on Heritage Montreal's list of endangered *landmarks*, but it is architecturally unremarkable. Expo 67 was indeed a watershed moment in Montreal's history, but more iconic *landmarks* stand in memoriam, such as Moshe Safdie's Habitat 67 and Buckminster Fuller's American pavilion—the geodesic dome that became the Biosphere.

As the prow of Ile Sainte-Hélène and an important witness of Expo 67, Place des Nations has been neglected for the past 30 years. Recognized as a *landmark* by Heritage Montreal, yet rejected by the politicians for the 2017 celebrations, Place des Nations faces an important design challenge to reinstate itself as an iconic urban design, landscape, and architectural statement to overcome its demolition. A critical look at the urban theater, its rehabilitation, future utilization, and redesign at all scales while strategically addressing political and economic viability was the main focus of the studio.

Students: Marissa Ashley Angell (MLA I), Rebekah Lynn Armstrong (MLA I), Ian Scott Brennick (MLA I), Christopher John Donohue (MLA II), Paloma Garcia Simon (MLA I), Siwei Gou (MLA I AP), B. Cannon Ivers (MLA II), Olivia Kaufman Rovira (MLA I), McKenna Dayan McKetty (MLA I), Leo Raphael Miller (MLA I), Tyler Mohr (MLA II), Pg Human Smit (MLAUD), Elizabeth Y. Wu (MLA I AP). ⊛

Figures. Rendered Plans (previous page). Ian Scott Brennick (MLA I). Sectional Perspective & Elevation (above). Tyler Mohr (MLA II).

See also BUILDING—see also FOLLY—see also ICON: Icons of Knowledge—see also OBJECT.

LANDSCAPE

Cultural *landscape*, environments: Designates land and water areas significantly altered or modified by human actions; used in contrast to "natural *landscapes*," that designate areas where human effects, if present, are not ecologically significant to the regions as a whole. *Landscape*, environments, settlements: Broadly used to describe portions of the Earth's surface that share common repeating characteristics that can be comprehended at a glance. *Landscapes* are more than scenery or political units; they are systems of natural and cultural contexts.

Landscape: An Evolution of Practice & Theory. Lecture. Gund Hall, Piper Auditorium. February 17, 2015. Mario Schjetnan. ❦

Poésie sur Alger. Publication. Éditions Falaize, 1950. Le Corbusier (author). Le Corbusier Research Collection, Frances Loeb Library. LeC NA 1588.2 Algi L496.

"Written in 1942 but published in 1950, Le Corbusier details his unsuccessful quest to obtain a commission during the 13 years he proposed several urban plans for the city of Algiers, which were consistently refused by the municipal authorities. 'Poetry' refers to the relationship he perceived between his proposed urbanism and the existing *landscape*. Le Corbusier understood his first project (and revised versions) for Algiers as an urbanism adapted to the local climate and to the particular topography. He saw in his plans for Algiers as the integration of man, architecture, and *landscape*. The gratte-ciel, with its bold front to the sea, symbolized the dialogue between water, land, and sky." —Inés Zalduendo. ❦

Theories of Landscape as Urbanism, Landscapes as Infrastructure: Paradigms, Practices, Prospects. DES 3241. Department of Landscape Architecture. Seminar. Fall 2014. Instructor: Pierre Bélanger.

Responding to contemporary urban patterns, ecological pressures, and decaying infrastructures, this course brought together a series of influential thinkers and researchers from the design commons across North America to discuss different methods, models, and measures of large-scale, long-range design for the 21st century. Organized around a sequence of weekly topics and readings, guest presentations focused on the future of the region, with the predominance of *landscape* ecology and the revival of geography worldwide, challenged the laissez-faire dogma of neoliberalist economics, Fordist forms of civil engineering, and Euclidean planning policies that marked the past century. From Geddes to Gottmann, Mackaye to Mumford, Olmsted to Odum, the first part of the course reexamined a series of influential plans, projects, and practitioners to trace a cross section through the history of urbanization in North America and the industrialized world to chart the trajectory of an emergent regional paradigm. Foregrounding the nascent reciprocity between ecology, economy, and energy, the second part of the course opened a horizon on pressing issues facing cities today to recast the infrastructural and geopolitical role of *landscape* as an operating system for future urbanism. ❦

Vast Minute Landscapes. Exhibition. Kirkland Gallery. December 1–12, 2014. Miranda Elizabeth Mote (MDes, HPD) & Jaime Daroca Guerrero (MArch II).

Vast: Vast embraced the intensity of the American *landscape* with a selection of black-and-white photo-graphs captured on a road trip through the northeastern United States. These instances materialized a continuous search for the American *landscape*—the magnificence of the vast space and endless mutable atmosphere that gives light and contrast to those moments.

Minute: Minute magnified the mundane and often overlooked Italian *landscapes* with a pressed display of botanical specimens, stamps, and photography. Their composition was designed to call attention to *landscapes* held within small frames of view often traversed or transported without notice—the stamp on a letter, lichen on a rock, and discarded blossoms. Within the mossy notions of this exhibit was a conscious investigation of material, scale, and composition. ❦

See also CULTURE—see also DISCIPLINE—see also ENVIRONMENT—see also GAME: Immersive Landscapes—see also LAND—see also MODERN: Making the Modern Landscape—see also PAINTING: Landscape as Painting—see also PRESERVATION: A History of Nature Conservation and Cultural Landscape Preservation—see also PROCESS—see also RADICAL: The Grounds of Radical Nature—see also REPRESENTATION—see also RESEARCH—see also SETTLEMENT—see also SUPERMARKET: Paper or Plastic—see also SURFACE: Superficial Surfaces—see also TOPOLOGY: On Sensing & Conceiving Landscape—see also URBAN—see also URBANISM: Master in Design Studies (MDes) Urbanism, Landscape, Ecology—see also WATER.

LANDSCAPE ARCHITECT

Landscape architect, people in the visual arts, people by occupation: People who specialize in designing the scenic environment on a relatively large scale, including the layout of plants and accompanying structures.

Figure. Photograph (above). Cornelia Hahn Oberlander.

LANDSCAPE ARCHITECTURE

Landscape architecture, discipline: Branch of *architecture* that deals with the design of the scenic environment, including the development and planting of all types of planned outdoor green spaces, often with accompanying structures and roadways, outdoor public areas, landmarks, and structures with the aim of creating a natural setting for human structures and settlements. For the planning discipline concerned with the physical environment and any and all human involvement with it, with the objective of assuring proper habitat for people, animals, and plants and the resources on which they depend, use "environmental design." For the development and decorative planting of gardens and grounds in particular, use "*landscape* gardening."

Harvard GSD Department of Landscape Architecture. The Department of *Landscape Architecture* at the Harvard GSD is home to the oldest and most distinguished academic program in *landscape architecture* in the world. Since its founding in 1900, it has played a singular role in the development of *landscape architecture* as a profession, an academic discipline, and as a medium of design that engages urbanism, environmentalism, and culture. Its mission is to advance research and innovative design practices in the natural and built environments, as they intersect with processes of urbanization. Candidates in the Master in *Landscape Architecture* program work with an internationally recognized faculty and explore the multiple ways that landscapes positively contribute to the complexities of the contemporary city, to a more equitable distribution of ecological and environmental resources, and to the creation of better futures across all regions of the world.

List of Degrees: Master in *Landscape Architecture* (MLA I), Master in *Landscape Architecture* Advanced Placement (MLA I AP), and Master in *Landscape Architecture* Post-Professional (MLA II). Department Chair: Charles A. Waldheim. Program Director: Anita Berrizbeitia. Program Coordinator: Erica George. Executive Assistant to the Chair: Sara Gothard. Department Administrator: Caroline P. Newton. Students: 113 MLA I candidates, 53 MLA I AP candidates, and 18 MLA II candidates. ❧

On The Theoretical & Practical Development of Landscape Architecture. Olmsted Lecture. Gund Hall, Piper Auditorium. October 28, 2014. Joseph Disponzio. ❧

LASER

Laser, optical instruments, equipment for science & technology: Devices that generate electromagnetic radiation in the ultraviolet, visible, or infrared spectrum, in the form of a very narrow continuous or intermittent beam. Originally an acronym for "light amplification by stimulated emission of radiation," the first functional *laser* was built by Theodore H. Maiman (1927–2007), and demonstrated in 1960. *Lasers* have multiple applications. They are used as components in information retrieval and transmission devices and systems, cutting, measuring, and medical tools, and as entertainment devices.

LASER CUTTER

Laser Cutters. Gund Hall, Rooms L40 & L40e. The Harvard GSD has an Epliog Laser System and Universal Laser Systems solid state *laser cutters*, useful for etching patterns or cutting virtually any two-dimensional shape from a wide variety of thin materials such as acrylic, chipboard, wood veneer, and thin plywood. There are a total of eight computer-controlled *laser cutters* available: four in the Fabrication Lab and two on the north ends of the 3rd- and 5th-floor studio trays. These machines typically require simple CAD software and drawing plot files for operation. ❧

LAUNCH

1: An act or instance of *launching*. 2: (a) To throw forward, hurl; (b) to release, catapult, or send off a self-propelled object <*launch* a rocket>. 3: (a) To set a boat or ship afloat; (b) to give a start <*launched* her on a new career>; (c) to put into operation or set in motion, initiate; (d) to get off to a good start; (e) to load into a computer's memory and run <*launch* a program>.

Grounded Visionaries, Campaign Launch. Memorial Hall, Sanders Theater. September 12–13, 2014.
At the Campaign *Launch*, the Harvard GSD not only celebrated design and the school's impact in the world, but also gave students and alumni a chance to reconnect with classmates, colleagues, faculty, and others. The Grounded Visionaries weekend kicked off as Dean Mohsen Mostafavi, Harvard University President Drew Gilpin Faust, Jeanne Gang, Rem Koolhaas, Fumihiko Maki, Thom Mayne, Michael Van Valkenburgh, and other featured speakers engaged with an audience of faculty, students, and alumni. ❧

GSD History & Philosophy Launch. Student Group. GSD History & Philosophy *Launch* is an academic group for students interested in topics related to the study of architecture history and theory. ❧

See also BOOK—see also CHALLENGE: Launch—see also LAND-SCAPE—see also SPACE—see also VISIONARY.

LAWN

Lawn, landscaped grass, landscape elements, site elements: Areas of cultivated grass or other ground cover maintained for aesthetic quality or recreation.

Harvard GSD Lawn. Nicknamed the "backyard," the Harvard GSD *Lawn* is a plaza and grassy *lawn* on the east side of Gund Hall. The lawn is the site of a number of class meetings, social events, and outdoor installations. ❧

LEADERSHIP

1: The office or position of a *leader*. 2: Capacity to *lead*. 3: The act or an instance of *leading*. 4: *Leaders* <the party *leadership*>.

Global Leadership in Real Estate & Design. SES 5405. Department of Urban Planning & Design. Seminar. Spring 2015. Instructors: A. Eugene Kohn & Bing Wang.
In today's constellation of increasingly connected urban centers, shifts in cultural preferences, design thinking, and spatial significations often reflect and parallel transitions in capital forces and economic realities, locally and across the globe. This course began with the premise that globalization imposes forces and tensions that di-

rectly impact the formation and production of the urban built environment, and that future real estate and design professionals will have a competitive advantage if they are well-prepared to understand, navigate, and indeed lead amidst the vicissitudes of cultural and economic disequilibrium and disruptions of the global realm. For these challenges, this project-based course encouraged a forward-looking examination of and exposure to complexity in today's real estate design, development, and investment process, through students' hands-on experience, creative propositions, risk-taking judgment training, and the exercise of *leadership* in real estate and design projects in the real world. The course integrated domestic and international field studies, lectures, and class discussion, and encouraged students to rethink, anticipate, and reinvent practice paradigms in both the real estate and design fields that respond to exigent and projected transformative environmental, market, economic, and cultural changes, while fully leveraging highly interactive, semester-long engagement with accomplished real estate and design *leaders*. ⑨

Le Corbusier (author). Le Corbusier Research Collection, Frances Loeb Library. LeC NA 29 L496.

"*Précisions sur un état présent de l'architecture et de l'urbanisme* includes the ten *lectures* Le Corbusier delivered in Buenos Aires between October 3 and 19, 1929, and one delivered in Rio de Janeiro on December 8, 1929. Aboard the *Lutétia* (off Bahia) on his way back to Paris, he writes his prologue to these *lectures* on December 10, 1929. This introductory essay describes the impact of the journey on his thinking (some of his first short trips by plane took place during this visit). Two appendixes outline his thoughts on contemporary Parisian and Soviet urban planning. Here, Le Corbusier's schematic diagrams serve as visual translations of the basic ideas he discussed in his *lectures*. It is here that Le Corbusier describes Buenos Aires, arriving at night by steamboat, as 'that phenomenal line of light …the simple meeting of the pampa and the ocean in one line.' His experience of the view from above recognizes the impact of landscape, and the need for site-specific responses in urbanism, as opposed to a universal proposal applicable worldwide." —Inés Zalduendo. ⑨

LEARNING

Learning & scholarship concepts: Concepts related to education, *learning*, and teaching. For specific branches of inquiry, use "disciplines."

Design for Learning. DES 3494. Department of Architecture. Seminar. Instructor: Derek Ham.

When Walter Gropius discussed the "training of an architect" he identified the very first years of formal education—nurseries and kindergartens. In truth, the early years of play are critical in establishing a pathway for individuals to become creative thinkers. Friederich Fröbel recognized this as well, and embodied a pedagogy of "playful *learning*" when he developed his "gifts"—a set of creative *learning* manipulatives for children. Fröbel was not only an educator, but also a designer of objects. These artifacts, although simple in nature, held great educational potency, which in time influenced an entire generation of artists and designers. This seminar looked beyond spatial concerns for educational environments and took a critical look at how we craft *learning* objects with *learning* experiences to bring improvements to K–12 education. Play itself became an object of study. Participants designed *learning* objects throughout the semester. Designers were asked to think like educators and educators were asked to think like designers. Students were introduced to seminal *learning* and design theories: constructivism, algorithmic thinking, visual calculation, and tangible *learning*. ⑨

See also IMPACT: Learning from the Americas—see also INITIATIVE: Harvard Initiative for Learning & Teaching.

LECTURE

Lecture, speeches, documents, visual & verbal communication: Documents containing the text of expositions of a given subject delivered before an audience or class, especially for the purposes of instruction.

Précisions sur un état présent de l'architecture et de l'urbanisme. Publication. Éditions G. Crès, 1930.

LETTER

1: A symbol usually written or printed representing a speech sound and constituting a unit of an alphabet. 2: (a) A direct or personal written or printed message addressed to a person or organization; (b) a written communication containing a grant—usually used in plural. 3: The strict or outward sense or significance <the *letter* of the law>. 4: (a) A single piece of type; (b) a style of type.

Open Letters (OL). Student Publication. Open *Letters* is a biweekly experimental literary journal, whose fundamental purpose is to stimulate earnest, personal, and thoughtful conversation about architecture through the publication of first-person correspondence. Each print issue presents one open *letter* (i.e., addressed to a particular party, but

intended for publication)—or a response to a previous issue—that focuses on a specific topic related to the built environment. The OL editorial staff accepts submissions from students, faculty, staff, and outside correspondents. The editors encourage liberal interpretations of the submission framework and welcome a variety of media—as long as it can be placed in a no. 10 envelope. ▒

Figure. Open Letters Publication (previous page).

See also COMMUNICATION—see also PUBLICATION—see also REPRESENTATION—see also WRITING.

LIBRARY

Academic *library*, institutions by activity: *Libraries* which serve an academic institution, such as a college or university, and develop their collections to support the programs of their parent institution. Digital *library*, institutions by activity: Refers to archival repositories of digital materials that are made accessible to individuals.

Cold Storage (2015). Film Screening. Harvard *Library* Strategic Conversation. Gund Hall, Piper Auditorium. February 6, 2015. Matthew Battles, Noam Dvir, Haden Guest, Eric Höweler, Cristoforo Magliozzi, Daniel Vladimir Rauchwerger (MDes, RR), Jeffrey Schnapp, and Sarah Thomas.
Cold Storage (2015), a documentary short directed by Cristoforo Magliozzi and produced and written by Jeffrey Schnapp, Matthew Battles, and the metaLAB team, portrays the dislocated heart of Harvard University's *library* system and one of the largest book depositories in the world. Organized in conjunction with the exhibition "Icons of Knowledge," this screening was the film's on-campus premiere. Following the screening, Jeffrey Schnapp lead a roundtable discussion on the ways space makes place, delving into the ways changing spaces reflect new *library* culture and how user perceptions of *libraries* are transformed by changes in the physical spaces. ▒

Frances Loeb Library. The Frances Loeb *Library* at the Harvard GSD houses a book and journal collection of some 300,000 volumes and hundreds of thousands of individual images and original materials related to the fields of architecture, landscape architecture, urban design, and urban planning. In addition, hundreds of e-resources are available through the online catalogue HOLLIS (Harvard On-Line *Library* Information System), which also includes the holdings of the entire Harvard University *library* system. The online catalogue of printed resources is complemented by Visual Information Access (VIA), the university's image database, and Online Archival Search Information System (OASIS), which includes manuscripts and archival and special collections inventories. ▒

See also BOOK—see also EXHIBITION—see also ICON: Icons of Knowledge—see also LANDFORM: Landformation Catalogue — see also SOFTWARE: From Drones to Data Portals and Maps—see also WRITING.

LIFESTYLE

1: The typical way of life of an individual, group, or culture.

Redefining Urban Living. STU 1318. Department of Architecture. Option Studio. Spring 2015. Instructors: Anne Lacaton & Marcos Rojo. Teaching Assistant: David Wolf Himelman (MArch I).
This studio dealt with contemporary urban conditions, exploring optimal ways to live in the city, but also the meaning of overused terms such as densification and transformation. The quality of housing must be based on the idea of well-being (pleasure), variety of spaces and atmospheres, a conception of comfort other than that normalized by standards, calculations, or models. The city should provide an exceptional quality of life: a large range of facilities, proximities, and pleasures resulting in a high quality of livable space. In a first quick assignment, the students developed their own definitions of what living—luxurious, public, and infrastructural— mean in qualitative terms. The definitions were approached in this essentially qualitative manner to allow each student to capture the spatial or organizational essence that lies behind them. This initial act demanded a critical way of thinking to produce a personal statement and assume a recognizable position regarding (but not reduced to) the following questions: what produces good conditions for life? Which are the qualities that make a space desirable, luxurious, liveable, and sustainable? What is my responsibility as an architect? What am I advocating for? Attempting to answer these questions will inevitably lead to a fragmentary way of thinking, covering different scales and ideas. The results were condensed and expressed through any possible media that activated these definitions as self-imposed constraints.
Students: Sofia Blanco Santos (MArch II), Hayrettin Gunc (MAUD), Daniel Alexander Hemmendinger (MArch II), Tamotsu Ito (MArch II), Michael Joseph Johnson (MArch II), Elizabeth Anna Lee (MArch I), Nupoor Monani (MAUD), Erin Jennifer Ota (MArch II & MDes, RR), David John Pearson (MArch II), Orcun Tonyali (MAUD), Rex Tzen (MArch I), Tzyy Haur Yeh (MLA I AP & MArch I). ▒

Figure. Rendered Plans (opposite page). Daniel Alexander Hemmendinger (MArch II).

See also CULTURE—see also HEALTH—see also SUBURB: The Storm, the Strife, and Everyday Life.

LIGHT

1: (a) Something that makes vision possible; (b) the sensation aroused by stimulation of visual receptors; (c) electromagnetic radiation of any wavelength that travels in a vacuum with a speed of about 186,281 miles (300,000 kilometers) per second, specifically radiation that is visible to the human eye. 2: (a) Daylight; (b) dawn. 3: A source of *light*, such as (a) a celestial body; (b) a candle; (c) an electric *light*. 4: (a) Spiritual illumination; (b) inner *light*; (c) enlightenment; (d) truth. 5: (a) Public knowledge <facts brought to *light*>; (b) a particular aspect or appearance presented to view <saw the matter in a different *light*>. 6: A medium through which *light* is admitted. 7: A set of principles, standards, or opinions <worship according to one's *lights* —Adrienne Koch>. 8: A noteworthy person in a particular place or field <a leading *light* among current writers>. 9: A particular expression of the eye. 10: (a) Lighthouse, beacon; (b) traffic *light*. 11: The representation of *light* in art. 12: A flame for *lighting* something.

Light Structures I. DES 3453. Department of Architecture. Seminar. Fall 2014. Instructor: Toshiko Mori.

Lightness is an attribute that spans structure, performance, materiality, assembly, transportation, as well as experiences and perceptions of the built environment. This seminar considered the environmental impact of *light* buildings, infrastructures, and systems from multiple angles. For example, from the perspective of structures, we studied the weight of buildings, a structure's impact on energy consumption, and its carbon footprint. The concept of *lightness*, its perception and meaning, has been studied within various cultural contexts, such as literature and film. These media have ascribed its meaning and value. The seminar questioned building typology, from housing and concert halls, to cultural centers and education facilities. The course explored whether mobility, temporality, and nomadic programming can be used to produce a new paradigm. *Light* Structures also dealt with perceptions of transparency and release from gravity. When the *lightness* of a structure is considered, economy of means and efficiency become an issue. There were many ways that one can contribute toward *lightness* through innovation. One can consider the scale and efficiency of its use—how multiple tasks can be handled by fewer elements—techniques, and engineering. ▨

Light Structures II. DES 3454. Department of Architecture. Seminar. Spring 2015. Instructor: Toshiko Mori.

The course focused on the analysis, survey, history, theory, and technology of *light* structures, questioning conventional building typologies to transform them into *light* structures. In particular, the course focused on membrane and textile-based structures due to the seminar's collaborative partner, Taiyo Kogyoes. Their expertise includes deployment, assembly, and reassembly transportation logistics. The course also examined how resource deployment may affect *lightness* through studies of materials, fabrication, and assembly. The seminar also questioned building typology to see how and which building types can become portable, nomadic, temporal, and mobile. ▨

LIGHTING

Architectural *lighting, lighting* by function, object groupings & systems: *Lighting* systems for the illumination of building elements, spaces, or exteriors for visual effects. Daylighting, *lighting* by methods of illumination: *Lighting* systems that employ daylight, including the arrangements and installation of such systems. *Lighting*, systems by function: Arrangements and installation systems of *lighting* devices for particular effects.

Light-Emitting Diode (LED). A LED light bulb can span 50,000 hours at 90 lumens per watt and use 11 kilowatt-hours per year with an annual operating cost of $1.00.

Compact Fluorescent Lamp (CFL). A CFL light bulb can span 8,000 hours at 45 lumens per watt and use 26 kilowatt-hours per year with an annual operating cost of $2.55.

Incandescent Light Bulb. An incandescent light bulb can span for 1,200 hours at 11 lumens per watt and use 110 kilowatt-hours per year with an annual operating cost of $10.95.

See also DAYLIGHTING—see also EXHIBITION—see also GALLERY—see also INSTALLATION—see also SYSTEM—see also SUSTAINABILITY.

LIMINAL

1: Of or relating to a sensory threshold. 2: Barely perceptible. 3: Of, relating to, or being an intermediate state, phase, or condition, in-between, transitional <in the *liminal* state between life and death —Deborah Jowitt>.

Liminal Space: Transforming the Taylor Yard G2 Parcel. STU 1401. Department of Landscape Architecture. Option Studio. Fall 2014. Instructors: Gerdo P. Aquino & Ying-Yu Hung. Teaching Assistant: Vi Vu (MLA I).

While the Los Angeles River may drift and turn before dispensing its waters into the Pacific Ocean, the sound of its rushing flows reverberate through California's capital, and across the country, in the halls of Congress. As staunch supporters raise one billion dollars for restoring the nation's most iconic streams, the Los Angeles Mayor, with the backing of the Army Corps, worked through the federal channels to bring this long-awaited vision to reality. A former Union Pacific rail yard, affectionately called the "crown jewel" of the Los Angeles River, the 42-acre Taylor Yard G2 Parcel is one of the largest remaining undeveloped lands along the river. Ironically, as the public celebrated the acquisition of this highly prized open space, California is undergoing the worst drought of the century. Transforming the G2 Parcel calls for a new paradigm for the reestablishment of historic riparian habitats and challenges the notion of a 21st-century urban park and its role in contemporary urbanism. Set within a politically charged context, the complex issues of water, ecology, infrastructure, and urbanism at the G2 Parcel warrant urgent explorations and design resolution. The objective of the studio was to reassess well-established approaches to ecological restoration, and to propose innovative design solutions for a highly volatile urban context defined by severe droughts and flash floods.

Students: Yichen An (MArch II), Chungseok Baek (MLA I AP), Xiaoran Du (MLA I AP), Michelle Arevalos Franco (MLA I), Yinjia Gong (MLA I AP), Xinjun Gu (MLA I AP), Meng Jia (MLA I AP), Weimao Kong (MLA I AP), Maria Catalina Picon (MLA I AP), Flavio Stefano Sciaraffia Marquez (MLA I AP), Vi Vu (MLA I), Han Yang (MLA I), Tzyy Haur Yeh (MLA I AP & MArch I). ▨

Figure. Sectional Perspective & Axonometric Renderings (opposite page). Vi Vu (MLA I).

See also PARK—see also SPACE—see also THRESHOLD—see also TRANSFORMATION.

LINE

Line, artistic concept, *linear* form, form & composition concepts: As an artistic concept, strokes or marks, long in proportion to breadth, traced upon a surface or implied through imaginary joining of points in a composition. *Line*, geometric concept, mathematical concepts: In mathematics, the trace of a moving point in continuous extent, either straight or curved, having length but

without breadth or thickness. In geometry, the concept of a *line* can vary with the definition of geometry; for example in analytic geometry, a *line* is the set of points on a plane having coordinates that satisfy a given *linear* equation; in incidence geometry, a *line* may be an independent object distinct from the set of points which lie on it. Property *line*, zoning concepts, legal concepts: The boundary *lines* between pieces of property. Sight *lines*, visual & representation concepts, formal concepts, artistic concepts: *Lines* that define an unimpeded field of vision, as within rooms or open spaces or along city streets.

See also COMPOSITION—see also CONTOUR—see also DRAFT-ING—see also DRAWING—see also GEOMETRY—see also HORI-ZON—see also HORIZONSCOPE—see also OBSERVATION—see also REPRESENTATION—see also SPACE—see also TOOL—see also VERTICAL.

LINK

1: A connecting structure, such as (a) a single ring or division of a chain; (b) one of the standardized divisions of a surveyor's chain that is 7.92 inches long and serves as a measure of length; (c) an intermediate rod or piece for transmitting force or motion, especially a short connecting rod with a hole or pin at each end; (d) the fusible member of an electrical fuse. 2: Something analogous to a *link* of chain, such as (a) a segment of sausage in a chain; (b) a connecting element or factor <found a *link* between smoking and cancer>; (c) a unit in a communication system; (d) an identifier attached to an element (as an index term) in a system in order to indicate or permit connection with other similarly identified elements, especially one <as a *hyperlink*> in a computer file.

Link, computer networking concepts, information technology: In hypertext, embedded instructions or codes that connect units of data. *Links* may take the form of highlighted text, images, or other indicators.

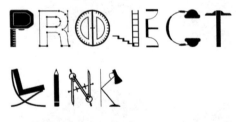

Project Link. Student Group. Project *Link* is a student-run organization at the Harvard GSD whose goals are to expand awareness and interest in design by offering introductory design workshops and lessons to Boston area youth. The program strives to foster the development of a broad range of design skills and to put students on track to explore their creative ideas at the collegiate level. The goal of the program is to cultivate greater diversity in the next generation of designers in order to expand the scope and influence of the profession itself. ⊛

Figure. Project Link (above).

See also CONNECTION—see also FENCE—see also PROJECT—see also WATER: Water, Aquatic Ecology, and Land-Water Linkages.

LISTEN

1: To pay attention to sound <*listen* to music>. 2: To hear something with thoughtful attention, give consideration <*listen* to a plea>. 3: To be alert to catch an expected sound <*listen* for his step>.

Symphony of the Air. Thesis. Timothy James Carey (MArch I), advised by Grace La.

"The ritual of *listening* today leads a double existence. Despite the history of the concert hall as a civic monument capable of condensing a crowd into a community, the custom of attending a performance of orchestral music as social and intellectual entertainment has ossified into a set of conventions at odds with contemporary life in the city. While the concert hall was conceived as a secluded auditorium that would awaken periodically to admit a devoted audience, the ability to *listen* to music outside of the concert hall through recordings has fostered a culture of solitary *listening* and omnivorous consumption, of which concert-hall attendance is only one component. In addressing this divide between the audience and the dispersed *listening* public, many orchestras now split their time between the public experience of the concert hall and the private experience of the recording studio. As a space within the city, the studio must sequester itself as a means of reaching a broader audience, while allowing the experience of music to become a personal and peripatetic one. The concert hall, on the other hand, faces the necessity of modulating into a model that addresses the dispersed *listening* public born through recording technology. This thesis investigates the ways in which a venue for orchestral music might reimagine itself in the face of a contemporary culture of *listening* that relies on both the auditorium and the recording studio as centers of production, using the radio and recording orchestras of the Czech Republic as a test case and the city of Prague as a site for design investigation." ⊛

Figure. Section Elevations (opposite page). Timothy James Carey (MArch I).

LIVELIHOOD

1: Means of support or subsistence.

Livelihoods & Urban Form: Mumbai in a Comparative Perspective. ADV 9129. Department of Urban Planning & Design. Seminar. Instructors: Rahul Mehrotra & Martha Chen.

Small-scale manufacturing in workshops and homes, small-scale trading on street corners or makeshift markets, car guarding, waste collecting, among a myriad of informal activities, is what characterizes as work and employment in most cities of the Global South. Statistics demonstrate that informal work, rather than being the exception, is one of the dominant modes of work in these cities. In India, 80 percent of the urban workforce is engaged in the informal economy and although individual incomes are low, cumulatively these activities contribute significantly to GDP.

Planners and designers have played a crucial role in both facilitating and hindering the *livelihood* activities of the working poor. Developing design imaginations for supporting these activities is an important contemporary challenge to local authorities, urban planners,

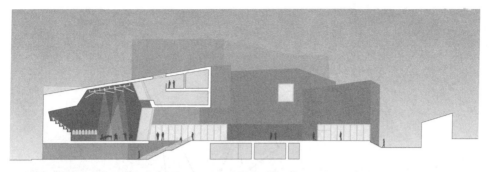

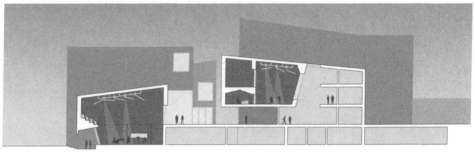

and designers across the globe. Much of the planning literature addresses the issue of "informality" very broadly, referring not only to forms of income generation but also modes of settlement, housing, and general modes of negotiating life in the city. This course specifically examined informal economies and their relationship to urban form. Mumbai was the focus of the course. The size and significance of the informal economy, a critical analysis of its nature, the role it plays in development, and how planning has and could potentially respond, were the central themes. ֎

LOBBY

Lobby, entrance spaces, rooms & spaces by function, components: Large halls serving as entrance spaces in public buildings or as anterooms, especially to legislative chambers. For entrance spaces in private houses, use "entrance halls."

See also BUILDING—see also CIRCULATION—see also CIVIC: Starbucks & Spiderman—see also DONUT—see also ELEMENT— see also HOUSING—see also SPACE.

LOTTERY

Lottery, contests, events, activities: Gambling contests in which prizes are distributed to the winners among those persons who have paid for a chance to win them.

Limited-Enrollment Lottery. At the beginning of each semester, students submit their top three choices for limited enrollment courses. Results, including wait lists, are posted online several hours after the *lottery* closes. Students are automatically enrolled in any courses successfully *lotteried* into. ֎

Studio Lottery. The Harvard GSD studio *lottery* occurs at the beginning of the semester, before the first day of classes. Students indicate their preferences for option studios by participating in the *lottery*. *Lottery* results are posted online by the end of the day. ֎

LUNAR

Lunar eclipse, astronomical, natural events: Occasions when the Moon is obscured to observers on Earth by the Moon passing through the Earth's shadow.

LYRICISM

1: The quality or state of being *lyric*, songfulness. 2: (a) An intense personal quality expressive of feeling or emotion in an art; (b) exuberance <the sort of author who inspires *lyricism* or invective, not judicious interpretation —*Time*>.

Le lyrisme des temps nouveaux et l'urbanisme. Publication. *Le Point*, no. 20, 1939. Le Corbusier (author). Le Corbusier Research Collection, Frances Loeb Library. LeC NA 2430 L496t.

"Here, Le Corbusier writes about beauty and artistic composition as being characterized by a system of proportion in harmony with the new Machine Age. Function and organization are imbued with a spiritual quality that expresses that synthesis. This synthesis is present at all scales—from volume to architecture to urbanism—and therefore poetically embodies the spirit of the times, a *lyricism* beyond the pure function and mechanics of the machine. A *lyricism*, a sensuality of expression, that goes beyond utility and encompasses beauty. Le Corbusier believes the architect is best equipped for this task at all scales of artistic intervention." —Inés Zalduendo. ֎

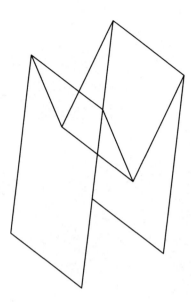

MACHINE

Machine, equipment by general type: Devices for applying mechanical power, replacing or assisting manual labor.

Propos d'urbanisme. *Publication.* Éditions Bourrelier et Cie, 1946. Le Corbusier (author). Le Corbusier Research Collection, Frances Loeb Library. LeC NAC 250 L496 1946.
"This is the last in a series of books on urbanism written by Le Corbusier during the postwar years (publications were architectural projects in the absence of built urban commissions). Here, he argues that the innovations of the *Machine* Age caused significant change (from trains and aircraft, to telegraph, telephone, and radio communication), which resulted in a civilization of production—over land, water, rail, and air. The effects are evident in patterns of settlement, which he describes in units of agricultural production, linear towns of industrial manufacturing, and concentric cities of business and administration. This requires studies of land distribution, population density, and new modes of occupying the land. Le Corbusier argues a new synthesis—for the need to reestablish harmony with the environment—and that architecture (as one of the arts) has agency in that synthesis." —Inés Zalduendo. ▓

See also CITY—see also COMPUTER—see also COMPUTATION: Paradigms in Computing—see also ERGONOMICS—see also FABRICATION—see also LASER—see also SHOP—see also TOOL.

MAGAZINE

Magazine, periodicals, serials, publications: Periodicals containing articles, essays, poems, or other writings by different authors, usually on a variety of topics and intended for a general reading public or treating a particular area of interest for a popular audience.

Harvard Design Magazine. *Publication.* Harvard GSD. Jennifer Sigler (editor in chief), Leah Whitman-Salkin (associate editor), and Meghan Ryan Sandberg (publications coordinator).
Relaunched in 2014, the twice yearly *Harvard Design Magazine* probes beyond the established design disciplines to enrich and diversify current discourse. Scholarly, poetic, and visually lush, each issue triggers new interpretations of the role of design today. Distinguished and unexpected voices from the fields of architecture, landscape architecture, and urban planning meet those from the realms of art, science, literature, and beyond. A space for dialogue, speculation, and surprise, *Harvard Design Magazine* opens a door onto the applied device of design, and the people, places, and politics it engages. ▓

See also HEALTH: Harvard Design Magazine No. 40—see also OCEAN: Harvard Design Magazine No. 39—see also PUBLICATION—see also WRITING.

MAKING

1: The act or process of forming, causing, doing, or coming into being. 2: A process or means of advancement or success. 3: Something *made*, especially a quantity produced at one time. 4: (a) Potentiality—often used in plural <had the *makings* of a great artist>; (b) the material from which something is to be made.

Figure, Photograph (opposite page). Brian Y. Chu (MArch II).

See also COMPUTATION: Paradigms in Computing—see also MATERIAL—see also MODEL—see also MODERN: Making the

Modern Landscape—see also PRACTICE—see also PROCESS—see also REAL ESTATE—see also SPACE: Spaces of Living for the Subsystem Human Being—see also SYSTEM—see also TECHNIQUE—see also TIME.

MALL

Pedestrian *mall*, walkways, open spaces by function: Open public areas, walks, or plazas, often lined with trees, shrubs, or shops, reserved for use by pedestrians. Shopping *mall*, shopping centers, commercial complexes: Structure or series of structures, either under a single roof or in open air, designed to house multiple retail outlets and to allow free passage of pedestrians on one or more levels.

See also BUILDING—see also CIRCULATION—see also PROMENADE—see also STRUCTURE—see also WALKING.

MANAGEMENT

Management, organizational functions, functions by general context: Functions including organizing, supervising, and carrying out the activities of a person, group, organization, or enterprise, and controlling its human and material resources, involving primarily the application rather than the formulation of policy. When the formulation of policy is the primary aspect, use "administration."

A Sustainable Future for Exuma: Environmental Management, Design, and Planning. Engagement Report. Publication. Harvard GSD, 2014. Mohsen Mostafavi & Gareth Doherty (authors). HT395.B24 2014.

This multiyear ecological planning project is a collaboration among the Government of the Bahamas, the Bahamas National Trust, and the Harvard GSD. The goal is to facilitate the design and *management* of a sustainable future for the Exuma archipelago and the Bahamas generally. The project has two parallel and mutually informing components: research and education. These components work to inform the development of proposals and interventions as well as the building of capabilities for local empowerment. ֍

See also BUILDING—see also COLLECTION—see also DATA—see also ENVIRONMENT—see also POLICY—see also RISK—see also SUSTAINABILITY—see also URBAN—see also WASTE—see also WATER.

MAP

Digital *map*, computer-assisted *maps*: Refers to *maps* that are stored in digital form, which is data recorded by digits or similar discrete elements compatible with storage and manipulation in a computer. *Map*, documents, cartographic materials: Refers to graphic or photogrammetric representations of the Earth's surface or a part of it, including physical features and political boundaries, where each point corresponds to a geographical or celestial position according to a definite scale or projection. The term may also refer to similar depictions

of other planets, suns, other heavenly bodies, or areas of the heavens. *Maps* are typically depicted on a flat medium, such as on paper, a wall, or a computer screen. For similar depictions on a sphere, use "globes (cartographic spheres)."

See also CARTOGRAPHY—see also CIRCULATION—see also CITY—see also CLIMATE—see also CONTOUR—see also DATA—see also DIGITAL—see also GEOLOGY—see also HYDROLOGY—see also INFORMATION—see also REPRESENTATION—see also RISK—see also SOFTWARE: From Drones to Data Portals and Maps—see also SOIL—see also SURFACE—see also TOPOGRAPHY—see also TRANSPORTATION.

MAPPING

Digital *mapping*, cartography, discipline: Cartography in which the points and lines that comprise a map are digitized as computer data. Texture *mapping*, digital imaging, electronic imaging: Texture *mapping* is the application of a two-dimensional image file containing texture, color, or surface detail to a three-dimensional model or computer-generated graphic.

Digital Mapping & Design Choices for International Development. Lecture. Gund Hall, Room 517. November 14, 2014. Harvard Urban Planning Organization, Master in Design Studies Risk & Resilience program, and the Center for Geographic Analysis. Joseph Agoada. ֍

Mapping Cultural Space: Sites, Systems, and Practices Across Eurasia. ADV 9137. Department of Urban Planning & Design. Seminar. Fall 2014. Instructors: Eve Blau & Julie Buckler.

The seminar explored the significance of cultural space as both an object and a tool of analysis focusing on Eurasia, an area of the world where political and cultural boundaries have been repeatedly reconfigured. Overlapping geographical and cultural interests were brought together in the *mapping* theme, as students considered practices of *mapping* cultural space in different disciplinary modes and examined *mapping* practices as forms of cultural politics. Cultural space, in this understanding, denoted cultural zones, physical or virtual, geographical or imagined, that are produced, sustained, monitored, and contested by human practices. ֍

Mapping: Geographic Representation and Speculation. SCI 6322. Department of Urban Planning & Design. Seminar. Spring 2015. Instructor: Robert Gerard Pietrusko.

Maps do not represent reality, they create it. As a fundamental part of the design process, the act of *mapping* results in highly authored views of a site. By choosing what features, forces, and flows to highlight—and implicitly, which to exclude—the designer first creates the reality into which their intervention will be situated and discussed. Furthermore, the usage and materiality of space is increasingly measured, categorized, and circulated by all manners of institutions; these competing data representations often become the primary way of understanding and responding to a site. Designers are in the difficult position of approaching these geographic data sets critically while simultaneously employing them in their work. It is not enough to represent complicated networks of site forces and interactions as a neutral backdrop to one's design; we are

tasked with actively shaping them. It is within the framework of a highly authored design process that this course presented the fundamentals of geographic analysis and visualization.

Over the course of a semester, students worked extensively with techniques of geospatial analysis in Geographic Information System (GIS). Using ESRI's ArcMap software, students explored data sources, data models, topological overlays, map algebra, spatial statistics, terrain analysis, and suitability modeling. ֎

Figure. Model (previous page). Seunghoon Hyun (MAUD) & Boram Lee Jung (MDes, ULE).

See also ATLAS—see also CARTOGRAPHY—see also CATALOGUE—see also COMPUTER—see also CONNECTION—see also DATA—see also DIGITAL—see also DRONE—see also GEOGRAPHY—see also INFORMATION—see also LANDSCAPE—see also MEGA: Kumbh Mela—see also MODEL—see also PROCESS—see also REPRESENTATION—see also SITE—see also SOFTWARE—see also SPACE—see also TECHNIQUE—see also SYSTEM—see also 2-D—see also 3-D.

MARKET

Market, structures, mercantile buildings, commercial buildings: Buildings or outdoor areas where trade is conducted, often optimized for a gathering together of people for the purchase and sale of produce and livestock. *Markets* typically have booths or stalls for individual merchants, either in open air or under a single large roof.

Harvard Farmers' Market. Harvard Dining Services organizes two farmers' *markets* during the summer—one in the Science Center Plaza on Tuesdays and another in Allston on Fridays. ֎

Quincy Market. Quincy Hall was constructed between 1824 and 1826 and was named in honor of Josiah Quincy III, the former Mayor of Boston, who organized its construction. The *market* complex is adjacent to Faneuil Hall in downtown Boston.

See also AGORA—see also BUILDING—see also ECONOMIC—see also STRUCTURE—see also SUPERMARKET.

MATERIAL

Building *material, materials* by function: Structural products, manufactured as standard units, intended for use in building construction. *Material* culture, anthropology, behavioral sciences: Study of the physical objects made by a people for satisfaction of their needs, especially those articles required for sustenance and perpetuation of life.

Material Ecologies Workshop. SCI 6327. Department of Landscape Architecture. Seminar. Spring 2015. Instructor: Jane Hutton.

Landscapes are shaped by continuous flows of *materials* and energy driven by anthropogenic and nonanthropogenic forces. Designers participate in this reorganization of *materials* around the globe, the great majority of which is bound as urban parks, buildings, and highways. In landscape architecture, these *mate-*

rials range from abiotic to biotic composition from simple to complex manufacturing processes, and from local to distant sources. While *materials* are selected for ecological, structural, and aesthetic performance characteristics desired for a particular site, their production is linked to a network of distant forests, quarries, and factories. Through *material* specifications, designers inadvertently transform remote landscapes, concealed and abstracted through the commodification of natural resources. Typically outside of the designer's purview, these relationships are critical to reconceptualize the present and future of landscape construction.

This seminar aimed to expand the consideration of *materials* in design beyond a single-state, incorporating multiscalar, sociometabolic lenses to better grasp the scope of *material* practice for design. The course simultaneously examined theories and metrics associated with *material* practice, including urban metabolism, *materialism,* and labor history, through spatial and temporal frameworks. Structured as a collaborative research workshop, the course was driven by reading discussions, lectures, and site and archival research, and the Harvard GSD *Materials* Collection. ֎

Material Performance: Composite Morphology & Fibrous Tectonics. STU 1307. Department of Architecture. Option Studio. Fall 2014. Instructor: Achim Menges.

A new understanding of the *material* in architecture is beginning to arise. No longer are we bound to conceive of the digital realm as separated from the physical world. Instead, we can begin to explore computation as an intense interface with *material* and vice versa. Thus *materiality* no longer remains a fixed property and passive receptor of form, but transforms into an active generator of design and adaptive agent of architectural performance. Accordingly, and in contrast to linear and mechanistic modes of fabrication and construction, *materialization* now coexists with design as explorative robotic processes. This presents a radical departure from both the trite Modernist truth to *materials* and the dismissal of *material* altogether as emblematic for the previous generation of digital architecture.

The studio explored the notion of *material* performance, its manifold and deep interrelations with technology, biology, and culture as a central field of architectural inquiry. It sought to trace the emergence of new *material* cultures within the context of the ever-accelerating integrative technologies of design computation and robotic fabrication with a particular focus on advanced fiber composite *materials.* Students were introduced to a design approach that bridged between the cultural and technical dimension of fibrous *materials* in architecture and the rich repertoire of fibrous *material* organizations in nature. Most biological systems are natural fiber composite structures, and their astounding level of performative capacity and *material* resourcefulness unfolds from morphological differentiation, which is the process of each element's response and adaptation to its specific environment. Based on an understanding of microscale *material* makeup, mesoscale *material* systems, and macroscale architecture as reciprocal and instrumental relationships, students investigated biological and technological fibrous systems, experimented with robotic fiber lay-up and filament winding processes, and pursued the development of fibrous tectonics in architecture as novel spatial, structural, and ecological potentials. They engaged with a computational design approach that conceived of *materiality* and *materialization*

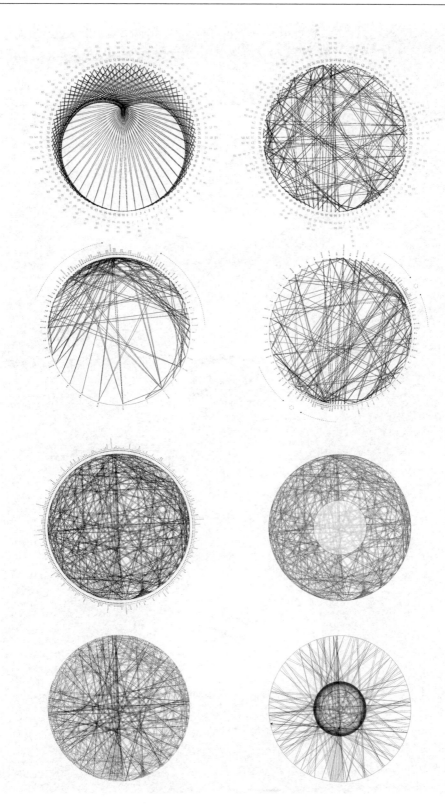

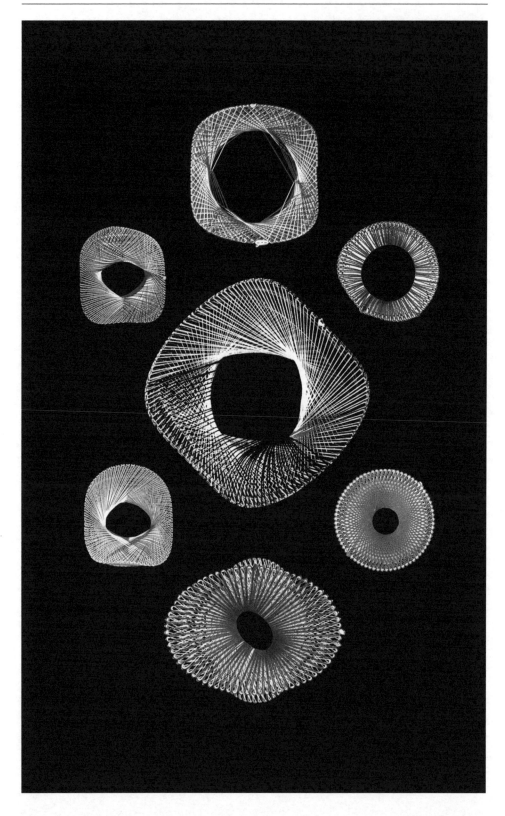

as active generators of form, space, and structure, uncovering novel, performative capacities and hitherto unexplored architectural possibilities.

Students: Alice Wan Chai (MArch II), Erin Golden Cuevas (MArch II), Niccolo Dambrosio (MArch II), Iman Salam Fayyad (MArch I), Joshua Bremner Feldman (MArch I), Michael Joseph Johnson (MArch II), Wenling Li (MLA II), Ping Lu (MArch II), Jana Marie Masset (MArch II), Christopher Michael Meyer (MArch II), Nancy Ellen Nichols (MArch I), Chase Addison Pitner (MArch II), Stefan Stanojevic (MArch II). ֍

Figures. Diagrams (previous page). Erin Golden Cuevas (MArch II), Michael Joseph Johnson (MArch II), and Jana Marie Masset (MArch II). Models (opposite page). Iman Salam Fayyad (MArch I) & Joshua Bremner Feldman (MArch I).

Material Processes & Systems (MaPS) Group. Design Lab. Martin Bechthold, Leire Asensio Villoria, and Panagiotis Michalatos. The *Material* Processes & Systems Group pursues the understanding, development, and deployment of innovative technologies in the promotion of design as an agent of change and in the quest for a better future. ֍

See also ASSEMBLY—see also AUDIOVISUAL: Six Microphones—see also BUILDING—see also COLOR—see also CONSTRUCTION—see also CULTURE—see also DISTRIBUTE: Material Distributions—see also ENERGY—see also ERGONOMICS—see also EXERGY: Low-Exergy Communities—see also FABRICATION—see also HABOOB: Dust Kingdom—see also HYPEROBJECT: The Proximities of Nuclear Waste—see also INSULATION: Insulating Modernism—see also LANDFORM: Landformation Catalogue—see also MECHANISM: Expanded Mechanisms/Empirical Materialisms—see also MODEL—see also NUCLEAR: Fatal Vitality—see also OBJECT—see also PLANT—see also POWER: Cambridge Talks IX—see also PRACTICE—see also PROCESS—see also PROJECT—see also PROTOTYPE—see also SKYSCRAPER: Wood Skyscraper—see also SURFACE—see also TECHNIQUE—see also WALL: Working Matter.

MATTER

1: (a) A subject under consideration; (b) a subject of disagreement or litigation; (c) the events or circumstances of a particular situation; (d) something of an indicated kind or having to do with an indicated field or situation <this is a serious *matter*> <as a *matter* of policy> <*matters* of faith>; (f) something to be proved in law; (g) a source especially of feeling or emotion; (h) problem, difficulty. 2: (a) The substance of which a physical object is composed; (b) material substance that occupies space, has mass, and is composed predominantly of atoms consisting of protons, neutrons, and electrons, that is interconvertible with energy; (c) a material substance of a particular kind or for a particular purpose. 3: (a) The indeterminate subject of reality, especially the element in the universe that undergoes formation and alteration; (b) the formless substratum of all things which exists only potentially and upon which form acts to produce realities. 4: A more or less definite amount or quantity <cooks in a *matter* of minutes>. 5: Something written or printed.

Architecture Matters. South America Project Lecture. Gund Hall, Piper Auditorium. March 23, 2015. Jean Pierre Crousse with Felipe Correa.

In a talk titled "Architecture *Matters*," Jean Pierre Crousse, principal of Barclay and Crousse, argued that architecture is fabricated by *matter*—not only the physical *matter* that shapes the ways in which a project becomes a building, but also the cultural, personal, social, technological, and local background. Crousse showed that in projects of Barclay and Crousse, a multidimensional approach emerged naturally and nurtured each project differently, at the scale of both the landscape and the detail, for the sake of local pertinence. ֍

Black Lives Matter. Installation. Gund Hall, Studio Trays. May 2015. GSD African American Student Union.

The African American Student Union, in conjunction with numerous volunteers, showcased a Black Lives *Matter* installation on the Gund Hall studio trays. Photographs displayed a small fraction of Black and Brown people who lost their lives due to instances of police brutality. The length of Gund Hall was transformed into a timeline of the previous nine months—from Michael Brown in Ferguson, Missouri, to Freddie Gray in Baltimore, Maryland. The installation served as an acknowledgment of each of these lives lost, with the hope of confronting the systemic inequities and poor race relations that are pervasive across the United States. Institutionalized racism has disenfranchised entire populations and directly resulted in the death of countless Black men and women. In the wake of the 2015 protests in Baltimore, and the resurgence of the Black Lives *Matter* movement, the installation attempted to address the role of designers in the American landscape of race relations. ֍

MATRIX

1: Something within or from which something else originates, develops, or takes form. 2: (a) A mold from which a relief surface is made; (b) an engraved or inscribed die or stamp; (c) an electroformed impression of a phonograph record used for mass-producing duplicates of the original. 3: (a) The natural material in which something is embedded; (b) material in which something is enclosed or embedded. 4: (a) The extracellular substance in which tissue cells are embedded. 5: (a) A rectangular array of mathematical elements that can be combined to form sums and products with similar arrays having an appropriate number of rows and columns; (b) something resembling a mathematical *matrix* especially in rectangular arrangement of elements into rows and columns; (c) an array of circuit elements for performing a specific function. 6: A main clause that contains a subordinate clause.

MEASURE

Measure, board rules, rulers by function: *Measuring* devices, usually in the form of flat sticks, bearing various scales for computing board feet. *Measure,* safety: The condition of being safe, free from danger.

Seven Studies. Exhibition. Kirkland Gallery. November 6–12, 2014. Joanne K. Cheung (MArch I) & Farhad Mirza (MArch I).

Measurement is an exercise in comparison, communication, and translation. To *measure* is to presuppose

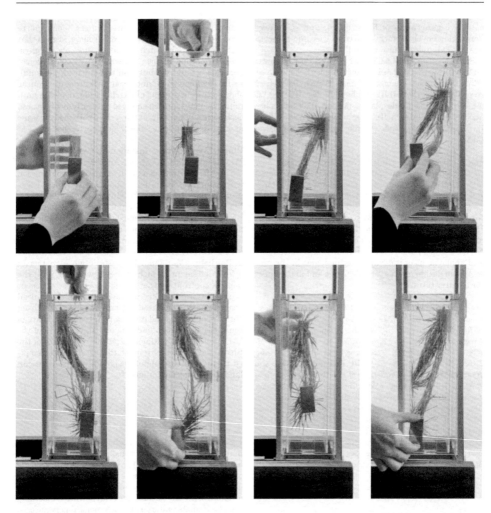

a certain contiguity between fields that are immeasurable. "Seven Studies," an exhibition at the Kirkland Gallery, documented its own making—a study that unfolded over the course of one week. 🔊

See also BODY—see also ERROR: The Architecture of Error—see also STUDY—see also TOOL.

MECHANISM

1: (a) A piece of machinery; (b) a process, technique, or system for achieving a result. 2: *Mechanical* operation or action. 3: A doctrine that holds natural processes to be *mechanically* determined and capable of complete explanation by the laws of physics and chemistry. 4: The fundamental processes involved in or responsible for an action, reaction, or other natural phenomenon.

Expanded Mechanisms/Empirical Materialisms. SCI 6436. Department of Architecture. Seminar. Instructor: Andrew Witt.

Machines and material are vitally connected and reciprocally constrained. Each responds dynamically to the other through a range of geometric, chemical, and physical events that the designer must choreograph to deliberate effect. Today, this dynamic interaction can be automated, but its full spatial and formal potential can only be interrogated through active invention. Just as scripting allows designers to make new tools, hacking enables the creation of new machines and, perhaps, new modes of material operation.

In this class, students made machines to create new material effects. The horizon of the class was bounded by the physics of materials themselves. The rules of material change—bending radii, elastic limits, viscosity, and so forth—were instrumental in the machine design, becoming geometric laws and ultimately *mechanical* rules that shaped elastic design ambitions. There was a particular interest in formed materials and parametric molds: the bending, forming, stamping, casting of concrete, glass, metal, Plexiglas, and wood. But machine operation may also be chemical or even geomorphic, and the class researched processes such as accelerated weathering, erosion, deposition, corrosion, and state change. The machines operated on typical materials up to and exceeding their elastic limit—to breaking, shredding, shattering—to open the possibility for reconstitution in a transformed state. The course

encouraged material hacking, or the evocative discovery of alternative systems through radical experimentation. The specific tactile and textural qualities of the result was an integral part of the experiment.

The course drew on a library of historical precedents for automatic form-making over the last two centuries including drawing machines, model machines, fabrication machines, and machines for simulating sensations as precedents to our current digital tools. With each historical evolution of machinery—for drawing, glass forming, metal bending, concrete shaping, and so forth—students deconstructed and diagrammed the parametric motions that defined their kinetic transformations, and traced the *mechanical* limits of form as a limit of design itself. ⊛

Figure. Models (opposite page & above). Julia Michalski (MArch II) & Catherine Soderberg (MArch II).

MEDIA

Media, artists' materials, materials by function: The materials that are applied to a support in the making of a work of art, such as ink on paper or oil paint on canvas; often a particular technique or techniques are closely associated with the *media*. *Media*, information storage: The physical material or substance or electronic components upon and by which information can be recorded or stored, including electronic and physical materials. Mass *media*, culture-related concepts: Means of communication designed to reach large numbers of people, such as hard copy or online newspapers, radio, and television, regarded collectively.

Designed Porous Media. SCI 6453. Department of Architecture. Seminar. Spring 2015. Instructor: Salmaan Craig.

How do trees get their shape and why is this shape so similar to other natural forms such as river deltas, lungs, and lighting strikes? Focus on the form too hard and you will miss the process that generated it. Instead, think of the currents that flow through the form and how those currents interact with the surrounding medium. Think of a tree as a splaying bundle of pipes, whose purpose is to transport water from the ground to the atmosphere. In return for the water (and with the help of sunlight), the pipe-bundle extracts carbon dioxide from the air, which it uses as a construction material

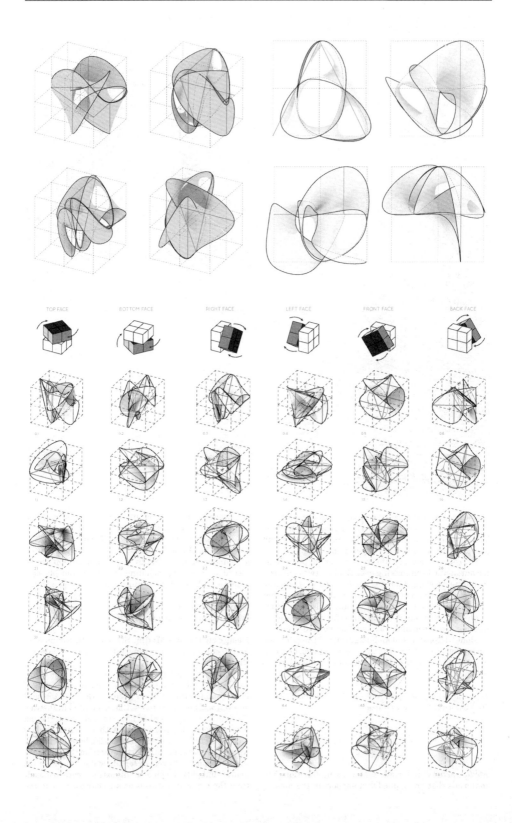

TOP FACE   BOTTOM FACE   RIGHT FACE   LEFT FACE   FRONT FACE   BACK FACE

to add new pipes and build the existing pipes taller. The deeper the pipe-bundle penetrates and splays into the atmosphere, the wetter the atmosphere gets. So a tree is an upward flow of water, supported by a material made from the thin air that surrounds it, and plastered into a shape that reads as a physical transcript of the amplifying communication between two *media*—the ground and the air.

This course was about reconfiguring materials and buildings to better orchestrate the currents of heat and mass that flow through them. The starting point was to recognize that the space we inhabit is not empty, but filled with a fluid called air and streams of photons from different places. The first two sessions were a mix of lectures and exercises to encourage students to think about the inner architecture of materials and the sculpting of thermal flows. The next five sessions were dedicated to different types of designed porous *media*, with a mix of contextual and technical lectures, class exercises, and short hands-on assignments employing a variety of imaging, analysis, and testing techniques to understand how each of the material-technologies work. The final project was a design project—a self-regulating and habitable "organ" for a desert climate, which combined the different designed porous *media*.

Digital Media I. VIS 2223. Department of Architecture. Seminar. Fall 2014. Instructor: Christopher Charles Hoxie.

This course sought to position the role of digital *media* within the broader context of digital practice and to examine the generative capacities of the *medium* to design and communicate ideas in the virtual realm. The goal of the course was to establish a core visual literacy in digital *media* by considering work across a range of disciplines, including: photography, film, lighting design, synthetic imaging, and animation. The course examined the construction and representation of environments through the integration of form, light, material, color, atmosphere, and photography. Investigations varied in scale from one-to-one virtual simulations of materials and details, to interior and architectural scales, to urban and landscape scales. This course was aimed at developing foundational skills in still-image development, lighting design and analysis, material exploration and prototyping, site modeling and scene population, photography, compositing and post production.

Although the emphasis was on still-image development, there was an extensive use of animation, serialized imagery, and iterative workflows to develop dynamic representations of the built environment across a range of perceptual models. Software use was based on a Rhino modeling workflow, with scene management, population, and rendering development in 3ds Max and V-Ray, and a postproduction workflow based on Adobe After Effects and Photoshop.

Digital Media II. VIS 2224. Department of Architecture. Seminar. Fall 2014. Instructor: Andrew Witt.

This class explored the design and science of logical form making, examined through geometry, parametric control, algorithms, and digital tools. The point of departure was a cumulative sequence of fundamental topics and problems in design geometry, which have recurring impact on the history of form. These problems provided a context and pretext for a rigorous introduction to parametric modeling, algorithmic automation, and the mathematical principles underpinning them.

These logical investigations of modeling cultivated a certain objective approach to form that explored the application of parametric approaches that were both deductive (i.e., topological classifications, surface characteristics, and pattern logics) and empirical (i.e., material deformation and generative detailing). Thematically, the course fostered an integrated understanding of topics such as parametric geometry definition, surface geometry qualification, and the converse dynamics of packing and subdivision. As a part of the course, students learned to use the parametric design tools Grasshopper, Python, and Digital Project to interrogate and permute these design problems.

Figure. Diagrams (opposite page). David Benard Hamm (MArch I) & Davis Shimon Owen (MArch I).

See also COLOR—see also COMMUNICATION—see also COMPUTER—see also CULTURE—see also DATA: Data Across Scales—see also FILM: Assistance Moretelle—see also MATERIAL—see also METHODOLOGY: Media as Method—see also POWER: Cambridge Talks IX—see also REPRESENTATION—see also TECHNIQUE—see also WORKSHOP: Digital Media Workshops—see also WRITING.

MEGA

1: Vast <a *mega* electronics store>. 2: Of the highest level of rank, excellence, or importance <a number one hit made her *mega*>.

Kumbh Mela: Mapping the Ephemeral Mega-City. Exhibition. Loeb House & the Center for Government and International Studies, Knafel Building. April–July 2015. Harvard South Asian Institute. Rahul Mehrotra, Luis Felipe Vera Benitez, Megan Panzano, Joshua Jonathan Mauch, and Joanna Vouriotis.

In 2013, over 50 Harvard University professors, students, administrative staff, and medical practitioners made the pilgrimage to the Kumbh Mela site in Allahabad, India, to analyze issues that emerge in large-scale human gatherings. The *Kumbh Mela: Mapping the Ephemeral Mega-City* exhibition and book consolidated the research findings and serves as an example of interdisciplinary research conducted at Harvard University.

See also CITY: Unplugged City—see also METABOLISM—see also TYPOLOGY: Air Frontier.

MEMORIAL

Memorial, structures, ceremonial structures, single built works by function: Structures built to preserve the memory of beings or events. For other objects created, issued, or worn to commemorate persons or events, use "commemoratives."

Abstracted Geologies: Disseminated Substrate Galleries to Memorialize Internment Experience. Thesis. Megan Jones Shiotani (MLA I), advised by Jill Desimini.

"This thesis proposes sectional terrain non-sites to be disseminated in a global *memorial* exchange with Topaz, Utah, one of ten sites of Japanese American internment from 1942 to 1945. The topological surface at Topaz illustrates the forced isolation of a cosmopolitan commu-

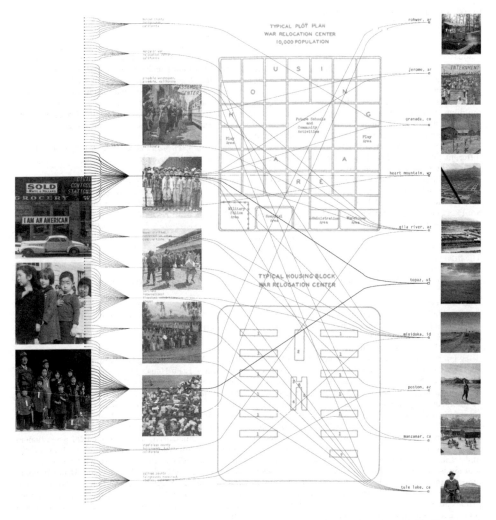

nity into a temporary prison city within a remote alkaline desert. Microbial soil crusts and minute lichen blooms wrap a carpet of construction remnants and abandoned internee possessions.

How can design foster terrain interpretation on a global scale when a site is defined by its remoteness? The *memorial* is driven by confinement and dispersal. Large-scale earthworks are dug from Topaz and placed in distant locations connected to internment history. These relocated non-sites are galleries and deposition areas for new activity layers that encourage audiences to interpret and engage with each palimpsest. In exchange, material markers at Topaz connect the vacant voids with the distant constructions. The duration of the exchange follows the timeline of exclusion—from February 19, 1942, to March 20, 1945—four years, one month, and one day. After this length of time, each earthwork is placed back in Topaz, altered by its past internment.

The thesis has three components: (1) a design strategy for Topaz, offering plans for circulation, voids, and methods of extraction; (2) a design strategy for the dislocated earthworks; and (3) a guide for the continual exchange of confinement *memorials*, including exchange

markers, priority origin locations within Topaz, and potential destinations worldwide." §

Figure. Diagram (above). Megan Jones Shiotani (MLA I).

See also LANDSCAPE—see also PALIMPSEST—see also PROJECT—see also STRUCTURE.

MEMORY

Memory, psychological concepts, social science concepts: The mental capacity or faculty of retaining and recalling facts, events, impressions, or recognizing previous experience.

Dirty Stories. Installation. Kirkland Gallery. March 23–31, 2015. Vero Rose Smith (MDes, ADPD).

To recapture some of the mysticism of earthly closeness, and to remind visitors that one's footsteps (environmental and otherwise) are usually heavier than intended, *memories* of soil were reconstituted in dirt on the gallery floor. Visitors were invited to read, write, and reimagine their own relationship with the world. "Dirty Stories" was a reminder of the imminent extinction of experience. ⊛

Ecologies of Memory: Landscape Architectural Methods in an Expanded Consideration of Culture. Thesis. Sara Zewde (MLA I), advised by Anita Berrizbeitia.

"Ecologies of *Memory* proposes a methodological framework for analyzing and designing for spatial cultures and aims to expand landscape architectural traditions and typologies. The framework is tested and evolved through the act of designing for the Pequena Africa region of Rio de Janeiro, Brazil, where excavation for an urban development project led to the 2011 discovery of the ruins of an infamous slave port. Using the proposed methodological framework, the project extracts a set of spatial strategies from local manifestations of Afro-Brazilian ecologies of *memory* and applies them the design of a constellation of everyday spaces in the region." ⊛

We Exist! We Exist! (We're Really Happy). Performance. Kirkland Gallery. April 3–4, 2015. Sophie R. Maguire (MLA I) & Lily Ockwell.

"We Exist! We Exist!" was a performative interlude exploring the segmented manifestation of the *memories* we hold and the *memories* we bury. ⊛

See also ART—see also COMPUTER—see also CULTURE—see also EXPERIENCE—see also GALLERY—see also HISTORY—see also HUMAN—see also INSTALLATION—see also PERFORMANCE—see also PROCESS—see also TIME—see also WELL-BEING.

META

Metadata, information: A data set that describes and provides information about other data.

metaLAB. Berkman Center for Internet & Society. The *metaLAB* is a program of the Berkman Center for Internet & Society that serves as an institutional hub for Harvard University's digital art, design, and humanities' communities while actively collaborating with partners both locally and worldwide.

METABOLISM

Metabolism, biological concept, scientific concept: The sum of all chemical and physical processes within a living organism and also the energy made available for various forms of work. *Metabolism*, design styles and movements: Japanese architectural movement of the 1960s and 1970s, dedicated to urban-scale issues based on biologic principles of dynamic growth and change.

New Geographies 06: Grounding Metabolism. Publication. Harvard University Press, 2014. Daniel Ibañez Moreno (DDes) & Nikolaos Katsikis (DDes) (editors). HT169.55.N46 2014.

The design disciplines have always recognized the potential of urban *metabolism* to shape spatial strategies, from Patrick Geddes's Valley Section to the megastructures of the Japanese *Metabolists*. Historically confined to the regional scale, today's generalized urbanization

is characterized by an unprecedented complexity and planetary upscaling of *metabolic* relations. Most contemporary discussions of *metabolism* have failed to integrate formal, spatial, and material attributes. Technoscientific approaches have been limited to a performative interpretation of flows, while more theoretical attempts to interrogate the sociopolitical embeddedness of *metabolic* processes have largely ignored their formal spatial registration. Within this context, the design disciplines—fascinated by the fluidity of *metabolic* processes—have privileged notions of elasticity without regard for the often sclerotic quality of landscapes and infrastructures. *New Geographies 06* aims to trace alternative, synthetic routes to design through a more elaborate understanding of the relation between *metabolic* models and concepts and the formal, physical, and material specificities of spatial structures across scales. This required addressing the planetary dimension of contemporary *metabolic* processes and critically examining the long lineage of discussions and approaches on *metabolism*. ⊛

Figure. New Geographies 06: Ground Metabolism Publication (above).

Urban Metabolism. Student Group. In recent years the concept of *metabolism* has increasingly mobilized in a diverse range of debates as a means to analyze and theorize the city. Generally, these debates coincide with the need to provide analytic frameworks and methodologies to understand urbanization as a process, with particular emphasis on the relations between biophysical and social processes. ⊛

See also CITY—see also DISCIPLINE—see also FLOW—see also GEOGRAPHY—see also PROCESS—see also TRANSFORMATION—see also URBANISM.

METHODOLOGY

Methodology, multidisciplinary concepts: A body of *methods*, procedures, working concepts, rules, and postulates employed by a science, art, or discipline.

Research Methods in Landscape Architecture.
ADV 9644. Department of Landscape Architecture. Seminar. Spring 2015. Instructor: Edward Eigen.

This seminar offered an overview of various types and practices of research *methodology* in contemporary landscape architecture. Central to the ambitions of the course was the belief that landscape architecture has cultivated a series of research modalities that are simultaneously unique to the discipline and at the same time reflective of universal issues in social science and environmental science-based research. Consequently, the course positioned contemporary practices in the broader context of historical evolutions and epistemological questions. Practices explored included displacement and representation, occupation, observation, social survey, crowdsourcing, inventory, morphological measurement, and additional qualitative and quantitative *methods*. ⑨

Media as Method.
ADV 9660. Departments of Architecture, Landscape Architecture, and Urban Planning & Design. Seminar. Spring 2015. Instructors: Pierre Bélanger & Kiel Moe.

Today, the models of thought and levels of cognition that underlie the tools and technologies we use on a daily basis, and over long periods of time, remain fundamentally misunderstood or overlooked. From the measures and materials to the techniques and technologies upon which we preconceive ideas, there is an underlying imperative to reconsider the models of research that precondition our motivations in design. The course served as an introduction and advanced inquiry into research *methods*, means, and media. With attention to media and documentation, the course looked at different representational *methodologies* associated with contemporary projects to establish advanced modes of research through representation. From the basics of writing, to the advancements of publishing, to the complexities of making, the course encouraged the formulation of contemporary, experimental, and risky projects where design opens new and unprecedented possibilities of collaboration and practice. Documentation therefore played an important role in the course in order to extend longevity of research, build impact, and grow public audiences over time. ⑨

See also CITY: Unplugged City—see also COPY: Copy As Method—see also DISCIPLINE—see also MEDIA—see also MEMORY: Ecologies of Memory—see also PRACTICE—see also PROCESS—see also QUANTITATIVE—see also QUALITATIVE—see also TECHNIQUE—see also UNDISCIPLINED.

MIGRATION

Migration, function by general context, activities: The function of moving from one country, region, or place to settle in another. *Migration*, journeys, events, activities: Occurrences of populations or groups traveling from one locality or habitat to another, usually for specific purposes such as resettlement, feeding, or breeding. With regard to human beings, refers to the changing of permanent residence (conventionally understood as being for at least one year) by discrete populations.

Migration: Storytelling the City/Alienation. The Sadness of Cities.
Lecture. Gund Hall, Piper Auditorium. October 22, 2014. Harvard South Asia Institute. Suketu Mehta.

Writer Suketu Mehta looked at the urban human being, exploring themes of *migration*, loneliness, and community in the world's cities. Mehta is the author of *Maximum City: Bombay Lost and Found.* ⑨

See also DIASPORA—The Diasporic Return of Capital.

MIXED-USE

Mixed-use, use, functional concepts: Use to describe projects or buildings when there is a highly site-intensive mixture of several different, major, revenue-producing functions involved. *Mixed-use* development, complexes by development practice: Relatively large-scale real estate projects incorporating several revenue-producing functions, having a highly intensive use of land, and developed from a coherent plan.

See also BUILDING—see also DEVELOPMENT—see also GRID: Rethinking Urban Grids in Hangzhou—see also PROJECT—see also REAL ESTATE.

MODEL

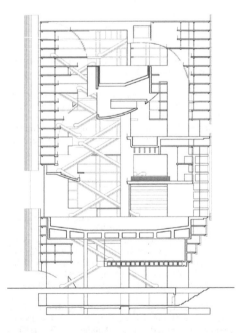

Architectural *model*, scale *models*, visual & verbal communication: Representations that visualize architectural projects in three dimensions, often including a representation of the surrounding site or context, and often, but not necessarily, built to scale. *Model*, concepts relating to the creative process, artistic concepts: Something that serves as an ideal, a pattern to follow or copy, or source of inspiration to a creator. Digital terrain *modeling*: Computer software technique for rendering virtual *models* of three-dimensional terrain. Historical *model*, visual works by function, visual & verbal communication: *Models* that are intended to represent how something, as a building, a ship, or a city, looked at a previous time. For drawings or full-scale new objects or structures made with similar intent, use "reconstructions." *Model* city, settlements by planning concepts, built environment: Urban areas or communities whose design incorporates innovative attempts at solving specific social and physical problems; often applied to the redesign of existing settlements in the 19th and 20th centuries. For 19th-century cities built with prescribed forms to fulfill specific military or economic ideals, use "ideal cities." *Model*-making, object-making processes & techniques: The creation of scaled representations of objects or structures, usually three-dimensional and made of hard, non-malleable material such as wood or stone. For the creation of malleable material such as wax or clay to create a form which is three-dimensional, see "*modeling*." *Model*, visual works by function, visual & verbal communication: Refers to scaled representations of objects or structures, usually three-dimensional. Scale *model*, visual works by function, visual & verbal communication: Representations or copies of an object that are larger or smaller than the actual size of the object being represented, and manufactured precisely according to relative size. Typically, the scale *model* is smaller than the original and used for illustrating the object, for a toy or collectible, or as a guide to constructing it in full size. Scale *models* may be one- or two-dimensional. Scale *models* are generally built according to a standard scale for the particular product; *model* ships may be 1:500 scale and doll house furniture may be 1:12 scale. Study *model*: Architectural *models* made to help clarify and visualize aspects of a project during the design process.

Architecture & the Territory: Models for Scholarship & Practice. Aga Khan Program Lecture. Gund Hall, Piper Auditorium. January 29, 2015. Shahira Fahmy & Diane Singerman. 🕮

Spectacular Simplicity: New Models for Design Research. Grounded Visionaries Design Weekend Lecture. Gund Hall, Piper Auditorium. September 13, 2014. Ann Forsyth, Michael Hooper, Jane Hutton, Grace La, Ali Malkawi, Farshid Moussavi, Antoine Picon, and Andrew Witt. 🕮

Figure. Section (opposite page). Chang Su (MArch I AP). Photograph (next spread). Relate: Fourth Semester Architecture Core Studio Review.

See also CAMPUS: A Campus for the 21st Century—see also CITY—see also COLOR—see also COMMUNICATION—see also COMPUTATION: Paradigms in Computing: Making, Machines, and Models for Design Agency in Architecture—see also DWELLING: Poor But Sexy—see also EXTRUSION: City of Artificial Extrusions—see also FABRICATION—see also GLOBAL WARMING: Nescient Hues / Meltwater—see also GRID: Rethinking Urban Grids in Hangzhou—see also HEALTH: Life-Styled—see also HISTORY—see also IDEA—see also IMPACT: Learning from the Americas—see also LISTEN: Symphony of the Air—see also MAKING—see also PLANNING: Perceptions of Physical Space and the Planning Process in Camp Azraq, Jordan—see also PRACTICE—see also PROCESS—see also PROJECT—see also REPRESENTATION—see also SCALE—see also TECHNIQUE—

see also URBANISM: Extreme Urbanism III—see also WORK: Work Environments I—see also 3-D.

MODERN

Modern, generic time frame, generic styles, periods & cultures: Being in existence at this time; although the time frame varies depending upon context, the term generally refers to a person, place, thing, or event dating no earlier than 75 years from the present time. *Modern*, style or period: Period and styles of painting, sculpture, graphic arts, and architecture dating from the late 19th century to the present date and characterized by a rejection of traditional artistic forms and conventions. It typically reflects changing social, economic, and intellectual conditions. *Modern* art includes numerous movements and theories. It differs from contemporary art, which does not carry the implication of a nontraditional style, but instead refers only to the time period in which the work was created. *Modern* and contemporary are inherently fluid terms. The term *modern* sometimes more narrowly refers to art up until the 1960s or 1970s.

Making the Modern Landscape. GSD Talks. Frances Loeb Library. September 11, 2014. Cornelia Hahn Oberlander and Susan Herrington, with Sonja Dümpelmann (moderator).

Cornelia Hahn Oberlander and Susan Herrington engaged in a conversation about Oberlander's life as a landscape architect, her education at Harvard University, and her career, in which she developed socially responsible and ecologically sensitive plans and designs for public landscapes, including sites in New York, Philadelphia, Vancouver, Seattle, Berlin, Toronto, and Montreal. 🕮

More than Mere Practicality. Exhibition. Gund Hall, Frances Loeb Library. November 3, 2014–January 20, 2015. Elizabeth Bacon Eager & Bryan Norwood (PhD).

Embracing the rise of second-wave *modernism* in midcentury America, Harvard transformed its campus and its design curriculum in the midst of what John Coolidge (the director of the Fogg Museum from 1948 to 1972) called "an unprecedented moment for visual arts in America." From *modern* art exhibitions to *modern* campus expansions and the establishment of a new urban design curriculum, the university was a hotbed of design activity, encouraging a wide range of collaborations and experimentation across the arts. This exhibition focused on the expanded concerns of university planning and design school pedagogy at midcentury, which went beyond functionalist pragmatics to address the emotional and spiritual impact of architectural and urban form. Through case studies of three Harvard buildings—The Architects Collaborative's Harkness Graduate Center (1948–1950), Josep Lluís Sert's Holyoke Center (1958–1966), and Minoru Yamasaki's William James Hall (1961–1965)—the exhibition explored a dynamic and evolving relationship between art and architecture that was central to this new, more humanist functionalism. 🕮

Women, Modernity, and Landscape Architecture. Publication. Routledge, 2015. Sonja Dümpelmann & John Beardsley (editors). SB469.375 .D86 2015.

Modernity was critically important to the formation and evolution of landscape architecture, yet its histories in the discipline are still being written. This book looks closely at the work and influences of some of the least

studied figures of the era: established and less well-known female landscape architects who pursued *modernist* ideals in their designs. The women discussed in this volume belong to the pioneering first two generations of professional landscape architects and were outstanding in the field. They not only developed notable practices, but some also became leaders in landscape architectural education as the first professors in the discipline, or prolific lecturers and authors. As early professionals who navigated the world of a male-dominated intellectual and menial work force, they were exponents of *modernity*. In addition, many personalities discussed in this volume were either figures of transition between tradition and *modernism* (like Silvia Crowe, Maria Teresa Parpagliolo), or they fully embraced and furthered the *modernist* agenda (like Rosa Kliass, Cornelia Hahn Oberlander).

See also CONTEXT—see also FUNDAMENTAL: 14th International Architecture Exhibition—see also HISTORY—see also INSULATION: Insulating Modernism—see also STYLE—see also TIME—see also WOMAN.

MODULAR

Modular construction, construction by form, assembling: Construction that utilizes prefabricated units and for construction based on the combination of similar subcomponents. *Modular* wall, walls by form: Interior walls made up of standardized *modules* or units which are the basis for construction and allow for flexible arrangement.

See also ASSEMBLY—see also CONSTRUCTION—see also PROPORTION: Modulor 2—see also SCALE: Modulor.

MOIRE

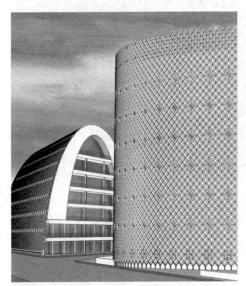

Moire effect, optical illusion, visual & representational concepts: Visual phenomena derived from the French word for "watered" that is produced when a set of straight or curved lines spaced equally apart is superimposed onto another set at a particular angle, resulting in a distinct geometrical design; used to represent and identify fluid flow, wave motion, and optic and magnetic field patterns and flows. *Moire*, patterns by specific type: Patterns having a watered or rippled look. Where this produces an illusion of movement, use "*moiré* effect."

Figure. Rendering (left). David Wolf Himelman (MArch I).

MONTAGE

Montage, image-making processes & techniques: Refers to the technique of making compositions from portions of existing images, such as drawings or photographs, arranged into somewhat unified images. When pieces of various relatively flat materials are pasted together to form less unified images, use "collage." Used also in film when two or more shots are superimposed to form a single image. *Montage*, visual works by material or technique: Works produced by the technique of *montage*. If photographs dominate the composition, use "photomontage."

MORPHOLOGY

Morphology, attributes & properties by specific type: Refers to the physical form of a thing or a material, often regarding shapes and arrangements of parts.

Mexico City: Between Geometry & Geography— Entre geometría y geografía. Publication. Applied Research & Design, 2014. Felipe Correa & Carlos Garciavelez Alfaro (authors). HT169.M62 C67 2014.

Mexico City: Between Geometry & Geography examines—through photography, archival material, and analytical drawings—the urbanistic evolution of Mexico City. The volume focuses specifically on the relationship between major public works projects and the urban fragments they have created in order to construct a visual analysis of the most dominant urban *morphologies* at play in the city. Organized in seven topical chapters—from Lake to City, from City to Metropolis, Mobility Networks, Logistical Footprints, Housing Stock, Hydrological Landscapes, and Urban Visions—the book tests the ability of design to confront and break down the perceived immensity of Mexico City by singling out and analyzing key urban projects that have shaped the city over 600 years.

See also AIRPORT: Dwelling in Stop-Over City—see also FORM—see also LANDFORM: Landformation Catalogue—see also TYPOLOGY.

MOVEMENT

Movement, artistic concept, formal concepts: As an artistic concept, the characteristic of a composition that causes the eye to pass from place to place, or from one form or area to another, through the composition. Earth *movement*, natural events: Differential *movements* of the Earth's crust or parts of its surface, or elevations or subsidences of land.

See also ANIMATION: Animating Material—see also COMPOSITION—see also GESTURE: Trace of Emotion—see also HISTORY—see also TIME.

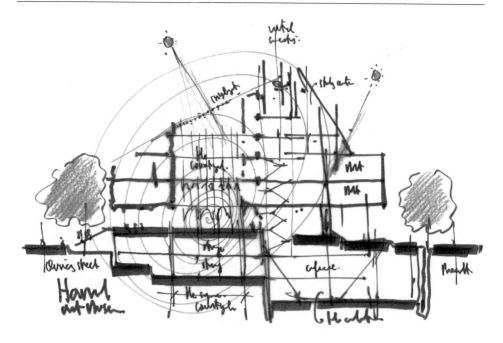

MUSEUM

Art *museum*, building, *museum* buildings by subject, built environment: Buildings, groups of buildings, or spaces within buildings where works of art are housed and displayed for public benefit. For stores in which works of art are displayed for sale, see "art galleries (buildings)." *Museum*, buildings, exhibition buildings, single built works by function: Refers to buildings, groups of buildings, or spaces within buildings where objects of value such as works of art, antiquities, scientific specimens, or other artifacts are housed and displayed for public benefit.

Collection of Historical Scientific Instruments. Science Center, Room 371. The Collection of Historical Scientific Instruments is a remarkable collection of objects dating from about 1400 to the present—related to navigation, electricity, medicine, surveying and more.

Harvard Art Museums. In 2014, Harvard University's three art *museums*—the Fogg *Museum*, the Busch-Reisinger *Museum,* and the Arthur M. Sackler *Museum*—were consolidated into one reorganized and upgraded facility, the Harvard Art *Museums*. The restored historic courtyard of the Fogg *Museum* became the heart of 200,000 square foot new *museum* space. The new facility combines the Fogg's protected 1920s Georgian revival building, with a new addition on its east side along Prescott Street. A new glazed rooftop structure bridges the old and the new, and was designed with sensitivity to surrounding historic structures. It allows for controlled natural light into the Conservation Lab, study centers, galleries, as well as the courtyard below. The original 1920s building by Coolidge, Shepley, Bulfinch & Abbot Architects was the first of its kind, combining *museum* space, teaching, and conservation in one facility to promote scholarship. Following this tradition, the new center designed by Renzo Piano Building Workshop was

designed to make the collection of 250,000 objects more accessible for teaching and learning.

Figure. Sketch Section (above). Harvard Art Museums Renovation & Expansion (2006–2014). Courtesy of Renzo Piano Building Workshop.

Harvard Museum of Natural History. Harvard *Museum* of Natural History is home to comparative zoology, mineralogical and geological material, and the Harvard Herbarium, including the world-famous collection of glass flowers made by father and son Leopold and Rudolph Blaschka.

How Did You Do It, Mr. Piano? Lecture. Gund Hall, Piper Auditorium. November 6, 2014. Renzo Piano with Thomas W. Lentz & Kenneth Frampton (moderator).

The Harvard Art *Museums* building, which opened November 16, 2014, consolidated three *museums* into a single volume capped by an art study center and state-of-the-art conservation laboratory. ❀

Peabody Museum of Archaeology & Ethnology. The Peabody *Museum* is among the oldest archaeological and ethnographic *museums* in the world with one of the finest collections of human culture, from towering Native American totem poles and large Maya sculptures to precious artifacts of the ancient world.

MUTATION

1: A significant and basic alteration, change. 2: (a) A relatively permanent change in hereditary material involving either a physical change in chromosome relations or a biochemical change in the codons that make up genes, also the process of producing a *mutation*; (b) an individual, strain, or trait resulting from *mutation*.

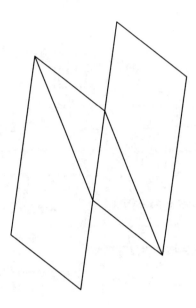

NANO

1: One billionth (10^{-9}) part of *<nanosecond>*. 2: *Nanotechnology* *<nanomachine>*. 3: *Nanoscale* *<nanoparticle>* *<nanotube>*.

NARRATIVE

Narrative, artistic device, artistic concepts: The technique of storytelling. *Narrative*, document genres for literary works: Literary work emphasizing a story or sequence of events.

NATURE

Nature, philosophical concepts: Refers to the concept of the physical world, including the forces at work in it and the nonhuman life inhabiting it, perceived by human beings as separate and independent from themselves, their activities, and civilization. For aggregates of physical things, conditions, and influences surrounding and affecting given organisms or communities of organisms at any time, use "environments (object groupings)." For the branch of biology dealing with the relations and interactions between organisms and their habitat, use "ecology."

Another Nature. Studio Reports. Publication. Harvard GSD, 2015. Junya Ishigami (studio instructor). NA 1555.6.I74 2015.
   In Spring 2014, the Another *Nature* studio investigated new views on place and the role of architecture, challenging the distinctions created through program, enclosure, and formal organization. The studio considered these three relationships in the context of contemporary Tokyo, a city where rapid and extensive urbanization has increasingly alienated individuals from their *natural* surroundings. Although Japan as a whole is relatively affluent, it faces persistent economic stagnation compounded by an aging population, rising state expenditures, and a diminishing tax base. These larger issues call into question existing approaches toward development and provide an opportunity for new conceptions of building and public space. ⊛

See also AIR—see also CITY: Expeditions in the Contemporary City—see also ECOLOGY—see also INSPIRATION: Natural & Unnatural—see also PLACE—see also PLANT—see also PRESERVATION: A History of Nature Conservation & Cultural Landscape Preservation—see also RADICAL: The Grounds of Radical Nature—see also SUSTAINABILITY: The Return of Nature—see also VENTILATION: Supernatural Ventilation—see also WATER.

NEGATIVE

Black-and-white *negative*, *negatives* by color, visual & verbal communication: Refers to *negatives* whose images are composed of gray tones, black, and white or clear areas; may include one hue as a result of process, toning, or discoloration. Color *negative*, *negatives* by color, visual & verbal communication: Photographic *negatives* that record on a single base the hue and lightness of a scene in values that are complementary in relation to the scene's actual perceived values (e.g., light blue is recorded as dark yellow). See "color separation *negatives*" for images in which each color is recorded on a physically separate *negative*. *Negative* perspective, perspective & shading techniques: Refers to a system of perspective designed to counteract the effect of objects appearing

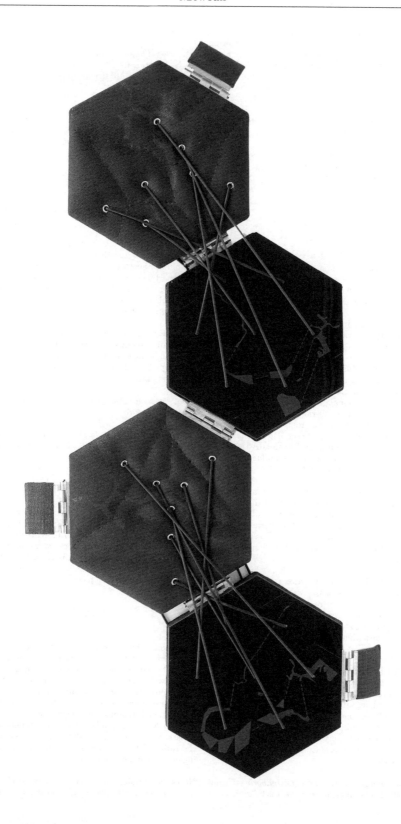

smaller at a distance. It employs the use of lines of sight to adjust proportions, typically in large-scale lettering and decorations, the effect being that all lettering or decoration appears to be the same scale from the vantage point of the viewer. The system was described in ancient times by Plato and others, and it was discussed by Dürer and other Renaissance artists. *Negative* space, space, form & composition concept: Describes an enclosed empty space in architecture, sculpture, or painting which makes an essential contribution to the composition.

See also COLOR—see also COMMUNICATION—see also COM-POSITION—see also FIGURE-GROUND—see also FORM—see also HUE—see also PERSPECTIVE—see also PHOTOGRAPHY—see also PROCESS—see also SPACE—see also TECHNIQUE.

NEIGHBORHOOD

Neighborhood, residential districts, land use, districts, built environments: Residential areas within a larger town or city, more or less cohered into integral communities having their own shops and other facilities, and other distinguishing characteristics.

Allston. Allston is directly south of the Charles River and home to the Harvard Business School and Harvard Innovation Lab.

Cambridgeport. Hugged by the Charles River to the south, this primarily residential *neighborhood* is a picturesque parade of triple-decker homes, children-strewn parks, and the occasional grade school or academic research building. Commerce ranges from the unironic industrial (vintage electronics repair), to the vaguely suburban (three major supermarkets), to the charmingly earnest (a tuxedo boutique). In the late 1800s the iconic Fig Newton cookie was first manufactured here at the F. A. Kennedy Steam Bakery.

East Cambridge. The *neighborhood's* main aorta, Cambridge Street, has access to some of the best fish markets, Portuguese bakeries, bars, and shopping centers including the Cambridgeside Galleria, Twin City Plaza, and Cambridge Antique Market. The residential makeup is richly diverse, anchored with strong Irish and Portuguese communities.

North Cambridge. Strewn along Massachusetts Avenue are small businesses and authentic ethnic restaurants, as well as a restaurant supply store, a boutique Italian foods retailer, an Indian bridal showroom, a bygone-era steakhouse, a legit donut hut, and a tree-lined bike path leading to Alewife Brook Parkway.

Somerville. Somerville is a city located in Middlesex County, Massachusetts, just two miles north of Boston. Occupying slightly over four square miles, its population of 75,754 (as of the 2010 census) and a myriad of immigrants from all over the world make this city the most densely populated community in New England and one of the most ethnically diverse *neighborhoods* in the nation. Rich in both history and culture, the city houses numerous intriguing sites, businesses, and restaurants for every style.

West Cambridge. This sprawling *neighborhood* is not easily defined by a single persona as it is by its relative preponderance of green land. Between Fresh Pond Reservation (a 155-acre kettle hole lake surrounded by 162 acres of land and a nine-hole golf course), the meditative Charles River Reservation, and bird-watchers' paradise Mount Auburn Cemetery, there is plenty of room to roam.

See also CAMPUS: A Campus for the 21st Century—see also CITY—see also COMMUNITY—see also HEALTH: Life-Styled—see also PHOTOGRAPHY: The Neighborhood Ketchup Ad—see also SETTLEMENT—see also SUBURBAN—see also URBAN.

NETWORK

1: A fabric or structure of cords or wires that cross at regular intervals. 2: A system of lines or channels resembling a *network*. 3: (a) An interconnected or interrelated chain, group, or system; (b) a system of computers, peripherals, terminals, and databases connected by communications lines. 4: (a) A group of radio or television stations linked by wire or radio relay; (b) a radio or television company that produces programs for broadcast over such a *network*. 5: A usually informally interconnected group or association of persons.

Network, computers: System of interconnected computers or any instances of two or more organizations or individuals engaged in a common pattern of information exchange through automated, online, or on air communications links.

Figure. Model (previous page). Igor Ekstajn (PhD) & Namik Mackic (MDes, RR).

See also COMPUTER—see also IMAGINATION—see also INFRA-STRUCTURE—see also URBANISM: Networked Urbanism.

NEUTRALITY

Neutrality, chemical properties, attributes & properties by specific type: Exhibiting neither acid nor alkaline qualities, having a pH value of 7.0. *Neutral* colors, hues or tints: Colors without hue: black, white, and the grays. *Neutral* zone, administrative districts: Areas that are *neutral*, not claimed by any political power, often created as buffer zones between powers.

NEWS

News agency, business enterprises by function: Business enterprises, including private companies and those owned by nations or international organizations, that gather, write, and supply *news* reports and photographs from around the world or a nation to *newspapers*, magazines, radio and television broadcasters, government agencies, and other users who subscribe to their services. *Newsbook*, serials, publications: Forerunners of *newspapers*, consisting of more than one leaf, published in the 16th and 17th centuries. For similar items consisting of one leaf, use "corantos."

Newswall. Student Group. *Newswall* is a student group that manages the student exhibition wall located on the

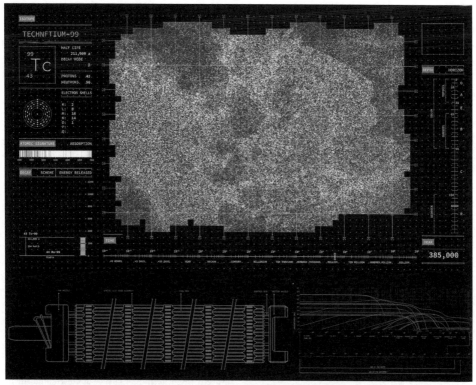

2nd floor of Gund Hall. This wall offers Harvard GSD students the unique opportunity to prominently present their thoughts, research, and projects to the rest of the school in the form of a curated exhibit. ❧

See also COMMUNICATION—see also DATA—see also INFORMATION—see also PUBLICATION.

NOTATION

1: Annotation, note. 2: (a) The act, process, method, or an instance of representing by a system or set of marks, signs, figures, or characters; (b) a system of characters, symbols, or abbreviated expressions used in an art or science, or in mathematics or logic to express technical facts or quantities.

NUCLEAR

1: Of, relating to, or constituting a nucleus. 2: (a) Of or relating to the atomic *nucleus* <*nuclear* reaction> <*nuclear* physics>; (b) used in or produced by a *nuclear* reaction <*nuclear* fuel> <*nuclear* waste> <*nuclear* energy>; (c) being a weapon whose destructive power derives from an uncontrolled *nuclear* reaction; (d) of, produced by, or involving *nuclear* weapons <the *nuclear* age> <*nuclear* war>; (e) armed with *nuclear* weapons <*nuclear* powers>; (f) of, relating to, or powered by *nuclear* energy <a *nuclear* submarine> <the *nuclear* debate> <a *nuclear* plant>. 3: Crazy, berserk, usually used in the phrase "go *nuclear*."

Fatal Vitality. Thesis. Grga Basic (MDes, ULE), advised by Robert Gerard Pietrusko.

"Regardless of its particular purpose, every *nuclear* activity generates radioactive byproducts. *Nuclear* waste, scattered across the globe and currently weighing more than 250,000 tons, will remain hazardous to humans for thousands of years. Taking into account the time frame for radioactivity to be reduced to harmless levels— which in most instances surpasses the timescale of human civilization—the issues of management and confinement of such material introduce scales and temporalities that are wholly beyond our cognition.

One example of such limitations—our attempts to develop a communication system capable of signaling danger and deterring human incursion into *nuclear* waste repositories for thousands of years—epitomizes the extent to which we are limited by current cultural conditions. Rather than maintain an anthropocentric perception of the world—one guided only by human self-interest, which is often shortsighted—my thesis aims to develop an experimental approach to conceptualizing the world according to *nuclear* waste by reversing the emphasis on our limited capacity to act upon things and focusing instead on more potent and vibrant engagements of radioactive material and its environment.

By shifting the focus from communicating danger to visualizing the process of *nuclear* decay within the environment, this project renders radioactivity itself as a communication system and an ecological process." ❧

Figure. Diagram (above). Grga Basic (MDes, ULE).

See also COLOR—see also HYPEROBJECT: The Proximities of Nuclear Waste—see also WASTE.

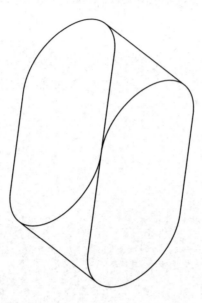

OBJECT

Man-made *object*, *object* genres by cultural or intellectual valuation, *object* classifications: *Objects* that are made by humans rather than being natural. Used primarily in the context of distinguishing man-made *objects* from natural *objects*. *Object* genres: Material things that can be perceived by the senses. In the context of art history or art information, the term may be restricted to works of art or cultural heritage, including architecture, artworks such as paintings, drawings, graphic arts, sculpture, decorative arts, photographs, and other cultural artifacts. An *object* may be a single item or it may be made up of many physical parts.

Common Objects. Thesis. Duncan Christopher Henry Scovil (MArch I), advised by Florian Idenburg.

"Scotland almost left the United Kingdom this past September. To many watching beyond its borders, the near success of the nation's independence referendum came as a surprise, not due to Scotland's desire for sovereignty, but rather from the revelation that the United Kingdom is, in fact, a construction that can be disassembled. Lacking a single written constitution, the United Kingdom instead governs through an assemblage of documents, conventions, spaces, and traditions. Its seemingly permanent form has emerged only through practice, both political and architectural. With parliamentary power concentrated at the Palace of Westminster in London for over 700 years, this model of development has slowly codified itself into a set of entrenched customs and rituals.

Today, however, a growing desire for separate, devolved local, regional, and national governments—exemplified by Scotland's referendum—has once again required the practice of parliament to become both flexible and mobile.

This thesis operates between the twinned states of assembly and disassembly to propose that it is the interpretive relationship of parts—of *objects* and furniture—to their immediate surroundings, rather than the immutable form of any single encompassing building or document, that serves as the primary medium through which to practice parliament. Explored through a set of common *objects*, the architectural model that emerges from this investigation is a dynamic one requiring both negotiation and transformation." ◊

Figure. Catalogue (opposite page) & Perspective (next spread). Duncan Christopher Henry Scovil (MArch I).

Object Studio. STU 1319. Department of Architecture. Option Studio. Spring 2015. Instructor: Josep Lluis Mateo. Teaching Assistant: Jaime Guerrero Daroca (MArch II).

The studio's objective was to precisely define projects based on three conditions: place, content, and material. Place: Here, it is the city, at the border, with the presence nearby of nature. Surrounded, dialogue with the exterior in continuity or in opposition. The exterior. Content: Use. Interior. Conventional briefs seen from a special viewpoint that aims to discover the magic of the everyday. To analyze, observe and propose new conditions of use. Material. Projects, always starting with abstract visions, take form, become intelligible, by means of material. Architecture as the expression of physical, material culture. Every project, beginning as an abstract vision, takes form and becomes intelligible by means of material. Architecture is an expression of physical, material culture. The studio set out to relate idea and material, to define the *object*, and to study its phenomenological conditions and potentials. Form—as a variable to be discovered (rather than the starting point) in relation to its exterior, to its content, and to the material—was the objective the studio.

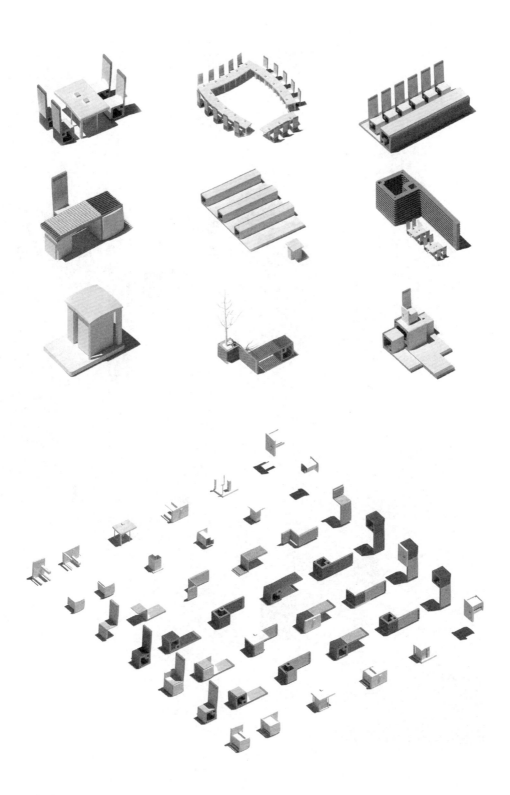

Students: Majda AlMarzouqi (MArch I), James Thomas Barclay (MArch II), Daniel Carlson (MArch I), Jose Pablo Cordero (MArch II), Jamie Gina Lee (MArch I), Aaron C. Menninga (MArch I), Yina Ng (MArch I), Lance Smith (MArch I), Xin Su (MArch II). ✤

Figure. Perspective (opposite page). Lance Smith (MArch I).

See also ART: Post Facto—see also ARTIFACT—see also AS-SEMBLAGE—see also BOX: Boxes for America—see also CON-STRUCTION—see also CULTURE—see also GAZE: Subverting the Gaze—see also HYPEROBJECT: The Proximities of Nuclear Waste—see also INFORMATION—see also MATERIAL—see also VISIONARY: Grounded Visionaries.

OBLIQUE

Oblique, axonometric projections, images: *Oblique* drawings, or works in another media, in which a vertical plane is parallel to the plane of projection, and receding planes are drawn at a scale that is somewhere between the same scale as and one half the scale of that vertical plane. *Oblique* perspective, perspective views: Refers to drawings, or works in another medium, that are made using *oblique* perspective, which is a system of linear perspective in which rectangular objects are set at an angle to the picture plane rather than parallel to it. *Oblique* perspectives may be two-point perspectives, three-point perspectives, or they may use another scheme. For drawings that use *oblique* projection, where parallel lines remain parallel rather than converging as they recede in space, use "*oblique* projections." *Oblique* projection, axonometric projections, images: Refers to drawings, or works in another medium, created by *oblique* projection, in which parallel lines remain parallel. Typically two spatial axes are parallel to the plane of projection or drawing surface, and a third axis is projected at an angle other than 90 degrees to the plane. For drawings in which objects are depicted at an angle to the picture plane but parallel receding lines converge, use "*oblique* perspectives." Plan *oblique* drawing, *oblique* projections, axonometric projections, images: Refers to drawings in *oblique* projection in which the horizontal plane is parallel to the plane of projection or drawing surface, and the plan is rotated to any convenient angle so that verticals may be drawn. They are characterized by typically having a higher angle of view than an isometric drawing, and orthographic plans may be depicted on the horizontal surfaces.

See also AXONOMETRIC—see also DRAWING—see also ELEVATION—see also PLAN—see also PROJECTION—see also SECTION—see also TECHNIQUE.

OBSERVATION

Observation, functional concepts: The action or practice of *observing*, watching, or noticing.

OCEAN

Ocean, marine bodies of water by biome: Category of marine body of water comprising the main water areas of the Earth, lying in basins; for shallow salt water areas lying on the margins of continents, use "seas."

Harvard Design Magazine No. 39: Wet Matter. Publication. Harvard GSD, 2014. Pierre Bélanger (guest editor) & Jennifer Sigler (editor in chief).

The *ocean* remains a glaring blind spot in the Western imagination. Catastrophic events remind us of its influence—a lost airplane, a shark attack, an oil spill, an underwater earthquake—but we tend to marginalize or misunderstand the scales of the *oceanic*. It represents the other 71 percent of our planet. To characterize the *ocean* as catastrophic—imperiled environment, coastal risk, or contested territory—is to overlook its potential power. The *oceanic* project—like the work of Marie Tharp, who mapped the seafloor in the shadows of Cold War star scientists—challenges the dry, closed, terrestrial frameworks that shape today's industrial, corporate, and economic patterns. Reexamining the *ocean's* historic and superficial remoteness, this issue profiles the *ocean* as contemporary urban space and subject of material, political, and ecologic significance, asking how we are shaping it, and how it is shaping us. ✤

OEUVRE

Oeuvre, masterpieces, visual works by function: Works used as test-pieces, often by apprentices, and presented to a guild to determine whether the makers were qualified to rank as masters. *Oeuvre*, object groupings by general context: The works produced by an artist or composer regarded collectively. For the collective body of works by a writer, use "corpora."

Steve Reich in Conversation with Mohsen Mostafavi. Gund Hall, Piper Auditorium. March 25, 2015. Steve Reich & Mohsen Mostafavi.

Steve Reich spoke about his work and played sample recordings from his *oeuvre*, including *WTC 9/11* (2009). From his early compositions in taped speech, *It's Gonna Rain* (1965) and *Come Out* (1966), to his digital video opera *Three Tales* (2002) with video artist Beryl Korot, Reich has evolved a distinctive style marked by simple melodies and pronounced rhythm, repetition, and variation. His music has sources in the Western classical tradition but also in non-Western and vernacular structures, harmonies, and rhythms.

See also ART—see also COLLECTION—see also PRACTICE—see also TECHNIQUE—see also WORK.

OFFICE

Office building, single built works by function: Buildings constructed or used primarily for *offices*, which are spaces where business, administrative, or professional activities are conducted. *Office*, work and instructional spaces, rooms & spaces by function: Rooms where business, administrative, or professional activities are conducted.

De-Construct: Office & the City. Thesis. Lily Wubeshet (MArch I), advised by Iñaki Ábalos.

"What is the *office* type of today, and what is its role in the regeneration and re-imagination of a city? The *office* has existed in one form or another throughout history. The first commercial *offices* appeared in industrial cities in the late 19th century, characterizing their central business districts, while heavy industry clustered along rivers and rail lines. By the second half of the century, *office* blocks were a major part of urban life.

The influence of technology on work culture has caused the corporate model of the *office* building to become obsolete and its relation to the city to be blurred. How disconnected has the *office* gotten from the urban core? Specifically, the *office*-campus type adopted by tech giants, such as the Googleplex in Mountain View and the Apple Campus in Cupertino, demonstrates such a shift. By reproducing functions characteristic of urbanity yet introverted and limited to the use of employees, the *office*-campus type ignores existing urban infrastructure and hopes to render its own removed and alienated community. So why the need to replicate when functions provided in an *office* campus can merge, borrow, and, where needed, add to the growth and richness of a city core? This thesis seeks to redefine today's *office* type through the redefinition of its relationship to the city." ◈

OLFACTORY

1: Of or relating to the sense of smell.

Fossa Olfactoria. Exhibition. Kirkland Gallery. April 6–17, 2015. Katie MacDonald (MArch II) & Erin Anne Pellegrino (MArch II).

"Fossa *Olfactoria*" was an installation that manifested smell as both an *olfactory* and tactile experience. While scent is often unexplored or completely omitted from serious discussions of architecture, the spatial consequences of scent and odor are powerful sculptors of experience, occupancy, and comfort. The installation brought the viewer into the epicenter of *olfactory* experience—the spatial cavity where the *olfactory* bulb is located, playing on notions of scale, phenomena, and bodily experience. An immersive, fleshy fabric membrane pulsed, undulating as 1,000 scent-dispensing balloons rose and fell behind its walls. ◈

See also BODY—see also EXPERIENCE—see also INSTALLATION—see also PHENOMENON—see also SCALE—see also SENSE.

ONTO-CARTOGRAPHY

Cyborg Coasts: Responsive Hydrologies. ADV 9139. Department of Landscape Architecture. Seminar. Spring 2015. Instructor: Bradley Earl Cantrell.

The interface between constructed environments and ecological systems is slowly blurring strategies in urbanism, biological engineering, and technological interface. These strategies encourage the application of responsive technologies to create new relationships through sensing and feedback, developing novel ecological systems. These new ecologies demand a deconstruction of the industry, settlement, infrastructure, and biological systems framing the constructed landscape as a synthesizer of biotic and abiotic processes. The interstices of these new relationships become the medium in which this course examined new potentials for sensing, monitoring, and automation as a starting point to reimagine coastal infrastructure.

The course unpacked the coastal landscape through the construction of what Levi Bryant calls an *onto-cartography*. This refers to a cartographic mode that maps objects (machines) and the connections between these objects. The resultant framework was then continually modified to test methods of sensing and feedback through mock-ups and prototypes. The course engaged prototyping, virtual models, and physical models as the primary modes of exploration. ◈

Figure. Diagrams (opposite page). Andrew Gregory Boyd (MLA I) & Tyler Mohr (MLA II).

OPENING

Opening, activity, physical activities by general context: The action of moving or turning a door, gate, window, tap, lid, or other component away from its closed position so as to allow passage or access. *Opening*, architectural elements, *openings* & *opening* components: Generally denotes apertures or breaks in the surface of a wall or other architectural element. *Opening*, events, activities: Events by which something new is put officially into operation, often but not always formal, public, and invitational.

See also ACTION—see also APERTURE: The Aperture Analyzed—see also DOOR—see also ELEMENT—see also EXHIBITION—see also LAUNCH—see also PROCESS.

OPERATION

1: Performance of a practical work or of something involving the practical application of principles or processes. 2: (a) An exertion of power or influence <the *operation* of a drug>; (b) the quality or state of being functional or operative <the plant is now in *operation*>; (c) a method or manner of functioning. 3: A procedure performed on a living body usually with instruments especially for the repair of damage or the restoration of health. 4: Any of various mathematical or logical processes of deriving one entity from others according to a rule. 5: (a) A usually military action, mission, or maneuver including its planning and execution; (b) the office on the flight line of an airfield where pilots file clearance for flights and where flying from the field is controlled; (c) the agency of an organization charged with carrying on the principal planning and *operating* functions of a headquarters and its subordinate units. 6: A business transaction especially when speculative. 7: A single step performed by a computer in the execution of a program. 8: A usually small business or establishment.

See also ASSEMBLY—see also CONSTRUCTION—see also LANDFORM: Landformation Catalogue—see also PROCESS—see also SPECULATION: Rare New Species—see also VISIONARY: Grounded Visionaries.

OPPORTUNITY

1: A favorable juncture of circumstances <the halt provided an *opportunity* for rest and refreshment>. 2: A good chance for advancement or progress.

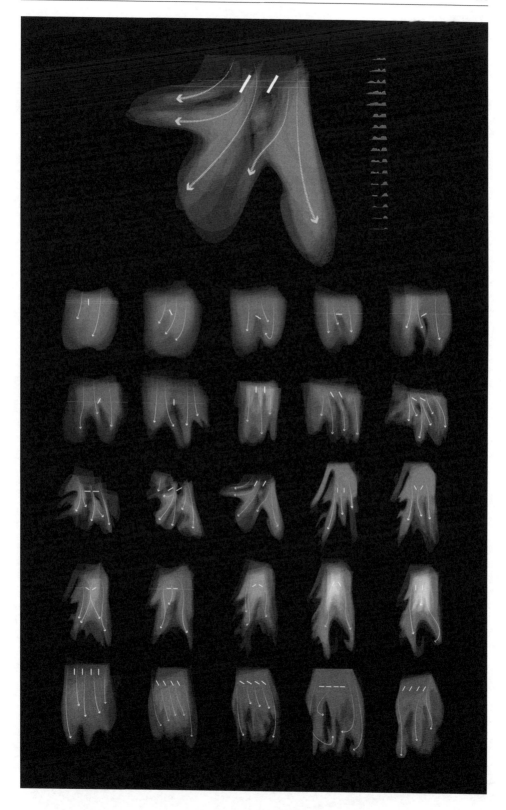

Innovate. GSD Talks. Gund Hall, Stubbins. September 9, 2014. Wolfgang Rieder with Salmaan Craig, Špela Videcnik with Iñaki Ábalos (moderator).

Innovation occurs at multiple scales, frequently crosses disciplines, and occasionally changes lives, cities, and culture. It is not a science, but requires design skills and must be informed by an eye for *opportunity*. *Innovate* is a noontime talk series featuring 20-minute presentations followed by discussions with faculty and students. 🖐

ORDER

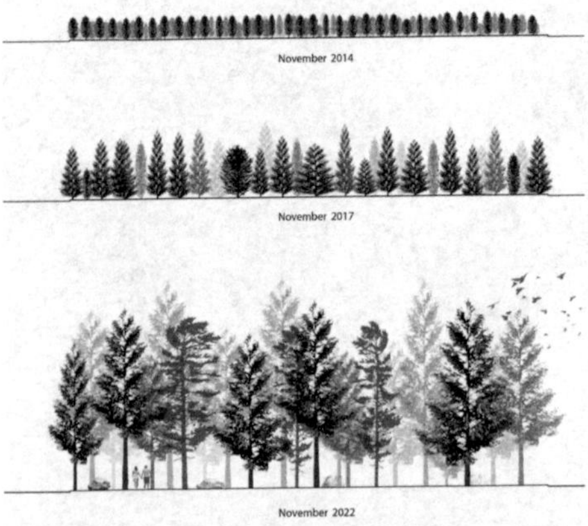

November 2014

November 2017

November 2022

Architectural *orders*, structural assemblies, structural elements: In classical architecture, a particular ensemble of column with its entablature, having standardized details. Corinthian *order*, architectural *orders*: Refers to the architectural *order* characterized by a capital having a bell-shaped echinus decorated with a combination of spiral and plant, usually acanthus, motifs. *Order*, concept, metaphysical concepts, philosophical concepts: The condition in which each thing is clearly distinguished and properly disposed with reference to other things, and performs its proper function. Doric *order*, architectural *orders*: Refers to the architectural *order* characterized by columns generally without bases, relatively simple capitals, and a frieze composed of alternating triglyphs and metopes. Ionic *order*, architectural *orders*: Refers to the architectural *order* characterized by capitals with volutes, richly carved moldings, and columns with bases.

Le poème de l'angle droite. Publication. Éditions Tériade, 1955 (No. 182/270). Le Corbusier (author). Le Corbusier Research Collection, Frances Loeb Library. LeC Oversize NA1053.J4 L328 1955.

"*Le poème de l'angle droite* consists of 19 lithographs and corresponding texts. Like a table of contents, they are arranged into seven rows, each with a dominant theme and corresponding color. Le Corbusier represents them in a hopscotch pattern with a single trunk and horizontal branches for each theme. The topics of the poem are as follows: environment (green), spirit (blue), flesh (violet), fusion (red), character (clear), offering (yellow), and tool (purple). The lithographs and text are about natural cycles: spirit relates to nature, architecture and the universe, flesh to primal creative capacities. The symbol of the open hand appears here for the first time as an offering. The poem was written between 1947 and 1953." —Inés Zalduendo. 🖐

Figure. Diagrams (above). Johanna Rose Cairns (MLA I).

See also ARCHITECTURE—*see also* ASSEMBLY—*see also* BUILDING—*see also* COLOR—*see also* COLUMN—*see also* COMPOSITION—*see also* CONCEPT—*see also* DETAIL—*see also* ELEMENT—*see also* FORM—*see also* NATURE—*see also* PROPORTION—*see also* SCALE—*see also* STRUCTURE.

ORGANIC

Organic, attributes & properties by specific type: In the general sense, describes substances containing carbon compounds, ultimately derived from living organisms. In a more specific sense, with reference to food and other consumer products, produced with no artificial materials, fertilizers, or additives, and, with regard to livestock, in a non-factory setting with room to move around. *Organic* material, materials by composition: Material containing carbon, including those derived from living organisms.

See also BIOPHILIA: Suspicious Biophilia—see also CARBON— see also MATERIAL—see also NATURE.

ORGANIZATION

Organization, groups: Groups of people *organized* for a purpose, typically characterized by a more or less constant membership, a body of officers or functionaries, and a set of regulations governing their activities and conduct.

ORIENTATION

Orientation, positional attributes, attributes & properties by specific type: The relative position of something, usually as regarding relative direction.

ORNAMENT

Architectural *ornament*, surface elements: Decoration used to embellish parts of a building; usually in and of itself having no function, although it may decorate functional members. *Ornament*, object genre by function, object classification: Decorative forms or embellishments that are an integral part of a building or object but are not essential to its structure. Refers also to decorative objects attached to or worn by humans and animals. For objects signifying an honor bestowed upon an individual, usually worn on the person, see "decorations." Regarding techniques of embellishment in general, see "decoration (process)." *Ornament*, object genres by function: Decorative forms or embellishments that are an integral part of a building or object but are not essential to its structure. Refers also to decorative objects attached to or worn by humans and animals.

Structure, Infrastructure, and Ornament. HIS 4435. Department of Architecture. Seminar. Spring 2015. Instructor: Antoine Picon.

With the rise of digital design and fabrication, *ornament* is back. Its return is accompanied by recurring interrogations to redefine tectonics, and more generally, to critically revisit the link between architecture and structure. Once thought essential, this link appears weaker today. Paradoxically, while the fundamental role that modernism had attributed to structure is being challenged, the relationship between architecture and infrastructure has intensified. Many contemporary projects play on the blurring of architecture and infrastructure.

The seminar examined the past and present interactions between these three components of architecture and the built environment. On the one hand, despite their apparent opposition, *ornament* and structure share a number of common characteristics. On the other hand, structure and infrastructure are more different than one assumes. The play between these three concepts—between *ornament*, structure, and infrastructure—raises fundamental issues regarding the way architecture is understood. ❦

ORTHOGRAPHIC

Orthographic, images: Drawings, prints, or other media in which the projectors are perpendicular to the plane of projection (drawing surface), that is, a three-dimensional object is shown frontally at all points, with no indication of recession into depth. *Orthographic*, technique, parallel projection: Refers to a technique for representing three-dimensional objects in two dimensions by using parallel projecting lines that are perpendicular to the plane of projection or picture surface. Principal surfaces of objects are parallel to the picture plane. It does not include foreshortening, shifts in scale and proportion, or other distortions that would be caused by employing linear perspective. It is often used for technical and architectural drawings, including plans, sections, and elevations. It is also used to create azimuthal projections of the Earth or another heavenly body as seen from space.

OUTLINE

Outline, linear form, form & composition concepts: Visual boundaries of a form, without regard to internal features; distinct from a contour, which may bound a form within an *outline*. *Outline*, summaries, versions of documents: General descriptions covering the main points of a subject, such as summaries of written works or speeches expressed as headings and subheadings.

OUT-MIGRATE

1: To leave one region or community in order to settle in another especially as part of a large-scale and continuing movement of population.

On the Edge: A Nissological Approach to Planning & Design in Newfoundland. Thesis. Matthew Austin John Brown (MDes, ULE), advised by John R. Stilgoe.

"For over half a century, the island of Newfoundland, Canada, has been plagued by *out-migration* and rural decline. It is estimated that, to date, more than 220,000 Newfoundlanders have left in search of employment and a means to support their families. This translates

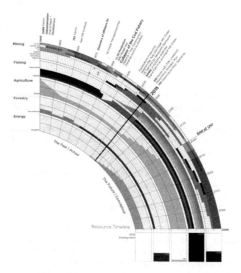

into the demise of over 250 out-port communities and with them the loss of history, culture, and tradition. The remaining population of Newfoundland continues to fight for a viable way to remain, while the majority of those who have left retain hope that they may one day return. It is evident that at the root of *out-migration* lies the island's lack of a diversified economy and a supportive infrastructure. Another critical factor is the absence of contemporary large-scale planning and design. This thesis critiques current planning theory and practice in Newfoundland and suggests a new nissological approach to effectively inciting positive change. It then offers a master plan, designed to create a strategy for infrastructure, landscape, and ecology with the aim of diversifying the economy and ending *out-migration*." ❦

Figure. Diagrams (above). Matthew Austin John Brown (MDes, ULE).

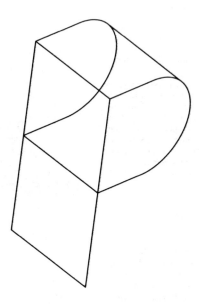

PAINTING

Painting, image-making, discipline: The art and practice of applying pigments suspended in water, oil, egg yolk, molten wax, or other liquid to a surface to create an expressive or communicative image. For the application of *paint* primarily to protect a surface or add a general color, use "*painting* (coating)."

Landscape as Painting. VIS 2448. Department of Landscape Architecture. Seminar. Spring 2015. Instructor: Ewa Harabasz.

The course objective was to advance the students' visual skills in artistic representation and creative imagination through *painting*. The course attempted to master visual sensitivity to detail and the capacity to articulate and convey detail through *painting* in a visually convincing and evocative form. Assigned and generated by students, the projects focused on emotional perception, bodily experience, and a metaphoric interpretation of landscape. The projects addressed both natural and built environments and included work in outdoor and indoor situations and places as well as drawing and *painting* live models. *Painting* assignments focused on the world of colors, textures, composition, mood, light effects, shape, shade, and values. Students used various tools, materials, and artistic techniques including acrylic and oil paint, watercolor, ink, gouache, and other wet media later combined with the application and transformation of media imagery—the use of cameras, computer renderings, etc. In the assignments, emphasis was made on playful experimentation that involved and encouraged a creative use of innovative combinations of various *painting* materials, methods, and techniques. ֎

See also ART: Post Facto—see also COMMUNICATION—see also DRAWING—see also MATERIAL—see also PROCESS—see also REPRESENTATION—see also SURFACE—see also TECHNIQUE.

PALIMPSEST

Palimpsest, manuscripts, document genres by conditions of production: Writing material, usually parchment, that has been written upon more than once; the previous text may have been imperfectly erased, thus remaining partly legible.

Landscape Architecture II. STU 1112. Department of Landscape Architecture. Core Studio. Spring 2015. Instructors: Anita Berrizbeitia (coordinator), Jill Desimini, Rosetta S. Elkin (coordinator), Shauna Gillies-Smith, Ewa Harabasz (workshop instructor), Martha Schwartz (workshop instructor), and Peter Del Tredici (workshop instructor). Teaching Assistants: Marissa Ashley Angell (MLA I), Ian Scott Brennick (MLA I), Bradley Paul Howe (MLA I), and Leo Raphael Miller (MLA I). The second semester core studio explored the research and design methods associated with interventions in complex urban conditions: sites layered with multiple interventions across a long span of history that present issues of connectivity, accessibility, identity, and the need for contemporary programs. The students learned to apply various forms of research—historical, social, material, spatial, and technical—to the formulation of project arguments and strategies. Emphasis was placed on exploring the relationship between documentation, analytical research, and design through diverse conceptual frameworks and projective representational techniques.

Students: Jonathan James Andrews (MLA I), Emily Anne Ashley Blair (MLA I), Lanisha Blount (MLA I), Laura Faith Butera (MLA I), Jenna Lee Chaplin (MLA I), Timothy Pittman Clark (MLA I), Tiffany Kaewen Dang (MLA I), Emily Ballou Drury (MLA I), Ellen E. Epley (MLA I), Siobhan Elizabeth Feehan (MLA I), Hannah P. Gaengler (MLA I), Ana Cristina Garcia (MLA I), Sophia Georgine Benet Geller (MLA I), Emma Freeman Goode (MLA I), Jeremy

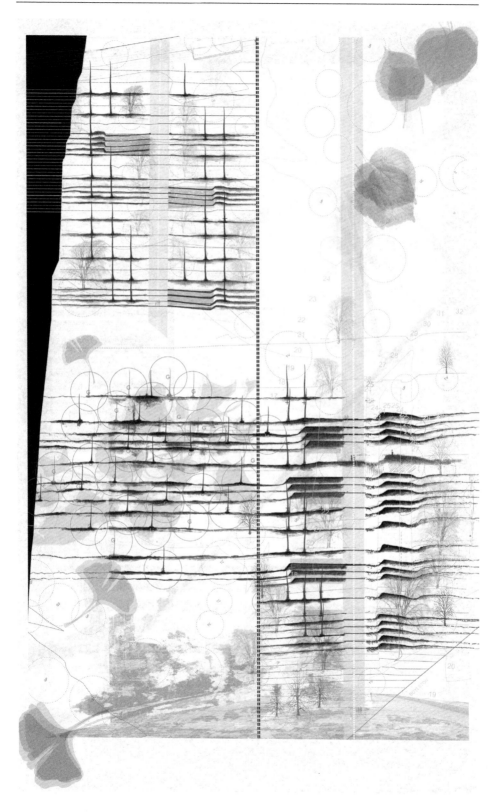

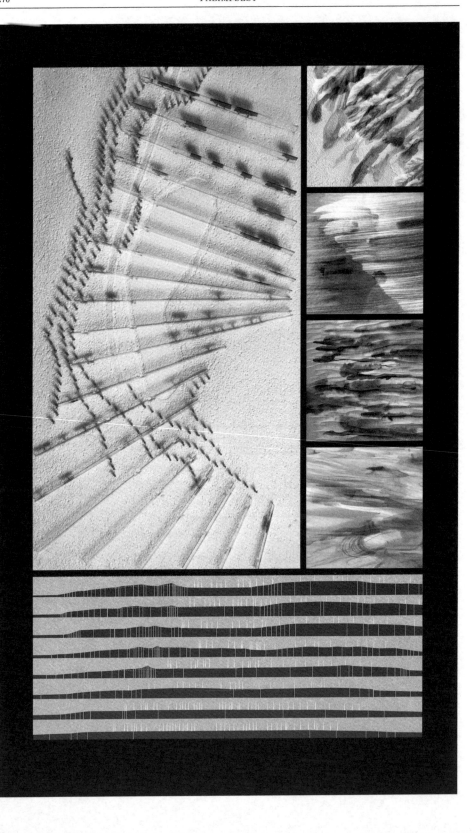

Kamal Hartley (MLA I), Aaron David Charles Hill (MLA I), Rayana Purnata Hossain (MLA I), Dana E. Kash (MLA I), Qi Xuan Li (MLA I), Annie J. W. Liang (MLA I), Rebecca A. Liggins (MLA I), Ho-Ting Liu (MLA I), Sophie R. Maguire (MLA I), Maria Gloria Robalino (MLA I), Louise Shannon Roland (MLA I), Kira Maria Sargent (MLA I), Keith L. Scott (MLA I), Yun Shi (MLA I), Jonah Susskind (MLA I), Diana Tao (MLA I), Carlo P. Urmy (MLA I), Yifan Wang (MLA I), James Toru Watters (MLA I), Eunice Wong (MLA I), Yuan Xue (MLA I), Xin Zhao (MLA I & MDes, ULE). ⸙

Figures. Serial Sections (previous page). Annie J. W. Liang (MLA I). Model (opposite page). Carlo P. Urmy (MLA I). Drawings & Sections (opposite page). Yuan Xue (MLA I). Section (below). Xin Zhao (MLA I & MDes, ULE).

See also MEMORIAL: Abstracted Geologies—see also PARK: Botanical Park at the Epang Palace.

PANEL

1: (a) A schedule containing names of persons summoned as jurors; (b) jury. 2: (a) A group of persons selected for service <a *panel* of experts>; (b) a group of persons who discuss before an audience a topic of public interest, also *panel* discussion; (c) a group of entertainers or guests engaged as players in a quiz or game on a radio or television program.

Paneling, wall coverings by form: Wall coverings consisting of *panels* of wood or other material joined in a continuous surface. *Panel,* wood by form or function: In art, the term refers to wood in the form of broad, thin, flat, or sometimes curved pieces. In architecture and other constructive arts, use "*panels* (surface components)" to refer to a *panel,* whether of wood or another material, that is typically a compartment of a surface either sunken below or raised above the general level and set in a molding or other border as a frame.

See also DOOR—see also ELEMENT—see also IMAGINATION: Architectural Imagination After May '68—see also IMPLEMENT: The Urban Design Group—see also MATERIAL—see also PHOTOGRAPHY—see also PRACTICE: Practice Platform Panel—see also SURFACE—see also WALL—see also WOOD.

PAPER

Arches *paper, paper* by form: Various acid-free, 100 percent cotton watercolor *papers* made in Lorraine,

France. The *paper* is mold-made, gelatin-sized, air-dried, and pH neutral. Sheets have deckle edges and are watermarked. It has a warm white color and is produced in hot-pressed, cold-pressed, and rough varieties. Although "Arches" is a registered trademark, the term has become generic through common usage and is typically spelled without the trademark symbol. The company was founded in 1492 and is still in operation. Carbon *paper,* transfer *paper*: A type of lightweight *paper* used for duplicating typewriting, pencil, or pen writing. The *paper* is coated on one side with dark pigment and a medium, typically a mix of waxes and oils, that is transferred to a copying surface such as *paper* by the impact of writing pressure or typewriter keys. Smudge-proof carbon *paper* has an additional coating of plastic lacquer. Copy *paper*: *Paper* designed for photocopying which may or may not be sensitized. Drawing *paper*: Heavy *paper,* typically white or buff in color, used for making drawings; it can be either smooth or rough, the smooth being hot-pressed. Good grades of drawing *paper* should allow considerable erasure without destroying its appearance. *Paper,* fiber product: Refers generally to all types of thin matted or felted sheets or webs of fiber formed and dried on a fine screen from a pulpy water suspension. The fibers may be animal, such as hair, silk or wool, or mineral, such as asbestos, or synthetic. However, most *paper* is made from cellulosic plant fiber, such as from wood pulp, grass, cotton, linen, and straw. Kraft *paper,* wood pulp *paper, paper* by composition or origin: A very strong *paper,* usually a light brown in color, which was originally made from rope but now is produced from unbleached sulfate wood pulp. Tracing *paper,* drawing *paper*: Any translucent *paper* which, when laid over an existing image, permits the image to be seen and traced.

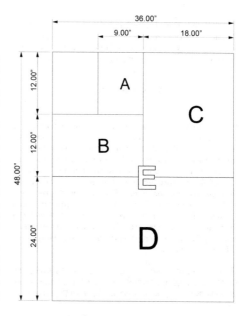

Figure. Standard Architectural Drawing Sizes (above).

Paper. Harvard University purchases 2,000 tons of *paper* each year totaling 13,333 feet—almost as high as the tallest peak in the Rocky Mountains. The Harvard GSD community uses 644,000 sheets of *paper* per semester. ⸙

See also ANIMATION—see also COLOR—see also DRAWING—see also PLOT—see also PRINT—see also SURFACE.

PAPERCUT

Cut-paper work, paperwork, visual work: Designs, patterns, or images created by removing small portions from the interior or edges of a piece of paper.

PaperCut. The Harvard GSD uses a print management software called *PaperCut* to track print job status, manage printers, and calculate printing costs. ❦

PARADIGM

1: Example, pattern, especially an outstandingly clear or typical example or archetype. 2: An example of a conjugation or declension showing a word in all its inflectional forms. 3: A philosophical and theoretical framework of a scientific school or discipline within which theories, laws, and generalizations and the experiments performed in support of them are formulated; broadly, a philosophical or theoretical framework of any kind.

See also COMPUTATION: Paradigms in Computing—see also LANDSCAPE: Theories of Landscape as Urbanism, Landscapes as Infrastructure—see also ROBOTICS: Informal Robotics.

PARALLEL

Parallel, positional attributes by relative position: Extending in the same direction and everywhere equidistant; usually said of lines and linear objects and structures. For the corresponding noun, use "*parallelism.*"

PARAMETER

1: (a) An arbitrary constant whose value characterizes a member of a system, also a quantity that describes a statistical population; (b) an independent variable used to express the coordinates of a variable point and functions of them—compare *parametric* equation. 2: Any of a set of physical properties whose values determine the characteristics or behavior of something <*parameters* of the atmosphere such as temperature, pressure, and density>. 3: Something represented by a *parameter*, a characteristic element, broadly characteristic, element, factor <political dissent as a *parameter* of modern life>. 4: Limit, boundary.

See also COMPUTATION—see also DATA—see also INFORMATION—see also QUALITATIVE—see also QUANTITATIVE—see also SOFTWARE—see also SYSTEM—see also TYPE: Blob Block Slab Mat Slat.

PARCEL

Parcel, lots, lands, open spaces by location or context: *Parcels* of land with fixed boundaries occupied or capable of being occupied by one building or use, including accessory buildings, and not divided by any public highway or alley. Distinguished from "plats (land)," because plats tend to be somewhat larger than lots and are often in the countryside, while lots are typically smaller and located within a settlement.

See also DEVELOPMENT—see also LAND—see also LIMINAL: Liminal Space—see also REAL ESTATE—see also SETTLEMENT—see also TERRITORY.

PARK

Amusement *park*, recreation areas: Commercially operated areas containing rides, stalls, and shows, and other entertainment attractions intended to attract a large number of visitors. Community *park*, *parks* by location or context: *Parks*, usually over 20 acres in extent, offering a wider range of activities and considerably more open space than "neighborhood *parks.*" Cultural *park*, *parks* by location or contexts: Heritage sites and the lands related to them committed to providing a cultural, recreational, and cultural resource for the public at large. *Park*, grounds, open spaces by location or context: Enclosed, preserved, and extensive woodland and pasture attached to substantial residences; especially in England and British colonies. Industrial *park*, industrial complexes, complexes by function: Refers to areas zoned and planned for so-called clean industries, developed and managed as a unit, where plots are offered fully equipped with transport and installation facilities, often already including a number of multi-use buildings. National *park*, *parks* by ownership or administration: Areas of special scenic, historical, or scientific importance set aside and maintained by a national government especially for recreation or study. Office *park*, office complexes, complexes by function: Areas of land or property where many office buildings may be grouped together and developed specifically to attract corporate offices. Skateboarding *park*, sports complexes, recreation areas: Areas designed or used primarily for the sport of skateboarding, including straight tracks as well as a variety of slopes and banked surfaces for sudden turns and stunts. Urban *park*, *parks* by location or context: Small *parks* serving central business districts, highly urban areas (including new towns), or commercial districts.

Botanical Park at the Epang Palace: Curating a Chinese Collection and Palimpsest. Thesis. Yi Lun Yang (MLA I), advised by Anita Berrizbeitia.
"The protection and preservation of both natural and cultural heritage sites in Xi'an, China, faces challenges as the city undergoes rapid industrialization and urbanization. This design thesis identifies the Epang Palace relic (212 BCE) as an important cultural infrastructure in Xi'an and transforms it into an urban botanical *park*. Botanical gardens as urban *parks* can engage with neighborhoods and act as mediators between past and future, the city and botany. In order to preserve this fragile and urbanistically contested site, this project envisions and curates botanical collections of Chinese soils. The *park's* four corners will act as new urban anchors. The project also integrates the process of archaeological excavation to create an active layer of palimpsest on the ancient ground, accruing new productive qualities and potentials in the process. Taking into account ecological, historical, and conservation param-

eters, the botanical approach experiments with new hybrids of ownership and stewardship of the land. The goal of this project is to provide a framework for diversifying both vegetal composition and human occupation over time. The *park* offers a holistic approach to designing a Chinese cultural heritage site that can be applied to similar sites around the city to create a cultural and botanical *park* system and reintegrate the city's profound history with its urban development and the daily lives of its inhabitants." ⊛

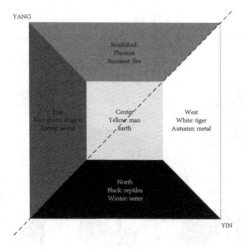

YANG

SouthRed;
Phoenix
Summer; fire

East
blue-green: dragon
Spring: wood

Center
Yellow: man
earth

West
White: tiger
Autumn: metal

North
Black: reptiles
Winter: water

YIN

Figure. Diagram (above). Yi Lun Yang (MLA I).

Urban Parks: The Battleground in Reviving City. Loeb Fellowship Lecture. Gund Hall, Piper Auditorium. May 8, 2015. Inga Saffron.
Distinguished journalist and architecture critic Inga Saffron illustrated the complexities of creating *park* policy that will contribute to reviving 21st-century cities. ⊛

See also AVIATION: Flights of Imagination—see also COMMUNITY—see also CULTURE—see also EDGE: The Barracks of Pion—see also GARDEN—see also NEIGHBORHOOD—see also OFFICE—see also TYPOLOGY—see also URBAN.

PARKING

Parking garage, vehicle storage buildings: Stacked *parking* structures comprising a building or part of a building having several stories and designed or used specifically for *parking* automobiles. *Parking* lot, motor vehicle lots, transportation spaces: Plots of ground used for the *parking* of vehicles.

PARTY

Party, events, activities: Occasions of celebration or merrymaking by groups of people. For larger and more formal occasions of celebration, use "festivals." *Party* wall, walls by location or context: Walls used jointly by two *parties* under easement agreement, erected upon a line dividing two parcels of land or between two dwelling units.

Beaux Arts Ball. Student Event. The Liberty Hotel. March 28, 2015. ⊛

Halloween Party. Student Event. Cyclorama Boston, Boston Center for the Arts. October 31, 2014. ⊛

See also BUILDING—see also CONSTRUCTION—see also DWELLING—see also EXPERIENCE—see also WALL.

PATTERN

Pattern, design elements: Ornamental designs, usually on a flat surface or in relief and composed of repeated or combined motifs. Distinguish from "motifs," which are distinct or separable design elements occurring singly as individual shapes. *Pattern*, guides, shaping & guiding tools: Forms or models, made from a variety of materials, cut to the size or profile of the finished article and used as a guide during its construction. Traffic *pattern*, transportation-related concepts: The passage of people or vehicles along routes of transportation. Also, vehicles or pedestrians in transit.

Innovate: R. Buckminster Fuller, Pattern Thinking. GSD Talks. Gund Hall, Stubbins. March 3, 2015. Ingrid Bengston (MArch I), Hanif Kara, Daniel Lopez-Perez, Andrew Witt with Iñaki Ábalos (moderator).
In celebration of what would be R. Buckminster Fuller's 120th anniversary (1895–2015), "*Pattern* Thinking" explored the relationship between artifacts and inventions in his work and their legacy in contemporary practice. Fuller's explorations into the physical *pattern* of shelter, structure, cartography, and even the universe was juxtaposed with his conceptual thinking of terms such as Dymaxion, Geodesic, and Tensegrity as a way to argue for their irreducibility. Through the lens of Fuller's transversal *pattern* thinking, a number of artifacts and inventions were explored from their literal to their most conceptual manifestations: Dymaxion as a mathematical, projective, cartographic, and political model of efficiency; Geodesic as a formal, structural, environmental, and social model of shelter; Tensegrity as a structural, natural and universal model of order.
Innovate is a noontime talk series, featuring 20-minute presentations followed by discussions with faculty and students. ⊛

See also CIRCULATION—see also CONSTRUCTION—see also DRAWING—see also ELEMENT—see also FORM—see also GEOMETRY—see also MATERIAL—see also MODEL—see also MOIRE—see also ORNAMENT—see also SCALE—see also SETTLEMENT—see also SURFACE—see also SYSTEM.

PAVILION

Pavilion, building divisions, components by specific context: Refers to both for the parts of buildings that project outward from the rest, especially common as corner, central, or terminal features in French architecture, and the detached or semidetached units into which a building (as a hospital) is sometimes divided. *Pavilion*, garden structures, single built works by location or context: Light, sometimes ornamental, structures in gardens, parks, or places of recreation that are used for entertainment or shelter.

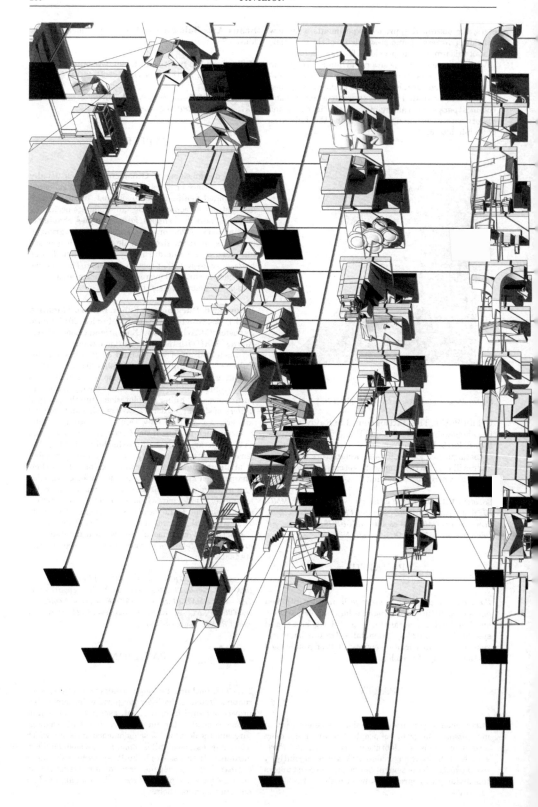

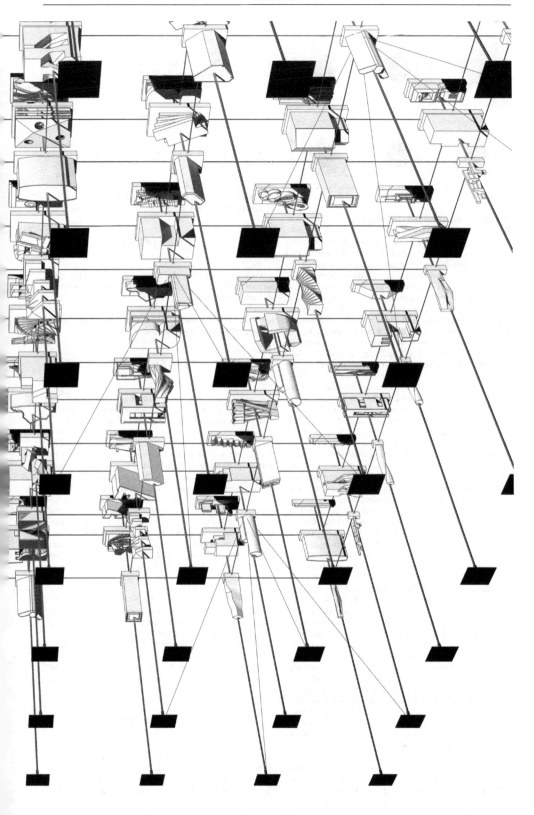

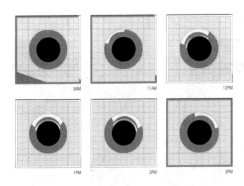

Design Miami/ Harvard GSD Pavilion. Competition. Spring 2015. Design Miami/ & Harvard GSD.

The annual Design Miami/ fairs are developed with the intent of creating a convergence of culture and commerce, inciting design enthusiasts and connoisseurs from around the world to engage with gallery exhibitions, commissions, talks, and installations celebrating avant-garde industrial and conceptual design. Design Miami/ has become the premier venue for collecting, exhibiting, discussing, and creating collectible design. Each December, Design Miami/ commissions young architects and designers to build a designed environment at the entrance to the fair. The Design Miami/ *Pavilion* acts both as a segue to the fair and a refuge for the more than 50,000 visitors who come to Miami for fair week, acting as a public installation that marries the practical requirements of shelter and seating to innovative architectural ideas. Past recipients of the *pavilion* commission include studios: Aranda\Lasch, Moorhead & Moorhead, Snarkitecture, formlessfinder, and Jonathan Muecke. The 2015 *pavilion* commission furthered Design Miami/'s goal of offering opportunities to young designers by collaborating with the Harvard GSD, and the 2015 *pavilion* was the first designed by students. All Harvard GSD students were eligible to propose designs for a temporary structure that responds to this unique environment with a bold public statement. A jury of Harvard GSD faculty—including Preston Scott Cohen, Grace La, Patrick Sean McCafferty, Mohsen Mostafavi, and Chris Reed—selected five finalists from the 32 submissions. The finalists presented their round-two designs to a jury of Design Miami/ representatives and Harvard GSD faculty and staff on May 12, 2015.

Finalists: *ICE*—Mark Turibius Jongman-Sereno (MLA I AP), Timothy Nawrocki (MLA I AP), Christopher James Reznich (MLA I AP) with Charles A. Waldheim (faculty advisor). *Melt Down*—Mark William Eichler (MArch II), Akihiro Moriya (MAUD), Phi Yen Nguyen (MArch I) with George L. Legendre (faculty advisor). *Oasis*—Brian Y. Chu (MArch II), Conor Coghlan (MArch II) with Toshiko Mori (faculty advisor). *Pitch*—Mikhail Thomas Grinwald (MArch II & MDes, HPD), Katie MacDonald (MArch II), Erin Anne Pellegrino (MArch II), Jake Peter Rudin (MDes, Tech) with Hanif Kara (faculty advisor). *Unbuilt*—Jennifer Lixian Shen (MArch I), Yiliu Chen Shen-Burke (MArch I), Douglas Robert Harsevoort (MArch I), Steven T. Meyer (MArch I), Joanne K. Cheung (MArch I) with Luis Callejas (faculty advisor). ❧

Figures. Drawing (previous spread). Joanne K. Cheung (MArch I), Douglas Robert Harsevoort (MArch I), Steven T. Meyer (MArch I), Jennifer Lixian Shen (MArch I), and Yiliu Chen

Shen-Burke (MArch I). Shadow Study Diagrams (left). Brian Y. Chu (MArch II) & Conor Coghlan (MArch II).

See also BUILDING—see also COMPETITION—see also CON- STRUCTION—see also EXHIBITION—see also GARDEN—see also INSTALLATION.

PEDAGOGY

1: The art, science, or profession of teaching, especially education.

See also ACADEMIA—see also ATLAS: Form & Pedagogy—see also FACULTY—see also MODERN: More than Mere Practicality—see also RESEARCH—see also VISIONARY: Grounded Visionaries.

PEDESTRIAN

1: Commonplace, unimaginative. 2: (a) Going or performed on foot; (b) of, relating to, or designed for walking <a *pedestrian* mall>.

See also BODY—see also CIRCULATION—see also MALL—see also PROMENADE—see also WALKING.

PERCEPTION

Figure-ground *perception*, visual & representation concepts, formal concepts: In an image, the way in which an object or shape is related to the background against which it is seen. *Perception*, psychological concepts, social science concepts: The process of becoming aware of objects, qualities, or relations via the sense organs; involves the reception, processing, and interpretation of sensory impressions. Space *perception*, psychological concepts: Refers to the awareness or consciousness of an organism to the relative position and orientation of its body and to the objects around it; based on recognition of depth and distance and other external stimuli. The concept also describes the compensatory capacity to use limited perceptual clues to orient oneself or predict and construct an environment's spatial field. Visual *perception*, psychological concepts: The process of receiving and interpreting sensory impressions attained by sight.

See also CONCEPT—see also DRAWING—see also FIGURE- GROUND—see also FORM—see also HOLOGRAM: Fragments of a Hologram House—see also HYPEROBJECT: The Proximities of Nuclear Waste—see also OBJECT—see also OBSERVATION—see also PATTERN—see also PHENOMENON—see also PLANNING: Perceptions of Physical Space and the Planning Process in Camp Azraq, Jordan—see also REPRESENTATION—see also SENSORY—see also SPACE—see also WORK: Perceiving & Working.

PERFORMANCE

Performance, entertainment events, activities: Instances of the execution of an action, operation, or process in *performing* a literary, artistic, or other creative work. *Performance* art, time-based works, visual works by material or technique: Refers to works of art that unfold over time and that combine elements of theater and object-oriented art. *Performance* specification, contract documents: Specifications written according to recognized standards within the building industry, such as the American Society for Testing & Materials (ASTM) and containing a complete description of the project including materials, products, designs, functions, and the *performance* to be expected.

GSDance. Student Group. GSDance connects the Harvard GSD community through the medium of dance. The group is open to all members of the Harvard GSD and provides a space of inclusion free of competition or judgment. Group activities include, but are not limited to, a weekly open level, multistyle dance class, specialized dance workshops, and opportunities for *performances* and recitals. ֎

GSDrag Show. Student Event. Gund Hall, Piper Auditorium. April 10, 2015. Queers in Design. ֎

Restless Legacy Performance & Finale. Event. Memorial Hall, Sanders Theater. September 12, 2014. Korea GSD.
   A fun-filled *performance* concluded the opening night of the Grounded Visionaries Design Weekend & Campaign Launch featuring dancers from Korea GSD and K. Michael Hays. ֎

High-Performance Design Group. Student Group. The High-*Performance* Design Group is a platform for students who are interested in sustainability and high-*performance* building design. The intention of the group is to aggregate, share, and improve our knowledge, experience, and research in the subject across the disciplines at the Harvard GSD. The High-*Performance* Design Group positions itself as a student consulting group where members provide skills and resources for the entire student body and research fellows at the Harvard GSD. ֎

See also ART—see also BUILDING—see also CONSTRUCTION—see also CREATIVITY—see also HISTORY: Temporary Accumulations—see also INTEGRATION: High-Performance Buildings and Systems Integration—see also LISTEN: Symphony of the Air—see also MATERIAL: Material Performance—see also MEMORY: We Exist! We Exist!—see also PARAMETER—see also PARTY—see also PROJECT—see also PROJECTION—see also TECHNIQUE—see also WALL: Working Matter.

PERMEABILITY

Permeability, physical properties, attributes & properties by specific type: Property of porous material which is measured by the rate by volume at which a fluid passes through a cross section of the material. Soil *permeability*: The extent to which gases, liquids, or plant roots penetrate into or pass through a layer of soil.

PERSPECTIVE

Anamorphic *perspective*: Refers to a system of *perspective* that is based on orthodox linear *perspective* but exploits the extreme degradation of forms on the picture plane at very wide angles of view. It uses the optical trick of anamorphosis, in which a form depicted on the picture plane is subject to such extreme lateral stretching that it is unrecognizable from the front, but legible when viewed from a very shallow angle. Bird's-eye *perspective*: Refers to *perspective* drawings having a viewpoint well above normal eye level; for other nonphotographic depictions from a high viewpoint, where *perspective* is not used or is not emphasized, use "bird's-eye views." For photographs taken from high locations, use "aerial views" or "aerial photographs." Cavalier oblique drawing, elevation obliques, oblique projections: Drawings in oblique projection in which the vertical plane is parallel to the plane of projection (drawing surface), and all three spatial axes are drawn to the same scale. Linear *perspective*, technique: Refers to the system of perspective in which orthogonals converge toward one or more vanishing points. In Western art, the term often refers to the system of one-point *perspective* that was developed in the Italian Renaissance, but based on ancient Greek and Roman models. One-point *perspective*: Refers to drawings, or works in another medium, that are made using one-point *perspective*, which is a system of linear *perspective* using one vanishing point to give the illusion of recession into space. The vanishing point is generally placed at or near the center of the composition. *Perspective* view, images: Refers to drawings or works in any other two-dimensional medium that employ *perspective*, meaning that they are executed by a systematic technique that creates the illusion of recession from a two-dimensional surface. *Perspective, perspective* & shading techniques: Refers to any graphic method concerned with conveying an impression of depth, usually on a two-dimensional surface, by means of geometric projection using one or more vanishing points, foreshortening, and/or atmospheric effects. Techniques include receding lines, gradients of color, tone and texture, and degrees of clarity. In Western art, the term generally refers to the geometrical technique of linear *perspective* that was invented in the early Renaissance, based on ancient Greek and Roman models. Although its meaning overlaps somewhat with "projection," "projection" is typically used for technical and architectural drawings that emphasize the mathematical properties of objects that are preserved in the images; "*perspective*" is used for art works and renderings that include the distortions of lengths, angles, shapes, and straightness of lines that optically appear to occur as objects recede into space. Two-point *perspective*: Refers to drawings, or works in another medium, using two-point *perspective*, which is a system of linear *perspective* in which there are two vanishing points, one at either side of the composition, and where rectangular objects are generally set at an angle to the picture plane. Three-point *perspective*: Refers to drawings that are made using three-point *perspective*, which is either a system of linear *perspective* using three vanishing points where rectangular objects are set at an angle to the picture plane or a depiction where there are three points of view. Worm's-eye *perspective*: Refers to *perspective* drawings having a station point well below normal eye level, typically depicted as if seen from the surface of the Earth or the floor, as if the viewer is lying down and looking straight up. For photographs or other images with low viewpoints, but where precise calculation of *perspective* is not employed or not emphasized, use "worm's-eye views."

See also AERIAL—see also AXONOMETRIC—see also COMPETITION: The Design Competition—see also DRAWING—see also

ELEVATION—see also LINE—see also OBLIQUE—see also PRO-JECTION—see also SECTION—see also SPACE—see also TECH-NIQUE—see also 2-D.

PHENOMENON

1: An observable fact or event. 2: (a) An object or aspect known through the senses rather than by thought or intuition; (b) A temporal or spatiotemporal object of sensory experience as distinguished from a noumenon; (c) a fact or event of scientific interest susceptible to scientific description and explanation. 3: (a) A rare or significant fact or event; (b) an exceptional, unusual, or abnormal person, thing, or occurrence.

See also ATMOSPHERE—see also CLIMATE—see also EX-TREME: Housing in Extreme Environments—see also HABOOB: Dust Kingdom—see also HORIZONSCOPE—see also OBJECT: Object Studio—see also OBSERVATION—see also OLFACTORY: Fossa Olfactoria—see also POST-SUBURB—New Landscape Ter-ritories—see also SENSE.

PHILOSOPHY

Philosophy, humanities, disciplines: Critical examination of the grounds for fundamental beliefs and analysis of the basic concepts, doctrines, or practices that express such beliefs.

See also CONCEPT—see also ETHICS—see also HISTORY: Mas-ter in Design Studies History & Philosophy—see also PRACTICE—see also THEORY.

PHOTOCOLLAGE

Photocollage, photographic compositions, visual works by material or technique: *Collages* in which photographs dominate the composition.

See also COLLAGE—see also COMPOSITION—see also HIKING: Wanderwege—see also MATERIAL—see also TECHNIQUE.

PHOTOGRAPHY

Composite *photograph*, manipulated *photographs*: *Photographic* prints in which two or more negatives are printed as one unified image. For combinations of images, such as *photographs* with architectural drawings, use "photomontage." When pieces of *photographs* or other relatively flat materials are pasted together into less unified images, use "collages." Digital *photographer*, artist by medium or work type: *Photographers* who primarily use digital cameras, which are cameras that acquire images via an electronic sensor and store them as digital information on a memory device. *Photography*, visual works by material or technique: Refers to still images produced from radiation-sensitive materials (sensitive to light, electron beams, or nuclear radiation), generally by means of the chemical action of light on a sensitive film, paper, glass, or metal. *Photographs* may be positive or negative, opaque or transparent.

DeTour Photography. Boston-area *photographer* Adam DeTour *photographed* Harvard GSD faculty for *Platform 8*.

The Neighborhood Ketchup Ad: Housing in American (and Tim Davis') Photography. Lecture. Gund Hall, Room 124. November 19, 2014. Tim Davis.

Tim Davis delivered a lecture on American *photogra-phy's* complex relationship with housing and the built environment, exploring, through a historical survey and a presentation of his own work, how the differences and clashes between residential and commercial environments inform how Americans understand their landscape. ❦

See also AERIAL—see also CHURCH: Nicholas Hawksmoor—see also COLLAGE—see also COMMUNICATION—see also COMPOSITE—see also EXHIBITION—see also LAB—see also LIGHTING—see also MATERIAL—see also PAPER—see also PHOTOMONTAGE: Composite Landscapes—see also REPRE-SENTATION—see also TECHNIQUE.

PHOTOMONTAGE

Photomontage, montages, visual works by materials or techniques: Refers to combinations of photographic images such as architectural drawings, usually arranged into a somewhat unified image. For photographs pro-duced by printing two or more negatives as one unified image, use "composite photographs." When pieces of photographs or other relatively flat materials are pasted together into less unified images, use "collages."

Composite Landscapes: Photomontage & Land-scape Architecture. Publication. Hatje Cantz, 2014. Charles A. Waldheim & Andrea Hansen (editors). TR660 .F54 2014.

Composite Landscapes examines one of landscape architecture's most recognizable representational forms, the montage view. The volume gathers work from a select group of influential contemporary artists and a dozen of the world's leading landscape architects. These compos-ite views reveal practices of *photomontage* depicting the conceptual, experiential, and temporal dimensions of landscape. *Composite Landscapes* illustrates the analog origins of a method now rendered ubiquitous through digital means. In revisiting the composite landscape view as a cultural form, *Composite Landscapes* illuminates the contemporary status of the photographically con-structed image for the design disciplines and beyond.

Croisade ou, Le crépuscule des académies. Publication. Éditions G. Crès, 1933. Le Corbusier (author). Le Corbusier Research Collection, Frances Loeb Library. LeC NA 27 L496b.

"*Croisade ou, Le crépuscule des académies* was a re-sponse to the lecture given by Beaux-Arts architect and academic Gustave Umbdenstock on March 14, 1932, attacking Le Corbusier for his alleged internationalism as contrary to nationalist beliefs and traditional build-ing crafts. Here, Le Corbusier openly defends modern architecture as an art and argues for its deep roots in humanism, positioning himself against both national regionalist sentiments and reductive functionalist ide-ologies. As described by Catherine de Smet, the strength of his written argument was visually paralleled with the use of *photomontage* (used here for the first time by Le Corbusier), to emphasize the polemical impact of the

publication. The *photomontage* emphasize the difference in the aesthetics and effects of both positions: one embracing future progress, the other entrenched in the past." —Inés Zalduendo. ֎

See also ART—see also COLLAGE—see also COMPOSITE—see also CRAFT—see also DIGITAL—see also DRAWING—see also HISTORY—see also MATERIAL—see also MONTAGE—see also PHOTOGRAPHY—see also PRACTICE—see also REPRESENTA-TION—see also SOFTWARE—see also TECHNIQUE.

PICTURESQUE

Picturesque, aesthetic concepts, philosophical concepts: Aesthetic concept or expression, arising in Europe, first in painting of the 18th century and later in architecture of the 19th century, characterized by rough, curious, or irregular forms; it applies particularly to rustic landscapes and crumbling buildings having neither the awe-inspiring grandeur of the Sublime nor the order and regularity of beauty.

The Endless Landscape: Observations on the Hudson River. STU 1402. Department of Landscape Architecture. Option Studio. Fall 2014. Instructors: Eelco Hooftman & Bridget Baines. Teaching Assistant: Olivia Kaufman Rovira (MLA I).

In recent years, the studio explored the iconography and scenography of the American landscape through studies of Frederick Law Olmsted's Central Park and Henry Thoreau's Walden. This year, the studio extended its research further into the dark hinterland and traveled upstream along the Hudson River searching for the origin of the American landscape psyche. The Endless Landscape studio explored notions of a new radicalized *picturesque* as a stimulus and provocation to compose visionary and cinematic landscapes. Departing from two stories by Edgar Allan Poe—"The Domain of Arnheim" (1846) and its pendant "Landor's Cottage" (1848), which reveal an exquisite discourse into landscape aesthetics inspired by the *picturesque* movement in both Britain and America—and informed by paintings by artists from the Hudson River School—such as Thomas Cole, Frederick Church, and Asher Durand—the outdoor laboratory and field of experiment for the studio was a series of distinctive sites along the Hudson River. Each was selected for their evocative nature such as a former power station, abandoned quarry, dismantled car factory, and the exquisite surreal ruins of Bannerman Island: a former munitions facility built as mock baronial castle.

Students: Marissa Ashley Angell (MLA I), Lisa Jane Caplan (MLA I), Olivia Kaufman Rovira (MLA I), Gregory Joseph Logan (MArch I), Lara Elisabeth Mehling (MLA I), Nuith Morales (MLA I), Raphael Stahelin (ETH), Jeronimo Van Schendel Erice (MArch II), Evelyn McLaurin Volz (MLA I), Allyssa Petrina Williams (MLA II), Yi Lun Yang (MLA I), Hannes Zander (MLA II), Simon Zemp (ETH). ֎

Figures. Maps & Plan (previous page). Olivia Kaufman Rovira (MLA I). Site Plan (opposite page). Yi Lun Yang (MLA I).

See also COMPOSITION—see also CONCEPT—see also FORM—see also HISTORY—see also LANDSCAPE—see also OBSERVA-TION—see also PAINTING—see also PARK—see also PERSPEC-TIVE—see also STYLE.

PINUP

1: Something fastened to a wall, such as (a) a photograph or poster of a person considered to have glamorous qualities; (b) something designed for wall attachment.

Studio Pinup. *Pinups* are informal presentations that take place periodically during studio. Students present their work in progress before faculty and their classmates. *Pinups* give students a chance to observe peer approaches to the same project and also to practice presentation skills. It is typical to have three to four *pinups* per project, but this number can vary depending on the critic and the needs of the student. ֎

See also COMMUNICATION—see also PRACTICE—see also RE-VIEW—see also WORK.

PLACE

Place, environmental psychology concepts, psychological concepts: The concept of a space or area within the lived world of daily experience, perceived as distinct and unified, and possessing emotional, purposive, and social connotations along with physical features and characteristics. For the concept of purely physical position in the universe, precisely definable in terms of geographic or astronomic measurement, or situation relative to geographic or astronomic features or elements of the built environment, use "location." Inhabited *place*, settlements & landscapes: General term for *places* or areas occupied, modified, or planned to be inhabited by communities of human populations and that contain enough societal functions to be relatively self-sufficient. They are characterized by inhabitants living in neighboring sets of living quarters and by the *place* having a proper name or a locally recognized status. Workplace, *place*, environmental psychological concepts: Locale where work is done, usually when referring to a *place* of employment.

See also AGE: Aging & Place—see also BUILT—see also COM-MUNITY—see also CONSERVATION: Critical Conservation—see also DWELLING—see also EDGE: The Barracks of Pion—see also ENVIRONMENT—see also HEALTH: Healthy Places—see also INITIATIVE: Health & Places Initiatives—see also LANDMARK: Montreal is Back—see also OBJECT: Object Studio—see also PLANNING: Planning and Design Guidelines and Prototypes for Healthier Places—see also POST-SUBURB—see also SETTLE-MENT—see also SPACE—see also WORK.

PLAN

1: A drawing or diagram drawn on a plane, such as (a) a top or horizontal view of an object; (b) a large-scale map of a small area. 2: (a) A method for achieving an end; (b) an often customary method of doing something, procedure; (c) a detailed formulation of a program of action; (d) goal, aim. 3: An orderly arrangement of parts of an overall design or objective. 4: A detailed program <pension *plan*>.

Area *plan*, orthographic projections: Orthographic *plans* portraying buildings, topography, plantings, roads, and other features of an area. Block *plan*, site *plans*, area *plans*: Small-scale, simplified *plans* of a building or building site, with features or structures indicated by simple outlines or shapes. Building *plan*, orthographic projection: Orthographic drawings, prints, or sketches that depict a building, or sections of a building, on a horizontal plane. Comprehensive *plan*, reports, *plans* by function: Organized, detailed proposals that are comprehensive in scope and lay out strategies and schemes of action for something to be done. Examples include land use control law, zoning, and urban redevelopment omnibus *plans* of cities or towns for housing, industry, commercial, and recreational facilities and their impact on environmental factors. Floor *plan*, building *plans*, *plans*, orthographic projection: Drawings or works in another two-dimensional medium that represent a horizontal section through a building taken above a floor to diagrammatically illustrate the enclosing walls, interior spaces, doors, and windows of a building. Grading *plan*, site *plans*, area *plans*, orthographic projection: *Plans* that show the ground surface of a building site or other site, generally including grade elevations and contours. Master *plan*, orthographic projections: Overall *plan*, usually graphic and drawn on a small scale, into which the details of other specific *plans* are fitted. A master *plan* is frequently supplemented by written material. For *plans* having to do with land use control law, zoning, and urban redevelopment used to describe the omnibus *plans* of cities or towns for housing, industry, commercial, and recreational facilities and their impact on environmental factors, use "comprehensive *plans*." Plan, formal concept, form & composition concepts: The formal concept of the layout of spaces and elements in the built environment, such as of a building or city. *Plan*, maps by form: Refers to maps depicting a relatively small district or region, such as a town or city, drawn on a large scale and with considerable detail. For maps of larger regions, use "topographic maps" or "chorographic maps." For depictions of smaller plots of land, particularly as related to the planning of architecture, use "site *plans*." *Plan*, orthographic projection: Refers to drawings, sketches, prints, computer graphics, or works in other media depicting a building or any object viewed from above, geometrically represented as projected on a horizontal plane. The term is particularly used to refer to drawings or other images showing the relative positions of all the parts of a building, or of the parts of any one floor, roof, or other part of a building in horizontal section; it is thus distinguished from vertical sections or elevations. The term can also be used collectively to refer to sets of drawings or other images for a project, including *plans* as well as other drawings, such as sections. For general reference to depictions or photographs showing structures or sites seen from directly above, use "*plan* views." For representations of portions of the Earth's surface use "maps" or "*plans* (maps)." Planting *plan*, landscaping *plans*, site *plans:* Refers to *plans* indicating the layout of trees, shrubs, and other plants on a building site or for garden or landscape design. Site *plan*, area *plans*, orthographic projection: Drawings or works in another medium laying out the precise arrangement of a structure on a plot of land. It may also refer to *plans* for gardens, groups of buildings, or developments, where the layout of buildings, roadways, utilities, landscape elements, topography, water features, and vegetation may be depicted. For drawings or other representations on a horizontal surface of cities or larger areas, particularly when such representations are not part of a design process, use "*plans* (maps)."

First Semester Core Urban Planning Studio. STU 1121. Department of Urban Planning & Design. Core Studio. Fall 2014. Instructors: Manisha Bewtra, Ann Forsyth (coordinator), Ana Gelabert-Sánchez (coordinator), Peter Park, Robert Gerard Pietrusko (workshop instructor), and Kathy Spiegelman. Teaching Assistants: Young Ae Chung (MUP), Irene Figueroa Ortiz (MArch I & MUP), Margaret Elizabeth Scott (MUP), Jonathan Springfield (MUP), and Robert William Wellburn (MUP).

The first semester core studio introduced students to the fundamental knowledge and technical skills used by urban planners to research, analyze, and implement *plans* and projects for the built environment. The studio used the City of Boston as the students' planning laboratory and students were expected to understand the city through the lenses of planning elements such as demographics, economic attributes, market forces, character and built form, and public and private stakeholder interests, all of which shape the city and inform decisions about land use, development, and infrastructure. The studio was organized into three parts, each representing a fundamental stage of the urban planning process. Part one explored the research skills and analytic tools used by urban planners to understand the built environment. Part two explored the importance of ideas as the basis for urban planning. An emphasis was placed on identifying sources of creative thinking, how ideas are expressed, and how they result in urban planning outcomes. Part three explored the making of *plans* for the built environment. Using the creative and research skills developed in parts one and two of the studio, students prepared functional urban *plans*, addressing land use, related building types, infrastructure requirements, open space needs, and other aspects of physical *plans*. It focused on the strategies that planners use to implement their ideas. Students explored the range of implementation tools necessary to realize a *plan*, including zoning, development guidelines, phasing, sources and uses of funds, public engagement, and roles and responsibilities, among others. Throughout the semester the principles of urban planning with regard to equity, environment, and economics were explored in planning proposals.

Students: Faisal bin Ayyaf Almogren (MUP), Maira A. Blanco (MUP), Elena Chang (MUP), Sohael Chowfla (MUP), Katherine Anabel Curiel (MUP), Isabel Margarita De Leon Cantada (MUP), Megan Mahala Echols (MUP), Marco Luigi Gorini (MUP), Fernando Granados Franco (MUP), Carolyn J. Grossman (MUP), Warren Everett Alexis Hagist (MUP), Tamara Jafar (MUP), Nathalie Maria Janson (MUP), Elliot Kilham (MUP), Russell P. Koff (MUP), Francisco Lara Garcia (MUP), Samuel Pike LaTronica (MUP), Alexander C. Lew (MUP), Paul Andrew Lillehaugen (MUP), Stephany Yu-Zhu Lin (MUP), Xinwei Liu (MUP), John William Curran McCartin (MUP), Dana Elise McKinney (MUP & MArch I), Meghan L. McNulty (MUP), Marcus Antone Walter Mello (MUP & MArch I), Andres E. Mendoza Gutfreund (MUP), Alexander John Mercuri (MUP), Vanessa Park Moon (MUP), Yvonne G. Mwangi (MUP), Paige E. Peltzer (MUP), Nina Denise Phinouwong (MUP & MLA I), Carlos Felipe Reyes (MUP), Aline Elizabeth Reynolds (MUP), Jennifer Athena Saura (MUP & MLA I), Emma L. Schnur (MUP), David Schoen (MUP), Laurel M. Schwab (MUP), Courtney Dominique Sharpe (MUP), Apoorva Narayan Shenvi (MUP), Brodrick Charles Spencer (MUP), Annie White (MUP), Sarah Madeleine Winston (MUP & MLA I). ❧

Figures. Maps (opposite page). Apoorva Narayan Shenvi (MUP). Aerial Perspective Diagram (next page). Vanessa Park Moon (MUP).

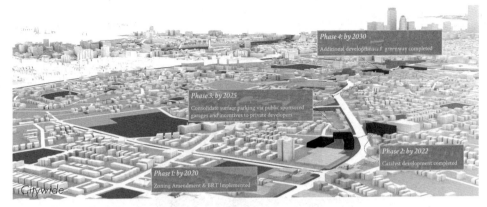

La ville radieuse. Publication. Éditions de l'Architecture d'Aujourd'hui, 1935. Le Corbusier (author). Le Corbusier Research Collection, Frances Loeb Library. LeC NAC 5550 L496.

"Published in this book, and as described by Stanislaus von Moos, La ville radieuse (an ideal urban master *plan* never realized) epitomizes the idea of the freestanding slab in a wide-open green space. The proposed city, in spite of the radical terms of its actual realization (its tabula rasa approach would have required extensive demolitions), influenced modern urban planning, and led to the generation of planning principles and development of high-density urban building typologies. The new city, a Cartesian grid of skyscrapers on a vast open space, was devised as a result of repetition and standardization as vehicles of a new urban form. This new urban form would be guided by zoning legislation and the segregation of functions in the modern city: dwelling, work, recreation, and transportation. These four functions were promoted by the Congrès International d'Architecture Moderne (CIAM) and defined the Athens Charter." —Inés Zalduendo. ❧

Les plans de Paris. Publication. Éditions de Minuit, 1956. Le Corbusier (author). Le Corbusier Research Collection, Frances Loeb Library. LeC NAC 6898 L496a.

"This is a compilation of Le Corbusier's urban proposals for Paris, beautifully illustrated with sketches of his architectural and urban ideas. What is unique in this publication is the integration of the text with the book design itself: it includes a *piste verte*, a color motif that suggests a parallel reading that clarifies concepts along the way. The book also incorporates ideas developed in *plans* elsewhere in the world and relates these ideas to his *plans* for Paris. The *piste verte* provides an aesthetic, visual dimension to the book as a designed object itself; and represents the path (with its accompanying advances and trepidations) to better understand Le Corbusier's conceptualization of the city as a *ville verte*." —Inés Zalduendo. ❧

See also ACTION—see also BUILDING—see also CITY—see also COLLECTION—see also COMMUNICATION—see also COMPOSITION—see also DETAIL—see also DRAFTING—see also DRAWING—see also EXTRUSION: City of Artificial Extrusions—see also FORM—see also GRID—see also GROUND—see also LANDSCAPE—see also LINE—see also MAPPING—see also MEASURE—see also MODERN—see also OBLIQUE—see also ORTHOGRAPHIC—see also PLANT—see also PUBLICATION—see also REPRESENTATION—see also SCALE—see also SECTION—see also URBAN.

PLANE

Plane wood, hardwood: Wood of trees belonging to the genus Platanus, pale brown in color with an even texture and fine grain. It is used for making handles for brushes, pallets, paneling, and veneer. Miter *plane*, grooving *planes*, tools: Planing tools used for preparing the surfaces of miter or butt joints. *Plane*, mathematics, geometric concepts: Flat surfaces in three dimensions such that all points on a line joining any pair of points also belong to the surface. *Plane*, tools for wood cutting & finishing: Tools having a sharp edge and used for leveling and smoothing the surface of wood or another material by paring shavings from it.

PLANNER

Architectural *planner*, people in engineering, building trades & planning, people by occupation: People training or working in the planning field having to do with the establishment of objectives, procedures, and resources for architectural projects. *Planner*, people in engineering, building trades & planning, people by occupation: Those trained or working in any of the planning fields, which have to do with the establishment of objectives, procedures, and resources. Urban *planner*, people in engineering, building trades & planning, people by occupation: Those who specialize in designing and improving the spatial organization and content of urban areas. For those who work in the overall management of urban areas, encompassing the setting of objectives for urban life, the establishment of policies, and the planning, development, operation, and maintenance of the urban environment and services, use "urban managers."

See also ARCHITECTURE—see also DISCIPLINE—see also PRACTICE—see also PROCESS: Communicating Architecture—see also URBAN—see also WORK.

PLANNING

Planning, analytical functions, functions by general context: The activity of determining objectives and outlining or arranging the procedures and resources for attaining them, especially in a formal project proposal or scheme. Regional *planning*: That field of *planning* concerned with the development of entire regions, particularly with the coexistence of human communities and facilities with the rural environment. Space *planning*, social sciences: Discipline focusing on the composition of spaces, often but not always interior architectural spaces. It includes plans for the flow of the inhabitants or users of the space, adherence to building codes, environmental factors, and other such concerns. Urban *planning, discipline:* Long-term *planning* for additions and improvements to the spatial organization and content of urban areas. It concerns *planning* for interaction between people, businesses, government, transportation infrastructure, mass transit, water and power infrastructure, pollution, waste management, and other broad and long-term interests in an urban setting. For the overall management of urban areas, encompassing the setting of objectives for urban life, the establishment of policies, and the *planning*, development, operation, and maintenance of the urban environment and services, use "urban management." For the field concerned with designing the specific appearance and function of cities, use "urban design."

Perceptions of Physical Space & the Planning Process in Camp Azraq, Jordan: Lessons for Time-Sensitive Camp Planning. Thesis. Joyce Lee (MUP), advised by Rahul Mehrotra & Anya Brickman Raredon (MIT).

"In April 2014, the Jordanian government and the United Nations High Commissioner for Refugees opened Camp Azraq, the second major refugee camp established in response to the Syrian conflict. Government and United Nations officials developed Camp Azraq over the course of several months and incorporated spatial and procedural lessons from earlier camp models. At full capacity, the camp can host 130,000 refugees and spans over six square miles in the Zarqa Governorate. Jordanian officials and the international media herald the camp as more advanced, secure, and orderly than previous refugee-management efforts. The camp employs a new form of camp *planning*, one that incorporates flexible space, mini-villages, and other community-oriented elements that help create a sense of normalcy among the displaced population.

Despite these improvements, the overwhelming majority of Syrian refugees do not reside in camps, and Camp Azraq remains relatively empty at 13 percent occupancy. This thesis asks: in what ways have newly applied spatial lessons and institutional processes been successful or changed the perceptions of the camp after occupation? Furthermore, given that timing is a prominent concern in physical *planning* and institutional processes, how can experiences from Camp Azraq inform time-sensitive *planning* practices for current and future camps?

This research relies on qualitative interviews, spatial analysis, and secondary research to bring more visibility to the nuanced perspectives of Camp Azraq's different stakeholders." ◈

See also CITY—see also DEVELOPMENT—see also DISCI-PLINE—see also HEALTH: Planning and Design Guidelines and Prototypes for Healthier Places—see also MANAGEMENT: A Sustainable Future for Exuma—see also MODERN: More than Mere Practicality—see also OUT-MIGRATE: On the Edge—see also RETAIL: Prestige Retail—see also SPACE—see also TRANSPORTATION: Transportation Policy and Planning—see also URBAN—see also URBANISM: Extreme Urbanism III.

PLANT

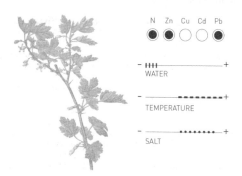

Annual, herbaceous *plants*, woody *plants:* Designates *plants* that complete their cycle from seed to seed in a single year. Assembly *plant*, factories by function: Factories where parts for a complete unit are put together, as in automobile manufacturing. Biennial, herbaceous *plants*, woody *plants: Plants* that spring and vegetate during one growing season and flower then perish the next. Bulb, herbaceous *plants*, woody *plants: Plants* with swollen, underground food-storage organs ringed with fleshy scalelike leaves enclosing next year's buds. Herbaceous *plant*, woody *plants*: Perennial *plants* that have no woody stem, and which can be divided into three types—annuals, biennials, and herbaceous perennials. Perennial, herbaceous *plants*, woody *plants: Plants* which remain green and leafy throughout the year, usually with new herbaceous growth from perennating parts. There are over 300,000 living species of *plants*. Woody *plant:* Term used to describe trees, shrubs, and vines; *plants* that have lignified secondary xylem in their stems.

Francis D. Pastorius' Garden: A Botanical Cosmos in a Howling Wilderness. Thesis. Miranda Elizabeth Mote (MDes, HPD), advised by Sonja Dümpelmann.

"Francis D. Pastorius described Pennsylvania as Germany's 'howling wilderness,' a place of freedom for German Pietists. He believed all living beings had souls—including the hundreds of species of flowers, herbs, grapevines, and fruit trees that he cultivated in his six-acre Germantown garden, orchard, and vineyard. *Plants* bound his faith with Pietist and Quaker theologies. His *Monthly Monitor Briefly Showing When Our Works Ought to Be Done in Gardens, Orchards, Vineyards, Fields, Meadows, and Woods* and his poetry imagined a botanical cosmos as a pious animate entity in America. Through it, he contemplated and cultivated an egalitarian alchemic existence through astrology, lunar effect, and *plant* material for the benefit of human physical and metaphysical health.

To a Pietist, a woman was a metaphor derived from the prophetic scripture of Revelations and described an androgynous spiritual ideal of divine wisdom. To Pastorius, *plants* were essential for human health. He also understood them to be a text that decoded the divine secrets of his celestial and terrestrial cosmos. Pastorius considered his garden a woman that measured the wisdom of his cosmos and mediated his own mortal existence in nature. His *Monthly Monitor*, dated 1701, accounts for this relationship and comprehensively documents a 17th-century garden in eastern Pennsylvania. Most significantly, it documents how Pastorius' formative horticultural practice and *plant* trade, which predated John Bartram's endeavors, was bound with practical and metaphysical purpose." ✤

Seven Plants to Improve Work & Living Space. The Harvard Office for Sustainability recommends these seven *plants* to improve work and living spaces: gerbera daisy, snake *plant*, chinese evergreen, english ivy, spider *plant*, peace lily, and bamboo palm.

Figure. Diagram (previous page). Chris Bennett (MDes, ULE) & Elaine Tyler Stokes (MLA I AP).

See also AFFORESTATION: Colony & Homeland—see also ASSEMBLY—see also BUILDING—see also CANOPY—see also COMMUNITY—see also ECOLOGY—see also INFRASTRUC-TURE—see also LANDSCAPE—see also POWER—see also PROCESS—see also REFUGE—see also RESILIENCE: Ocean State—see also SYSTEM.

PLATFORM

1: Plan, design. 2: A declaration of the principles on which a group of persons stands, especially a declaration of principles and policies adopted by a political party or a candidate. 3: (a) A usually raised horizontal flat surface, especially a raised flooring; (b) a device or structure incorporating or providing a *platform*; especially such a structure on legs used for offshore drilling; (c) a place or opportunity for public discussion. 4: (a) A usually thick layer between the inner sole and outer sole of a shoe; (b) a shoe having such a sole. 5: (a) A vehicle used for a particular purpose or to carry a usually specified kind of equipment; (b) operating system, also the computer architecture and equipment using a particular operating system.

Platform mound, earthworks, engineering works: Artificial earthen mounds with a flat summit, intended to support a structure or activity. They were particularly prominent in the pre-Columbian American cultures. *Platform*, object genres by form: Flat surfaces, blocks, or floors, generally raised above the adjoining floor.

Platform. Publication. ActarD & Harvard GSD, 2009–2015. The Harvard GSD has always recognized the indispensable importance and values of architecture, landscape architecture, urban planning, and urban design, yet has transcended their individual aspirations through intellectual cross-fertilization and collaboration. The Harvard GSD *Platform* series is reviewed and edited by a different faculty member every year. ✤

See also FLOOR—see also INSTALLATION—see also LAND-FORM—see also PRACTICE: Practice Platform Panel—see also PROJECT: South America Project—see also PUBLICATION—see also ROOF—see also SCALE—see also SURFACE—see also STRUCTURE.

PLEASURE

Pleasure, sensation, psychological concepts: The state of emotional, mental, or physical gratification. Also refers to the source of joy or amusement.

See GARDEN—see also SENSORY—see also USE: Freedom of Use—see also WELL-BEING.

PLOT

1: (a) A small area of planted ground <a vegetable *plot*>; (b) a small piece of land in a cemetery; (c) a measured piece of land, lot. 2: Ground plan, plat. 3: The plan or main story. 4: A secret plan for accomplishing a usually evil or unlawful end, intrigue. 5: A graphic representation.

Plot, drawings by material or technique: Computer drawings when emphasizing that they were produced on a *plotter*.

See also BUILDING—see also COMPUTER—see also DIGITAL—see also DRAWING—see also GROUND—see also PAPER—see also PAPERCUT—see also PLAN—see also PRINT—see also TOPOGRAPHY.

POLICY

Environmental *policy*, government *policy*, political concepts: A course or principle of action adopted or proposed by a government to protect wildlife and endangered species and habitats, and to decrease the threat to planetary systems posed by pollution, deforestation, desertification, and other effects of human activity. Public *policy*, political concepts, social science concepts: Governing principles that serve as guidelines for decision making and action as embodied in legislative and judicial enactments.

See also ACTION—see also DISPLACEMENT: Global Displacement—see also ENVIRONMENT—see also GUIDELINE—see also HOUSING: Institutional Strategies for Upholding Affordable Housing Agreements—see also PARK: Urban Park—see also POLITICS—see also TRANSPORTATION: Transportation Policy & Planning.

POLITICS

Comparative *politics*, *political* science, social sciences: Study of the ways in which different societies establish and work with their *political* structures and government, with the goal of developing general theories concerning government based on the analysis of the differences and similarities among *political* units. *Politics*, *political* concepts, social science concepts: The art or science of government or governing, especially the governing of a *political* entity, such as a nation, and the administration and control of its internal and external affairs.

See also CITY: Identity, Sovereignty, and Global Politics in the Building of Baghdad—see also COMPARATIVE—see also GEO-POLITICS—see also HOUSING: Craft, Politics, and the Production of Housing in Oaxaca, Mexico.

POLLUTION

Pollution, environmental concepts: The introduction of or condition of having harmful or otherwise undesirable substances or products in the environment; for the substances themselves use *"pollutants."*

See also AIR—see also CLIMATE CHANGE—see also CONNEC-TION—see also ENVIRONMENT—see also FLUX—see also

SOIL—see also SYSTEM—see also TRANSFORMATION—see also WATER.

POPULATION

Population, demographics, social & economic geography concepts: The total number of individuals of a given species or other class of organism in a defined area. *Population* change, demographics, social & economic geography concepts: The fluctuations that occur in the numbers of individuals in plant and animal *populations* in time and space. *Population* decline, *population* change, demographics: A decrease in the total number of individuals of a given species or other class of organism in a defined area. *Population* density, demographics, social & economic geography concepts: The ratio of a number of individuals to a given unit of the area in which they live. *Population* growth, *population* change, demographics: An increase in the total number of individuals of a given species or other class of organism in a defined area.

See also AGE: Aging & Place—see also CULTURE—see also DENSITY—see also DIASPORA—see also FLUX—see also GEOGRAPHY—see also MAP—see also MIGRATION—see also OUT-MIGRATE: On the Edge—see also SKYSCRAPER: Wood Skyscraper—see also SUBURB: The Storm, the Strife, and Everyday Life—see also TRANSFORMATION—see also URBANIZATION.

PORTRAIT

Portrait, visual works by subject type, visual & verbal communication: Representations of real individuals that are intended to capture a known or supposed likeness, usually including the face of the person. For representations intended to be anonymous, or of fictional or mythological characters, see "figures (representations)." *Self-portrait,* visual works by subject type, visual & verbal communication: An artwork in which the artist produces a likeness of himself or herself.

L'atelier de la recherche patiente. Publication. Fage Éditions, 1960. Le Corbusier (author). Le Corbusier Research Collection, Frances Loeb Library. LeC NA 2500 L496mf.

"This is Le Corbusier's last book, also published by Gerd Hatje. It is a true *self-portrait* of his life and work, which he divides chronologically into three stages: 1900–1918; 1919–1939; and 1940–1960 (both World War I and II define these stages). As to his métier, he describes it as a patient search that encompasses not only his built work, but also his painting, sculpture, urbanism, and written work. He uses a visual language rather than extensive texts when describing his métier. It is not a detailed description of his work, but rather a survey of his approaches to work. It reveals the interests and thoughts that guided him, rather than his work, as the result of a profession. It also includes the bibliography used for this homage." —Inés Zalduendo. ֍

Figure. Portraits (left). Emily Eleanor Russell (MArch I).

POST

1: (a) After, subsequent, later <*postdate*>; (b) behind, posterior, following after <*postlude*> <*postconsonantal*>. 2: (a) Subsequent to, later than <*postoperative*>; (b) *posterior* to <*postorbital*>.

Post, mail, document genres by function: Material that is physically sent or carried in the *postal* system, or in modern usage, by electronic means. *Post*-and-beam structure, structural frames, structural systems: Structures based on upright *posts* or columns supporting horizontal beams or lintels; these exclude balloon frames and platform frames, in which support is by stud walls. *Post* road, roads by function: More recently, refers to roads over which mail is carried. Historically, roads with stations providing for horses for postriders, mail coaches, or travelers. *Post,* structural elements, supporting & resisting elements: In architecture or other construction, refers to stiff, vertical, relatively isolated members of considerable length. *Posts* are typically round, square, or rectangular in cross section and are used in building as supports for a superstructure or to provide a firm point of lateral attachment. They are characteristically relatively undecorated and made of a single timber, but may be made of stone, metal, another material, or composite materials. The term is particularly used for any main vertical support in a timber frame structure. For square uprights in classical style, and for square and rectangular masonry uprights, use "piers (supporting elements)"; for most cylindrical uprights, and for all uprights in steel and concrete frames, use "columns (architectural elements)."

See also ASSEMBLY—see also CIRCULATION—see also ELEMENT—see also HISTORY—see also PAPER—see also POST-CONFLICT—see also POST-DISASTER—see also POST-SUBURB—see also PRACTICE—see also STRUCTURE—see also SYSTEM—see also TIME—see also TRANSPORTATION—see also WALL.

POST-CONFLICT

May Kabul Be without Gold, Rather without Snow: Establishing Infrastructure within the Post-Conflict City. Thesis. Zannah Mae Matson (MLA I), advised by Jane Hutton.

"Increasingly, contexts of persistent conflict are defining urban sites of intervention. In the wake of war

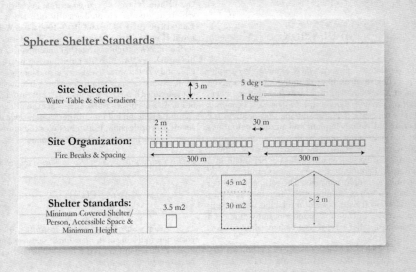

and widespread destruction, the pervasive question has become: How should the city be rebuilt?

This thesis contends that this traditional approach to urban reconstruction is unsuited to the aftermath of contemporary urban warfare. It suggests that the city is not an artifact to be restored after a conflict. It is instead a dynamic and active character, fundamentally altered by protracted conflict and the processes of urbanization that are accelerated by war. Within this framework, the urban landscape can be understood through processes of remediation that ameliorate the deficiencies of its *post-conflict* existence, without necessarily restoring conditions to a fixed former state.

Working within the context of Kabul as a prototypical site of *post-conflict* urban landscape, this thesis establishes a system of connected interventions to address the insufficiencies of existing water infrastructure within the city. Situated within the city's hillside informal settlements, these interventions seek to address existing social hierarchies. Protracted warfare has not only severely damaged the city's physical infrastructure, it has also exacerbated social tensions and inequality throughout the city. Although buildings across the city are being rebuilt, the public water infrastructure has remained in disrepair since the civil war of the 1990s and cannot provide for the growing urban demand." ֍

See also CONFLICT—see also CULTURE—see also HISTORY—see also TIME—see also TRANSFORMATION.

POST-DISASTER

Understanding Tension around the Application of Global Standards in Post-Disaster Scenarios. Thesis and Urban Planning & Design Thesis Prize. Martha Elizabeth Pym (MUP), advised by Michael Hooper.

"Urban *disasters* are an increasingly common phenomenon. The rapid growth of urban settlements in disaster-prone settings, combined with the increasing frequency of natural *disasters*, has enhanced the vulnerability of urban populations. This growing phenomenon has been addressed within the humanitarian field over the last five years, with a number of reports focusing on the urban context of *disasters*. What is less understood is how well existing universal standards for humanitarian response and engagement are able to respond to this changing context for *disasters*. My research focuses on how the Sphere Standards have been applied in the urban context, using Haiti as a case study, and seeks to understand what their lack of implementation indicates about their applicability and the tensions around their use." ֍

Figure. Diagrams (above). Martha Elizabeth Pym (MUP).

Under One Roof: New Findings from USAID Post-Disaster Shelter Projects Evaluations. Event. Gund Hall, Room 109. April 17, 2015. Master in Design Studies Risk & Resilience (RR). Charles A. Setchell. ֍

POST-SUBURB

Post-Suburb: Nashua, New Hampshire—New Landscape Territories. STU 1404. Department of Landscape Architecture. Option Studio. Fall 2014. Instructor: Peter Beard. Teaching Associate: Megan Jones Shiotani (MLA I).

The old mill buildings of northern Massachusetts and southern New Hampshire are striking both in their scale and number. An extended sequence of mills stretches along the Nashua and Merrimack rivers taking in the cities of Manchester, Nashua, Lowell, Lawrence, and Haverhill, a distance of some 50 miles. The vast brick buildings are set within a highly engineered fluvial landscape of weirs and sluices, holding ponds, channels, and canals overlaid on the natural river course. The industries, which originally created this landscape, are long gone, replaced by new industrial *suburbs* remote from the river. The resulting fallow urban-landscape

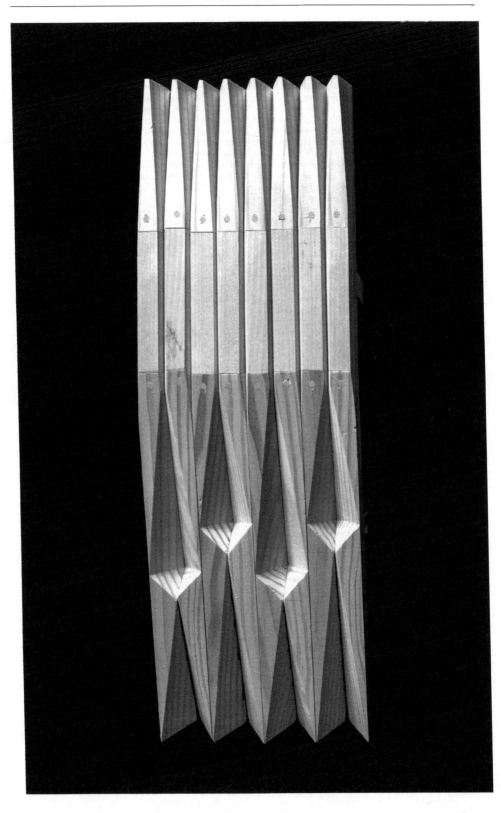

condition has only partially been resettled in the intervening years. Addressing scales ranging from hand and pace, to yard, lot, mill, and field, the studio developed design proposals for the postindustrial riverine landscape of Nashua, New Hampshire. A sequence of new open grounds will transform the loosely structured landscape territories close to the city's core, challenging common assumptions around use, proximity, scale, and settlement. Programmatic themes developed in response to the found conditions of relict industrial infrastructures, wild nature, and the everyday life of the city included: rewilding—the support of territories of slack nature as a substitution of former industrial lots; a new urbanism of the trail—the recalibration of local movement networks and modes in response to needs and imagination; a revalidation of the civic—a new public realm designed around events and temporary uses; and, new productive landscapes—alternative forms of food and nonfood agriculture considering a range of scales from the individual to the collective. The work of the studio was underpinned by a situated, syncretic understanding of place, in respect to both physical conditions and social narratives.

Students: Jordan Boan (MLA I AP), Joshua Ackermann Brown (MLA I), Dane Graham Carlson (MLA II), Vineet Divgi Diwadkar (MUP & MLA I AP), Christopher John Donohue (MLA II), Megan Jones Shiotani (MLA I), Timothy Robert Logan (MArch II), McKenna Dayan McKetty (MLA I), Craig Michael Reschke (MLA I AP), Zhuangzhuang Song (MAUD), Aliza Sovani (MLA I AP), Héctor Ignacio Tarrido-Picart (MLA I AP & MAUD). §

Figure. Model (previous page). Dane Graham Carlson (MLA II).

See also HISTORY—see also TIME—see also TRANSFORMATION—see also URBANIZATION.

POWER

Power, energy resources, resources concepts, environmental concepts: Available supplies or means of producing energy, whether natural, such as fossil fuels or hydroelectric *power,* or man-made, such as nuclear fuel. *Power,* culture-related concepts: The property of strength, influence, and dominance over others, which can be personal, political, or national. *Power* tool, equipment by mode of operation: Tools *powered* by electric motors or by gasoline engines. Solar *power,* energy resources: The use of the sun's energy to provide heating or to generate electricity. Tidal *power* plant, hydroelectric *power* plants, *power* plants: Facilities designed to extract and store energy, employing one or more of the following methods, or other methods—harnessing energy from the differences between high tides and low tides by employing a "barrage" or type of dam to block receding water during ebb periods, the subsequent release of the water through a turbine generating electricity as the tide rises (similar to the workings of hydroelectric dams); using tidal stream *power* by utilizing ocean currents to drive turbines, particularly in areas around islands or coasts where these currents are fast, including systems that employ tidal fences where turbines are stretched across a channel or tidal turbines that resemble underwater wind turbines; using wave *power* systems to harness energy from the up-and-down motion of waves to drive energy production, installed in shoreline areas as well as offshore. Wind *power,* energy resources: The use of wind energy to generate electricity.

Cambridge Talks IX: Inscriptions of Power; Spaces, Institutions, and Crisis. Cambridge Talks Conference. Gund Hall. April 2–3, 2015.

Over two days, fostering dialogue between social scientists and spatial thinkers, an interdisciplinary gathering of scholars explored the relationship between physical and institutional structures. How is institutional *power* manifested in the built environment? How does space bear the mark of bureaucratic networks, typological assumptions and lived experiences? How are different forms of *power*—aesthetic, political, economic, even insurgent—manifest across boundaries and scales?

Cambridge Talks is an annual conference organized by students in the Doctor of Philosophy program at the Harvard GSD. §

Community Power & Leadership. Meet the Loebs Week Seminar. Gund Hall, Stubbins. September 18, 2014. Gísli Baldursson, Jamie Blosser, LaShawn Hoffman, and Marc Norman. §

See also AGENCY—see also CULTURE—see also ENERGY—see also ENVIRONMENT—see also GEOTHERMAL—see also MACHINE—see also MODEL: Architecture & the Territory—see also SOLAR—see also TECHNIQUE—see also TOOL—see also WATER.

PRACTICE

1: (a) Actual performance or application <ready to carry out in *practice* what they advocated in principle>; (b) a repeated or customary action <had this irritating *practice*>; (c) the usual way of doing something <local *practices*>; (d) the form, manner, and order of conducting legal suits and prosecutions. 2: (a) Systematic exercise for proficiency <*practice* makes perfect>; (b) the condition of being proficient through systematic exercise <get in *practice*>. 3: (a) The continuous exercise of a profession; (b) a professional business; especially one constituting an incorporeal property. 4: (a) To perform or work at repeatedly so as to become proficient <*practice* the act>; (b) to train by repeated exercises <*practice* pupils in penmanship>. 5: To do repeated exercises for proficiency. 6: To pursue a profession actively. 7: To do something customarily.

From Roots to Routes: Challenging the Knowledge Industries that Spatialize Race. Thesis. Annie Boehnke (MArch I), advised by Jana Cephas & Mack Scogin.

"This thesis is a tool to investigate how architecture presses myths of race into service and a mechanism to challenge how architecture strives to consolidate something essential. A specter looms over Fulton Street Mall in downtown Brooklyn, where spatial *practices* subvert broader notions of what it is to engage a commercial district. Fulton Street has long been the commercial heart of Brooklyn, and for the past 30 years it has thrived as a place of community and dignified shopping for low- and middle-income black residents. Without the help of the city or its economic development corporation, Fulton Street Mall is the third-largest shopping district in New York City and is emblematic of a larger condition of successful commercial districts whose livelihoods are threatened by cities and developers who seek to enforce normative spatial patterns. The thesis is not an architecture of race; it is an architecture that reveals decisions in building *practice.* It endeavors to upend how architecture presses damaging myths about racialized bodies into service." §

Material Practices & Design Representation. GSD Talks, Gund Hall, Stubbins. November 18, 2014. Zaneta H. Hong & Charles A. Waldheim.

Designers are paradoxically generalists and specialists. We are trained and *practiced* in creating organizations and logistics, and across disciplines and manners of *practice*, investigations can take on many forms. Even though research and design projects can vary greatly in their modalities, they are all part of a larger body of work built on the ideas of iterative processes that deal with material information and composite forms of communication. In a public lecture at the Harvard GSD, Zaneta H. Hong presented her past work and introduced her current research, the *Landformation Catalogue*. §

POSTGSD. Student Group. POSTGSD explores traditional and alternative models of professional *practice*, focusing on the stories and experiences of emerging designers who have opened their own *practices*. Through talks and interviews with professionals ranging from recent graduates to established practitioners, the group aims to better understand the realities of starting an independent *practice* and what comes after the Harvard GSD. §

Practice Platform Panel: Talking Practice. Panel Discussion. Gund Hall, Piper Auditorium. November 4, 2014. David Benjamin, Elena Manferdini, Ashley Schafer, Aaron Sprecher with Grace La & Paul Nakazawa (moderators).

This event addressed expanded modes of contemporary design *practice* and the disciplinary potential of these innovative models. Representing some of the new forms of design *practice*, from hybrid and curatorial *practice* to open platform and corporate acquisition, the speakers reflected on the how and why of their *practices*, sharing concepts, processes, methods, and techniques. §

See also ALTERNATIVE: Alternative Spatial Practices in Istanbul—see also ARCHITECTURE: Architecture for Everyone—see also CHALLENGE: Launch—see also CITY: Expeditions in the Contemporary City—see also COMPUTATION: Paradigms in Computing—see also CONTEMPORARY—see also CULTURE—see also DISCIPLINE—see also ECOLOGY: Projective Ecologies—see also EDUCATION: Talca, Matter of Education—see also ELEMENT—see also FABRICATION: Material Practice as Research—see also FRAMEWORK: Frameworks of Contemporary Practice—see also GEOGRAPHY: New Modes, Models, and Geographies of Practice—see also INNOVATION: Innovation in Practice—see also LANDSCAPE—see also LANDSCAPE ARCHITECTURE—see also MAPPING: Mapping Cultural Space—see also MODEL: Architecture & the Territory—see also MODERN: Women, Modernity, and Landscape Architecture—see also POWER: Cambridge Talks IX—see also PROGRESS—see also PROJECT—see also SPECULATION—see also SURFACE: Superficial Surfaces—see also TECHNIQUE—see also URBAN DESIGN—see also URBAN PLANNING—see also URBANISM—see also VISIONARY—see also WORLDCRAFT—see also WRITING.

PRECEDENT

1: An earlier occurrence of something similar. 2: (a) Something done or said that may serve as an example or rule to authorize or justify a subsequent act of the same or an analogous kind <a verdict that had no *precedent*>;

(b) The convention established by such a *precedent* or by long practice. 3: A person or thing that serves as a model.

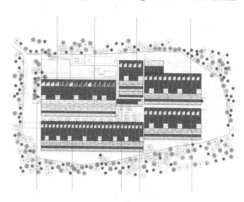

Figure. Plan (above). Ivy Pan (MLA I) & Foad Vahidi (MLA I).

PRECISION

1: The quality or state of being *precise*, exactness. 2: (a) The degree of refinement with which an operation is performed or a measurement stated—compare to accuracy; (b) the accuracy with which a number can be represented usually expressed in terms of the number of computer words available for representation <double *precision* arithmetic permits the representation of an expression by two computer words>.

See also ASSEMBLY—see also BLOCK—see also CONSTRUCTION—see also DRAFTING—see also ERROR: The Architecture of Error—see also FABRICATION—see also TECHNIQUE.

PRESERVATION

Digital *preservation*: Refers to *preservation* of all digital materials, and of digital heritage generally, which aims to ensure access to such content over the long term. Historical *preservation*: Refers to actions taken to promote the protection and continued use of the built environment for cultural, aesthetic, or historic reasons. For actions taken specifically to return an object, site, or structure to a state of historical correctness, see "restoration (process)." For actions taken generally to prevent further changes or deterioration in objects, sites, or structures, see "preservation." For actions taken to return an already deteriorated structure to sound condition, see "rehabilitating." For changes that return an object or structure to a state of historical correctness, see "restoration (process)." For the activity of keeping people and things safe from harm or deterioration generally, see "protection." More generally, for the treatment, preventive care, and research directed toward the long-term safekeeping of cultural and natural heritage, see "conservation."

A History of Nature Conservation & Cultural Landscape Preservation. HIS 4446. Department of Landscape Architecture. Seminar. Spring 2015. Instructor: Mark Laird.

Historic Urban Landscape (HUL) is a new approach to integrating urban *preservation* within the three pillars of sustainability: economy, ecology, and society. In 2011, UNESCO adopted HUL, the first instrument on the historic environment issued by UNESCO in 35 years. This course explored backgrounds to HUL, asking how the new approach can aid urban biodiversity resilience in the face of multiple pressures, including climate change. Since cultural landscapes were introduced into the World Heritage Convention in 1992, nature conservation and the conservation of cultural heritage have found common ground in forest, agricultural, and wildlife management; now HUL promises more. While the writings of Marsh (*Man and Nature*, 1864) are foundational in environmental history, such thinking has roots in the early modern writings of Gilbert White (*The Natural History of Selborne*, 1789). Laird's *A Natural History of English Gardening: 1650–1800* assesses White's place in that history. Tracing the history of cultural landscape *preservation* alongside the history of cultural geographies over 100 years, the course is also a history of Laird's evolving engagement with heritage landscapes. In this course, some of the nearly 1,000 World Heritage Sites were considered, exploring what is left out of protections as much as what is protected. Its themes were activism, urbanism, sustainability, and globalism, and, with discussion of the fast-changing world of climate change, it offered scope for speculation. §

Tax Credits & Adaptive Reuse—The Key to Preservation. Lecture. Gund Hall, Room 318. October 23, 2014. Lawrence Curtis. §

See also COLLECTION—see also CONSERVATION—see also DIGITAL—see also HISTORY—see also PARK: Botanical Park at the Epang Palace—see also TIME.

PRINT

Blueprint, reprographics copies, visual & verbal communication: Reproductive *prints* of architectural plans, maps, mechanical drawings, and other technical drawings, characterized by having white images on blue backgrounds and produced by the blueprint process. For blue images on white backgrounds, use "blueline *prints*." For blue-toned photographs produced by the blueprint process, use "cyanotypes." Color *print, prints* by process or technique: Images *printed* in two or more colors; if color is applied after *printing*, use "colored" (alternate of "coloring") and "*prints*." For color photographs, see "color *prints* (photographs)." Copy *print*, photography *prints*, positives, photographs, visual & verbal communication: Photographic *prints* produced by photographing a two-dimensional work, such as a drawing or painting, or by rephotographing another photograph. Digital *print, prints* by process & technique, visual & verbal communication: Broadly describes physical manifestations made from digital image files that are achieved by the application or generation of colorant to a substrate, and that are not struck directly from a material master matrix. This is in contrast to traditional *prints* struck from matrices such as *printing* plates, blocks, negatives or transparencies, though these may be the primary origin of imagery. Digital *prints* have as their immediate source electronic signals that drive any of a variety of *printing* mechanisms. *Fingerprint*, conditions & effects by origin: The impression of the markings from the inner surface of the finger. *Print*, visual works by material or technique: Pictorial works produced by transferring images by means of a matrix

such as a plate, block, or screen, using any of various *printing* processes. When emphasizing the individual *printed* image, use "impressions."

PRINTER

Dot matrix *printer*, impact *printer*, *printers* by mode of operation: *Printers* that create each character from an array of dots that are usually formed by transferring ink by mechanical impact. Inkjet *printer*, nonimpact *printers*, *printer* by mode of operation: *Printers* that form images by projecting droplets of ink onto paper or other media. Laser *printer*, nonimpact *printers*, *printer* by mode of operation: Electrophotographic *printers* in which a laser is used as the light source. Nonimpact *printer*, *printers* by mode of operation: *Printers* in which the image is formed without use of mechanical impact with the printed surface material. *Printer*, people in the printing industry: Refers to people in the commercial printing trade. For artists who make prints, see "printmakers." *Printer*, output devices, peripherals: Output devices that convert coded information from the processor into a readable form on paper.

See also COLOR—see also COMMUNICATION—see also COMPUTER—see also DIGITAL—see also DRAWING—see also NEGATIVE—see also PAPER—see also PAPERCUT—see also PHOTOGRAPHY—see also PLAN—see also PRINTING—see also PROCESS—see also SURFACE—see also TECHNIQUE—see also 2-D—see also 3-D.

PRIVATE

1: (a) Intended for or restricted to the use of a particular person, group, or class <a *private* park>; (b) belonging to or concerning an individual person, company, or interest <a *private* house>; (c) restricted to the individual or arising independently of others <*private* opinion>; (d) carried on by the individual independently of the usual institutions <a doctor in *private* practice>, also, being educated by independent study or a tutor or in a *private* school <*private* students>; (e) not general in effect <a *private* statute>; (f) of, relating to, or receiving hospital service in which the patient has more privileges than a semi-*private* or ward patient. 2: (a) Not holding public office or employment <a *private* citizen>; (b) not related to one's official position, personal <*private* correspondence>; (c) being a *private*. 3: (a) Withdrawn from company or observation <a *private* retreat>; (b) not known or intended to be known publicly, secret; (c) preferring to keep personal affairs to oneself, valuing *privacy* highly; (d) unsuitable for public use or display. 4: Not having shares that can be freely traded on the open market <a *private* company>.

See also BODY: The Room for Hiding the Body In—see also DWELLING: Poor But Sexy—see also LAND USE—see also PRACTICE—see also SPACE—see also STUDY.

PRIZE

Prize, social recognition, sociological concepts: Things offered to be competed for, or sometimes won by chance; may include objects, privileges, money, honors, or tokens.

Harvard GSD Fellowships, Prizes & Travel Programs. Numerous donors have established endowed awards and traveling fellowships at the Harvard GSD. Awards are also granted by the recommendation of the department faculty and awarded to students in recognition of significant achievement throughout the relevant program's design sequence. In addition, thesis commendations are awarded each year before commencement to degree candidates who have demonstrated outstanding work on their thesis projects. ❦

Alpha Rho Chi Medal. Natsuma Shigeo Imai (MArch I). The Alpha Rho Chi Medal is awarded to the graduating student who has achieved the best general record of leadership and service to the department, and who gives promise of professional merit through his or her character. ❦

American Institute of Architects (AIA) Certificate of Merit. Joanie Tom (MArch I). The AIA Certificate of Merit is awarded to a student in recognition of excellence of achievement in his or her studies. ❦

American Institute of Architects (AIA) Medal. Yun Fu (MArch I AP) & Meng Li (MArch I AP). The AIA Medal is awarded to a professional degree candidate in the Master in Architecture graduating class who has achieved the highest level of excellence in overall scholarship throughout the course of his or her studies. ❦

American Institute of Certified Planners (AICP) Outstanding Student Award. Matthew V. Furman (MUP). The AICP Outstanding Student Awards recognizes outstanding achievement in the study of planning by students graduating from the Planning Accreditation Board during the academic year of the award. ❦

American Society of Landscape Architects (ASLA) Certificate of Honor. Peichen Hao (MLA I) & Dima Rachid (MLA II). On nomination by the faculty in the Department of Landscape Architecture, the ASLA awards a Certificate of Honor and a Certificate of Merit to students enrolled in the Master in Landscape Architecture program who have "demonstrated a high degree of academic scholarship and accomplishment in skills related to the art and technology of landscape architecture." ❦

American Society of Landscape Architects (ASLA) Certificate of Merit. Lara Elisabeth Mehling (MLA I) & Timothy Yung Wei (MLA I). ❦

Award for Excellence in Project-Based Urban Planning Work. Robert William Wellburn (MUP). ❦

Award for Excellence in Urban Design. Clayton C. Strange (MAUD) & Dimitris Venizelos (MAUD). ❦

Award for Outstanding Leadership in Real Estate. Brian Patrick Vargo (MDes, REBE). ❦

Charles Eliot Traveling Fellowship. Lara Elisabeth Mehling (MLA I). Established in 1914 by a gift to honor Harvard alumnus Charles Eliot, this traveling fellowship is awarded annually on recommendation by the faculty in the Department of Landscape Architecture to a Harvard GSD graduate who has received the Master in Landscape Architecture degree within three years of the date of the award. It is the highest honor the department can bestow on its graduates. ❦

Daniel L. Schodek Award for Technology & Sustainability. Olga Lucia Mesa (MDes, Tech).

Department of Architecture Faculty Design Award. Nelson Byun (MArch II) & Benjamin Richard Ruswick (MArch I). The Department of Architecture Faculty Design Award was established by the faculty of the Department of Architecture with the aim of recognizing significant achievement within a body of design work completed by a student at the Harvard GSD. This award is given to graduating students from each of the department's two programs. ❦

Dimitris Pikionis Award. Grga Basic (MDes, ULE). The Dimitris Pikionis Award is awarded in recognition of outstanding academic performance in Master in Design Studies Program. ❦

Druker Traveling Fellowship. Clayton C. Strange (MAUD). Established in 1986 by Ronald M. Druker (Loeb Fellow, 1976) and by the Trustees of the Bertram A. Druker Charitable Foundation, this fellowship is open to all students at the Harvard GSD who demonstrate excellence in the design of urban environments. The fellowship offers students the opportunity to travel in the United States or abroad to pursue study that advances urban design. ❦

Gerald M. McCue Medal. Laure Anne Katsaros (MDes, HPD). The Gerald M. McCue Medal is awarded in recognition of the highest overall academic record among the post-professional programs at the Harvard GSD (MArch II, MAUD, MDes, MLA II, MLAUD). ❦

Jacob Weidenman Prize. Craig Michael Reschke (MLA I AP). The Jacob Weidenman *Prize* is awarded annually to the landscape architecture student who has shown outstanding ability and talent in design. It was established by a bequest from the daughter of Jacob Weidenman, who devoted himself to the study and practice of landscape architecture. ❦

James Templeton Kelley Prize. Chloe Natanel Brunner (MArch II) & Meng Li (MArch I AP). The James Templeton Kelley *Prize* recognizes the best final design project submitted by a graduating student in the architecture degree programs. ❦

Julia Armory Appleton Traveling Fellowship. Jessica Lynn Wilcox (MArch I). The Julia Amory Appleton Traveling Fellowship is given to a student in the Department of Architecture on the basis of academic achievement as well as the worthiness of the project to be undertaken. ❦

Kevin V. Kieran Prize. Nelson Byun (MArch II). The Kevin V. Kieran *Prize* recognizes the highest level of academic achievement among students graduating from the post-professional Master in Architecture program (MArch II). ❦

Master in Landscape Architecture Thesis Prize. Timothy Yung Wei (MLA I). ❦

Norman T. Newton Prize. Ken Chongsuwat (MLA I). The Norman T. Newton *Prize* is awarded annually to the graduating landscape architecture student whose work best exemplifies achievement in design expression as realized in any medium. ❦

Public space offers relief from the interiors, the governed and surveyed, and the "off-limits" of the city. And yet, by definition, public spaces are adjacent, connected, and in contrast to these opposites: the administered. The boundary between public space and the city is significant, guaranteeing the individual and collective liberties, access, and amenities that every other urban boundary attempts to restrict. Public spaces are democratic spaces without a conscious agenda otherwise. They thrive, like all other democratic systems, on constant opposition, on a constant and stable difference of multiple and simultaneous programs, uses, politics and occupants. Traditionally, public spaces are large voids within the density of cities.

In the figure-ground, they are read as the ground —
as the opposite of the built city, yet an opposite within and as an essential part of, and therefore

a persisting answer to its persisting issues.
From February to June 2011, protestors opposing the "Wisconsin Act 10" bill, including new budget-reform legislation that would affectively restrict the collective bargaining rights and disband most public sector unions, occupied the Wisconsin State Capitol building. Wisconsin was the first state to legislate collective bargaining for public employees in 1959 for the negotiation of terms of employment and publically funded pensions and benefits. The proposed cuts were seen not only as a threat to the individual pubic-sector employees whose pensions were defended, but also to Wisconsin's history of progressive politics. Wisconsin is one of only two states with a capitol open 365 days a year, and at the time maintained a law that allowed for the building to remain open as long as public debate was held about a pending bill within the Capitol itself. The State Senate had not set a limit on the number of speakers for debate on Act 10, and thousands of individuals were signed up by labor groups and organizations to keep the debate, and therefore the capitol, open indefinitely. A microphone was set up in the rotunda of the building and used in a 24-7 "speak-out" lasting several weeks. At the height of the demonstrations, an estimated 100,000 people occupied the capitol grounds. During the 3-month demonstration, small groups of Tea Party activists demonstrated in favor of the budget reform at the capitol.

The Wisconsin Capitol Occupation transformed the conception of the forum, in building as an iconic public space into an active and accessible, budget reform and which to voice the diverse opinions and grievances on. protests were seen as austerity in the United States generally. Importantly, proceedings and services, an example of how and why to insist on parliamentary employees and services, political process, budget reform and cuts to public with broader Wisconsin and allowed for public-sector unions to connect sector jobs and the probable communities around the importance of public sector disbanding public-sector party power and political leverage ensured by building itself organized unions. Both the process of occupation and the gue around Act 10 and created demonstrators trying to unite the State in div. to voice common concerns. a space for diverse groups to work together. people united diverse opinions and Filling the space with "the voices" of the bot. made them heard as a critical mass; bot.

activating and activating by an architecture.

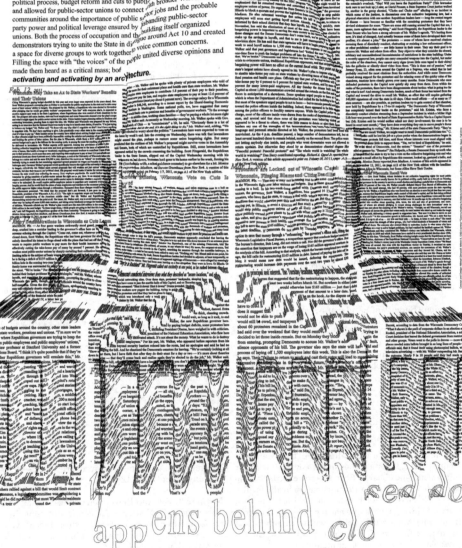

Peter Rice Prize. Jeonghyun Kim (MArch II). The Peter Rice *Prize* recognizes students in the architecture and advanced degree programs who have proven their competence and innovation in advancing architecture and structural engineering. ⚐

Peter Walker & Partners Fellowship for Landscape Architecture. Michelle Arevalos Franco (MLA I). The fellowship is granted to support travel that extends the learning experience of the formal educational program by providing young landscape architects an opportunity to spend a concentrated period of time studying landscape design in various parts of the world. Each holder of the fellowship is expected to deliver a lecture or participate in a symposium or other event, sharing his or her travel studies with the Harvard GSD community. ⚐

Urban Planning & Design Thesis Prize. Martha Elizabeth Pym (MUP). ⚐

Urban Project Prize. Miranda Elizabeth Mote (MDes, HPD). ⚐

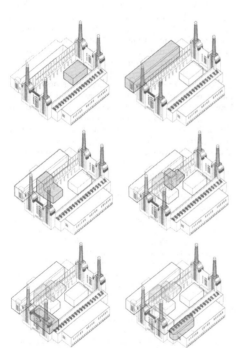

PROCESS

Processes & techniques by general type: Actions or procedures followed to produce some end, and for the actions or changes that take place in materials or objects. When emphasis is on the manner or method by which actions or procedures are performed, use "techniques."

Basel Study Abroad Seminar: Communicating Architecture—The Planner and Architect as Active Participants in Democratic Processes. VIS 2602. Department of Architecture. Seminar. Fall 2014. Instructor: Lars Müller.

Based on an analysis of the media (posters, brochures, publications) that have accompanied selected landmark referendums, the seminar sought to understand the dynamics and mechanisms behind political *processes*, looking at how the planner and architect can intervene and present convincing arguments. On the basis of the analytical findings, students designed a poster or pamphlet for an actual or fictional project with the goal of verbally or visually assisting the citizen, who is only vaguely aware of the matter at hand, in reaching an informed decision. This practical work provided the framework for a study of the conceptual foundations of design and the treatment of images and typography. In the *process*, students developed greater awareness of how their disciplines can be integrated into social and democratic contexts, learning to see themselves as both political stakeholders and citizens. ⚐

Figures. Drawing (opposite page). Mikhail Thomas Grinwald (MArch II & MDes, HPD). Diagrams (left). Ingrid Kestrel Bengtson (MArch I).

See also ACTION—see also COMMUNICATION—see also ECOLOGY—see also MATERIAL: Material Processes & System Group (MaPS)—see also PRACTICE—see also PRODUCTION: Tactics for a Coproduced City—see also REPRESENTATION—see also SYSTEM—see also TECHNIQUE—see also TRANSFORMATION—see also VISIONARY: Grounded Visionaries.

PROCESSION

Procession, cultural ceremonies: Occasions consisting of a group of people moving in orderly succession in a formal ceremonial context. For large public *processions* of a festive nature, often including floats and marching bands and held in honor of an anniversary, person, or event, use "parades."

See also CIRCULATION—see also CULTURE—see also FLOAT: Floating Cities—see also MIGRATION—see also PARTY.

PRODUCTION

1: (a) Something *produced, product*; (b) a literary or artistic work; (c) a work presented to the public; (d) something exaggerated out of proportion to its importance. 2: (a) The act or process of *producing*; (b) the creation of utility, especially the making of goods available for use. 3: Total output especially of a commodity or an industry. 4: Often attributive, something not specially designed or customized and usually *mass-produced* .

Tactics for a Coproduced City. GSD Talks. Gund Hall, Stubbins. November 12, 2014. Doina Petrescu & Constantin Petcou.

Doina Petrescu and Constantin Petcou, of Atelier d'Architecture Autogérée, discussed the notion of co*production* in the context of their recent participatory projects in Paris. They spoke about the tools, spaces, and agencies needed for citizens to co*produce* their cities in times of crisis and austerity and about the political role of architects in facilitating such processes. ⚐

See also DWELLING: Poor But Sexy—see also FOOD: Surviving, Sustaining, and Shaping Urbanization—see also GRID: Rethinking Urban Grids in Hangzhou—see also HOUSING: Craft, Politics, and the

Production of Housing in Oaxaca, Mexico—see also LISTEN: Symphony of the Air—see also POST-SUBURB—New Landscape Territories.

PROFILE

Profile, orthographic projections: Orthographic drawings or works of another medium depicting an object or structure seen in a vertical plane. In architecture, most often sections; in shipbuilding may be sections or elevations, but always showing the vessel broadside. *Profile*, figures, view by vantage point or orientation, visual & verbal communication: Refers to side views of figures, especially when a clear outline is emphasized. For certain orthographic drawings of objects or structures, use "*profiles* (orthographic drawings)." Soil *profile*, orthographic projections, visual & verbal communication: Vertical sections of soil showing the nature and sequence of the various layers, as developed by deposition, weathering, or both.

See also COMMUNICATION—see also DRAFTING—see also DRAWING—see also ELEVATION—see also MODEL—see also ORIENTATION—see also ORTHOGRAPHIC—see also PROJECTION—see also SECTION—see also SOIL.

PROGRAMMING

Architectural *programming*, organizational functions: Refers to that part of the architectural design process in which requirements, conditions, goals, and methods of a building project are defined and documented. Computer *programming*, computer-use functions, information handling functions: Composing precise, logical sequences of instructions that direct the actions of a computer or computer system. *Programming*, function, organizational functions: Planning and establishing a sequence or system of actions, events, or instructions.

See also COMPUTER—see also DATA: Data Across Scales—see also DIGITAL—see also INFORMATION—see also PARAMETER—see also PROCESS—see also PROJECT—see also REPRESENTATION—see also SOFTWARE—see also SYSTEM.

PROGRESS

1: (a) A royal journey marked by pomp and pageant; (b) a state procession; (c) a tour or circuit made by an official; (d) an expedition, journey, or march through a region. 2: A forward or onward movement, advance. 3: Gradual betterment, especially the *progressive* development of humankind—in *progress*, going on, occurring.

OMA: On Progress. Lecture. Memorial Hall, Sanders Theater. September 13, 2014. Rem Koolhaas. 🔊

PROJECT

Project, artistic concepts, concepts relating to the creative process: Use generally for proposed undertakings or creations, including the creation of works of art or architecture, or for the actual carrying out of such proposals. When emphasis is on specific conceptual schemes for the organization or appearance of graphic works, objects, structures, or systems, use "designs." Housing *project*, housing complexes by development practices: Planned residential developments, generally publicly built and operated, intended for low- and moderate-income tenants. Unbuilt *project*, artistic concepts: Refers to planned works of architecture that were never physically produced. For works other than architecture, use "unexecuted designs."

Project: First Semester Core Architecture Studio. STU 1101. Department of Architecture. Core Studio. Fall 2014. Instructors: Iñaki Ábalos, Mariana Ibañez (coordinator), Kiel Moe (coordinator), Nerea Calvillo, Megan Panzano, and Cameron Wu. Teaching Assistants: Lauren Malane Bordes (MArch I), Iman Salam Fayyad (MArch I), Natsuma Shigeo Imai (MArch I), Rossitza Dimitrova Kotelova (MArch I), and Christopher J. SooHoo (MArch I).

Project is the first core studio of the four-semester sequence of the MArch I program. With a multiplicity of references, *project* may refer to fundamental modes of architectural representation, the mapping of the subject in the larger objective context, or a conceptual foray into unknown territory. In the first semester, architectural conventions and typologies are taught by means of anomalies: extreme or exceptional conditions of space and form that elicit a heightened awareness of the norms that are customarily taken for granted. The aim is to bring architecture to heightened consciousness and to confront it at a deeply conceptual level while learning the fundamental tools of the architect's craft. The exceptional nature of each *project* highlighted specific architectural constraints, which lead to the discovery of unexpected solutions. The *projects* tested the limits of possibility within the medium of architecture and in so doing defined terms of the medium. The four *projects* throughout the semester were each conceived as a conundrum, a seemingly insoluble or paradoxical problem that spurred ingenuity and inventiveness by drawing from manifold perspectives and fields of knowledge.

The first *project* began not with a functional program but rather with an idea: architecture exists between subjective perception and objective reality. The focus was the relationship between the exterior, the interior, the conspicuous, and the inconspicuous at the scales of intimate and large rooms. On the one hand, the hypothesis required consideration of the relationship between the sensorial and the conceptual bases of architecture. On the other hand, it elicited the act of interpretation and the processes by which an idea is given three-dimensional form and represented in architectural drawings and models. The second *project* called attention to the interrelationship between the discrete building and its extended context. The *project* investigated the means to make interdependent the individual building, its interior, and the collective landscape as defined by an urban morphology. It was a study of the unique, the repeatable, and the mutually determinative elements of private and public forms and space. The third *project* focused on the charged relationship between the interior dynamics of a building and its outward appearances. It was at once a study in circulation, perimeters, and typologies as codeterminants in the elaboration of a building. The final *project* was a study of various intensive and extensive properties of architecture. The premise was that a single architecture might have multiple manifestations or states. This *project* was slightly longer, thus demanding greater

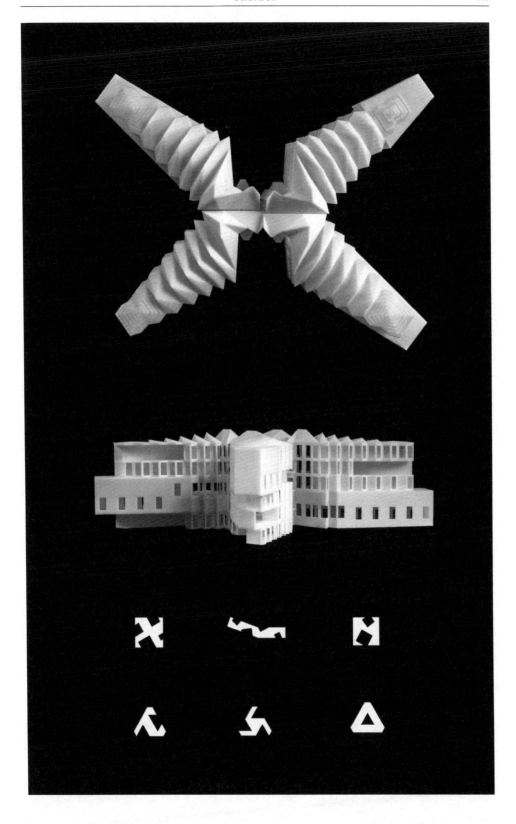

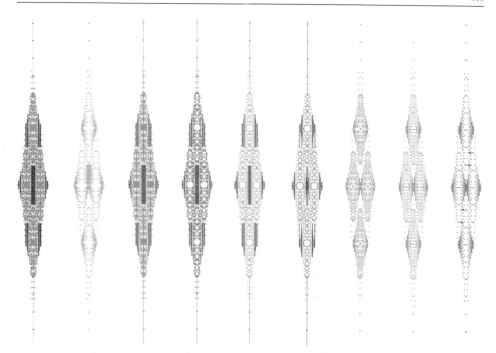

resolution of the topics, and incorporation of the representations and techniques, studied in the course of the semester.

Students: Alice Marie Armstrong (MArch I), Rekha Auguste-Nelson (MArch I), Esther Mira Bang (MArch I), Sasha S. Bears (MArch I), Jeffrey David Burgess (MArch I), Nathan Jon Buttel (MArch I), Kathryn Hanna Jansen Casey (MArch I & MUP), Shiyang Chen (MArch I), Joanne K. Cheung (MArch I), Chieh Chih Chiang (MArch I), Valeria Fantozzi (MArch I), Ya Gao (MArch I), Douglas Robert Harsevoort (MArch I), Carlos Ignacio Hernandez-Tellez (MArch I), Yousef Awaad Hussein (MArch I), Tomotsugu Ishida (MArch I), Michael Clyde Johnson (MArch I), Danielle Marissa Kasner (MArch I), Gerrod M. Kendall (MArch I), Min-Gyu Kim (MArch I), Haram Hyunjin Kim (MArch I), Shaina Sunjin Kim (MArch I), Wyatt Komarin (MArch I), Hyojin Kwon (MArch I), June Lee (MArch I), Madeline Jane Lenaburg (MArch I), Ethan J. Levine (MArch I), Naomi K. Levine (MArch I), Keunyoung Lim (MArch I), Shao Lun Gary Lin (MArch I), Kirby Liu (MArch I), Naureen Mazumdar (MArch I), Grace McEniry (MArch I), Steven T. Meyer (MArch I), Farhad Mirza (MArch I), Chit Yan Paul Mok (MArch I), Bryant Huybao Nguyen (MArch I), Matthew Okazaki (MArch I), Meric Ozgen (MArch I), Andy Byung Kwan Park (MArch I), Aeri Park (MArch I), Yen S. Phoaw (MArch I), David Mark Pilz (MArch I), Philip Wing-Chung Poon (MArch I), Alexander Searle Porter (MArch I), Irene Cecilia Preciado Arango (MArch I), Lane Raffaldini Rubin (MArch I), Santiago Serna (MArch I), Jennifer Lixian Shen (MArch I), Yiliu Chen Shen-Burke (MArch I), Tianze Tong (MArch I), Roger W. Tran (MArch I), Ho Cheung Tsui (MArch I), Isabelle Verwaay (MArch I), Madelyn A. Willey (MArch I), Hanguang Wu (MArch I), Huopu Zhang (MArch I), Monica Zhou (MArch I), Eric C. Zuckerman (MArch I). ⊛

Figures. Models (previous page, above). Bryant Huybao Nguyen (MArch I). Diagrams (previous page, below). Shiyang Chen (MArch I). Diagram (opposite page, above). Chit Yan Paul Mok (MArch I). Diagrams & Sections (opposite page, below). Bryant Huybao Nguyen (MArch I). Diagrams (above). Yousef Awaad Hussein (MArch I).

Inevitable Errors. Installation. Kirkland Gallery. March 8–13, 2015. Elad Horn (MDes, CC) & Emily Marie Kappes (MArch I AP).

"What is it like, when you start a *project* and you do not know what it will become? You are out of control— it might collapse, it might explode. What is it like, if you embrace the errors, endorse the mistakes? Make it your own endeavor, name it your *project*." ⊛

Nose-to-Nose. Kenzo Tange Lecture. Gund Hall, Piper Auditorium. October 7, 2014. Sir Peter Cook.

Sir Peter Cook presented a selection from his 50 years of *projects*, emphasizing his recent work with Gavin Robotham and the Cook Robotham Architectural Bureau (CRAB Studio), with forays into the seaside, kiosks, not-quite-architecture architecture, the continual observation of people, cartoons, the essential silliness of daily life; and the construction of cheerful buildings (Graz Kunsthaus), blue buildings (Vienna Law Faculty, Australian Architecture School), the Archigram memory lingering, and a vehement disinterest in abstraction. Cook was the 2015 Kenzo Tange Visiting Professor at the Harvard GSD. ⊛

Project Room. Gund Hall, Room L31. The *Project* Room is open 24 hours a day, seven days a week and is the primary student work space in the Fab Lab. It is equipped with work tables, a wire foam cutter, sink, and spray booth. The use of materials such as plaster, resin, concrete, as well as any painting, staining or sealing of wood is conducted in this space rather than in the Wood Shop or studio trays. Space for temporary material storage and *project* workspace can be reserved. ⊛

To Be Determined. Lecture. Gund Hall, Piper Auditorium. April 10, 2015. Florian Idenburg.

Florian Idenburg discussed the *projects* of SO–IL, the New York-based architectural design firm of which he is a founding partner with Jing Liu. ⊛

South America Project (SAP). Research *Project.* Felipe Correa & Ana María Durán Calisto. The South America *Project* is a transcontinental applied research network that proactively endorses the role of design within rapidly transforming geographies of South America. SAP specifically focuses on how a spatial synthesis best afforded by design can provide alternative physical and experiential identities to the current spatial transformations reshaping the South American hinterland, in particular, fast-paced modes of resource extraction and an unprecedented regional integration at a continental scale (primarily through roads, energy grids, fluvial corridors, and telecommunication networks).

Launched by Felipe Correa and Ana María Durán Calisto with the support of the Department of Urban Planning & Design at the Harvard GSD, the David Rockefeller Center for Latin American Studies (DRCLAS), and the Loeb Fellowship Program, the *project* brings together a broad host of academic institutions, scholars, and designers from diverse fields in order to create a projective platform that can allow for architecture and the diverse disciplines affiliated with the constructed environment to actively partake in proposing more comprehensive models of urbanization for South America. 🔸

See also ARCHITECTURE: Architecture for Everyone—see also BUILT—see also CAMPUS: A Campus for the 21st Century—see also CITY—see also CONTEMPORARY—see also DESCRIPTION: Innovate—see also DEVELOPMENT—see also DISCIPLINE—see also DUALISM—see also HOUSING—see also INSPIRATION: Natural & Unnatural—see also LANDSCAPE: An Evolution of Practice & Theory—see also LANDSCAPE ARCHITECTURE—see also LINK: Project Link—see also MUSEUM: How Did You Do It, Mr. Piano?—see also PRACTICE—see also PROCESS—see also PRODUCTION: Tactics for a Coproduced City—see also SPECULATION: Rare New Species—see also SYSTEM—see also TEA: Project TEAhouse—see also UNBUILT—see also UNDISCIPLINED—see also URBAN DESIGN—see also URBAN PLANNING—see also VISIONARY: Grounded Visionaries—see also WORK: Perceiving & Working—see also WORLDCRAFT.

PROJECTION

Digital *projection*: Methods for *projecting* cinematic materials digitally first set forth in the Digital Cinema System Specification, a proposal authored by the Digital Cinema Initiatives (DCI), a group of six Hollywood studios, in 2005. Traditional film containing the movie is replaced by an electronic copy contained on a storage device. Instead of *projecting* light through print film, digital cinema uses technologies such as Digital Light Processing (DLP) and Liquid Crystal on Silicon (LCOS) to accomplish the task. The DCI has mandated industry-wide compliance with digital *projection* standards by January 2014. Mercator *projection*, technique: Refers to a system of *projection* generally used in cartography and named for Gerardus Mercator, who introduced this *projection* on a map in 1569. It is generally classified as a cylindrical *projection* even though it is actually derived mathematically. It is characterized by having parallels of latitude represented as straight horizontal lines and meridians of longitude represented as vertical straight lines at right angles to the equator. It is often used for navigation charts because any straight line is a line of true bearing that allows navigators to plot a straight-line

course; it is often considered impractical for world maps because the scale is distorted and areas farther away from the equator appear disproportionately large. *Projection*, perspective & shading techniques: Refers to a system based on *projective* geometry and used in art, architecture, cartography, and other disciplines for representing three-dimensional objects or spaces on a two-dimensional surface by following strict conventions by which imaginary sight lines project from the observer's eye to the object, transmitting an image of the object to an intervening transparent surface, which is the picture plane. Although its meaning overlaps somewhat with "perspective," *projection* is used for technical and architectural drawings that emphasize the mathematical properties of objects that are preserved in the images; "perspective" is used for artworks and renderings that include the distortions of lengths, angles, shapes, and straightness of lines that optically appear to occur as objects recede into space. *Projection*, visual works by material or technique: Refers to images cast on a surface or in space by optical means, generally by placing an object between a light source and the surface or a designated point in space. They include images created with slides or film, digital images or other computer files, or shadows cast from opaque objects; *projections* on surfaces may be cast from the front or the rear of the surface. They also include holograms cast onto a point in space.

John Harvard Projection. Art Installation. Harvard Yard. April 20–27, 2015. Krzysztof Wodiczko.

John Harvard Projection was a large-scale *projection* installation by artist and Professor in Residence of Art, Design and the Public Domain Krzysztof Wodiczko. The public *projection*, commissioned by the Harvard Committee on the Arts, animated the John Harvard statue with the faces, voices, words, and gestures of Harvard University students from a series of recorded video interviews conducted by Wodiczko. The interviews were edited, compiled, and *projected* onto the statue making it appear as though John Harvard spoke, superimposing contemporary reflections by students and connecting the historical statue with the present moment.

Projection/Installation/Intervention. VIS 2481. Department of Architecture. Seminar. Spring 2015 Instructor: Krzysztof Wodiczko.

The course focused on the ways in which designers and artists can help monuments entrenched in the past become enlivened for the living—be relevant, meaningful, and critically useful in the present and for the future. Blank facades and blind eyes of lofty civic monuments face the speechless and estranged residents living in their shadows. City monuments and city residents need to be animated, even reanimated. In this way, the art of animating monuments may include the animation of ourselves as existential and political subjects, the reactualization and critical mobilization of built symbolic structures among which we live, thereby developing our more conscious and meaningful relations to them. 🔸

See also ART—see also AUDIOVISUAL—see also AXONOMETRIC—see also COMMUNICATION—see also DIGITAL—see also DRAFTING—see also DRAWING—see also EXHIBITION—see also INSTALLATION—see also ISOMETRIC—see also LIGHTING—see also MATERIAL—see also OBLIQUE—see also ORTHOGRAPHIC—see also PARALLEL—see also PERSPECTIVE—see also REPRESENTATION—see also SCREEN—see also SPACE—see also SURFACE—see also TECHNIQUE.

PROJECTIVE

1: Relating to, produced by, or involving geometric projection. 2: Of or relating to something that indicates the psychodynamic constitution of an individual <*projective* tests>.

Projective Representation in Architecture. VIS 2122. Department of Architecture. Seminar. Instructor: Cameron Wu.

This course examined the history, theory, and practice of parallel (orthographic) and central (perspective) projection. The objective was to provide the tools to imagine and represent with precision, dexterity, and virtuosity a continually expanding repertoire of three-dimensional architectural form. The focus of the lectures was twofold: first, to trace key historical developments of projection in architecture from the Renaissance through the Enlightenment into the 20th century, and second, to explain the comprehensive codification of descriptive geometry and the means by which it is practiced. *Projective* systems have affected relationships between masons, carpenters, engineers, mathematicians, cartographers, painters, and architects. The impact of the computer on architecture's perennial oscillation between the three and two dimensions of projection come into focus. ▧

See also CARBONURBANISM: Projective Futures—see also ECOLOGY: Projective Ecologies.

PROMENADE

Promenade photograph, card photographs: Photograph introduced in 1875 as a variation of the cabinet photograph. Measuring approximately 9.5 centimeters by 19 centimeters, the size was meant to allow for photos of standing figures. *Promenade*, walkways, open spaces by function: Places for strolling; public walks.

PROPERTY

Property, characteristics: Refers most often to characteristics that suggest how a substance, or sometimes a grouping of items or entities, will respond under certain conditions. Often quantifiable, though often not apparent without analysis or testing. Intellectual *property*, legal concept: Intangible assets that include patents, trademarks, copyrights, and registered and unregistered design rights. *Property*, legal concept: Anything that can be owned, tangible or intangible. Physical *property*: Measurable *properties* that can be experienced through sight, sound, touch, taste, smell, or detected through a measuring tool, including color, brightness, length, height, width, mass, volume, density, hardness, solubility, ductility, malleability, heat conduction, melting and boiling points, electrical *properties*, etc. *Property* line, zoning concepts, legal concepts: The boundary lines between pieces of *property*. *Property* right, *property*-related concepts: Rights, constitutionally protected in some nations, to make contracts, conduct business, earn income through one's labor, and own real and personal *property*.

See also ADVOCACY—see also DISPLACEMENT: Global Displacement—see also IDEA—see also LINE—see also MATERIAL—see

also MEASURE—see also QUALITATIVE—see also QUANTITATIVE—see also REAL ESTATE—see also SENSORY—see also TERRITORY—see also ZONING.

PROPORTION

Proportion, form & composition concepts, artistic concepts: Relation between respective parts or between parts and the whole, in a building or any work of art, whether considered purely visually or numerically.

Modulor 2. Publication. Éditions de l'architecture d'aujourd'hui, 1955. Le Corbusier (author). Le Corbusier Research Collection, Frances Loeb Library. LeC NA 2750 L496a 1955.

"The search for harmonic *proportions* in Le Corbusier is simultaneously linked to ideal modules and serial measurements, the construction industry and building materials (and components), universal standards, and a mathematical basis for reconstruction. The positive reception of his first book on this system of measurement prompted this second book on the subject in which he argues for his Modulor as an instrument of design. Both *Modulor* and *Modulor 2* are works on the relationship between architecture and mathematics, in the tradition of Alberti and others. He demonstrates its use in several of his own projects, and includes letters of critique and support for the proportioning system. Le Corbusier mentions that, when he visited Princeton, Albert Einstein commented that the Modulor was a scale of *proportions* that 'makes the bad difficult and the good easy.'" —Inés Zalduendo. ▧

PROSTHETIC

1: Of, relating to, or being a *prosthesis* <a *prosthetic* device> <*prosthetic* limbs>, also of or relating to *prosthetics* <*prosthetic* research>. 2: Of, relating to, or constituting a nonprotein group of a conjugated protein.

Architecture of Cultural Prosthetics: Tools for Communication and Expression in the Public Space. STU 1310. Department of Architecture. Option Studio. Fall 2014. Instructor: Krzysztof Wodiczko. Teaching Associate: Anne Liu.

An important function of public space and architecture is to operate as inclusive, discursive, and communicative environment. To fulfill such a task, socially committed architecture must not only focus on creating permanent city structures, but also engage in the design of tools, equipment, instruments, and other communicative interfaces and media-enhanced architectural supplements for cross-cultural communication, public dialogue, individual and collective expression, and civic engagement: the architecture of cultural *prosthetics*. This studio provided a chance for architecture students to design, build, and test experimental communicative tools: mobile, wearable, or parasitically appropriating architectural sites. Students developed skills in human-scale design and fabrication, innovative use of technology, as well as social and critical knowledge: valuable cross-disciplinary experience. Students' ergonomic, psychological, and social research was consulted with potential users and fabricators. The students used creative software, 3-D printing, physical modeling, and hardware design/integration (sensors, microprojectors, speakers,

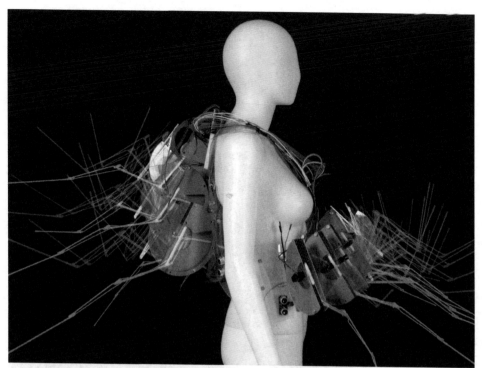

display screens, and other input and output devices). The studio included visits to groups who are working on *prosthetics*, artificial intelligence, and robotics at Harvard University, the MIT Media Lab, and the Boston area.

Students: Clare Adrien (MArch I), James Thomas Barclay (MArch II), Shaunta Rene Butler (MLA II), Lauren Nicole Friedrich (MArch I AP), Joshua Michael Jow (MArch II), Chrisoula Kapelonis (MArch II), Hanul Kim (MLA I), Ramzi Naja (MArch II), Michael C. Piscitello (MArch II), Joshua Stanton Smith (MArch II), Andrey A. Yakovlev (MArch I), Yufeng Zheng (MArch I AP). ◈

Figures. Model (opposite page). Michael C. Piscitello (MArch II).
Model (above). Chrisoula Kapelonis (MArch II).

PROTOTYPE

Prototype, object genres by function: A manufactured object that serves as the working model for the production of subsequent copies. The term is most often associated with three-dimensional objects that are functional: furniture, buildings, and machines, and less often with painting, drawing, or sculpture. Use *"prototypes"* to describe sculpture only if the works conform to other completed works in size, shape, and detail. For small-scale three-dimensional renderings for sculpture, use "maquettes," and for more finely detailed sketches for sculpture or painting, use "bozzetti."

(Re)fabricating Tectonic Prototypes. SCI 6423. Department of Architecture. Seminar. Spring 2015. Instructor: Leire Asensio Villoria.

The course was motivated by a general ambition to develop explorations in digital design, fabrication, and parametric tools that was informed and enriched by

historical precedent while still maintaining a speculative and novel outlook. The primary focus was the development of skills, techniques, and both conceptual and technical understandings of the application of digital processes and tools to the development of tectonic and construction systems in architecture. Students developed a semester-long project that took advantage of a number of emerging and established digital techniques and processes to develop new *prototypes* for construction systems that took inspiration from and expand on the analysis of a number of exemplary construction and tectonic systems. Precedents of construction and tectonic systems were studied and reconsidered during the course in order to inform and inspire the development of each project. These projects were encouraged to rethink these existing systems in order to produce and incorporate novel expression as well as performance. A period of analysis and document-ation of existing systems and their associative geometric and material relationships informed the development of a rigorous analytical knowledge of specific construction and tectonic systems, as well as a proficiency in applying this knowledge to the construction of associative and parametric digital models. This *prototype* fabrication exercise allowed students to gain knowledge in and explore the new potentials and capabilities afforded by the emerging field of digital fabrication in architecture. ◈

Figures. Models (next page). Aaron C. Menninga (MArch I) &
Joshua Bremner Feldman (MArch I). Models (page 311). Hamed
Bukhamseen (MAUD) & Ali Ismail Karimi (MArch I).

See also ASSEMBLY—see also BUILDING—see also CONSTRUC-
TION—see also FABRICATION—see also HEALTH: Planning and
Design Guidelines and Prototypes for Healthier Places—see also
LAB—see also LANDFILL: Systematic Landfill Reclamation—see
also MATERIAL—see also MODEL—see also SCALE—see also
SKYSCRAPER: Wood Skyscraper—see also 3-D.

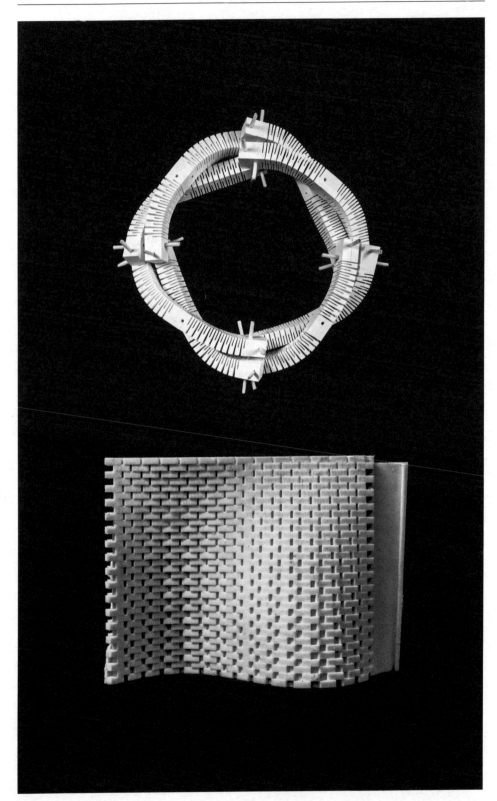

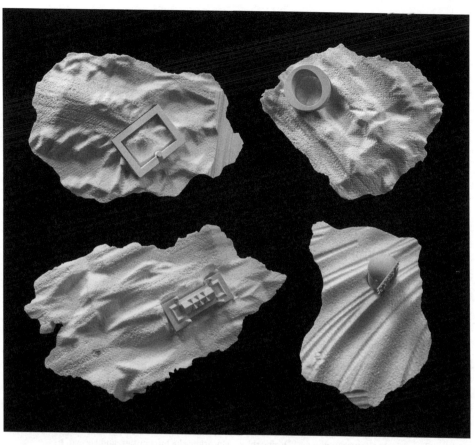

PROXY

1: The agency, function, or office of a deputy who acts as a substitute for another. 2: (a) Authority or power to act for another; (b) a document giving such authority, specifically a power of attorney authorizing a specified person to vote corporate stock. 3: A person authorized to act for another, procurator.

Proxy Series. Installation. Boston Society of Architects Space. June 17–October 4, 2015. Michael Leighton Beaman & Zaneta H. Hong with Ivy Pan (MLA I) & Foad Vahidi (MLA I).

Proxy No. 15 was a lightweight, translucent suspension structure built from recyclable polypropylene and nylon. The installation was derived from the architectonic language, assembly process, manufacturing techniques, and material effects of *Proxy No. 10*, an installation created for the American Institute of Architects (AIA) National Emerging Practitioners Exhibition in 2012. The use of a series of custom-coded digital modeling algorithms to rationalize, structure, and generate all the parts was required to build the pavilion in a single day. *Proxy No. 15* was designed by reprogramming those algorithms, inverting many of the original pavilions characteristics; whereas *Proxy No. 10* was oriented vertically, configured through two minimal surfaces, operating in compression, resting on the floor and rising to a height of seven feet, *Proxy No. 15* was a synclining symmetrical landscape, oriented horizontally, operating in tension, and suspended 12 feet above the floor.

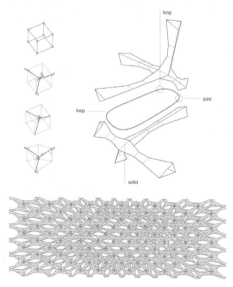

Figure. Diagrams (above). Michael Leighton Beaman, Zaneta H. Hong, Ivy Pan (MLA I), and Foad Vahidi (MLA I).

PSYCHOGEOGRAPHY

1: An approach to geography that emphasizes playfulness and "drifting" around urban environments. It has links to the Situationist International.

GSDerive. Student Group. GSDerive responds to the ubiquity of Google Maps, its top-down cartographic representation, and the screens that are used to guide people's existence, by experiencing space without a plan. The group is reviving *psychogeography* to shed light on the ways in which space is affected, used, and reappropriated, exploring different kinds of cultural mapping practices to represent the uncanny and its relationship to overly determined landscapes. GSDerive places the highest value on journeying, a hypersensitization to the everyday, and the multiplicity of narratives that coexist in place. ֍

PUBLIC

Public domain, legal concepts, social science concepts: Land owned and controlled by the state or federal government. Also, the status of publications, products, and processes that are not protected under patent or copyright.

Assessing Human Comfort in Urban Public Places in China. Health & Places Initiative Webinar Series. March 4, 2015. Jack Spengler & Jianxiang Huang.
Content research is focused on the modeling and measurement of thermal comfort in *public* places. The CityComfort+ model can be used to assess factors of building massing, shading, vegetation on radiant heat balance, and the sensation of human comfort. Using climate forcing methods, future conditions of *public* places can be used to evaluate alternative designs.ZDuring this webinar, Jack Spengler and Jianxiang Huang reviewed case studies and publications: assessing the relationship between efficient energy use and levels of resident satisfaction in China, including the psychological, health, and behavioral impact of urban lifestyle in China. ֍

See also ART—see also BOUTIQUE: America's Boutique City— see also COMPETITION: The Design Competition—see also DEVELOPMENT: Public & Private Development—see also DO- MAIN—see also DWELLING: Poor But Sexy—see also GARDEN: Third Natures—see also LAND USE—see also POLICY—see also PROSTHETIC: Architecture of Cultural Prosthetics—see also SPACE—see also SYSTEM: Resilient Modular Systems—see also TRANSPORTATION—see also ZONING.

PUBLICATION

Publication, serials, document genres by conditions of production, visual & verbal communication: *Publications* in any medium issued in successive parts bearing numerical or chronological designations and intended to be continued indefinitely, such as periodicals, newspapers, annuals (reports, yearbooks, etc.), journals, memoires, proceedings, transactions, etc., of societies and numbered monographic series.

Backpocket Projects. Student *Publication. Backpocket Projects* is an alternative, student-run *publication* that

gives greater and more immediate exposure to student works while they are being produced without respect to polish or the judgment of faculty.
The *publication's* purpose is to bring all disciplines of the Harvard GSD into greater contact with one another, through the discourses that arise from a shared *publication*. The *publication* has both an online presence and a physical *publication*, which is printed twice per year and reflects the work submitted from each semester. All work is published anonymously. ֍

Harvard Journal of Real Estate (HJRE). Student *Publication.* The *Harvard Journal of Real Estate* is an annual journal published on behalf of the Master in Design Studies Real Estate & the Built Environment program. Each publication focuses on a specific contemporary topic in real estate and includes several articles written by students, faculty, and fellows from across the university, as well as professionals in the industry. This open platform encourages an interdisciplinary approach and transparent process in the development of each journal, which takes place throughout the academic year. ֍

Newsroom at the Design School. Student Group. Newsroom at the Design School is a student-initiated editorial program based at the Harvard GSD that draws from Harvard University and beyond to offer an array of theories, beliefs, and verdicts about issues facing design and the contemporary built environment. The main product of this editorial program is the student journal, *Very Vary Veri*; the first issue was released in Spring 2014.
VVV sets forward a unique view on the the built environment by examining the breadth of authorship responsible for its form. Any innovation in contemporary design practice is impossible without perspectives from law, finance, government, real estate, public health, education, the humanities, and beyond. ֍

Poetry GSD. Student Group.

"Why not poetry
Leave the GSD sometimes
Wiser than before." ֍

SAMPLE. Student *Publication. SAMPLE* is an expression of the amateur voice lost in the contemporary discourse on architecture and ecology. *SAMPLE* operates outside of the constricting channels of closed academic systems and inspires students to denature their assumptions, absorb their surroundings, and practice nimble contemplation.
Each edition investigates the particularities of a specimen's relationship to its territory as a source of inspiration for stories, drawings, maps, photographs, texts, and inquiries. By deconstructing the boundaries that define these specimens, the *publication* hopes to relocate their relationships and interactions, as interiors and exteriors, and as an integral part of an ever changing whole. *SAMPLE* is a quarterly *publication* dedicated to the wide-eyed observations and explorations of the nonprofessional: part field guide, part wunderkammer, part menu. ֍

See also ADVOCACY—see also ART—see also COMMUNICA- TION—see also EXHIBITION—see also LETTER—see also PROJ- ECT—see also WORK.

QUALITATIVE

Qualitative analysis, analysis & testing techniques: Chemical analysis aimed at examining the nature of a material's chemical constituents.

See also ANALYSIS—see also EXERGY: Low-Exergy Communities—see also MATERIAL—see also PROCESS—see also TECHNIQUE.

QUALITY

Air *quality*, environmental concepts: Degree to which air is polluted, such that air *quality* is deemed to be high when air pollution levels are low. Archival *quality*, physiochemical attributes & properties: Property of materials, such as paper or mat board, or processing methods that are expected to allow items to be stored for extended periods of time without loss of *quality*. *Quality*, aesthetic concepts, philosophical concepts: Use in the context of aesthetic judgment for the concept of inherent merit, worthiness, or excellence in something. Image *quality*, aesthetic concepts: Use with reference to photographic and electronic images, usually pertaining to the clarity of details, often relating to the degree of resolution. *Quality* of life, social issues, sociological concepts: The degree of well-being felt by an individual about his or her lifestyle, often defined in terms of social indicators, such as nutrition, air *quality*, crime rates, etc.

Designed for Evaluation: Treatment & Control. Thesis. Jim Peraino (MArch I), advised by Iñaki Ábalos & Allen Sayegh.

"Quantity of life. Medicalized architecture: How can we tap into a growing body of evidence that suggests design strategies affect health outcomes? Evidence &

evaluation: how can we design a building that can produce knowledge, that holds itself accountable to its hypothesis and allows itself to be evaluated?

Quality of life. Desubjectification: what are the shortcomings of an approach driven entirely by evidence? What are the subjective experiences that cannot be quantified, cannot be proven, and where can they infiltrate the machine?" ☙

Figure. Diagrams (next page). Jim Peraino (MArch I).

See also AIR: Innovate—see also COMMUNITY—see also DETAIL—see also ENVIRONMENT—see also LIFESTYLE—see also MATERIAL—see also PHOTOGRAPHY—see also REHABILITATION—see also WELL-BEING.

QUANTITATIVE

1: Of, relating to, or expressible in terms of *quantity*. 2: Of, relating to, or involving the measurement of *quantity* or amount. 3: Based on *quantity*, specifically of classical verse, based on temporal *quantity* or duration of sounds.

Quantitative analysis, chemical analysis, analysis & testing techniques: Chemical analysis aimed at determining the proportions of the substances present in a sample of a material.

The Fisher Lab & Its Legacy. Exhibition. Gund Hall, Frances Loeb Library, Special Collections. April 9–May 15, 2015. Stephen McTee Ervin & Matthew Wilson.

1965 was a seminal year in the history of Geographic Information Science (GIS), as the Harvard Laboratory for Computer Graphics (subsequently Computer Graphics and Spatial Analysis) was founded by Howard

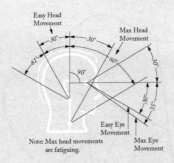

Easy Head
Movement

Max Head
Movement

90°

Easy Eye
Movement

Note: Max head movements
are fatiguing.

Max Eye
Movement

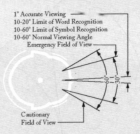

1" Accurate Viewing
10-20° Limit of Word Recognition
10-60° Limit of Symbol Recognition
10-60° Normal Viewing Angle
Emergency Field of View

Cautionary
Field of View

Adopted from Humanscale, Henry Dreyfuss Associates

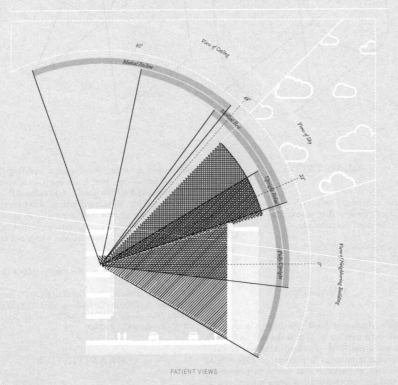

View of Ceiling

80°

Medial Recline

View of Sky

48°

Medial Rise

22°

Upright Recline

Fully Upright

0°

View of Neighboring Building

PATIENT VIEWS

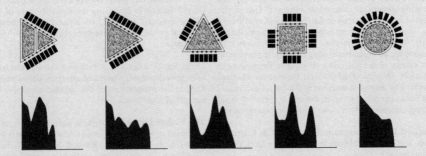

Fisher with support from the Ford Foundation and the Harvard GSD. Harvard University had been the home of a robust geography department in the 1930s and 1940s, until 1948 when the department was disbanded. In the 1960s, several North American geographers had become interested in the application of the new technology of digital computing to the management of geographic data and the creation of maps. Against this background, Fisher and a small team of researchers and programmers, starting in the basement of Memorial Hall, embarked on a more than 20-year journey of research and development in theoretical geography, computer cartography, and spatial analysis, which gave us many of today's essential ideas and early versions of tools now embedded in commercial GIS, remote sensing, geospatial science, and today's ubiquitous online culture. At the same time, early collaborations with Harvard GSD faculty, primarily in planning and landscape architecture, demonstrated the use of these emergent technologies in landscape planning and environmental design and laid the foundations for the emergence in the current decade of the discipline of geodesign. This exhibition showcased computer-generated maps and graphics surrounded by images, texts, artifacts, and correspondence, mostly from 1965 to 1985, that illustrate the various disciplines, viewpoints, and individuals who contributed to those heady days of experimentation and development. One wall of the exhibition was devoted to works by contemporary researchers and developers, building upon, and going beyond, the foundation laid by the lab, half a century ago. ✸

See also ANALYSIS—see also EXERGY: Low-Exergy Communities—see also MATERIAL—see also METHOD—see also PROCESS—see also TECHNIQUE—see also URBAN: Analytic Methods of Urban Planning.

RADICAL

1: Of, relating to, or proceeding from a root, such as (a) of or growing from the root of a plant <*radical* tubers>; (b) growing from the base of a stem, from a rootlike stem, or from a stem that does not rise above the ground <*radical* leaves>; (c) of, relating to, or constituting a linguistic root; (d) of or relating to a mathematical root; (e) designed to remove the root of a disease or all diseased and potentially diseased tissue <*radical* surgery> <*radical* mastectomy>. 2: Of or relating to the origin, fundamental. 3: (a) Very different from the usual or traditional, extreme; (b) favoring extreme changes in existing views, habits, conditions, or institutions; (c) associated with political views, practices, and policies of extreme change; (d) advocating extreme measures to retain or restore a political state of affairs <the *radical* right>. 4: Excellent, cool.

The Grounds of Radical Nature. Lecture. Gund Hall, Piper Auditorium. April 22, 2015. Eva Castro & Jose Alfredo Ramirez.

In the context of today's generic urban developments and the eradication of public space by market forces and power structures, does landscape as a discipline have any capacity to challenge those mechanisms that produce contemporary urbanization as opposed to its conventional role in producing their aesthetic component? Eva Castro and Jose Alfredo Ramirez explored this question in their understanding of the landscape discipline and

their *radical* utilization of infrastructure. These ideas represent a paradigm in the construction of their own political position not only in respect to questions of identity and public space but in the construction of an approach toward nature.

Nature and ecology began to serve as a mechanism of depoliticizing discourses linked to territorial planning and design as an effect of the mainstream ecological urbanism related practices. This professional shift toward pretended neutrality, in terms of both its social and political context, further reached the domain of spatial design. As a counterargument, beyond the romanticist, apolitic, altruist, protectionist or mimetic conceptions of nature of the so-called ecologic or sustainable urbanism, Castro and Ramirez understand nature as an artifice, along the lines of an artificial construct, reinforcing rather than minimizing its political power. They argued that a spatial definition of the concept of ground can turn nature into a *radical* component of a morphologically-driven urban discourse, signaling ways in which the discourse around the concept of ground and nature can be recentered as a source of a *radical* approach to engineered landscapes. ✸

Radical Cities. GSD Talks. Gund Hall, Frances Loeb Library. October 10, 2014. Justin McGuirk.

Ever since the mid-20th century, when the modernist utopia came to Latin America to die, the continent has been a testing ground of *radical* ideas in city-making. Here, in the most urbanized continent on the planet, extreme cities have bred extreme conditions, from vast housing estates to sprawling slums. But after decades of political and architectural failure, a new generation has returned to the problems of the city to address the poverty and inequality. This is a generation of activists, pragmatists, and social idealists, and together they are testing new ideas that the rest of the world can learn from. ✸

RAM

Random-Access Memory (*RAM*), computer components: Computer memory which acts as the primary storage for programs and data. Hydraulic *ram*, pumping machinery: Automatic pumps that use the kinetic energy of descending water to raise the water above its original height. *Ram*, animals: Adult male uncastrated sheep. *Ram*, warships, naval ships: Steam-driven warships of the 19th and early 20th centuries equipped with an armored prow to be used as a primary weapon against other ships; for rowed warships equipped with ramming prows, use "galleys (watercraft)."

RAMP

Ramp, circulation elements, architectural elements: Inclined planes or slopes that are constructed of earth, stone, cement, metal, wood, or another material, and used to connect two different levels, or to connect one level to the air or water. Examples include sloping floors or walks in architecture, sloping construction used in highway engineering, movable sets of stairs used when boarding or leaving an airplane, and movable slopes to allow access to a bus or other type of vehicle. Wheelchair *ramp*, circulation elements: Inclined planes that are constructed instead of or in addition to stairways in order to allow wheelchair users and people pushing carts or other small wheeled devices to access buildings, parts of buildings, curbs, or other locations where it is necessary to go from one level to another.

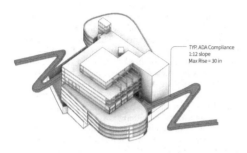

TYP. ADA Compliance
1:12 slope
Max Rise = 30 in

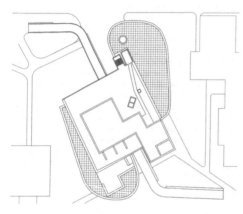

Figure. Diagram & Plan (above). Christopher Michael Johnson (MArch I AP).

RARE

1: Marked by wide separation of component particles, thin <*rare* air>. 2: (a) Marked by unusual quality, merit, or appeal, distinctive; (b) superlative or extreme of its kind.

Rare book, books by condition of production: Books that are valuable due to their actual or prospective rarity, specifically books distinguished by an early publication date, limited issue, historical interest, or a special characteristic of the edition or binding, for example having been signed by the artist or containing special illustrations. This designation typically includes books that are collected by a special collections department, archives, or museum, as opposed to books that are available to casual readers on the shelves of a public library. *Rare* earth element, materials by chemical form: Any of the group of metallic elements whose oxides are classed as *rare* earths. These include the lanthanide series, yttrium, and scandium.

See also BOOK—see also COLLECTION: Special Collections—see also EXTREME—see also GEOLOGY—see also PLANT—see also QUALITATIVE—see also SPECULATION: Rare New Species.

RATIO

Aspect *ratio*, proportion, form & composition concepts: The *ratio* of width to height of an image frame. The term is generally used in reference to motion pictures and other screen-oriented technologies including computer graphics. Floor Area *Ratio* (FAR), zoning concepts, legal concepts: Refers to the ratio of the permissible total floor area of a building on a zoning lot to the total area of the lot. Golden section, proportion, form & composition concepts: Canon of proportion based on the *ratio* between two unequal parts of a whole when the proportion of the smaller to the larger is equal to that of the larger to the whole. *Ratio*, mathematical concepts: The values obtained by dividing one number by another; often used for comparison.

See also COMPUTER—see also FILM—see also GEOMETRY—see also GRID—see also MEASURE—see also PROPORTION—see also ZONING.

REAL ESTATE

Real estate, property, legal concept: Property consisting of freehold land or certain rights over freehold land.

Master in Design Studies (MDes) Real Estate & the Built Environment (REBE).
    In the contemporary global economy, architecture, landscape architecture, and urban planning and design must confront the complex mechanisms of finance and economics. *Real Estate* & the Built Environment engages both by considering design and investment as integrally connected. Mirroring the experience many graduates encounter in practice, this Master in Design Studies concentration places design within the crucible of finance, examining the ways one can add value to the other. As part of a design discourse, financial analyses—feasibility studies, economic models, and investment strategies—acquire added social, cultural, and aesthetic dimensions. The transdisciplinary program positions *real estate* development as a collaborative process, allowing students to enroll in courses from across the Harvard GSD as well as throughout the university—including Harvard Business School, Kennedy School of Government, and Harvard Law School. ⊛

Greater China Real Estate Investment Association. Student Group. The Greater China *Real Estate* Investment Association aims to provide a strong platform for *real estate* professionals from mainland China, Hong Kong, Macau, and Taiwan. By bridging the gap across these areas, the association shares information about the *real estate* industry with all the members who are eager to work and invest in *real estate* in China. ⊛

Disruptive Innovation in Real Estate. Harvard *Real Estate* Conference & Panel Discussion. Gund Hall, Piper Auditorium. October 16, 2014. Bing Wang & Raymond Torto (moderators). ⊛

Real Estate Development (RED) Club. Student Group. The *Real Estate* Development Club at the Harvard GSD is a student organization that provides students with an interest in *real estate* with the resources to further their knowledge of and pursue careers in the *real estate* industry. In addition, the RED Club seeks to establish and foster a strong *real estate* community between the Harvard GSD, alumni, other academic institutions, and the global *real estate* network. The group accomplishes its mission through a variety of events such as its speaker series, organized networking events with other *real estate* clubs and national organizations, global *real estate* treks and local site visits, and skill-building training sessions. ⊛

Real Estate, Finance & Development: Fundamentals for Public and Private Participants. SES 5492.
Department of Urban Planning & Design. Seminar. Fall 2014. Instructor: Edward Henry Marchant.

This course provided an analytical framework for understanding *real estate* finance and development fundamentals from both public and private perspectives. The topics addressed included: establishing investment and development objectives, structuring ownership entities, evaluating and controlling prospective development sites, creating sound development plans, understanding the public entitlement process, preparing market and feasibility studies, securing debt and equity financing, coordinating the design and construction process, and marketing and managing *real estate* assets. Students learned principles that are globally applicable to private, public, NGO, and not-for-profit participants in policy planning for or implementation of *real estate* development, community redevelopment, and disaster relief activities. ⊛

See also DEVELOPMENT—see also INITIATIVE: Real Estate Academic Initiative—see also LAND USE—see also LEADERSHIP: Global Leadership in Real Estate & Design—see also RETAIL: Prestige Retail—see also ZONING.

REALITY

Reality, psychological concepts, social science concepts: The aggregate of real things and actual existence as opposed to what is theorized, imagined, or desired. *Reality* is that which underlies and is the truth of appearances or phenomena.

See also AUGMENTED REALITY—see also CITY: Unplugged City—see also PHENOMENON—see also VIRTUAL.

RECLAMATION

Land *reclamation* work, hydraulic structures by function: Dikes, canals, pumps, and other structures and equipment used to create dry land in an area that otherwise would be flooded. *Reclamation*, maintenance, functions by general context: Making areas of the natural landscape available for human use by changing natural conditions.

See also BROWNFIELD—see also LANDFILL: Systematic Landfill Reclamation.

RECONSTRUCTION

Reconstruction, construction by function: Use only to refer to *construction* of new objects or structures built to re-semble old ones based on historic, archaeological, or other similar evidence. *Reconstruction*, visual works: Drawings that propose how something may have looked at a previous time, and for full-scale new objects or structures based on historical, archaeological, or other similar evidence. For models made to represent how something looked at a previous time, use "historical models."

See also ADAPTIVE REUSE—see also POST-CONFLICT: May Kabul Be Without Gold, Rather Without Snow—see also STRUCTURE—see also TRANSFORMATION.

RECYCLING

Recycling, waste management, maintenance: Recovery and reuse of materials and energy from waste.

Single-Stream Recycling. The following items may be *recycled* at the Harvard GSD following the guidelines of Harvard University's single-stream *recycling* program: Paper items (white and colored paper, shredded paper, paper bags, paper plates and bowls, paper clamshells, wrapping paper, newspaper, magazines and catalogs, phone books and junk mail, coffee cups, books), plastics (plastic items no. 1–7, stiff plastic containers, shampoo bottles, milk cartons, juice boxes, large plastics), metal cans and foils (empty aerosol cans, aluminum cans, aluminum foil and trays, metal food cans, spiral cans), glass jars and bottles (beverage bottles, food jars, wine bottles), and cardboard (cardboard boxes, pizza boxes, paperboard). ⊛

See also COMPOST—see also ENERGY—see also GREEN—see also MATERIAL—see also PAPER—see also PROCESS—see also SUSTAINABILITY—see also TECHNIQUE—see also WASTE.

REDEVELOPMENT

Redevelopment, urban renewal, urban development, community development: Activity of clearing, rebuilding, restoring, or refurbishing urban areas.

See also COMMUNITY—see also DEVELOPMENT—see also POST-DISASTER—see also POST-SUBURB—see also URBAN—see also VISION: Toulouse.

REFUGE

1: Shelter or protection from danger or distress. 2: A place that provides shelter or protection. 3: Something to which one has recourse in difficulty.

Wildlife *refuge*, nature reserves, open spaces by function: Areas set aside for feeding, roosting, nesting, breeding, and habitat protection for species of animals and plants native to the region; also offering protection from hunting, and sometimes protection from predation and competition.

Refugia: Boundary between the Binaries. Thesis. Eri Yamagata (MLA I), advised by Gary R. Hilderbrand.
"*Refugium*, meaning place of *refuge*, refers to an isolated fragment of habitat removed from regional ecological patterns often associated with glaciation,

climatic change, geography, and human activities. This project recognizes two sites of *refugium* in Wellfleet, Massachusetts. The first is the Atlantic White Cedar Swamp, a unique ecosystem consisting of an ombrotrophic (cloud-fed) bog that is hydrologically isolated from the stream system and springs; the second is Lieutenant Island, cut off and made inaccessible by high tides and sea-level changes. This thesis addresses matters of climate change and ongoing geological transformations, that have impacted the Outer Cape dramatically (especially after the intensive extraction of resources for habitation, which has also altered the Cape's landscape). These fragile conditions are progressively disappearing through alterations caused by inevitable forces of erosion and rising tides.

While ennobling the intimate and intricate experience of these distinct places, the operation of precise design and focused planting techniques at the edges of the *refugia* must consider long-term transformative energies of the sea and the wind. We are unable to prevent forces, whether anthropogenic or natural; in design, we must instead embrace that which constantly changes the landscape. This project frames the constant struggle for the ecosystem: the path of entropy or the hand of design." §

Figure. Perspective (previous spread). Eri Yamagata (MLA I).

See also CLIMATE CHANGE—see also COLOR—see also DWELL-ING—see also HYDROLOGY—see also ISLAND—see also PLAN-NING: Perceptions of Physical Space and the Planning Process in Camp Azraq, Jordan—see also TERRITORY.

REGIME

1: (a) Regimen; (b) a regular pattern of occurrence or action; (c) the characteristic behavior or orderly procedure of a natural phenomenon or process. 2: (a) Mode of rule or management; (b) a form of government <a socialist *regime*>; (c) a government in power; (d) a period of rule.

Destin de Paris. Publication. Éditions F. Sorlot, 1941. Le Corbusier (author). Le Corbusier Research Collection, Frances Loeb Library. LeC NAC 6898 L496.

"This small book summarizes Le Corbusier's principles of and experiences in urban planning as of 1922, and advocates for housing as the key solution for the well-being of families and, therefore, the nation. Le Corbusier had drafted master plans for Rio, Buenos Aires, Paris, and Algiers, and had been invited to Moscow, but none of these resulted in actual commissions. With boots on the ground across Europe, Le Corbusier joined the collaborationist Vichy *regime* under Pétain, believing (opportunistically) that his alliance would open doors to actual commissions and even to the reconstruction of Paris under his direction: 'I enter the ranks after six months of doing nothing and 20 years of hopes,' he writes. Several iterations for Algiers were developed during his association with the Vichy *regime*, but his attempts to promote them were unsuccessful and he left soon after." —Inés Zalduendo. §

REGULATION

Building code, *regulations*, visual & verbal communication: Laws, ordinances, or government *regulations* concerning fitness for habitation setting forth standards and requirements for the construction, maintenance, operation, occupancy, use, or appearance of buildings, premises, and dwelling units. *Regulation*, executive records by function: Use broadly for principles, rules, or laws designed to control or *regulate* behavior of individuals, corporations, or other entities. Height restriction, zoning concepts, legal concepts: Limitations placed, usually by the government, on the vertical distance from the base to the top of structures.

See also ADVOCACY—see also DEVELOPMENT—see also HOUS-ING: Institutional Strategies for Upholding Affordable Housing Agreements—see also LAND USE—see also POLICY.

REHABILITATION

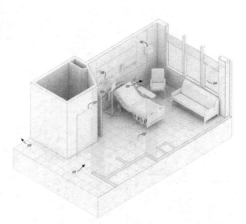

Rehabilitation, maintenance, functions by general context: Refers to the function of restoring people to physical or mental health or good repute. Refers also to the activity of returning to good condition deteriorated objects, structures, neighborhoods, or public facilities; may involve repair, renovation, conversion, expansion, remodeling, or reconstruction. For actions taken to prevent further changes or deterioration in things, see "preservation." When deterioration has not occurred, see "renovation" for actions taken to improve the quality of structures.

Figure. Diagram (above). Jim Peraino (MArch I).

See also CONSERVATION—see also HISTORY—see also INFRA-STRUCTURE—see also LANDMARK: Montreal is Back—see also PRESERVATION—see also STRUCTURE—see also TRANSFOR-MATION—see also WELL-BEING.

RELATE

1: To give an account of, tell. 2: To show or establish logical or causal connection between <seeks to *relate* crime to poverty>. 3: To apply or take effect retroactively—usually used with back <the law *relates* back to the initial date of decision>. 4: To have relationship or connection <the readings *relate* to his lectures>. 5: To have or establish a relationship, interact <the way a child *relates* to a teacher>. 6: To respond especially favorably <can't *relate* to that kind of music>.

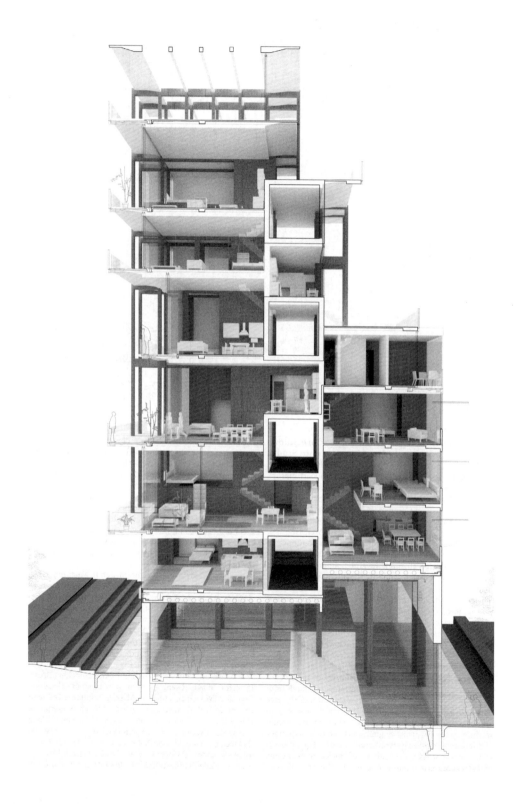

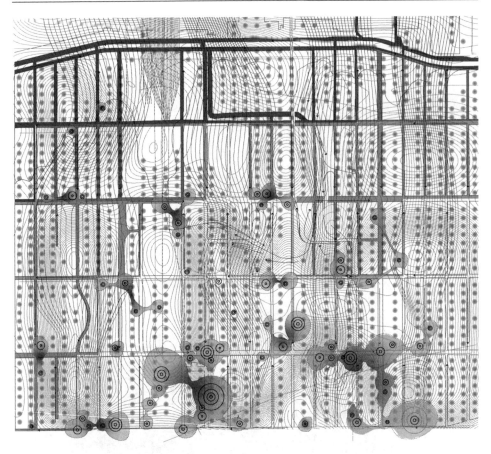

Relate: Fourth Semester Architecture Core Studio.
STU 1202. Department of Architecture. Core Studio.
Spring 2015. Instructors: Vincent Bandy, Eric Höweler,
Mariana Ibañez, Max Kuo, Carles Muro (coordinator),
and Renata Sentkiewicz. Teaching Assistants: Chris
Bennett (MDes, ULE), Kathryn Leigh Blackstock (MArch
I), Matthew Joseph Conway (MArch I), Patrick Kramer
Herron (MArch I), José Ramón Sierra Gómez de León
(MArch II), and Alexander R. Timmer (MArch I).

Relate was the last of a four-semester sequence of
studios that was aimed at introducing students to architectural design through specific pedagogical lenses.
The studio introduced students to the complexity of the
urban condition and the different forms of negotiation
between architecture and the city across multiple scales,
and explored the role of housing as a central component
of the physical fabric of the city and the fundamental
site of negotiation between the individual and collective
in search of new forms of inhabitation. Cities are extremely complex social and spatial organizations made
of streets and squares, blocks and buildings, but also
dwellers. The city is the field of inquiry of many contemporary disciplines, but the uniqueness of the designer's approach consists in the understanding of the city
through its transformation. We generate knowledge
when actively transforming the urban fabric. When
working in the city, the designer has to address a number
of different and often contradictory factors. The physical
structure of the city, a specific set of block configurations
and street organizations is informed by the local climate,

the networks of infrastructures of mobility, energy supply
and waste collection, the availability of construction
materials and technologies, the topography and the
geography of the area, and also its people, history, and
culture. All of these factors are at odds with one another
and one of the tasks of the designer is to set priorities
and preferences in a continuous process of negotiation.
It could be argued that the design process is always a
form of negotiation, but the very understanding of the
city as a complex system with many interrelated variables calls for a form of design that takes negotiation
at its core.

Students: Cari A. Alcombright (MArch I), Nastaran Arfaei
(MArch I), Sofia Balters (MArch I), Taylor John Brandes
(MArch I), Jacob Joseph Bruce (MArch I), Yaqing Cai
(MArch I), Maria Carriero (MArch I), Ruth H. Chang (MArch
I), Sean Chia (MArch I), Shani Eunjin Cho (MArch I), Collin
Stephens Cobia (MArch I AP), Stephanie Kristina Conlan
(MArch I), Allison C. Cottle (MArch I), Elizabeth Marie
Cronin (MArch I AP), Carly Linda Dickson (MArch I), Anna
Rose Falvello Tomas (MArch I), Evan Robert Farley (MArch
I), Johanna Marja Faust (MArch I), Justin Gallagher (MArch
I), John Morris Going (MArch I), Christian Alexander
Gonzalez (MArch I), Yun Gui (MArch I), Fabiola Guzman
Rivera (MArch I), Michael Haggerty (MArch I), Benjamin
David Halpern (MArch I), David Benard Hamm (MArch
I), Spencer Taylor Hayden (MArch I), Olivia Jiang Yi Heung
(MArch I), Gu Jia (MArch I), Justin Jiang (MArch I), Chase
Mitchell Jordan (MArch I), Sarah Kantrowitz (MArch I),
Andrew Wade Keating (MArch I), Jason Hwan Kim (MArch

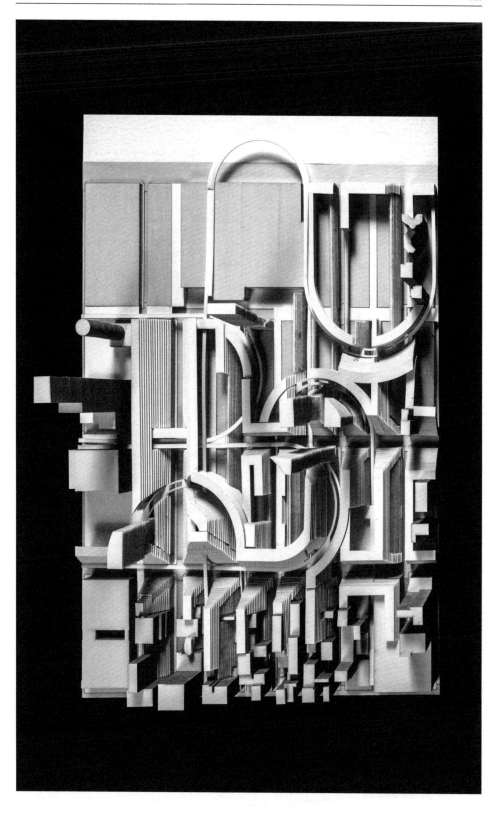

I), Yurina Kodama (MArch I & MLA I AP), Claire Kuang (MArch I), Yixin Li (MArch I), Yanchen Liu (MArch I), Yan Ma (MArch I & MLA I), Emily Margulies (MArch I), Patrick Alexander McKinley (MArch I & MLA I), Thomas Michael McMurtrie (MArch I), Dasha Draginia Mikic (MArch I), Niki Murata (MArch I), James Francis Murray (MArch I), Duan Ni (MArch I), Felipe Oropeza (MArch I), Kimberly Orrego (MArch I), Davis Shimon Owen (MArch I), Sophia Panova (MArch I), Maia Sian Peck (MArch I), Haibei Peng (MArch I), Jiayu Qiu (MArch I), Benzion Isaac Rodman (MArch I), Gavin Ruedisueli (MArch I), Anne MacDonald Schneider (MArch I), Anita Sellers Helfrich (MArch I), Scott March Smith (MArch I), Kathryn Leigh Sonnabend (MArch I), Constance Blair Storie Johnson (MArch I), Chang Su (MArch I AP), LeeAnn Liang Suen (MArch I), Lilian Mae Taylor (MArch I), Xuezhu Tian (MArch I AP), Enoch Wong (MArch I), Bryan Yang (MArch I), Guowei Zhang (MArch I), Snoweria Zhang (MArch I). ℘

Figures. Sectional Perspective (page 321). Justin Gallagher (MArch I), Yurina Kodama (MArch I & MLA I AP), Dasha Draginia Mikic (MArch I), and Fabiola Guzman Rivera (MArch I). Plan (page 322). Chase Mitchell Jordan (MArch I), James Francis Murray (MArch I), and Kimberly Orrego (MArch I). Model (previous page). Stephanie Kristina Conlan (MArch I), David Benard Hamm (MArch I), Kathryn Leigh Sonnabend (MArch I), and Xuezhu Tian (MArch I AP).

See also ANALYSIS—see also OBSERVATION—see also PRO-CESS—see also TYPE: Blob Block Slab Mat Slat.

RELEVANCE

1: (a) Relation to the matter at hand; (b) practical and especially social applicability, pertinence <giving *relevance* to college courses>. 2: The ability to retrieve material that satisfies the needs of the user.

Relevance & Revelation. Conversation. Gund Hall, Piper Auditorium. September 13, 2014. Mack Scogin & Preston Scott Cohen. ℘

RELIEF

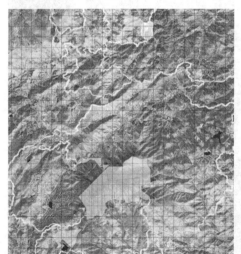

Relief, sculptures by technique: Sculptures in which the ornaments or figures are attached to a background from which they stand out to a greater or lesser degree. *Reliefs* are often used as architectural decoration and because of their capacity for narration they are often used for pictorial narrative purposes. *Relief* map, maps by form, visual & verbal communication: Maps showing land or sea bottom *relief* in terms of height above or below a datum by any method, such as contours, Hatchures, shading, or tinting. *Relief* printing, printing & printing processes & techniques: Printing processes in which the nonprinting areas of the block or plate are carved, engraved, or etched away, leaving the original plane surface raised so that ink is deposited and transferred to paper. Traditionally a woodcut technique, *relief* printing developed into letterpress for the printing of text and wood engraving to provide accompanying illustrations. It is one of the oldest printing techniques known. Shaded-*relief* maps, maps by form, visual & verbal communication: Maps on which *relief* is made to appear three-dimensional by the use of graded shadow effect.

Figure. Map (left). Christina Leigh Geros (MLA I AP & MAUD).

See also ART—see also COMMUNICATION—see also CON-TOUR—see also LAND—see also MAPPING—see also PLANE—see also PRINT—see also PROCESS—see also REPRESENTA-TION—see also SURFACE—see also TECHNIQUE—see also TOPOGRAPHY—see also WATER.

RENDERING

Rendering, drawing techniques: Creating a technical drawing, such as an elevation, with an indication of light and shadow, and sometimes of color. *Rendering*, drawings by material or technique, visual works: Architectural drawings or drawings of other subjects, characterized by the depiction of shadows, textures, sometimes colors, often executed with watercolor washes, and showing some setting. Intended as visualizations of the full conception of a project or as an accurate record of the work depicted.

Digital Drawing for Landscape Architecture: Contemporary Techniques & Tools for Digital Re-presentation in Site Design. Publication. John Wiley & Sons, 2015. Bradley Earl Cantrell & Wes Michaels (authors). SB475.9.D37 C36 2015.

Digital *rendering* is more efficient, flexible, and fast than traditional *rendering* techniques, causing offices to adapt digital *rendering* techniques into their daily workflow. Deconstructing the design image explores specific techniques, like creating digitally *rendered* plans, perspectives, and diagrams.

Figure. Rendering (opposite page). Gavin Ruedisueli (MArch I).

See also DRAWING—see also LIGHTING—see also PROJECT—see also REPRESENTATION—see also TECHNIQUE.

REPETITION

Repetition, formal concept: As an artistic concept, the characteristic within a composition where a form, line,

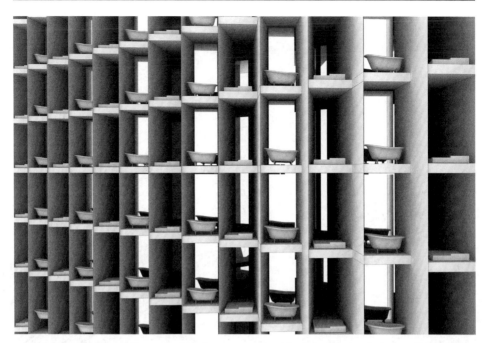

color, or other compositional element is *repeated* to cause unity or for another purpose. *Repetition*, process and techniques by specific type: The action of saying or doing something over again which one has already said or done. The term may be used in the context of visual images, the spoken or written word, performances, music, and other contexts.

See also COMPOSITION—see also CONCEPT—see also ELE-MENT—see also HARMONY—see also ITERATION—see also LINE—see also OEUVRE—see also PRACTICE—see also PROCESS.

REPRESENTATION

Representation, form of expression: A manner of expression by the artist in which the subject matter is presented so that the observer is reminded of actual visible forms. However, the subject *represented* may or may not exist in the visible world. For example, *representations* may include presentations of subject matter that are invisible to the eye, such as emotions or imaginary events, as if they are visible. *Representing*, governmental functions, functions by context: Serving in a legislative body by authority delegated by persons subject to the laws enacted by that body, usually by election, to *represent* their wishes and interests.

Dweller on the Threshold. Thesis & James Templeton Kelley Prize. Chloe Natanel Brunner (MArch II), advised by Mack Scogin.

"*Misrepresentation* introduces an alternative perspective and generative process to architecture. Here, *misrepresentation* describes two interrelated design processes: first is the intentional and methodical distortion of the context by digital mismapping; second is the disturbance of both the context and the architecture through a structural coupling. Structural coupling, a term from systems theory, refers in this instance to the reciprocal relationship in which the architecture and the context observe each other and make use of each other's properties in order to build complexity in their own internal structures (of form, material, and program). While the initial *misrepresentation* of the context proceeds through a systematic recoding of the map, the second-order structural coupling requires an intuitive interpretation of properties assigned by the inhabitants. The specific environment of Google Earth exposes the generative potential of technical errors in its *misrepresented* images of bridges. Five sites are constructed from distorting perspective and projection of these initial data in such a way as to generate hitherto unimagined locations. Each site houses a construction, a vacation home for an idiosyncratic resident, carrying with them a suite of spatial phobias and philias. Together, these sites are offered as an entry to Alberto Manguel and Gianni Guadalupi's catalogue of world literature's fantastical lands, *The Dictionary of Imaginary Places*." §

Figure. Drawing (next spread). Chloe Natanel Brunner (MArch II).

See also ART—see also AXONOMETRIC—see also COLLAGE—see also COMMUNICATION—see also CONCEPT—see also DIGITAL—see also DISCIPLINE—see also DRAFTING—see also DRAWING—see also FILM: Assistance Moretelle—see also FORUM—see also GAME: Immersive Landscapes—see also HOLOGRAM: Fragments of a Hologram House—see also IDEA—see also INFORMATION—see also METHODOLOGY—see also OBLIQUE—see also ORTHOGRAPHIC—see also PERSPECTIVE—see also PHOTOGRAPHY—see also PHOTOMONTAGE: Composite Landscapes—see also PRACTICE—see also TECHNIQUE—see also WRITING: Writing Architecture.

RESEARCH

Research, function, analytical functions: Conducting diligent and systematic inquiry or investigation into a

subject or question, especially in order to discover or revise facts or theories.

See also CENTER—see also COLLECTION—see also COMPUTA-TION: Paradigms in Computing—see also DESIGN—see also INI-TIATIVE—see also LAB—see also LIBRARY—see also METHODOL-OGY—see also MODEL: Spectacular Simplicity—see also PARK—see also PLAN: First Semester Core Urban Planning Studio—see also PRACTICE—see also SYSTEM—see also TECHNIQUE—see also THEORY—see also WRITING.

RESILIENCE

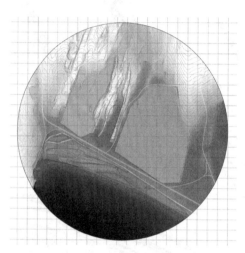

1: The capability of a strained body to recover its size and shape after deformation caused especially by compressive stress. 2: An ability to recover from or adjust easily to misfortune or change.

Coastal Resilience: Sustainable Development of the Spanish Atlantic Coast. Student Event. Spain GSD & GSD Ecological Thinking. Miriam García.

The Coastal Management Plan of Galicia is a landmark project in the Spanish context. It proposes adaptive and anticipatory planning, and elaborates strategies for the protection and planning of sustainable growth of the coastal region. Thus, it challenges the traditional urban planning approach and proposes an alternative reading of the landscape as a system of superimposed dynamics requiring a comprehensive and holistic approach. This professional project is closely linked with a broader dissertation exploring innovative practices in planning for coastal *resiliency* by critically reflecting on the cultural and political meaning of landscape as an infrastructure. ֍

Creating Resilient Cities: Future Cities, Future Coasts, and Spatial Analysis of Cities at Risk. SES 5342. Department of Urban Planning & Design. Seminar. Fall 2014. Instructor: Joyce Klein Rosenthal.

Coastal cities are undergoing environmental changes at a scale and pace that challenges traditional cultures, disciplinary methods, experience, histories, and techniques. The same could be said about social change and economic transformation in many of these cities, and their interactions exacerbate the challenges of governance and response in planning and design. Cities have re-

sponded by developing new institutions, planning processes, and design approaches aimed at promoting *resilience* to the impacts of climate change and variability.

This course examined the impacts of environmental change on cities, and explored planning and design approaches that foster development under these conditions. The course examined the urban risk and *resilience* paradigm and the integration of hazard risk reduction and climate action planning and focused on social equity and vulnerability, the merger of chronic and episodic shocks at the urban scale, the analysis of *resilience* as a paradigm in planning, and the development of professional responses. ֍

Master in Design Studies (MDes) Risk & Resilience (RR). The world faces unpredictable challenges at increasing intensities—natural disasters, ecological uncertainty, public health crises, extreme social inequity, rising violence—and yet counters and absorbs risk through acts of *resilience*.

Risk & *Resilience*, a concentration area within the Master in Design Studies, sets out to support novel approaches to sociospatial planning through design. Design as a discipline provides cities, communities, and individuals with tools to effectively prepare for, cope with, and anticipate rapid change within the spatial, social, and economic vulnerabilities it produces. While the program is grounded in the physical and tectonic realities of location, it is the social and political conflicts that emerge as sites of investigation. ֍

Ocean State. Exhibition. Gund Hall, Experiments Wall. November 2, 2014–January 20, 2015. Rosetta S. Elkin & Michael Van Valkenburgh.

Resilience is typically a value associated with the scale of an ecosystem. This view overlooks the potential of *resilience* as an embedded microcondition, which amalgamates, through biological evidence. By nature, competitive, plants emerge and spring back based on regimes of disturbance that warrant their use and exploitation along the urbanized coastline, contrary to the ideology of native or restorative environmentalism. A strategy that realizes the potential for plants to shape the environment provides a foundation to develop a design that can be manipulated and measured alongside typical construction materials.

The Harvard GSD, working in conjunction with a consortium of universities, as well as the Rockefeller Foundation and the United States Army Corps of Engineers, has developed a set of generalizable storm surge mitigation strategies in order to provide a cohesive estuarine-based approach for addressing the growing concerns over sea-level rise and storm surge. The application of vegetal infrastructure is being expanded, crafting a wider role in which plants are the primary wave attenuating agents, using disturbance regimes to cultivate rhizomatic structural components. ֍

Figure. Ocean State Exhibition (left). Rosetta S. Elkin & Michael Van Valkenburgh.

The Resilience Dividend. Lecture. Sackler Museum, Lecture Hall. March 24, 2015. Judith Rodin with Jerold S. Kayden.

Resiliency for the 21st Century. Lecture. Loeb Fellowship Program. Gund Hall, Stubbins. September 16, 2014. Scott Campbell, Maria Jaakkola, and Edwin Thaddeus Pawlowski. ֍

RESPONSIVE

Responsive, smart materials, materials by property: Materials with adaptive capabilities that react to external stimuli such as load, heat, and vibrations. Examples of smart materials include self-healing concrete which releases reserves of a strong adhesive when under stress, mending cracks; shape-memory alloys and polymers which can undergo deformation by heat or stress thanks to pseudo-elasticity; or chromogenic systems which change their color.

Responsive Environments & Artifacts Lab. Allen Sayegh. The *Responsive* Environments & Artifacts Lab takes an interdisciplinary look at the design of the physical environment with regard to technologically augmented experiences. ⊛

Socio-Environmental Responsive Design. STU 1304. Department of Architecture. Option Studio. Fall 2014. Instructors: Belinda Tato & José Luis Vallejo.

This studio considered the complexity of the human ecosystem and the interpenetration of natural and artificial elements that are embedded within it. People, nature, and the built environments we have constructed all influence one another in a complex system of reciprocal interaction. Human ingenuity in developing techniques to improve climatic comfort has allowed us to inhabit extreme climate zones, where artificial conditions impose over the natural ones. Adaptation strategies have evolved from the adoption of clothing and the construction of simple shelters, to the complex arrangements and technologies that facilitate physical survival and large-scale settlement in cities today. The studio focused on the atmospheric conditions of the contemporary city and how they affect the use of public space. Using the city of Manama as a case study, the students explored the potential of *responsive* design, where nature and artifice could establish a creative dialogue, to design new environments that can improve social life.

Students: Shahab Yousuf Al Bahar (MLA I AP), Hayrettin Gunc (MAUD), Yoonjee Koh (MArch II), Joyce Lee (MUP), Chen Ling (MAUD), Nan Liu (MAUD), Thien Nguyen (MAUD), Carolina Sendoda Yamate (MAUD), Adelene Yu Ling Tan (MArch I), Haotian Tang (MArch II), Tiantian Wei (MArch II), Haoxiang Yang (MArch II), Meng Zhu (MArch II). ⊛

Figure. Axonometric Details (right) & Perspective Collages (next page). Haotian Tang (MArch II) & Tiantian Wei (MArch II).

Vital Signs. Thesis. Drew Gregory Seyl (MArch I), advised by Andrew Witt.

"What would a Fun Palace for 2020 look like? Not an experimental theater, an urban adult playground, or a public exhibition hall/library, but probably something like a public-private health and wellness hub—a centerpiece for a modern, diffuse healthcare system in which personal data is collected everywhere and analyzed continuously (and available for a price). If the Internet of Things grows as predicted, its network of inexpensive, integrated, and ubiquitous sensors will transform our environments, with or without the input of architects.

Pioneers of cybernetic architecture in 1960s London were among the first to explore the possibilities of *responsive* environments. Their interests are just as relevant today: impermanence, programmatic flexibility,

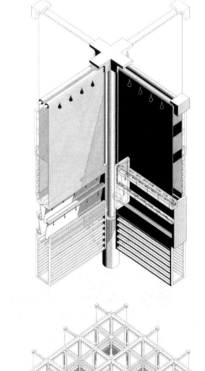

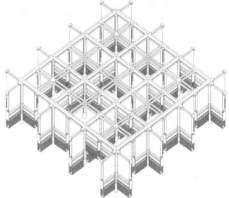

user determination, and *responsiveness*. Their ideas about what constituted user *responsiveness*, however, differ markedly from contemporary technologists' optimized, friction-free, behind-the-scenes vision. The (mostly) paper projects of architects like Cedric Price and Archigram often elaborated large public cultural centers for the masses. Today, we work in a different context. The idea of a new publicly funded cultural center seems quaint and the complete commodification of personal data by corporations (unanticipated by early cybernetic architects) looms large.

The J. Edgar Hoover Building in Washington, DC., the soon-to-be-vacated headquarters of the FBI, is another artifact of the 1960s. Widely reviled, the hulking Brutalist building embodies the associations of its tenant almost too perfectly. By transforming it into Washington's health hub, this project aims to open a dialogue with both the optimistic, public-minded, and user-oriented attitude of the 1960s and the realities of today." ⊛

See also ADAPTIVE REUSE—see also ANIMATION: Animating Material—see also COLOR—see also MATERIAL—see also ONTO-CARTOGRAPHY: Cyborg Coasts.

RETAIL

Retail store, stores by merchandising practice: Places of business where goods are sold directly to the ultimate consumers.

Prestige Retail: Design & Development Perspective on the High-End, Luxury Goods Market. Publication. International Council of Shopping Centers, 2014. Richard Peiser & Bing Wang (authors). HF5430 .P64 2014.

Prestige Retail: Design and Development Perspectives on the High-End Luxury Goods Market is a study of the interdependence of the design and development of *retail* real estate and the luxury *retail* market that reviews how luxury *retail* markets have grown and survived historically and continue to flourish today. Included are case studies of successful luxury *retail* buildings along with essays written by prominent luxury design and development scholars and professionals.

REVIEW

Design *review*, analytical function: The evaluation of proposals for development or for changes to existing structures or spaces, typically by a board representing the community where the activity is to take place. *Review*, document genre by function: Periodicals, reports, or essays giving critical estimates and appraisals of art, a performance, or event. For other critical descriptions and analyses, use "criticism."

Midterm & Final Reviews. Midterm and final *reviews* are formal pinups and presentations given before a panel of guest critics, which can include those from within the Harvard GSD as well as outside professionals and academics. The final *review* is the culmination of the students' studio work during the semester. It is a chance for students to present the context and rationale of their projects and to make a case for their merits. Final *reviews* are typically held as all-day events and are open to visitors. Final *review* schedules are posted on the Harvard GSD website several weeks before the end of the semester. ⑧

See also COMMUNICATION—see also CRITICISM—see also EX-HIBITION—see also PERFORMANCE—see also PINUP—see also PRACTICE—see also PROCESS—see also WRITING.

RGB

RGB, color systems, color & color-related phenomena: Color model used for televisions, computer monitors, and in other situations where light produces the color. It is an additive model in which *Red*, *Green*, and *Blue* are combined in various ways to produce other colors.

RHYTHM

Rhythm, artistic concept, formal concept: In art, a flow or sense of movement achieved by repetition of regular or patterned units.

See also COMPOSITION—see also CULTURE: Chamamé—see also EXPERIENCE: Choose Your Own Adventure—see also HARMONY—see also IMAGINATION: Architectural Imagination After May '68—see also OEUVRE—see also PATTERN—see also REPETITION.

RISER

1: One that *rises*. 2: The upright member between two stair treads. 3: A stage platform on which performers are placed for greater visibility. 4: A vertical pipe or a vertical portion of an electric wiring system. 5: One of the straps that connects a parachutist's harness with the shroud lines.

RISK

Risk assessment, analytical functions: Analyzing the potential loss, failure, injury, or other damage involved in or resulting from any activity or project. *Risk* management, analytical functions: Planning how to conduct affairs by assessing, minimizing, and preventing potential losses, injuries, or other damages. *Risk* map, maps by function: Maps used by insurance companies and emergency management agencies such as the Federal Emergency Management Agency (FEMA) in assessing *risk* to property. In conservation and heritage management contexts, maps used in vulnerability analysis, assessing *risk* to cultural heritage areas.

See also COMMUNICATION: Interactive Games for Risk Communication—see also CONFLICT—see also ENVIRONMENT—see also HOUSING—see also IMPACT—see also MAP—see also PROJECT—see also RESILIENCE.

RIVER

River, riverine bodies of water: Bodies of water flowing in direct course or a series of divergent or converging channels.

New River. Thesis. Michelle Arevalos Franco (MLA I), advised by Rosetta S. Elkin.
"A pilgrimage happens at night, at this country's southern border. It happens here, and now, because the physical imprints of power on this stretch of desert have left peculiar apertures. One of those is the New *River*, flowing northward from Mexico and carrying a multitude of wastes from the Imperial Valley's great prosperity. The *river's* toxicity momentarily protects northbound pilgrims, its currents a safe zone from apprehension. The informal movements of crossing this border exist in an invented landscape sculpted by economic pressures and political will and are rooted in the individual's passage from water to land. The ritual holds a potent connection to the landscape. By tapping into its overlooked leaks, this project seeks to subvert the infrastructure of territorial control and attend to pilgrims navigating the New *River's* passage northward." ⑧

Figure. Plan (above). Michelle Arevalos Franco (MLA I).

See also CULTURE: Chamamé—see also LAND—see also LIMINAL: Liminal Space—see also SETTLEMENT—see also TOPOGRAPHY—see also WATER.

ROBOTICS

Robotics, engineering, science: Refers to the science of *robot* design, construction, and use.

Informal Robotics/New Paradigms for Design & Construction. SCI 6478. Department of Architecture. Seminar. Fall 2014. Instructor: Chuck Hoberman.
Today new materials and fabrication techniques are transforming the field of *robotics*. Rather than rigid metal parts connected by mechanical components, *robots* can now be made of folded paper, carbon laminates, or soft gels. They can be formed fully integrated from a 2-D or 3-D printer rather than assembled from individual com-

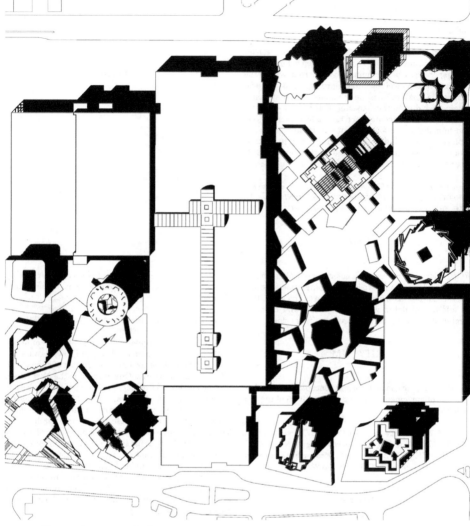

ponents. These techniques are leading to entirely new configurations where programmable behavior is closely coupled with material composition. Light, flexible, compliant, highly customized—we are seeing the emergence of a new design paradigm. The class was organized along four primary topics: kinematics, fabrication, controls, and applications. Students explored informal *robotics* from multiple perspectives, with an aim to design and fabricate original devices displaying animated intelligence in real-time. Going beyond traditional engineering approaches, the students sought new opportunities for design at the product, architectural, and urban scales. Informal *Robotics*/New Paradigms for Design & Construction was the first collaboration between the Wyss Institute's Bioinspired *Robotics* platform and the Harvard GSD. ֍

Robotic Arm. Gund Hall, Room L19. The Harvard GSD has two industrial six-axis *robotic* arms. One is an ABB IRB 140 industrial *robot*, a six-axis multipurpose *robot* that handles a payload of six kilograms with long reach. The other, larger *robot* is an ABB 4400-L30 with a load capacity of 60 kilograms. An extremely fast, compact

robot for medium to heavy handling, it is equipped with a waterjet and milling spindle. ֍

ROM

CD-*ROM*, compact discs, optical disks: Compact discs on which a large amount of digitized read-only data can be stored. *Read-Only Memory* (*ROM*), computer components: Computer memory that contains fixed information, such as a program, that does not change, and cannot be written to, only read from.

ROOF

Barrel *roof*, *roofs* by form, interior shape: *Roofs* that are semicircular in section or, sometimes, *roofs* that incorporate a semicircular ceiling. Mansard *roof*, curb *roofs*, pitched *roofs*: Curb *roof* with all four sides sloping, usually enclosing habitable spaces, and therefore having dormers. Pitched *roof*, *roofs* by form, exterior shape: Designates *roofs* with one or more surfaces that have a pitch greater than 10 degrees from the horizontal. *Roof*, enclosing structural elements: Outside, overhead enclosures of buildings or other structures, including the *roofing* and its structural framing.

Figure. Plan (opposite page). Ingrid Kestrel Bengtson (MArch I), Dong ah Cho (MArch II), Jaime Daroca Guerrero (MArch II), Julian Ryan Funk (MArch I), Gunho Kim (MArch II), Dayita Sanjay Kurvey (MArch II), Erin Jennifer Ota (MArch II & MDes, RR), Jim Peraino (MArch I), Harsha Sharma (MArch II), José Ramón Sierra Gómez de León (MArch II), Isaac James William Smith (MArch I), Han Wang (MAUD), and Dana Yao Yao Wu (MArch I).

See also BUILDING—see also ELEMENT: Architecture at the Human Scale—see also STRUCTURE.

ROOM

1: An extent of space occupied by or sufficient or available for something <*room* to run and play>. 2: (a) Obsolete, an appropriate or designated position, post, or station; (b) place, stead. 3: (a) A partitioned part of the inside of a building, especially such a part used as a lodging; (b) the people in a *room*. 4: A suitable or fit occasion or opportunity, chance <no *room* for doubt>.

Room, interior spaces: Refers to the interior portions of buildings or other structures fully separated and divided off from the other portions by a floor, ceiling, and walls or partitions.

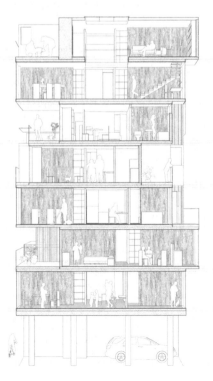

Figure. Sectional Perspective (left). Charlotte Morrow Lipschitz (MArch I).

See also BODY: The Room for Hiding the Body In—see also BUILDING—see also INITIATIVE: Harvard Initiative for Learning & Teaching.

RUIN

1: To reduce to *ruins*, devastate. 2: (a) To damage irreparably; (b) bankrupt, impoverish. 3: To subject to frustration, failure, or disaster. 4: (a) The state of being *ruined* <the city lay in *ruins*>; (b) the remains of something destroyed <the *ruins* of an ancient temple>. 5: A cause of destruction. 6: (a) The action of destroying, laying waste, or wrecking; (b) damage, injury. 7: A *ruined* building, person, or object.

Artificial *ruin*, follies, single built works by design: Constructions, usually in large gardens or grounds, meant to imitate *ruined* buildings for aesthetic effect. *Ruin*, single built works by condition: The remains of buildings or groups of buildings that have been destroyed or are in a state of great disrepair or decay.

See also AESTHETIC: The Ruin Aesthetic—see also BUILDING—see also CONSERVATION—see also FOLLY—see also HISTORY—see also PRESERVATION.

RULER

Ruler, measuring devices, linear distance: Straight-edged strips or cylinders of medium size, usually of wood, metal, or plastic and having demarcations to indicate units of measurement, used for measuring and for guiding a pen, pencil, or other marking-instrument in forming straight lines upon paper or another material. They are used in geometry, drafting, drawing, carpentry, building, interior design, crafts, and other disciplines. For very long bars or strips of wood or metal having straight and true edges and used for a variety of purposes, including cutting or establishing the evenness of surfaces, use "straightedges." *Ruler*, people in government & administration: Refers to people who *rule* or govern, specifically sovereigns.

See also BODY—see also DRAFTING—see also EDGE—see also FORUM—see also LINE—see also MEASURE—see also PARALLEL—see also POWER—see also TOOL—see also UNIT.

RURAL

Rural area, districts by location or context: Settlement areas characterized by country life or agriculture. *Rural* community, settlements by location, inhabited place: Communities, usually small in size, located outside urban areas in isolated or undeveloped areas. *Rural* development, community development: Basic development of *rural* regions emphasizing improvements in the standard of living and the active participation of the local population.

See also AGRICULTURE—see also COMMUNITY—see also DEVELOPMENT—see also LAND USE—see also MIGRATION—see also PLANNING—see also SETTLEMENT—see also URBAN.

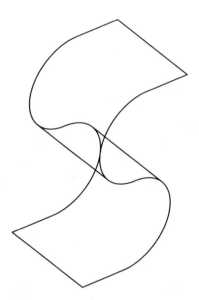

SCALE

Architects' *scale*, rules, rulers by function: Flat beveled or triangular bars, usually of wood or plastic, with a variety of graduations so that *scale* drawings can be drawn and measured. *Scale*, rules, rulers by function, measuring devices: Rules with proportioned graduations for measuring or making *scale* drawings. The term refers to a graduated strip of metal or wood used for measuring length as well as to a rule drawn or otherwise indicated on an architectural drawing, map, or other work. Balance, *scales*, weighing devices by form: *Scales* with a horizontal bar pivoting about a central fulcrum, creating equal-length arms; suspended from the ends of the arms are pans or baskets, in one of which is placed the item being weighed and in the other, a premeasured weight. Bar *scale*, *scales*, rulers by function: *Scale* that is shown by a line that is labeled to represent a stated distance. Engineers' *scale*, rules, rulers by function: Flat beveled or triangular straightedges, usually of wood or plastic, graduated in multiples of ten parts per inch allowing drawings to be drawn or measured to *scale* in decimal values. *Full-scale* drawing, *scale* drawings, images by method of representation, visual & verbal communication: Drawings at the same size as the object. Geological time *scale*, styles, periods & cultures: An internationally recognized time *scale* of Earth's history since the planet's formative period subdivided into eons, eras, periods, and epochs. *Grayscale*, color-related attributes: Describes the representation of monochrome continuous-tone digital images. *Grayscale* images differ from one-bit black and white images in that they are composed of levels of intensity in stages from black to white, not merely black or white. *Scale*, relative size, form & composition concepts, formal concepts, artistic concepts: An expression of the ratio between the size of the representation of something and that thing, such

as the size of the drawn structure in an architectural drawing and the actual built work. May also refer in general to the concept of relative size. *Scale* drawing, representations, visual & verbal communication: Refers to drawings or works in other media that are *scaled* representation of physical objects, meaning they represent the object and its parts in precisely the same proportion as the original, although it may be larger or smaller than the original. *Scale* model, representations, visual & verbal communication: Representations or copies of an object that are larger or smaller than the actual size of the object being represented, and manufactured precisely according to relative size. Typically, the *scale* model is smaller than the original and used for illustrating the object, for a toy or collectible, or as a guide to constructing it in full size. *Scale* models may be two- or three-dimensional. *Scale* models are generally built according to a standard *scale* for the particular product; for example, model ships may be 1:500 *scale*, and dollhouse furniture may be 1:12 *scale*.

Le Modulor. Publication. Éditions de l'architecture d'aujourd'hui, 1950. Le Corbusier (author). Le Corbusier Research Collection, Frances Loeb Library. LeC NA 2750 L496 1950.

"Le Corbusier developed two *scales* of measurement closely related to both the height of a human and the golden section (more accurately, using the Fibonacci Sequence), which he intended to be applied in projects such that all dimensions relate to a universal human proportion. The so-called red and blue *scales* were based first on a 108-centimeter unit, and then later doubled to a 216-centimeter unit. Further development adjusted these dimensions to 113 centimeters (height of the navel of a man with his arm raised) for the red series and 226 centimeters (height of the fingertip of his raised hand) for the blue series. These *scales* were intended to derive universal laws of harmonic proportion and to be

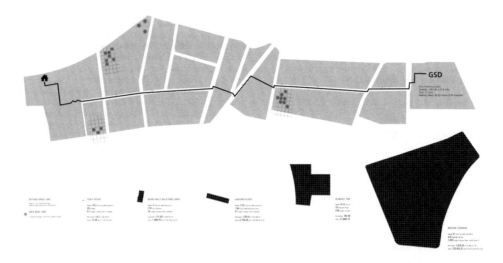

used in the standardization of building components."—
Inés Zalduendo ❀

Figure. Diagram (above). Yun Shi (MLA I).

See also BALANCE—see also BODY: Standard Deviations—see also CAMPUS: A Campus for the 21st Century—see also COLOR—see also COMMUNICATION—see also COMPOSITION—see also CONFLICT: Ad Absurdum—see also CULTURE—see also DATA: Data Across Scales—see also DETAIL—see also DRAFTING—see also ELEMENT: Architecture at Human Scale—see also FORM—see also GEOLOGY—see also HISTORY—see also ICON: Icons of Knowledge—see also INTENSITY: Urban Intensities—see also MATERIAL—see also MEASURE—see also MEGA—see also MODEL—see also MORPHOLOGY: Mexico City—see also NANO—see also OPPORTUNITY: Innovate—see also POST-SUBURB—see also PROJECT—see also PROTOTYPE—see also REPRESENTATION—see also SCALE—see also STYLE—see also TERRITORY: Territorialism—see also TIME—see also TOOL.

SCENOGRAPHY

Scenography, discipline, design, arts-related disciplines: The discipline of design for the stage, including design of all visual aspects of a stage production, such as scenery, properties, lighting, costume, and makeup.

See also ART—see also EXPERIENCE—see also LIGHTING—see also REPRESENTATION—see also SURFACE: Superficial Surfaces.

SCHOLARSHIP

Learning & *scholarship* concepts: Concepts related to education, learning, and teaching. For specific branches of inquiry, use "disciplines." *Scholarship*, student aid, subsidies: A need-based or merit-based financial award given to a student, usually from the funds of a school, college, or university, for the purpose of defraying the cost of education.

See also ACADEMIA—see also DISCIPLINE—see also EDUCATION—see also MODEL: Architecture & the Territory—see also PRIZE.

SCREEN

Screen process, additive color processes, photography: Photographic processes that produce an additive color image using a *screen* of minute red, green, and blue filters to record the relative intensity of each hue on a panchromatic, black-and-white emulsion which is processed to form a transparency. When viewed through a similar filter, each filter contributes its hue with its intensity modulated by the silver image. *Screen*, furniture: Refers to furniture in the form of an upright partition that can be used to embellish, partition, shelter, and provide privacy. *Screens* are often highly decorated. *Screen*, projections, image-projecting equipment: A white, vertical, flat surface on which images are projected, made of reflective material. Generally used for motion picture, video, or photographic slide projection. Touch *screen*, input devices, peripherals, computers: A computer interface that behaves as both an input and output device. The surface of the monitor *screen* is overlaid with sensors of various types that allow the user to trigger software tasks.

See also COMPUTER—see also FILM—see also FILTER—see also LIGHTING—see also MATERIAL—see also PHOTOGRAPHY—see also PRIVATE—see also PROCESS—see also PROJECTION—see also SOFTWARE—see also SURFACE—see also TECHNIQUE—see also TECHNOLOGY.

SEA LEVEL

Sea level, earth sciences concepts, physical science concepts: The *level* corresponding to the surface of the *sea* at mean *level* between high and low tides, used as a standard for the measurement of heights. *Sea-level* rise, environmental concepts: A rise in the surface of the sea due to increased water volume of the ocean or sinking of the land. There is concern that the rate in *sea-level* rise may increase markedly in the future owing to global warming.

See also CLIMATE—see also CLIMATE CHANGE—see also ENVIRONMENT—see also FLUX—see also SURFACE—see also WATER.

SEASONALITY

Seasonality, attributes & properties by specific type: The quality or condition of accompanying or varying with particular *seasons* of the year.

See also CLIMATE—see also TIME—see also WINTER.

SECTION

Cross *section*, orthographic projections, visual & verbal communication: Orthographic drawings that depict a building, object, or site as if cut transversely. Longitudinal *section*, orthographic projections, visual & verbal communication: *Sections* taken along the principal organizational axis of a structure or object. *Section*, orthographic projections, images: Orthographic drawings or works in another media depicting a building, object, or site as if cut through and exposed at one specific plane. *Sectional* elevation, orthographic projections, visual & verbal communication: Orthographic drawings that show a structure as partly an exterior elevation and partly an interior elevation. If only a small portion of exterior is taken away, use "broken-out *sections*." For smaller, symmetrical objects shown as half exterior and half interior, use "half *sections*." *Sectional* perspective, perspective views, images by method of projection, visual & verbal communication: Refers to drawings in which a structure or object is cut away in orthographic *section*, and a perspective is projected back from this plane. *Section*, general, components by general context: Parts or subdivisions separated or divided off from the remainder; portions into which a thing is cut or divided.

See also COMMUNICATION—see also DETAIL—see also DRAWING—see also DRAFTING—see also ELEVATION—see also MODEL—see also OBLIQUE—see also PERSPECTIVE—see also PLANE—see also REPRESENTATION.

SECURITY

Security, safety-related concepts: The state of being *secure* against violation such as theft or vandalism, and for the precautions taken to assure such a state.

See also FRINGE: Homeownership on the Fringes—see also SYSTEM.

SEDIMENTATION

1: The action or process of forming or depositing *sediment*, settling.

See also EROSION—see also HABOOB: Dust Kingdom—see also LANDFORM—see also TOPOGRAPHY—see also WATER.

SEED

Seed, material, plant material: Material comprising the *seed* of a plant, which is the nutrient material for development after germination that is enclosed in a protective coat. *Seeds* may be processed in various ways for use as materials, or they may be used whole as elements in a design. *Seed*, plant components, biological components: The characteristic reproductive bodies of both angiosperms (flowering plants) and gymnosperms (conifers, cycads, and ginkgos) and the ovary that encloses it. A *seed* consists of a miniature undeveloped plant (the embryo), which, alone or in the company of stored food for its early development after germination, is surrounded by a protective coat (the testa). *Seeds* are frequently small in size and suited to perform a wide variety of functions, such as multiplication, perennation (surviving seasons of stress such as winter), dormancy (a state of arrested development), and dispersal.

SEMINAR

Seminar, educational events, activities: Use generally for conferences or courses of instruction for specialists. Use in an academic context for meetings of small groups of advanced students studying a subject in depth under a professor, each student doing some original research, and all exchanging results.

See also ACADEMIA—see also EDUCATION—see also RESEARCH.

SENSE

Sense, biological concepts, scientific concepts: The five faculties by which stimuli from outside or inside the body are received and felt.

Remote Sensing in Mumbai: Disturbed Habitat in Urban Settlements. Thesis. Héctor Ignacio Tarrido-Picart (MLA I AP & MAUD), advised by Robert Gerard Pietrusko & Jill Desimini.
    "This thesis intends to study novel vegetation and coastal slums in Mumbai through the use of remote *sensing*. It uses the coastal slum of Malad as a case study in which vegetation and people interact in a disturbed habitat. The thesis introduces new methodologies for first-source data acquisition, which can be used to speculate, plan, design, and manage ecosystem and infrastructure services in settlements near tropical estuaries." ⁂

Sensory Media Platform. Krzysztof Wodiczko, Silvia Benedito, Chris Reed, Allen Sayegh, and Christopher Charles Hoxie. The Harvard GSD Sensory Media Platform offers a series of lectures and workshops for the first-year students from each department. These events provide complementary ways to examine the relation between the body, environment, and space by means of other arts and expressions including dance, film, performance, video, and photography. ⁂

See also BODY—see also COLOR—see also IMAGINATION—see also PERCEPTION—see also TOPOLOGY: On Sensing & Conceiving Landscape.

SENSIBILITY

1: Ability to receive sensations, sensitiveness <tactile *sensibility*>. 2: Peculiar susceptibility to a pleasurable or painful impression. 3: Awareness of and responsiveness toward something. 4: Refined or excessive sensitiveness in emotion and taste with especial responsiveness to the pathetic.

See also MODERN: Making the Modern Landscape—see also SENSE.

SEQUENCE

Sequence, object groupings by general context, object groupings & systems: Groups of objects, images, or data elements arranged in a specified order. For photographs taken in chronological order to record motion or change, use "chronophotographs" or "motion photographs."

See also CIRCULATION—see also DATA—see also EXPERIENCE: Choose Your Own Adventure—see also FILM—see also GASTRONOMY: The Architecture of Taste—see also PATTERN.

SERVICE

Public *service, service*, work-related events: The activity or condition of being employed or otherwise working as a primary endeavor in the government or other public function. *Service*, organizations, groups: Ministerial offices, branches of public employment, or bodies of public servants concerned with some particular kind of work or the supply of some particular need in a society. *Service*, work-related events: The activity, condition, or employment of a domestic servant, a public servant, or in the military.

Building Services. Gund Hall, Room L30. Building *Services* is the administrative office that organizes room scheduling, security, keys, parking, mail, safety, and lost and found at the Harvard GSD. ֎

Career Services. Gund Hall, Room 422. The Harvard GSD offers career programs designed to help students during their time at school and beyond. Career *Services* offers individual advising, experiential programs, career workshops, and special events throughout the year. ֎

Community Service Fellowships. The Harvard GSD supports four domestic Community *Service* Fellowships: the Doebele Community *Service* Fellowship, funding to work in a nonprofit setting with a current or former Loeb Fellow in the United States; the Greater Boston Community *Service* Fellowship, funding to work in a nonprofit setting with preference given to the Greater Boston area; the Harvard Club of New York Community *Service* Fellowship Program, funding to work in a nonprofit setting in New York; and the Joint Center for Housing Studies Community *Service* Fellowship. ֎

Service Desk. Gund Hall, Frances Loeb Library. The staff at the *Service* Desk help students make the most of the wealth of Harvard's library resources. Circulation *services* include support for course reserves, circulation of library materials, inter-library loan and Harvard-wide Scan & Deliver document delivery, help with library copiers and scanners, and more. The reference staff assist with research by offering an array of tours and training sessions as well as individual and small group consultations. ֎

Student Services. Gund Hall, Room 422. The Office of Student *Services* is responsible for admissions procedures, funding, course registration, student life, special programs, and career advising—interacting with students from the time they first become interested in studying at the Harvard GSD, through graduation, and beyond.

The Dean of Students, Laura Snowdon, is the primary resource for all Harvard GSD students with academic or personal concerns and is the school's coordinator for students with disabilities. She serves in an advisory role and provides support and information about counseling as well as other *services* for students. ֎

See also BUILDING—see also COMMUNITY—see also FELLOW-SHIP: Community Service Fellowship Program—see also INFORMATION—see also PUBLIC—see also WELL-BEING.

SETTLEMENT

Settlement house, health & welfare buildings: Buildings that house a variety of individual and family social, educational, and recreational facilities provided for recent immigrants or residents of underprivileged neighborhoods; especially in England and the United States since the late 19th century. *Settlement* of structure, structural analysis concepts, engineering concepts: Gradual subsidence of structures, caused by the compression of soil below foundation level. *Settlement* pattern, demographics, social & economic geography concepts: Spatial arrangements and distributions of populations and human *settlements* across the landscape.

See also AGRICULTURE—see also COASTAL—see also COMMUNITY—see also CONSTRUCTION—see also DWELLING—see also GEOGRAPHY—see also HEALTH—see also HOUSING—see also INFRASTRUCTURE: Lively Infrastructures—see also MIGRATION—see also PATTERN—see also STRUCTURE—see also WELL-BEING.

SHELTER

Shelter, single built works by function: General term for structures providing some degree of protection, refuge, or defense; if possible, use a more specific term.

Les constructions "murondins." Publication. Éditions. Etienne Chiron, 1942. Le Corbusier (author). Le Corbusier Research Collection, Frances Loeb Library. LeC NA 7199 L496.

"When Le Corbusier closed his office during the war, he devoted time to a project for refugee housing made with rammed earth. This book outlines the methods and techniques for occupants to build their own units with materials found at hand: earth, wood, and sand. According to Mary McLeod, Le Corbusier actively promoted the 'murondins' ('mur' and 'rondins' or 'wall' and 'logs') as projects for the Vichy government to mobilize French youth in the construction of these temporary *shelters*." —Inés Zalduendo. ֎

See also BUILDING—see also CONSTRUCTION—see also EVALUATION: Under One Roof—see also HOUSING—see also PATTERN: R. Buckminster Fuller, Pattern Thinking—see also REFUGE—see also STRUCTURE.

SHOP

Machine *shop,* accessory industrial buildings: Places where metal and other substances are cut and shaped by machine tools. *Shop* drawing, working drawings, visual & verbal communication: Working drawings that are usually produced by the manufacturer of a building element, and approved by the architect.

Machine Shop. Gund Hall, Room L33a. The Machine *Shop* is equipped with two metal working machines, a lathe, and CNC mill, primarily for the fabrication of the robotic manipulators, custom-end effectors, and workpiece holding. Custom tooling and fixtures are achievable with the application of these precise tools. The three-axis CNC mill is also available to students who have undergone advanced training with Fab Lab staff for the machining of precise parts in a range of materials including metals, hardwood, and machinable plastics. ₪

Metal Shop. Gund Hall, Room L31a. Equipment in the Metal *Shop* includes a horizontal band saw, compound shear/break/roller, abrasive saw, sandblaster, mig welder for mild steel, and a spot welder. ₪

Wood Shop. Gund Hall, Room L35. The Wood *Shop* is available to all students during the school year and is commonly used for scale models, research and prototyping work, and full-scale projects. The workshop provides most of the necessary tools and equipment for executing school-related projects using wood or other relatively soft and machinable materials such as plastics, foam, and all manner of sheet stock. Tools may be signed out for short-term use elsewhere. In general, students must purchase their own materials, however, small scraps are commonly available as is a limited amount of hardware. A variety of traditional woodworking hand and power tools are available, including a Saw Stop table saw, drill press, jointer/planer, band saws, pedestal sanders, miter saw, and panel saw. Portable tools may be borrowed on a daily basis for use in the Project Room. ₪

See also DRAWING—see also MALL—see also MATERIAL—see also PROJECT: Project Room—see also TOOL—see also WORKSHOP.

SHRUB

Shrub, woody plants, Plantae kingdom, living organisms: Low-growing, woody perennials characterized by several branches at the base and by a lack of conspicuous trunks; generally restricted to plants under six meters high.

SIMULATION

Simulation, computer-use functions, information handling functions: The representation of the behavior or characteristics of one system through the use of another system, especially a computer model; often used to forecast or predict the behavior of a dynamic system when real-world experimentation is not feasible.

Adventure & Fantasy Simulation, 1871–2036. HIS 4305. Department of Landscape Architecture. Seminar. Spring 2015. Instructor: John R. Stilgoe.

Visual constituents of high adventure since the late Victorian era, emphasizing wandering woods, rogues, tomboys, women adventurers, faerie antecedents, halflings, crypto-cartography, Third-Path turning, martial arts, and post-1937 fantasy writing as integrated into contemporary advertising, video, computer-generated *simulation,* and private and public policy. ₪

See also BUILDING: Building Simulation—see also ENERGY—see also EXPERIMENT—see also METHODOLOGY—see also PROTOTYPE—see also REPRESENTATION.

SITE

Construction *site,* locations, complexes by function: Places where construction is occurring, particularly construction of a building. For the more general meaning of a *site* where a building is or was located, whether or not the building is under construction, use "building sites." *Site* analysis, analysis & testing techniques, processes & technique: Includes the complete examination, investigation, and testing of surface and subsurface soil and conditions at a *site. Site* interpretation, analytical functions: An interpretation of a heritage *site* offered to the public through display and communication. *Site* location, exploring & investigating techniques: The process of discovering an archaeological *site* to be excavated by aerial photography, remote sensing, or by other means such as statistically predicting archaeological *sites* from environmental variables. *Site,* locations, complexes by function: Pieces of land or other physical positions on which something is located, particularly where human habitation or activities have taken place, especially in archaeological or other historical contexts.

See also AERIAL—see also AGORA: Reimagining La Merced Market—see also ANALYSIS—see also BROWNFIELD—see also COMMUNICATION—see also ELEMENT—see also ENVIRONMENT—see also GEOGRAPHY—see also HISTORY—see also LAND—see also LANDSCAPE—see also PHOTOGRAPHY—see also PLAN—see also REPRESENTATION—see also SENSE—see also TECHNIQUE—see also TERRITORY.

SITUATE

1: To place in a site, *situation,* context, or category, to locate.

Situate: Second Semester Architecture Core Studio. STU 1102. Department of Architecture. Core Studio. Spring 2015. Instructors: Jeffry Burchard, Luis Callejas, Grace La (coordinator), Victor Navarro Rios, Elizabeth Lee Whittaker, and Cameron Wu. Teaching Assistants: Iman Salam Fayyad (MArch I), Joshua Bremner Feldman (MArch I), Paul Daniel Fiegenschue (MArch I), Ali Ismail Karimi (MArch I), and Aaron C. Menninga (MArch I).

The pedagogical agenda for the second semester architecture core studio was to expand upon the design methodologies developed in the first semester such that students acquired an understanding of the interwoven relationship between form, space, structure, and materiality. This semester extended the subject matter to include the fundamental parameters of site and program, considered foundational to the discipline of architecture.

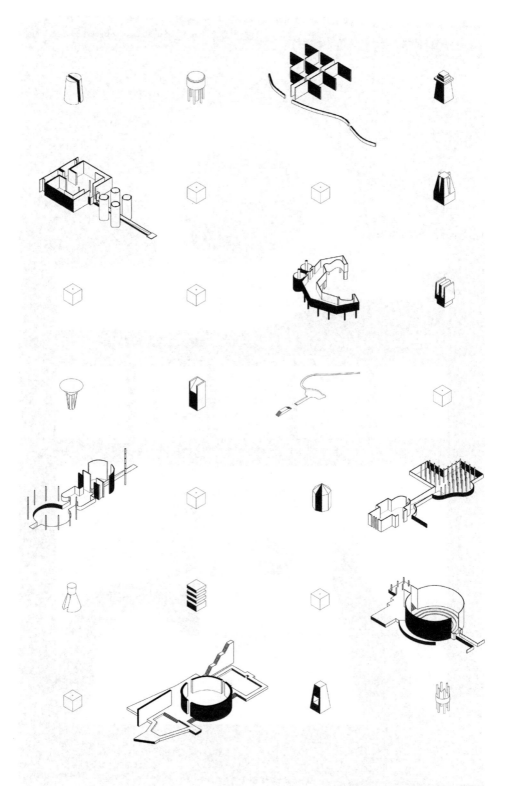

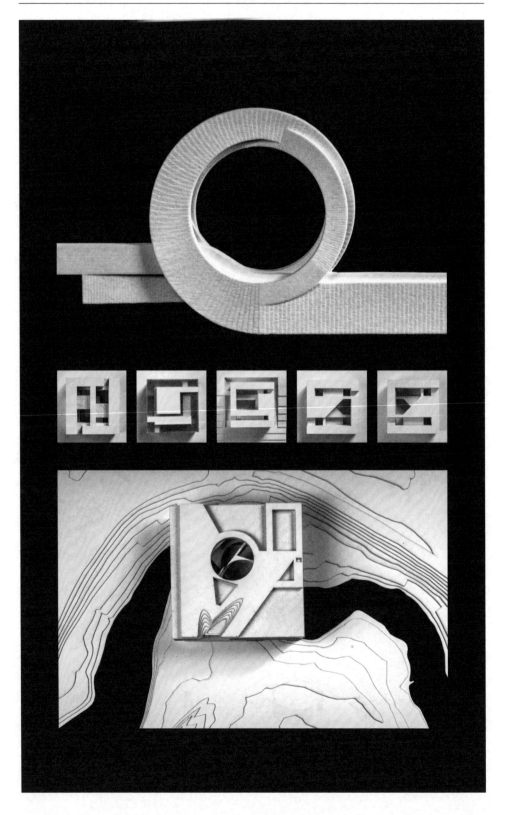

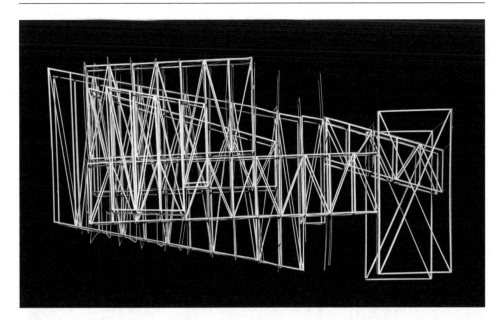

Through the design problems, students engaged in the multiple modes of analytical processes that inform and inspire the study of mass, proportion, and tactility.

While seemingly pragmatic in orientation, *Situate* proposes the potency of site—its physical, conceptual, contextual, environmental, historical, and morphological state—as a generative and inspirational condition. Equally, *Situate* proposes the critical engagement with program—its investment in purpose, social frameworks, relational capacities, and function—as a primary driver of form-making and organization. Both factors, site and program, require meditation and speculation on performative and projective agendas that provide rich opportunity to *situate* the project at numerous physical and metaphysical levels.

By this effort, we imply the architect's desire to *situate* the human body in space: to ground and transform the physical realities of the site; to position the project relative to historical and contextual understandings; to mine the cultural conditions of place and time; to locate programmatic potential; to orient and reorient spatial cognition. To *situate*, then, is as much to unearth the hidden, imagined topologies as it is to articulate what is seemingly obvious, tangible, or banal. In this way, the authorial tradition of design is thoroughly leveraged to embody and include the intellectual construction of site and program.

Students: Alice Marie Armstrong (MArch I), Rekha Auguste-Nelson (MArch I), Esther Mira Bang (MArch I), Sasha S. Bears (MArch I), Jeffrey David Burgess (MArch I), Nathan Jon Buttel (MArch I), Kathryn Hanna Jansen Casey (MArch I & MUP), Shiyang Chen (MArch I), Joanne K. Cheung (MArch I), Chieh Chih Chiang (MArch I), Valeria Fantozzi (MArch I), Ya Gao (MArch I), Douglas Robert Harsevoort (MArch I), Carlos Ignacio Hernandez-Tellez (MArch I), Yousef Awaad Hussein (MArch I), Tomotsugu Ishida (MArch I), Danielle Marissa Kasner (MArch I), Gerrod M. Kendall (MArch I), Min-Gyu Kim (MArch I), Shaina Sunjin Kim (MArch I), Haram Hyunjin Kim (MArch I), Wyatt Komarin (MArch I), Hyojin Kwon (MArch I), June Lee (MArch I), Madeline Jane Lenaburg (MArch I), Naomi K. Levine (MArch I), Ethan J. Levine

(MArch I), Keunyoung Lim (MArch I), Shao Lun Gary Lin (MArch I), Kirby Liu (MArch I), Naureen Mazumdar (MArch I), Grace McEniry (MArch I), Steven T. Meyer (MArch I), Farhad Mirza (MArch I), Chit Yan Paul Mok (MArch I), Bryant Huybao Nguyen (MArch I), Matthew Okazaki (MArch I), Meric Ozgen (MArch I), Andy Byung Kwan Park (MArch I), Yen S. Phoaw (MArch I), David Mark Pilz (MArch I), Philip Wing-Chung Poon (MArch I), Alexander Searle Porter (MArch I), Irene Cecilia Preciado Arango (MArch I), Lane Raffaldini Rubin (MArch I), Jennifer Lixian Shen (MArch I), Yiliu Chen Shen-Burke (MArch I), Tianze Tong (MArch I), Roger W. Tran (MArch I), Ho Cheung Tsui (MArch I), Isabelle Verwaay (MArch I), Madelyn A. Willey (MArch I), Hanguang Wu (MArch I), Huopu Zhang (MArch I), Eric C. Zuckerman (MArch I). ⊛

Figures. Axonometric Catalogue (previous page). Yousef Awaad Hussein (MArch I). Model (opposite page, above). Steven T. Meyer (MArch I). 5 Models (opposite page, middle). Chit Yan Paul Mok (MArch I). Model (opposite page, below). Esther Mira Bang (MArch I). Model (above). Chit Yan Paul Mok (MArch I).

SKYSCRAPER

Skyscraper, high-rise buildings, multistory buildings: Exceptionally tall buildings of skeletal frame construction.

Quand les cathédrales étaient blanches, voyage au pays des timides. Publication. Éditions Plon, 1937. Le Corbusier (author). Le Corbusier Research Collection, Frances Loeb Library. LeC NA 2500 L496.

"Mardges Bacon described the cover of this book as an assemblage of images that offers two conceptual models: the walled European medieval city overlaid on the rational gridiron plan of New York, representing the new world—with Le Corbusier asserting himself as the one who would unite the two. Advocating for high-density living in cities (as opposed to suburbanization), New York *skyscrapers* seemed much too small for Le Corbusier. This emerging new world was too timid

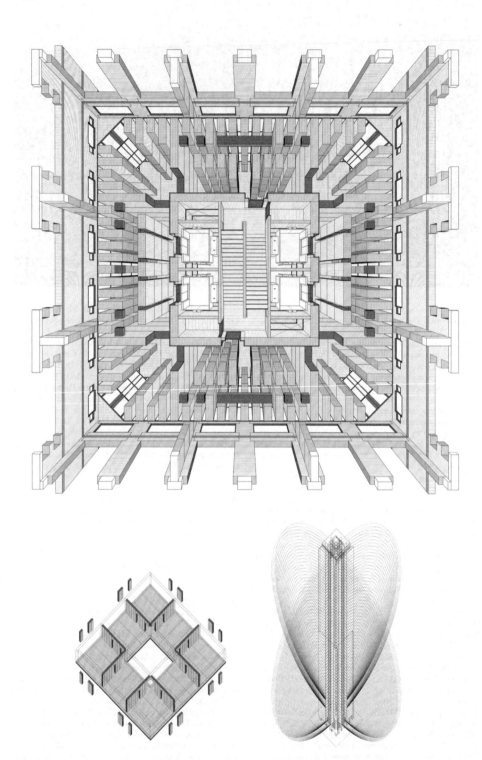

in his eyes. The *skyscraper*—an American invention—large-span bridges, and highways together lacked the collective conscience to embody the cultural change that this new world demanded. Le Corbusier saw himself as the messenger of a direction toward morality and social values, and his program of lectures at American architecture schools focused on the need for spiritual reawakening." —Inés Zalduendo. ※

Wood Skyscraper. Thesis. Nelson Byun (MArch II), advised by Hanif Kara.

"This thesis investigates wood as a material for a *skyscraper*. Wood's natural ability to sequester carbon and recent advancements in engineered-wood products are repositioning wood as a sustainable and structural alternative to steel and concrete, and as the primary material for building *skyscrapers*. The following can be achieved: (1) a sustainable housing prototype to accommodate the global urban population, set to increase by 2.5 billion people in 2050; (2) the tallest wood building in the world, by analyzing the structural limits of the material in collaboration with engineers; and (3) a design aesthetic appropriate for wood. When *skyscrapers* transitioned from masonry to steel construction, there was a transformation of building aesthetic from heavy to transparent. Such qualities are expressions of a material's particular strengths. Therefore, since wood has different properties than masonry and steel, it will yield a unique aesthetic." ※

Figure. Perspective Plan & Diagrams (opposite page). Nelson Byun (MArch II).

See also AIR—see also BUILDING—see also CONSTRUCTION—see also HOUSING—see also MATERIAL—see also SUSTAINABILITY—see also TYPOLOGY—see also ZONING.

SLOPE

Slope, geometric concepts, mathematics concepts: Inclined surfaces, *slopes*, or declivities; a *slope* is the numerical measure of a line's inclination relative to the horizontal. In analytic geometry, the *slope* of any line, ray, or line segment is the ratio of the vertical to the horizontal distance between any two points on it. Given a straight line in a plane, the constant value $m=(y_2 - y_1)/(x_2 - x_1)$, where (x_1, y_1) and (x_2, y_2) are any two points on the line. *Slope* stability, attributes & properties by specific type: In soil mechanics, the study of static and dynamic stability of soil in natural *slopes* and other forms of embankment. *Slope*, landforms, terrestrial: Deviations from the horizontal or perpendicular, particularly stretches of rising or falling ground, including any portion of the Earth's surface marked by a gradual ascent or descent, whether natural or artificial.

See also CONTOUR—see also LANDFORM—see also RAMP—see also STAIR—see also SURFACE—see also TERRAIN: Mountain Valley Urbanism—see also TOPOGRAPHY.

SLUM

Slum, neighborhoods, residential districts: Densely populated usually urban areas characterized by crowding, run-down housing, poverty, and social disorganization.

Slums in Architectural & Planning History. HIS 4477. Department of Urban Planning & Design. Seminar. Fall 2014. Instructor: Alejandro de Castro Mazarro.

When and why did informality become an urban and architectural issue? Contemporary projects developed within precarious settlements and overcrowded areas are often interpreted as epitomes of the modernist project's aim to house the masses. This seminar questioned the characterization of definitions such as informality, housing deficit, substandard living, or *slums*, and built a thread of historical precedents that link urban informality with mainstream urban planning and design history. By relating planning and design to a broader political and economic context, the seminar sought to define the role of spatial strategies in proposing accurate solutions to urban poverty and inequality.

See also DENSITY—see also DWELLING—see also FRINGE: Homeownership on the Fringes—see also HOUSING—see also SENSE: Remote Sensing in Mumbai—see also URBAN.

SOCIAL

1: (a) Marked by or passed in pleasant companionship with friends or associates <an active *social* life>; (b) *sociable*; (c) of, relating to, or designed for *sociability* <a *social* club>. 2: Of or relating to human society, the interaction of the individual and the group <*social* institutions>. 3: (a) Tending to form cooperative and interdependent relationships with others; (b) of a plant, tending to grow in groups or masses so as to form a pure stand. 4: (a) Of, relating to, or based on rank or status in a particular society; (b) of, relating to, or characteristic of the upper classes; (c) formal. 5: Being such in *social* situations <a *social* drinker>.

Social issue, sociological concepts: Important subjects of debate or litigation having to do with an organized and interdependent community. *Social* service, organizations: Organized assistance provided by public or private agencies and organizations to individual community members. For essential ongoing services provided by the government relating directly to the protection and maintenance of the lives and property of community members as a whole, use "public services."

See also AGENCY: Social Agency Lab—see also CLUB—see also COMMUNITY—see also CONFLICT—see also CONTEXT: King's Cross—see also DEMOCRACY—see also ENVIRONMENT—see also ETHICS—see also GEOGRAPHY: Geographies of Social Conflict and Cohesion—see also INFRASTRUCTURE: Lively Infrastructures—see also MEDIA—see also PARTY—see also SERVICE—see also WELL-BEING—see also WORK.

SOFTSCAPE

1: Vegetation that is incorporated into a landscape—compare to hardscape.

SOFTWARE

Software, electronic documents, documents genres by form: Computer system programs, procedures, and associated documentation concerned with the operation of data processing systems, and which require hardware for use to be made of them. For individual collections or sequences of code provided by a user to perform a particular task, use "programs." For programs that serve a particular purpose and that may be packaged and sold by a manufacturer use "applications." Open-source *software*, electronic documents, visual & verbal communication: Programming whose source code is open to all rather than proprietary.

Design Software. The Harvard GSD provides students with an extensive collection of network-licensed design *software*. When *software* is launched, it checks out a license from a license pool hosted on an internal server. It can be used with the Harvard GSD network or remotely with a VPN. Students use a range of design *software* including: Adobe Creative Cloud, ArcGIS, Arduino, AutoCAD, Catia, Cinema4D, Ecotect, Grasshopper, MODO, Onyx, Processing, RealFlow, Rhino, V-Ray, and 3ds Max. ✸

From Drones to Data Portals and Maps: A Brief History of GIS at Harvard Library. Exhibition. Gund Hall, Frances Loeb Library. Harvard Center for Geographic Analysis. Janina Mueller & Michalis Pirokkas.

Over the past two decades, Geographic Information System (GIS) has become an integral part of many academic disciplines. This exhibition showcased the many different ways the Harvard Library provides GIS services to students and scholars. Until the early 1990s, GIS at the Harvard Library was limited to a small collection of geospatial data sets on CDs. As a result of training initiatives, more formal GIS support services were introduced at the Harvard Map Collection in the mid-1990s. Soon thereafter, librarians began to make geospatial data sets more accessible through web-based discovery tools, which eventually led to the creation of today's online data portal, the Harvard Geospatial Library (HGL). In 2013, the Frances Loeb Library at the Harvard GSD hired a Design Data Librarian and began offering GIS support services. In addition to regular GIS workshops and office hours, the library purchases data sets and collaborates in the creation of geospatial data. The Harvard GSD's first Unmanned Aerial Vehicle (UAV) was purchased by the Frances Loeb Library in 2014. It has been used to create remotely-sensed data that are highly accurate and current. The data products created using the UAV include customized color-referenced 3-D landscapes, tree canopy height maps, and aerial photos.

This exhibition illustrated the innovative research, teaching, and learning support that libraries provide in an ever-changing information environment. Through collaborations and partnerships, librarians create and make accessible new digital collections. ✸

See also COMMUNICATION—see also COMPUTER—see also DATA—see also DIGITAL—see also GLITCH—see also LAB: The Fisher Lab & Its Legacy—see also REPRESENTATION.

SOIL

Earth, *soil* by form or function: Refers to *soil* in the context of building materials. *Soil*, combination inorganic & organic material, materials by composition: Unconsolidated material on the Earth's surface formed

by the weathering of rock and that portion of the Earth's surface that can support plant life.

See also AGRICULTURE—see also GROUND—see also LAND—see also LANDFORM: Landformation Catalogue—see also MAPPING—see also MATERIAL—see also PLANT—see also PROFILE—see also SURFACE—see also TERRAFORM—see also TERRAIN.

SOLAR

1: Of, derived from, relating to, or caused by the sun. 2: Measured by the Earth's course in relation to the sun <a *solar* year>, also relating to or reckoned by *solar* time. 3: (a) Produced or operated by the action of the sun's light or heat <*solar* energy>; (b) utilizing the sun's rays especially to produce heat or electricity <a *solar* house>, also of or relating to such utilization <*solar* design>.

Solar, interior spaces, spaces by location: Certain upper floor rooms in medieval houses that are smaller than halls and reserved for private family use. Sunlight, daylight, light, energy: Use with reference to the direct light of the sun; for the light of day in general, use "daylight."

See also BUILDING—see also CLIMATE—see also ENERGY—see also LIGHTING—see also ORIENTATION—see also POWER—see also ROOM—see also SPACE—see also SUSTAINABILITY.

SOUND

Sound, acoustics, acoustic concepts, physics concepts: Mechanical disturbance from a state of equilibrium that propagates energy through air, water, or another elastic medium. It is responsible for the sensation of hearing, although it also includes energy waves that cannot be heard by the human ear but can be detected by sonar equipment and other devices. *Sound*, bodies of water, natural landscapes: A long arm of the sea or relatively narrow channel between the mainland and an island or islands or connecting two larger bodies of water.

GSDj. Student Group. GSDj aims to create a collective for the musically-inclined with a focus on contemporary trends in electronic music. The group also aims to explore the relationship between music production software and hardware and architecture. In tandem with producing auditory environments, GSDj experiments with real time visualization and its relationship to space-making and entertainment. The group sends out a mix every month on *SoundCloud*—listen online at /gsddj. ✸

See also ACOUSTICS—see also AUDIOVISUAL: Six Microphones—see also COMMUNICATION—see also EXHIBITION—see also INSTALLATION—see also SYSTEM—see also TOOL—see also WATER.

SOVEREIGNTY

Sovereignty, political concepts, social science concepts: Supreme and independent authority of a political unit to make and apply laws within its own boundaries and to conduct international relations.

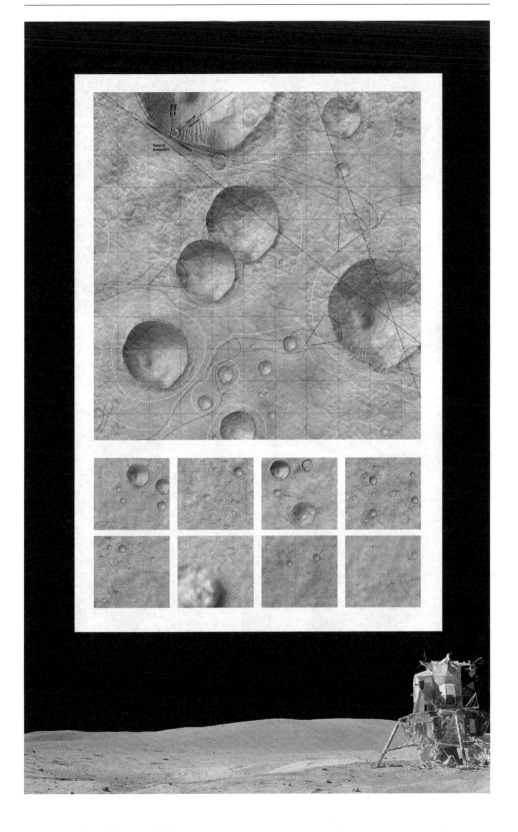

See also CITY: Identity, Sovereignty, and Global Politics in the Building of Baghdad—see also POLITICS.

SPACE

Open *space* & site elements, built environment: *Spaces* in urban environments designed as passages for pedestrians, and as social *spaces*, not as clearly delimited as parks, but sharing some of the same characteristics. Often these function as utilitarian connecting *spaces* between buildings, or simply as an open area designated by a municipal authority, but without the amenities or formality of a park. Public *space*: Open *spaces* designed for public use or accessible to the public, often designed to foster a sense of community. *Space*, form & composition concepts: In art and architecture, a compositional element comprising the two- and three-dimensional areas around, above, below, beside, between, and within objects, whether the area is actual or simulated. Included is *space* occupied by architecture, a work of art, other object, or things depicted in a work. *Space*, natural or built world: Physical extent or area, in two or three dimensions, in the natural world or built environment. Typically used in the context of *space* being applied to or sufficient for a purpose or action. *Space* station, extraterrestrial structure, single built works by location: Manned artificial satellites designed to revolve in a fixed orbit and to serve as a base for specific functions (e.g., scientific observations or the refueling of spaceships). For manned installations established on natural extraterrestrial bodies for specific functions, use "extraterrestrial bases." For larger communities established in *space* or on natural extraterrestrial bodies, use "*space* colonies."

Designing Garments for Space Travel: Space Suits for the 21st Century. Lecture. Gund Hall, Room 111. April 23, 2015. *Space* GSD. Ted Southern.

Ted Southern, president of Final Frontier Design, a private design firm crafting aerospace safety garments for the future of *space* travel, discussed his transition from the field of costume design and art into designing *space* garments, the creation of Final Frontier Design and the work they have produced, and general trends in *space*-suit design. ֍

Interlaced Spaces: A Live Portal between the Harvard GSD & the American University of Iraq-Sulaimani. Event. Gund Hall, Chauhaus. April 20–24, 2015. Alexander Matthias Jacobson (MArch I) & Tamara Jafar (MUP).

On April 20, 2015, two students at the Harvard GSD opened a portal between Iraq and the United States. The interactive digital installation intermittently interlaced the cafeteria at the American University of Iraq, Sulaimani, with the Chauhaus at the Harvard GSD over four days. The project was the serendipitous culmination of several years of work, and the first iteration of an ongoing experiment empowering civilians to directly connect despite of preconceived spatial, national, or cultural barriers. ֍

New World of Space. Publication. Reynal & Hitchcock, 1948. Le Corbusier (author). Le Corbusier Research Collection, Frances Loeb Library. LeC NA 45 L496.

"In *New World of Space*, Le Corbusier defines *space* in terms of occupation and associates position in *space* with the awareness of being. For him, architectural *space* tran-

scends physical dimensions and is capable of producing an aesthetic emotion. For example, he writes that the Parthenon has a spiritual energy of its own. Le Corbusier coins the phrase 'ineffable *space*' (espace indicible) for the aesthetic emotion produced by architecture and its surroundings. Air becomes a material capable of transmitting this newly discovered quality of *space*." —Inés Zalduendo. ֍

Space GSD. Student Group. *Space* architecture challenges the way we design, build, and think. Harvard University was a pioneer in outer *space* habitat research in the 1970s. Today, the challenge of living and traveling in outer *space* is becoming increasingly concrete. *Space* GSD encourages designers to think critically and build a network of people from diverse fields who enrich each other's ideas through discussions and meetings—toward the conquest of *space*. ֍

Spaces of Living for the Subsystem Human Being: Design of a Space Station. Thesis. Patricia Semmler (MArch I), advised by Iñaki Ábalos.

"In 1961, the first human was launched into orbit by the Soviet Union. Since then, humans have been living in outer *space*. Different structures have been developed, launched, and inhabited, each one redefining the needs and position of human beings within their environment—that is, their *spaces* of living. Currently, a *space* station, such as the International *Space* Station, is an agglomeration of purely utilitarian *spaces* within which humans are regarded as one of the subsystems that the structure must accommodate: the subsystem Human Being. Although a number of scientific studies have recognized aesthetics as necessary for the performance and psychological well-being of the crew, it has been left out from most designs due to the fact that the definition of beauty or pleasantness within architecture has been considered cultural and historical. An unquestioned part of our architectural language relies on signs and symbols established throughout our culture and history; architectural *spaces*, the *spaces* our bodies inhabit, are materializations of certain cultures at certain points of history. What does architecture become when it is regarded as a technological interface between humans and their environment, instead of being designed as an embodiment of culture and history? Premised upon the idea that technological objects are the outcome of a society's cultural development, this thesis questions the current signs and symbols of architecture by placing it in the most fundamentally different environment from earth architecture: in a zero-gravity environment, the ideal site to study the meaning-making potential of architectural *spaces*." ֍

Figure. Models (opposite page). Patricia Semmler (MArch I).

Terrestrial Analogues: Design Fiction & Imagined Geographies. Thesis. Ken Chongsuwat (MLA I), advised by Silvia Benedito.

"This thesis proposes the design of landscapes, environments, and atmospheres of a celestial body, such as the Moon, within the confines of Earth. The site is used in the frames of *space* exploration (training and simulation), research (education), and tourism to study the geological and biological processes observed on other planets, thus enhancing our understanding of our own planet." ֍

Figure. Plans (page 345). Ken Chongsuwat (MLA I).

See also AIRPORT: The New London Airport—see also APERTURE: The Aperture Analyzed—see also AUDIOVISUAL: Six Microphones—see also *BOX: Outside the Box—see also COMPOSITION—see also CON-TEMPORARY—see also EXPERIENCE—see also EXTRASTATE-CRAFT—see also FIGURE-GROUND—see also FORM—see also GEOGRAPHY—see also HYPEROBJECT: The Proximities of Nuclear Waste—see also IMAGINATION: Architectural Imagination After May '68—see also INITIATIVE: Harvard Initiative for Learning & Teaching—see also LIBRARY: Cold Storage—see also LIMINAL: Liminal Space—see also MAPPING: Mapping Cultural Space—see also MEASURE—see also MEDIA—see also NEGATIVE—see also PERCEPTION—see also PLANNING: Perceptions of Physical Space and the Planning Process in Camp Azraq, Jordan—see also PRODUCTION: Tactics for a Coproduced City—see also PROSTHETIC: Architecture of Cultural Prosthetics—see also SENSE—see also SPECULATION: Rare New Species—see also SUPERFICIAL: Superficial Spaces—see also WALKING.*

SPATIAL

Spatial analysis, analysis & testing techniques: Statistical technique in which the *spatial* locations, distributions, and relations of designated factors are analyzed.

See also ALTERNATIVE: Alternative Spatial Practices in Istanbul—see also ANALYSIS—see also COMPOSITION—see also PLANNING.

SPECTACLE

Spectacle, performances, entertainment events: Performances and displays on a large scale that are specially prepared or arranged for viewing, usually by the public, with the intent of forming an impressive or interesting show or entertainment. *Spectacles*, eyeglasses: Eyeglasses kept in place by sidepieces passing over the ears.

Functional Spectacle: Reimagining Trade Fair Architecture in Emerging Chinese Cities. Thesis. Weishun Xu (MArch I AP), advised by Grace La.

"Trade fairs often present a materialized imagination of a city. But from world's fairs to local emerging markets, quite often this kind of showing is criticized for demonstrating a superficial *spectacle*, in which image represents reality in such an idealized manner that the *spectacle* is completely isolated from its subject. This phenomenon is especially conspicuous in rapidly urbanizing small Chinese cities, where large-scale local events are expected to greatly swing the emplacement of their identities, while both their social and physical environments manifest the isolation of the *spectacles*, rendering efforts futile.

This thesis takes on the architectural struggle of trade fair halls in emerging Chinese cities as a problematic typology of suburban megasheds. By systematically breaking down its programs to match existing urban fabrics, the design attempts to reestablish the physical and social emplacement of trade fairs within the city. The site of a trade fair should be a place of negotiation between citizens, goods, and spaces rather than a homogeneous playground for exhibit stands and banners. The resulting event is an active *spectacle* that both manifests the city's identity transition and serves its actual community—locals and visitors alike."

Figure. Models (opposite page). Weishun Xu (MArch I AP).

SPECULATION

1: An act or instance of *speculating*, such as (a) an assumption of unusual business risk in hopes of obtaining commensurate gain; (b) a transaction involving such *speculation*.

Speculation, business, commercial function: Engaging in business transactions in the anticipation of profit from changes in the economic situation.

Practices in the Turbulent City: Land Speculation in Mumbai. Thesis. Vineet Divgi Diwadkar (MUP & MLA I AP), advised by Rahul Mehrotra & Robert Gerard Pietrusko.

"This project uses *speculation* as a category to analyze land conversion and occupation practices in post-1991 Mumbai and represents these landscape economies as alternatives for working with risk and the unknown in the city. Human activity has transformed Mumbai through successive land reclamations from sea, wetlands, and refuse into a landscape of intensifying trading, industrial activity, and real estate investment. Twentieth-century Mumbai was locked by the sea and also by restrictive urban policies, intense demand for space, and strained municipal-planning capacity. Policies stemming from economic liberalization in 1991 have reconfigured and recategorized relationships between people, land, space, and economies, and have increased volatility. A flood of domestic and foreign investment has taken advantage of loopholes in the dominant planning mechanism, spurring new markets for the architectural currencies of people, transferable development rights, and spatial allotments. The abstraction and commodification of people and space disassociates occupants from the ways they relate with land and turns their attention to the volatility of the land-conversion process.

Over the past 25 years, land occupiers, land converters, and professional intermediaries have developed *speculative* practices to harness uncertainty toward new possibilities from inside and outside state-legitimized categories. Dharavi, M-Ward, and Dahisar are wet frontiers where slums persist as a pattern for coastal urbanization in Mumbai's history, generating wet-specific models through which land occupiers drain and fill terrain to support habitation and labor. Over the long term, land converters seek to capture this drier land and to reclassify and redevelop it for higher exchange-value outcomes. This thesis analyzes four ecology-based workflow settlements in their relation with wet terrain, spatial interactions, economies, and valuations of this landscape, as well as the ways the practices of landscape *speculating* maximize their possibilities."

Rare New Species. Lecture. Gund Hall, Piper Auditorium. October 16, 2014. Cristina Díaz Moreno & Efrén García Grinda.

Cristina Díaz Moreno and Efrén García Grinda presented 15 years of speculations, projects, and built proposals by their Madrid and London-based practice and collaborators.

The lecture was organized according to concepts from the speakers' own vocabulary in an attempt to convey the range of their projects and the main fields of operation: the space of mediation between people, objects, natural species, and built environments.

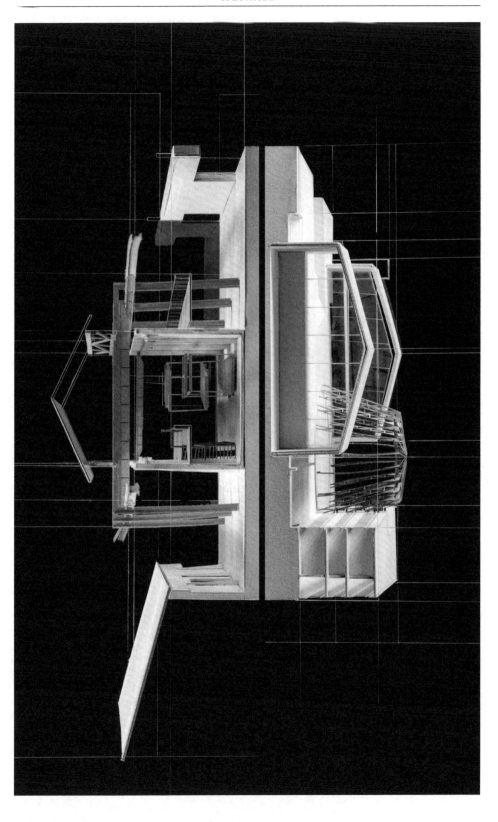

SPECTRUM

Spectrum, physical sciences concepts, scientific concepts: Generally an array of the components of an emission or wave separated and arranged in the order of some varying characteristic, as wavelength, mass, or energy. Specifically, the colored band into which a beam of light is decomposed by means of a prism or diffraction grating.

SPHERE

Sphere, geometric figures, solids: A geometrical figure comprising the set of all points in three-dimensional space lying the same distance (the radius) from a given point (the center), or the result of rotating a circle about one of its diameters.

See also FOLLY: Torqueing Spheres—see also FORM—see also GEOMETRY—see also SPACE—see also 3-D.

SPRAWL

Urban *sprawl*, social issues, sociological concepts: The spreading of urban developments (such as houses and shopping centers) on undeveloped land near a city.

Figure. Plan of Boston (above). Vanessa Park Moon (MUP).

See also CITY—see also FRAGMENT: Ilium—see also HOUSING: Craft, Politics, and the Production of Housing in Oaxaca, Mexico— see also UNBUILT: Achtung: die Landschaft—see also URBAN.

SQUARE

Carpenters' *square*, tools, shaping & guiding tools: Flat, metal, L-shaped tools that constitute an accurate right angle and are engraved with divisions and markings useful to a carpenter in laying out and erecting framing.

Square, open spaces by form: Open public spaces in cities or towns, usually rectilinear, surrounded by buildings, and located at the junction of two or more thoroughfares. *Square*, shape: Having the form or outline of a *square*, a four-sided plane figure with four equal sides and four right angles. *Square*, open spaces by form: Open public spaces in cities or towns, usually rectilinear, surrounded by buildings, and located at the junction of two or more thoroughfares.

Central Square. Central *Square* lies one T stop inbound from Harvard *Square* and anchors a cluster of music venues, bars, eateries and clubs.

Davis Square. Davis *Square* is equal parts Cambridge and Somerville. Students living in Davis *Square* commute to the Harvard GSD by cycling and taking the T. A mix of trendy new restaurants and working-class diners surround the historic Somerville Theatre.

Harvard Square. Harvard *Square* is very close to the Harvard GSD. Restaurants, bars, chain stores, and local boutiques fill the *square's* commercial spaces. Students make up the majority of the surrounding neighborhood's inhabitants, while tourists and street performers usually populate the *square* itself.

Inman Square. Inman *Square* is home to a number of bars and restaurants that are worth the short walk from Gund Hall. Inman *Square's* diverse resident population of locals, families, and students lends it a neighborhood feel.

Kendall Square. Kendall *Square* is adjacent to MIT. The City of Cambridge has invested heavily in making it a destination.

Porter Square. Porter *Square* is a great option for Harvard GSD students looking for an affordable place to live. It is a five to ten-minute bike ride from Gund Hall and one T stop outbound from Harvard *Square*.

Union Square. Union *Square* is up Kirkland Street from Gund Hall. It is not accessible by the T, but buses and bicycles make the commute quick and convenient.

See also ASSEMBLY—see also BLOCK—see also CITY—see also CONSTRUCTION—see also FORM—see also GEOMETRY—see also LANDMARK: Montreal is Back—see also PLAN—see also PUBLIC— see also T—see also T-SQUARE—see also TOOL—see also 2-D.

STAFF

Staff, personnel, people by occupation: The people employed by or active in a business, organization, or service, it is a collective term and never refers to an individual. *Staff*, walking sticks: Long sticks carried in the hand for support in walking.

Harvard GSD Staff. Each school at Harvard University has a full contingent of staff providing many of the services that in other universities are delivered more centrally. The staff at the Harvard GSD are organized into two divisions, headed by the Executive Dean and the Associate Dean for External Relations.

Functions reporting to the Executive Dean include: Academic Services, Student Services, Faculty Planning, Human Resources, Communications, the Frances Loeb

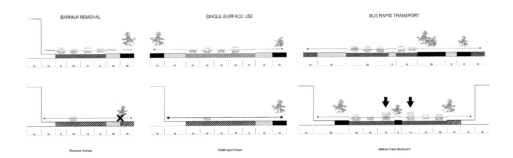

Figure. Sections (above). Andres E. Mendoza Gutfreund (MUP).

Library, Computer Resources, Fiscal Services, Building Services, the Joint Center for Housing Studies, and Executive Education. External Relations includes Development and Alumni Relations.

STAIR

Flight, *stair* components: Continuous series of steps with no intermediate landings. Landing, *stair* components: The platforms between flights of *stairs*, or at the termination of a flight of *stairs*. Stair, *stair* components: Ascending series or flights of steps, sometimes connected by landings, leading from one level to another; typically used for passing from one floor to another in a house or other building. *Stairwell*, circulation spaces, rooms & spaces by function: Spaces, extending through one or more floors, that contain staircases.

See also CIRCULATION—see also ELEMENT: Architecture at the Human Scale—see also LANDFORM—see also MOVEMENT—see also SLOPE—see also THRESHOLD—see also TOPOGRAPHY.

STORE

Store, mercantile buildings, commercial buildings: Buildings offering merchandise for sale, usually on a retail basis.

Shop Store. Gund Hall, Room L43. The Shop *Store* provides students convenient access to materials and tools for use in the Fab Lab. Chipboard, acrylic sheets, polystyrene foam, expanding urethane glue, bondene, and wood glue are available for purchase. The Shop *Store* is open for one hour each day and accepts Crimson Cash only. A list of available inventory and current prices is available online.

STORYTELLING

Storytelling, performing arts, disciplines: Telling or writing *stories*, especially recounting *stories* aloud to others, either from memory, ex tempore, or reading from notes or a book.

See also COMMUNICATION—see also EXPERIENCE: Choose Your Own Adventure—see also MIGRATION—see also PUBLICA-TION—see also WRITING.

STREET

Pedestrian *street*, *streets* by function: Urban *streets* lined with storefronts and closed off to most automobile traffic. *Street*, roads by form: A road in a city, town, or village, characterized by usually being paved and comparatively wide (as opposed to a lane or alley), and generally running between two rows of houses or other buildings.

Figure. Sections (above). Andres E. Mendoza Gutfreund (MUP).

See also AUTONOMOUSMOBILE—see also CIRCULATION—see also CITY—see also CURB: The Re-Rise of the Curb—see also TRANSPORTATION—see also URBAN.

STRUCTURE

Structure, attributes & properties by specific type: The elements or parts of an entity and their interrelations, often with reference to the manner in which they are organized or constructed. *Structure*, single built works by general type: Refers to constructions of any kind artificially fabricated of parts joined together in some definite manner, and which may or may not provide enclosure or shelter. Includes not just buildings, but other *structures*, for example oil wells, bridges, docks, and railroads. The term normally applies to *structures* built by humans, but may also apply to those built by other species.

Structural Design I. SCI 6227. Department of Architecture. Seminar. Fall 2014. Instructor: Patrick Sean McCafferty.

The course introduced the discipline of *structural* engineering as a means of unlocking hidden architectural design potential. Students developed the skills necessary to make informed decisions about geometry and material selection through a detailed understanding of statics, force flow, strength, stiffness, and material durability. The course began with the fundamentals of *structural* analysis, the design of engineering components (columns, beams, trusses, arches, etc.), and *structural* materials (*structural* steel, timber) as a means of introducing the design of more complex *structural* systems (funicular systems, bridge design, high-rise building design, etc.). Case studies of historic and recently completed projects from around the world were used throughout the course to demonstrate first principles of engineering design and construction. In the process, students developed an understanding of the collaborative design process necessary among engineering and architectur-

al design professionals in the pursuit of real-world design applications. ֍

Structural Design II. SCI 6229. Department of Architecture. Seminar. Spring 2015. Instructor: Paul Edward Kassabian.

This course was a continuation of *Structural* Design I and, after an overview introduction, furthered understanding of more developed *structural* systems and materials in architectural design. Systems included frames and floor-system behavior, lateral systems, tall buildings, and bridges. Materials included reinforced concrete, *structural* glass, and composites. The course focused more on a qualitative understanding than quantitative. This prioritized *structures* from a design, rather than analytical, perspective. Personal case studies were used to tell the real story of project development, *structural* concepts, and construction. ֍

Figure. Section (above). Ingrid Kestrel Bengtson (MArch I).

See also BUILDING—see also CONSTRUCTION—see also ELEMENT—see also FABRICATION—see also INFRASTRUCTURE—see also LIGHT: Light Structure—see also OEUVRE—see also ORNAMENT: Structure, Infrastructure, and Ornament—see also SKYSCRAPER: Wood Skyscraper—see also SURFACE: Structural Surfaces.

STUDENT

Student, people by degree of qualification: People who are attending school, or otherwise engaged in study.

Entretien avec les etudiants des ecoles d'architecture. Publication. Éditions Denoel, 1943. Le Corbusier (author). Le Corbusier Research Collection, Frances Loeb Library. LeC NA 2500 L496t 1943.

"In this message to *students,* Le Corbusier sought to breach the gap between youth and learning and his own experience, which he describes extensively. He further proposes that, amidst the chaos of war, an era of construction centered on people is necessary. He argues that the house, as a machine for living, must be thought of hand-in-hand with an urbanism that responds to man's physical and spiritual needs, and which also relates man to his environment. He develops ideas related to climate, site, scale, and notions of promenade, proportion, and intention in architecture, concluding that technique and sensibility are intricately tied together. The first is rational and can be learned, whereas the latter is cultivated and must be experienced." —Inés Zalduendo. ֍

Harvard GSD Students. The total number of *students* at the Harvard GSD during the 2014–2015 academic year was 893, including: 32 DDes candidates; 238 MArch I candidates; 36 MArch I AP candidates; 89 MArch II candidates; 64 MAUD candidates; 13 MDes, ADPD candidates; 7 MDes, CC candidates; 20 MDes, EE candidates; 11 MDes, HPD candidates; 29 MDes, REBE candidates; 21 MDes, RR candidates; 26 MDes, Tech candidates; 18 MDes, ULE candidates; 113 MLA I candidates; 53 MLA I AP candidates; 18 MLA II candidates; 7 MLAUD candidates; 80 MUP candidates; and 32 PhD candidates. 18 HAA concentrators were enrolled in the undergraduate studios at the Harvard GSD. 35 *students* were dual-degree candidates. ֍

See also ACADEMIA—see also ARCHITECTURE—see also DISCIPLINE—see also LANDSCAPE ARCHITECTURE—see also RESEARCH—see also STUDIO—see also STUDY—see also STUDY ABROAD—see also URBAN DESIGN—see also URBAN PLANNING.

Ingrid Kestrel Bengtson (MArch I, 2015)
Peter Rice Internship Program at Renzo Piano Building Workshop & Women in Design

Benjamin Graham Burdick (MArch I, 2015)
Backpocket Projects

Allison Craig Burrell (MArch I AP, 2015)
Harvard x-Design

Irene Chin (MDes, HPD, 2015)
Backpocket Projects, Grounded Visionaries Campaign & Exhibition, Kirkland Gallery, Newswall, Open Letters

Timothy Pittman Clark & Tiffany Kaewen Dang (MLA I, 2017)

Jose Luis Garcia del Castillo (DDes, 2017)
Code Without Frontiers & Parametric Camp

Daniel Ibañez Moreno (MDes, 2012 & DDes, 2017)
New Geographies 06: Grounding Metabolism & Wood Urbanism Colloquium

Chase Mitchell Jordan (MArch I, 2017)
Queers in Design, Student Forum, and YogaGSD

Xiaoxuan Lu (MLA I, 2012 & PhD, 2016)
From Silk Road to Gas Road Kickstarter Campaign

Dana Elise McKinney (MUP & MArch I, 2017)
African American Student Union, Dean's Diversity & Urban Planning Diversity Committees, and InForming Justice Symposium

Lara Elisabeth Mehling (MLA I, 2015)
Backpocket Projects, Horizonscopes, and Open Letters

Taraneh Meshkani (DDes, 2015)
Graduate Consortium on Energy and Environment & New Geographies 07: Geographies of Information

Pablo Pérez Ramos (DDes, 2016)
New Geographies 08: Island & Office for Quito's Metropolitan Master Plan

Héctor Ignacio Tarrido-Picart (MLA I AP & MAUD, 2015)
African American Student Union & InForming Justice Symposium

Gabriel Buxton Tomasulo (MArch I, 2015)
Projection GSD & Working GSD

Annie Yuxi Wang (MArch I, 2015)
Elements, Grounded Visionaries Campaign & Venice Biennale Central Pavilion

Jessica Lynn Wilcox (MArch 1, 2015)
Julia Armory Appleton Traveling Fellowship & Working GSD

Lily Wubeshet (MArch I, 2015)
Design Carnival & Project Link

Eri Yamagata (MLA I, 2015)
Japan GSD

Tim Daniel Zeitler (MArch I, 2015)
Fabrication Lab

STUDIO

Design *studio*, organization: *Studios* in which one or more master designers create designs, supervise assistants, and instruct pupils. *Studio* apartment, combination of rooms: Apartments containing one spacious room, often with large windows, which is or resembles an artist's *studio*, and serves as both a sitting area and sleeping area, and with access to a separate bathroom and small kitchen. *Studio*, organizations: In the context of the visual and decorative arts, refers to groups comprising a master artist or architect and his or her assistants. A *studio* typically includes a number of assistants and pupils, who are usually talented or adept artists who are honing their skills under the direction of the master. The term is typically applied to groups active in the 17th century and later. The meaning of the term overlaps with "workshops (organizations)," although there is often a subtle distinction in usage. "Workshops (organizations)" typically refers to groups active prior to the mid-17th century, where the emphasis is on organized collaboration, smooth teamwork, a division of labor, and where apprentices are learning a trade rather than being trained as artists in the modern sense of the term. "*Studios* (organizations)" typically refers to later groups in which the master artist or architect took on pupils rather than apprentices, and the emphasis of the pupil was on honing his native artistic skills rather than on learning a trade. *Studio*, work & instructional spaces: Working places set aside for artists to work. The term is generally applied to workspaces used by artists and designers creating fine art, particularly art dating from the 16th century to the present. The characteristics of a *studio* may be dictated by the practical requirements of adequate light, ample space in which to create the work, and storage of materials. Display of the finished works and training may also be accommodated in a *studio*. Creation of a work may require a range of artistic processes; therefore, separate areas of work may be delegated in the *studio*. The term may also refer to spaces used by dancers, singers, musicians, and other performing artists to create or practice. The term "workshops" generally refers to spaces used by craftspeople, artists working prior to the 16th century, and industrial workers.

Core Studios. The core curriculum includes required *studio* and non-*studio* course work. It is tailored to create a foundation on which Harvard GSD students build their later semesters of option *studios* and elective courses. Core is a time of bonding between students, during which everyone in the same graduating class has at least a few of their classes together. The number of courses varies from program to program. Core *studios* are required for the completion of all professional degree programs. Each student takes one *studio* per semester to become familiar with the fundamental techniques and methods of design. 11 core *studios* were conducted at the Harvard GSD in the 2014–2015 academic year. ֍

Option Studios. After core requirements are completed, Harvard GSD students begin to take option *studios*. Eligible students indicate their preferences in a lottery system. Option *studios* address a wide range of issues, topics, and contexts. Many provide students the opportunity to work with prominent practitioners, who serve as visiting critics. Students may take option *studios* hosted by departments outside of their own as long as the number of *studios* does not exceed the limit set by their degree program: 39 option *studios* were conducted at the Harvard GSD in the 2014–2015 academic year. ֍

See also ACADEMIA—see also BUILDING—see also DISCIPLINE—see also FACULTY—see also HOUSING—see also LOTTERY—see also PRACTICE—see also REAL ESTATE—see also ROOM—see also SPACE—see also STUDENT—see also WORK—see also WORKSHOP.

STUDY

Study, rooms, reading & writing spaces: Rooms or spaces in domestic contexts used for reading, writing, and *study*. *Study*, visual works by function: Works in any medium of the visual arts that explore a subject or are preliminary to a separate, more finalized work; more finished than sketches. For representations or diagrams that clarify, usually accompanying a text, use "illustrations." *Study* model, architectural models, scale models, visual & verbal communication: Architectural models made to help clarify and visualize aspects of a project during the design process.

Étude sur le mouvement d'art decoratif en Allemagne. Publication. Impr. Haefeli, 1912. Le Corbusier (author). Le Corbusier Research Collection, Frances Loeb Library. LeC N6868 L496.

"*Étude sur le mouvement d'art decoratif en Allemagne* summarizes Le Corbusier's *studies* during his extended stay in Germany between April 1910 and May 1911 (almost half of which he spent working for Peter Behrens). He analyzed the innovations in the industrial and applied arts (he rarely used the term arts decoratifs in the text) in Germany compared to those of France. The Werkbund's program—to unite art, industry, and commerce—had a lasting impression on Le Corbusier. This is a significant text that reveals his struggle to resolve the tension between art and industry, which would later define much of his writing and practice." —Inés Zalduendo. ֍

See also DETAIL—see also GARDEN: Studies in the History of Gardens & Design Landscapes—see also INDEPENDENT—see also MODEL—see also PROCESS—see also ROOM—see also SCALE—see also SPACE—see also WRITING.

STYLE

1: Designation, title. 2: (a) A distinctive manner of expression as in writing or speech <writes with more attention to *style* than to content> <the flowery *style* of 18th-century prose>; (b) a distinctive manner or custom of behaving or conducting oneself <the formal *style* of the court> <his *style* is abrasive>, also a particular mode of living <in high *style*>; (c) a particular manner or technique by which something is done, created, or performed <a unique *style* of horseback riding> <the classical *style* of dance>. 3: A distinctive quality, form, or type of something <a new dress *style*> <the Greek *style* of architecture>. 4: (a) The state of being popular, fashion <clothes that are always in *style*>; (b) fashionable elegance; (c) beauty, grace, or ease of manner or technique <an awkward moment she handled with *style*>. 5: A convention with respect to spelling, punctuation, capitalization, and typographic arrangement and display followed in writing or printing.

  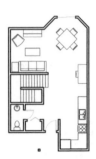

Style, critical concept: Configuration of artistic elements that together constitute a manner of expression peculiar to a certain epoch, people, or individual. A distinctive appearance or manner; a visual language.

The Function of Style. Publication. Harvard GSD & ActarD, 2014. Farshid Moussavi (author). NA2750.M68 2014.

During the 19th and most of the 20th century, discussions of *style* revolved around pure formalism or pure functionalism. *Style*, as the way of assembling forms, was trapped in producing consistency and sameness across architectural forms. *The Function of Style* is the third in a series at Harvard GSD which focus on researching a contemporary idea of *style* in architecture. The previous publication, *The Function of Form*, investigated the architecture of the latter part of the 20th century, which defied the senselessness and anonymity of the early 20th-century city. The aim was to establish whether the systems of differentiation identified earlier were exploring their *style* as formalism or were based on a new idea of *style* that would work with form and function simultaneously as a way to use form to subvert function. The book continues to interrogate the form-function relationship of those projects. It focuses particularly on the history of drawing techniques for describing different concepts of function. ⊗

See also AESTHETIC—see also AGENCY—see also FORM—see also FUNCTION—see also HISTORY—see also OEUVRE—see also ORNAMENT—see also SPACE—see also THEORY—see also TIME—see also WRITING.

SUBJECT

1: (a) One that is placed under authority or control, such as a vassal; (b) one *subject* to a monarch and governed by the monarch's law; (c) one who lives in the territory of, enjoys the protection of, and owes allegiance to a sovereign power or state. 2: (a) That of which a quality, attribute, or relation may be affirmed or in which it may inhere; (b) substratum, especially material or essential substance; (c) the mind, ego, or agent of whatever sort that sustains or assumes the form of thought or consciousness. 3: (a) A department of knowledge or learning; (b) motive, cause; (c) one that is acted on <the helpless *subject* of their cruelty>; (d) an individual whose reactions or responses are studied.

Subject analysis: Examining the content of documents, either textual or pictorial, in order to determine what they are about or of.

SUBJECTIVITY

1: Of, relating to, or constituting a subject, such as (a) of, relating to, or characteristic of one that is a subject especially in lack of freedom of action or in submissiveness; (b) being or relating to a grammatical subject, especially nominative. 2: Of or relating to the essential being of that which has substance, qualities, attributes, or relations. 3: (a) Characteristic of or belonging to reality as perceived rather than as independent of mind, phenomenal—compare to objective; (b) relating to or being experience or knowledge as conditioned by personal mental characteristics or states. 4: (a) Peculiar to a particular individual, personal <*subjective* judgments>; (b) modified or affected by personal views, experience, or background <a *subjective* account of the incident>; (c) arising from conditions within the brain or sense organs and not directly caused by external stimuli <*subjective* sensations>. 5: Lacking in reality or substance, illusory.

SUBURB

Suburb, settlements by location, inhabited places: Compactly developed or developing, usually residential, areas on the outskirts of a central city; distinguished from central cities by their more homogeneous socioeconomic and physical character, although rarely is there an identifiable boundary between *suburbs* and central cities.

The Storm, the Strife, and Everyday Life: Sea Change in the Suburbs. STU 1502. Department of Urban Planning & Design. Option Studio. Fall 2014. Instructor: Daniel D'Oca. Teaching Assistant: Irene Figueroa Ortiz (MArch I & MUP).

For many Long Islanders, the devastation caused by Superstorm Sandy was a wakeup call, adding urgency to a nascent discussion about Long Island's vulnerability to storm surge, sea-level rise, and heavy rain events that regularly overwhelm an antiquated sewer system. But when Sandy struck, Long Island—like many older *suburban* regions—had another sea change on its mind.

Consider the following: in 2011, population growth in urban centers outpaced population growth in *suburban* areas for the first time in 100 years. Between 2000 and 2012, the poor population in *suburbs* grew by 65 percent—more than twice the rate of growth in large cities. In the past decade, minorities have accounted for four-fifths of *suburban* growth. Statistics like these, plus peak oil predictions, reveals the overwhelmingly urban lifestyle preferences of millennials. Numerous other statistics pointing to a great inversion of wealth and opportunity from *suburbs* to cities, led many leaders on Long Island—host of the world's earliest and most iconic postwar, mass-produced, sitcom *suburbs*—to the realization that the *suburb* as we have known it might be reaching the end of its shelf life. Lewis Mumford's enduring image of "a multitude of uniform, unidentifiable houses, lined up inflexibly, at uniform distances, on uniform roads, in a treeless communal waste, inhabited by people of the same class, the same income, the same age group ...conforming in every outward and inward respect to a common mold," still strikes a chord, but there is little question that *suburbs* in the United States are witnessing a radical formal, demographic, and semantic shift. No longer the exclusive province of well-off, white, car-driving nuclear families, the *suburbs* are increasingly diverse, increasingly poor, and, in Long Island's case, increasingly wet.

What can an almost exclusively auto-based, *suburban* landscape of detached single-family homes, with a dearth of affordable housing and transportation options, a highly balkanized system of governance, and tremendous vulnerability to storm surge do to stay strong the 21st century? This interdisciplinary studio invited students to imagine a future for Long Island, America's first *suburb*. Drawing from an analysis of how things like sea-level rise, increased immigration, increased poverty, and the aging of the population are transforming everyday life in the *suburbs*, students worked with community-based organizations to envision futures for Long Island. Students developed a vision at a regional scale, and then zoomed in to articulate the vision on one of a dozen or so contentious development sites.

Students: Rebekah Lynn Armstrong (MLA I), Paloma Garcia Simon (MLA I), Andrew Richard Gipe (MArch I AP), Courtney Goode (MLA I), Allison Camille Green (MUP), David Jason Henning (MUP), Tamotsu Ito (MArch II), Yuxiang Luo (MArch II), Marcus Pulsipher (MLAUD), Rui Qian (MLA I AP), Stephen Sun (MArch II), Robert William Wellburn (MUP). ❀

Figures. Floor Plans (page 374) & Site Plan (previous page). Marcus Pulsipher (MLAUD).

See also COLLABORATION—see also COMMUNITY—see also HOUSING—see also POST-SUBURB—see also SETTLEMENT—see also URBAN.

SUPERMARKET

Supermarket, markets, structures, mercantile buildings: Large, self-service, retail markets which sell food, household goods, and household merchandise.

Paper or Plastic: Reinventing Shelf-Life in the Supermarket Landscape. VIS 2415. Department of Architecture. Seminar. Fall 2014. Instructor: Teman Evans.

The *supermarket* shelf is a highly volatile, hypercompetitive space. On this shelf, products struggle to max-imize every possible advantage, in a ruthless effort to lure consumers away from competitors. However, what may have once been merely a beauty contest of packaging has quickly become a much more complex issue. The modern consumer in today's strained economy demands tangible value from the products that he or she consumes. To survive, brands must negotiate issues that include the ergonomics of the hand, the complex geometries of the refrigerator, and even sustainable material innovations that determine a product's afterlife and its impact on the environment. These are multiscalar, spatial life problems that the architect is uniquely suited to address. This seminar asked students to operate as brand strategists. However, rather than invent new products, students instead innovated upon existing brands. Outdated *supermarket* products were considered from the top down (logo, tagline, advertising, etc.). Students were required to study their product's shelf competitors, and presented their efforts through visual rather than verbal arguments. ❀

SURFACE

Surface element, architectural elements: Architectural elements or components located on the *surface. Surface,* object portions or aspects: The outermost layers or areas of objects.

Dueling Surfaces. Thesis. Craig Michael Reschke (MLA I AP), advised by Bradley Earl Cantrell.

"The USDA's Conservation Reserve Program (CRP) spends two billion dollars each year to rent farmland for the purpose of taking it out of production in an effort to mitigate the environmental impact of farming and ranching. These sites are largely unseen, unmapped, and unoccupied by people—a managerial plus sign on a ledger filled with the negative externalities of farming. In the surrounding landscape, a suite of Global Positioning System (GPS) and Geographic Information System (GIS) technologies known as precision agriculture have dominated the agricultural industry with a single mantra: increase production and profits. However, the real-time feedback loop created by precision agriculture has set up a dual *surface* condition in the landscape that has gone unnoticed and unharnessed by users of precision agriculture. Landscape architecture can appropriate these systems and deploy them in a way that diversifies the agents for which they act. This project reconsiders the CRP and precision agriculture in the rural Midwestern landscape through the following questions: how can CRP react to real-time feedback loops generated with precision agriculture? Should these landscapes serve only as factories that deliver needed calories to cities? How can CRP more broadly interpret conservation? Is there a lifestyle in this environment that is as glamorous as the sort proposed for city dwellers, and does this culture need to be conserved?" ❀

Superficial Surfaces. Lecture. Gund Hall, Piper Auditorium. September 16, 2014. Martin Rein-Cano.

Topotek1 works with landscape at the intersection of architecture, urban design, music, and art. To illustrate aspects and strategies of the firm's philosophy and approach, which often involves a recontextualization of design features and scenography, Martin Rein-Cano's lecture examined one of the firm's large-scale projects and the urban ambiance for Superkilen in Copenhagen. ❀

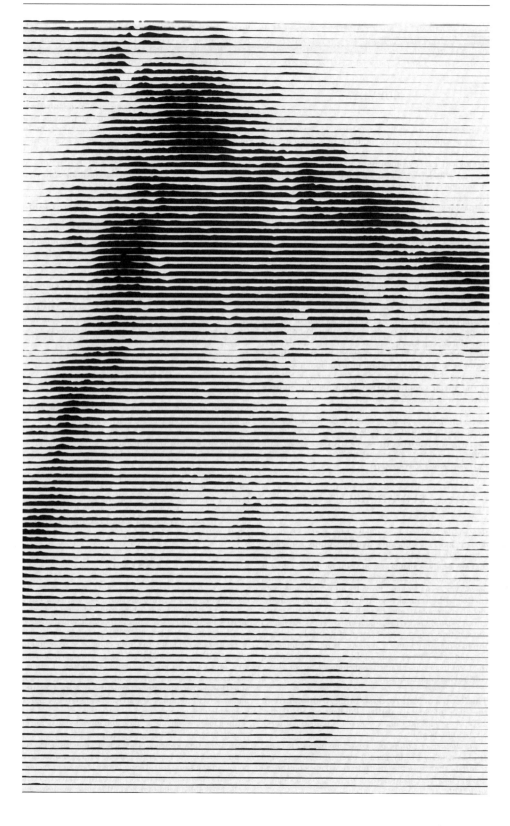

See also ELEMENT—see also GEOMETRY—see also LAND-FORM: Landformation Catalogue—see also MATERIAL—see also MEMORIAL: Abstracted Geologies—see also PATTERN—see also STRUCTURE: Structural Surfaces—see also 2-D.

SURVEY

Architectural *survey*, documents genres by function: *Surveys* which assess the condition of a set of historic buildings and prioritize preservation and repair. Geological *survey*, document genres by function: *Surveys* which investigate and determine the distribution and origin of mineral deposits and rock masses. Insurance *survey*, financial records by function: Collections of data gathered and examined for the purpose of formulating insurance policies. Land *survey*, document genres by function: Documents, often maps, which record the measuring and marking of land. *Survey*, questionnaires, document genres by form: Documents containing a set of questions for submission to a number of persons in order to obtain statistically useful information. *Survey*, documents, document genres by form: Documentation of examinations or inspections conducted in order to achieve a comprehensive view, as of a place, a group of related items, or to ascertain condition or value. For detailed lists of items on hand, or of items in a given category, use "inventories." For sets of questions submitted to a number of persons to obtain information, use "questionnaires." Topographic *survey*, land *surveys: Surveys* of the surface configuration of an area, including natural and man-made features.

See also BUILDING—see also CATALOGUE—see also COLLECTION—see also COMMUNICATION—see also CONTOUR—see also DATA—see also GEOLOGY—see also LAND—see also LANDFORM—see also MAP—see also MEASURE—see also PRESERVATION—see also TOPOGRAPHY.

SUSTAINABILITY

Sustainable architecture, architecture genre: Structure design that is specifically environmentally conscious, taking into account construction methods and materials that are locally available as well as the building's efficient use of resources, including systems of heating, cooling, power, water, and waste. Provides affordable, adequate shelter with minimal negative effect on the local and global environment; may be replicated and locally maintained. *Sustainability*, use, functional concepts: Ecological concept referring to preservation of natural resources through responsible use and stewardship. A component of *sustainable* development. In the conservation context, the term has been extended to include *sustainability* of cultural heritage resources.

The Return of Nature: Sustaining Architecture in the Face of Sustainability. Publication. Routledge, 2014. Preston Scott Cohen & Erika Naginski (editors). NK1520.R534 2014.
   The Return of Nature is a collection of detailed case studies and essays by practitioners, historians, and theorists that presents multiple viewpoints on the relations between architecture, nature, green design, *sustainability*, technology, and culture.

Sustainable Exuma. Research Project. The *Sustainable* Exuma project is a collaboration among the Government of the Bahamas, the Bahamas National Trust, and the Harvard GSD. The goal is to facilitate the design and management of a more *sustainable* future for the Exuma archipelago, and the Bahamas more generally. The project has two parallel and mutually informing components: research and education. These components work to inform the development of proposals and interventions as well as the building of capabilities for local empowerment. In addition, the project seeks to understand local issues through various forms of public engagement. Public forums, workshops, and conferences are part of the process, in addition to fieldwork that facilitates the connection of researchers with residents. §

Paul Zofnass Program for Sustainable Infrastructure. Research Program. The Zofnass Program for *Sustainable* Infrastructure develops and promotes methods and tools to quantify the *sustainability* of infrastructures and facilitate the adoption of *sustainable* solutions. §

See also CONSERVATION—see also CONTEXT: King's Cross—see also DEVELOPMENT—see also ECOLOGY—see also ENVIRONMENT—see also ETHICS—see also GREEN—see also MANAGEMENT: A Sustainable Future for Exuma—see also RESILIENCE: Coastal Resilience, Sustainable Development of the Spanish Atlantic Coast—see also URBANISM.

SYMPOSIUM

Symposium, conferences, meetings: Formal meetings at which several specialists deliver short addresses on a topic or on related topics. *Symposium*, parties, events: Parties, specifically those in ancient Greece, which featured drinking and intellectual conversation.

See also AGE: Aging & Place—see also COMPETITION: The Design Competition Conference—see also CONFERENCE—see also DATA: Data Across Scales—see also MEGA: Kumbh Mela—see also PARTY—see also POWER: Cambridge Talks IX—see also SURVIVAL: Design As Survival—see also TECHNIQUE—see also URBANISM: Ecological Urbanism.

SYSTEM

Cataloging *system*, information *systems*, computer *systems: Systems* for describing and indexing works or images, particularly in a collections management *system* or other automated *system*. Color *system*, color & color-related phenomena: Any three-component coordinate *system* with three variables of color such as hue, intensity, and value to represent the attributes of colors. Structural *system*: Architectural elements that consist of entire *systems* to support structures. *System*, equipment, object groupings & *systems*: Designates complex assemblies of equipment and activities, arranged according to some scheme or plan, and intended to perform specific functions. Transit *system*, infrastructural *systems*: Transportation *systems* of attached vehicles, such as trains, that make is possible to move large numbers of people in the same travel corridor with greater efficiency. Wall *system*, curtain walls, nonbearing walls: Curtain walls assembled from highly similar components, each

combining two or more of the traditionally separate elements of windows, external finish wall, internal finish wall, and insulation.

Environmental Systems in Architecture. SCI 6125. Department of Architecture. Seminar. Spring 2015. Instructor: Holly Samuelson.

The primary focus of the course was the study of ecological considerations in architectural design. These considerations include the thermal, luminous, and acoustic behavior of buildings. The course examined the basic scientific principles underlying these phenomena and introduced students to a range of technologies and analytical techniques for designing comfortable indoor environments. Students were challenged to apply these techniques and explore the role energy, light, sound, water, and materials can play in shaping architecture. Students gained a better understanding of global resource issues and the role of buildings in this context. The course also presented the principles of heat flow in and around buildings. Basic manual and computer-based methods to predict the energy performance of buildings were discussed. In addition, the course introduced the art and science of lighting buildings along with manual and computer-based methods for analyzing daylight design. ❦

Infrastructural Ecologies: Third Semester Core Landscape Architecture Studio. STU 1211. Department of Landscape Architecture. Core Studio. Fall 2014. Instructors: Steve Apfelbaum (workshop instructor), Steven Beites (workshop instructor), Pierre Bélanger (coordinator), Luis Callejas, Rosetta S. Elkin, Andrea Hansen, Niall G. Kirkwood, Robert Gerard Pietrusko (workshop instructor), and Sergio Lopez-Pineiro. Teaching Assistants: Marissa Ashley Angell (MLA I), Hillary Jane Archer (MLA I), Chris Bennett (MDes, ULE), Ken Chongsuwat (MLA I), Stephanie Hsia (MLA I), Leo Raphael Miller (MLA I), Jennifer Athena Saura (MUP & MLA I), and Vi Vu (MLA I). Workshop Teaching Assistants: Grga Basic (MDes, ULE), Lisa Jane Caplan (MLA I), Vineet Divgi Diwadkar (MUP & MLA I AP), Xiaoran Du (MLA I AP), Paloma Garcia Simon (MLA I), Peichen Hao (MLA I), and Yujun Yin (MArch II & MLA I AP). Modeling Teaching Assistants: Ian Scott Brennick (MLA I), Siwei Gou (MLA I AP), Tzyy Haur Yeh (MLA I AP & MArch I), Rituparna Simlai (MLA I AP), Bingjie Shi (MLA I AP & MAUD), and Timothy Yung Wei (MLA I).

Addressing the inertia of urban planning and the overexertion of civil engineering in the 20th century, this studio focused on the design of large, complex, contaminated, brownfield sites with a regional, ecological, and infrastructural outlook. Employing the agency

of regional ecology and landscape infrastructure as the dominant drivers of design, the studio involved the development of biodynamic and biophysical *systems* that provide flexible yet directive patterns for future urbanization. Through a series of contemporary mapping methods, field measures, case studies, readings, and design investigations, the studio resulted in a series of collaborative exercises leading to a large-scale design project and future scenarios. Drawing from canonical case studies on regional reclamation strategies from around the world, the studio further enhanced a robust, regional representation program. Focusing on the metrics of geospatial representation and remote sensing, two intensive workshops throughout the term didactically dealt with the interrelated subjects of regional cartography and site topography as operative and telescopic instruments of design across scales. Contributing to a complex, multilayered profiling of the site as *system* and the reformulation of program as process, the studio established a base platform for engaging an array of complex issues related to site contamination, biophysical *systems*, regional ecology, land cover, urban infrastructure, and economic geography.

Students: Weaam Husain Alabdullah (MLA I AP), Rawan Aaah Alsaffar (MLA I AP & MDes, ULE), Maria Isabel Arroyo (MLA I), Rachel Nara Bedet (MLA I), Larissa Lea Kristina Belcic (MLA I), Christianna Bennett (MLA I AP), Elise N. Bluell (MLA I AP), Lee Ann Sheridan Bobrowski (MLA I), Sarah Marcela Bolivar (MLA I), Jessica Booth (MLA I), Andrew Gregory Boyd (MLA I), Sarah Morgan Canepa (MLA I), Alexander Louis Cassini (MLA I), Azzurra Shani Cox (MLA I), Devin Dobrowolski (MLA I), Alberto Embriz de Salvatierra (MLA I AP & MDes, ULE), Leif Tobias Estrada (MLA I AP & MDes, ULE), Enrico Evangelisti (MLA I), Yufan Gao (MLA I), Matthew Joseph Gindlesperger (MLA I AP), Jia Joy Hu (MLA I AP), B. Cannon Ivers (MLA II), Clementine InHye Jang (MLA I), Mark Turibius Jongman-Sereno (MLA I AP), Brett Keese (MLA I AP & MArch I), Gyeong Wanee Kim (MLA I AP), Lyu Kim (MLA I AP), Yong Uk Kim (MLA I), Bradley Kraushaar (MLA I), Liza Langer (MLA I AP), Qiyi Li (MLA II), Ruichao Li (MLA I AP), Xinhui Li (MLA I), Yuanjie Li (MLA I), Ambrose Ka Yiu Luk (MLA I), Simon Peter Madigan (MLA I AP), Mailys Meyer (MLA I AP), Alica Meza (MLA I), Mary Catherine Miller (MLA I AP), Tyler Mohr (MLA II), Timothy Nawrocki (MLA I AP), Thomas Nideroest (MLA II), Althea Jane Northcross (MLA I), Ivy Pan (MLA I), Linh Kim Pham (MLA I AP), Natasha Emily Polozenko (MLA II), Christopher James Reznich (MLA I AP), Antonia Rudnay (MLA II), Rachel Louise Schneider (MLA I), Max Elliot Sell (MLA I), Michelle Shofet (MLA I), Vipavee Sirivatanaaksorn (MLA I), Samantha Maria Solano (MLA II), Elaine Tyler Stokes (MLA I AP), Chella

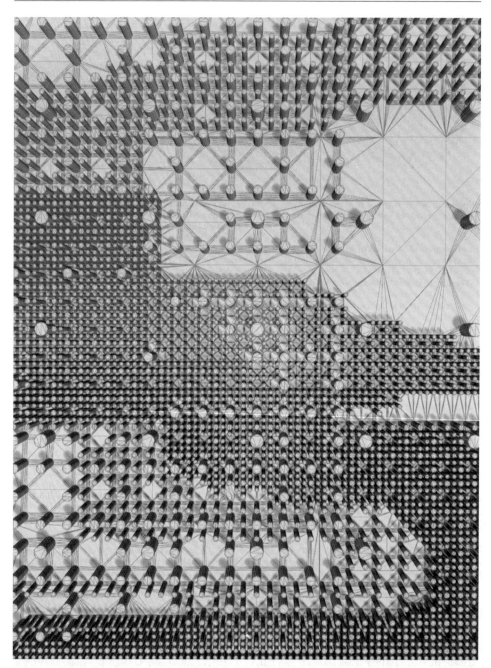

Jade Strong (MLA I), Carly Alexandra Troncale (MLA I), Foad Vahidi (MLA I), Gege Wang (MLA I), Hui Wang (MLA I), Daniel Widis (MLA I), Zehao Xie (MLA I), Han Xu (MLA I), Xiaodi Yan (MLA II). 🕮

Figures. Serial Sections (page 377), Log Sections (page 379), Diagram (above), and Planting Diagram (opposite page, below). Mark Turibius Jongman-Sereno (MLA I AP), Antonia Rudnay (MLA II), and Foad Vahidi (MLA I). Worm's Eye View Perspective (opposite page, above). Devin Dobrowolski (MLA I), B. Cannon Ivers (MLA II), and Mary Catherine Miller (MLA I AP).

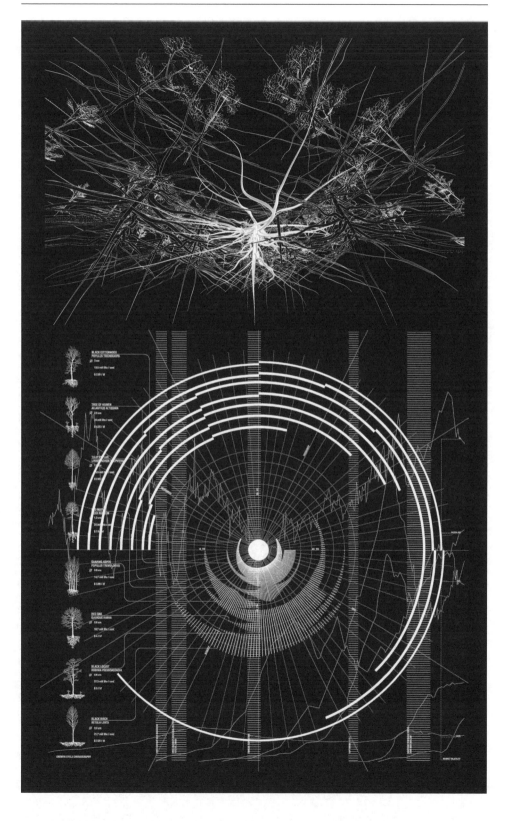

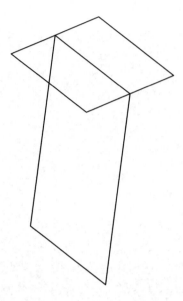

T

1: (a) The 20th letter of the English alphabet; (b) a graphic representation of this letter; (c) a speech counterpart of orthographic *t*. 2: A graphic device for reproducing the letter *t*. 3: One designated *t* especially as the 20th in order or class. 4: Something shaped like the letter *t*. 5: *T* formation. 6: Technical foul.

The T. Boston has the oldest underground subway system in the United States. The Massachusetts Bay Transportation Authority, often referred to as the MBTA or The *T*, is the public operator of most bus, subway, commuter rail, and ferry routes in the greater Boston, Massachusetts area. Locals call it "The *T*", after its logo, the letter *T* in a circle, adopted in the 1960s and inspired by the Stockholm metro.

The five subway lines—Red, Green, Blue, Orange, and Silver—meet at six transfer stops in downtown Boston: Park Street, Government Center, Downtown Crossing, South Station, Boylston Street, and State Street. The Red Line (colored so because of its proximity to Harvard University) is the line that runs through parts of Cambridge and Somerville. The Red Line transfers to the Green Line at Park Street, to the Orange and Silver Lines at Downtown Crossing, and to the Silver Line at South Station. Its terminus stations are Alewife (northwest), Ashmont (south, Dorchester), and Braintree (south).

See also CIRCULATION—see also CITY—see also COLOR—see also DRAFTING—see also FLOW—see also FORM—see also HISTORY—see also LINE—see also MAPPING—see also NEIGHBORHOOD—see also NETWORK—see also ORTHOGRAPHIC—see also REPRESENTATION—see also SQUARE—see also SYSTEM—see also T-SQUARE—see also TOOL—see also TRANSPORTATION—see also URBAN.

T-SQUARE

T-square, squares, tools, shaping & guiding tools: Squares in the shape of a T, used in technical and architectural drawing. The short arm slides along the edge of a drawing board keeping the long arm in a parallel state.

See also DRAFTING—see also EDGE—see also GEOMETRY—see also LINE—see also PARALLEL—see also SQUARE—see also TOOL.

TABLE

Table game, games, public & interactive activities: Games that are played on *tables*, either generic *tables* or *tables* designed specifically for play of a particular game. *Table*, architectural elements, surface element components: A nonrepeating, often flat, rectangular, and usually stone surface, slab, or panel set into a wall or pedestal; and bearing inscriptions, paintings, or relief sculpture. For similar objects that are movable or that are not part of the structure of a wall or pedestal, use "tablet." *Table*, documents, graphic document genres by form: Condensed, orderly arrangements of data, especially those in which the data are arranged in columns and rows.

GSD Table Tennis. Student Group. GSD *Table* Tennis is a social *table* tennis group with the mission of reviving the passion for the sport that once flourished in Gund Hall. §

See also COMMUNICATION—see also DATA—see also ELEMENT—see also ERGONOMICS—see also GAME—see also INFORMATION—see also REPRESENTATION—see also SURFACE—see also WELL-BEING.

TACTIC

1: A device for accomplishing an end. 2: A method of employing forces in combat.

See also PRODUCTION: Tactics for a Coproduced City—see also VISIONARY: Grounded Visionaries.

TASTE

Taste, aesthetic concepts, philosophical concepts: The appreciative sensibility of observers who experience delight when disinterestedly observing or experiencing certain natural and man-made objects and events. *Taste*, senses, biological concepts: Sense by which the flavor or savor of things is perceived when they are brought into contact with the tongue.

See also AESTHETIC—see also ALIMENT—see also BODY—see also CHAUHAUS—see also EXPERIENCE—see also FOOD—see also GASTRONOMY: The Architecture of Taste—see also PERCEPTION—see also SENSE.

TEA

Tea, beverage, food, materials by function: Aromatic beverage prepared from selected dried leaves and buds of the *tea* plant, by infusion in hot water. For similar beverages made from various other plants and herbs, use "herbal *tea*."

Tea. 7,000 cups of *tea* are consumed at the Chauhaus annually. ⊛

Project TEAhouse. Installation. Kirkland Gallery. May 12–21, 2015. Tamotsu Ito (MArch II) & Andrew Michael Nahmias (MArch II).

"Project *TEA*house" was an installation reimagining a Japanese teahouse at the Harvard GSD. Mixing traditional Japanese construction techniques with familiar and recycled materials, the project translated the experience of the Japanese teahouse to the American context, giving visitors the chance to break out of the everyday, step into an unfamiliar world, and participate in the experience of a *tea* ceremony. The teahouse installation transitioned visitors from the context of the simple American living room into reimagined elements of a Japanese teahouse—the waiting pavilion, the *tea* garden, and the tearoom, where *tea* ceremonies were held.

"Project TEAhouse" was just as much about exposing the building process as the event itself. As architects with backgrounds in design-build projects in Japan and the United States, the installation team led workshops for students on traditional Japanese techniques like wood joinery, *tsuchi-kabe* earth-wall plastering, and materials common to American construction such as wood frames, Tyvek house wrap, coir mats, and Boston clay. The rules of traditional Japanese teahouse design were followed, while adapting the experience of the *tea*house to the American context. ⊛

See also CHAUHAUS—see also COFFEE—see also FOOD—see also PLANT—see also WELL-BEING.

TECHNIQUE

Technique, historical, theoretical & critical concepts: The manner in which an artist or craftsman uses the *technical* elements of a medium to achieve a desired aesthetic effect. Processes & *techniques* by general type: The manner or method by which an activity is performed. Use "processes" when referring generally to the activities or procedures followed to produce some end, and for the actions or changes that take place in materials or objects.

Design Techniques I. Symposium. Gund Hall, Piper Auditorium. October 30, 2014. Sharon Johnston, Jeannette Kuo, Mark Lee, Philippe Rahm, Camilo Restrepo Ochoa, with Iñaki Ábalos (moderator).

At a moment of dissolution in design, *technique* is all an architect can grasp. *Techniques* occupy a beautifully indeterminate void on the fault line between theory and practice. Spared of reductive allegiance to either, design *techniques* are uniquely powerful. A *technique* may disrupt, innovate, communicate, or surprise. At the same time, *techniques* stand as silent markers of membership—opaque envelops delimiting communities of colleagues.

This symposium, the first event in the series, interrogated the motivations, instruments, influences, justifications, effects, and origins of contemporary design *techniques*. Ultimately, *technique* is how novelty manifests itself in architecture, expanding and advancing the inner core of our discipline.

Design Techniques II. Symposium. Gund Hall, Piper Auditorium. February 19, 2015. Momoyo Kaijima, Tom Emerson, Kersten Geers, Florian Idenburg, Silvia Benedito, Antoine Picon, with Enrique Walker (moderator).

In a discipline reformulating the role of the architect, the question of *technique* has acquired a new priority. *Techniques* move with unexpected fluidity, circulating between individuals and collectives, calling the influence of each into question. Paradoxical and ambiguous, *techniques* simultaneously negate and open possibilities. A *technique* can be a subversive strategy, resisting apparently objective parameters or an appropriative gaze, reconstituting the world as an object of disciplinary knowledge.

This symposium, the second event of the series, interrogated the collectivity, authorship, effects, and deployment of contemporary design *techniques*.

See also ACTION—see also AESTHETIC—see also ANIMATION: Animating Material—see also DRAWING—see also GREEN: Design Techniques—see also MATERIAL—see also METHODOLOGY—see also PRACTICE—see also PROCESS—see also REPRESENTATION—see also TECHNOLOGY.

TECHNOLOGY

Technology, technology & related concepts: Generally refers to the application of science, particularly to commercial or industrial objectives. The term is sometimes used in an anthropological context to refer in a general sense to a civilization's knowledge regarding the making of implements, the collecting of goods, and the practicing of manual arts and skills.

Master in Design Studies (MDes) Technology (Tech). Coupling an intensive critical and theoretical approach with practical, lab-based projects, *technology* advances innovative methods for making and understanding form and *technologically*-driven design through *technological* experimentation. As a separate concentration area within the Master in Design Studies program, the *Technology* concentration allows post-professional students to pursue a broad spectrum of inquiries, including design computation, digital fabrication, robotics, and the exploration of responsive environments. Cutting across scales, students engage subjects from the level of a single artifact or building to landscapes and urban systems. Despite the range of scales and subjects, each project shares this in common: a commitment to challenge existing modes of practice and design through *technological* invention.

The program offers students full access to state-of-the-art facilities—fabrication labs, robotics, CNC equipment, and rapid prototyping—as well as courses and initiatives throughout the Harvard GSD and across the university. Underscoring its emphasis on innovation and empiricism, the concentration is closely aligned with several of the school's research initiatives, particularly Design Robotics, and Responsive Environments & Artifacts, where students can develop fully conceived prototypes. Within *Technology* there are four subareas of concentration: (1) Design Computation includes programming, algorithm design and scripting techniques, parametric modeling and dimensionally-driven design, advanced visualization and animations as well as other computational approaches to design. (2) Responsive Environments pursues the design of virtual and physical worlds as an indivisible whole. Recognizing the all-pervasive nature of digital information in buildings and in the public realm, students investigate new hybrid spaces and environments that seamlessly integrate digital information and communication within purposefully conceived physical environments. (3) Advanced Materials & Systems courses study smart materials and environments, high-performance materials and advanced structural materials and systems. Recent interests include high-performance ceramics and adaptive materials. (4) Digital Fabrication & Robotics leverages *technology* transfer in the investigation of new design opportunities that arise through the advent of cutting-edge computer-controlled and robotic fabrication approaches. Prototyping efforts are supported through our state-of-the art Fab Lab that includes industrial robots as well as several CNC tools, rapid prototyping, and other devices. Students often work closely with the Design Robotics Group. ֍

Science & Technology GSD. Student Group. Science & *Technology* GSD is focused on the role of science and *technology* in the fields of urban planning, architecture, and design. The group aims to bring together students from various departments at Harvard University and MIT who are interested in science and *technology* through social events and lectures. The group collaborates with other universities and labs such as the MIT Media Lab, the SENSEable City Lab, and the Berkman Center for Internet and Society at Harvard University. ֍

See also ANIMATION: Animating Material—see also COMPU-TATION: Adaptive Technologies—see also COMPUTER—see also CONSTRUCTION—see also DATA—see also ELEMENT—see also GAME: Immersive Landscapes—see also INFORMATION—see also INITIATIVE: Harvard Initiative for Learning & Teaching—see

also MATERIAL—see also SOFTWARE—see also SUSTAINABIL-ITY: The Return of Nature—see also THEORY—see also TOOL.

TECTONICS

Tectonics, architectural theory, theoretical & critical concepts for visual arts: In recent architectural theory, the consideration of loads and stresses in architectural designs. *Tectonics*, geology, earth sciences, disciplines: The study of the form, pattern, and evolution of large-scale units of the Earth's crust, such as basins, disturbed belts, forelands, and continental shelves. For the study of smaller, individual geological structures, use "structural geology."

See also ASSEMBLY—see also CONSTRUCTION—see also GE-OLOGY—see also MATERIAL: Material Performance—see also OBJECT: Object Studio—see also PROTOTYPE: Refabricating Tectonic Prototypes—see also STRUCTURE—see also THERMO-DYNAMICS: Ábalos + Sentkiewicz.

TEMPLE

Temple, buildings: Buildings housing places devoted to the worship of a deity or deities. In the strictest sense, it refers to the dwelling place of a deity, and thus often houses a cult image. In modern usage, a *temple* is generally a structure, but it was originally derived from the Latin "templum" and historically has referred to an uncovered place affording a view of the surrounding region. For Christian or Islamic religious buildings the terms "churches" or "mosques" are generally used, but an exception is that "*temples*" is used for Protestant, as opposed to Roman Catholic, places of worship in France and some French-speaking regions.

TEMPORAL

1: (a) Of or relating to time as opposed to eternity; (b) of or relating to earthly life; (c) lay or secular rather than clerical or sacred, civil <lords *temporal*>. 2: Of or relating to grammatical tense or a distinction of time.

TENSEGRITY

Tensegrity structure, space frames, trusses by construction: Stable, three-dimensional structures consisting of members under tension that are contiguous and members under compression that are not.

See also CONSTRUCTION—see also PATTERN: R. Buckminster Fuller, Pattern Thinking—see also STRUCTURE—see also 3-D.

TENSION

1: (a) The act or action of stretching or the condition or degree of being stretched to stiffness, tautness; (b) stress. 2: (a) Either of two balancing forces causing or tending to cause extension; (b) the stress resulting from the elongation of an elastic body. 3: (a) Inner striving, unrest,

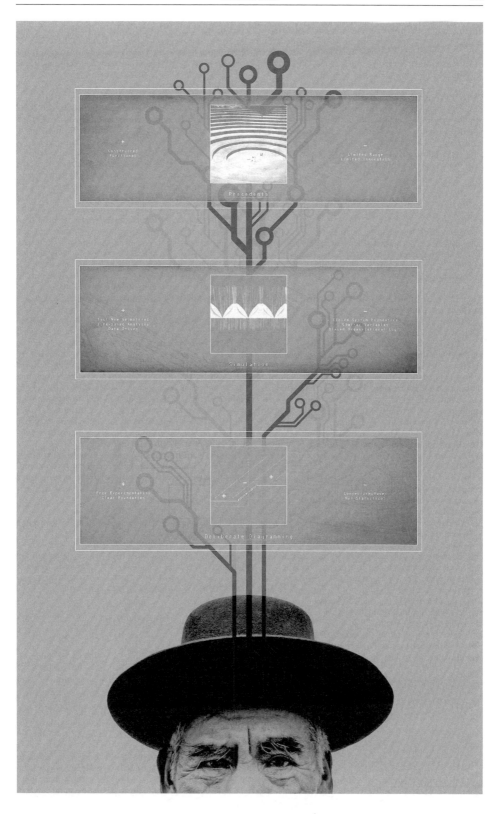

or imbalance often with physiological indication of emotion; (b) a state of latent hostility or opposition between individuals or groups; (c) a balance maintained in an artistic work between opposing forces or elements. 4: A device to produce a desired *tension*.

Tensile strength, mechanical strength, mechanical properties: The maximum pulling or ductile stress that a material can be subjected to without breakage. It is usually measured by taking a bar of the material and stretching it to destruction. The ultimate tensile strength is the maximum load divided by the bar's cross-sectional area and is measured in newtons per square meter.

TERRAFORM

Terraforming: Earth-shaping of a planet, moon, or other body with the hypothetical process of deliberately modifying its atmosphere, temperature, surface topography, or ecology to be similar to the environment of Earth and to make it habitable by Earth-like life.

Terraforming Cultivation: Landformations for Agricultural Continuity. Thesis & Master in Landscape Architecture Thesis Prize. Timothy Yung Wei (MLA I), advised by David Mah.

"Today, a gargantuan 35 gigatons of earth is moved annually, a number that rivals those of geomorphological processes. The sculpting of the planet's surface has fallen to human hands, as has the reshaping and reclamation of the uninhabitable. Although dominated by titans of industry and engineering, this is a crucial role that lies at the very foundation of the landscape discipline. From Capability Brown's Croome Park to Jean-Charles Alphand's Parc des Buttes Chaumont, adapting land for human use through large topographic moves has always been part of landscape architecture. In a twist of fate, present-day conditions have paved the way toward repossessing this act and pushing it to new levels. It is projected that, due to climate change, temperature will shift greatly over the next 200 years, placing many of the world's major agricultural production zones at risk. Enter *terraforming*: the design of dissipative multiscalar landformations to create viable microclimates for agricultural productivity. Through careful manipulation of geometry, agricultural risk can be mediated by curating specific microclimates and altering temperature, solar exposure, wind velocity, and hydrologic retention—from crop to landform, from *terraform* to a new form of agriculture settlement, from localized climate interventions to a catalogue of *terraform* typologies. This thesis is centered on the geometric composition, formation and implications of *terraforming* for agricultural productivity. The goal is a developed system of *terraforming*, applicable to multiple sites, that functions as a reference for the future landscape architect and as a tool for dissipative landformation." ◈

Figure. Collage (previous page). Timothy Yung Wei (MLA I).

See also AGRICULTURE—see also FORM—see also LAND—see also LANDFORM—see also TOPOGRAPHY.

TERRAIN

Digital *terrain* modeling, exploring & investigating techniques: Computer software technique for rendering virtual models of three-dimensional *terrain*. *Terrain* analysis, analysis & testing techniques, processes & techniques by specific type: The process of studying and interpreting the land surface and subsurface conditions of a geographical area using, for example, aerial photography or computer models.

Mountain Valley Urbanism: In Search of a New Paradigm of Urbanization in South Korea. Thesis. Won Joon Seol (MLAUD & MLA I AP), advised by David Mah.

"The historic evolution of cities in South Korea has been greatly affected by the country's topography; 68 percent of its *terrain* is mountainous. Flatter *terrain* (anything under a five-degree slope) occupies only 23 percent of South Korea and is mainly distributed throughout the west and south along the coast, though it is still blocked by major mountain ranges. South Korea has experienced incredibly rapid urban growth since the industrialization period in the mid-20th century. Today, it is in search of a new paradigm of urbanization that could accommodate its continuous urban growth and resolve the problems that have evolved from it. In the face of new spatial demands for further urban growth due to South Korea's population growth and its unusually high concentration of both physical and economic development—especially in the metropolitan regions—it is essential to understand the causes of this growth.

This thesis considers the mountain valleys in South Korea as a new lens through which the contemporary urbanistic problems caused by suburbanization and nonstop urban growth can be resolved at the same time that the lost environment and spirituality of the mountain is restored. Different methods of analysis examine how such extreme topographical conditions generate chaotic development patterns, monofunctional land use (low real estate value), massive infrastructural systems, and inefficient municipal boundaries.

In response, the thesis proposes a platform through which the reimaging of the valley strip between metropolis and satellite cities can respond to the contemporary urbanistic problems socially, ecologically, and strategically." ◈

Figure. Plan, Aerial Perspective, and Section (opposite page). Won Joon Seol (MLAUD & MLA I AP).

See also ANALYSIS—see also DIGITAL—see also GEOLOGY—see also LANDFORM—see also MEMORIAL: Abstracted Geologies— see also MODEL—see also PROCESS—see also SOFTWARE—see also STUDY—see also TECHNIQUE—see also 3-D.

TERRITORY

Territory, political divisions: Divisions under the jurisdiction of a nation, not vested with the full authority of provinces or states, but having some degree of local governing and legislative power.

Les trois établissements humains. Publication. Éditions Denoël, 1945. Le Corbusier (author). Le Corbusier Research Collection, Frances Loeb Library. LeC NA 9050 T76x.

"Le Corbusier's notion of architecture in relation to the environment is expanded in this book beyond the city itself and related to the broader scale of geography. To operate at this scale, he studies the formal configu-

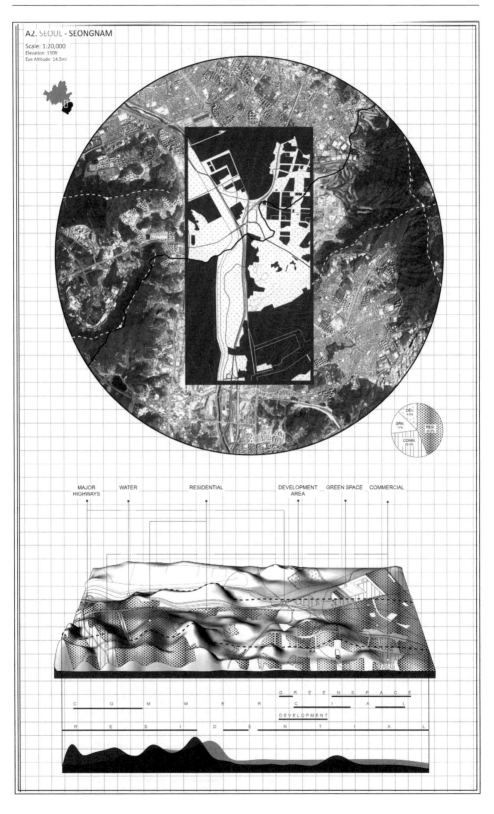

A2. SEOUL - SEONGNAM
Scale: 1:20,000
Elevation: 130ft
Eye Altitude: 14.5mi

DEV.
GRN.
COMM.
RES.

MAJOR HIGHWAYS   WATER   RESIDENTIAL   DEVELOPMENT AREA   GREEN SPACE   COMMERCIAL

G R E E N S P A C E
C O M M E R C I A L
D E V E L O P M E N T
R E S I D E N T I A L

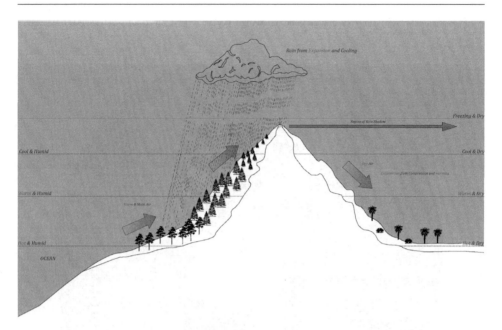

rations that *territorial* occupation entail. Relationships between housing and density, transportation and landscape, and concentric centers versus linear cities all speak to the occupation of *territory* at a larger geographic scale. Architecture and geography together define cities, their parameters, and those who inhabit them."
—Inés Zalduendo. ⊗

Territorialism. Studio Reports. Publication. Harvard GSD, 2014. Paola Viganò (studio instructor). HT 176. M37 T47 2014.

In Fall 2012 and Fall 2013, the *Territorialism* studios examined the *territorial* scale and the form of the *territory* as a basis to understand the contemporary city and the important modifications that have occurred in its spatial, economic, and social structure.

The studios were based on the premise that the urban field is changing and ecological rationality can offer fundamental opportunities to intersect and integrate various *territorial* layers. It is a means of directing or redirecting attention toward the *territorial* support in contemporary landscape architecture and urbanism. It focused attention on time, impermanence, and biotic relations, which, through natural dynamics, can permeate all environments. What we perceive as a *territory*, or as our *territory*, is above all a mental construction inside which *territories* can be created or erased. The studios investigated the role of design as a knowledge producer and as an active research tool in the understanding and construction of the contemporary *territory*. ⊗

See also BOX: Boxes for America—see also CITY: Expeditions in the Contemporary City—see also CONFLICT—see also DISCIPLINE—see also EDGE: The Barracks of Pion—see also INTELLIGENCE: Territorial Intelligence—see also INTENSITY: Urban Intensities—see also LANDSCAPE—see also MAPPING—see also MODEL: Architecture & the Territory—see also POST-SUBURB—see also POWER—see also TOWARD: Territorial Organization beyond Agglomeration—see also UNBUILT: Achtung: die Landschaft.

TERROIR

1: The combination of factors including soil, climate, and sunlight that gives wine grapes their distinctive character.

Built Climates. STU 1305. Department of Architecture. Option Studio. Fall 2014. Instructor: Philippe Rahm. Teaching Assistant: Baha Sadreddin (MDes, EE).

The concept of *"terroir"* (or "climates" in Burgundy) is popular in France in the term of *produits du terroir*, which means wine, cheese, or sausages whose taste is related to specific resources of geology, climate, and particular production methods such as fermentation (related to local bacteria) or smoking (burning wood growing in the region), giving them an irreproducible single, unique flavor. With a decline of its industries and technical knowledge, France is experiencing a crisis of its business and intellectual models in the face of globalization. Some sectors have nevertheless escaped this crisis, including *terroir* products (wine, champagne, cognac, etc.), luxury products, and gastronomic cuisine. It is this positive signal that the studio attempted to solve its future crises, and the process of globalization that will inevitably lead to a global homogenization of labor laws and wage scales. These results will then differentiate and qualify one region from another, bringing them closer to the concept of *terroir*, an idea where interest is growing worldwide through new food customs, the Slow Food movement, and urban farms. The studio proposed a project at the scale of a building, located in a particular French *terroir*. The goal was to design architecture by inventing new materials and a thermodynamic language, utilizing resources and production methods from the physical, chemical, and organic specification of a precise geology and climate.

Students: Hamed Bukhamseen (MAUD), Abigail Ann Chang (MArch I), Kevin Edwin Hinz (MArch I), Alexander Sarkis Karadjian (MArch I), Junyoung Lee (MArch II), Andrew Michael Nahmias (MArch II), Andreas Nikolovgenis (MArch

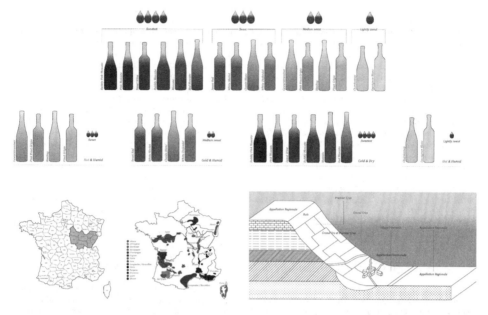

II), Ryan Thomas Otterson (MArch II), Christopher J. SooHoo (MArch I), Alexander R. Timmer (MArch I), Rex Tzen (MArch I), Emily Elizabeth Wettstein (MLA I AP & MArch I). ▨

Figures. Diagrams (opposite page & above). Junyoung Lee (MArch II).

THEORY

Theory, multidisciplinary concepts: Body of generalizations and principles developed in association with practice in a field of activity and forming its content as an intellectual discipline.

Urban Theory Lab. Design Lab. Neil Brenner. The Urban *Theory* Lab builds upon the notion of generalized urbanization to investigate emergent sociospatial formations under 21st-century capitalism. ▨

See also ARCHITECTURE—see also ART—see also CONCEPT—see also DISCIPLINE—see also HISTORY—see also IMAGINATION: Architectural Imagination After May '68—see also LANDSCAPE ARCHITECTURE—see also TECHNIQUE: Design Techniques I—see also TECHNOLOGY—see also URBAN.

THERMODYNAMICS

Thermodynamics, dynamics, mechanics concepts: The branch of science that is concerned with the study of energy and with the relationship of heat transfer and work to other forms of energy.

Ábalos + Sentkiewicz: Essays on Thermodynamics, Architecture, and Beauty. Publication. ActarD, 2014. Iñaki Ábalos & Renata Sentkiewicz (authors).
Ábalos + Sentkiewicz: Essays on Thermodynamics, Architecture, and Beauty is a book that unfolds argu-

ments and designs around the concept of *thermodynamic beauty*. This new aesthetic category opens up new and unexpected directions in the architect's work, connecting architecture and *thermodynamics* without giving up tectonic tradition. The book is a compendium of essays and projects that sets up new scenarios for the architecture of the next decade.

THESIS

Masters *thesis, theses*, school records: Papers, research results, or other documents presenting the author's research and submitted in support of candidature for a Masters Degree. *Thesis*, school records: Discourses advancing an original point of view as a result of research, especially as a requirement for an academic degree.

See also ACADEMIA—see also ADAPTIVE REUSE: Building Appreciation—see also AFFORESTATION: Colony & Homeland—see also AIRPORT—see also ANIMATION: Animating Material—see also ARCHITECTURE—see also AUTONOMOUSMOBILE: The (Love) Affair—see also BODY—see also BOX: Outside the Box—see also CIVIC: Starbucks & Spiderman—see also CONFLICT: Ad Absurdum—see also DIASPORA: The Diasporic Return of Capital—see also DISCIPLINE—see also DURATION: Indeterminately Bound—see also EGO—see also ENCLAVE: Leftover Moments—see also EXERGY: Low-Exergy Communities—see also EXPERIENCE: Choose Your Own Adventure—see also FOOD: Surviving, Sustaining, and Shaping Urbanization—see also FRAGMENT: Ilium—see also GESTURE: Trace of Emotion—see also HABOOB: Dust Kingdom—see also HOLOGRAM: Fragments of a Hologram House—see also HOUSING: Institutional Strategies for Upholding Affordable Housing Agreements—see also HYPEROBJECT: The Proximities of Nuclear Waste—see also INCUBATOR: Urbanity Incubator—see also ISLAND: Hydraulic Islands—see also LANDSCAPE ARCHITECTURE—see also MEMORIAL: Abstracted Geologies—see also NUCLEAR: Fatal Vitality—see also OBJECT: Common Objects—see also OFFICE—see also OUT-MIGRATE: On the Edge—see also PARK: Botanical

Park at the Epang Palace—see also PLANNING: Perceptions of Physical Space and the Planning Process in Camp Azraq, Jordan—see also PLANT: Francis D. Pastorius' Garden—see also POST-CONFLICT: May Kabul Be Without Gold, Rather Without Snow—see also POST-DISASTER: Understanding Tension around the Application of Global Standards in Post-Disaster Scenarios—see also PRIZE—see also REFUGE: Refugia—see also REPRESENTATION: Dweller on the Threshold—see also RESEARCH—see also RESPONSIVE: Vital Signs—see also RIVER: New River—see also SENSE: Remote Sensing in Mumbai—see also SKYSCRAPER: Wood Skyscraper—see also SPACE: Spaces of Living for the Subsystem Human Being—see also SPECTACLE: Functional Spectacle—see also SPECULATION: Practices in the Turbulent City—see also STUDENT—see also SURFACE: Dueling Surfaces—see also TERRAFORM: Terraforming Cultivation—see also TERRAIN: Mountain Valley Urbanism—see also TIME—see also URBAN DESIGN—see also URBAN PLANNING—see also UTOPIA: Glass Architecture—see also VALUE: Marrying Market Timing with Human-Centered Urban Design—see also VENTILATION: Supernatural Ventilation—see also WALL: Working Matter—see also WRITING.

THRESHOLD

1: The plank, stone, or piece of timber that lies under a door, sill. 2: (a) Gate, door; (b) end, boundary, specifically the end of a runway; (c) the place or point of entering or beginning, outset <on the *threshold* of a new age>. 3: (a) The point at which a physiological or psychological effect begins to be produced <has a high *threshold* for pain>; (b) a level, point, or value above which something is true or will take place and below which it is not or will not.

Threshold, doorway components: Strips fastened to the floor beneath a door, usually required to cover the joint when two types of floor materials meet; may provide weather protection on external doors; for the lower sides and bottom of doorways, use "doorsills."

See also BUILDING—see also CIRCULATION—see also CIVIC: Starbucks & Spiderman—see also DOOR—see also ELEMENT—see also ENCLAVE: Leftover Moments—see also FLOOR—see also LIGHTING—see also REPRESENTATION: Dweller on the Threshold—see also SEQUENCE—see also TIME.

TIME

Geologic *time* scale, periods, cultures by general era: An internationally recognized *time* scale of Earth's history since the planet's formative period subdivided into eons, eras, periods, and epochs. *Time*, physics concepts, physical sciences concept: A fundamental dimensional quantity defined by a nonspatial continuum in which events occur in apparently irreversible succession from the past through the present to the future. *Time* of day, earth sciences concepts, physical sciences concepts: Points or period in the course of a day or of the diurnal cycle.

Architecture between Remembering & Forgetting. Thesis. Jessica Lynn Wilcox (MArch I), advised by Grace La.

"*Time* is inherently spatial. We 'get lost in *time*,' we charge ourselves to 'be in the moment,' and we peer endlessly into our futures. It is no wonder that cities

and collective spaces are used as tools to construct a collective memory and therefore a collective, total present. And yet, through this construction we reject the multiplicity and immediacy of our past and present moments, seeking instead a stable past and a singular vision of the city. Presenting such a singular history is a fallacy; one history can never encompass all.

The apparent alternative, however—that of pure progress, forgetting, and tabula rasa—is equally a fallacy. It too rejects our backgrounds, our ancestors, refuses layers, and denies the literal earthly ground by leveling it and producing flatness. Friedrich Nietzsche alludes to this problem in *The Use and Abuse of History* and calls on us to live within the tension between the historical and the unhistorical in order to assess our present honestly and promote real progress. Architecture makes up our constructed collective spaces. How can it create a space between the historical and the unhistorical? This thesis argues that subtraction as a mode of architectural production allows us to reveal, critique, and discuss the contested ontological grounds of the city as well as the literal ground line of construction. The project takes as its site the historic town center of Krakow, Poland—a UNESCO World Heritage Site and a place of overlapping and often hidden spatial histories. Employing subtraction to adaptively reuse and compose a new space for the now existing International Cultural Center, it seeks to cut away the veneer of a monolithic and singular history, creating instead a space for multiple narratives." ❧

Tlön: A Zoo for Taxidermists. Thesis. Benjamin Richard Ruswick (MArch I), advised by Mariana Ibañez.

"We occupy a point in *time* along an ever-advancing continuum. It is anchored on one end by our static origin; on the other; a dynamic future. To stabilize ourselves and ameliorate the inherent discomfort of our displacement from these unknowable certainties, we seek the contextual nature of histories and the satisfaction of encapsulated fictions through the collection of memory and projection of futures. We obsess over the methodical integration of historical aggregate and fear the finality of irrecoverability. This thesis offers commentary on the contemporary act of history-making, which is making our world increasingly total, and the value of hoarding memorial fragments that can never reconstitute the foundations of our beginning's decaying edifice. Borrowing a title and an underlying conceptual structure from a fiction written by Jorge Luis Borges entitled 'Tlön, Uqbar, Orbis Tertius,' Tlön is a hyperbolic, anachronistic depiction of a future history positioned after the end of archaeological discovery and the severing of our tenuous hold on a common evidential past. It consumes the traces of history embedded within made things. Through the archival, the world is remade as an image of the self it destroyed in the act. *Time* is reconceptualized in terms of advancement toward an artifactual infinity—an ever-increasing collection divorced from the subjective nature of historical constructions." ❧

Figure. Drawings (opposite page). Benjamin Richard Ruswick (MArch I).

See also AIRPORT: The New London Airport—see also BOX: Outside the Box—see also COMPLEX: The Function of Time—see also DIMENSION—see also FILM—see also HYPEROBJECT: The Proximities of Nuclear Waste—see also MEASURE—see also PERCEPTION—see also SEED: Seeds of Time.

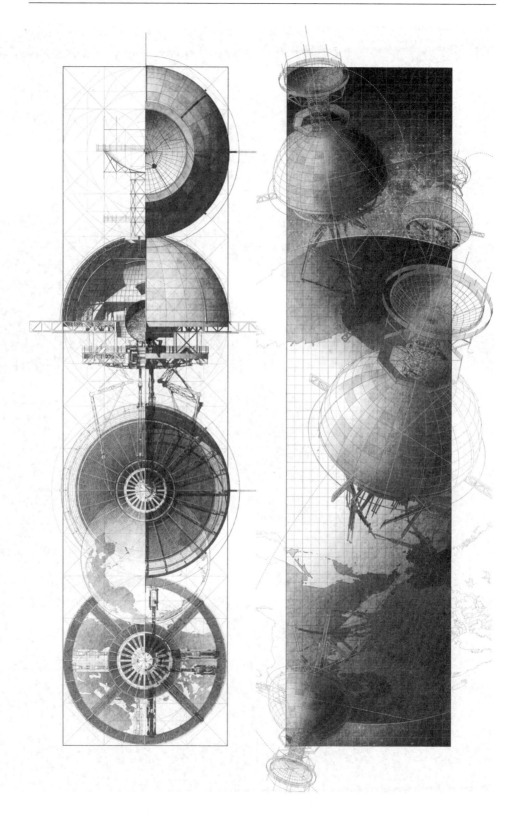

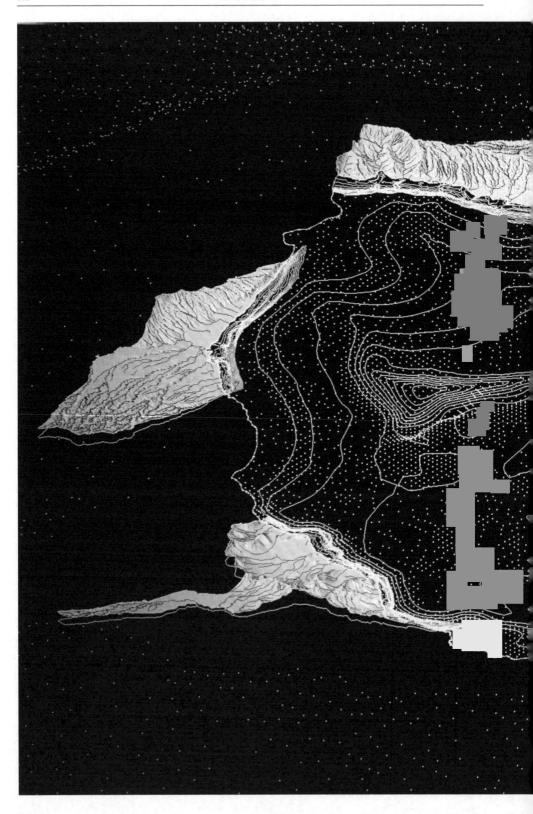

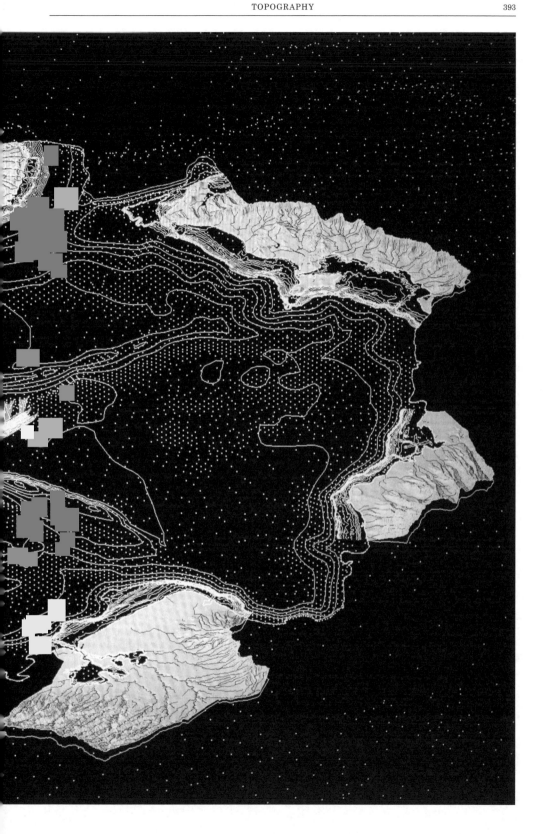

TOILET

Toilette, activity, personal & passive activities: Activities surrounding washing and attiring oneself. *Toilet*, plumbing fixtures: Plumbing fixtures consisting typically of a water-flushed bowl with a *toilet* seat.

See also BODY—see also ELEMENT: Architecture at the Human Scale.

TOOL

Tool, drawing instruments: Crafted instruments used for drawing and measuring, such as rulers, scales, protractors, pens, pencils, etc. *Tool*, equipment by general type: Objects, especially those handheld, for performing or facilitating mechanical operations.

Computer Hardware. Specifications for meeting the most basic performance requirements for design computing: HDMI port, for connecting to external displays; RAM/memory, 8GB minimum; strong graphics card, capable of displaying resolutions at or higher than 1280 by 720 pixels; i5 or i7 processor.

Drawing Tools. For drafting & measuring: 30-60 standard triangle, 12-inch; adjustable triangle, 8-inch; compass; drafting duster; drafting scales, metric, imperial (architectural), and imperial (engineering); drafting tape, 0.5 inch by 60 yards; eraser shield; flex steel ruler, 18 inch; flexible curve, 16-inch; French curves; rolling ruler. Graphite & pencils: drawing pencils; lead holders; lead refills, black (4H, 2H, H, HB); lead refills, red; lead sharpener; pencil sharpener; Prismacolor colored pencils; vinyl eraser, white. Pens & markers: felt-tipped pens, black, red, blue, green; Micron drawing pens, 6-piece set, black (0.05, 0.1, 0.3, 0.5, 0.8); Pentel sign pen, fiber-tipped, black.

Model-Making Tools. Soba glue; Olfa snap-utility knife, heavy-duty; Plastruct/plastic weld; X-Acto knife; Olfa and X-Acto replacement blades, No. 11.

See also DRAFTING—see also DRAWING—see also HEALTH: Planning & Design Health Assessment Tools—see also MACHINE—see also MODEL—see also OPERATION—see also POWER—see also PRODUCTION: Tactics for a Coproduced City—see also PROSTHETIC: Architecture of Cultural Prosthetics—see also REPRESENTATION.

TOPOGRAPHY

Topography, attributes & properties by specific type: Relief features or surface configurations of a place or an object, including its natural and man-made features. For the art or practice of the accurate graphic representation of the *topography* of a specific urban area, tract of land, or other place, use "*topography* (image-making)."

Figure. Plan (previous spread). Sean William Connelly (MDes, REBE).

See also CONTOUR—see also LANDFORM: Landformation Catalogue—see also MODEL: Digital Terrain Modeling—see also RELIEF—see also REPRESENTATION—see also SURFACE—see

also TERRAFORM: Terraforming Cultivation—see also TERRAIN: Mountain Valley Urbanism.

TOPOLOGY

1: Topographic study of a particular place, specifically the history of a region as indicated by its topography. 2: (a) A branch of mathematics concerned with those properties of geometric configurations which are unaltered by elastic deformations that are homeomorphisms; (b) the set of all open subsets of a *topological* space; (c) configuration <*topology* of a molecule> <*topology* of a magnetic field>.

Topology: On Sensing & Conceiving Landscape. Lecture. Gund Hall, Piper Auditorium. November 12, 2014. Christophe Girot.

The invention of landscape has always oscillated between a history of beliefs in nature, with its many representations, and a history of terrain measurements through various techniques of appropriation. In his talk, Christophe Girot considered the longstanding balance between culture and its instruments for sensing and conceiving landscape, noting that the particular representation of landscape that we hold true today has roots in the dialogue between *ars* and *techne* that characterized every epoch.

The aim of this talk and discussion was to open a window on *topology's* shifting point of view with regard to this form of interdependence which will considerably affect our ability to act and perform effectively on landscape's reality. §

TORQUE

1: A force that produces or tends to produce rotation or torsion <an automobile engine delivers *torque* to the drive shaft>, also a measure of the effectiveness of such a force that consists of the product of the force and the perpendicular distance from the line of action of the force to the axis of rotation. 2: A turning or twisting force.

See also FOLLY: Torqueing Spheres—see also INSTALLATION—see also ROTATION.

TOUCH

Touch, senses, biological concepts: The faculty of perception through physical contact, especially with the fingers.

See also BODY—see also HUMAN—see also PERCEPTION—see also SCREEN—see also SENSE—see also WELL-BEING.

TOURISM

Tourism, industry, economic concepts: The industry providing facilities and services to people traveling for recreation. *Ecotourism*, industry, economic concept: Branch of *tourism* aimed at providing responsible travel to natural areas, conserving the environment, and sustaining the well-being of local people.

See also CULTURE—see also DEVELOPMENT—see also ECO-NOMIC—see also ENVIRONMENT—see also WILDERNESS: So Urban | So Brave.

TOWARD

1: In the direction of <driving *toward* town>. 2: (a) Long a course leading to <a long stride *toward* disarmament>; (b) in relation to <an attitude *toward* life>. 3: (a) At a point in the direction of, near <a cottage somewhere up *toward* the lake>; (b) in such a position as to be in the direction of <your back was *toward* me>. 4: Not long before <*toward* the end of the afternoon>. 5: (a) In the way of help or assistance in <did all he could *toward* raising campaign funds>; (b) for the partial payment of <proceeds go *toward* the establishment of a scholarship>.

Soft Thought: Toward a Theory of Computational Design. DES 3362. Department of Architecture. Seminar. Spring 2015. Instructor: Neil Leach.

Within contemporary architectural design, a significant shift in emphasis can be detected—a move away from an architecture based primarily on visual concerns *toward* an architecture justified by its performance. Structural, constructional, economic, environmental, and other parameters—concerns that were once relegated to a secondary level—have now become primary and are being embraced as positive inputs into the design process from the outset. Architecture, it would seem, is now preoccupied less with style and appearance and increasingly with material processes and performance. It is as though a new architectural design sensibility has emerged. But how exactly might we theorize this new sensibility? The course tracked this new development from its origins in materialist philosophies to its implications within the field of design. It drew upon biomimetics and other aspects of scientific thinking, such as theories of emergence and swarm intelligence, that are informing recent developments in contemporary design thinking, and sought to link them to debates within critical theory. In particular, it delved into the issue of computational design thinking and considered the role of computation in this development, from new scripting techniques to fabrication technologies, from the scale of individual components to entire cities, and from terrestrial concerns to new robotic technologies being envisaged by NASA and the European Space Agency (ESA) for application on the Moon. ❦

Territorial Intelligence: Toward an Evidence-Based Design. SES 5360. Department of Urban Planning & Design. Seminar. Fall 2014. Instructor: Luis Marcos Valenzuela.

In this millennium of intense urbanization, cities have increasingly become spaces of conflict, ranging from urban violence to segregation. Yet, the city is also seen as a space of cohesion, a place for redistribution, and for new mobilities, improved life quality, modernity, and development. How can cities be mapped and documented throughout these changes and paradoxes? What is the relationship between city form and structure in such transformations? Does this new information necessitate a certain kind of new evidence-based design?

This course explored these and other related questions by bringing together diverse research approaches to explore four main scopes—(1) territories of conflict, (2) urban economies, (3) infrastructural mobilities, and (4) reconstructed urbanity—into a research debate of crit-ical issues in cities where even good design is not good enough. Fostering innovations in spatial analysis, city science, and GIS applications, the seminar looked to provide new insights into an evidence-driven approach to territorial quests through design research. ❦

TRADITION

1: (a) An inherited, established, or customary pattern of thought, action, or behavior; (b) a belief or story or a body of beliefs or stories relating to the past that are commonly accepted as historical though not verifiable. 2: The handing down of information, beliefs, and customs by word of mouth or by example from one generation to another without written instruction. 3: Cultural continuity in social attitudes, customs, and institutions. 4: Characteristic manner, method, or style <in the best liberal *tradition*>.

Oral *tradition*, culture-related concepts: The transmission of facts and cultural knowledge, rules, beliefs, and stories in oral rather than written form.

See also COMMUNICATION—see also CULTURE—see also INSPIRATION: Natural & Unnatural—see also MEMORY: Ecologies of Memory—see also PRACTICE.

TRAJECTORY

1: The curve that a body describes in space. 2: A path, progression, or line of development resembling a physical *trajectory* <an upward career *trajectory*>.

Trajectories. Student Publication. In each issue, *Trajectories* frames a specific image of an architectural project to elicit responses from different perspectives. The goal is to channel the disciplinary and cultural heterogeneity of the Harvard GSD student body to generate unforeseen ways of thinking about architecture. The specificity of this approach encourages students to engage in imaginative interpretation, either focusing on the image itself or bringing in external knowledge. The publication's emphasis is not on heavy research nor the discernment of the architect's original intent, but rather on the generation of unexpected conceptualizations of architecture. These prompts can be seen as brief, intensive exercises in perception and creativity. Each issue serves as a compilation of strategies for thinking about architecture according to wildly different logics, captured in written or other less traditional forms. This independent, interdisciplinary, and cross-cultural thinking will be instrumental in the act of design. ❦

TRANSFORMATION

1: An act, process, or instance of *transforming* or being *transformed*. 2: (a) The operation of changing one configuration or expression into another in accordance with a mathematical rule; (b) the formula that effects a *transformation*; (c) function; (d) an operation that converts one grammatical string into another. 3: Genetic modification of a bacterium by incorporation of free DNA from another bacterial cell, also a genetic modification of a cell by the uptake and incorporation of exogenous DNA.

Transformations Studio I. HAA 96A. Undergraduate Architecture Studio. Spring 2015. Instructor: Megan Panzano. Teaching Assistants: Justin Gallagher (MArch I) & Sofia Balters (MArch I).

This course introduced the basic architectural concepts and techniques used to address issues of form, function, ornament, and material, and provided instruction in project analysis, visualization, communication, and fabrication using both physical and digital modeling. Students proceeded through a series of progressively complex investigations of *transformational* processes, and of context, program, and material assemblage. As an introduction to architectural design, students explored comprehensive and foundational design principles, skill sets, and critical thinking and making.

Students: Connor Cook (FAS), Autumne Franklin (FAS), Abigail Harris (FAS), Joy Jing (FAS), Mathew Murray (FAS), Jonathan Palmer (FAS), Courtney Smith (FAS), Yaara Yacoby (FAS). §

Figure. Models (opposite page). Jonathan Palmer (FAS).

See also ACTION: Design as Survival, Resistance, and Transformative Action—see also CITY: Expeditions in the Contemporary City—see also CONFLICT: Ad Absurdum—see also CONNECTION—see also DURATION: Indeterminately Bound—see also INCUBATOR: Urbanity Incubator—see also ITERATION—see also LIFESTYLE: Redefining Urban Living—see also LIMINAL: Liminal Space—see also ORNAMENT—see also REFUGE—see also TECHNIQUE—see also VISION.

TRANSIT

Transit system element, transportation elements: Infrastructural components of systems that allow for the movement of large numbers of people. *Transit*, angle distance measuring devices: Surveying instruments designed primarily to measure horizontal and vertical angles and generally consisting of telescope, spirit level, graduated plates, verniers, various leveling screws, and often a compass.

See also CIRCULATION—see also INFRASTRUCTURE—see also MEASURE—see also ORIENTATION—see also SYSTEM—see also T—see also TRANSPORTATION—see also URBAN—see also VALUE: Marrying Market Timing with Human-Centered Urban Design.

TRANSITION

1: (a) Passage from one state, stage, subject, or place to another, change; (b) a movement, development, or evolution from one form, stage, or style to another. 2: (a) A musical modulation; (b) a musical passage leading from one section of a piece to another. 3: An abrupt change in energy state or level usually accompanied by loss or gain of a single quantum of energy.

Transition zone, land-use districts: Designates areas undergoing an orderly conversion from one predominant use to another, as from residential to higher-density residential plus commercial.

The Forms of Transition. STU 1311. Department of Architecture. Option Studio. Fall 2014. Instructor: Camilo Restrepo Ochoa. Teaching Assistant: Daniel Feldman (MAUD).

Architecture of *transition* is made by the built forms that emerge under extreme geographical, social, and environmental conditions. It has indeterminate borders and temporary, but intense use. It is not mechanically acclimatized. It is socially porous. Its space is the result of negotiation processes and exchange between policies for social transformation, communities, and their nearby geography. It is the space in between conditions, technologically mongrel and impure. It emerges from the variations of exchange between design methods, instruments for knowledge, available resources, and reality. The studio site was in the Medellin and Antioquia regions of Colombia, where the tropics meet the Andes, and where a wide range of biodiversity and specific microclimates emerge, creating diverse social idiosyncrasies and particular ways of using public space and architecture.

Students: Hillary Jane Archer (MLA I), Caio Caesar Barboza (MArch II), Joseph William Bivona (MLA II), Daniel Carlson (MArch I), Bradley Paul Howe (MLA I), Stephanie Hsia (MLA I), Kaitlin Meredith Kurs (MArch I), Christian Lavista (MArch II), Ilka Lin (MAUD), Aaron C. Menninga (MArch I), Leo Raphael Miller (MLA I), Ivan Ruhle (MArch I), Lance Smith (MArch I). §

Figure. Plan (next spread). Caio Caesar Barboza (MArch II).

TRANSLUCENCY

Translucency, optical properties, attributes & properties by specific type: The quality or state of a substance or body of transmitting light, but without allowing clear visibility.

TRANSMISSION

1: An act, process, or instance of *transmitting* <*transmission* of a nerve impulse across a synapse>. 2: The passage of radio waves in the space between *transmitting* and receiving stations, also the act or process of *transmitting* by radio or television. 3: An assembly of parts including the speed-changing gears and the propeller shaft by which the power is *transmitted* from an engine to a live axle, also the speed-changing gears in such an assembly. 4: Something that is *transmitted*, message.

Transmission, processes & techniques by specific type: Actions and methods performed by *transmitting* and receiving information.

See also COMMUNICATION—see also DATA—see also ENERGY—see also HOLOGRAM—see also INFORMATION—see also PROCESS—see also SYSTEM.

TRANSPARENCY

Transparency, visual works by material or technique: Images designed for viewing by transmitted light. Most often refers to *transparent* positive photographs; can also refer to *transparent* nonphotographic images that are designed for projection viewing or as intermediates for reproduction. *Transparency*, optical property: The

quality or state of a substance or body of transmitting light without appreciable scattering so that things lying beyond are entirely visible.

TRANSPORTATION

Transportation: The act of conveying or the process of being conveyed. *Transportation* infrastructure, *transportation* structures, single built works by function: General term for facilities that allow the movement of people and goods from one location to another, including air, rail, road, water, cable, pipeline, and space *transport* and travel.

Transportation Policy & Planning. SES 5302. Department of Urban Planning & Design. Seminar. Spring 2015. Instructor: José Antonio Gómez-Ibáñez.
    This course provided an overview of the issues involved in *transportation* policy and planning, as well as an introduction to the skills necessary for solving the various analytic and managerial problems that are peculiar to this area. The course was organized around seven problems: (1) analyzing the market for a service, (2) costing and pricing, (3) operations management, (4) controlling congestion and pollution, (5) *transport* and land use, (6) investment evaluation, and (7) the regulation of private carriers. Examples were drawn from both urban and intercity passenger and freight *transportation*. ֍

Transforming Urban Transport (TUT): The Role of Political Leadership. Research Project. Diane Davis & Onesimo Flores Dewey.
    This project seeks to advance our knowledge of how, when, and where political leadership has been critical to the successful implementation of path-breaking *transportation* policies. It will do so through case study research of eight to ten cities where political leadership has been central to the adoption and implementation of significant, transformative, and innovative *transportation* policies. By asking how, why, and under what conditions political leaders have been able to overcome obstacles—whether in the form of bureaucratic inertia, citizen opposition, *transport* provider intransigence, or other such factors—the research insights that emerged from this project had significant practical application. TUT aims to generate new scholarly insights about leadership, not just in *transportation* but more broadly in 21st-century urban governance. ֍

See also AIR—see also CIRCULATION—see also CURB: The Re-Rise of the Curb—see also DEVELOPMENT: Transportation Planning & Development—see also INFRASTRUCTURE—see also INITIATIVE: Transforming Urban Transport—see also MOVEMENT—see also PUBLIC—see also SPACE—see also SYSTEM—see also TRANSIT.

TRASH

1: Something worth little or nothing, such as (a) junk, rubbish; (b) empty talk, nonsense; (c) inferior or worthless writing or artistic matter, especially such matter intended purely for sensational entertainment; (d) *trash* talk. 2: Something in a crumbled or broken condition or mass, especially debris from pruning or processing plant material. 3: A worthless person, also such persons as a group, riffraff.

See also COMPOST—see also GREEN—see also LANDFILL—see also SUSTAINABILITY—see also WASTE.

TRIMETRIC

Trimetric projection, images, techniques: Refers to drawings created by *trimetric* projection, which is an axonometric projection where the three spatial axes are unequally inclined to the plane of projection or drawing surface, and the ratio of foreshortening is different for all three.

TWIPOLOGY

Twipology. Exhibition. Kirkland Gallery. March 23–31, 2015. Joëlle Yael Bitton (DDes).
    "Twipology" was a garden generated from Twitter conversations using the hashtags #whatever, #system, #control, #radical, #surface, #cigarette, #pink, #raw, #passage, #abstract, #kindergarten, and #superficial. Visitors were welcomed to walk, sit, dance, rest, contemplate, and spend hours or days in the space. *"Twipology"* was a comment on the uses of personal data for narrated digital fabrication. ֍

TYPE

1: (a) A person or thing believed to foreshadow another; (b) one having qualities of a higher category, model; (c) a lower taxonomic category selected as a standard of reference for a higher category, also a specimen or series of specimens on which a taxonomic species or subspecies is actually based. 2: A distinctive mark or sign. 3: (a) A rectangular block usually of metal bearing a relief character from which an inked print can be made; (b) a collection of such blocks <a font of *type*>; (c) alphanumeric characters for printing <the *type* for this book has been photoset>; (d) typeface <italic *type*>; (e) printed letters; (f) matter set in *type*. 4: Qualities common to a number of individuals that distinguish them as an identifiable class, such as (a) the morphological, physiological, or ecological characters by which relationships between organisms may be recognized; (b) the form common to all instances of a linguistic element; (c) a typical and often superior specimen; (d) a member of an indicated class or variety of people; (e) a particular kind, class, or group <oranges of the seedless *type*>; (f) something distinguishable as a variety, sort <what *type* of food do you like?>.

Typeface, *type* forms, script & *type* forms: Sets of printed characters, comprised of alphabets, numerals, and other symbols, that share certain characteristics of style or design. For the rectangular pieces, usually metal, having a character on one side, from which text is composed and set to be printed, use "*type*."

Blob Block Slab Mat Slat. STU 1315. Department of Architecture. Option Studio. Spring 2015. Instructor: George L. Legendre. Teaching Assistant: Weishun Xu (MArch I AP).
    Teased over the apparent lack of historical perspective in OMA's proposal for the extension of the Dutch Parliament, Rem Koolhaas quipped that the brief called

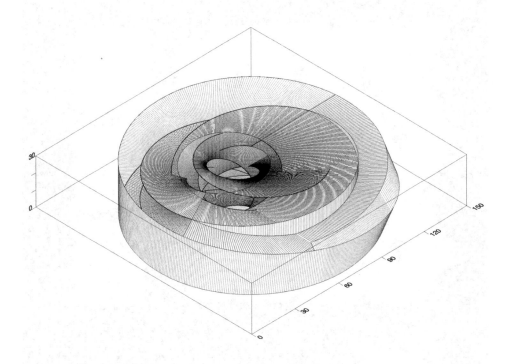

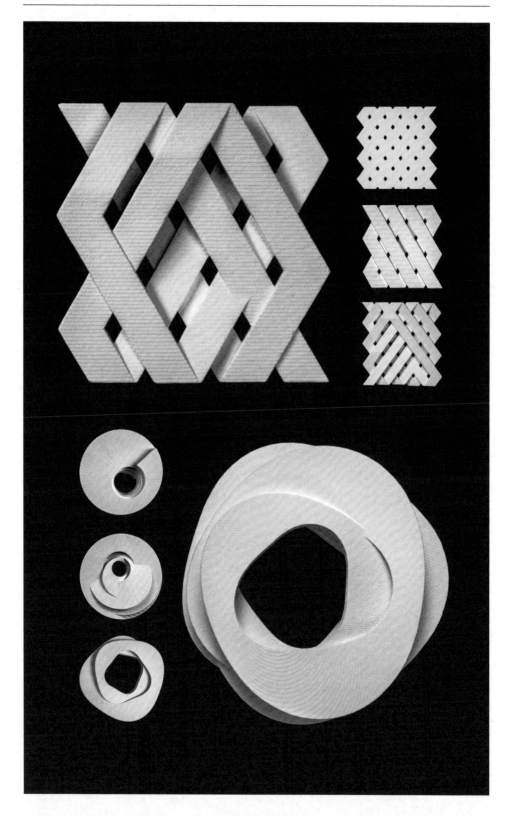

for an auditorium of 20,000 seats, for which requirement "there are no typologies." 35 years later, the 19th-century conceit that spaces ought to be planned according to some blueprint or *type* is, give or take the inevitable odd revival, almost universally extinct. In tandem with a free-for-all distrust of design discourse, the scale, variegation, and programmatic "monstrosities" called for in project briefs worldwide have turned the idea of a common repository ordained by similarities and differences (eventually merging into accepted practice), into a thing of the past. Or have they? Seemingly unrelated developments have recently imbued that improbable concept with new life. For one, we have the pressures of urbanization in places like China, where the prospect of housing 4,000 tenants in a single dwelling block has reawakened the historicist appeal of architectural *type,* which held sway over Europeans at the height of their own local postwar boom (in both instances, quantity seems to be the culprit). And then there is the black-swan event of parametric digital design. By its very nature—regardless of who is doing it or what the outcome looks like—parametric design fosters variation, variegation, and versioning. In other words, it create its own *types.* But the similarities end there. Unlike the figurative and conspicuous *types* of the past, the new *types* are abstract and invisible. They do not recombine building parts and figures to make new projects, as the old *types* did, but calibrate relationships, expressed for the sake of convenience in mathematical or computational terms. The studio systematically explored the exhilarating intersections of the old and new concept of typology to produce carefully calibrated programmatic and architectural proposals on a choice of urban sites across Western Europe.

Students: Niccolo Dambrosio (MArch II), Mark William Eichler (MArch II), Iman Salam Fayyad (MArch II), Arion Kocani (MArch I), Ping Lu (MArch II), Christopher Michael Meyer (MArch II), Akihiro Moriya (MAUD), Phi Yen Nguyen (MArch I), Fani-Christina Papadopoulou (MArch II), Jee Hyung Park (MArch I), Royce John Thomas Perez (MArch I AP), Meng Zhu (MArch II). ֍

Figure. Axon & Sectional Diagrams (page 401). Mark William Eichler (MArch II), Akihiro Moriya (MAUD), and Phi Yen Nguyen (MArch I). 4 Models (opposite page, above). Iman Salam Fayyad (MArch I), Ping Lu (MArch II), and Meng Zhu (MArch II). 4 Models (opposite page, below). Mark William Eichler (MArch II), Akihiro Moriya (MAUD), and Phi Yen Nguyen (MArch I). Diagrams (right). Fani-Christina Papadopoulou (MArch II) & Royce John Thomas Perez (MArch I AP).

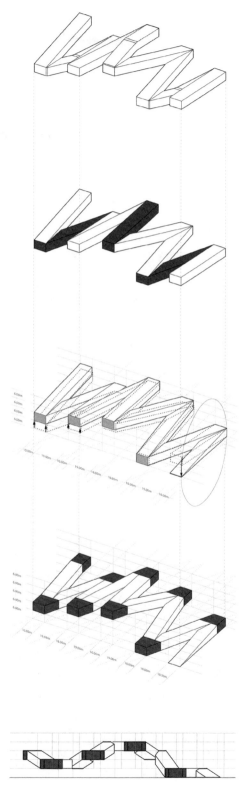

TYPOLOGY

Typology, multidisciplinary concepts: Generally, the comparative study and analysis of the characteristics of things, including their grouping into classes on the basis of common characteristics.

Air Frontier: Post-Aerotropolis. Thesis. Hung Lai Wesley Ho (MArch I), advised by Iñaki Ábalos.

"With the emergence of Vertical Take-Off Landing (VTOL) technology, silent superconductor engines, and a new supercommuter workforce, this thesis attempts to speculate on a new type of air infrastructure and urbanism. This new vision subverts the Aerotropolist notion of a centralized mega-airport by challenging the flat airport *typology* in order to reintegrate the airport as an international hub with the city as a regional in-

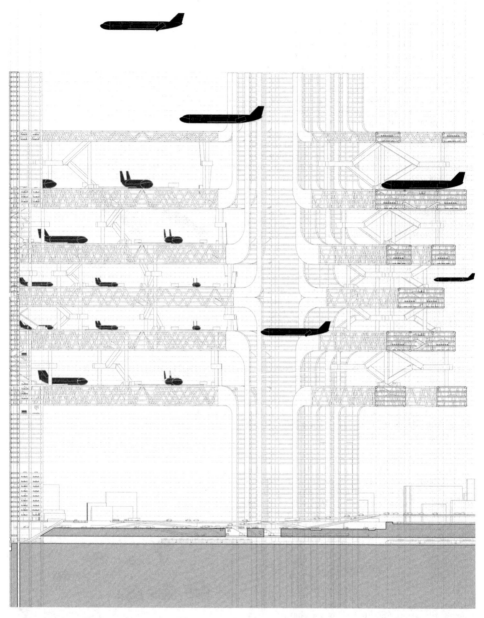

frastructural hub. It reconciles the dilemma of Aerotropolis—an intracompetition between airport expansion and downtown development within a city—without sacrificing socioeconomic exchange, accessibility, and proximity.

From airport as city to city as airport, it explores the possibility of creating a vertical air urbanism that resides in the core of our cities and incorporates airports that expand vertically with smaller footprints to create infrastructural superhubs. As air travel and long-distance commutes become an everyday issue, architecture must reinvent itself and propose prototypes to redefine the urbanity of the airport." ⊛

Figures. Section Elevation (above) and Diagrams (opposite page). Hung Lai Wesley Ho (MArch I).

The Fourth Typology: Dominant Type & the Idea of the City. ADV 9123. Department of Urban Planning & Design. Seminar. Fall 2014. Instructor: Christopher C. M. Lee.

Taking Anthony Vidler's *Third Typology* as a starting point, the seminar proposed the fourth *typology* as a common framework for the production of an architecture of the city in today's globalized context. Unlike the first three *typologies* that found their justification for sociality in nature, the machine, and the historical city re-

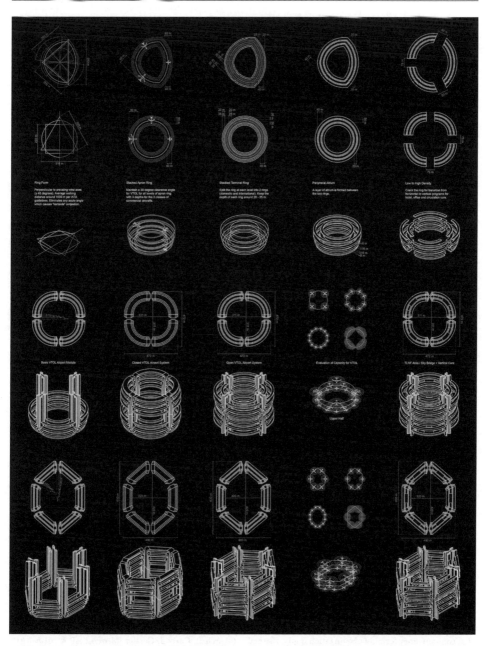

spectively, the fourth *typology* is rooted in the developmental city. The first half of the seminar began with the understanding of type from Quatremère de Quincy and J. N. L. Durand through the dialectics of idea and model. This renewed understanding of type and *typology* offered an alternative reading of the writings and projects of Aldo Rossi and Rem Koolhaas as attempts to revalidate architecture's societal and political role through the redefinition of the idea of the city. This idea of the city was discussed through Aristotle's polis, Schmitt's homogeneous demos, Mouffe's agonistic pluralism, Rossi's collective memory, Agamben's dispositif, and Koolhaas' heterogeneous containments. §

See also AIRPORT—see also AUTONOMOUSMOBILE: The (Love) Affair—see also CITY: The Countryside as a City—see also DWELLING: Poor but Sexy—see also EDGE: The Barracks of Pion—see also ELEMENT: Elements of Urban Design—see also EXTRUSION: City of Artificial Extrusions—see also FOOD: Surviving, Sustaining, and Shaping Urbanization—see also ICON: Icons of Knowledge—see also IMPACT: Learning from the Americas—see also INDETERMINACY: First Semester Core Landscape Architecture Studio—see also INTENSITY: Urban Intensities—see also LANDFILL: Systematic Landfill Reclamation—see also LIMINAL: Liminal Space—see also MEMORY: Ecologies of Memory—see also OBSERVATION—see also OFFICE: De-Construct—see also SPECTACLE: Functional Spectacle—see also STYLE.

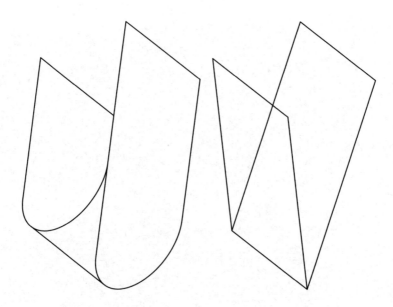

UNBUILT

Unbuilt project, artistic concepts: Refers to planned works of architecture that were never physically produced. For works other than architecture, use "unexecuted designs."

Basel Study Abroad, Achtung: Die Landschaft. STU 1312. Department of Architecture. Option Studio. Fall 2014. Instructors: Jacques Herzog & Pierre de Meuron. ETH Studio Basel Instructors: Lisa Euler, Metaxia Markaki, Charlotte von Moos, and Martino Tattara.

In 1955, Max Frisch, Lucius Burckhardt, and Markus Kutter published *Achtung: Die Schweiz*, a warning about the increasing sprawl throughout the Swiss landscape and a plea for a new and more controlled level of urbanity in the form of high-density settlements. 58 years later, the concern for urban sprawl has not diminished, and yet single-family houses and low-density settlements still cover the Swiss landscape. Alluding to the book, the studio project *Achtung: Die Landschaft* (Warning: The Landscape) attempted to offer a radical alternative to the problems of landscape and resource consumption that contemporary forms of urbanization imply. Instead of new dense settlements built outside of the existing cities, as in the 1955 project, the studio proposed to shift attention toward *Landschaft*—land, landscape, and the entire *unbuilt* territory as a deliberate choice to operate within the constraints of a modern democracy and the need to safeguard individual freedoms and lifestyles. The studio tackled different urban conditions in Switzerland as part of a larger project aimed at critically contributing to the debate on the future of the country.

Already central to the current political and public debate (i.e., the Zweitwohnungsinitiative and the recent Raumplanungsgesetz), the Swiss landscape became the lens through which students formulated an alternative

vision for the future of the city. The analysis, conceptualization, and representation of the *unbuilt* territories at stake were the prerequisites for interventions at the intersection of architecture, urban design, and landscape architecture at multiple scales. Students were asked to advance radical yet specific proposals that resolved and articulated of the limit between sprawling agglomeration and *unbuilt* territory. The studio's themes included the space of the limit, physical space of delimitation and separation between different conditions, and notions of place able to inform the experience of architecture. The hypothesis was that the space of the limit between built and unbuilt will be able to reintroduce an idea of place within an otherwise undifferentiated and generic urban condition. The project unfolded into the definition and transformation of existing settlements through new edges and borders by establishing unexpected territorial hierarchies, separating contiguous conditions, tracing new geographies, offering new scopes, and uncovering unprecedented routes.

Students: Majda AlMarzouqi (MArch I), Patrick James Baudin (MArch I), Eliana Dotan (MArch I), Paul Daniel Fiegenschue (MArch I), Arianna Mirielle Galan Montas (MArch I), Carly J. Gertler (MArch I AP & MLA I AP), Mikhail Thomas Grinwald (MArch II & MDes, HPD), Yuxin He (MLAUD), Mazyar Kahali (MArch I), Arion Kocani (MArch I), Helen Edith Kongsgaard (MLA I), Chong Ying Pai (MArch I AP). ◈

Figure. Aerial Perspective (opposite page). Eliana Dotan (MArch I) & Carly J. Gertler (MArch I AP & MLA I AP).

See also BUILDING—see also BUILT—see also DENSITY—see also GEOGRAPHY—see also HOUSING—see also LAND-SCAPE—see also PLACE—see also PROCESS—see also PROJECT—see also REPRESENTATION—see also SPRAWL—see also TERRITORY.

UNDISCIPLINED

Undisciplined. Lecture. Gund Hall, Piper Auditorium. March 4, 2015. Lola Sheppard & Mason White. ⊛

UNION

1: An act or instance of uniting or joining two or more things into one, such as (a) the formation of a single political unit from two or more separate and independent units; (b) a uniting in marriage; (c) the growing together of severed parts; (d) a unified condition, combination, junction <a gracious *union* of excellence and strength>. 2: Something that is made one, something formed by a combining or coalition of parts or members, such as (a) a confederation of independent individuals for some common purpose; (b) capitalized, the federal *union* of states during the period of the American Civil War; (c) capitalized, an organization on a college or university campus providing recreational, social, cultural, and sometimes dining facilities, also the building housing such an organization; (d) the set of all elements belonging to one or more of a given collection of two or more sets; (e) labor *union*. 3: (a) A device emblematic of the *union* of two or more sovereignties borne on a national flag typically in the upper inner corner or constituting the whole design of the flag; (b) the upper inner corner of a flag. 4: Any of various devices for connecting parts, especially a coupling for pipes or pipes and fittings.

Student *union*, social & civic buildings: Buildings on a college campus dedicated to social and organizational activities of the student body. *Union*, political entities: Political entities officially bound in agreement to a joint action or policy. The European *Union* is an example.

African American Student Union. The African American Student *Union* at the Harvard GSD is dedicated to supporting the advancements of African Americans in the areas of architecture, design, real estate, urban design, urban planning, and landscape architecture. The group is meant to be a source of unity and strength for the Harvard GSD with the specific goal of fostering a network and community that actively promotes the interests of the African American students, alumni, future students, and the professional fields. ⊛

See also ASSEMBLY—see also BODY—see also BUILDING—see also DEMOCRACY—see also FORUM—see also POLITICS—see also PROCESS.

UNIT

1: (a) The first and least natural number, one; (b) a single quantity regarded as a whole in calculation. 2: A determinate quantity adopted as a standard of measurement, such as (a) an amount of work used in education in calculating student credits; (b) an amount of a biologically active agent required to produce a specific result—compare international *unit*. 3: (a) A single thing, person, or group that is a constituent of a whole; (b) a part of a military establishment that has a prescribed organization; (c) a piece or complex of apparatus serving to perform one particular function; (d) a part of a school

course focusing on a central theme; (e) a small molecule especially when combined in a larger molecule <repeating *units* of a polymer>; (f) an area in a medical facility and especially a hospital that is specially staffed and equipped to provide a particular type of care <an intensive care *unit*>.

Shingle system lies outside of primary insulation layer, further reducing conduction of solar gains from shingles to interior

Pre-fabrication and standardized assembly allows tighter positioning tolerances between discrete elements, increasing the system's ability to repel precipitation and moisture

Continuous vertical channels formed by the shingle assembly system create ventilation and moisture drying channels

The standardized attachment system also features minimal contact area with the structural system behind it, reducing conduction heat transfer of solar gains back to the building interior

Shingles can be specified with varying angles of fin deflection, increasing or decreasing their self-shading capacity and propensity for convection cooling; a standardized attachment system allows shiNgles of several different angles to be used on the same facade or building

Figure. Detail Diagram (above). Sasha S. Bears (MArch I), Shiyang Chen (MArch I), Chieh Chih Chiang (MArch I), Grace McEniry (MArch I), Ho Cheung Tsui (MArch I), and Hanguang Wu (MArch I).

L'unité d'habitation de Marseille. Publication. *Le Point*, no. 38, 1950. Le Corbusier (author). Le Corbusier Research Collection, Frances Loeb Library. LeC NA 45 L496 L496c.

"L'unité d'habitation de Marseille was the first of five unités built by Le Corbusier (the others were at Nantes-Rézé, Briey-en-Forêt, Firminy, and Berlin) and is probably the project, as described in this book, where Le Corbusier's philosophy of the individual and the collective as an urban thesis is best achieved. This is an architecture defined by section, both of the *units* (with interior double-height spaces) and of the building (with its circulation, the street, or 'rue en l'air' that would influence the architecture of Alison and Peter Smithson). Le Corbusier described this vertical configuration as having an inherent human scale (designed according to the Modulor) and as an example of modern material techniques and architectural components—through the use of béton-brut and brise-soleil." —Inés Zalduendo. ⊛

See also HOUSING—see also MODEL—see also PATTERN—see also PROPORTION—see also REAL ESTATE—see also SCALE.

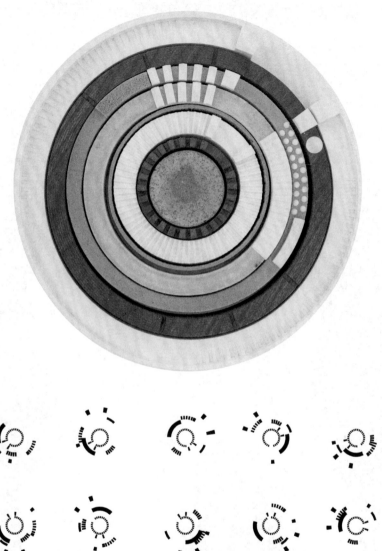

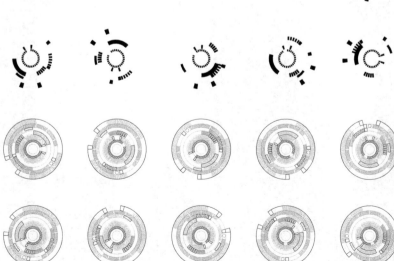

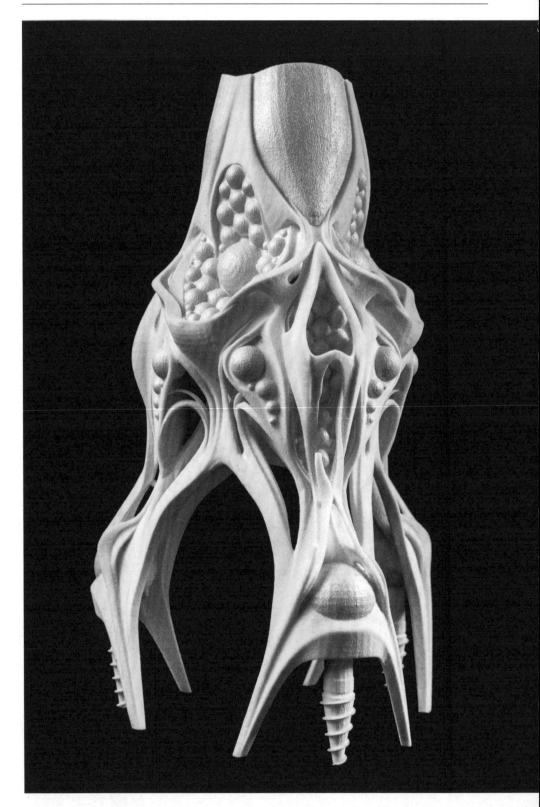

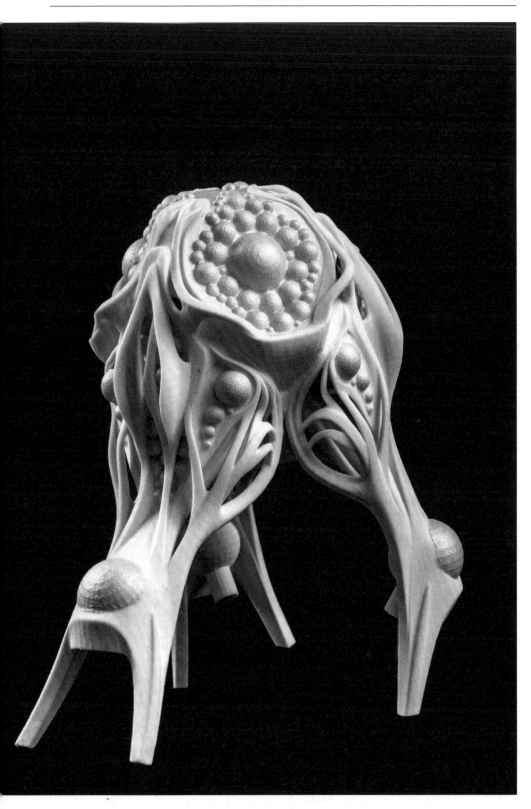

UNWONTED

Spartan Unwonted. STU 1320. Department of Architecture. Option Studio. Spring 2015. Instructor: Mack Scogin.
"I'll have the 'Spartan' Special
rare, please
with a side of straddle-ramp salad
just a touch of Boudoir sauce
and a cup of Balustrade soup.
See if you could substitute
the knobdeco for the pushpixels
and add a dollop of
congealed facadeics.
Oh—something sweet—maybe
a small section of horizontal
loos with a little bowl
of tassel-plasty
Drinks?
Let's have a bottle of
still polygel the Green
Label and
for after-meal a foyer
of molten swag."
    Students: Cheuk Fan Au (MArch I), Patrick Burke (MArch I AP), Sonya Chao (MArch I), Eliana Dotan (MArch I), Elena Cecilia Hasbun (MArch II), Chrisoula Kapelonis (MArch II), John Christopher Kirsimagi (MArch I), Ramzi Naja (MArch II), Xuanyi Nie (MArch I), Erin Anne Pellegrino (MArch II), Joshua Stanton Smith (MArch II), Haotian Tang (MArch II), Georgia Williams (MArch I). 🕮

Figures. Model & Diagrams (page 409). Patrick Burke (MArch I AP). Models (previous spread). Joshua Stanton Smith (MArch II).

URBAN

1: Of, relating to, characteristic of, or constituting a city.

Berlin Study Abroad Seminar: The Urban Architecture of Berlin—From Schinkel to the Present. HIS 4602. Department of Architecture. Seminar. Spring 2015. Instructor: Fritz Neumeyer.
    After abstract modernist planning lost contact with the physical aspects of the built environment, architects and designers returned to looking at the city at the scale of *urban* design and paid more attention to the capacities of architecture as a viable resource for *urban* culture. The question of what constitutes the specific *urban* capacities of architecture has therefore become a significant issue in theory and practice. It also relates to the idea of the city as a space of the performance of architecture. In Berlin, after the reunification of the city, this idea gained significance as vast open spaces in the middle of the city demanded reurbanization. The importance of architecture as an *urban* manifestation can be traced back to the 19th and 20th century when rapid industrial growth and social change challenged *urban* life. This makes Berlin a place with a rich tradition of *urban* architecture, reaching from the time of Schinkel, the reform movement of 1910, to the experiences of IBA, and up to the present. This seminar introduced and analyzed eminent examples of this tradition in order to investigate the *urban* capacities of architecture and its physical potential as well as the aesthetic qualities it produces in terms of bodily expression, surfaces, and spatial connections. 🕮

Korean & East Asian Urban Research Program. Research Project. Peter Rowe. The Korean & East Asian *Urban* Research Program focuses on the *urban* settlement dynamics in the evolving natural and regional contexts of Korea, China, and Japan aimed toward identifying and explaining optimal processes and arrangements. Emphasis is also given to the physical characteristics of *urban* settlement patterns involving planning, management, and design associated with land use and environmental issues, buildings, landscapes, and supporting infrastructure, as well as the social, economic, and environmental factors that bear on the physical environment. 🕮

See also CAMPUS: A Campus for the 21st Century—see also CITY—see also DATA: Data Across Scales—see also DEVELOPMENT—see also DWELLING: Poor but Sexy—see also EDGE: The Barracks of Pion—see also ENVIRONMENT—see also FORM—see also GEOGRAPHY—see also GRID—see also HISTORY—see also HOUSING—see also IMAGINATION—see also INFRASTRUCTURE—see also INTEGRATION—see also INTENSITY: Urban Intensities—see also LAND USE—see also LANDSCAPE—see also MORPHOLOGY—see also PARK—see also POST-CONFLICT: May Kabul Be Without Gold, Rather Without Snow—see also POST-DISASTER: Understanding Tension around the Application of Global Standards in Post-Disaster Scenarios—see also QUANTITATIVE: Analytic Methods of Urban Planning—see also SENSE: Remote Sensing in Mumbai—see also SYSTEM—see also THEORY—see also VISION: Toulouse.

URBAN DESIGN

Urban design, discipline: The field of study and practice of designing the specific appearance, integration, and function of cities, towns, and villages. It is an interdisciplinary field that works with many built environment professions, including urban planning, architecture, landscape architecture, and civil engineering.

Harvard GSD Urban Design. Department of Urban Planning & Design. The Master of Architecture in *Urban Design* (MAUD) program is intended for individuals who have completed a professional program in Architecture. Similarly, the Master of Landscape Architecture in *Urban Design* (MLAUD) program is intended for individuals who have completed a professional program in Landscape Architecture. Both the MAUD and MLAUD post-professional programs share a common curricular structure in foundational concepts and practices of *urban design*. As post-professional studio-based programs, the *urban design* programs at the Harvard GSD combine intense design instruction, extensive applied research, and knowledge of urban history and theory. The curricular structure encourages advanced individual and collective research and the possibility to develop an elective thesis.
    List of Degrees: Master of Architecture in *Urban Design* (MAUD) and Master of Landscape Architecture in *Urban Design* (MLAUD). Department Chair: Rahul Mehrotra. Program Director: Felipe Correa. Program Coordinator: Erica L. George. Executive Assistant to the Chair: Janessa Mulepati. Department Administrator: Caroline P. Newton. Students: 64 MAUD candidates & 7 MLAUD candidates. 🕮

See also IMPLEMENT: The Urban Design Group—see also MODERN: More than Mere Practicality.

URBAN PLANNING

Urban planning, discipline: Long-term *planning* for additions and improvements to the spatial organization and content of *urban* areas. It concerns planning for interaction between people, businesses, government, transportation infrastructure, mass transit, water and power infrastructure, pollution, waste management, and other broad and long-term interests in an *urban* setting. For the overall management of *urban* areas, encompassing the setting of objectives for urban life, the establishment of policies, and *planning*, development, operation, and maintenance of the urban environment and services, use "urban management."

Harvard GSD Urban Planning. Department of *Urban Planning* & Design. The Master in *Urban Planning* (MUP) program at the Harvard GSD draws on the strengths of the department, school, and university in four overlapping areas: sustainable development, social and critical concerns, international *planning*, and physical *planning*. *Urban planners* play a central role in fostering a productive, sustainable, and equitable built environment. The built environment encompasses private and public buildings, transportation and other infrastructure, and public spaces, all arrayed spatially as land-use and form-based patterns fundamentally affecting the quality of human experience.

List of Degrees: Master in *Urban Planning* (MUP). Department Chair: Rahul Mehrotra. Program Director: Ann Forsyth. Program Coordinator: Erica L. George. Executive Assistant to the Chair: Janessa Mulepati. Department Administrator: Caroline Paquette Newton. Students: 80 MUP candidates. ֍

URBANISM

1: The characteristic way of life of city dwellers. 2: (a) The study of the physical needs of urban societies; (b) city planning.

New *Urbanism*, modern North American architecture styles & movements: The planning movement in the United States of the 1990s espousing a return to traditional small-town design features for newly constructed suburbs or redeveloped urban neighborhoods.

Dense Urbanism. Lecture. Gund Hall, Piper Auditorium. September 13, 2014. Alex Krieger, Moshe Safdie, and Jerold S. Kayden. ֍

Ecological Urbanism. Second Edition. Publication. Lars Müller, 2014. Mohsen Mostafavi & Gareth Doherty (editors). NA9053.E53 E34 2014.

While climate change and sustainable architecture have become increasingly topical, issues surrounding the sustainability of the city are much less developed. This book brings together design practitioners and theorists, economists, engineers, artists, environmental scientists, and public health specialists, with the goal of reaching a more robust understanding of ecological *urbanism*.

Ecological Urbanism—Urbanismo Ecológico. Symposia. Santiago, Chile & São Paulo, Brazil. October 10 & 14, 2014. Diane Davis, Gareth Doherty, Mohsen Mostafavi, and Charles A. Waldheim.

Extreme Urbanism III: Planning for Conservation. STU 1507. Department of Urban Planning & Design. Option Studio. Spring 2015. Instructor: Rahul Mehrotra. Teaching Assistant: Vineet Divgi Diwadkar (MUP & MLA I AP). In collaboration with the Loeb Fellowship Program.

The South Asian city exemplifies contemporary challenges in planning, designing, and constructing the built environment with high population growth, overstressed and poorly-managed ecosystems, splintered financial and infrastructural investment, dense bureaucracies, and layered cultural histories. Extreme *Urbanism* III explored possibilities for Agra, India, at the intersection between critical conservation and urban planning and design. The studio examined connections between the forces and contingencies that have transformed Agra as a Mughal, British Colonial, and now Indian city and the imprint of the Taj Mahal on Agra's economy on account of the city's loss of industrial activity. The Yamuna River landscape within Agra has been a site and actor within histories of empire and state, fantasy and myth, livelihoods and crafts production, the performing arts, and water. The Yamuna River and sites along Agra's riverfront, have served functional, cultural, and religious needs for people living within its territory and imagination. The studio investigated the city's Yamuna riverfront and the 45 Mughal gardens and monuments strung along a six-kilometer stretch of the river's economic, cultural, and hydrologic field. By partnering with local, state, and central government departments, nongovernmental and academic communities, the studio developed possibilities for productive economic and administrative synergies. This studio investigated the potentials for more sustainable models of conservation, not only for the Taj Mahal, but for several other monuments lining the Yamuna River— telescoping outward from Agra's monuments and into larger scales of the river landscape and region. Students investigated these issues and developed design propositions with strategies, interventions, and sites for planning for conservation in Agra.

Students: Zhuo Cheng (MLAUD), Xinjun Gu (MLA I AP), Peichen Hao (MLA I), David Jason Henning (MUP), Seunghoon Hyun (MAUD), Jacob Liebman Koch (MUP), Shiyao Liu (MAUD), Nishiel R. Patel (MAUD), Mengchen Xia (MAUD), Ruoyun Xu (MAUD), Han Yang (MLA I), Bin Zhu (MAUD). ֍

Figure. Diagrams & Perspective (next page). Peichen Hao (MLA I).

Urbanisme. Publication. Éditions G. Crès, 1925. Le Corbusier (author). Le Corbusier Research Collection, Frances Loeb Library. LeC NAC 210 L496 1925a.

"*Urbanisme* is the first of Le Corbusier's books in which he delves into the urban context of architecture and addresses the city, including social and economic considerations. It is at the urban scale that Le Corbusier's writing is not only an instrument of cultural critique, but also the context for his urban practice, which remained largely on paper. It is here that he developed his urban ideas and theories, which, together with conferences and lectures, he disseminated in the 1920s and 1930s. Here, he denounces cities as inefficient and poorly affecting physical and spiritual well-being. The proposal (the first of many) that he puts forward at the urban scale is a plan for a city of three million. His initial urban ideas were opportunistically modified over the years and locales according to his changing political alliances." —Inés Zalduendo. ֍

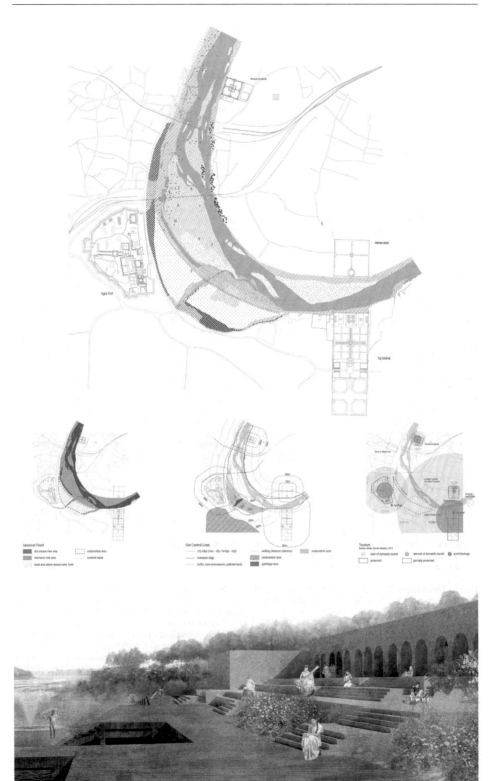

Master in Design Studies (MDes) Urbanism, Landscape, Ecology (ULE). Over the past decade, longstanding disciplinary divides between the urban and the ecological have given way to more fluid, polyvalent, and more productive relations. The challenges of the built environment have rarely corresponded to traditional disciplinary or professional boundaries. Today, contemporary practices of *urbanism* are shaped by thinking from subjects as diverse as landscape architecture, geography, and economics, while increasingly informed by sensibilities and knowledge broadly associated with the study of the natural world. In this milieu, the MDes program invites candidates to examine contemporary practices of design and modes of production as they inform and manifest *urbanism*. As model and metaphor on the one hand, and as applied science on the other, urban and architectural practices are increasingly engaged with ecological thinking. In this space of intellectual inquiry and the advancement of the design arts, the MDes program aspires to be a leading venue for post-professional studies of contemporary urban practice.

MDes candidates in the *Urbanism*, Landscape, Ecology concentration pursue advanced studies on topics related to contemporary *urbanism*, landscape, geography, or territory within the broader contexts of the global, social, and natural environment. Candidates are invited to construct their own program of study from among the course offerings at the Harvard GSD, across the university, and at MIT. ❦

Networked Urbanism: Design Thinking Initiatives for a Better Urban Life. Studio Reports. Publication. Harvard GSD, 2014. Belinda Tato & José Luis Vallejo (studio instructors). HM851.N38 2014.

Networked *Urbanism* was a series of studios taught between 2010 and 2014. This studio aimed to bring network-design thinking to the forefront of design disciplines, and strove to solve real-world problems on the ground, providing an alternative to the traditional approach of designing urban environments from a bird's eye view and a single designer's perspective. Networked *Urbanism* not only examined the physical dimension of the city, but also its social processes and fluxes, developing initiatives that generated spontaneous transformations and set up conditions for change. The studio provided the framework for students to pursue their own interests, find their own means of expression, and create their own paths. ❦

See also BOUTIQUE: America's Boutique City—see also CHURCH: Nicholas Hawksmoor—see also ECOLOGY: Projective Ecologies—see also LANDSCAPE ARCHITECTURE—see also MOVEMENT—see also PRACTICE—see also STYLE—see also TERRAIN: Mountain Valley Urbanism—see also TYPOLOGY: Air Frontier—see also URBAN DESIGN—see also URBAN PLANNING—see also VISIONARY: Grounded Visionaries.

URBANIZATION

Urbanization, development: To become densely populated and built up like towns and cities.

Urbanization in the East Asian Region. HIS 4329. Department of Urban Planning & Design. Seminar. Fall 2014. Instructor: Peter Rowe.

The purpose of this lecture course was to provide an overall account of *urbanization* in selected cities within the rapidly developing East Asian region from early beginnings, to characterize relevant political traditions and forms of planning administration and city management affecting *urbanization*, and to depict prevalent patterns of settlement. Generally, discussion moved from a macrolevel, including overall city plans, to the mesoscale of specific districts and the microlevel of particular building configurations and types. The questions being addressed were: is there a distinctive form of *urbanization* within East Asia, or is it largely a matter of satisfying demands within the ambit of internationally available building and infrastructural technologies? Are there common problems and opportunities accompanying urban development in the region, or is each place sufficiently different so as to defy unitary characterization?

The cities in question were Singapore, Hong Kong, Taipei, Tokyo, Seoul, Shanghai, Beijing, Suzhou, Wenzhou, and Wuhan. Lecture presentations began with a summary account of traditional city-making, as well as later Western influences, including those from the Soviet Union (in the case of China) followed by descriptions and analysis of patterns of urban formation in various East Asian national settings and questions of sustainability, particularly in the Chinese context. ❦

See also CITY—see also DENSITY—see also DEVELOPMENT—see also FOOD: Surviving, Sustaining, and Shaping Urbanization—see also HOUSING—see also LAND USE: Urbanization and the Changing Landscape—see also RADICAL: The Grounds of Radical Nature—see also TERRAIN: Mountain Valley Urbanism—see also URBAN.

USE

Use, functional concepts: The ability or permission to, or the method or manner of employing, occupying, applying, or exploiting the value of something.

Freedom of Use. Lecture. Gund Hall, Piper Auditorium. March 24, 2015. Anne Lacaton & Jean-Philippe Vassal.

This lecture by Anne Lacaton and Jean-Philippe Vassal of Lacaton & Vassal illustrated a continuous process of accumulation, addition, and reinterpretation, reformulating recurrent themes, such as capacity, flexibility, superimposition, climate, comfort, *use*, shells, structures, and economy. The projects presented spoke primarily about inhabiting, *use*, pleasure, and freedom. Inhabiting (beyond the functional) is about pleasure, generosity, and the freedom to occupy the space around and in front of oneself. Architecture means building multitudes of *usage* situations—connected, intersected, and mobile—that facilitate the appropriation of space. Economy is a tool of freedom that, far from restricting and diminishing, opens possibilities and provides margins for generosity and the extraordinary. Beyond any aesthetic and formal determination, beyond rules, standards, and programs, buildings are beautiful when people feel good in them, when the light inside is beautiful and the air is pleasant, when the exchange with the outside seems easy and gentle, and when *uses* and sensations are unexpected. ❦

See also ADAPTIVE REUSE—see also LAND USE—see also POST-DISASTER: Understanding Tension around the Application of Global Standards in Post-Disaster Scenarios—see also SUSTAINABILITY.

UTOPIA

Utopia, political concepts, social science concepts: Places of ideal perfection, especially with regard to laws, government, and social conditions.

Glass Architecture: Charles Fourier's Utopia of Total Visibility. Thesis. Laure Anne Katsaros (MDes, HPD), advised by Antoine Picon.
"This thesis maps an intellectual journey from the pyramid of the cosmos described in the final chapter of Leibniz's *Theodicy*, to the panopticon project proposed by Jeremy Bentham, and finally to Charles Fourier's plans for an ideal phalanstery. Centered on the writings of the French *utopian* philosopher Charles Fourier, it explores the link between visibility and architectural *utopias*. Starting with the premise that visibility—both as a principle of intelligibility and as a universal moral good—is the cornerstone on which Fourier built his ideal architecture, the thesis concludes that Fourier's obsession with visibility ultimately produces the opposite effect. An instrument of vision rather than an image to be seen, Fourier's phalanstery becomes immaterial to the point of near invisibility." ֍

VACUUM

Vacuum, pressure, physic concepts: A given space filled with a gas at pressure below atmospheric pressure. *Vacuum* forming, molding: Forming process in which heated plastic sheet is drawn against the mold surface by evacuating the air between it and the mold.

Vacuum Former. Gund Hall, Wood Shop. The *vacuum* former can be used to thermoform thin sheets of plastic (ABS, Acrylic, etc.) over a form (mold). The sheets are heated until soft, and then moved over a perforated plate onto which the mold is fixed, and then the *vacuum* draws the sheet tight around the mold. ֍

VALUE

Value, color properties: The degree of lightness or darkness of a hue, white having the lightest *value* and black the darkest. When referring generally to the relative degree of lightness or darkness of a surface, use "brightness." *Value*, economic concepts, social science concepts: An amount, as of goods, services, or money, considered to be a fair and suitable equivalent for something else. *Value*, philosophical concepts: Moral standards or principles held by a person, community, or participants in an enterprise which may philosophically inform the activities that these parties plan and undertake.

Alternate Design Values. Project Delivery Lecture. Gund Hall, Piper Auditorium. March 9, 2015. Phil Bernstein. ֍

Marrying Market Timing with Human-Centered Urban Design: How Investors and Municipalities Can Better Realize Transit-Oriented Development. Thesis. Jared Katseff (MUP), advised by Bing Wang.
"It has been shown that transit investments positively influence property *values* under certain circumstances. This thesis seeks to understand two missing pieces of this relationship: when in the investment cycle property goes from its pretransit to posttransit *value,* and what urban design features can amplify this change most. It focuses on three specific corridors: (1) the extension of the Massachusetts Bay Transportation Authority Red Line into Cambridge and Somerville; (2) the construction of the Metropolitan Area Express Yellow Line in Portland, Oregon; and (3) the extension of the Hudson–Bergen Light Rail into Bayonne and Hoboken, New Jersey.
For each corridor, market sales transaction data was collected for residential properties that were within a half-mile walkshed of each station, to calculate growth-rate premiums for property *values*. Surveys were also conducted in each of the corridors to document and quantify the existence of various characteristics associated with walkable human-centered urban design. This data was applied to the market-sales data in a multiple-regression analysis to determine which urban design features were most associated with higher property *value* growth rates. By making the financial case for walkable urbanism, and by providing more certainty on the timing of investment returns in Transit-Oriented Development (TOD), the thesis ultimately seeks to create more TOD, along with its attendant civic, environmental, and health benefits." ֍

See also ADAPTIVE REUSE: Building Appreciation—see also ECONOMIC—see also ETHICS—see also QUALITATIVE—see also QUANTITATIVE—see also PERCEPTION.

VARIATION

1: (a) The act or process of *varying*, the state or fact of being *varied*; (b) the extent to which or the range in which a thing *varies*. 2: Declination. 3: (a) A change of algebraic sign between successive terms of a sequence; (b) a measure of the change in data, a *variable*, or a function. 4: The repetition of a musical theme with modifications in such elements as rhythm, melody, harmony, key, tempo, and accompaniment. 5: (a) Divergence in the structural or functional characteristics of an organism from the species or population norm or average; (b) something that exhibits *variation*. 6: (a) A solo dance in classic ballet; (b) a repetition in modern ballet of a movement sequence with changes.

VAST

1: Very great in size, amount, degree, intensity, or especially in extent or range <*vast* knowledge> <a *vast* expanse>.

See also LANDSCAPE: Vast Minute Landscapes.

VEGETATION

Vegetation, natural landscapes: Plants collectively, usually referring to plants or *vegetal* growths in a defined area. For the kingdom of plants, use "Plantae (kingdom)."

See also CANOPY: Vegetal City—see also COMMON: The Holler—see also ENVIRONMENT—see also ESPALIER—see also

VEHICLE

Amphibious *vehicle*, transportation *vehicles*: Transportation *vehicles* capable of travel equally well in water and on land, or in water and in the air. Electric *vehicle*, *vehicles* freewheeled by method of propulsion: Road *vehicles* propelled by electric motors, drawing either their current from storage batteries or overhead cables. Light rail transit *vehicle*, transit railway *vehicles*: Transit railway *vehicles* used in an urban transit rail system. Motor *vehicle*, freewheeled *vehicles* by method of propulsion: Overland self-propelled devices for conveying people, materials, or goods or designed for specific transportation operations. Transit railway *vehicle*, guideway *vehicles*: Rail guideway *vehicles* that are part of a transit system.

Figure. Perspective (above). Peter Duncan Sprowls (MArch I AP).

VELLUM

Vellum, paper by form: Paper made from high-grade rag pulp with a treated surface generally in imitation of parchment. Tracing *vellum*, tracing paper, drawing paper: Translucent *vellum* paper often used for architectural drawings and tracings.

VENTILATION

Ventilation, processes & techniques by specific type: The motion of air or the act of causing a current of air through a space. An example is the admission of a proper supply of fresh air to a room, building, mine, or other place where the air readily becomes stagnant or unhealthy. *Ventilation*, systems, HVAC: Systems that introduce air into or remove air from spaces.

Supernatural Ventilation. Thesis. Alexander Matthias Jacobson (MArch I), advised by Iñaki Ábalos & Salmaan Craig.

"Architectural design can still learn from nature. These lessons should not be limited to incremental improvements; they should be systemic. They should supersede the state of our art. Instead of the fragmented outsourcing of *ventilation*, which is currently standard practice, recent developments in the neighboring fields of buoyancy-driven *ventilation*, eusocial animal behavior, and thermodynamic theory suggest an integrated strategy for *ventilation* design. The opportunity is literally inside of our noses. The buoyant force from heat we exhale drives the flow of air that delivers our next fresh breath. Instead of imposing an average temperature that forces building occupants to compromise at great expense, we should use air to thermally differentiate the interior, offering subtly warm and cool spaces that appeal to diverse preferences. Architects need to offer passive responses to social circumstances. Occupants spending time together in meetings need cooling, while individuals working alone need heating. This level of integration between occupant behavior and building performance should not be an afterthought relegated to consultants.

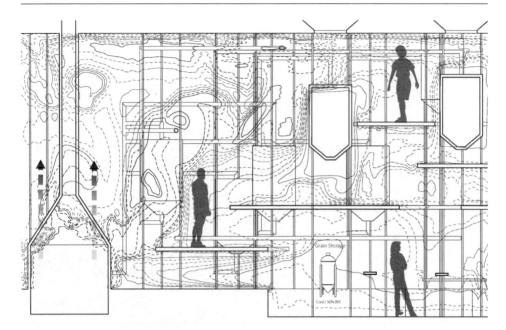

It should be embedded deeply in the design of the building itself—a series of microclimates defined in plan, section, and material detail. If architects focus on the relationships between technique, technology, and social organization, we can design truly sociotechnical buildings that will *ventilate* themselves." §

Figure. Drawing (above). Alexander R. Timmer (MArch I).

See also AIR—see also ENERGY—see also WELL-BEING.

VERNACULAR

Vernacular architecture, architecture genres: Architecture built of local materials to suit particular local needs, usually of unknown authorship and making little reference to the chief styles or theories of architecture.

See also ARCHITECTURE—see also CULTURE—see also MATE-RIAL—see also STYLE—see also TECHNIQUE—see also THEORY.

VERTICAL

Verticality, form & composition concepts: Parallel relationships to a *vertical* axis in designs for graphic works, objects, and structures.

VINEYARD

Vineyard, farms by function: Tracts of land on which grapevines are cultivated; plantations of vines.

Figures. Diagrams (opposite page, above). Alexander R. Timmer (MArch I). Diagrams (opposite page, below). Ryan Thomas Otterson (MArch II).

See also LAND—see also PLANT: Francis D. Pastorius' Garden—see also TERROIR.

VIRTUAL REALITY

Virtual reality, computer science concepts, scientific concepts: Use with regard to types of computer interface that produce compelling sensory output in response to user selections or movements. Distinguished from "cyberspace," which is the virtual place within the collective memories and networks of computers.

See also AUGMENTED REALITY—see also COMPUTER—see also HOLOGRAM—see also MEMORY—see also PERCEPTION—see also REALITY—see also REPRESENTATION—see also SENSE—see also SPACE.

VISIBILITY

1: The quality or state of being *visible*. 2: (a) The degree of clearness, specifically the greatest distance through the atmosphere toward the horizon at which prominent objects can be identified with the naked eye; (b) capability of being readily noticed; (c) capability of affording an unobstructed view; (d) publicity. 3: A measure of the ability of radiant energy to evoke visual sensation.

See also ANALYSIS—see also OBSERVATION—see also UTOPIA: Glass Architecture.

VISION

1: (a) Something seen in a dream, trance, or ecstasy, especially a supernatural appearance that conveys a revelation; (b) a thought, concept, or object formed by

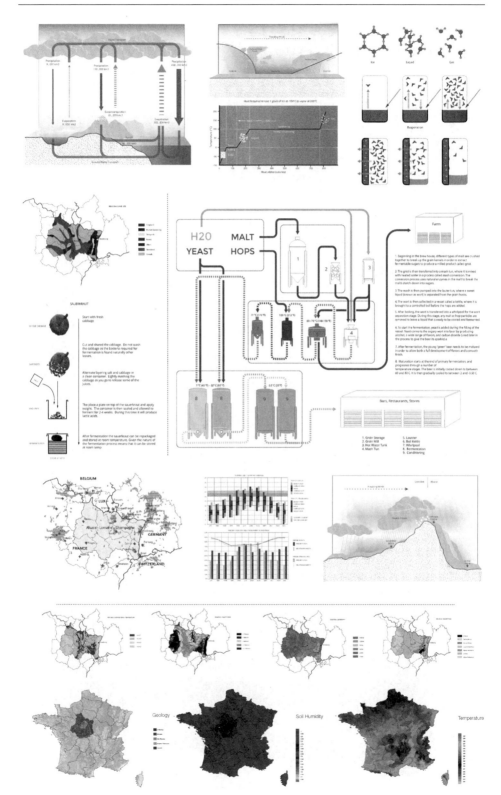

the imagination; (c) a manifestation to the senses of something immaterial. 2: (a) The act or power of imagination; (b) mode of seeing or conceiving; (c) unusual discernment or foresight <a person of *vision*>; (d) direct mystical awareness of the supernatural usually in visible form. 3: (a) The act or power of seeing, sight; (b) the special sense by which the qualities of an object constituting its appearance are perceived through a process in which light rays entering the eye are transformed by the retina into electrical signals that are transmitted to the brain via the optic nerve. 4: (a) Something seen; (b) a lovely or charming sight.

Vision, life events: Experiences in which a person, thing, or event appears vividly or credibly to the mind, although not actually present.

Toulouse: Identité et partage du centre-ville. Publication. Loubâtières, 2014. Joan Busquets (author). DC801.T726 B87 2914.

This book includes the work of Joan Busquets for Toulouse and establishes an urban *vision* for the city, modes of urban analysis to describe and articulate a transformation strategy, and a study of the proposals for the different phases.

See also CITY: Unplugged City—see also EXPERIENCE—see also IDEA—see also PERCEPTION—see also SENSE—see also VISIBILITY—see also VISIONARY.

VISIONARY

Visionary, people by ideology, philosophy or political activity: People who have visions, or have unknown things revealed to them in visions. *Visionary* architecture, fantastic architecture, architecture genres: Designs that are rhetorical, reflecting a theoretical or speculative architectural position on social or political issues, often considered ahead of their time, and usually not intended to be carried out; often applied, but not necessarily restricted, to designs by certain French architects of the late 18th and early 19th centuries.

Grounded Visionaries: Pedagogy & Practice. Exhibition. Gund Hall, Lobby. August 25–December 28, 2014.

The intellectual and imaginative contributions of the Harvard GSD are exemplary, global, and distinct. These contributions—whether by alumni, faculty, or students—engage with the realms of ideas and implementation, design and impact. We strongly believe in the value of learning from and caring for others. That is why our approach to the built environment is always attuned to cultural, social, economic, and physical global conditions. But for our projects and proposals to be effective, we must also be at the vanguard of disciplinary knowledge. It is this combination of knowledge and global purpose that forms the ethos and shapes the work of the school.

Inequity and risk are two of the defining characteristics of our contemporary society. From climate change to limited resources, inadequate housing, and lack of public infrastructure and amenities, it is our responsibility to imagine and design alternative proposals that are at once beautiful and just. This exhibition provided a glimpse into the world and unique investigations of the Harvard GSD. For us, the term Grounded *Visionaries* provides a framework, a dialectical strategy, that reinforce the op-

portunities and necessities that lie between vision and action. This is no small project, but one that calls on the full extent of our talents and commitment. ⦿

Grounded Visionaries: Writing Practice. Exhibition. Gund Hall, Frances Loeb Library. September 8–October 19, 2014.

Designers communicate their ideas not only through drawings and built works but also through writing. Throughout the centuries, books and essays have translated the ideals and understanding of the built environment worldwide. From the systematic exposition of principles and elements of architecture in the 16th century to the *visionary* speculations for the design of the 21st century, texts ground the design disciplines. They also define the theoretical landscape in relation to the discourse and practice of design today. While considering contemporary design demands, designers continue to build on the thinking behind these texts.

This exhibition was comprised of selected written works across time. Located on this wall was the *Elements of Architecture*, the 15-volume publication released as part of the 2014 Venice Architecture Biennale (curated and edited by Rem Koolhaas) and on the north wall were representative publications by Harvard GSD faculty from the last 20 years.

The exhibition continued downstairs in the Special Collections, highlighting 16th- to 20th-century book production and design-thinking, from *I Quattro libri dell'architettura* by Andrea Palladio, to Le Corbusier's *The Radiant City*. ⦿

Figure. Photograph (opposite page). Grounded Visionaries Campaign. Gund Hall.

See also COLOR—see also CREATIVITY—see also DESIGN—see also EXPERIMENT—see also FACULTY—see also FUTURE—see also LAUNCH—see also PICTURESQUE: The Endless Landscape—see also POLITICS—see also STAFF—see also STUDENT—see also THEORY—see also VISION—see also WORK.

VISUALIZATION

1: Formation of mental visual images. 2: The act or process of interpreting in visual terms or of putting into visible form. 3: The process of making an internal organ or part visible by the introduction of a radiopaque substance followed by radiography.

Visualization, computer-use functions, information handling functions: The use of computer graphics to make large amounts of complex data comprehensible.

Visualization. SCI 6472. Department of Architecture. Seminar. Spring 2015. Instructor: Alexander Lex.

The seminar was an introduction to key design principles and techniques for *visualizing* data. Design practices, data and image models, *visual* perception, interaction principles, *visualization* tools, and applications were covered. This seminar introduced students to web-based interactive *visualization* programming. ⦿

Figure. Diagrams (next page). Craig Michael Reschke (MLA I AP).

See also DATA—see also INFORMATION—see also REPRESENTATION—see also SOFTWARE.

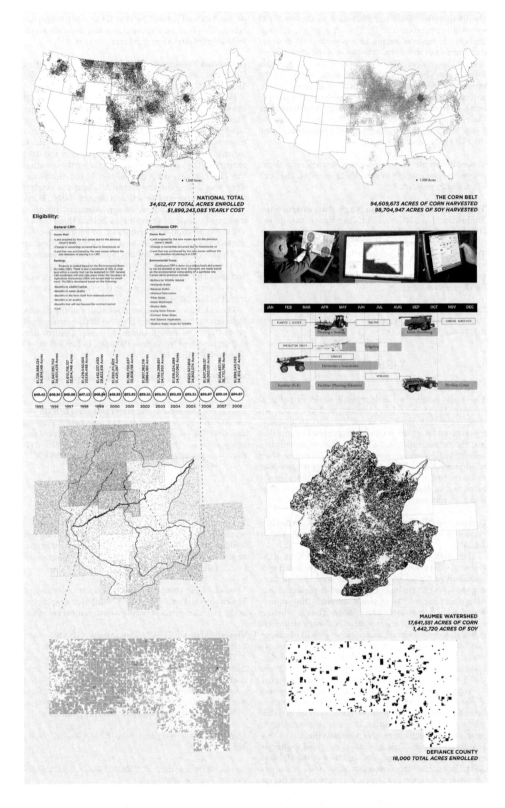

NATIONAL TOTAL
34,612,417 TOTAL ACRES ENROLLED
$1,899,243,083 YEARLY COST

THE CORN BELT
94,609,673 ACRES OF CORN HARVESTED
98,704,947 ACRES OF SOY HARVESTED

Eligibility:

General CRP:

Continuous CRP:

MAUMEE WATERSHED
17,641,551 ACRES OF CORN
1,442,720 ACRES OF SOY

DEFIANCE COUNTY
18,000 TOTAL ACRES ENROLLED

VOID

1: (a) Not occupied, vacant <a *void* bishopric>; (b) not inhabited, deserted. 2: Containing nothing <*void* space>. 3: Idle, leisure. 4: (a) Being without something specified, devoid <a nature *void* of all malice>; (b) having no members or examples, specifically of a suit, having no cards represented in a particular hand. 5: Vain, useless. 6: (a) Of no legal force or effect, null <a *void* contract>; (b) *voidable*.

See also MEMORIAL: Abstracted Geologies—see also NEGATIVE—see also SPACE.

arately bound portion or division of a written work or series that is divided into two or more sections, each contained in a separate binding; generally, multiple *volumes* of the same work or series are of similar dimensions and contained in similar bindings.

Figure. Perspective (above). Ashley Lynn Takacs (MArch I).

See also BUILDING: High-Rise, High-Density—see also COLLECTION—see also COLOR—see also DENSITY—see also FORM—see also MEASURE—see also OBJECT: Object Studio—see also PUBLICATION—see also QUALITY—see also QUANTITATIVE—see also WRITING.

VOLUME

Volume, quantity or mass, size/dimension by general type: The quantity or mass of an object or material that occupies space. *Volume*, document genres by form: Collections of written or printed sheets bound together so as to form a book. The term may also refer to a sep-

VPN

VPN. *Virtual Private Networking* (*VPN*) facilitates secure remote computing by providing remote access to the Harvard GSD network. With an active *VPN* connection, students can run network-licensed software and access file repositories that would otherwise be inaccessible. ⸿

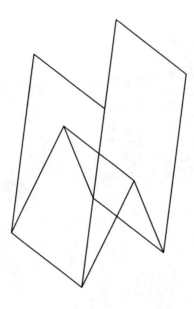

WALKING

See also CIRCULATION—see also GROUND—see also HIKING— see also MEMORY: Dirty Stories—see also PEDESTRIAN.

Walking, personal & passive activities: Traveling on foot at a moderate pace, proceeding by steps, and moving the feet alternately so that there is always one foot on the ground in bipedal locomotion and two or more feet on the ground in quadrupedal locomotion.

WALL

Wall system, curtain *walls*, nonbearing *walls*: Curtain *walls* assembled from highly similar components, each combining two or more of the traditionally separate elements of windows, external finish *wall*, internal finish *wall*, and insulation. *Walls* & *wall* components: Vertical architectural members used to define and divide spaces.

Working Matter: Optimizing Material Distribution for Thermal Performance. Thesis. Jared Friedman (MDes, Tech), advised by Salmaan Craig.

"Working Matter investigates the role of the building envelope as a mediator, rather than as a determinant, of the surrounding environment. Despite a growing wealth of information on materials and thermodynamics, contemporary design practice has maintained an ongoing reliance on existing technologies that are quick to assume the building as a closed system. Such assumptions often lead to a dependence on energy-intensive mechanical systems and poor material selections that are applied only after a predetermined building form has been generated. Nature, as well as many examples of vernacular architecture, suggests an alternative approach wherein material information and hierarchies play active roles in determining the overall form of a system. This project proposes a thermal-mass *wall*—specifically, a small earth-masonry structure—as a proxy for demonstrating the ways designers can work with inherent material properties to design building envelopes that mediate between interior and exterior environments. Like many of the vernacular mass-*wall* structures found in desert climates, the primary objective of the

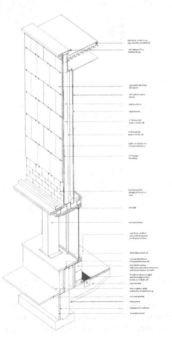

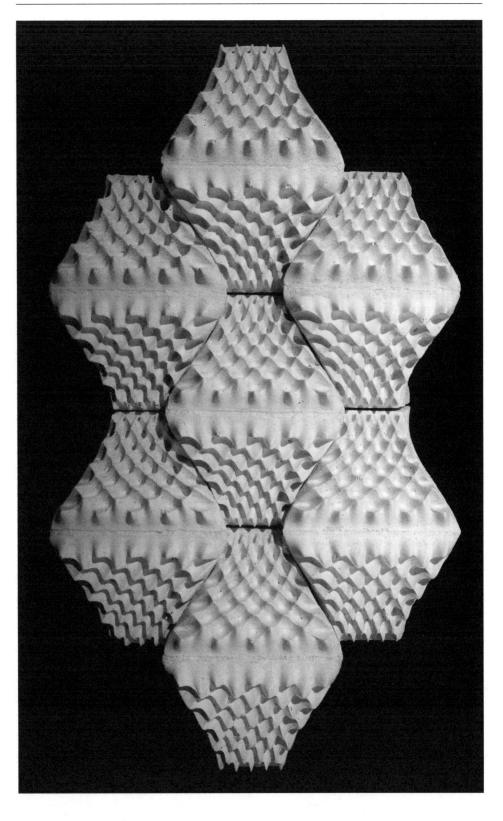

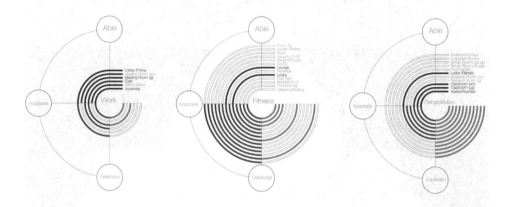

wall is to provide cooling by maximizing the thermal energy that is exchanged over a 24-hour cycle. The distribution of material throughout the *wall* responds to micro and macro flows of heat while maintaining basic structural and fabrication constraints. By applying modern principles from the fields of thermodynamics and material science to traditional construction methods, this research examines the capabilities of common materials to perform in complex ways." §

Figures. Detail Diagram (page 424). Yiliu Chen Shen-Burke (MArch I). Model (previous page). Jared Friedman (MDes, Tech).

See also BUILDING—see also CONSTRUCTION—see also ELE-MENT: Architecture at the Human Scale—see also FACE—see also STRUCTURE—see also SURFACE—see also SYSTEM.

WAR

War, armed conflicts, events: Open and declared hostile armed conflict between nations or parties within a nation.

Sur les quatre routes. Publication. Gallimard, 1941. Le Corbusier (author). Le Corbusier Research Collection, Frances Loeb Library. LeC NAC 250 L496s.

"Although also written during the *war*, this book has a different tone than that of *Destin de Paris*. Le Corbusier understood the *war* as a testimony to a greater crisis, that presaged a positive outcome through reconstruction. This would begin when the *war* ended with the construction of adequate housing. He introduced *Sur le quatre routes* with a history of his life, his practice, his urbanism, and alternative routes for when peace was restored: the routes are conveyed over land, rail, water, and air. The architect guides these routes through three tasks—the art of construction, administration, and planning." —Inés Zalduendo. §

WATER

Water, inorganic material: A liquid made up of molecules of hydrogen and oxygen (H_2O). When pure, it is colorless, tasteless, and odorless. It exists in gaseous, liquid, and solid forms; it is liquid at room temperature. It is the

liquid of which seas, lakes, and rivers are composed, and which falls as rain. *Water* is one of the most plentiful and essential of compounds. It is vital to life, participating in virtually every process that occurs in plants and animals. One of its most important properties is its ability to dissolve many other substances. The versatility of *water* as a solvent is essential to living organisms. The term "*water*" is typically used to refer to the liquid form of this compound; for the solid or gaseous forms, use "ice" or "*water* vapor."

Disposable Plastic Water Bottles. 17 million barrels of oil are consumed to make disposable plastic *water* bottles every year.

Water, Aquatic Ecology, and Land-Water Linkages. SCI 6333. Department of Landscape Architecture. Seminar. Spring 2015. Instructors: Betsy A. Colburn & Timothy John Dekker.

This course was intended to provide students with an understanding of *water* that will inform their professional approaches to landscape architecture, architecture, and planning, and contribute to protecting, improving, restoring, and sustaining *water* resources. The semester was broadly divided into two sections covering: (1) general characteristics of *water* on Earth, land-*water* interactions, hydrology and hydrologic calculations, and green *stormwater* management and design/Low-Impact Development (LID); and (2) aquatic ecosystems and ecology, emphasizing specific design problems in habitat creation and restoration. Topics were illustrated with examples and case studies from around the world spanning local to continental scales. §

See also ECOLOGY—see also FLOW—see also GLOBAL WARM-ING—see also HYDROLOGY—see also RIVER—see also SYSTEM.

WELL-BEING

1: The state of being happy, healthy, or prosperous, welfare.

The Entwinement of Housing & Well-Being. 15th Annual John T. Dunlop Lecture. Gund Hall, Piper Auditorium. September 29, 2014. Joint Center for Housing Studies (JCHS) and the National Housing Endowment. Jonathan F. P. Rose. §

Figure. Diagrams (opposite page). Christopher Michael Johnson (MArch I AP).

See also BODY—see also HEALTH—see also LIFESTYLE: Redefining Urban Living.

WHITE

White, color, neutrals: Universal Color Language (UCL) standard color name identifying *whitish* colors, such as the color of snow or milk. More specifically, *white* is the absence of color. It is the color produced by reflection, transmission, or emission of all kinds of light in the proportion in which they exist in the complete visible spectrum, without sensible absorption, being thus fully luminous and devoid of any distinctive hue.

WI-FI

1: Used to certify the interoperability of wireless computer networking devices.

IEEE 802.11: Refers to a family of networking technology standards developed to allow for high-speed data transfer via radio waves for abbreviated distances. "*Wi-Fi*" is a trademark of the *Wi-Fi* Alliance in the United States.

WILDERNESS

Wilderness, cultural landscapes by location or context: Designates *wild* and uncultivated regions that have been left untouched in a natural state by humans, with no human control or interference; distinct from "nature reserves" in which plant and animal communities are protected and controlled; distinct from "*wilderness* areas" which are lands where natural growth is protected by legislation, and recreation and industrial use are restricted.

So Urban|So Brave. Exhibition. Kirkland Gallery. May 4–9, 2015. Cristina Leigh Geros (MLA I AP & MAUD) & Zannah Mae Matson (MLA I).

"So Urban | So Brave" was a collaborative project bringing together the divergent narratives of image and existence within the northernmost state, Alaska. Set within a lodge in this last frontier, the work was a compilation juxtaposing frequently exported images of *wilderness*—now used to market adventure tourism and sport hunting—with the realities of daily life in Alaska. ◈

See also PLANT: Francis D. Pastorius' Garden—see also WILDING.

WILDING

1 (a) A plant growing uncultivated in the *wild* either as a native or an escape, especially a *wild* apple or crab apple; (b) the fruit of a *wilding*. 2: A *wild* animal.

WINDOW

Window, windows & *window* components: Openings in the wall of a building, serving to admit light, usually to permit vision, and often to admit air.

See also AIR—see also APERTURE—see also ELEMENT: Architecture at the Human Scale—see also LIGHTING—see also OBSERVATION—see also OPENING—see also VENTILATION.

WINTER

Winter, seasons, earth science concepts: Usually the coldest season of the year, occurring between autumn and spring.

Winter 2014–2015. The National Weather Service in Boston recorded Logan Airport as receiving 108.6 inches of snow, officially making the 2014–2015 *winter* the all-time snowiest for the city.

In the last 21 years, Boston had four of its top five snowiest winters (the period from July 1 through June 30, including snow in the fall and spring months). Over ten snowfall records were broken during this time, as reported by the National Weather Service and the

Weather Channel, including: (1) record 30-day snowfall: 94.4 inches from January 24–February 22, 2015, inclusive (previous record: 58.8 inches from January 9–February 7, 1978); (2) record snowfall for meteorological *winter* (December, January, and February): 99.4 inches (previous record: 81.5 inches in 1993–1994; of the 107.6 inches in 1995–1996, only 79.4 inches came in December, January, and February); (3) record snow depth: 37 inches on February 9 (previous record: 31 inches on January 11, 1996); (4) fastest six-foot snowfall: 72.5 inches in 18 days from January 24–February 10, 2015 (previous record: 73 inches in 45 days from December 29, 1993, to February 11, 1994); (5) four calendar days with at least 12 inches of snow, a first for any snow season (previously, only two seasons had as many as two such days, in 1977–1978 and 1960–1961); (6) at least 0.5 inch of snow had fallen six straight days through February 12, topping the previous such record stretch of five days in 1943. The record stretch of measurable snow (at least 0.1 inch) was nine straight days ending on March 10, 1916; (7) most days with measurable snow in a month: 16 in February, topping the record of 14 days in March 1916, January 1923, and January 1994. It also broke the record for the month of February, which was previously set in 1907 and 1967; (8) while not a snow record per se, part of the difficulty Boston has faced in dealing with the snow is the persistent cold weather, which has prevented any meaningful snowmelt. The city recorded 28 consecutive days with lows 20 degrees or colder from January 25 through February 21 (inclusive), breaking the all-time record of 27 consecutive days set January 12 through February 7, 1881.

Winter Storm Juno. January 26–28, 2015. 24.6 inches snowfall in Boston (Logan Airport). *Winter* storm Juno was the sixth heaviest snowstorm in Boston on record as of spring 2015. Harvard University closed on January 27, 2015 when *winter* storm Juno covered Cambridge in about two feet of snow.

Winter Storm Marcus. February 7–10, 2015. 23.8 inches snowfall in Boston (Logan Airport). *Winter* storm Marcus was the seventh heaviest snowstorm in Boston on record as of spring 2015. Harvard University closed on February 9, 2015.

Figure. Photograph (previous page). Gund Hall.

See also CLIMATE—see also CLIMATE CHANGE—see also GE-OGRAPHY: The Distributed Winter & Other Edible Geographies—see also PHENOMENON—see also SEASONALITY.

WOMAN

Woman, female humans, people by gender: Refers to female human beings from young adulthood through old age.

Women in Design. Student Group. *Women* in Design is a forum to instigate dialogue about diversity, inclusion, joint creativity, and interdisciplinary and collaborative practice in the design disciplines. Led by *women*, but open to all, the group advocates for the field to be more equitable and open in light of the under-representation of *women* in recognized leadership roles. *Women* in Design is a flexible association that can shift direction and focus in response to the interests of its current members, which include students, faculty, alumni, and staff. ❧

See also BALANCE—see also DESIGN—see also HUMAN—see also MODERN: Women, Modernity, and Landscape Architecture—see also PRACTICE—see also WORK: Perceiving & Working.

WOOD

Wood, plant material, *wood* & *wood* products: The principal tissue of trees and other plants that provides both strength and a means of conducting nutrients. *Wood* is one of the most versatile materials known.

Wood Urbanism. Colloquium. Gund Hall, Piper Auditorium & Stubbins. September 25–26, 2014. Betsy

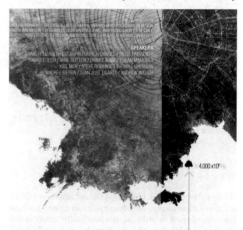

A. Colburn, Salmaan Craig, Ulrich Dangel, Billie Jo Faircloth, Tomas Folch, Jane Hutton, Daniel Ibañez Moreno (DDes), Sean Mahoney, Kiel Moe, Steve Roberge, Thomas Sherman, Andrés Sierra, Juan José Ugarte, and Andrew Waugh.

From under-considered thermal properties to emerging manufacturing possibilities, forestry regimes to larger ecosystem and carbon cycle dynamics, *wood* is uniquely positioned for ecological urbanization in the 21st century yet remains inadequately characterized in architecture, landscape architecture, and urbanism. As the unique material properties of *wood* operate at multiple, simultaneous spatial and temporal scales, so too should the

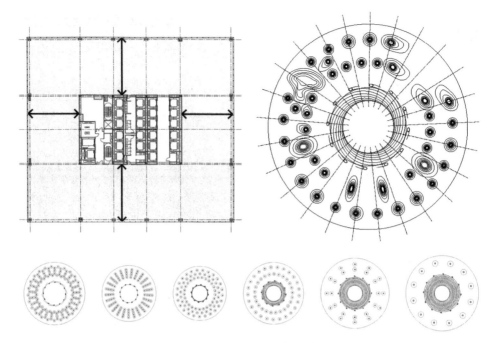

discussions surrounding *wood's* role as a critical material for design today. This event brought together scholars and practitioners in conversation, focusing on *wood* from a range of perspectives—from the working forest to the mid-rise building to the cell itself. The aim was to examine the implications and potentials of *wood* urbanism, drawing particular focus to the complex relationships between land use, *wood* production, and *wood* construction. While relying on the intelligence and depth of multiple disciplines, a more totalizing thermodynamic perspective on the role of *wood* in contemporary buildings, urbanism, and territories is needed: from the imperceptibly small to the imperceptibly large.

This event marked the initiation of a research collaboration between the Harvard GSD; the Energy, Environments, and Design Lab (EED); and the Centro de Innovación y Desarrollo de la Madera (CIDM), Universidad Católica de Chile. ⊛

Figure. Wood Urbanism (opposite page). Jane Hutton, Daniel Ibáñez Moreno (DDes), Kiel Moe, and Juan José Ugarte.

See also CONSTRUCTION—see also ECOLOGY—see also FABRICATION—see also LAB—see also MATERIAL—see also PLANT—see also SKYSCRAPER: Wood Skyscraper—see also SURFACE—see also WORK—see also WORKSHOP.

WORK

Work, general, creative: Objects, performances, or written or intellectual compilations, that are considered creative and require effort or labor. *Work* of art: *Works* of art in any medium, including performance art. A *work* of art may exist as a part of a larger object, e.g., a mural painting or a painting on a piece of furniture. When referring to the study or practice of the fine arts or the fine and decorative arts together, use "art."

Perceiving & Working. Lecture. Gund Hall, Piper Auditorium. April 14, 2015. Carla Juaçaba. ⊛

Work Environments I: Campus & Event. STU 1317. Department of Architecture. Option Studio. Spring 2015. Instructor: Florian Idenburg. Teaching Assistant: Abigail Ann Chang (MArch I).

This studio was the first of three studios to examine the disruptive transformations that take place globally in *work* environments. It looked at the United States, and explored two interrelated domains of *work*, namely the corporate campus and the industry-wide event.

A company—an enterprise growing through the input of *workers'* energy, knowledge, and time—tries to employ the best possible people and have them be as productive as possible at the most efficient cost. In a system that continuously forces companies to increase profits, the perpetual quest to optimize the *workforce* is essential. In this equation, the *workplace* is a key component. Many components that define this environment are quantifiable, but since a *workforce* is made up of human beings, individual sensitivities such as comfort, pleasure, and convenience are also part of this equilibrium.

Recent advancements in technology have not only led to a greatly reduced floor area per *worker*, but they have also liberated the *worker* from the office, and the physical environment from its structural role. Particularly in the United States, with relatively high mobility and individuality, a nomadic and independent *workforce* constantly redefines the place of *work*. Studies show that two-thirds of office *workers* are either temporarily or permanently on the move and *work* online. If the office of today can be anywhere, what do we need from the physical environment?

Technology has not only disrupted spatial orders, but also the way *work* is portrayed and experienced. Office *work* has changed from repetitive *work* to creative and innovative tasks. Terms as playbour, enterprise gamification, and hackathons suggest a general "ludification"

GX7148717B2

(12) **Google X Patent**
      (Formerly US Patent)

(10) **Patent No.:**   **GX7148717B2**
(45) **Date of Patent:**   Dec. 12, 2042

(54) ZERO GRAVITY MAGNETIC MOBILE WORK STATION

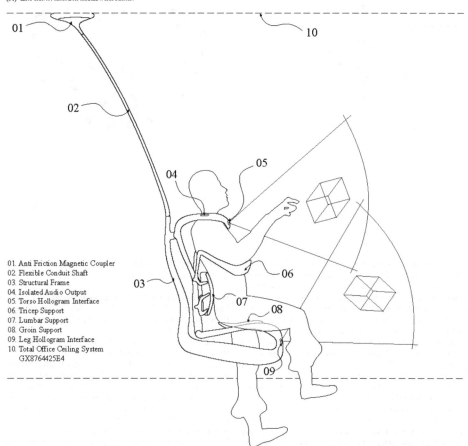

01. Anti Friction Magnetic Coupler
02. Flexible Conduit Shaft
03. Structural Frame
04. Isolated Audio Output
05. Torso Hologram Interface
06. Tricep Support
07. Lumbar Support
08. Groin Support
09. Leg Hologram Interface
10. Total Office Ceiling System
      GX8764425E4

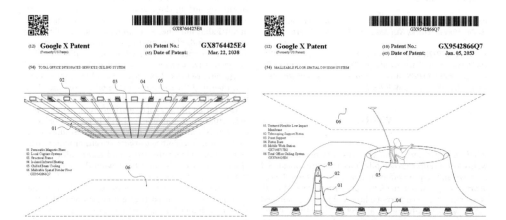

GX8764425E4

(12) **Google X Patent**
      (Formerly US Patent)

(10) **Patent No.:**   **GX8764425E4**
(45) **Date of Patent:**   Mar. 22, 2038

(54) TOTAL OFFICE INTEGRATED SERVICES CEILING SYSTEM

01. Permeable Magnetic Plane
02. Local Caption Systems
03. Structural Frame
04. Isolated Infrared Heating
05. Chilled Beam Cooling
06. Malleable Spatial Divider Floor
      GX9542866Q7

GX9542866Q7

(12) **Google X Patent**
      (Formerly US Patent)

(10) **Patent No.:**   **GX9542866Q7**
(45) **Date of Patent:**   Jan. 05, 2053

(54) MALLEABLE FLOOR SPATIAL DIVISION SYSTEM

01. Textured Flexible Low Impact
      Membrane
02. Telescoping Support Piston
03. Foot Support
04. Piston Base
05. Mobile Work Station
      GX7148717B2
06. Total Office Ceiling System
      GX8764425E4

of work, the merging of leisure and obligation. The *work-sphere* has become a big, social playground, its players a hybrid troop of nomadic urbanites accessorized with a menagerie of technologies. This studio examined two sites in the *work* environment where this convergence is most obvious: the corporate campus and the industry-wide event. Research ranged in scale from campus via chair to charger, and was undertaken to rethink and redesign the now and near future.

Students: Caio Caesar Barboza (MArch II), Abigail Ann Chang (MArch I), Michael Ryan Charters (MArch II), Lauren Nicole Friedrich (MArch I AP), Joshua Michael Jow (MArch II), Justin M. Kollar (MArch I AP), Dayita Sanjay Kurvey (MArch II), Yi Li (MArch I AP), Chenchen Lu (MArch II), Michael Ernest Meo (MArch I), Tianhang Ren (MAUD), Yi Ren (MArch I). ❀

Figures. Diagrams (page 429) & Patent Drawings (opposite page). Caio Caesar Barboza (MArch II) & Michael Ryan Charters (MArch II).

Working GSD. Student Group. *Working* GSD seeks to provide a resource and platform at the school for students with a range of financial needs. The organization *works* at a variety of scales, including the institutional (Harvard GSD), the professional (the world of practice), and the broader community (larger issues of student debt). *Working* GSD is an inclusive group that *works* toward positive and practical solutions without separating itself from the realities and limitations of the school and of practice, or from those who may not identify as being in financial need. ❀

See also OEUVRE—see also OFFICE: De-Construct—see also PERFORMANCE—see also PRACTICE—see also PROJECT.

WORKSHOP

Workshop, organizations, groups: In the context of visual and decorative arts, refers to groups of artists or craftsmen collaborating to produce works, usually under a master's name. The *workshop* typically included trained artists as well as a number of apprentices, who learned a trade by practicing progressively more sophisticated tasks associated with the production of art works or decorative objects. Different people in the *workshop* generally perform different tasks associated with producing a work. The term is typically applied to groups active prior to the mid-17th century. The meaning of the term overlaps with "studios (organizations)," although there is often a subtle distinction in usage. "Studios (organizations)" typically refers to groups active in the 17th century and later, when the master artist or architect took on pupils rather than apprentices, and the emphasis was on the pupil was on honing his native artistic skills rather than on learning a trade. "*Workshops* (organizations)" typically refers to earlier groups where the emphasis is on organized collaboration, smooth teamwork, a division of labor, and where apprentices are learning a trade rather than being trained as "artists" in the modern sense of the term. *Workshop*, seminars, education events: Refers to relatively small instructional sessions or classes emphasizing demonstration and practical application of skills and principles in a specialized field or occupation.

Digital Media Workshop (DMW). The Digital Media *Workshop* series is a set of *workshops* targeted at developing digital skills and techniques for the Harvard GSD community addressing a range of software and digital techniques and projects, including: Adobe Creative Cloud, Climate Consultant, digital photography, DIVA, GIS, Grasshopper, immersive modeling, LadyBug, Mastercam, online portfolios, Processing, Revit, Rhino, and the art of presentation. ❀

See also COLLABORATION—see also DIGITAL—see also DISCIPLINE—see also MATERIAL: Material Ecologies Workshop—see also PRACTICE—see also STUDIO—see also WORK.

WORLDCRAFT

Worldcraft. Lecture. Gund Hall, Piper Auditorium. September 4, 2014. Bjarke Ingels. ❀

WRITING

Writing, image-making process & techniques: Forming or producing letters to record the ideas which characters and words express or to communicate the ideas by visible signs. *Writing*, document genres by form, visual & verbal communication: Broadly used for the written works by an individual or a specific group of individuals. For the body of *writings* of a particular nation, region, period, or language, of a particular form or genre, on a particular subject, or for a particular audience, use "literature (*writings*)."

Writing Architecture. Lecture. Gund Hall, Piper Auditorium. February 3, 2015. Christopher Hawthorne, Florencia Rodriguez, Michael Sorkin, Oliver Wainwright, with K. Michael Hays (moderator).

Until recently, when the Internet emerged as the main conduit for information about design, a reader was normally led to understand design ideas through an author's critical response in print media, illustrated by project drawings and other representations and references. Today, the project of criticism is often close to reportage. What is the status of design criticism today in relation to the production of buildings and architecture? ❀

The Writings of Josep Lluís Sert. Publication. Harvard GSD & Yale University Press, 2015. Eric Mumford (editor). NA1313.S38 W75 2015.

This collection of architect Josep Lluís Sert's *writings* on urbanism highlights rare texts by the former Dean of the Harvard GSD. Of the 15 essays featured, ten were previously unpublished.

The other five were long forgotten: one first appeared in the rather obscure "Michigan Society of Architects Bulletin"; one in "Harvard Today," a rare and long-defunct alumni magazine; and one in the Harvard GSD proceedings of the Fifth Urban Design Conference, copies of which can now only be found in a few university libraries; and the other two were published commercially, but both in out-of-print books. ❀

See also COMMUNICATION—see also EXTRASTATECRAFT—see also FORM—see also IDEA—see also PAPER—see also PRACTICE—see also PROCESS—see also PUBLICATION—see also REPRESENTATION—see also RESEARCH—see also TECHNIQUE—see also THEORY—see also URBANISM—see also VISIONARY: Grounded Visionaries.

X

1: (a) The 24th letter of the English alphabet; (b) a graphic representation of this letter; (c) a speech counterpart of orthographic x. 2: Ten. 3: A graphic device for reproducing the letter x. 4: One designated x especially as the 24th in order or class, or the first in an order or class that includes x, y, and sometimes z. 5: An unknown quantity.

Harvard x-Design. Student Group. Harvard x-Design (pronounced "by Design") is a group dedicated to exploring a wide range of design careers and is committed to understanding the business of design. The group's goal is to understand how business and design work together to create successful enterprises, while also discovering the myriad possibilities open to design professionals. Looking beyond Harvard the GSD to learn about allied industries and careers, Harvard x-Design embraces networks across schools to better understand the value of design across disciplines. ∰

X-AXIS

1: The axis in a plane Cartesian coordinate system parallel to which abscissas are measured. 2: One of the three axes in a three-dimensional rectangular coordinate system.

XERISCAPE

Xeriscape, gardens by function, open spaces: Gardens or landscapes designed for low-water maintenance by planting selection and techniques, and irrigation systems tolerant of low-water input.

Y-AXIS

1: The axis of a plane Cartesian coordinate system parallel to which ordinates are measured. 2: One of the three axes in a three-dimensional rectangular coordinate system.

Z-AXIS

1: One of the axes in a three-dimensional rectangular coordinate system.

Z-CORP

Z-Corp 3-D Printer. The *Z-Corp* 3-D Printer was the first rapid prototyping tool brought to the Harvard GSD, and it remains the most widely used given the relative speed and consumable cost of the technology. Based on MIT's patented Three-Dimensional Printing (3DP), the powder-based build system employs ink-jet technology to apply binder to thin layers of gypsum-based powder, rapidly building objects from 3-D drawing files. It is useful for all types of models, but given the nature of the build material, it is limited to printing parts with larger wall thicknesses than the other two printer technologies available. After printing is complete, the models require at least two hours of additional time to cure in the machine, at which point a finished part must be carefully removed from the surrounding unbound powder supporting it. A variety of post-processing options are available to strengthen these powder-based models, including baking, Epsom salt water solution, cyanoacrylate, wax, epoxy-based resin, or paint.

Figure. Models (opposite page). David Benard Hamm (MArch I) & Davis Shimon Owen (MArch I).

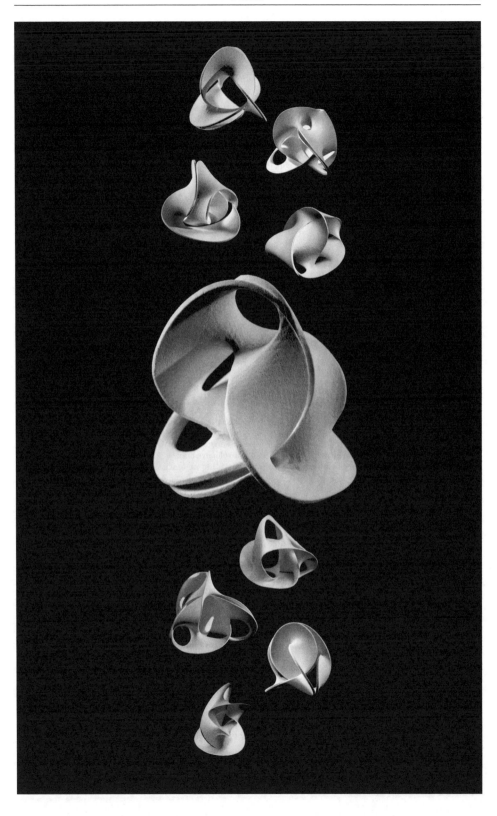

ZIGGURAT

Ziggurat, religious structures, ceremonial structures: Ancient Mesopotamian temple towers in the form of stepped pyramids.

ZOGRASCOPE

Zograsope, optical toys: Devices of the 18th century for viewing "perspective view prints," which are pseudo-stereoscopic images. These tabletop viewers consist of a wooden stand supporting a hinged mirror and lens, used to view a flat image placed on the table next to the stand. A perspective effect is created through a combination of image design and lens and mirror properties. Surviving examples are elegant and highly collectible pieces of mahogany furniture, designed for the drawing rooms of affluent homes.

ZOMBIFY

1: To turn (an active alert person) into a *zombie*.

ZONING

Zoning, governmental functions: Regulating land use for stated purposes. *Zoning*, legal concepts, social science

concepts: Legal concepts related to land use and planning restrictions. *Zoning* incentive, economic concepts, social science concepts: Ordinances that outline how land developers may be granted concessions in exchange for providing amenities a community feels are desirable, such as low-income housing.

ZOO

Zoo, built complexes by function: Gardens, parks, or other grounds in which wild animals, and sometimes also domestic animals, are kept for public exhibition, usually in enclosures. Animals in *zoos* can generally be given more intensive care than is possible in nature reserves or wildlife refuges. Marine invertebrates, fish, and sometimes marine mammals, are often kept in separate aquariums.

The Zoo License Manager. The *Zoo* organizes Rhino-compatible software licenses in one place and shares licenses with Rhino users over a network. The *Zoo* also generally refers to the collection of Rhino enabled plug-ins, many named after animals, including: Armadillo, Badger, Bumblebee, Dragon, Elk, Flamingo, Firefly, Grasshopper, Heron, Human, Kangaroo, Ladybug, Meerkat, Penguin, Platypus, Primate, Seahorse, Squid, Spider, Yeti, and Weaverbird.

Figure. Collage (above). Hannah P. Gaengler (MLA I).

See also *GARDEN*—see also *PARK*—see also *SOFTWARE*—see also *TIME: Tlön.*

2-D

1: A *two-dimensional* form <displayed in *2-D*>.

3-AXIS

1: A multiaxis around three axes.

3-Axis CNC Milling. The Fab Lab has four *3-axis* CNC milling machines and two robots with spindles capable of milling foam materials. ⌘

3-D

1: A *three-dimensional* form, also an image or a picture produced in it.

Three-dimensional, form attributes: Having, or appearing to have, the *three dimensions* of length, width, and height.

3-D PRINTER

3-D printer, nonimpact printers, printers by mode of operation: Machines used to create a physical object from a 3-D digital model, typically by laying down thin layers of a material in succession. *3-D printing*, printing and printing processes & techniques: The action or practice of creating physical objects from three-dimensional digital models or CAD files by means of *3-D printers*.

3-D Printers. Gund Hall, Rooms L40a–c. The most direct methods to make objects from 3-D digital files are 3-D rapid-prototyping processes including stereolithography, selective laser sintering, fused deposition modeling, laminated object manufacturing, and *3-D printing*. Printing with thermoplastics or powders and glues that use modified print heads to build up layers of material thousandths of an inch at a time are the technology of choice for rapid prototyping.

The Fab Lab has three types of rapid prototyping machines: two Z-Corp starch-based *3-D printers*, one Stratasys Dimension ABS fused deposition modeler, and one high-resolution Object polyjet printer. These machines model complex physical geometry—especially valuable for models that cannot be created with traditional techniques or tools. ⌘

See also FABRICATION—see also MATERIAL—see also OBJECT—see also PRINTER—see also PROTOTYPE—see also Z-CORP—see also 3-D.

3-D SCANNER

3-D Scanner. Gund Hall, Photo Lab. The David SLS *3-D Scanner* uses a projector and camera to bounce colored light off an object to determine the distance from visible surfaces to a calibrated plane. The object is rotated manually between the capture of individual scans. Users must strategically capture scans that can be fused together to describe the solid. The *3-D Scanner* comes with software that can rotate and align the individual scans and fuse them together, but holes and other artifacts will very likely need to be repaired in other software, such as Geomagic Studio, in order to make a clean mesh and a closed volume for digital modeling. ⌘

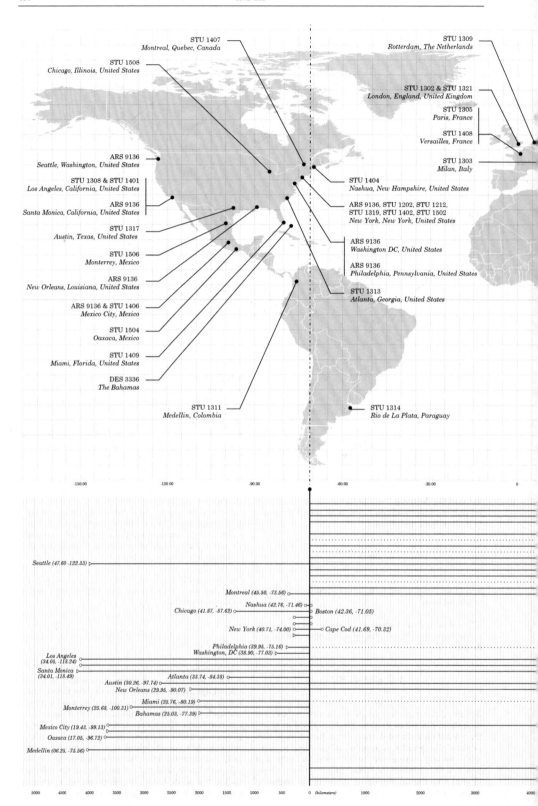

STU 1407
Montreal, Quebec, Canada

STU 1309
Rotterdam, The Netherlands

STU 1508
Chicago, Illinois, United States

STU 1302 & STU 1321
London, England, United Kingdom

STU 1305
Paris, France

STU 1408
Versailles, France

ARS 9136
Seattle, Washington, United States

STU 1303
Milan, Italy

STU 1308 & STU 1401
Los Angeles, California, United States

STU 1404
Nashua, New Hampshire, United States

ARS 9136
Santa Monica, California, United States

ARS 9136, STU 1202, STU 1212,
STU 1319, STU 1402, STU 1502
New York, New York, United States

STU 1317
Austin, Texas, United States

STU 1506
Monterrey, Mexico

ARS 9136
Washington DC, United States

ARS 9136
New Orleans, Louisiana, United States

ARS 9136
Philadelphia, Pennsylvania, United States

ARS 9136 & STU 1406
Mexico City, Mexico

STU 1313
Atlanta, Georgia, United States

STU 1504
Oaxaca, Mexico

STU 1409
Miami, Florida, United States

DES 3336
The Bahamas

STU 1311
Medellin, Colombia

STU 1314
Rio de La Plata, Paraguay

-150.00   -120.00   -90.00   -60.00   -30.00   0

Seattle (47.60 -122.33)

Montreal (45.50, -73.56)
Nashua (42.76, -71.46)
Chicago (41.87, -87.62)   Boston (42.36, -71.05)
New York (40.71, -74.00)   Cape Cod (41.69, -70.32)
Philadelphia (39.95, -75.16)
Washington, DC (38.90, -77.03)
Los Angeles
(34.05, -118.24)
Santa Monica
(34.01, -118.49)   Atlanta (33.74, -84.38)
Austin (30.26, -97.74)
New Orleans (29.95, -90.07)
Miami (25.76, -80.19)
Monterrey (25.68, -100.31)
Bahamas (25.03, -77.39)
Mexico City (19.43, -99.13)
Oaxaca (17.05, -96.72)
Medellin (06.25, -75.56)

5000   4500   4000   3500   3000   2500   2000   1500   1000   500   0 (kilometers)   1000   2000   3000   4000

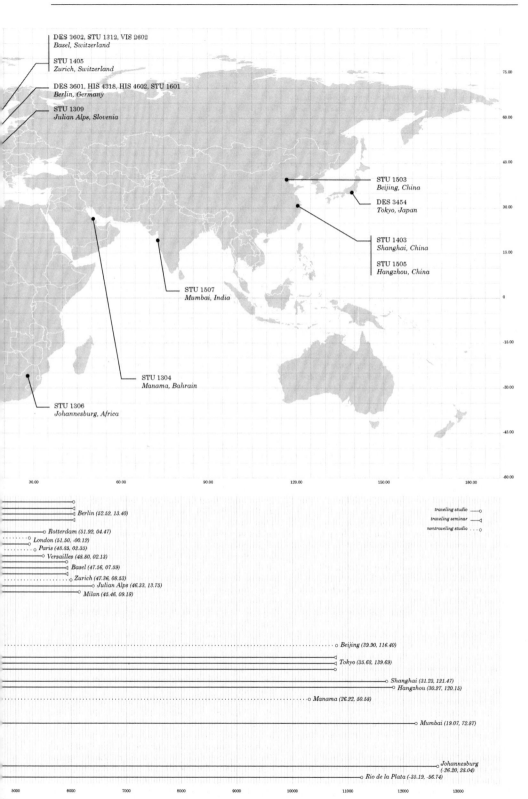

DES 3602, STU 1312, VIS 2602
Basel, Switzerland

STU 1405
Zurich, Switzerland

DES 3601, HIS 4318, HIS 4602, STU 1601
Berlin, Germany

STU 1309
Julian Alps, Slovenia

STU 1503
Beijing, China

DES 3454
Tokyo, Japan

STU 1403
Shanghai, China

STU 1505
Hangzhou, China

STU 1507
Mumbai, India

STU 1304
Manama, Bahrain

STU 1306
Johannesburg, Africa

75.00
60.00
45.00
30.00
15.00
0
-15.00
-30.00
-45.00
-60.00

30.00   60.00   90.00   120.00   150.00   180.00

traveling studio ———o
traveling seminar ———◁
nontraveling studio . . . —o

◁ *Berlin (52.52, 13.40)*
o *Rotterdam (51.92, 04.47)*
o *London (51.50, -00.12)*
o *Paris (48.85, 02.35)*
o *Versailles (48.80, 02.13)*
◁ *Basel (47.56, 07.59)*
◁ *Zurich (47.36, 08.53)*
o *Julian Alps (46.33, 13.75)*
o *Milan (45.46, 09.18)*

o *Beijing (39.90, 116.40)*
◁ *Tokyo (35.68, 139.69)*
o
o *Shanghai (31.23, 121.47)*
o *Hangzhou (30.27, 120.15)*
o *Manama (26.22, 50.58)*

o *Mumbai (19.07, 72.87)*

o *Johannesburg (-26.20, 28.04)*
o *Rio de la Plata (-35.19, -56.74)*

5000   6000   7000   8000   9000   10000   11000   12000   13000

2014–2015 LOEB FELLOWS

GUEST CRITICS & LECTURERS

ADMINISTRATION & STAFF

STUDENTS